Emma Goldman

DATE DUE

EMMA GOLDMAN
A DOCUMENTARY HISTORY OF
THE AMERICAN YEARS

Candace Falk, EDITOR
Barry Pateman, ASSOCIATE EDITOR
Jessica M. Moran, ASSISTANT EDITOR
Susan Wengraf, ILLUSTRATIONS EDITOR
Robert Cohen, CONSULTING EDITOR

1. *Made for America, 1890–1901*
2. *Making Speech Free, 1902–1909*

Emma Goldman

A DOCUMENTARY HISTORY OF THE AMERICAN YEARS

VOLUME TWO

Making Speech Free, 1902–1909

CANDACE FALK • EDITOR

BARRY PATEMAN • ASSOCIATE EDITOR

JESSICA M. MORAN • ASSISTANT EDITOR

SUSAN WENGRAF · ILLUSTRATIONS EDITOR

ROBERT COHEN · CONSULTING EDITOR

UNIVERSITY OF ILLINOIS PRESS

Urbana and Chicago

SPONSORS

The Emma Goldman Papers thanks all of our supporters, including these sustaining sponsors for the volumes, for helping to keep history alive through their generous contributions.

National Historical Publications and Records Commission

University of California, Berkeley

Leon F. Litwack, Alexander F. and May T. Morrison Professor of American History

Joseph Cerny, Vice Chancellor for Research and Graduate Dean (1994–2000)

Linda Fabbri, Assistant Vice Chancellor for Research

Susan Hirano, Budget Director

Edwin M. Epstein, Chair of Peace and Conflict Studies

John Lie, Dean of International and Area Studies

Joan Kask, Associate Dean of International and Area Studies

Charlene Nicholas, Mary Lewis, Susan Meyers, Budget and Personnel Officers of International and Area Studies

Lois Blum Feinblatt, Irving and Lois Blum Foundation

Cora Weiss, Samuel Rubin Foundation

Judith Taylor, The Murray and Grace Nissman Foundation

Stephen M. Silberstein

National Endowment for the Humanities (2002–2003)

Milken Family Foundation

Furthermore: A Project of the J.M. Kaplan Fund

Carol Amyx

The late Art and Libera Bortolotti

Ben and Ida Capes family:

Susan Chasson, David and Judith Capes, Bonnie Capes Tabatznik, and Albert and Marlene Chasson

Mecca Reitman Carpenter

The late Marcus and the late Harryette Cohn

Eric Alan Isaacson and Susan Kay Weaver

Carolyn Patty Blum

Yvette Chalom and Paul Fogel

Mariam Chamberlain

Patrick Coughlin

Barbara Dobkin, Ma'yan, The Jewish Women's Project

Martin Duberman

E. L. and Helen Doctorow

Elaine Feingold and Randall M. Shaw

Marilyn French

Mark Friedman and Marjorie Solomon

The Funding Exchange

Christina and John Gillis

Peter Glassgold and Susan Thibodeau

The list of donors to the Emma Goldman Papers Project as well as donations in remembrance of and in honor of others continues with Emma's List, *beginning on p. 575.*

CONTENTS

THE DOCUMENTS

FOREWORD

Lunching in Paris with Emma Goldman, Theodore Dreiser pleaded with her, "You must write the story of your life, E.G.; it is the richest of any woman's of our century." It had not been the first time a friend had suggested that she chronicle her life. With the assistance of her comrades, she heeded the advice, collected the necessary funds, and began to write her remarkable autobiography, *Living My Life*. Goldman wanted very much to share her life, thoughts, and struggles with the people she had sought to influence and change, and she hoped the publisher, Alfred A. Knopf, would charge a minimal sum for the book. "I am anxious to reach the mass of the American reading public," she wrote a friend, "not so much because of the royalties, but because I have always worked for the mass."

Emma Goldman succeeded in a variety of ways in reaching "the mass," both a reading and listening audience. *Living My Life* went through several editions, her life has been portrayed on film and in song as well as on stage, and numerous biographies have been written. None of these, however, is as critical as the publication of the four volumes of selected letters, speeches, government documents, and commentaries from the Emma Goldman Papers Project, making that vast and invaluable resource available to scholars, students, and a reading public throughout the world.

This is a truly remarkable achievement, the culmination of several decades of collaborative work, including an international search for documents, the identification of correspondents, and the preparation of biographical, historical, and bibliographical guides. To appreciate the magnitude of this task is to know that Goldman's papers were as scattered as her scores of correspondents, in private collections and archives here and abroad, even in places like the Department of Justice, whose agents had seized a portion of her papers before ordering her deportation. Only the commitment of many friends and comrades over many decades, and the untiring efforts of librarians, scholars, and archivists, have made these volumes possible.

In closing her autobiography, Emma Goldman reflected over her tumultuous years on this earth: "My life—I had lived in its heights and its depths, in bitter sorrow and ecstatic joy, in black despair and fervent hope. I had drunk the cup to the last drop. I had lived my life. Would I had the gift to paint the life I had lived!" It will now be left to scores of scholars, students, artists, and dramatists to use this extensive collection to enrich their accounts of an extraordinary career. This is more, however, than material for future biographers; it is an indispensable collection for studying the history of American social movements. That is clear from the moment one scans the list of Goldman correspondents and finds the names of some of the leading cultural and political figures of her time, alongside the names of less known but no less important men and women who shared—and did not share—her commitments.

Emma Goldman came out of a unique and expressive subculture that flourished in America in the late nineteenth and early twentieth centuries. The participants included some of the nation's most creative and iconoclastic artists, writers, and intellectuals, most of them libertarians, some of them revolutionaries. What drew them together was their rejection of the inequities of capitalism and the absurdities of bourgeois culture and politics. That led them to embrace such causes as the labor movement, sexual and reproductive freedom, feminism, atheism, anarchism, and socialism. They represented everything that was irreverent and blasphemous in American culture. In their lives and in their work, they dedicated themselves to the vision of a free society of liberated individuals. They were too undisciplined, too free-spirited to adapt to any system or bureaucratic structure that rested on the suppression of free thought, whether in Woodrow Wilson's United States or in Vladimir Lenin's Soviet Russia. "All I want is freedom," Emma Goldman declared, "perfect, unrestricted liberty for myself and others."

The economic depression of the 1890s introduced Americans to scenes that contradicted the dominant success creed—unemployment, poverty, labor violence, urban ghettos, and, in 1894, an army of the unemployed marching on the nation's capital. In that spirit, Emma Goldman engaged herself in these struggles, employing her oratorical powers to stir audiences and awaken them to the perils of capitalism and the violence of poverty. According to newspaper accounts of her address in 1893 to a crowd of unemployed workers in New York City's Union Square, Goldman implored them, "Demonstrate before the palaces of the rich, demand work. If they do not give you work, demand bread. If they deny you both, take bread. It is your sacred right." That statement was Goldman at her oratorical best, and it did not go unnoticed. For her exhortation she was arrested, convicted, and sentenced to a year's imprisonment. It would be only one of many arrests, whether for lecturing on anarchism, circulating birth control information, advocating workers' and women's rights, or opposing war and the military draft.

The life of Emma Goldman is a forcible reminder that the right to free expression in America has always been precarious. Intellectual inquiry and dissent have been perceived—often for good reason—as subversive activities, and they have, in fact, been known to topple institutions and discredit beliefs of long standing. To be identified as public enemies, to be hounded as disturbers of the peace, was the price Goldman and her comrades paid for their intellectual curiosity, expression, and agitation. During her lifetime, Emma Goldman was denounced for godlessness, debauchery, free thinking, subversion, and for exposing people within the sound of her voice to radical and unconventional ideas. Her life provides a unique perspective on the varieties of anarchist and feminist thought, radical and socialist movements in the late nineteenth and early twentieth centuries and the causes championed, the position of women in American society (and within radical organizations), and the political repression that followed the outbreak of World War I and the imprisonment and political exile of dissenters. In 1919, Goldman was deported to Soviet Russia, where she found something less than a revolutionary utopia. Her stay in Moscow provides an intimate glimpse of both the promise of the Russian Revolution to American radicals and their subsequent disillusionment with its betrayal. Her exile continued in Germany, France, Britain, and Canada, bringing her finally into the Spanish Civil War and still another chapter in the turbulent history of radicalism in the twentieth century.

Since the birth of the United States, Americans have struggled to define the meaning of freedom. That has often been a difficult and perilous struggle. For Emma Goldman, freedom required individuals to shake off the "shackles and restraints of government." The price of freedom, she came to recognize, was eternal vigilance, a wariness of those who in the name of protecting freedom would diminish freedom, and resistance to rules, codes, regulations, and censorship (no matter how well intended) that would mock free expression by restricting or penalizing it. Free speech meant not only the right to dissent but more importantly the active exercise of that right in the face of attempts to suppress it. And, perhaps most important of all, it insisted on the right of others to speak out on behalf of what the majority believed to be wrong, freedom for the most offensive and disturbing speech. That was the true test of freedom of speech. "Free speech," Goldman declared, "means either the unlimited right of expression, or nothing at all. The moment any man or set of men can limit speech, it is no longer free."

What Emma Goldman said provoked controversy, both within and outside the radical movement, and not all radicals were enamored with her political positions. Margaret Anderson, a radical editor and literary modernist, appreciated Goldman's sheer presence more than her ideological commitments: "Emma Goldman's genius is not so much that she is a great thinker as that she is a great woman." But whatever one might think of Emma Goldman's political views, actions, blind spots, and vision, few individuals in American society so exemplify the tradition of dissent and nonconformity. Few brought more passion, intensity, exuberance, perseverance, and self-sacrifice to the causes she espoused. Even when she failed to convert people to her positions, she compelled many of them to reexamine their assumptions and to question the accepted wisdom and elected leadership.

For much of her life in America, Emma Goldman defined the limits of political dissent. True loyalty to a nation, she believed, often demanded disloyalty to its pretenses and policies and a willingness to unmask its leaders. To Goldman, liberty was more than an ideology, it was a passion, to be lived and breathed each day. "Liberty was always her theme," said Harry Weinberger, her lawyer and close friend: "liberty was always her dream; liberty was always her goal . . . liberty was more important than life itself." And, as he went on to suggest, free expression has always led a precarious existence. "She spoke out in this country against war and conscription, and went to jail. She spoke out for political prisoners, and was deported. She spoke out in Russia against the despotism of Communism, and again became a fugitive on the face of the earth. She spoke out against Nazism and the combination of Nazism and Communism and there was hardly a place where she could live."

It must be said, however, that Goldman did not speak out with equal fervor about the most repressive and violent denial of human rights in her lifetime. She identified with the struggles of oppressed workers, and the New Declaration of Independence she issued in 1909 proclaimed that "all human beings, irrespective of race, color, or sex, are born with the equal right to share at the table of life." But in a time of racist terror and severe racial subjugation (political, social, and economic), far more severe than any of the violations of civil liberties she so courageously deplored and fought, Emma Goldman avoided the South and mostly ignored the struggle for black rights and racial equality, a struggle that involved not only black Americans but a coterie of progressive white allies. Perhaps she was trying to appease the racism pervading the labor and socialist movements. More likely, she was unconscious of this contradiction in her life's commitment to "the wretched of the earth." Whatever her personal feelings about these matters, they would occupy little space in her writings or speeches, and hence are mostly absent from these volumes.

The Emma Goldman Papers Project at the University of California at Berkeley, in selecting, editing, and annotating the documents for this valuable series under the direction of Candace Falk, has brought into our historical consciousness a most extraordinary woman, whose passion, spiritual qualities, and commitments illuminate a certain time in our history, even as the lesson she taught remains timeless: that social and economic inequities are neither unintentional nor inevitable but reflect the assumptions, beliefs, and policies of certain people who command enormous power over lives. Her life forces us to think more deeply and more reflectively about those individuals in our history— from the abolitionists of the 1830s to the labor organizers of the 1890s and 1930s to the civil rights activists of the 1960s—who, individually and collectively, tried to flesh out and give meaning to abstract notions of liberty, independence, and freedom, and for whom a personal commitment to social justice became a moral imperative. No better epitaph might be written for Emma Goldman than the one composed in 1917 by A. S. Embree, an organizer for the Industrial Workers of the World imprisoned in Tombstone, Arizona: "The end in view is well worth striving for, but in the struggle itself lies the happiness of the fighter."

LEON LITWACK,
MORRISON PROFESSOR
OF AMERICAN HISTORY,
BERKELEY, CALIFORNIA

RAISING HER VOICES: An Introduction

The paper tracings of a life are by definition incomplete. Cherished letters, crumbling into dust in stray boxes, betoken the secret murmurings of relationships long gone and nearly forgotten. A public life has more permanent print markers—newspaper clippings of interviews, reportage of the give and take of political meetings, possibly even trial transcripts and government surveillance records—but these cannot capture the totality of a person's lived experience any more than correspondence or diaries can disclose the complexity of their inner life. For a historian whose research is focused upon an individual, the quest for biographical insight into issues of intimacy and love excavates hints of what in the end must remain unknowable. When the historian's subject is a self-proclaimed revolutionary anarchist, who periodically broke the law in the name of a higher cause, the print record may be even more elusive and potentially misleading. *Making Speech Free, 1902–1909,* vol. 2 of *Emma Goldman: A Documentary History of the American Years,* suggests the existence of dimensions too dangerous to fully commit to writing in Goldman's lifetime, the hidden side of her public political world. Rather than jeopardize her own safety and that of her comrades, rather than betray the trust of those of her liberal friends who subscribed to her vision of harmony and social justice but had little or no knowledge of the extent to which she supported violent tactics in her anarchist circles to hasten that process, she deliberately created an enigmatic persona—as a woman who was both a force to reckon with and a mystery to unravel. Goldman, promoter of modern drama as "the dynamite which undermines superstition," may well have been the consummate actress in a play of intrigue, casting herself simultaneously in the role of very different characters.[1] The collection of documents in *Making Speech Free, 1902–1909* reconfigures Goldman's life and work in ways that challenge previous interpretations, displaying the shadowy edges

---

1. Emma Goldman, *The Social Significance of the Modern Drama* (Boston: Richard G. Badger, 1914), p. 8. Goldman's lectures on modern drama eventually evolved into popular evening series at women's clubs and sometimes as lunch talks to coal miners. She saw in the theater the potential to reach beneath the surface, to dramatize the larger context behind each individual's seemingly insignificant decisions and actions—and to address the social prejudices that she believed crippled the spirit of openness to change.

of a new montage of light and dark that suggest she may have harbored more violent sentiments during the first decade of the twentieth century than many historians previously assumed.[2]

A DISCORDANT OVERTURE
VARIATIONS ON THE THEME OF RESILIENCE

The first volume in this documentary history of Emma Goldman—*Made for America, 1890–1901*—begins and ends with violence. It charts Goldman's political awakening in an era marked by bloodshed between the forces of labor and capital. As an immigrant radical based in New York City's Lower East Side, she allied herself with the most militant anarchists in the United States.[3]

The second volume—*Making Speech Free, 1902–1909*—opens just after the 1901 assassination of President McKinley by Leon Czolgosz. The newspapers' portrayal of the assassin as an immigrant anarchist incited by Emma Goldman's radical ideas unleashed a public thirst for revenge against these "dangerous" outsiders. Overnight, the press transformed Goldman, a slight woman in her thirties, who was developing a following as an intelligent critic of law-and-order politics and an eloquent spokesperson for anarchist ideas, into a she-devil who had inspired an act of terror.[4]

Rocked by the assassin's deafening gunshot, America spent the next years turning inward, barricading itself against perceived threats from foreign intruders. Laws were passed to gag those who dared to break the silence and keep out those deemed undesirable and dangerous. In this unstable time, the authorities intermittently tried, though often failed, to suppress even the slightest whisper of anarchism.

In the years immediately following the McKinley assassination, exasperated lawmakers chipped away at the right to freely express and propagate radical political views, arguing that such openness, especially to anarchist ideas, had left the president, and in turn the nation, vulnerable to attack. During this volatile period from 1902 to 1909, in what was regarded as political self-defense on both sides, a crucial alliance was forged

---

2. Some historians portray Goldman ultimately as a pacifist; see for example Frederick C. Griffin, *Six Who Protested: Radical Opposition to the First World War* (Port Washington, N.Y.: Kennikat Press, 1977). Others indicate that she eschewed violence after the arrest of Alexander Berkman; see editorial in *Ramparts* 10, no. 8 (February 1972); David Waldstreicher, *Emma Goldman* (New York: Chelsea House Publishers, 1990); and Kathryn Gay and Martin Gay, *The Importance of Emma Goldman* (San Diego: Lucent Books, 1992). Still others identify the use of individual violence as a consistent political tactic for achieving social change; see Cliff Hawkins, "Assassination, Self-Expression, and Social Change: Emma Goldman and Political Violence," *Anarchist Studies*, no. 7 (1999).

3. Her first alliances, in the 1890s, were with German and Jewish anarchists. Later, especially from 1906 to 1919, she would ally herself with militant Italian immigrant anarchists, even as she extended to others outside immigrant and anarchist circles.

4. See vol. 1, *Made for America, 1892–1901*, pp. 460–70. Also see introduction, vol. 1, p. 73–81, esp. pp. 73–74.

between many anarchists, socialists, and liberals[5] to uphold the principles of the First Amendment right to free speech and to prevent erosion by laws drafted in difficult times and crafted out of fear. Goldman protested the laws that banned anarchism and treated all anarchists as "criminals," laws that for the first time in the nation's history made entry into the country contingent on political ideology. She fostered temporary tangents of mutual concern, creating a braid of solidarity in adversity that would strengthen the on-going movement for free expression in America. Goldman built coalitions that overrode disparate strategies for change and permanently set the template for her integrative style of political action.

Goldman was a rebel in a social war, embedded in a culture that sanctified martyrdom, but her public weapon of choice was the spoken word. A Russian Jewish immigrant who came to America at age sixteen, she first immersed herself in the German-speaking anarchist community but determined to master the language of her adopted country. As a propagandist profoundly influenced by the radical aristocratic culture of her native revolutionary Russia, she became a translator of intention—a spokesperson for the ideals of militant anarchists in America who otherwise kept a silent distance from the respectable edges of American liberalism and the radical reformers who offered Goldman much of her financial support. The ease with which Goldman traversed seemingly contradictory political worlds is displayed throughout this volume. Originally intent on protecting anarchist speech, she became a tireless advocate of free expression for all.

BETWEEN RESPECTABLES AND OUTCASTS

"I am a rebel, a revolutionist, a heretic at heart, but my associations and background have given me a technique of life that only partially discloses it. I am always therefore, between the respectables and the outcasts, damned by sections of both."—Roger Baldwin, 1931

There is often an attraction to those who are daring—who seem unafraid to stand for that which common sense dictates as just, but from which practicality steers the cautious away. Goldman made personal connections to radicals and left liberals that made it possible for them to vicariously experience each other's way of life. In this way she created a synergy between diverse political groups, who, in friendship, validated other perspectives without compromising their own. Goldman's allegiance to militant anarchists, with whom she associated covertly, and her genuine appeal to liberal audiences, on whom she had a mollifying influence, gradually became her signature political style. During a period of

---

5. The term "liberal" encompassed a wide variety of political activists, some of whom identified most closely with the establishment (including future president Woodrow Wilson), while for others the term was conflated with free speech and radicalism. For some, "liberal" and "liberal club" were code terms for anarchists. See also entry on liberal clubs, pp. 560–61.

repression when there was good reason for anarchists to fear being crushed by the state, her bifurcated strategy for survival served Goldman and her cause well.

The capacity to be present in different worlds is to some degree critical to all who engage in public life. Meetings that address strategy are often secret, separating the organizers from the organized. Trust among those in the inner circle creates its own closeness and intensity. When backroom planning sessions included discussions of violence, Goldman's ability to divide her expressed and covert loyalties had to be refined to a high art. The consequences, if she failed, would be dire: imprisonment or worse. She protected her comrades and left few paper trails that could be used as evidence in their prosecution. Secrecy, by necessity, became a way of life—often used to wield power, specifically the power of knowledge over those not engaged in clandestine activity. By separating her worlds, Goldman stepped outside the conspiratorial tenets of anarchism while at the same time advancing its causes. Without experiencing any contradiction, she could speak, write, and fund-raise for her anarchist comrades, without revealing the full spectrum of her own roles in the theater of politics.

A compelling orator, Goldman merged politics and aesthetics. She never turned away from the grisly injustice of her times, nor was she ever far from those who believed that only with the destruction of the old was the construction of a new order possible. When state violence against strikers and their families was commonplace, when immigrants killed in labor battles were not given the dignity of a name or number, the thrust for revenge often went hand in hand with the desire for justice.

In response to repressive anti-labor and anti-immigrant sentiments and the passage of immigration laws and anti-anarchist statutes, Goldman took a public stand for free expression and gradually gathered support well beyond anarchist circles. Her whole-hearted belief that anarchism was a philosophy of life as well as of politics, with personal freedom at its center, gave Goldman an authentic voice with which to address audiences more diverse than she could have imagined when she first set foot in the United States. Her message reflected the breadth of her vision—a belief that inequality went beyond class conflict to encompass the whole person. In "The Tragedy of Woman's Emancipation" (see Essay in *Mother Earth*, March 1906), she addressed the need to engage in the long battle to free oneself from internal tyrants, the "jailers of the human spirit." And then she challenged women to relinquish the habit of subservience to men. In contrast, when addressing the most militant of her comrades at the anarchist congress in Europe in 1907, she emphasized support for terror tactics, especially with regard to the revolution brewing in Russia. When she returned to the United States, she rallied support for sending guns to Russia from the same liberal constituency that might have been appalled had they known that she also supported such tactics in their own country. Even when challenged on the subject of individual violence (an act directed at a single official perceived as an aggressor against the people), Goldman was often able to elicit sympathy and even defense funds from audiences who often opposed such political tactics but upheld the rights to a fair trial and to free speech (see, for example, "Emma Goldman Blames Police," Article in the *Chicago Tribune*, 29 March 1908). Interestingly when she addressed immigrant anarchists in her native German in the 1890s, Goldman felt free to shout insults far more militant than most she would use when lecturing to Engish-speaking audiences. When speaking to American liberals and progressives, she often cited Thomas Jefferson's belief in the necessity for a free people to exercise the right to depose tyrants and thus, she forged links between anarchism and the concept of universal freedom separate from the state and inherent in the American ideal of individual liberty.

Her work as a propagandist required tremendous personal skill and acute political instincts. Goldman was among the few who persuasively linked the private and public spheres. As she questioned the authority of existing social, political, and economic mores, she was also able to intuit and address her audiences' concerns. Very consciously, she chose to use her growing fluency in English to serve the anarchist movement—often to provide the context for the acts of those—like Czolgosz—who lacked the capacity to explain them.

In anarchist circles, intimacy—like violence—generated heated debate. As a political figure Goldman tried to shield herself from both the curious and the damning, reserving a place in her life for pleasures hidden from public gaze. Goldman, whose first commitment was to anarchism, chose never to bind herself to a lover or a child, or allow anyone to possess her. Her passionate devotion to anarchist communism, which she exalted as her "beautiful ideal," came at a price: longing secretly for a committed relationship, she could count on only fleeting moments with her lovers. Politically opposed to possessiveness but emotionally yearning for constancy in love, she felt "condemned before the bar of my own reason." An early critic of marriage, Goldman idealized free love, believing that love given in complete freedom created the strongest bonds. While her life, especially on the lecture trail, had its share of adventure and connectedness, it was also permeated with displacement and loneliness. Her vow to devote herself fully to the cause of anarchism also required what she considered a woman's ultimate sacrifice—the disavowal of motherhood, her "most glorious privilege."[6] The infusion of the personal with the political created an authenticity and powerful resonance also in Goldman's writings. The narrative that she created of her life in her autobiography, and in many of her interviews with the press, is however distinctly different from the documentary evidence presented in these volumes. Her distinct cadences appear side by side in this book, exposing multifaceted truths and fictions and inviting new interpretations of Goldman's life.

In some of her earliest essays written in German in 1893 for her own community of

---

6. For Goldman's praise of motherhood, see "The Tragedy of Woman's Emancipation," Essay in *Mother Earth*, March 1906.

mostly Russian Jewish and German anarchists, Goldman lashes out vituperatively at the police, the government, capitalists, and emergent imperialists. Although some of the essays published later in her magazine, *Mother Earth,* carried a militant message, others written to reach a wider American audience placed more emphasis on her social critique. These discrepancies exemplify Goldman's agile political balancing act. Her correspondence during these years also ranges from straightforward requests for funds or attendance at her meetings to communiques written in code to escape the gaze of prison and post office censors. Letters written during the late 1920s reveal the extent of Goldman's links to clandestine activities and violence.[7] Also included in this second volume are complex political tracts addressing differences of opinion among anarchists. Goldman's many voices reverberate through this volume, with her growing attempts to reach out to left liberals sympathetic to her desire to make speech free.

Goldman's capacity to bridge disparate worlds evolved most strongly from 1902 to 1909 as she attempted to safeguard a place for dissent. During this period, both free speech rights and the development of anarchism in America were shaped in part by laws barring entry to those who identified with anarchist ideas. Goldman became a go-between, able to exercise her oratorical skills across the continents. At the same time, her effectiveness as an organizer began to reap rewards, reinforcing patterns of political behavior and private life that had only just begun to take form.

Goldman's political orientation, and its life consequences, provided the vantage point from which to see the underside of the Progressive era, generally described as an age of liberal reform against corporate abuse, of protective legislation, and of heightened sensitivity to injustice. The documents in *Making Speech Free* reveal a time when the struggle for tolerance and protection against corporate greed and labor abuse was waged most daringly, not only by lawmakers and labor unions through strikes and negotiations, but paradoxically by lawbreakers on the margin, like the anarchist Emma Goldman.[8]

THE LURE OF FREEDOM AND SPECTER OF ANTI-ANARCHIST IMMIGRATION LEGISLATION

Free expression—an ideal encoded in the U.S. Constitution, draped in the American flag, and waved across the seas—attracted political exiles and bestowed dignity to free-born citizens. And yet within the country's own borders, a constant battle raged to prevent the

---

7. See for example EG to AB (22 July 1927), *EGP,* reel 18 (also in Alexander Berkman Archive, IISH), in which she discusses Claus Timmerman's knowledge of the plot to kill Frick; and Modest Stein to EG (20 September 1929), *EGP,* reel 21 (also in Alexander Berkman Archive, IISH), regarding his plan to finish up Berkman's failed attempt to assassinate Frick (instead, an informer foiled the plan, forcing Stein to hide out at Robert Reitzel's house in Detroit).

8. Anarchists and other activists and lawyers who fought for economic and social justice included Clarence Darrow and Edgar Lee Masters (for the Turner case), and Lincoln Steffens, Gilbert Roe, and Theodore Schroeder, all three members of the Free Speech League.

banner of free speech from becoming a meaningless mantle protecting only the most conformist political and cultural views.

Among the hundreds of thousands who sought refuge in America at the beginning of the twentieth century, political exiles in particular found a country gripped by fear and a government intent on banishing them for the very same convictions that drew them to its shores. Within the "huddled masses yearning to breathe free,"[9] those refugees who had fled political repression against anarchism and sailed toward the welcoming figure of the Statue of Liberty would soon be barred for harboring forbidden ideas.

In 1901, Leon Czolgosz, an American citizen born in Detroit of Polish immigrants and a self-proclaimed anarchist, assassinated William F. McKinley, the president of the United States. Politicians immediately conjured up threatening images of foreign anarchists forcing their way into an otherwise idyllic land of the free. By the following year, in a frantic attempt to heal the festering national wound left by the assassin's bullet and to assuage the American public's sense of vulnerability and undercurrent of rage, the U.S. Congress passed laws designed to protect the nation from the threat of further political violence.[10] Legislators, especially in New York, the nation's principal port of entry for immigrants, rushed to stockpile anti-anarchist statutes. At the federal level, a restrictive new immigration law targeting anarchists was cast as a barricade against future harm—with seemingly little awareness that the attraction to anarchism for many of those already in the country was a direct response to the perceived injustice and violence of America.

The legal firewall against the threat of individual acts of violence was intended to repel all anarchists—whether or not they advocated individual acts of terror. The new laws thus left those who identified only with the social theories of anarchism as vulnerable as those who in fact believed in (and perhaps practiced) violence. Such laws further threatened to erode the free speech of nearly everyone who dared to question the justness of the nation's social, political, or economic organization. Although the First Amendment to the U.S. Constitution prohibited the making of laws to restrict free speech, at this time the courts offered few meaningful protections for the enforcement of this right. For immigrants, entitlement to such rights was tentative, irregularly honored both within and at the point of entry to America's borders. The passage of legislation barring the admission of alien anarchists to the United States immediately burst open national boundaries to the struggle for free speech. And, even through anarchist literature was readily available, without a steady flow of lecturers to breathe life into the latest developments in anarchist political thought from Europe, the law arguably altered the evolution of anarchism in America. Whether anarchist ideas—which posited social harmony without government and the destruction of the old as the prerequisite for the construction of a new social order—could be contained, kept out, or quarantined would remain a contested arena in

---

9. See Emma Lazarus's poem, "The New Colossus," inscribed at the foot of the Statue of Liberty in New York City's harbor.

10. See introduction, vol. 1, p. 75, for observations on similar reactions following the Haymarket affair.

the world of law and order, far beyond the parameters of Emma Goldman's life, to be challenged over time again and again.

STEPPING BACK

In 1902 Emma Goldman was thirty-three years old and still reeling from the political aftershocks of the assassination the previous autumn. No longer protrayed as "an eloquent woman"[11] whose style was both emotionally and intellectually evocative, she was cast as a dangerous public enemy. Suddenly this compelling advocate of anarchist ideas and biting critic of the hypocrisy of the politics of law and order was subjected to a level of political persecution she had never imagined before. Within days of the 6 September 1901 assassination of President McKinley by a man she barely knew, the newspapers printed an unsubstantiated claim that Goldman had colluded in Czolgosz's act. They claimed that the lecture in which she expressed admiration for those who took it upon themselves to avenge political wrongs especially rife in Europe at the time had been his determining catalyst.[12]

It wasn't that she didn't remember, just four months prior to the McKinley assassination, delivering a provocative talk in that crowded Cleveland auditorium where the would-be assassin evidently hung on her words; nor did she deny her respect for the particular kind of courage it took to actually pull the trigger and face whatever punishment the state might mete out for such a violent act.[13] She had admired since her youth the courageous revolutionary heroes and heroines of Russian novels and had been galvanized by the martyrdom of the Haymarket anarchists—whose executions marked her political birth.[14] She too had pledged her life to the struggle for spiritual, political, social, and economic freedom.

In 1892, as a young activist in her twenties inspired by the spirit of those she considered to be martyrs of the 1886 Haymarket affair, Goldman and her comrade-lovers Alexander Berkman and Modest Stein literally sealed a pact in blood to devote themselves to the cause of anarchism and to die, if necessary, in its pursuit.[15] Later in that fateful year, Pinkerton guards shot striking workers at a steel plant in Homestead, Pennsylvania. With a sense of urgency, the threesome and others, including Claus Timmerman, the editor of *Der Anarchist*, conspired to avenge the laborers' deaths. Berkman went to the Homestead plant where he wounded but did not suceed in his attempt to kill the company manager,

---

11. See vol. 1, p. 95, for an early newspaper reference to Goldman's eloquence.
12. See "Defends Acts of Bomb Throwers," Article in the *Cleveland Plain Dealer*, 6 May 1901, vol. 1, pp. 452–54, and introduction, vol. 1, p. 73, for context on her talk "Modern Phases of Anarchy" delivered in Cleveland in May 1901.
13. See, for example, Goldman's essays in vol. 1: "Gaetano Bresci," pp. 455–56, and "The Tragedy at Buffalo," pp. 471–77.
14. See Paul Avrich, *The Haymarket Tragedy* (Princeton: Princeton University Press, 1984).
15. *Living My Life* (reprint, New York: Dover Publications, 1970), p. 62; pagination of 1970 edition replicates 1931 edition of Goldman's autobiography (abbreviated hereafter as *LML*). See also introduction, vol. 1, p. 22, on their ménage à trois.

Henry Clay Frick—an accident of fate that saved not only Frick's life but also Berkman's. Goldman, who was accused but not charged as his accomplice, remained unflinchingly loyal to her jailed comrade. As she found her own political voice, she raised it in praise of those who risked their lives for the freedom of others. Still, it is unlikely that years later, in 1901, she meant to incite a young man in her audience to kill the president of the United States, but nonetheless, given her history, it was not an unreasonable assumption and drew international attention to the power of her oratorical skills and the threatening underside of her political message.

When she broached the complex subject of political violence on the lecture platform the young, attractive Goldman's mix of sexuality and aggression terrified not only those wary of anarchism but also those accustomed to relegating women to the background of political debate. Never malleable, accommodating, or passive, she defied conventional constructs of womanhood. Though flirtatious, her charm had an edge: she excited her audience and taunted them with her cultural-political dares. As a Russian Jewish immigrant and anarchist living in the hotbed of radicalism in New York City, the threat she posed to the country's growing nativism loomed larger as the fear of Eastern Europeans coalesced after the president's assassination. Wrongly accused, Goldman nevertheless would be linked forever to the act that took the life of America's chief executive—and it would take years to wipe away the tarnish of this disturbing association from her name.

PROTECTING THE THORNY EDGES OF FREE EXPRESSION

In the aftermath of the McKinley assassination—with newspapers stories day after day delving into the mysteries of anarchism—the public thirsted for the blood of those who espoused tactics known as "propaganda by the deed." Some within the anarchist ranks (including Goldman and Max Baginski at the International Anarchist Congress in Amsterdam in 1907) construed the press attention as positive exposure (regardless of its outcome) for inadvertently raising the visibility of their ideas. Nonetheless, it was the most nightmarish episode of Goldman's life.[16] Goldman recognized the horrors of political violence, no matter which side perpetuates it, no matter how satisfying the pleasure of revenge. She was terrified by the experience of being demonized and targeted as the designated muse of an assassin—and feared for her life as the angry mob searched for a person to blame rather than a system of injustice to transform.

Goldman survived the emotional challenges of this time in part by tapping into what she considered the resilience of her Jewish race. She also had the shield of a small circle of comrades from a variety of nationalities reconstituted themselves as a chosen family— including Alexander Berkman who, even behind bars, remained her closest comrade; Max Baginski, who would later co-found the magazine *Mother Earth* with her; and Ed Brady, her intermittent lover and mentor. This constellation of like-minded revolutionary friends cushioned her from loneliness, enlivened her with the force of their convictions,

16. See *LML*, pp. 295–320 for more detail; see also introduction, vol. 1, pp. 73–77.

and anchored her amidst the storms and political turmoil of the times, sparking her love and affection.

Tucked into the intricate fabric of the Lower East Side's neighborhood enclave of Russian Jews and German radicals, Goldman had forged her place. Hungry for knowledge, she read incessantly—in German, Russian, Yiddish, and in the English of her adopted country—expanding her understanding of the intellectual and literary traditions of a variety of cultures as one who hoped to become an integrating force between immigrant and native-born Americans in their struggle for economic and social justice. Her contemporaries recognized her among the great humanitarians of her time, while Goldman's favorite humanitarians of the nineteenth century evinced a rare blend of cultures and included writers, anarchists, activists, and abolitionists, heroes and heroines from France, Russia, and America. Her guiding spirits included prominent European-born anarchists Louise Michel, Élisée Reclus, Peter Kropotkin, Catherine Breshkovskaya, Albert Parsons, Alexander Berkman, and Vera Figner, as well as prominent figures in America's political history including John Brown, William Lloyd Garrison, and Henry David Thoreau.[17]

Goldman, who admired and emulated many of the great anarchist orators of her time, was acutely aware of the potential hazards of new laws proposed in Congress that would deny entry to all foreign anarchists and thereby also deprive her movement access to Europe's most eloquent anarchist speakers, including Errico Malatesta and Louise Michel. Only a few years earlier, the visiting Russian anarchist theorist Peter Kropotkin was among the most sought after lecturers in the United States. The danger the American anarchist movement would face if new restrictions succeeded in curtailing the flow of anarchist ideas across the continents prompted Goldman to lift her voice on behalf of anarchists like Kropotkin, who were now barred from America's shores for their political ideals—and silenced by absence—although their works in print were easily accessible.

Goldman, who had been arrested in 1893 for urging the poor and unemployed to take bread as their sacred right, and who upon her release from almost a year in prison had proclaimed jokingly that no court order could ever stop women from talking, mounted her next major legal battle in 1903 in defense of alien anarchists' right to political speech. But first she would have to fight her own desperate battle for free speech.

LIVING IN THE WAKE OF THE McKINLEY ASSASSINATION

Absolved of any prosecutable guilt by association, Goldman acted as if she had never met Czolgosz (even though he had attended her lecture, asked for advice on good anarchist

---

17. Vera Figner (1852–1943), a Russian anarchist and member of Narodnaya Volya, was involved in planning the 1881 assassination of Alexander II. In his *Symposium on Humanitarians,* Victor Robinson describes Goldman as "by all odds the most famous Anarchist in America . . . a very brainy woman . . . powerful orator . . . for the last three years she has been publishing *Mother Earth*" (New York: The Altrurians, 1909, p. 21). Alexander Berkman's list of humanitarian influences begins with Karl Marx, Élisée Reclus, Robert Owen, Henrik Ibsen, Louise Michel, Errico Malatesta, Peter Kropotkin, Sophia Perovskaya, William Lloyd Garrison, and ends with Emma Goldman.

books to read, and was among those who had accompanied her to the train station in Chicago not long before his deadly act). Informal contact with all varieties of anarchists and radicals was not unusual for one who traveled widely and addressed so many audiences across the country—and yet in this case, it was not until 1906 that Goldman would risk even a hint at her scant acquaintance with McKinley's assassin. Goldman, who recognized and spoke of Czolgosz as a troubled young man ("a soul in pain . . . impractical," "inexpedient, lacking in caution") yet considered him an extraordinarily rational and sensitive martyr in the service of justice to whom she could not "help but bow in reverenced silence." She found herself genuinely fearful of the public's insidious thirst for revenge.[18]

Arrested and denied contact with friends and family, Goldman was besieged by an avalanche of hate letters in jail.[19] Angry accusations seared into her memory: "You damn bitch of an anarchist," one of them read; "I wish I could get at you. I would tear your heart out and feed it to my dog." "Murderous Emma Goldman," another wrote; "you will burn in hell-fire for your treachery to our country." A third sadistically promised: "We will cut your tongue out, soak your carcass in oil, and burn you alive." Others expressed perverted sexual fantasies that Goldman suspected "would have astounded authorities on the subject."[20] Upon her release from her two weeks in jail, she continued to be hounded by a faceless public desperate to vent their anger and assuage their fears. Unable to use her own name in the open, she disguised her identity and stayed close to friends she knew and trusted. Vulnerable to attack by those who held her guilty and feared everything she represented, it was clear that the struggle ahead was not only for her political survival, but also for her own life.[21] Whatever spirit of openness associated with the Progressive

18. For further details on the contact between EG and Czolgosz, see Max Baginski, "Leon Czolgosz, Stray Leaves in Commemoration of the 29th October 1901," *Mother Earth*, October 1906, pp. 4–9; also see note 1 to "Defends Acts of Bomb Throwers," Article in the *Cleveland Plain Dealer*, 6 May 1901, vol. 1, p. 452. For one of EG's descriptions of Czolgosz, see her "The Tragedy at Buffalo," Essay in *Free Society*, 6 October 1901, vol. 1, p. 476.

19. Thirty years later, Goldman would recount in her autobiography the severe personal cost of being implicated in the assassination of President McKinley. Even though no sustainable legal grounds existed for her arrest, she endured a tremendous public outpouring of ostracism and personal attacks. And yet, Czolgosz's fatal act did occur four months after he attended Goldman's powerful public lecture in praise of the personal courage of anarchists who sacrificed themselves by taking individual "action" against representatives of injustice, and three months after he read Goldman's essay in *Free Society* (2 June 1901) praising Gaetano Bresci, the Italian American anarchist who assassinated King Umberto of Italy to avenge victims of repression. Only a week before Czolgosz's act, C. L. James published "The Monster Slayer" in *Free Society* (1 September 1901). This sequence raised legitimate questions about the impact of inflammatory spoken and written political speech. And in the face of a government desperate to legislate law and order, it flags the principled courage of those who strongly disagreed with Goldman's ideas but upheld her right to express them.

20. *LML*, p. 301.

21. Along with such death threats, Goldman realized that her life might be in danger when her comrades at *Freie Arbeiter Stimme* were attacked by an angry mob just after the McKinley assassination, and others, like Guiseppi Ciancabilla, the editor of *L'Aurora* in Springfield, Illinois, were run out of town.

era—in 1901 and 1902 Goldman experienced the complex undercurrents of violence fueling both government reform and labor militancy.

TORTUROUS INTROSPECTION

McKinley's assassination tested Goldman's stamina, leaving her vulnerable to her own inner demons and a feeling of emptiness during her brief incarceration. For Goldman this period of relative inactivity loomed like a dark cloud over her life. She lamented even the slightest temptation to succumb to despair as tantamount to a betrayal of her comrades and herself. Plagued by the unsettling feeling that she had "left the movement at its most critical moment, had turned my back on our work when I was most needed, that I had begun to doubt my life's faith and ideal,"[22] she set the lives of those who had martyred themselves for the anarchist cause as a standard by which to judge all others. In contrast to the regrets and self-castigation she expressed in her autobiography, at the actual time of the assassination, she focused on Czolgosz's state of mind—on his compulsion to assassinate President McKinley. In retrospect, she wondered whether Czolgosz may in fact have been provoked to prove his loyalty to anarchism; he may have read a notice in *Free Society* warning its readers that his general behavior, based on word from a comrade in Detroit about Czolgosz's many insistent queries about guns, was suspicious enough to warrant posting a government spy alert. This notice also casts doubt on *Free Society*'s editors, who may have been covering their own complicity by the charade of distancing themselves from one who possibly acted in concert with their ideas. Yet, in spite of her awareness of the political complexity of the circumstances surrounding his *attentat* and her public acknowledgment at the time that Czolgosz appeared to some anarchists as having an uneasy nervous manner, in her 1901 essay "The Tragedy at Buffalo" reprinted in October 1906 in *Mother Earth,* she would label his "crime" the result of "too sensitive a social consciousness." By the time she wrote her autobiography, she linked Czolgosz's sacrifice to the deaths of the Haymarket anarchists, who had always been her beacon: "The qualities I had most admired in the heroes of the past, and also in Czolgosz, the strength to stand and die alone, had been lacking in me. Perhaps one needs more courage to live than to die. Dying is of a moment, but the claims of life are endless—a thousand small and petty things which tax one's strength and leave one too spent to meet the testing hour." Although her retreat from the podium in the face of repression—only for a few months—may have been a prerequisite for her political and personal survival in that horrible time, Goldman emerged from her "torturous introspection as from a long illness, not yet in possession of my former vigour, but with a determination to try once more to steel my will to meet the exigencies of life, whatever they might be."[23]

22. *LML,* p. 329.
23. *LML,* pp. 329–30. Goldman's memory of this time was one of great inner torment, although the documents in vol. 2 track only her outer resilience and defiant determination, and include an invitation from the Manhattan Liberal Club, whose commitment to free expression spurred them to ask the

RAISING THEIR VOICES IN PROTEST

Given the level of labor violence and repression that followed the McKinley assassination, it is fitting that vol. 2 begins with a talk Goldman prepared but never delivered to Italian American silk workers, on strike and under attack, in Paterson, New Jersey. Translated into Italian and published in *La Questione Sociale,* her address rails at the widespread prejudice against immigrant anarchists whose labor activism left them vulnerable to violent reprisals by government militias, with all too few native-born citizens raising their voices in protest (see "To the Strikers of Paterson," 5 July 1902, in *La Questione Sociale*). Later, in her autobiography, she explained her sudden decision not to speak to the striking silk workers in Paterson as a response to a traumatic nightmare she had the night before in which she imagined that as she spoke the sea of people that comprised her audience were suddenly engulfed and swept away, leaving her alone on the platform. A giant apparition moved ominously toward her. As it came closer, in shock she recognized it as the ghost of Czolgosz, who had been electrocuted, and shouted his name. Awakened, disturbed, and in a sweat, Goldman took this dream as a strong premonition that she should stay away from Paterson.[24] Succumbing to such fears was highly uncharacteristic for Goldman, and thus raises the possibility that this account in the autobiography may not have revealed the full story. In her memoir she admitted that when she found out that William MacQueen and Rudolph Grossman, her anarchist comrades who had invited her to address the striking workers, were arrested, she felt ashamed to have allowed a nightmare to intimidate her. Her autobiography recorded her belief that Czolgosz was pressured by a prison guard to confess to Goldman's collusion in his act.[25] Goldman struggled to free herself from the residues of guilt she associated with Czolgosz's rushed electrocution and the accompanying accusations that she had inspired him.

Yet she defended Czolgosz's act and continued to assert, in the spirit of the German philosopher Max Stirner, that "Anarchism claims the right of Defence against Invasion and Aggression of every shape and form and no one, who has his eyes open will and can deny that those in Power are the Invadors."[26] Thus when she found herself thrust into an awkward correspondence with a psychiatrist who labeled Czolgosz clinically insane, invalidating the veracity of his connection to anarchism, Goldman challenged this judgment, claiming that Czolgosz assassinated the president in self-defense, as the act of one of "the Exploited and Disinherited Millions, who lead a life of darkness . . . one of the Victims of the McKinley regime" (see Letter to Walter Channing, 18 October 1902).

---

controversial Goldman to speak in their lecture series in October 1901, shortly after President McKinley's death. See also the original text of "The Tragedy at Buffalo," vol. 1, pp. 471–78.

24. *LML,* p. 328. This account, so vividly portrayed in Goldman's autobiography, is not directly recorded in the documents in vol. 2.

25. *LML,* p. 317.

26. Based on Stirner's idea that "every personal invasion of another's sphere revolts the civic sense"; see *The Ego and His Own* (reprint, New York: Dover Publications, 1973), p. 108.

Provocative comments that sought to justify revenge by the victims of Russian brutality set the stage for a Chicago lecture in which two hundred policemen lined the halls, as she bewailed to the audience of mostly Russian Jews—already experiencing a clampdown on their freedoms, a feeling of being watched, and scapegoated—that America was "fast being Russianized," and that even native-born citizens would feel its effects. Even though her message may have been melodramatic, her experiences with repression as an immigrant prompted her to warn others that it would not be long until such meetings would take place "in cellars, or in darkened back rooms with closed doors, and [we will have to] speak in whispers lest our next door neighbors should hear that free-born American citizens dare not speak in the open." With these pressing caveats in mind, she called upon "all advanced people [to] unite in protesting against such brutal invasion . . . to maintain the right of freedom of speech, of press and of assembly" (see "Free Speech in Chicago," in *Lucifer, the Lightbearer,* 30 November 1902). Not cowed by the police show of force, Goldman led the festivities, including a round of the revolutionary songs of the Paris commune and the raffle of a portrait of the Russian anarchist and pacifist author Leo Tolstoy.[27]

Goldman stepped back to the political podium in January 1902, in a world that had been shaken by assassinations, the revolution fomenting in Russia, and by violent strikes, intent on playing a role in leading the mounting public outrage about the "Russification" of America. In November 1902, she was summarily warned by a Chicago police officer as he prevented her from speaking at one of her many scheduled talks,[28] acting on a common concern of conservatives and liberals alike that her critique of Russia should not seep into the soil of her adopted country: "Say what you please about Russia, but you must not attack OUR institutions."

For her comrades in Russia and her friends at home, the harsh rule of the Tsar, marked by the violent quelling of student, worker, and peasant protests, bred fierce reactions. The vicious pogrom in Kishinev during Easter 1903 with its murder of forty-seven Russian Jews, injury to over ninety others, and looting of hundreds of Jewish homes and shops, led to similar horrors across southern Russia. The atrocities wrought a small militant subculture among Jews there—most of whom had a cultural-political critique of religious orthodoxy. They became drawn to the most violent edge of the revolutionary movement,

27. See "Police Eyes on Anarchy," *Chicago Tribune,* 17 November 1902, *EGP,* reel 47. Tolstoy had eschewed his attachment to his renowned novels *War and Peace* and *Anna Karenina,* seeking instead to write stories and novels that promoted the values of Christian anarchism—and thus became a symbol of anarchist pacifism.
28. See chronology entries in both vols. 1 and 2 for account of talks by Goldman suppressed by the police or other local officials.

creating a core of anarchists and socialist revolutionaries for whom terror against terror had become the strategy of choice. To most Americans, including conservatives, whose sense of superiority rested on the belief that free speech and the right of dissent were the distinguishing hallmarks of their country, the violence against protest movements in Russia represented everything they despised.

With split loyalties between the United States and Russia, Goldman identified with the American ethos of freedom and casual social openness (in stark contrast to the repressiveness of its laws) but valued her birthright's link to the revolutionary and literary tradition of Mother Russia—in spite of her homeland's long history of anti-Semitism. Goldman's attraction to anarchism was in part rooted in a Jewish culture that survived by adopting clandestine ways of practicing its religion, by maintaining its distinct identity through a cohesive system of beliefs ballasted by the study of critical texts and a lively tradition of questioning authority that eschewed reliance on the governance of a nation state. As a girl she admired the biblical Judith, who cut off the head of the tyrant Holofernes to avenge the wrongs of her people. Goldman, who cared deeply about the wrongs committed around her, believed that freedom for one depended upon freedom for all and that every instance of injustice had a ripple effect on others, especially in Russia. Goldman's closest comrade, Alexander Berkman, asserted that, although there was lots of "talk of government-incited riots," he and Goldman knew from their own experience in Russia "that the hatred of Jews is a deep-set R[ussian] instinct" and impossible to erase through "a mere constitution." He predicted that it would take "two or more generations of real enlightenment and education to eradicate the long-inbred racial prejudices of the R[ussian] peasant." And yet he believed that "The only real salvation of the R[ussian] Jew lies in the Liberty of R[ussia]" (see Letter from Alexander Berkman, 11 February 1906). With remarkable self-knowledge, Berkman articulated the plight of men and women who like himself and Goldman live with a vision of a grander future within the confines of present possibility.

Goldman shared the general outrage against the despotism of the tsarist regime and focused her efforts on the parallels to anti-labor violence in America without acknowledging that the free-wheeling police repression—though devastating rarely matched the vicious racist lynchings in America and the day-to-day experience of African Americans—nor did she call attention to the fact that the experience of white Americans paled in comparison to the brutality and lack of recourse in Russia. Although American freedoms were unevenly protected, on the whole the most horrific violations of free speech in the United States were quite different in nature from the pogroms and the generalized terror in Russia. Among the many causes she championed, Goldman warned audiences of the horrors that crushed the lives of workers in American factories and mines, whose labor struggles were disregarded and whose deaths were barely reported in the news.

The characterization of Russia as a country gripped by a despotic regime supplied Goldman with an easy foil for dramatic comparisons between repression in Russia and in the United States. Like the canary in the mine, she believed that if her voice was silenced, others' would be too.

"CRIMINAL ANARCHY" DEFINED

New York state in 1902 was the first to pass anti-anarchist laws. Federal immigration law would incorporate the spirit of such state laws, while municipal authorities did so informally. New York took the lead because it was the state where McKinley's assassination took place and because the city of New York received the country's largest influx of immigrants. A New York criminal anarchy act made it a felony to express "by word of mouth or writing" the "doctrine that organized government should be overthrown by force or violence, or by assassination of the executive head or of any of the executive officials of government, or by any unlawful means."[29]

The passage of this law provoked Goldman to educate the public and to expand their understanding of anarchism and of free speech. On her lecture tour in 1903, she challenged her audiences' prevalent and narrow misconceptions of anarchism by repeating a variant of her talk "Modern Phases of Anarchism," which addressed aspects of anarchism, clarifying each position simply and coherently. With this strategy, Goldman clung to her legal right to discuss the philosophical underpinnings of anarchist ideas and, by so doing, indirectly challenged any ban on open advocacy of militant anarchist tactics.

Goldman found it increasingly difficult to book space for her lectures. Intimidated owners of lecture halls chose to give up revenue from Goldman's speaking events rather than risk punishment at the hands of the new law that levied two years of imprisonment and fines of up to $2,000 for the "crime" of facilitating anarchist speech.[30] The hall keepers' legitimate fear of police harassment and large fines for renting Goldman a speaking venue added a new level of vulnerability to her lecture career. Previously, her talks had often been thwarted primarily by arrests ordered by mayors and police chiefs. Now she also was faced by landlords who refused to rent halls to the noted anarchist. Thus in these years, Goldman's habit of carrying a good book into the lecture halls to offset the possibility of long nights in jail with nothing to read, served her well.

During these repressive months and years following the McKinley assassination, Goldman could not even rely on a secure home base. In April 1902, her landlord evicted her from her First Street apartment. By January 1903, public sentiment against anarchists was so pervasive that, in New York City, police arrested Goldman and Max Baginski, the German-born anarchist-communist editor, just "on general principles."[31]

---

29. Criminal Anarchy Law, sec. 468-a, passed 3 April 1902. See also Theodore Schroeder, *The Criminal Anarchy Law and On Suppressing the Advocacy of Crime* (New York: Mother Earth Publishing Association, 1907).
30. Criminal Anarchy Law, sec. 468-e.
31. Max Baginski would serve as Goldman's first editor on her magazine *Mother Earth,* from March 1906 to March 1907.

Shortly after anti-anarchist legislation was enacted in New York state, Congress adopted even more sweeping national anti-anarchist legislation codifying America's rising anti-immigrant impulses and adding a new dimension to existing exclusion laws.[32] In 1903, Congress officially barred entry to alien anarchists—mandating that all immigrants swear upon arrival that their political persuasion was not anarchism.[33] Defining "anarchist" narrowly and in its most pejorative sense, according to the first edition of *Century Dictionary*'s interpretation, Section 2 of the Immigration Act of 3 March 1903 excluded from the country anarchists or any other persons who believed in the overthrow of government (even outside the United States), categorizing them with criminals, the insane, diseased, mentally retarded, polygamists, and "paupers." Another segment, Section 38, denied admission not only to those who advocated the violent overthrow of the state but also to those who did not believe in or were opposed to "organized government" or were affiliated with any group holding these tenets. As with the 1902 New York Criminal Anarchy Act, in practice purely philosophical anarchists who entertained such ideas only in the abstract were rarely prosecuted.

The 1903 Immigration Act had moved swiftly through Congress, in hopes of filtering out alien anarchists from the flood of immigrants entering the country. The law was rooted in part in an erroneous belief that assassins were never American citizens (although in fact Czolgosz had been born in the United States) and that only the impoverished and uneducated would be drawn to anarchism, especially those who were vulnerable to envy, suspicion, and the hatred of order from which it was presumed that anarchism sprang. Theodore Roosevelt, President McKinley's successor, in late 1901 and early 1902, endorsed this legislation in order to limit U.S. entry to those immigrants believed capable of appreciating and living by the standards set by American institutions.[34] Well aware that these new laws could not easily keep out immigrants he categorized as the intellectual criminal class, Roosevelt focused his efforts on those he considered more susceptible to anarchist ideas. In his December 1903 State of the Union address

32. A congressional law proposed by David Hill in August 1894 didn't pass, in part because of discomfort at designating an abstract political idea rather than conduct as grounds for exclusion. Despite the pervasive anti-radical undercurrent in Congress, this bill stirred conflict over the issue of fairness owing to the lack of a uniform definition of an anarchist that could encompass both ideas and practices.

33. Government representatives anxious to display their power to quell the public's fears pulled one of many defeated proposals out of the legislative dustbin, modified it slightly and placed it back on the floor; the Ray bill was passed with very little debate.

34. Among the many proposals debated on the Senate floor in 1902 was one to include a clause intended to deter future assassinations—judging all threats on a president's life, whether or not they succeeded, as treasonous acts punishable by death. During the debate, Senator Hawley declared publicly that he "would give a thousand dollars to get a shot at an anarchist." Voltairine de Cleyre, the renowned anarchist, offered herself as a target, free of charge, suggesting that if he really wanted to pay such a high price he might consider giving it directly to anarchist propaganda. Many in Congress raised serious

he called anarchism "criminal . . . seditious and treasonable"—barring entry to the most indigent immigrant-hopefuls by mandating payment of a "head tax" (the distinguishing element of the law for which it was later known) and weeding out the illiterate with a stringent written entrance exam.

ALIEN ANARCHISTS AND THE TURNER CASE

The first application of the provision of the 1903 Immigration Act,[35] barring admission to foreign anarchists, occurred within six months of its passing and elicited a small but significant battle for free expression that would curb its enforcement. Apart from the intimidation factor of a law that required all to answer the question of whether they practiced anarchy or polygamy, immigrant anarchists generally declined to reveal their actual political persuasion. Because the coordination of entry and exit visas from one country to another was inconsistent, either for lack of sophisticated surveillance techniques or for actual disagreement about the validity of the law among its enforcers, anarchists (even assassins) generally had no problem coming to the United States. But for those who were well-known speakers who could draw a broad following in the United States, like anarchist Peter Kropotkin,[36] the doors were definitely barred. In fact, in an age in which ideas were most forcefully conveyed on the speakers' platform, a law that guaranteed the exclusion of Europe's most persuasive and sophisticated voices of anarchism placed an enormous burden of responsibility on Emma Goldman to synthesize the thinking of anarchists abroad and bring them to America. Had the law been in place years earlier, the prominent German-born anarchist speaker and theorist Johann Most[37] would never have been allowed to enter the country; nor could he have helped establish the firm base of German American anarchists or brought a strong militant strand of European anarchist ideas to the United States. Goldman, in some sense a home-grown anarchist,

---

questions about whether a law mandating uniform punishment regardless of the outcome implicitly favored the life of a high official over that of a private citizen. Congress ultimately considered this attempt to secure heightened protection for the president too "un-American"—too reminiscent of British protective measures to safeguard the royal family—and thus dropped it from the broader anti-anarchist legislative proposal. Except for the special provision to safeguard the life of the president, the language recommended on the floor to bar entry to alien anarchists in the Immigration Act of 1903 was adopted almost verbatim from the Ray bill passed in the House in 1902, just after the McKinley assassination.

35. Sec. 38, Immigration Act of 3 March 1903 (32 Statutes-at-Large 1213).
36. Kropotkin had toured America in 1897 and 1901. EG helped arrange several of his New York meetings during the 1901 tour. He was, in many respects, Goldman's primary ideological mentor. See Paul Avrich, "Kropotkin in America," *Anarchist Portraits* (Princeton, N.J.: Princeton University Press, 1988).
37. Johann Most, editor of *Freiheit*, formerly had been Goldman's mentor and lover. He and Goldman fell into mutual disagreement on issues of anarchist tactics for change, especially diverging on the efficacy of Berkman's *attentat*. See introduction, vol. 1, pp. 18–19, for more detail on Most's influence on EG, and *LML*, esp. pp. 29–30, 38–40, 53–54, 62–66, 76, 77.

whose citizenship papers were acquired through her ex-husband, was not subject to this law, although various government agents would do everything in their power to find a way to use it against her.[38]

John Turner was a choice subject for contesting the anti-anarchist clause of the Immigration Act of 1903. Turner had lectured widely in the United States in 1896, relatively unhindered. He was a cultured Englishman "of semi-Quaker descent"[39] and an anarcho-syndicalist who believed in the general strike and the necessity for labor to overthrow capitalism, but he did not advocate assassination. Turner, who was recruited by Goldman, claimed to have come to the United States on vacation, purportedly to give occasional organizing advice to retail clerks based on his experience with the Amalgamated Shop Assistants Union in England. Goldman, in fact, had arranged many of his meetings during his previous trip and thus learned the critical skills of road tour management. She knew that it was much easier to elicit outrage at the ill-treatment of an English-speaking lecturer in the United States, where many were still in thrall to the gentility of the British, than it would have been to muster equal enthusiasm for the defense of a German- or Italian-speaking lecturer.[40]

The Turner case tapped into a particularly potent cultural embarrassment, especially by exposing an unwarranted use of force in the arrest of an Englishman. Turner described the brutish manner in which he—who came from a country where police rarely carried guns—was taken into custody after a lecture in which he had identified himself an anarchist. At first he was herded into "a patrol wagon filled with armed attendants." Later, at Ellis Island, he was "taken down to the basement of the immigration station and locked in the center one of three cages . . . like those for wild animals in a zoological garden, with open bars back as well as front, a cement floor and a pair of rungs . . . strong enough to hold an elephant, and guarded night and day." Some perceived such treatment as absurd excess and reason enough to rally the Free Speech League to Turner's case.

---

38. Targeting anarchism was an insidious part of the 1903 Immigration Act, which would later be transformed to bar whatever political persuasion was deemed most threatening to the security of the nation. Also see two government documents: P. S. Chambers to Richard K. Campbell, 18 March 1908, and P. S. Chambers to Charles J. Bonaparte, 22 April 1909; both in *EGP*, reel 56.

39. John Turner, "The Protest of an Anarchist," in *The Independent*, 24 December 1903.

40. The German anarchist Johann Most, for example, had been prosecuted in 1901 under art. 575 of the New York state penal code and defended by socialist lawyer and labor activist Morris Hillquit, for publishing an article tending to disturb the public peace. His ill-timed page filler "Murder Against Murder" was reprinted in his paper, *Freiheit*, immediately preceding McKinley's assassination. Although many had rallied to his defense, helping to appeal a decision that was ultimately upheld by the courts, the content of the article plus Most's reputation for direct advocacy of assassination limited the number of his supporters, even among free speech advocates. Most, who never sought support outside his own anarchist ranks (apart from a few socialists), was sentenced to one year, released on appeal, then imprisoned in June 1902 and freed in April 1903 for good behavior—without a groundswell of public backing for his cause.

ANARCHISTS AND LIBERALS—THE FREE SPEECH CONNECTION

Anarchists, socialists, and liberals organized the Free Speech League in 1902 to counter increased repression especially against anarchist and freethought papers. Fighting against the newly reinvoked 1876 Comstock Act, which prohibited "obscenity in the mails," was a stronger base for a broad coalition than simply opposing anti-anarchist statutes and became a critical organizing tool for those who challenged cultural norms and engaged in political dissent.[41] With its vague terminology, the Comstock Act was open to interpretation and subject to the winds of political prejudice. Entire publications could be squelched with the rescinding of the affordable second-class mailing rate, closing lines of communication on the left forever.

The Free Speech League was a continuation of the National Defense Association, a group formed when sex radicals were arrested for publishing explicit materials for sexual educational purposes. The group defended the anarchist Ezra Heywood, who was arrested in 1878 for publishing the pamphlet *Cupid's Yokes,* which advocated intimate partnerships without the state sanction of marriage and explicitly described the mechanics of sex and reproduction. Many, though not all, in the National Defense Association were freethinkers. Being accused of obscenity seemed like a natural progression from the charge of blasphemy they suffered for their outspoken atheist beliefs. Relatively small but tremendously effective, the National Defense Association obtained over 50,000 signatures on a petition to Congress demanding a repeal of the Comstock Act as "an instrument of moral and religious persecution." Even after a hiatus of almost fifteen years in their activity, the group was able to quickly reconstitute themselves as the Free Speech League to once again counter the ire of the conservators of traditional beliefs in God and marriage. For E. B. Foote, Jr., Benjamin Tucker, A. C. Pleydell, and Edward Chamberlain, the core carry-over members, the September 1901 arrest of the editors of *Discontent* for reprinting an 1890 article that linked marriage to prostitution was just the latest in a series of attempts to limit free expression and control the content of the press. Elder anarchist and exponent of sex radicalism Moses Harman had printed a call in *Lucifer* for the establishment of a free speech league in response to the 1901 arrest of the editors of *Discontent*. The trial took place in April 1902, and although the judge dismissed the charges that morning, later the post office at Home, Washington (the *Discontent* anarchists' colony) was closed, effectively terminating their publication.

The Comstock Act provided legal grounds to harass anarchists on sex issues, which some authorities considered a more immediate threat than the subject of political violence. The act functioned as a stop-gap measure while officials awaited the passage of more strin-

41. For an interesting discussion of the Comstock laws and their historical and legal context, see David Rabban, *Free Speech in its Forgotten Years* (Cambridge: Cambridge University Press, 1997), esp. pp. 27–32. See also entry on Free Speech League, pp. 557–58.

gent laws against anarchism.[42] Extending censorship against advocates of sexual freedom and free speech to anarchist trade-union organizer John Turner ultimately strengthened the opposition by forging ties between anarchists and concerned liberals who worked in partnership on a free-speech platform. Prominent members of the Manhattan Liberal Club, including some who defended the single land tax—a replacement for income tax based on the theory that private land ownership was the fundamental source of social and economic injustice—joined forces with anarchists who defended the editors of the journal *Discontent*. Goldman considered such single-taxers "the bravest and staunchest champions of liberty in the widest sense" (see "The End of the Odyssey," Article in *Mother Earth*, April 1909)—and closer to anarchists in sensibility than to socialists.[43] In part, from these beginnings, a significant core group was primed, by 1903, to effectively oppose the new immigration act legalizing the arrest and deportation of alien anarchists.

OMINOUS LEGAL PRECEDENT

The Chinese Exclusion Acts of 1882, 1886, and 1892 set legal precedents for regulating immigrant entry and expulsion on the basis of race and national origin. The 1903 Immigration Act[44] extended the notion of exclusion on the basis of political beliefs. With precedents set for denial of entry based on political ideology, the Naturalization and the Denaturalization Act of 1906 followed,[45] which required petitioners for citizenship to sign a Declaration of Intention, swearing they were not anarchists, and allowed the cancellation of citizenship obtained in an illegal or fraudulent manner within three years of entering the United States. In 1907, the regulations for residency became more stringent, thus marginalizing immigrant radicals even further.[46]

In 1903, Goldman helped transform the New York City–based Free Speech League (a group that included anarchists Benjamin Tucker, Ernest Crosby,[47] and socialist Mo-

---

42. By 1908, an amendment to sec. 3893 of the Comstock Act (on matter excluded from the mails) expanded the definition of "indecent" to include "matter of a character tending to incite arson, murder, or assassination" (Records of the Sixtieth Congress, sess. I, ch. 206, 1908, p. 416).

43. In spite of a significant split with single-tax leader Henry George, who rescinded his support for the Haymarket anarchists in the 1880s (see Letter to Joseph A. Labadie, 18 May 1909) and Tucker's written response that labeled George a traitor, the bonds between the two relatively underrecognized groups remained strong. Anarchists George Seldes and Bolton Hall, for example, were also active single-taxers.

44. See 32 Statutes-at-Large 1213. See also Roger Daniels, *Not Like Us* (Chicago: Ivan R. Dee, 1997).

45. 34 Statutes-at-Large 596.

46. 34 Statutes-at-Large 898.

47. Among the committee supporters was Ernest Crosby, a social reformer and the leading proponent of Tolstoyan anarchism in the United States. His 1903 pamphlet *How the United States Curtails Freedom of Thought* argued against the deportation of John Turner and echoed the sentiments of Victor Hugo's frequently reprinted poem "The First Anarchist." The poem boldly suggested that the definition of anarchism had become so broad that the religious martyr Jesus Christ—who aimed "to annihilate wealth and power, not to grasp them"—could easily have been prosecuted as an anarchist. Crosby evoked the spirit of the Free Speech League's predecessors and argued that even the esteemed abolitionist William Lloyd Garrison—who in his 1838 "Declaration of Sentiments" expressed distrust

ses Oppenheimer, among others) from an informal lobbying group with branches in Washington, D.C., and Chicago into the temporarily renamed Turner Defense Committee. Goldman, who organized large public meetings for Turner, was designated by the committee to act as its agent—largely by collecting funds for the defense of Turner (see facsimile of memo from E. B. Foote, Jr., 24 March 1904).

Turner was arrested and charged on 23 October 1903 under the anti-anarchist clause of the 1903 Immigration Act. After a formal hearing the next day before the Board of Special Inquiry, a deportation order was issued. He was interrogated without a lawyer—on grounds that his was an administrative rather than a judicial hearing. His arrest was based on a warrant that had been issued even before he spoke. From his detention cell, he issued a formal protest, arguing that he was arrested "simply because I am an anarchist—because I believe it possible for the highest social order to be developed without territorial government. . . . apparently, the country that once rebelled against England's tyranny can show her how to introduce political discrimination, which, if successful, must end in the extinction of liberty. The spirit of inquisition is by no means dead. Every steamship company sailing to United States ports now asks intending passengers, among other questions, 'Are you an anarchist?' If any one replies 'Yes' they will refuse to carry him. . . . If this goes unchallenged, how long before other opinions will be placed on the list?"[48]

Turner's appeal rose to the Supreme Court, where it was argued by Clarence Darrow and Edgar Lee Masters (*Turner v. Williams*, 194 U.S. 279).[49] Darrow contended that the law under which Turner was ordered to be deported was contrary to the First Amendment's guarantee of free speech and free press, "independent of whether such law relates

---

of a government that compelled its people "to do right on pain of imprisonment or death" and encouraged others to "exclude [themselves] voluntarily from every legislative and judicial body, and repudiate all . . . worldly honors and stations of authority"—might have been barred from entry into the United States had the new immigration laws been in place during his lifetime. With some irony, Crosby suggested that Henry David Thoreau, who declared that "that government is best which governs not at all," certainly "must get into the prison-van alongside of Garrison." Crosby asserted that to "shut out 'beliefs' is not only unjust, undesirable and inexpedient, but impossible. Beliefs spring up uncensored and uncensorable in the mind of every one of our eighty millions of population." He then surmised that the Turner case was a culmination of the narrow thinking that thwarts visionary change, and that the law barring entry to alien anarchists ultimately toppled any illusion of the United States as a bastion of freedom. With imagery Goldman would later adopt, Crosby urged the American public to shed the mystique of the Statue of Liberty: "Let us take down . . . that brazen lie which now casts its beams upon Ellis Island and its prison, and let us put up in its place an ogre of iron, grasping a gnarled and knotted club, and casting its baleful shadow upon the immigrant,—an image no longer of Liberty Enlightening, but of Despotism Darkening, the World."

48. Turner, "Protest of an Anarchist."
49. The appeal procedure began on October 26 with Secretary of Labor and Commerce Oscar S. Straus who, after his denial, issued the warrant for Turner's deportation. Turner, once released on bail, petitioned the U.S. Circuit Court to adhere to a narrower definition of anarchist—which would exclude those like himself who did not believe in the forceful overthrow of the government. He also contested the original denial of his rights to due process of the law. In April 1904, after the court denied all pending motions, he filed an appeal.

to a citizen or an alien." Along with case precedents, he cited John Stuart Mill's *Essay on Liberty*. Among other issues, Darrow challenged the lack of due process—the ways in which Turner was never informed of his rights upon arrest, treated like chattel, subject to confinement too harsh for the crime for which he was accused—and the importance of a public trial.[50]

By May 1904, Turner's appeal was summarily rejected—and the original deportation orders reinstated. During his release on appeal, even before the U.S. Secretary of Commerce and Immigration had signed his deportation order, Turner's vacation leave had run out, and he decided to return home, where he was free to organize and speak publicly as an anarcho-syndicalist.[51] Turner's experience with the new anti-anarchist provision of the immigration law was an ominous sign of what the future would hold for Goldman.

Anarchists in Europe, including Peter Kropotkin (see Letter from Peter Kropotkin, 16 December 1903), were puzzled by the attention of American anarchists to the Turner case and wondered why anarchists expected anything from a repressive and conservative nation state, believing as Kropotkin did that a capitalist democracy could never be reformed. Kropotkin understood that "bourgeois Society is doing exactly what we expected it to do; throws its hypocritical liberties over-board, tears them to pieces,—as soon as it sees that people use these liberties for fighting that cursed Society." Kropotkin urged Goldman to leave such naïve protests to the liberals, who had little understanding of the inherent injustice of governments and their laws. Goldman, however, believed that Kropotkin and many other European anarchists had little understanding of the power and ethos of free speech in America and the grand opening it offered for the circulation of a multitude of ideas, including, and especially, anarchism. The chorus of protest the Turner case elicited was proof enough that her instincts about its significance as a propaganda exercise would resonate well beyond her circle of anarchists (see Letter to Abe Isaak, 4 December 1903).

For Goldman, the added political benefit of her work on the Turner case was that it allowed her to extend her ties beyond the immigrant anarchist community firmly into a world of English-speaking liberals and radicals of many persuasions. Although she had arranged many of the large rallies on Turner's behalf, she generally remained out of the spotlight, sometimes under her pseudonym, E. G. Smith, to avoid scaring those who

---

50. Darrow also distinguished "the commerce clause," with its implied right to conduct business with foreign nations, from the First Amendment guarantee of the right to free speech. In this period when the tension between federal and state regulations was high, he warned that if these concepts were treated as if there were no meaningful distinction between them, it would set a precedent that could prevent citizens from passing from one state to another simply based on their political beliefs, reversing the thrust of the post–Civil War interpretation of the Constitution.

51. When Turner shifted his lecture topic from "Trade Unionism and the General Strike," which had been the occasion for his arrest, to an address "On the Signs of the Times," he met no restriction from the police in New York, Buffalo, and Chicago. He appreciated the significance of the organizing work on his behalf and was grateful to have the opportunity to serve the cause. Turner had just turned down a candidacy for Parliament because of his anarchist disavowal of government and organized structures of power.

would be appalled to work with "wild-eyed anarchists."[52] For the most part she had found real friends among the liberals, who had no hesitation about their association with her and gladly hosted meetings in her own name. She worked with civil-liberties-oriented liberal reformers to advocate free speech and found them remarkably open to her ideas about the centrality of freedom in all realms of life. By her early thirties, many perceived her less as a young feisty rebel and more as an articulate spokesperson for freedom. Goldman became adept at moving from one social-political milieu to another and reached a point of acceptance as an equal among both civil-liberties-oriented liberals and the older communist- and individualist-anarchists. While Turner was only five years her senior, those within the Free Speech League were generally much more advanced in years.[53] Among many civil-liberties-oriented liberals, Goldman was respected as someone who had suffered with dignity and withstood the ire of a public thirsty for revenge in the wake of the McKinley assassination, and who had the moral stature and experience to stand up for others whose rights were transgressed. The reach of this free-speech fight was a bold step for her—from her community of immigrant radicals into the most radical edge of American liberals—marking the potential for authentic commonality without betraying her anarchist roots.

DRAWN TO THE STORMS OF REVOLUTION IN MOTHER RUSSIA

Far away from the intermittent waves of reproach that threatened to destabilize Goldman's life in America and to bar her comrades from visiting its shores, storms of revolution in "Mother Russia" were gathering force.[54] Goldman, who had never completely severed her ties to her birthplace, laced her life in America with threads of devotion to the Russian revolution—and wove its story into her own. Back in the 1890s, her small commune modeled itself after the fictive group in Chernyshevsky's novel *What Is to Be Done?*[55] She and her live-in comrades had hoped to earn enough money to return to their Russian homeland, eager to support the battles they were too young to join before their emigration. But the labor struggles that raged around them in the United States, with growing violence against workers, diverted their plans to return to Russia and stirred them to respond to the social war in America—the battle between capital and labor, not just of classes but of conflicting social ideas—and to avenge their adopted country's wrongs in the style of their Russian counterparts.

Furthermore, Goldman would not leave the United States until Alexander Berkman,

---

52. *LML*, p. 349.
53. Anarchist E. B. Foote, Sr., was forty years older than Goldman; his son, E. B. Foote, Jr., was fourteen years older, and Edward Chamberlain was twenty-three years older.
54. See "The Stormy Petrel," chap. 1 in Paul Avrich, *The Russian Anarchists* (New York: W.W. Norton, 1978), pp. 9–34, on the emergence of anarchism in Russia.
55. See introduction, vol. 1, pp. 13–14, for discussion of Goldman's emulation of the Russian revolutionary elite, evidence that the dual role she began to assume between 1902 and 1909 fit a pattern rooted in the tales and experiences building up to the Russian revolution.

her closest comrade, was out of prison. Berkman, who believed in the efficacy of justice through revenge, had in 1892 carried out an assassination plan against Carnegie Steel plant manager Henry Clay Frick. His failed attempt, which was misunderstood even by many of the steelworkers, left Berkman relatively isolated and facing a long prison sentence rather than the martyr's death for which he was prepared.[56] Goldman, one of several who had been complicit in his act, never abandoned her "Sasha"—not even for Russia. Seared into her memory was the night she and Claus Timmerman stayed up waiting with anxious anticipation to read the news about Berkman's *attentat* in the papers—knowing that she, Timmerman, Modest Stein, Carl Nold, Henry Bauer, and Robert Reitzel all had conspired to effect his "deed."[57] For fourteen years, she would always remain loyal, even conspire in his fouled escape plan, and ultimately wait and work for his release, staying relatively close by even as she continued to engage in the politics of the day, especially in support of Russian revolutionary activity.

She was drawn first to the militant wing of the Russian Socialist Revolutionaries—a group with many strategies in common with the U.S. anarchist movement. The Socialist Revolutionary Party, which came together in 1901, had evolved from nineteenth-century dissident groups, like Narodnaya Volya, that embraced violence, including political assassination, in its philosophy and tactics. Over time, the party vacillated on the use of terror as a means to an end; the left and right extremes of the party advocated violence as a political tool, while moderates took a public stand against it. Although Goldman seemed less concerned about the details and internal discussion among the Socialist Revolutionaries in Russia and in exile—their identification with agrarianism and industrialism, Marxism and even Populism—she so wanted to be part of the struggle that she actually briefly joined the party in what was truly an uncharacteristic act for one who would forever pride herself as acting first and foremost as an individual. Goldman raised money for her Russian comrades and reveled in the international intrigue of this association. She seems to have been influenced in turn by the growing differentiation between the Socialist Revolutionaries' public and private strategies for change as her own style of political action evolved.

Goldman's role was in part a culmination of previous contacts and desires. In London in 1900, she had ushered in the new century in the company of some of the foremost Russian revolutionary exiles—including Peter Kropotkin, Varlaam N. Cherkezov (the Georgian anarchist and revolutionary), and Nikolai Chaikovsky—for whom she became a bridge between anarchists in Europe and in the United States. Especially in the period just before the 1905 Russian uprising, Goldman was closely associated with efforts to internationalize the American movement. To this end, she hosted various Russian emissaries of the most militant wing of the Socialist Revolutionaries while remaining, above all else, an anarchist.

56. See introduction, vol. 1, pp. 25–27.
57. EG to AB, 22 July 1927, *EGP*, reel 18 (also in Alexander Berkman Papers, IISH).

For many Anglo and Eastern Europeans living in America, transgressions of freedom in America in the first decade of the twentieth century were measured against the despotism of tsarist Russia, with its pogroms and attacks on students, peasants, and workers. As early as 1891, the American Society of the Friends of Russian Freedom[58] became a rallying point for prominent liberals, including author Mark Twain, civil libertarian William Lloyd Garrison, Jr., and Russia-watch expert and author George Kennan. After a brief hiatus, the group was reconstituted in 1904 by Russian exiles and joined by the next generation of leading American liberals, including Robert Ely and many radical Russian immigrants eager to renew their ties to the old country and help the struggle they had left behind. Those with strong affinities to the anarchist position affirmed "that any sane man, knowing the facts, who pronounces it wrong to assassinate the Czar, deliberately lies."[59] With accounts of horrific atrocities and pogroms in Russia published almost daily in both mainstream and radical presses, even the most respectable and socially conservative critics approved of the militant activities of the Russian revolutionaries.

Interest in Russia's political struggles did not, however, extend to approval of the more unconventional social practices of its representatives, as was especially apparent in 1906 when the society summarily rejected the Russian playwright Maksim Gorky for traveling to the United States with a lover who was not his wife.[60] In contrast, in Russia, Gorky's 1902 arrest for his poem "The Song of the Storm Finch" (often translated as "The Stormy Petrel") opposing the Tsar and upholding instead the struggles of the country's revolutionaries, had elicited an outpouring of international support. In deference to Gorky, Goldman published his poem in the very first volume of her magazine. But, when he arrived in the United States to appeal to middle-class liberals for funds, Gorky's behavior besmirched his public image as the purist harbinger of Russian revolutionary ideals; he not only continued the charade with his lover (which didn't actually offend most of the readers of *Mother Earth*) but also blackened his name in Goldman's circles by labeling the Tsar an anarchist because he employed terror tactics. He then brazenly rejected the request of poor Russian Jewish anarchists for a discount to his high-priced event because he claimed he had come to the United States primarily to bring back as much money as possible to Russia. Gorky's unethical maneuvering on issues so central to anarchists threw into relief by contrast Goldman's integrity and compassion, qualities for which she had become well known. While Goldman's magazine included several protests[61]

---

58. Goldman often claimed, including at a meeting with Lenin in Russia in 1920, that the American Society of the Friends of Russian Freedom needed a Russian counterpart, "The Russian Society of Friends of American Freedom."

59. Victor Robinson, *Comrade Kropotkin* (New York: The Altrurians, 1908), pp. 102–103n.

60. For expository and satiric commentary on the incident, praising Gorky and criticizing his treatment, see John Coryell (writing under his pseudonym Margaret Grant),"This Man Gorky," *Mother Earth* 1, no. 3 (May 1906): 8–16.

61. Voltairine de Cleyre published "An Open Letter" in *Mother Earth* 1, no. 7 (August 1906), attacking Gorky for his cowardly behavior in running away from New York City and especially for his deleterious comments about anarchists, who were among his greatest supporters.

and satiric accounts of the hoopla around Gorky's visit, it also benefited by publishing a translation of one of his stories in the same issue that bore a critique of his conduct.[62]

Left liberals, even with their conflicts over social mores, came to believe that in Russia violence was necessary to counteract the extreme violence of the Tsar, and thus did not flinch at the thought of supplying money for guns to support the fomenting revolution, a position they seemingly never considered transposing to their own country. Anarchists, often frustrated with the distance between the here and now and their vision of the future, were drawn to the Russian situation, even to the voting process which they rejected in America. This sentiment was taken a step further by many Russian Jews, who felt the chill of anti-Semitism so strongly wherever they went (and horrifyingly prevalent in Russia) that the wish for a secure nation of their own—outside the United States or Russia—became more and more appealing to some who otherwise eschewed the validity of a nation state (see Letter from Alexander Berkman, 12 March 1905). Still, general support for the struggle within Russia would become a rallying point, with tacit approval of brutal and ruthless methods of revenge, including random bombings.

Outside of Russia, these well-meaning supporters of the brewing revolution were not always fully aware of the differences among various internal groups. At this time, Goldman herself knew little of the Russian anarchists (see Letter to Marie Goldsmith, 14 April 1905). She allied herself with the Socialist Revolutionaries, a primarily socialist political organization that shared the tactics of some anarchists—including terrorism—but not the anarchist conviction that to construct a new equitable society ultimately necessitated purging all structures of power. In 1904, Catherine Breshkovskaya, the "Grand Old Lady of the Revolution," who had been chosen by the Socialist Revolutionaries to woo American audiences to the Russian cause, visited Goldman in New York, where the two women cultivated a friendship and camaraderie based on their many social and political affinities. With Grigorii Gershuni, Breshkovskaya, known as the grandmotherly architect of the Socialist Revolutionary Party's agrarian terror strategy (which included violent attacks on landowners), was a master at reaching out to the liberal public while carrying out the most clandestine of activities. Goldman felt validated by the presence of her elder female mentor, who mirrored and encouraged the development of the two seeming extremes of Goldman's own political activity. She admired Breshkovskaya as a great humanitarian and, in some ways, emulated the woman, who found no contradiction between creating tearooms for Russian workers and formulating strategies for terror against the tsarist autocracy.

Angry protests spread into the streets of Russia, initiating violent demonstrations, popular petitions, and widespread outrage against the extreme brutality of the tsarist regime both within Russia and around the world, signaling that the 1905 revolution was

---

62. "Comrade" by Maksim Gorky, *Mother Earth* 1, no. 3 (May, 1906): 17–22; and "The Masters of Life," *Mother Earth* 1, no. 11 (January 1907), the latter among the first pamphlets of the Mother Earth Publishing Association in 1907.

imminent. Especially for Russian Jews who had fled the despotism of the Tsar and the anti-Semitism that permeated the country, hopeful news of the uprisings in Russia vindicated their experience of injustice. In this period before 1905, the Socialist Revolutionaries' practice of terrorist activities that included the selective assassinations of government officials in Russia (which continued until 1917) was backed by international defenders of the left including Goldman, who was relied upon to convey the noble intent of horrific acts committed in the name of the revolution. She reinforced the general mood among left liberals and radicals who tacitly approved of violence and among some anarchists and socialists who openly supported it.

The differences in Goldman's and Breshkovskaya's theories melted in the warmth of friendship, and their commonalities merged in the desire to take action against injustice. Goldman looked to Breshkovskaya as a role model and shared her desire to bridge their movements—an effort that proved indispensable to promoting public awareness, tolerance, and raising financial support for the revolution. Ironically, given Goldman's initial support of the Bolsheviks and her questioning of Breshkovskaya's antagonism toward them, Goldman too would become a prominent international critic of Bolshevism.

Although she would never abandon her friendship and loyalty to Breshkovskaya—"whatever my attitude towards her party may be, I shall always love and revere her, in fact we all shall"—Goldman summarily resigned from the Socialist Revolutionary Party and pledged her support to her Russian anarchist comrades (see Letter to Marie Goldsmith, 14 April 1905). Goldman explained the situation to Breshkovskaya and genuinely thanked "dear Babushka" who had "given us so much that is good and useful and we will never forget you." At the same time, although both women believed in the efficacy of individual *attentats,* Goldman distinguished her ideas from those of Breshkovskaya, who like the Socialist Revolutionaries supported socialism achieved through a democratic republic based on the vote and the conversion of Russia into a federated state. Goldman, on the other hand, believed that anarchism and its individual methods of organization were "just as important and useful" (see Letter to Catherine Breshkovskaya, 14 April 1905).

Although on the surface Goldman's and Breshkovskaya's letters on the subject of collective versus individual organization appeared benign, theirs was in fact a loosely veiled exchange of ideas on violence. Goldman affirmed the anarchist position that individual *attentats* committed by "one of such a sensitive nature that he will feel a wrong more keenly and with greater intensity than others" were as effective and valid as those designed by a political organization or by small clandestine groups. These positions reflected differences in their demographic and geographic realities.[63] There was also a steady flow back and forth of militants from Russia to Europe and the United States—especially after the failure of the 1905 revolution—militants who imported the tactics of

63. Quote on *attentaters* from "The Tragedy at Buffalo," *Mother Earth* 1, no. 8 (October 1906). For background on Berkman's *attentat* and the debate that ensued among the anarchists, see introduction, vol. 1, pp. 25–27, and also esp. pp. 119–21, 349–52.

terror, some of whom would work closely with Berkman on the 1914 Lexington Avenue bombing. In some ways, although several steps removed from what was actually happening in Russia, her conversations with Breshkovskaya, Goldsmith, and Kropotkin signaled that Goldman's engagement with party politics, even that of the Socialist Revolutionary Party, had been reined in by her new awareness of, and overarching allegiance to, the ideas and needs of her anarchist comrades in Russia and in America. Goldman, for whom friendship was an immutable gift that transcended political difference, reiterated her devotion to Breshkovskaya, even as she distanced herself from organizational political work: "I hope, my darling, that you will understand that I love you and your work, but I must help those who are closer to me in principles and ideas" (see Letter to Catherine Breshkovskaya, 14 April 1905).

HEALING THE WEARY

Goldman, exhausted from her work as a night nurse, decided in December 1904 to engage in an easier trade that would enable her to earn a living and still have the time and energy to serve the revolution. While ruling heads actually were being toppled, she opened a scalp and facial massage business, which would conveniently double as an inconspicuous "cover for the Russian work we were to go on with."[64] Operating under the pseudonym "E. G. Smith," her legal business entity was useful for laundering money collected from a growing group of affluent liberals who were outraged at Tsarist atrocities.[65]

Goldman's intermittent massage work gave her access to a steady stream of weary radicals and liberals—including Bolton Hall, a single-tax anarchist and writer who would provide her with a country retreat for her writing. The get-away spot in Ossining, New York, would later become a desirable destination for local anarchists eager to escape the summer heat of New York City. Most likely, given her supporting role to the steady flow of Russian Socialist Revolutionaries in hiding, it also doubled as a relatively safe place to harbor Russian exiles and to mastermind the gathering of ammunition. Her massage clients, many of whom she had met during her work for the Turner Defense Committee, sometimes helped Goldman either by directly contributing to the Russian cause or by providing her with new referrals for her night nursing work. E. B. Foote, Sr., a medical doctor and free-speech advocate whose *Dr. Foote's Monthly* popularized medical information, proved to be among her best sources for recommendations; ulti-

---

64. See *LML*, p. 365, for an intimation of this as a cover operation. Documents in the Goldman Papers archive indicate that Eric B. Morton, who had been a key figure in the plan to help Berkman escape from prison, was chosen by Goldman, the mastermind of the endeavor, as a reliable transporter of guns to Russia. See EG to Catherine Breshkovskaya, 14 May 1905 (*EGP*, reel 1), which discusses EG's role in shipping guns to Russia for the Socialist Revolutionaries. In her *Tomorrow Is Beautiful* (New York: Macmillan, 1948), pp. 39–41, Lucy Lang implicates Morton with Goldman.

65. See Goldman's letters to prominent liberals, soliciting support for the Russian revolution, especially Letter to Robert Erskine Ely, 2 February 1905, and Letter to Lillian Wald, ca. 14 March 1905

mately both he and his son, E. B. Foote, Jr., also a physician, provided financial support to Goldman.[66]

Goldman came to view her professional work as a healer as an expression of her desire to promote individual and general health and well-being. She worked intermittently as a midwife to the poor, as a prison nurse, and as a night nurse. She loved the small pleasures of night duty—the breeze of an open window, the ability to focus on the patient without the interference of a doting and concerned family, a strong cup of coffee, and the time to read a good book.[67] She was equally drawn to the sensuousness of bodywork but grew tired of its strain on her own body. Instead she opted for the less taxing specialty of scalp and facial treatments upon the recommendation of a manicurist friend of hers who convinced Goldman that it was an efficient and pleasant way to make a comfortable living and still have time for political engagement. These, and other kinds of paid work—including tutoring and cooking—proved expedient and satisfying.

Her nursing and massage work was a practical expression of her yearning to lessen the pain around her. With infections and fevers abounding in an era before antibiotics, meticulous care was often critical to recovery. Scalp and facial massage was known to alleviate headaches and nervous disorders. Goldman's seemingly limitless empathy for human suffering, her intuitive power, emotional intelligence, and stamina served her patients well—whether they were ailing, giving birth, or just coming to relax through what must have been, given the force of her personality, a very intense massage. Whether she was healing the sick, helping impoverished women through the birthing process, or muting the physical barriers between people with a restorative touch, she imbued her work with political meaning—as an extension of her public agenda. Still, the varieties of her professional healing work functioned mostly as a means to support her ceaseless political activities for her anarchist ideal, the most central element of her life.

MOTHER LIBERTY

Goldman's desire to nurture others and, by extension, to heal the world might be thought by some to be part of a generalized woman's impulse to mother—and yet she clearly weighed in on the side of those who chose not to bear or raise children, who instead gave their all to the cause. For one whose life was centered around her ideal of anarchism, who revered martyrs for justice, giving up the promise of becoming a mother—"the sacred right of womanhood"—required disciplined resolve. For Goldman such a life choice was an expression of woman's sacrifice for the cause. In her memoir and in letters to friends and lovers, she theorized about the roots of her conflicted desire for a

---

66. EG memorialized E. B. Foote, Jr., as "a man who *really* believed in freedom of speech—for everyone, including those whom he considered in the wrong" (*Mother Earth* 7, no. 9, November 1912, p. 277).

67. *LML*, p. 327.

child, while underscoring the importance of such a decision in the life of a woman who chose to take the political road.

Although her memoir included extraordinarily vivid descriptions of many of the most intimate details of her personal and political life, Goldman routinely concealed that which she considered the most sensitive details—not only to shield others from the gaze of a potentially censorious public, but also to guard her own dignity. Encoded allusions and unnamed accomplices in sub-rosa political activities left hints with no answers, impressions easily erased by time; yet the emotional intimacy of the narrative style and content of her autobiography seduced most readers into believing that Goldman told all and hid nothing.

Generally historians, biographers, and documentary editors face the dilemma of accounting for both the seemingly benign spaces as well as the abrupt ruptures between chronological texts and must rise to the task of formulating a reasoned commentary on that which is unspoken. Those who rely completely upon the written record often inadvertently omit nuanced life choices and decisions that bear no paper trail. Those who opt for a largely speculative approach to history—privileging the hearsays of the past—risk seeming to be untrustworthy narrators who stray too far afield from the documentary evidence. And yet to deny strong historical clues and suppress the intuition of seasoned biographers (of which documentary editors could be considered a subset) accustomed to decoding the writings of their subject and following identifiable trace elements until they coalesce into a textured whole, would present a different kind of omission from the historical record—a falsification in its own right. Such documentary exclusionism constitutes a refusal to acknowledge the many tributaries of the life force that may never be known. Investigation into significant events and relationships often deliberately underreported remains as worthy of consideration as those committed to writing.

Somewhere between 1902 and 1904, in a period quickly passed over in her autobiography, Goldman may have given birth to and given up a child. Based on inconclusive and unproven family stories, this intriguing possibility offers an opportunity to reframe Goldman the public woman and her varying stands on childbearing and motherhood. During her youth, when all possibilities seemed open, it is interesting to ponder how and why, on the issue of children, Goldman closed the door.

In the pages of her autobiography, *Living My Life,* Goldman recounts the details of her love live—and the life circumstances that would have dictated against following through on childbearing or child rearing. These issues were most acute in the early years of her relationship with Ed Brady (in the mid-1890s), when he taunted her with doubts about her womanhood and tried desperately to lure her into a more stable and less dangerously "impetuous" life on the lecture trail. In *Living My Life,* she retraces the steps of their arguments on the issue. "He was sure that the strongest motive in my devotion to the movement was unsatisfied motherhood seeking an outlet. . . . My starved motherhood— was that the main reason for my idealism? He had roused the old yearning for a child. But I had silenced the voice of the child for the sake of the universal, the all-absorbing passion of my life. Men were consecrated to ideals and yet were fathers of children. But man's physical share in the child is only a moment's: woman's part is for years—years of absorption in one human being to the exclusion of the rest of humanity. I would never give up the one for the other. Surely it must be possible for a man and a woman to have a beautiful love-life and yet be devoted to a great cause."

Yet throughout her life, she felt waves of desire for a child, a palpable ache for what she had left behind; she consoled herself that, unlike so many of her anarchist comrades, she was not responsible for bringing an apolitical child into the world. Ultimately the cause of justice and freedom, framed by Goldman's vision of anarchism, was the center of her life. A child fit into this life only as a recipient of the better world which she, as the messenger editor of *Mother Earth*, her "child born of love," would hasten to bring. Still, she was aware that she was "not hewn of one piece"; her vulnerability, her longings, would forever leave her feeling "tossed between yearning for a personal life and the need for giving all to my ideal."

In the early 1890s, Goldman had been advised by her doctor of the need for surgery should she ever wish to conceive a child. She believed that her "inverted womb"—a variant on endometriosis—precluded the possibility of pregnancy. She recounted her decision to decline this surgery as a turning point in her life. Her friend and comrade Dr. Hillel Solotaroff counseled her to submit to the procedure "because if you have the operation, you will be able to have a child. So far your condition has made that impossible." Although on the surface a free-love advocate might welcome such a condition as a convenient form of carefree birth control, she recalled her decision to forgo the operation as a political act of loyalty, an affirmation of her desire to serve the cause completely and without restraint: "Years of pain and of suppressed longing for a child—what were they compared with the price many martyrs had already paid? I, too, would pay the price, I would endure the suffering. I would find an outlet for my mother-need in the love of *all* children." An unplanned baby would not have been perceived as a gift of nature. By the time she was in her thirties, set in her path, she felt in no position to bear or raise a child.

The true story is unknown. It is difficult to discern the authenticity of her multiple proclamations about unwanted children, or whether her repeated denials in the autobiography were part and parcel of a clever approach to keeping a secret by taking her readership along a path away from that which she hoped to keep private. On the other hand, her protests also may have been her way of reinforcing her decision to give up a child—to herself—and to maintain the validity of being a single and childless woman, especially at a time when women primarily defined themselves, even if they worked outside the home, in relation to family and parenting.

Goldman continued to live, and viewed herself, as a woman without a child, a woman who experienced both the intermittent agony of desire for the connectedness of motherhood, and the ecstasy of unencumbered freedom. Openly she pined more for a partner than for a dependent, and frequently expressed her feelings of vulnerability and isolation. Driven to extend her communal family, having no easy fallback to a consistent, tithed 'other,' she reveled in an intensity of personal bonds with comrades and lovers unmediated by the daily caretaking of the young—finding strength to go against the norm through intimacy and her unwavering commitment to an ideal.

Goldman's writings and lectures (see "The Tragedy of Woman's Emancipation," Essay in *Mother Earth,* March 1906) swung between exalting and demeaning childbirth and mothering. She claimed that her devotion to the anarchist cause necessitated that she cast off the "most glorious privilege" of womanhood and "overcome the strongest and most primitive craving of a woman—the desire for a child." Yet often she referred to "motherhood, in general, [as] that blind, dumb force that brings forth life in travail, wasting woman's youth and strength, and leaving her in old age a burden to herself and to those to whom she has given birth," claiming that it was "this helplessness of motherhood that had made me recoil from adding to its pain."[68] Her ambivalence, which came in spurts, had been most pronounced in her twenties, when countering the norm of childbearing took tremendous internal courage.

THE RUSSIAN POLITICAL STAGE

Once Breshkovskaya left the United States, in 1905, Goldman reaffirmed her devotion to the Russian cause by promoting the creative work of the Pavel Orlenev theater troupe. On tour and desperately needing the services of a manager, the Russian troupe accepted Goldman's offer to use her superb organizing skills and personal ties to gather audiences for the new theater. Their production of Evgenii Nikolaevich Chirikov's *The Chosen People* was especially popular in the Lower East Side for its damning portrayal of the antisemetic pogroms sweeping Russia, designed to deflect the government's problems onto the Jews. With Goldman's samovar in constant use and her rolling Russian "r's" percolating, she felt completely in her element. Although she would never leave the United States permanently while Berkman was still in jail, they both anticipated an eventual return to their mother country. She may even have been building her future community in Russia from her home base in New York. The steady flow of Russians in and out of her apartment also provided an easy cover for those who were either escaping or were about to smuggle arms back into Russia—most likely both Russian anarchists and Socialist Revolutionaries. Her engagement with the theater group, however arduous, lifted her spirits and familiarized her with the precursors of the Russian free-theater movement.

Managing the theater troupe was a form of cultural political work that allowed her to be in contact with creativity and an acting process she respected, in part because she too identified herself as a performer. Just as the theater tapped into her love and interest in the modern drama, acting capitalized on her belief in the power of the medium to shake

68. EG's comments on children and childbirth all from *LML*, pp. 58, 61, 153–54, 340.

people out of their complacency. Goldman worked hard as the American representative of the Russian troupe, exposing many audiences to challenging plays and helping to create cultural ties across continents that would promote sympathy for the plight of the Russian people.

Some of the plays she promoted were chosen especially for the Jewish community of the Lower East Side, including *Petty Persecution,* performed as a benefit "for victims of the recent Jewish massacres"; *The Family Tsvi,* about Jewish identity written in response to the antisemetic Kishinev pogroms; as well as Henrik Ibsen's *Ghosts* and plays by August Strindberg and Maksim Gorky. Yet, what seemed like a seamless link between Goldman's cultures of origin ended in a disaster when their plays were boycotted in response to rumors that some of the actors belonged to the notorious antisemitic organization known as the Black Hundreds—a charge that may or may not have been true. Gradually the finances and coherence of the troupe collapsed, its luster tarnished by debt, dissension, and public doubt about its integrity—an accusation eventually entertained by Goldman herself, who joined with others in the Chirikov Society in an aborted attempt to sue Orlenev for damages along the way.

While Orlenev's troupe was thriving, the spectacle of its elaborate costumes and ornate scenery drew curious as well as politically motivated crowds. The theater troupe combined traditional staging with a choice of plays that indicated its movement toward the sensibilities of the emergent "free theaters" which had sprung up at the end of the nineteenth century in Germany, France, England, Norway, and Sweden. The free-theater troupes translated and performed each other's work, encouraging each other to enact the real, the common, and the accessible. In a departure from the hectoring, stylized delivery of previous stage performance, the Moscow Art Theater, under the direction of Constantin Stanislavsky and Vladimir Nemirovich-Danchenko, produced many of the great plays of Tolstoy, Chekhov, and Gorky, even developing a method of acting that evoked the "inner truth . . . of feeling and experience. 'Method acting' reflected a desire to extend the reach of the theater by utilizing its capacity to arouse emotions and reinforce the power of ordinary people" on stages that included everyday props and furniture.[69] The Orlenev troupe partook of the free-theater tradition to address challenging political themes while retaining the stylized spectacle of nineteenth-century drama. It is possible that these ideas influenced the more direct and informal, though no less theatrical, approach Goldman took in addressing her audience on the political stage.

An admirer of Ibsen and Strindberg, Goldman, like many anarchists (especially European anarchists), integrated these two playwrights' ideas into the content of her lectures on the modern drama and allowed them to influence the form of her delivery. Although Goldman's speaking style shared many qualities with her oratorical colleagues, whose booming voices projected across a wide expanse, as a political understudy of the new

---

69. Kenneth Macgowan and William Melnitz, *The Living Stage* (Englewood Cliffs, N.J.: Prentice-Hall, 1955), pp. 399–432.

theater, Goldman strove for, and eventually succeeded in, creating a sense of intimacy and an authentic connection to her audience. These qualities, along with her fine sense of timing as her lectures built toward their dramatic crescendo—as well as the technique of countering the formality of her talks with humorous, playful, and quick-witted interchanges with her audience during the question-and-answer periods—made lectures by Emma Goldman guaranteed entertainment. Eventually, Goldman would perfect her delivery and enter into a league of the most powerful political orators of her time—of all persuasions—including Eugene V. Debs, Alice Stone Blackwell, Mother Jones, Big Bill Haywood, and Voltairine de Cleyre. Her emotiveness was, in part, gender specific and linked to the trends in the new theater that most excited her. Unlike some of her colleagues on the lecture trail, however, she sent a bold message about the significance of the relationships between the personal and the political aspects of life. She appreciated the power of the dramatic form to awaken the emotions and the intellect concurrently. The speaker's platform would become Goldman's political stage, and the theatrics of free expression an integral part of her own performance.[70]

By 1909, after her road manager (and erstwhile lover) Ben Reitman claimed that Goldman "was the best-informed person in America" on the subject of modern drama, a hesitant reporter for the *San Francisco Bulletin* agreed to interview Goldman. Entering a room he assumed to be "the crowded headquarters of the annihilators," the journalist found himself genuinely surprised (and impressed) by Goldman: "Her costume answered the requirements of decency and warmth, but scorned any weak impulse toward adornment. Back of her glasses, however, glitters the light of an acute intelligence and there is a distinct personal magnetism about her as she frames her thoughts in quick and highly expressive words." He dutifully recorded her thoughts on the history and permutations of modern drama—in Germany where avant-garde playwrights had succeeded in disseminating challenging ideas about social problems that Socialists had worked on for years with little avail, then in Scandinavia, then in Mother Russia, highlighting the revolutionary ideas of the Orlenev troupe that included bringing many peasants from the countryside into their performance group, as actors in the service of sending an authentic message of social revolution. Goldman also described developments among Italian, French, and Spanish dramatists. She predicted that America, with its inborn optimism, would gradually be influenced by European drama and would no longer be able to "evade the tragic contrasts and misadjustments of life." In spite of his intentions, the reporter, who believed that he had successfully avoided discussing Goldman's "subversive doctrine, unrelated to the drama, which I refrain from using because I do not care to advertise a cause which I believe is fundamentally wrong and am positive is immediately dangerous"—inadvertently imparted the essence of her ideas in depth and with great

70. Candace Falk, "Emma Goldman: Passion, Politics, and the Theatrics of Free Expression," *Women's History* 11, no. 1 (2002): 11–26.

respect for her authority and intelligence (see "Priestess of Anarchism Becomes Dramatic Seer," Interview in the *San Francisco Bulletin*, 16 January 1909).[71]

"SUNSHINE INTO THE DARKNESS OF YOUR NIGHTMARE"

Freedom to speak was intertwined with freedom to write. In 1906, any publication that combined direct and graphic references to sexuality, especially if it intimated an endorsement of anarchism, was a prime target for government censorship. When the seventy-five-year-old Moses Harman, editor of *Lucifer, the Lightbearer,* was sentenced to a year of hard labor in federal prison under the Comstock Act for publishing letters addressing the sexual health and rights of married women—Goldman, Carl Nold, and the recently released Alexander Berkman sent him greetings and support: "our hearts go out to the Nestor of free expression, the many-time victim of governmental hypocrisy and persecution. May our love cast a ray of sunshine into the darkness of your nightmare" (see Letter to Moses Harman in *Lucifer, the Lightbearer,* 21 May 1906). The magazine *Lucifer,* devoted to sex radicalism, and Goldman's *Mother Earth,* intended as a journal of literary radicalism, each expressed complementary elements of the desire to promote a world of complete freedom and harmony. Although Goldman chose to advocate sexual freedom without explicit discussions of sexual technique and birth control methods (just as she addressed issues of political violence without including manuals on how to carry out such acts), she stood beside those who did, raising public support and legal funds when necessary. In fact, in 1910 when Harman died, unexpired subscriptions from his *American Journal of Eugenics* transferred to *Mother Earth* even though the eugenics movement's ideas on race and birth control differed from Goldman's. Still, Goldman met the formidable challenge of choosing her battles and avoiding unnecessary arrests, while maintaining her commitment to anarchist principles.

Goldman had always relied on Berkman as a political and emotional sounding board. Their letters, especially those smuggled out away from the eyes of prison censors, represent history's closest window into their souls. While reading her letters, sometimes written in German script, Berkman remembered that they had never conversed in English on the outside: "when I read your letters it is like hearing you talk; for you are all there . . . your whole self, the true one."

His letters were written in English, his Russian and German being "rusty, from lack of use." He mused that the best remedy for their ailing movement would be an East Side anarchist school of oratory and sociology conducted entirely in English. The graduates, trained public speakers, would tour only to those places where their ideas, rooted in organizations, could lay seeds for ongoing discussion groups. His emphasis

---

71. The *San Francisco Bulletin* article, which addressed only the issue of modern drama, in fear of collusion with Goldman's efforts to spread anarchist ideas, appeared two days after Goldman and Reitman's arrest on charges of conspiracy against the government.

on staying close to one group, one place, and working from within the community, as opposed to Goldman's talent as an itinerant lecturer, represented the greatest tactical difference between them. However, he and Goldman believed that "it is of far more immediate importance, and will prove of more real and lasting influence in the long run, to win for our ideas Americans of the intelligent middle class, rather than the masses. It is in this direction that our main efforts should be aimed. The ways are many; one of the most important of them is the higher class periodicals-route" (Letter from Alexander Berkman, 12 March 1905).

On the issue of class, they continued a Russian tradition of valuing the role of the intelligentsia. They shared their profound insights into the critical role of the concept of freedom to the American psyche, regardless of social or economic class, and their belief that America was a fertile field for the realization of their ideas—only if they remained open and inclusive.[72] Both surmised, and Berkman articulated, that "no people living are ready for [Anarchy]. . . . though many are for Anarchism. . . . when we begin, as individuals, to live our An[archist] ideas in our everyday lives, then—and no sooner—will the sun rise and shine on the first day of a germinating social Anarchy." Berkman expounded in his letter: "Anarchism is not comprehended in a certain platform or set of theories; it is neither political, nor economical. . . . Anarchism is a philosophy of social life, its ideals apply to all the phases of man's intellectual, physical and psychical life. . . . ideals grow . . . very slowly . . . they must take root in the social mind and, spread [and] choke off the weeds of outlived old ideas and old-time preconceptions and prejudices. The struggle, then, is not between rich and poor, nor between the people and their government; these struggles are more apparent than real. The real struggle is far greater, far more important; it is the titanic [life and death] struggle of an outlived barbarism against a new Civilization; the struggle of two diametrically opposed 'civilizations.'" Berkman added that a social vision is never a fixed point: "Ideals are never realised; as we approach our ideal, it grows and expands and appears farther away; it is a changed, a different ideal . . . [a progr]essive march" (Letter from Alexander Berkman, 12 March 1905).

Though the solitude of his prison confinement had given Berkman the privacy to engage in long philosophical discussions, upon his release in May 1906, the hustle of renewed personal contact with friends and comrades and the gradual escalation of his editorial work on Goldman's new magazine *Mother Earth* overwhelmed him. In hopes of re-energizing Berkman, Goldman arranged for him to go on a lecture tour to promote her magazine, but halfway through, he disappeared. Rumors circulated that he had been kidnapped, but in fact his depression had incapacitated him. Obsessed with getting away, he couldn't tolerate the presence of others. Goldman, harried and protective, announced to the curious and concerned readers of her magazine, *Mother Earth,*

72. For a discussion of Golman's ideas about class, see introduction, vol. 1, pp. 50–52.

that Berkman realized that "one can never find the strength to live outside of himself and that to find oneself at all, one needs absolute harmony and peace. He has therefore decided to retire for a time" (see "To the Readers of Mother Earth," Notice in *Mother Earth*, November 1906). Goldman would see her comrade through his mood swings, over and over again, and eventually he would bolster Goldman through her political and personal struggles, applying his considerable skills as an editor and political theorist to enhance her written work.

"A CLUB INSTEAD OF A TORCH"

Berkman and Goldman's challenges also included braving the storms of police brutality. In a 30 October 1906 public meeting in New York City, called on the fifth anniversary of Czolgosz's death, several mostly very young people were arrested just for daring to discuss whether or not Czolgosz, the assassin of President McKinley, was an anarchist. Goldman herself was struck in the back by the police and immediately arrested. Such experiences prompted her to taunt that "If we as a nation were not such unspeakable hypocrites, we should long since have placed a club instead of a torch in the hand of the Goddess of Liberty" (see "Police Brutality," Essay in *Mother Earth*, November 1906).

Berkman emerged from his long depression to join Goldman in rallying support for the case, bringing himself back to political life as he defended both of them against attacks from other anarchists who believed that the issue of Czolgosz's association with anarchism was a subject too raw and dangerous even to broach. Although praising the the president's assassin as a hero was enormously provocative, and pushed the boundaries of free speech, Goldman and many other anarchists considered this dramatic example of the use of the New York criminal anarchy law, "which makes almost every Anarchistic utterance a crime, punishable with $2000 fine and 10 years prison" an indication of the fears within and outside of the anarchist movement about reexamining the issue of President McKinley's assassination. The criminal charges against Goldman extended beyond holding a public meeting to commemorate the fifth anniversary of Czolgosz's death to the "crime" of having published an issue of *Mother Earth* devoted to Czolgosz's memory—with many provocative articles praising him and his act.

Goldman and Berkman used the publicity around the case as an opportunity to distribute the Czolgosz issue more widely and as a means to raise money and awareness about the upcoming trial. Goldman, Berkman, and the other *Mother Earth* editor, Harry Kelly, pointed out that there was relatively little self-censorship among anarchists on "the sex question" yet warned that free speech within the movement was threatened whenever the subject of violence came to the fore. They defied any one "to produce a single line from any English Anarchist paper or magazine published in this country within the last twenty-five years where assassination is advocated or even implied." With no hint of justification or apology, the three editors of *Mother Earth* attempted to clarify their position, distinguishing their sympathy for Czolgosz as "a soul in pain" and suggesting that they merely intended to foster understanding—"and for the rest, let posterity judge" (see "As to 'Crammers of Furnaces,'" Article in *Mother Earth*, December 1906).[73]

Mother Earth was inaugurated in March 1906 with lofty visions of becoming a literary radical magazine whose words and ideas would be woven into the fabric of American culture. By October, however, with the publication of the Czolgosz memorial issue, the police went on the offensive. Goldman reported that the police "raided two meetings, clubbed the audiences, arrested twelve persons and confiscated many copies of the October issue of 'Mother Earth.' Not satisfied with this arbitrary and highhanded proceeding, the police have since kept up their brutal persecution, closing radical meetings, terrorizing hall keepers and audiences, and threatening them with arrest." In this atmosphere of fear, fewer people dared attend their meeting, although the Czolgosz memorial issue of the magazine was much in demand not only among many of the staunchest anarchists but also attracted interest among a small group of progressives and liberals. Still, some anarchists stopped selling *Mother Earth* at their meetings, fearing police intervention, putting the journal's future in jeopardy. In a plea to her supporters Goldman asserted, "All this, however, shall not influence in the least my determination to continue the magazine. Neither shall police persecution nor personal danger deter me from voicing my ideas. Are the readers and friends of 'Mother Earth' willing to assist me?" (see "To My Readers," Editorial in *Mother Earth*, December 1906). In the meantime, Goldman arranged for others to publish the magazine should she be faced with a long bout in jail. By necessity, *Mother Earth* now focused more on political activism than on literary criticism. In reaction to the threat of incarceration, the issue of free speech became more central than she and her co-editors had originally conceived.

At this time, a major champion of free speech died. Goldman was honored to be asked to write the obituary for Ernest Crosby in the Italian-language newspaper published in Barre, Vermont; she describes Crosby as "one of the most selfless sons to have sprung from the loins of this cynical America . . . a great intellect and noble heart had been stilled forever" ("Ernest Crosby," Obituary in *Cronaca Sovversiva*, 16 March 1907). In writing Crosby's obituary, Goldman expounded upon the social history of the complex ties between socialists and anarchists, theorists and political activists, joined together in respectful homage to a man who, for Goldman, held the attributes of the active and the reflective life she so admired—and who had also won her eternal favor for his support for Berkman's pardon and earnest work for Turner's right to speak freely on anarchism.

"A RIGHT TO TALK TO MY FELLOW AMERICANS"

It was not only the Czolgosz issue of *Mother Earth* that alerted the public and police to the threat implicit in the persuasive writer and orator's ideas. Inevitably, when Goldman was on the road, newspaper reporters queried her and listened for her statements

---

73. Also notes the complex labor and racial issues raised in this article.

on whether she supported violence. During her lecture swing through Ohio in March 1907, the *Ohio State Journal* reported her emphatic and perhaps somewhat disingenuous denial, a denial she calibrated to her audience's degree of receptivity: "I never advocated violence. . . . It is contrary to the teachings of anarchism. Violence comes from a few individuals who cannot wait for the conditions for which we are working to come about in a natural way. The pressure and grinding of the authorities makes them wild for relief. They imagine that the removal of two or three persons will change conditions." Such general assertions to the press were often modified in her own publication, *Mother Earth,* which, along with its cultural critiques and espousal of freedom in all areas of life, also applauded the impact and curiosity about anarchism peaked by dramatic, targeted acts of violence.

In an attempt to counter the demonization of anarchists and to diffuse the fears associated with anarchism, Goldman asserted that "The doctrine of anarchy taught in this country was founded by Americans" and claimed that many of the values imparted by the nation's literary icons—Thoreau's civil disobedience and Emerson's individualism and undercurrent of anti-statism—were forms of indigenous anarchism. Identifying herself as an American, she believed that "each country must work out its own salvation . . . foreign anarchists who come here work among their own people [and] talk to those of their own language and customs about the conditions at home. Only Americans, or those who have become Americans, attempt to talk in English, or about our country. . . . I was in this country ten years before I ever appeared in public. I have been here 22 years now. I know conditions here as they are, and I would like to know if I have not a right to talk to my fellow Americans" (see "High Priestess of Anarchy Here," Interview in *Ohio State Journal,* 8 March 1907). Goldman actually had begun to lecture in 1890, within five years of her coming to the United States. Thus, Goldman's preference for addressing her audiences in English was not only a strategy for gathering a readership, attracting newspaper coverage, and embedding her magazine into the annals of American radical culture, but was also her way of proclaiming that—in mind and spirit—she had become an American.

For Goldman, anarchism was the harbinger of freedom and the underlying political spirit of the nation—a sentiment she shared with the Haymarket anarchists who preceded her, and with Berkman, her closest comrade and political advisor.

MOTHER EARTH TAKES ROOT

Goldman had long imagined how exciting it would be to create a monthly journal as a steady platform for her work. Although Goldman was a woman with a talent for words and a reputation for attracting and inspiring an audience, few magazines outside the anarchist ranks dared to publish her ideas. One rejection after another proved that she was still considered too dangerous for mainstream publications. "It is not my wish to write as an agitator, but only as a heart-sore actor and spectator," wrote Goldman in a letter to the editor of *Metropolitan Magazine,* 4 December 1905. Even so, some considered her ideas too radical, while others may have perceived them as too simplistic to print.[74]

In her own magazine, she would expound a uniquely American form of anarchist communism, positing a blend of individual freedom and the promise of ample resources to be distributed according to the needs of the people. Its articles would address both cultural and political issues and appeal both to her anarchist comrades and to a wider pool of interested supporters of her work. The potential for wide distribution of her ideas in print also overrode the many obstacles to attendance at her lectures, whether by happenstance or by the deliberate suppression by police, who were more fearful of her persuasive oratorial talents than the government was of her pen.

As originally conceived, the magazine would also serve Goldman's covert activities. It was a convenient cover for concealing her role as messenger and defender of the underground movement as well as strategizer for crafting the cadence of a public message that would keep them out of jail. The magazine was also a base for fundraising for strikers and other militant groups in need of legal aid. She hoped to broaden her public reach to represent "all truly radical elements in the United States [who] see the only hope for struggling humanity in the reorganization of our social and economic life upon a basis of freedom and justice" (see "The Open Road," Letter to Max Metzkow, 20 January 1906).

Inspired by the spirit of the American poet Walt Whitman, the journal was originally to be called *The Open Road*, but in deference to another magazine of the same name, Goldman launched her magazine in March 1906 as *Mother Earth*.

The name "Mother Earth," rooted in Goldman's desire to ground her readers in the real condition of the world, framed its mission as a "good mother sees the bleeding feet of her children, she hears their moans and she is ever calling to them that she is theirs." Conjuring images of nurturance, protection, and the potential for unconditional love, the all-inclusive title embraces the idea that social and environmental harmony was a natural condition whose attainment was possible.

Invoking, as she had in many of her lectures, George Washington, Tom Paine, and Thomas Jefferson for whom the terrain of America appeared "vast, boundless, full of promise," the magazine's statement of intent in its inaugural issue of March 1906 lamented that America's riches were seized by the "privileged few to monopolize every material and mental resource." Although the magazine reached out to an American readership, given its editor and primary constituency, the title also evoked the familiar name for Goldman's native "Mother Russia."

Its subtitle, a journal "devoted to social science and literature," identified the magazine in generic terms used within her circles to attract the general public to discussions of social issues from an anarchist perspective. It also included poetry, literature, and

---

74. Both Sara Bard Field, suffragist and poet, and Margaret Anderson, the avant-garde writer and editor, would later complain in letters that Goldman's literary criticism was one-dimensional, telling the story rather than analyzing the artfulness of the texts.

reviews of recently published books. *Mother Earth* announced its intention to include cutting-edge poetry and fiction alongside political articles. Although poetry and fiction never fully materialized in its pages, *Mother Earth,* published from 1906 to 1917, took its place among the longest-running anarchist periodicals, grounding not only the movement but also Goldman herself.

Mother Earth began when a small group of friends and potential supporters met at Goldman's apartment on East 13th Street and talked into the small hours of the night about the many paths the journal might take. A formal meeting followed at Hillel Solotaroff's office on East Broadway where Goldman and her collaborators created a plan for the financing and conceptual shape of her magazine. With scant seed money generated by an Orlenev theater group benefit performance, supplemented by in-house donations, within months Goldman's publication took root—and blossomed intellectually and politically. Among the earliest "little magazines," its reputation far exceeded its circulation of roughly three thousand.

Meanwhile, Goldman's apartment, already the site of meetings with Russian revolutionaries and Greenwich Village radicals, became the makeshift office for *Mother Earth,* where Goldman slept in a bed tucked behind a bookshelf, as a whirlwind of publishing activity took place around her. She became the publisher of *Mother Earth* when she was thirty-seven years old, a perfect age at which to solidify her talents and anchor her life's work within a chosen family (an editorial board of similar political persuasion). Goldman's magazine established her as a writer—in a medium that she hoped would be more lasting than the transient words spoken on the lecture stage or reported in newspapers.

She modeled her magazine after Augustin Hamon's *L'Humanite Nouvelle*[75]—an international review of science and arts which had been published in Paris and Brussels until 1903.[76] *Mother Earth* attracted an interesting mix of radicals, trade unionists, feminist intellectuals, left liberal reformers, and militant anarchists from whom Goldman solicited advance subscriptions. During her lecture tours, she distributed the magazine and raised money for its production and its causes—publicly, support committees for strikers or legal fees for arrested anarchists—but also for more clandestine activities, including prison escapes and the purchase of arms for Russia. At sixty pages and produced in a small five-by-eight-inch format, the publication fit in a worker's pocket. Well printed on relatively high-quality paper, *Mother Earth* was a visual representation of an intrepid, literate, and enterprising association of anarchists.

At first Goldman published travel reports in *Mother Earth* as well as many of her

75. According to a reminiscence written by fellow editor and friend Harry Kelly, who was present at one of the inaugural meetings; see Harry Kelly, "Mother Earth 1905–1915," *Mother Earth* 10, no. 1 (March 1915): 408–10.
76. *L'Humanite Nouvelle* (New Humanity) was published between 1897 and 1903. Edited by Augustin Hamon and others, it attracted a wide range of contributions from leading political and cultural figures, including Peter Kropotkin, Havelock Ellis, George Bernard Shaw, Victor Dave, and the Russian playwright Leonid Andreyev.

speeches. She then sold copies of her talks in pamphlet form to the thousands of people who attended her lectures.[77] Her pamphlets sold more copies than did the magazine—in part because of her immense popularity beyond anarchist circles and in part because the group lacked the funds for a large print-run of the magazine itself.

The character of the magazine also took its shape from five men who worked formally and informally as its editors—Max Baginski, Harry Kelly, John Coryell, Hippolyte Havel, and Alexander Berkman, who in March 1907 became the sole editor. Each editor had his own political emphasis, and several assumed aliases to freely publish a variety of political ideas and literary works or to help create the illusion of a broader group of contributing writers. *Mother Earth* took on a different voice when one or the other editor dropped out or was replaced. Although it was a collaborative effort of the Mother Earth group, overall the magazine's tone reflected Goldman's mix of militancy with political and literary theory. The magazine became a template for her ability to maintain and contain her dual identity as a militant revolutionary and a broad-based cultural critic.

Skeptical about the possibility of finding readers in the United States to match the general intellectual and political caliber of its European readership, the magazine's founders nonetheless strove to address topics which would be important to the international anarchist movement. Like *L'Humanite Nouvelle, Mother Earth* updated its readers about developments in anarchist theory and activism in Europe, Asia, Latin America, and the United States. Unlike its European counterpart, however, Goldman's magazine, rather than striving to be highly theoretical, favored the accessible style of her lectures.

A typical issue included an opening poem, notes and comments on current issues, an article or tour report by Goldman, a literary piece, and several essays on anarchist theory, along with reports on strikes and solicitations and tallies of funds received. The magazine's international notes covered key developments in the anarchist community, almost any act of resistance to governments, or the exercise of government tyranny, across the globe. Initially, the editors called for "articles, essays, and notes, treating of the development and growth of Anarchistic ideas, in various phases of human life . . . international reports of the struggle of new ideas against the old, of the various movements of the oppressed against the oppressors, and the methods employed by them, such as the general strike, trade unionism, and the co-operative movement. Every endeavor . . . literary, artistic, social, or economic . . . the serious side of life, but with its humorous, satirical and ironical phases as well" (see Letter to Max Metzkow, with Enclosure, "The Open Road," 20 January 1906).

Within three months after the publication of the first issue of *Mother Earth,* Alexander

---

77. Ben Reitman commented in "Three Years" (*Mother Earth,* May 1911) that "during the time that I have been with Emma Goldman about a half million cards have been distributed announcing our meetings, most of them containing some Anarchist quotation or definition." Over the years, the numbers who attended her lectures increased, culminating in the massive anti-war rallies of 1917 that would lead to her arrest and eventual deportation.

Berkman was released from jail, met Goldman in Detroit and shortly after, arrived in New York. It had been fourteen years since his *attentat* on Frick. As one of the uncharged accomplices, Goldman had taken on the role of explaining to the public the significance of Berkman's act, working tirelessly to have his sentence shortened. His release freed her of the survivor-guilt that may, in part, have fueled her sympathetic preoccupation with prison and violence. For their personal and political relationship, *Mother Earth* marked a new beginning. Gradually he would become integral to the shaping of its content and the managing of its production and distribution.

But, Sasha's reentry was rocky. Goldman stood by him during his harrowing mood changes and his many moments of panic and terror. She hoped that offering him the possibility of taking primary responsibility for the editorship of the magazine would divert him from his past and put his remarkable literary ability to good use. Berkman was an excellent editor and elegant writer, and his political acuity and organizing experience added a special depth to the magazine. His work complemented Goldman's. Her editorial stalwarts, Max Baginski and Hippolyte Havel, wrote for the journal and managed the typesetting, printing, and distribution tasks—skills that were especially critical when Berkman lapsed into the abyss of prison memories or when Goldman was overwhelmed by legal battles or harassed by police in her peripatetic life along the lecture trail.

In the pages of *Mother Earth*, Berkman wrote about his rededication to anarchism: "Though the bloodthirsty hyena of the law has, in its wild revenge, despoiled me of the fourteen most precious blossoms in the garden of my life, yet I will, henceforth as heretofore, consecrate what days are left to me in the service of that grand ideal, the wonderful power of which has sustained me through those years of torture . . . and it shall be more than my sufficient reward to know that I have added, if ever so little, in breaking the shackles of superstition, ignorance and tradition."[78] Whether Goldman and Berkman took equally militant positions on the question of anarchist tactics or whether Sasha's were the more overtly violent of the two comrades remains unclear.[79] New research, combined with rediscovered documents referenced and published for the first time in this volume, piece together written remembrances that shed light on clandestine activities too dangerous to commit to paper at the time. These documents reveal the extent of Goldman's awareness of a range of covert violent acts committed by fellow anarchists. The documents further suggest that Goldman and Berkman played different, but not exclusive, roles. In recounting these days later, Goldman spoke directly to the press, explaining that Berkman "actually undertook to shoot Frick because she was better able to explain the reasons for the deed."[80]

78. Alexander Berkman, "A Greeting," *Mother Earth* 1, no. 4 (June 1906): 3–6.
79. Berkman, the veteran anarchist organizer, continued to function in a quasi-clandestine manner, working closely with the Anarchist Federation of New York City, whose member Selig Silverstein blew himself up at the 1908 Union Square bombing. Berkman was the secretary of the Anarchist Federation.
80. "Woman Anarchist Is a Super Cook," 4 January 1933, *EGP*, in-house third-party newspaper file.

Whatever political tactics or forms of direct action they may have condoned or even participated in, it is also clear that Goldman and Berkman valued and relied on the power of the written word to articulate their shared vision of anarchism. Moreover, whether the readers shared Goldman's sense of what needed to be done is not clear; the magazine attracted a mix of radicals, trade unionists, feminist intellectuals, left liberal reformers, non-socialist radicals, and militant anarchists, each authentically linked to the idea of social change and radicalism and to Goldman, though in all likelihood not to each other.

SYNTHESIZING A WORLD OF IDEAS

An extension of the magazine, the Mother Earth Publishing Association printed Goldman's essays and a wide variety of pamphlets on political and cultural subjects of interest to anarchists, radicals, and trade unionists—works that advanced the theory of anarchist communism. The magazine distributed material otherwise available only in Europe, including works by Peter Kropotkin, tracts by the American free-speech advocate Theodore Schroeder, and writings on a range of social and scientific topics, including the more readily accessible works by Charles Darwin on the theory of evolution.

In its early years, *Mother Earth* magazine advertised, and the Mother Earth Publishing Association distributed, a variety of rare books and pamphlets on both political and literary topics. Many of its core anarchist texts (including almost all of the works of Kropotkin, along with selected material from C. L. James, Leo Tolstoy, and Jean Grave, the French anarchist editor and writer) were imported from London's Freedom Press. Titles from the fields of anthropology, literature, philosophy, and education and those advertised by booksellers from radical bookstores, were eventually dropped.[81] By 1909, the list was limited to the works of Kropotkin, some new writing by Émile Pouget, and some by William Morris and Élisée Reclus, as well as the story "Schopenhauer in the Air" by Sadakichi Hartmann. The magazine featured works by John Coryell, prolific author of Nick Carter mystery stories, often writing articles in *Mother Earth* under the pseudonym Margaret Grant.

Pamphlet versions of Goldman's essays—including "The Tragedy of Woman's Emancipation," "A Beautiful Ideal," "Patriotism: A Menace to Liberty," "What I Believe," "A New Declaration of Independence," and her analysis of the phenomena of prostitution, "The White Slave Traffic"—incorporated much of what Goldman had been reading. The classics of anarchist theory became increasing apparent in her thinking and writing: in part, she took her sense of anarchist morality from Peter Kropotkin's *Appeal to the Young* but did not hesitate to draw upon the works of the anti-religious "egoist" Max Stirner—especially after the 1907 release of the first English translation of *The Ego and His Own*—to

81. Anthropology texts like Otis Tufton Mason's *Women's Share in Primitive Culture* (New York: D. Appleton, 1894) were offered along with Oscar Wilde's *De Profundis,* John Meslier's *Superstition in All Ages* (New York: Anna Knoop, 1898), an early freethought classic, and Friedrich Nietzsche's *Thus Spake Zarathusa.* Among the books advertised were those of Ernest Crosby and Bolton Hall. Max Maisel's radical bookstore in New York offered the collected works of Charles Darwin and Herbert Spencer.

repudiate any need for creating or articulating a collective sense of morality in defense of the actions of individual *attentaters* like Czolgosz and others, who acted independently against a perceived aggressor in what Stirner referred to as the psychological moment of individual action against invasion. Goldman also drew on Henrik Ibsen's characters as vehicles for encouraging others to stand up against the masses and restrictive social convention. She was exposed to French syndicalism at the 1907 Anarchist Congress in Amsterdam, which may have influenced her shift back to labor and to the Industrial Workers of the World as it was evolving in the United States, ruminating on its ideas and tactics for later writings. As she developed a compelling critique of the concept of patriotism, the French anti-militarist Gustave Hervé's ideas thread through her essays and lectures, sometimes almost verbatim.

During these years from 1902 to 1909, in her quest for a more nuanced understanding of anarchism, Goldman read widely and—a brilliant synthesizer—created a patchwork of ideas that were at once derivative and original. Along with the influences of the philosophical texts of Max Stirner, the dramatic works of Henrik Ibsen, and the anti-militarist treatises of Gustave Hervé, she stayed current in the writings and debates among the socialists—referencing the works of Antonio Labriola and Karl Kautsky though rarely referring to careful readings of Karl Marx. She did, however, keep up to date on anarchist theoretical writings, including Arnold Roller's (Siegfried Nacht) *The Social General Strike* and J. Blair Smith's *Direct Action Versus Legislation*. She studied the social theories of single-tax anarchists like Bolton Hall and socialist Ernest Crosby and theories of sexuality by Edward Carpenter. She also read works that concentrated on the "scientific" development of humanity, including Wilhelm Boelsche's *The Triumph of Life* and Otis Tufton Mason's *Women's Share in Primitive Culture*—works that challenged religion and its disavowal of evolution and asserted women's importance to the dynamics of community. Goldman also steeped herself in anti-religious freethought literature, including Volney's *Ruins* and Jacob Wilson's *The New Dispensation at the Dawn of the Twentieth Century*. Often she exchanged subscriptions to her magazine *Mother Earth* with other anarchist publications from Europe, which familiarized her with the latest works by Errico Malatesta and Peter Kropotkin as well as syndicalist theories emerging from the movement in France, especially the work of Pierre Monate, among others. Many of her essays—particularly "The Tragedy of Women's Emancipation"—were geared to the growing suffrage movement and displayed her use of literary works as metaphors for exposing the limitations of the concept of the New Woman. She extended the definition of emancipation, referencing works by George Sand, Laura Marholm-Hansson's *Woman, A Character Study*, and Jean Reibrach's *New Beauty*, among others. The writings of Edward Carpenter and Havelock Ellis informed her ideas, especially about homosexuality. For someone like Goldman, who strove to be a public intellectual, in part by acquainting others with the ideas in circulation that challenged convention—reading was a critical component of her political life.

As a lecturer, especially after 1906 when *Mother Earth* became the vehicle for her national tours, her quest to gather current theories from all fields, pulling them creatively into her anarchist political construct, kept both her talks and her mind alive and lively.

She was constantly learning and teaching, and no doubt her love of great literature—especially in English—informed her own words, infusing her with an eye and an ear for a turn of phrase that would have lasting resonance, in both her ideas and their graceful expression.

Goldman added her strong interests in the political dimension of personal life, especially with respect to woman's independence. Many issues of her magazine included forthright articles about sexuality and marriage, which may have raised some eyebrows among "proper" liberals, and even among some in her own ranks, but definitely increased sales—especially among the radical edge of the New Woman movement and of the left liberal middle class. Goldman's insightful commentary about her trials and tribulations as a woman traveling on her own across the nation was a steady feature in the magazine. *Mother Earth* was widely read by anarchists and served as a monthly cohesive force for anarchists in disparate locations, as well as a source of interest for immigrants who enjoyed the vicarious exposure to the vast expanse and diverse character of their adopted country.

EMANCIPATING HERSELF

The very first issue of *Mother Earth* included one of Goldman's most significant essays—"The Tragedy of Women's Emancipation," a synthesis of her speeches on a subject she had addressed before in lectures. In the essay, Goldman articulated why women's freedom could never be legislated by a vote. As a jab against separatism and the war of the sexes, she reiterated her belief that "Peace and harmony between the sexes and individuals does not necessarily depend on a superficial equalization of human beings." Instead, she asserted that the deeper problem confronting women and men is "how to be oneself, and yet in oneness with others, to feel deeply with all human beings" (see "The Tragedy of Women's Emancipation," Essay in *Mother Earth, March* 1906).

In a compelling indictment of the illusions that full equality could be achieved through the law and that women were intractible pillars of morality and peace incorruptible by economic or political influence, Goldman took on the gathering force of the suffrage movement. She counseled women to first confront "the necessity of emancipating herself from emancipation." Goldman bemoaned the contradictory progress of a world in which few women ever achieved professional status—or, if they did, often became "professional automatons" exchanging "the narrowness and lack of freedom of the home . . . for the narrowness and lack of freedom of the factory, sweat-shop, department store, or office." She warned that such "independence is . . . but a slow process of dulling and stifling women's nature, her love instinct and her mother instinct . . . [as her] inner life is growing empty and dead." Goldman caricatured suffragists as puritanical, humorless, and limited in life experience, women who mistakenly "banished man as a disturber and doubtful character out of emotional life . . . except perhaps as the father of a child." The crescendo of her argument and the refrain that she would repeat in many forms thereafter was that "woman's freedom is closely allied to man's freedom" and that "true emancipation begins neither at the polls nor in the courts. It begins in woman's soul." Goldman claimed that such ideas often branded her "fit for the stake." Ultimately Goldman strove "to do away with the absurd notion of the dualism of the sexes, or that man and woman represent two antagonistic worlds. She counseled suffragists not to be prudish but rather to remain open to the experience of surrender to another, and to "joy, limitless joy." A significant minority within the increasingly liberal public—primed in cultural radicalism—was ready to receive the challenge of her hopeful though perhaps idealized vision of the joyful harmony of the sexes (see "The Tragedy of Women's Emancipation," Essay in *Mother Earth*, March 1906).

Goldman routinely tailored her underlying anarchist message to fit the language of the mass movements of her time—the suffrage movement, the labor movement, and the free speech movement—acting as a gadfly, prodding them on to shift their position further to the left. She sought to catalyze independent thought, encouraged her audiences to question their assumptions, and rarely compromised her ideas to gain acceptance. Time after time, she prided herself in standing alone against the crowd, as part of an enlightened minority. Her ideas and the inclusion of articles of specific interest to women often served as anchors for those who might otherwise feel unacknowledged amid the journal's more militant anarchist writings. In spite of her alternatively hostile and friendly sparring, she offered professional discounts to suffragists for her services—for troubles of the scalp, hair, and face "through a very thorough system of massage and electricity [and] a special method of shampooing"—in the *Women's Journal*, the official publication of the American Women Suffrage Association (see "Emma G. Smith, Vienna Scalp and Face Specialist," Advertisement in the *Women's Journal*, 28 September 1906).[82]

DISPATCHES FROM THE LECTURE TRAIL

Among the most popular essays in *Mother Earth* were Goldman's travelogues of her cross-country tours, documenting encounters with police and offering a taste of the local flavor of politics and of the activities and challenges faced by her comrades as they hoped to ride on Goldman's coattails to affect change in their own communities. These picturesque reports provided fascinating vignettes of civic life in many American cities and small towns, though their tone was generally sarcastic and sometimes mocked the same reformers from whom she sought support. For example, she poked fun at the respectable Jane Addams and her soup-kitchen philanthropy in Chicago by reporting that Addams was happier to host the fictitious E. G. Smith than the actual Emma Goldman. She chastised some of the young anarchists in Cleveland for setting the "bad example of applying for protection [of their right to free assembly] from the city authorities," and mocked the police captain in Buffalo as "ignorant of the provisions of the American Constitution" for declaring "any other language than English a felony" (see "A Sentimental Journey—Police Protection," Essay in *Mother Earth*, April 1906).

With too few English-speaking anarchist lecturers, Goldman wrote to her comrades

---

82. Goldman had probably closed her scalp and facial massage parlor by the time the advertisement appeared.

across the country asking for help in arranging meetings on behalf of *Mother Earth* (see Letter to Leon Malmed, 7 April 1906). She also elicited suggestions for the magazine, which she believed had the potential of becoming the only "good literary radical Magazine" in America (see Letter to Joseph A. Labadie, 11 April 1906). Boasting of its success—with 3,000 copies of the first issue sold out and 1,000 more printed—she felt less threatened by even her enemies within the anarchist ranks: "I do not consider myself at fault when people speak ill of me, nor do I think myself [virtuous], if they say kind things. In either case they are following their own desires, why should I then express thanks, or sorrow" (see Letter to Joseph A. Labadie, 11 April 1906).

The magazine helped her create a new image and broaden her audience. Reaching out beyond the limits of the immigrant Jewish and German enclave, Goldman lectured more and more often in English, in part due to her lack of adequate Yiddish-speaking skills (and her sense that those who spoke "Jargon"—a commonly used term for Yiddish—also understood German and English as well) but also because of her desire "to interest the people all over the Country" in her magazine (see Letter to Nunia Seldes, 18 May 1906). Carefully calibrating her speeches to her broader, English-speaking audiences, Goldman had high expectations for her "little magazine" as she attempted to forge her way into the collective conscience of America.

Goldman's lively columns from the road were read not only by the curious general reader but also most likely by government agents eager to document presumed transgressions of the law. More often than not, her encounters with the police forged an alliance between anarchists and various progressive, liberal, and radical strands of a movement unified by a common commitment to making speech free. Mainstream newspapers began to devote Sunday features to the woman who seemed to be as much a curiosity as a threat.

The early years of *Mother Earth* magazine, from 1906 to 1909, marked a turning point in Goldman's political evolution and gave her new exposure to a reading audience. Although she hoped to use the magazine to link the ideas and practice of politics, literature, and social science, it was often difficult to solicit outside writers. For this reason, its essays leaned more toward anarchist propaganda, especially when comrades in trouble needed support, which definitely limited the magazine's popularity outside anarchist circles.

Support for militant actions and ideas at home and abroad, evident from the magazine's beginnings, eventually led to Goldman's deportation. In a consistent thread, Goldman continued to write extensively about police brutality, analogizing the suppression of free speech in America with the extreme persecution of dissent in tsarist Russia, in praise of those who dared to perform individual acts of violence. The broad spectrum of ideas and essays in the magazine allowed less militant readers to find a comfort zone for themselves in relation to their projected vision of Goldman. What unified the articles in the magazine was the editors' challenging anarchist belief that government hindered rather than helped enhance the potential of the individual and society.

The editorial board of *Mother Earth* never hid its support of various militant acts and actively raised money for the resulting legal cases. The first issue, for example, coincided with the indictment of Western Federation of Miners representatives Charles Moyer, William Haywood, and George Pettibone, as co-conspirators in the bombing by Harry Orchard on 30 December 1905 that killed ex-governor of Idaho Frank Steunenberg (in retaliation for his anti-union actions against strikers in the Coeur D'Alene labor disputes of 1899). A *Mother Earth* article championed the cause of the accused miners, claiming they had been framed.[83]

As the magazine became more established, its editors became more adept at transmitting political ideas and cultural critiques without getting the magazine banned. Although in the end its blatant references to and support for violence would contribute, in part, to Goldman and Berkman's deportation, the magazine was much more circumspect in its discussions of sexuality—direct descriptions of which would have exposed the magazine to prosecution under the anti-obscenity laws enforced through the mails. The Progressive era espoused openness, protection, and regulation for the public good but in fact was a fragile period in the history of dissent in America—with mass lynchings of African Americans and violence against labor all too commonplace. Anarchists and radicals moved from one medium to the other, depending upon which afforded more freedoms—often determined by the culture, custom, and prejudice of a place rather than any formal discrepancy in the law.

"Free speech means either the unlimited right of expression or nothing at all. The moment any man or set of men can limit speech, it is no longer free," proclaimed Goldman to the readers of *Mother Earth*. Goldman embodied two dimensions of the free-speech issue—as an editor of an anarchist magazine and as a frequent lecturer on the topic, alerting her readers to assaults on the right of free speech that she regularly experienced on the road. In this period of extremes, when government officials backed industrial greed with violence against striking workers, she warned, "Let all reformers and radicals realize, once for all, that to love liberty means to become lawless, since freedom and law can never harmonize" (see "En Route," Letter to *Mother Earth*, 30 April 1908).

"CARRYING TRUTH TO THE BARRACKS"

One of the most dramatic events of Goldman's tours took place in 1908 in a crowded hall in San Francisco where a soldier in uniform came up across the stage, shook her hand, and thanked her just moments after she delivered her talk "Patriotism"—her critique of the rationale of nationhood with its boundaries for which one was expected to fight and die. For this act, which was perceived as treason by the soldier's commanding officers, William Buwalda was court-martialed, dishonorably discharged, and sentenced to five years in a military prison. His case provoked an uproar in government bureaucratic

---

83. For further discussion on the Haywood, Moyer, and Pettibone case, see J. Anthony Lukas, *Big Trouble* (New York: Simon & Schuster, 1997).

circles and among Goldman's audiences, and proved to be a far more powerful critique of patriotism than her lecture on the subject. Goldman roused the public in protest, gathering support wherever she spoke (see "Too Large an Army Now," Article in the *Portland Morning Oregonian*, 27 May 1908).

At his trial, Buwalda denied applauding the remarks of the speaker. He said that the arrangement of chairs made crossing the platform to the stage door the easiest way to exit the building. He testified that as he passed the speaker, she smiled and extended her hand, which he took and said, "'How do you do, Miss Goldman?' He denied making the remark to which the police officer testified" (see George B. Davis to William Howard Taft, 19 June 1908).

Buwalda's perfectly plausible story, coupled with his having fought in the Spanish-American War in 1898 in the Philippines and almost unanimous record of "excellent" character ratings, led the military court under the direction of Brigadier General Frederick Funston to conclude that Buwalda's offense was "not of opinions deliberately formed, but of a mind temporarily thrown off its balance by the words of an anarchist orator." Funston accordingly decided to reduce his sentence from five to three years.

The Buwalda case stirred up dissension among top-ranking military officials and a difference of opinion about how their harsh punishment would be viewed by the public. General Funston, who considered Buwalda "too good a man to have his life ruined," recommended an executive pardon and was careful to warn against giving the public the impression that this case could be considered a precedent (see Frederick Funston to Fred C. Ainsworth, 30 June 1908). Ultimately, President Theodore Roosevelt granted Buwalda a pardon—lest a more severe punishment cede even greater influence to Emma Goldman and the righteous indignation of her cause. Upon his release, however, the disillusioned Buwalda, claiming that he had never been guilty of any crime, returned the medals he had received for service in battle in the Philippines—a symbolic act of defiance and pride.

The subjects of patriotism and national boundaries were difficult to address for an anarchist and internationalist like Goldman, who viewed patriotism not as benign love of place but as a dangerous force charged with the hazardous ingredients of "conceit, arrogance, and egotism." In a litany of examples of veiled economic interests fueling wars, she asserted that "the greatest bulwark of capitalism is militarism. The very moment the latter is undermined, capitalism will totter." She predicted that the boundaries between nations would eventually disintegrate as the working people of the world recognized their source of commonality: "the centralization of power has brought into being an international feeling of solidarity among the oppressed nations of the world . . . a solidarity which fears not foreign invasion because it is bringing all the workers to the point" of refusing to fight for their masters. Recognizing militarism as a looming threat—and taking a stance against it that echoed the tactic of the general strike advocated by the French syndicalists and that would eventually lead to the suppression of her magazine and to Goldman and Berkman's arrest—Goldman believed that to achieve a truly free society and an international brotherhood, "it is probably even more important to carry the truth into the barracks than into the factory" (see "Patriotism: A Menace to Liberty," Pamphlet, October 1908).

"FREE SPEECH . . . GRABBED BY THE THROAT"

In almost all her talks that followed Buwalda's arrest until his pardon, Goldman continued to draw on the themes of his case and what it signified about the government's fear of anarchism even though its own founding fathers ascribed to similarly violent tactics against national despotism. In Spokane, the newspapers reported her proclamation that "the right of rebellion when government becomes tyrannical" was guaranteed by the Declaration of Independence. Deflecting and denying any connection between bombings and anarchists, Goldman also equated misunderstandings about the true nature of anarchism to early Christians who at first "were persecuted by those who did not know of their beliefs, and that continued for centuries. Anarchists are martyrs in the same way. People are willing to accept what others say about anarchists, but will not try to understand them." In an energetic response to a journalist's queries, she expanded her topics of discussion to include religion, the state, violence, marriage, and the military, drawing particular attention to injustice in the Buwalda case (see "Goldman Traces Anarchy to 1776," Article in the *Spokesman-Review,* 31 May 1908).

With regard to religion, she had always been especially provocative, having derived much of her thinking from Michael Bakunin, who believed that religious dogma was the result of "man's mental inability to solve natural phenomena." During this period, the frequency of her talks on anti-religious themes increased. In a 1907 lecture, reported in a transcript made by a government agent in the audience, Goldman blamed religion for fossilizing the hierarchical order of things, serving the interests of capital: "The Church is always with the rich and the successful. They preach to you about loyalty to your country. Whose country? The country of the Rockefellers, the Morgans, the Astors and the Vanderbilts?" In the same speech, in what amounted to a racial slur, Goldman cautioned her "civilized" audiences that they were "losing [their] sense of hearing and seeing" by their obliviousness to industrial greed: even "the savage Indian" could "put his ear to the earth and can hear the hoofs, and the sound of his enemy coming on miles distant but you hear not nor do you see beyond your noses" (see Louis J. Domas to George B. Billings, 12 December 1907).

Such lectures were carefully transcribed by government agents, who were eager to prove that Goldman provoked the poor to steal from the rich. From this same December 1907 lecture, agent Domas of the Immigration Service records her pronouncement that "no man, woman or child has any right to go hungry or go without shelter as long as there are mansions and houses enough to shelter all of us, and the warehouses are full . . . I am not telling you to steal, I am merely telling you to help yourselves to what by every right belongs to you" (see Louis J. Domas to George B. Billings, 12 December 1907). At a lecture a few weeks later, she is recorded as saying "The real thieves, the men who do their stealing on a large scale, under the mantle of business operations, they go free . . . laws actually protect and legalize their robberies. I think the man who steals my pocketbook is a harmless person compared to the man who steals my chances of employment and ruins the possibilities of my making a living for myself and my family" (see F. W. Maasch to Robert Watchorn, 24 December 1907).

Because of her critique of what were considered the pillars of societal stability—trust in god, government, law, capitalism, marriage, and the family—it was no wonder that blocking the very persuasive Goldman from speaking was such a frequent occurance. Excuses for barring her ranged from invoking official city ordinances against disturbing the peace to health and safety regulations. She was exasperated when Spokane, Washington, officials took her to headquarters, fined her, and mandated her departure after a crowd of sympathizers broke the lock on the hall door. When she was similarly constrained from speaking in Everett, she issued a resolution: "Resolved, that the city of Everett, in the state of Washington, should be taken off the American map and turned over to the dominion of the Russian czar." A reporter quoted Goldman's resolution, which proclaimed that the city's decision was "backed by the power of the club, and might being right, free speech was grabbed by the throat and choked to death." Goldman went on to assert that it was not herself but rather the freedom to express ideas about anarchism that was stopped—ideas that she defined as standing for human development against stagnation and for freedom and noninterference as opposed to enforcement of restrictive laws by club-wielding police (see "Emma Goldman Says Everett Ought to Be Annexed to Russia," Article in the *Everett Morning Tribune,* 15 December 1908).

Her dramatic departure from Everett, where the authorities claimed that they were in fact protecting Goldman from violent vigilantes, was followed by an equally charged encounter in Bellingham, Washington. There, she and Ben Reitman were arrested and accused of inciting treason when they attempted to address an anarchist gathering. Faced with the possibility of being charged with insanity, she decided to leave town rather than fight in court. Then, as they headed toward Vancouver, Canadian authorities pulled them off the train, only to put them right back again, lacking the authority to bar their entry. Constant harassment, however, was better than being jailed or silenced completely.

When, in 1909, the recently pardoned Buwalda attempted to attend a Goldman lecture in San Francisco, he, along with Goldman and Reitman, was arrested for disturbing the peace. Spontaneous protests erupted, prompting a quick release on bail, followed by yet another arrest for Goldman on the charge of unlawful assembly. She warned that if her defense failed in California, the next victims might be Socialists, Single-Taxers, Mormons, Prohibitionists, or any minority movement and counseled that "piece-meal the enemy can cut us into mince-meat, but working together we are invincible" (see Circular Letter, 26 January 1909).

The fight for free speech was not always an obvious fit for anarchists, who viewed it as neither god-given nor something the state had the authority to grant. Some anarchists feared that free speech fights obscured the vicious battle between labor and capital, or contradicted their anti-government stance. Nonetheless, Goldman's attunement to free speech and her spirited fight to defend it, remains among her greatest legacies. Although a critic of Progressive reform as a seductive but doomed palliative intended to cover a multitude of horrendous transgressions by an evasive government that turned the other cheek to violence against labor and to lynchings of the American Negro, she also relied on the protection of civil liberties to deliver her message. Goldman and her associates, partially out of self-interest, helped roll back the tide of repression set in motion after the assassination of the president in 1901. And, through persistance and courage, she was able to exercise her freedom of expression, reaching thousands of people each year as she spread her ideas about the promise of anarchism. But not even Emma Goldman could stop the torrents of repression that would overtake the country prior to its entry into the First World War. The underside of liberalism, which squelched labor and barred admission to anarchists after the McKinley assassination, would find its dramatic symbol in 1919, with the deportation of Emma Goldman—one of the nation's boldest advocates for free speech.

ANARCHISTS VS. SOCIALISTS

Staged debates between anarchists and socialists were frequent events during the first decade of the twentieth century, especially because the Socialist Party was the largest group within the American Left. In an era of Progressive reform, socialists carried the idea of protective legislation several steps further by countering the profit-motive, competition-driven forces of capitalism with a vision of benevolent socialist governance in the interests of meeting the immediate needs of the people. Anarchists spurned all hierarchical power structures as inherently corrupting, opting instead for confederations of self-governing groups that held individual freedom at the core of their definition of the social good. Debates between spokespersons for the warring tendencies on the left were sure to attract a large audience—sometimes up to 300 (see Letter to Peter Kropotkin, 31 May 1907)—from both camps, with many there just to witness the spectacle of clever sparring. Goldman argued that "socialism and anarchy are as far apart as the poles" and that "humanity is suffering from two evils: first, capitalism, and [second] organized government which protects capitalism in its robbery of the rights of the individual. In their desire to abolish capitalism . . . anarchy and socialism stand on common ground, [but] the latter stands for and advocates government and centralization, while anarchy stands for 'liberty' and 'voluntarism.'" She rejected the socialist presumption that a "working man's state would be an entirely different thing." Goldman's socialist opponent ridiculed her self-definition as an "anarchist-communist," claiming that "the individualism of the anarchist and the social instinct of communism were incompatible"—although for Goldman communism called for the tending to the basic needs of the people and was completely compatible with the optimal development of the individual (see "Goldman-Bauer Debate," Article in *Common Sense,* 16 May 1908). These debates raised issues already circulating among many who would never think of identifying with one "ism" or the other.

Still, Goldman's success as a lecturer was not only attributable to her eloquence and bite, but often depended on the presence of a strong labor movement for whom the issues of exploitation were fought on a daily basis and on the hard work of a local cluster of effective anarchists, alongside a preponderance of progressive politicians in a receptive and politically open town. Goldman was often welcomed in places that had most recently undergone intense labor strife, where she could offer her immediate fundraising support for strikers and engage the community in political debate, pitting the anarchist perspective against the various socialist strategies on unionization and the rights of workers. Although dominated in its early years by socialists, the labor organization often associated with anarchism was the Industrial Workers of the World (IWW).

The distinguishing characteristic of the IWW was its attempt to break down the boundaries between craft unions and unskilled workers, women's and men's unions, and to break through the barriers of racial and ethnic exclusion that permeated the early labor movement (especially toward African American and Chinese laborers). Although it had a distinctly American character, the movement around the IWW, which constituted the radical fringe of the growing labor movement, later bore traces of European industrial unionism—especially in its organizing tactics, which included sabotage as an important element in its array of strike techniques. The majority of the early members of the IWW believed that an organized union based on class struggle was a necessary step toward socialism. The issue of whether or not the IWW should take part in electoral activity was too volatile for its uneasy mix of socialists and anarchists—and personal tensions around these and other political differences added to the turmoil of the organization's infancy, especially in its first three years.

Perhaps not surprisingly, Emma Goldman kept her distance from the IWW in its early years. In fact, as the group was sorting out its tactics and embroiled in various factionalized power struggles, mostly among its socialist membership trying to make it their stronghold, Goldman was even antagonistic—and noticeably absent from its founding convention in 1905. However, many other prominent anarchist militants allied themselves with industrial unionism and were represented in Chicago—Jay Fox, Lucy Parsons, Joseph Peukert, Florecio Bazora (Spanish anarchist and close associate of Ricardo Flores Magón), *Free Society* editorial group member Julia Mechanic, and Al Klemensic, longtime contributor to *Free Society* from Colorado. The majority of the initial organizers were driven by a variety of frustrations and desires. Some believed that the American Federation of Labor (AFL) was unable to meet the needs of many of its members (seconded later by the Western Federation of Miners and various trade branches of the AFL that objected to the perceived East Coast bias of the AFL). Others, especially left-wing socialists (including Eugene Debs and Algie Simons) and Socialist Labor Party members and their trade union organization, the Socialist Trade and Labor Alliance, believed that a labor organization whose central organizing principle was class struggle as well as labor negotiations was essential for the ultimate emancipation of the working class. The founding convention held the craft-based AFL most accountable for its collusion with management, for creating elitism in the workforce that obscured the encroaching technology that they believed would have an impact on all.

Goldman's magazine *Mother Earth*—which was established the year after the 1905 IWW convention—covered the IWW but never, during this early period, with the enthusiastic support common then among other anarchist papers, including *The Liberator* and *The Demonstrator*. Although Goldman vigorously spoke out against the imprisonment of William Haywood, Charles Moyer, and George Pettibone as militants of the Western Federation of Miners, she never acknowledged their active membership in the IWW.[84] In fact, in the October 1907 *Mother Earth* (vol. 2, no. 8), in the Observations and Comments section, she counseled anarchists in the IWW about the dangers of becoming a front group for—in her words, an "appendage of the Socialist Labor Party" of Daniel De Leon—if they did not quickly "act independently on their own initiative." In the magazine's reprint of her report to the International Anarchist Congress in Amsterdam entitled "The Situation in America," Goldman described the IWW as "considerably impaired by internal strife, jealousy and legal investigation" as well as by "strikebreakers."[85] Although Goldman returned from Amsterdam with a proposed series of talks on the "General Strike" and "Direct Action," not until 1910 during the IWW's dramatic free speech fights would she support the organization in any meaningful way—and then only sporadically. Goldman's interest in the group's direct-action tactics (and horrendous violence to which IWW activists were subjected) coincided with the IWW's official decision to abandon any attempt to take part in supporting political candidates or in other aspects of electoral politics in the United States.

The movement attracted both enthusiasts for the vast number of unskilled laborers drawn to the spirited IWW groups across the nation and antagonists who would later claim its initials were an abbreviation for the "I Won't Work" force. During this period, however, the news media reflected more fear of the growing strength of the unruly IWW than of the previously demonized Goldman. Still, withstanding violent police harassment and maintaining a consistent focus on the right to organize labor and to break down the hierarchies of the workplace signaled a lasting affinity between the spirit of the IWW and the anarchists.[86]

84. The Western Federation of Miners left the IWW between 1908 and 1909 over the many conflicts that arose with the union's leadership, who were more conservative than most IWW members.

85. The charge that the IWW was permeated with "strikebeakers" was angrily refuted by IWW anarchist Jean Spielman in the December 1907 *Mother Earth*.

86. Recent studies of the IWW include Nigel Anthony Sellars, *Oil, Wheat, and Wobblies: The IWW in Oklahoma 1905–1930* (Norman: University of Oklahoma Press, 1998); and Howard Kimeldorf, "Radical Possibilities? The Rise and Fall of Wobbly Unionism on the Philadelphia Docks," in Calvin Winslow, ed., *Waterfront Workers: New Perspectives on Race and Class* (Urbana: University of Illinois Press, 1998). For the most thorough review of literature on the IWW, see David Montgomery, "What More to Be Done?" *Labor History* (August 1999). On the relationship between anarchists and socialists, see Salvatore Salerno, *Red November, Black November* (Albany: State University of New York Press, 1989).

By the end of 1909, "Wobbly" free speech fights ensued, for example in Missoula, Montana, and Spokane, Washington—attracting sympathizers who flooded the jails and overwhelmed the courts. In this charged atmosphere, city officials were especially wary of Goldman and, in some cities, she was considered too dangerous to the public to be allowed to utter even one word.

As early as 1907, Goldman wrote to her mentor Kropotkin that, in spite of the significant setbacks due to police harassment, she believed that the impact of the Wobblies on the American consciousness made her current tour the first of any consequence since 1898: "You can not begin to imagine the tremendous growth of interest in Anarchism since that time. Halls were packed in every City, too small to hold the people [who were] eager to listen and to be informed." She reported that her lectures on misconceptions of anarchism, the modern drama, and the preference for tactics of direct action "aroused the greatest interest." Goldman attributed her lecturing successes in the West to the frustrations of labor and to the well-publicized case against the IWW and Western Federation of Miners (see Letter to Peter Kropotkin, 31 May 1907).[87] The lack of protection offered to the worker and the quick call for militia to quell strikes stood out as among her strongest indictments of government.

The agent who trailed her was part of a larger campaign and a growing coordination between surveillance arms of various government agencies. He began to find the labor message in her lectures repetitive—especially her espousal of the general strike and her disdain for the gradualism of trade unionism—but he feared her expressed desire for an "international brotherhood of workingmen." According to the agent's transcript, Goldman urged trade unionists to organize the unemployed and counseled them to "greet [the unemployed] as your brothers and promise to share with them while they are out of work, so that they could not be used by your enemies the capitalists as scabs in case of a strike."

The agent report included her insensitive jabs at the tactics of some of the trade union organizations, ignoring the movement's sacrifices and victories, discounting its attempt to solidify its demands into law—"Get a few more pennies for your labor, that is far from bringing around the millennium, as long as there is somebody to direct you to work, even four hours a day or even four minutes a day." Although some union members found her message counterproductive and offensive, others appreciated the underlying truths of Goldman's controversial perspective even though they too labeled her ideas strategically impractical and her tactics often too volatile to advocate in the open. The surveillance report described an enthusiastic crowd in Lowell, Massachusetts, that frequently ap-

---

Standard texts include Melvin Dubofsky, *We Shall Be All* (New York: Quadrangle/The New York Times Book Co., 1969) and Philip S. Foner, *History of the Labor Movement in the United States,* vol. 4: *The Industrial Workers of the World, 1905–1917* (New York: International Publishers, 1965).

87. The original letter from Goldman to Kropotkin written during her thirty-six-hour train ride from San Francisco to Portland was released to the public in 1989 from the Peter Kropotkin Collection of the Central State Archive of the October Revolution in Moscow.

plauded both her direct and her coded messages about violence (including her linking trade unionism with the efforts of the Haymarket anarchists) (see Louis J. Domas to George B. Billings, 12 December 1907).

Goldman's critique seared through what she considered the hypocrisy of the labor movement itself and the ways in which it did not honor the unemployed. In a Labor Day address prepared for delivery at Cooper Institute, she railed, "Hundred thousand men out of work in the city of New York—homeless, shelterless, clothless, foodless, in this city of wealth and affluence. Who dares speak of Labor Day in the face of this awful spectacle? . . . Labor Day marks the end of holiday and idleness. You men have had a holiday and have been idle, not by choice, but by grim, iron necessity. . . . where is that all powerful, omnipotent God—Labor—that will give you a chance?"(see "Labor Day," Address, September 1908).

THE PERSEVERANCE OF A GAMBLER

It was enormously difficult to keep *Mother Earth* consistently funded in a time of national economic instability and, in spite of Goldman's many free-speech victories in the constant uphill back-and-forth, win-or-lose battles with the police, there remained various, more mundane obstacles to filling halls on the lecture trail. Expressing her frustrations to the readers of her magazine, Goldman identified the times that presented the biggest challenges to an anarchist lecturer: November, with its "Electiomania, America's greatest malady," and December, "the month of glad tidings. . . . Christmas—a howling, pushing, scrambling, obsessed bargain huntress with no interest or time for anything"—as well as those unpredictable times in which one was foiled by "the Conspiracy of Circumstance," including inclement weather (see "The End of the Odyssey," Article in *Mother Earth*, April 1909).

Goldman compared herself to a gambler who knows that "he is losing, that if he goes on, it means complete distruction. But he is driven on by an irristible force, until he has lost his last shirt." Her compulsion and the necessity to continue lecturing, combined with her dedication to the anarchist vision of a future order without government, left her without institutional support and dependent upon the generosity of friends and associates to tow her and the magazine through these inevitable, cyclical low tides (see Letter to Meyer Shapiro, 20 February 1909, and Letter to James H. Barry, 4 March 1909).

Keeping the magazine afloat took constant effort and the ability to coordinate not only the content and production of the magazine but also to find the financial resources to carry it all through. Goldman raised the lion's share of operating expenses for *Mother Earth* and also solicited funds for strike committees, legal challenges, and for obscure anarchist groups who otherwise had no access to outside support. A financially vulnerable radical journal like hers could be terminated with little fanfare just by the government's rescinding its second-rate postage privileges as part of the blanket application of the Comstock Act. But more often she feared the financial shortfall of *Mother Earth* would force her to give up the magazine—"it would be like killing my own child" (see Letter to Meyer Shapiro, 12 August 1908)—and obliterating the core constellation of her life and the constant focus of her unconditional loyalty and devotion.

Alexander Berkman's desire for an even more effective form of communication among anarchists combined with his frustration over the limitations of the monthly publication format of *Mother Earth*, "whose work is theoretical, literary and educational" and in some ways distant from labor and working-class America, prompted him to lead a campaign to fund "a practical weekly, a fighting champion of revolutionary labor" that would, in a timely manner, openly address the specifics of the propaganda of direct action and the general strike and would "point out the real cause of [labor] dissatisfaction, misery and oppression" (see "In Favor of an Anarchistic Weekly," Appeal in *The Demonstrator,* 2 October 1907). Although in 1907 when the idea first started to circulate with serious intent, finding financial support for such an endeavor proved too overwhelming and Berkman's weekly did not materialize. However, by 1915 Berkman would move to San Francisco where he would satisfy his yearning for a militant, labor-oriented news weekly with the publication in January 1916 of *The Blast*.

MILITANT UNDERCURRENTS

Loosely representing their readership as the editors of *Mother Earth*, Goldman and her co-editor Max Baginski traveled to Amsterdam in 1907 to attend the International Anarchist Congress. There they expressed their unmediated militancy and jumped into the debates by boldly initiating a motion for "individual action," countering the prevalent singular focus of European anarchists on syndicalism. Eventually they compromised with their European counterparts by affirming a strategy of collective insurrection. Goldman and Baginski's advocacy of political violence against the oppressive force of the state in solidarity with a wave of assassinations in Russia represented the most extreme constituents of the already charged atmosphere of the meetings.

Among other items of mutual interest, the Anarchist Congress addressed the issue of individual and collective terror—asserting "the right of rebellion on the part of the individual, as well as on that of the masses. . . . [and that] terroristic acts, especially those directed against representatives of the State and the plutocracy, must be considered from a psychological viewpoint . . . as the socio-psychological consequences of an unbearable system." The situation in Russia formed the context of the discussion and was seen to wholly justify "terrorism . . . directed against the most brutal and hated agents of despotism" (see "The International Anarchist Congress," Article in *Mother Earth*, October 1907).

The discussion of anti-militarism included support for those who refused to serve in the military, for soldiers who disobeyed orders to shoot at strikers, and for workers who abstained from manufacturing "articles of wholesale slaughter." On the last day of the congress, the discussion, led by Goldman, who had been given the honor of chairing the last session ranged from cooperative societies, co-education, Esperanto, and alcoholism, to greetings of solidarity sent to anarchists serving time in prison. A resolution was passed on behalf of Russian revolutionaries, supporting their right to direct action and confirming their creation of a revolution on which "the international proletariat depends."

Strategic general strikes and "refusing to carry [government] arms or other sinews of war into Russia" were agreed upon by all except two Christian anarchists (who refused to vote), and the consensus confirmed "the necessity of furthering Anarchism in Russia and the Russian Revolution."

Goldman stood firmly with the most militant anarchists of the congress, and like many others, she never allowed it to eclipse her cultural critiques or her firm stand on sexual freedom, a stand she also adamantly asserted at the congress. This was an opportunity for Goldman to reveal herself more fully. Despite the European view that advocacy of violence (the subject of the day) and advocacy of free expression (a concept central to Americans that Europeans often found baffling) represented diametrically opposite poles of political thought, in Goldman's anarchist lexicon, these paradoxical positions were absolutely consistent. In the company of her European comrades, Goldman, stood out as an intriguing and powerful cultural hybrid; moreover, her magazine legitimated her stature and her presence at the 1907 Anarchist Congress, offering her a new format to bridge the varied ideas and activities of anarchists from many continents—by representing a country with a native pull toward both individual liberty and the common good but where anarchism was still relatively marginal. As a participant in theoretical discussions at the sessions, she influenced the evolution of anarchist communism with its advocacy of distribution of goods to meet the particular needs of the people while interpreting its principles in a way that seemed distinctly American—incorporating Jeffersonian guarantees of the right to rebel against a tyrannical government and an ideology that held freedom at its core.[88] Her wariness of a movement that privileged the working class over others in part was based on the relatively small inroads made by the anarchists at that time into the U.S. labor movement and also Goldman's strong conviction, rooted in her Russian experience, that the middle class held the strongest revolutionary potential. At the congress, she also contributed to the international conversation by crystallizing insights from America— especially with regard to a recent shift in public awareness of issues of sexual inequities and harsh racial prejudice. In light of the recent barring of European anarchists from entry to the United States, her relative isolation there was muted by the solidification of her relationship to Malatesta and other prominent figures of the movement at the congress, which proved not only to be a source of camaraderie but also an opportunity for her to absorb and eventually transmit what these comrades had to offer. Goldman returned from the congress invigorated and satisfied at having assumed a more central role as the foremost American anarchist theorist in the shaping of the next phase of international anarchist activity—which would be anarcho-syndicalism.

Just after leaving Amsterdam, Goldman traveled to London where she spoke to "an eager, expectant audience" from a lecture platform presided over by John Turner, the English anarchist-syndicalist who only a few years before had been the plaintiff in the

88. See introduction, vol. 1, pp. 8–9, 13–19, 20.

1903–1904 free-speech fight against his deportation from the United States. He introduced her warmly and with great respect and appreciation as one of the "few people . . . qualified to speak on the subject of the American Labour Movement." Holding the audience's attention for over an hour, Goldman contended that other than the Russian refugees "fleeing from the Black Hundreds, the pogroms, and all the tortures of the cowardly and bloody Czardom," most emigrated to the United States only for "material gain." Expressing frustration with the labor movement and its alliances with bosses and politicians, she voiced her hopes for the eventual success and awakening to the tactic of the general strike (see "Emma Goldman's Lecture," Article in *Freedom,* November 1907). The U.S. Secret Service agent who trailed Goldman to London reported that the audience's response to her lecture was "not enthusiastic"; in his report, he quoted only her sarcastic contention that the U.S. government's trial against William Haywood "failed because the Western miners know how to handle dynamite" (see Maurits Hymans to John E. Wilkie, 11 October 1907).

CROSSING BOUNDARIES IN THE NAME OF FREEDOM

The support Goldman felt from, and provided to, her anarchist comrades knew no national boundaries or limitations on the range of subjects an anarchist could address. After attending the 1907 Anarchist Congress in Amsterdam, Goldman built on her interest in the political impact and significance of childhood education[89] by visiting the pathbreaking La Ruche (Beehive) school community outside of Paris inspired by Sebastien Fauré. The Beehive was a small experimental educational institution akin to Francisco Ferrer's Escuela Moderna (Modern School) in Spain. During the Neo-Malthusian Conference in Paris in 1900, her interest in the subject had been piqued by her encounter with Paul Robin of the Cempius experiment in education in France. Ferrer's attempt to honor the child's independence and creativity away from the halls of religious indoctrination, in a devoutly Catholic country, was a bold revolutionary action. True to the state and the church's wildest projections, the schools doubled as meeting halls and organizing venues for militant anarchists: in 1906, Ferrer's associate Mateo Morales, who worked in its publishing house, threw a bomb at the Spanish royal family. The school and its circle were targeted by those who felt threatened by its underlying challenge, especially because Ferrer funneled his wealth to anarchist causes and bankrolled their publication *Solidaridad Obrera* in Spain. Ferrer was executed on 13 October 1909 for a crime in which he seemed to have little involvement but which was definitely in synchrony with the pervasive violence erupting across Europe and the United States.

The horrific image of this gentle pillar of education, shot to death and thrown into a ditch in Montjuich Prison, sent shock waves across the world and signaled the coming of a new round of brutality against anarchists. Overnight, Ferrer became a martyr—

89. EG had recently published her essay "The Child and its Enemies" in *Mother Earth* (April 1906).

although questions of just how closely he was involved in violent direct actions linger even today.[90] Anarchists, socialists, and liberals primarily in Europe and America united to pay homage to his memory by canonizing him as one of a long line of martyrs. Goldman was no exception, proclaiming that Ferrer's death "awakened human consciousness" (see "Francisco Ferrer," Essay in *Mother Earth*, November 1909). The end of his life prompted Goldman to reflect on her own fate and the profound risks of a small movement against the larger forces of power—no matter how inspiring the successes of her *Mother Earth* circle: "When I too, shall walk the path of Ferrer it will be no new experience. . . . I am broken in spirit and body. I feel weary, just weary. My struggle never seemed more useless, a lone voice, against a multitude"(see Letter to Ben Reitman, 13 October 1909). And yet in spite of her dire fears, the battering club of the police in America paled in comparison to the horror of the firing squad that killed the secular anarchist educator of Spain.

Following Ferrer's execution, the modern school movement that he inspired began to spread in Europe and America. The schools honored Ferrer's efforts by promoting creativity in education and giving the younger generation an experience of freedom they would eventually believe was worth fighting for. Goldman helped launch a modern school and initiated a Modern School Association in the United States in Ferrer's memory. The cross-pollenization of "free" ideas and the web of international support the schools facilitated became critical to the survival of the anarchists, for whom personal risk was often an inevitable consequence of their grand political design.

INTERNATIONAL NOTES

In an effort to create solidarity and comradeship among anarchists across national boundaries, *Mother Earth* regularly reported on developments in anarchist theory and practice, highlighting significant anarchist events and personalities in Europe, Asia, and Latin America.

Against the backdrop of increased interest in anarchist trade unionism in Europe, Goldman and other anarchist communists in the United States—who believed that it was possible to meet basic economic needs in the context of completely free association— deliberately refrained from engaging too closely with their socialist contemporaries on either side of the Atlantic. Their aversion was shared by many socialists who had spurned anarchists since the 1896 London congress of the Second International. Among the European anarchists she solicited was Victor Dave, an anarchist-collectivist, friend of Michael Bakunin, and associate of Johann Most in England, whose contribution to her magazine she hoped would add to "a useful and educational literature in America." Using their fondness for each other to encourage the elderly Dave (without success) to write for her, she ended her letter to him with a flirtatious coaxing: "if you like the magazine half

90. See, for example, J. Romero Maura, "Terrorism in Barcelona and its Impact on Spanish Politics, 1904–1909," *Past and Present* (December 1968).

as well as you like the publisher, you will surely not refuse my request, especially so since it is really very important to us here" (see Letter to Victor Dave, 27 August 1908).

Mother Earth became a conduit for transmitting information about the atrocities committed, especially against workers in Mexico in 1907. The plight of political exiles who were attempting to organize the overthrow of the harsh regime from across the border became a rallying point for both liberal and left support. Goldman, motivated by international solidarity and recognizing the implicit anarchist-communist undercurrents of the Mexican Liberal Party (PLM), took an interest in the fate of Mexican revolutionaries and *Regeneración,* the PLM's official newspaper, which had been forced to move its operation to the United States in 1905. She published the PLM manifesto in *Mother Earth,* kept its readers informed of the developments of the struggle in Mexico, raised money as well as awareness of the plight of Mexican radicals paying special interest in the political fate of the brothers Enrique and Ricardo Flores Magón.

Her help had been solicited in 1905 when Ricardo Flores Magón and a small band of Mexican exiles announced the formation of the Junta Organizadora del Partido Liberal Mexicano (the organizing board of the Mexican Liberal Party) and again in 1906, when *Regeneración* published the party's program to implement land and economic reforms and to limit the term of the Mexican president. Although it is commonly thought by historians that Goldman first met the Magón brothers in 1905 in St. Louis and that it was she who influenced their political trajectory toward anarchism,[91] documents discovered trace their meeting to 1907 in Los Angeles during her lecture tour. This meeting is confirmed in Goldman's letter to Kropotkin. She wrote to Kropotkin to alert him to their interest in his books and ideas, and to her hope to "work out a plan to arouse the radical American element" (see Letter to Peter Kropotkin, 31 May 1907). In February 1908 *Mother Earth* translated and published the PLM manifesto, although it deliberately masked its anarchist-communist tendencies.

When a detective agency hired by the Mexican ambassador to the United States arrested Ricardo Flores Magón and his associates in Los Angeles in 1907 and charged them with violating the neutrality law, Goldman reported on their case and on political developments in Mexico. The PLM sent updates on their activities to those influential political figures in the United States who they believed could best assist them—anarchist Emma Goldman, socialist Eugene Debs, and labor leader Samuel Gompers. Honored by the PLM's trust in her and set on supporting revolutionary movements across national boundaries, Goldman raised funds for the Magón brothers' defense—and perhaps also for clandestine Mexican guerilla units, even after Ricardo Flores Magón was released in 1910. Goldman's efforts on the Magón brothers' behalf widened the circle of sup-

91. See for example: Diego Abad de Santillan, *Ricardo Flores Magón: el apostol de la revolución social Mexicana* (Mexico, D.F.: Gruppo Cultural "Ricardo Flores Magón," 1925; Florecio Barrera Fuentes, *Historia de la Revolution Mexicana: la etap precursora* (Mexico, 1955); and James D. Cockcroft, *Intellectual Precursors of the Mexican Revolution, 1900–1913* (Austin: University of Texas Press, 1968).

port for the Mexican revolution among radicals and left liberals in the United States, helping to keep the Magóns funded and out of jail as they worked for the cause from across the border.

Transnational alliances proved to be an effective means for supporting vulnerable political figures (including Kōtoku Shūsui of Japan) and movements (often the initiators of sweeping transformations), for overcoming censorship, and possibly even for smuggling weapons. The crossing of national boundaries, so integral to Goldman's anarchist vision, was also critical to the long-term impact of her political work.

PARALLEL BORDERS OF OPPRESSION

Equating the Mexican situation with Russian despotism, *Mother Earth* labeled Mexican president Porfirio Díaz, the Mexican tsar who "throttled free expression in Mexico," "a hangman of this country."[92] Goldman's international comparisons appealed to Russian Jewish readers, for whom Mexico must have seemed exotic (some of whose relatives would later migrate to Mexico). Such readers reveled in *Mother Earth*'s cosmopolitanism, sharing its perspective on "national atavism" among Jews: "Owing to the lack of a country of their own, they developed, crystallized, and idealized their cosmopolitan reasoning faculty."[93] Vicariously, *Mother Earth*'s readership crossed borders, traveling to places in the United States and across the world, where most likely, by virtue of their ethnic or national identities, they might not be welcome.

Meanwhile, pockets of injustice across the country continued to repel Goldman, often but not always keeping her away. She wrote, for example, of the horrors that befell the Negroes of the South, the Mexicans in the Southwest, the immigrant Wobblies in the Pacific Northwest, and the immigrant workers in sweatshops in the Northeast. Though she evinced an awareness of race—of lynching and race feuds—she rejected her own primary identification with the "Jewish race."[94] Opting instead for a more universal identity, she also bypassed the centrality of race inequality as an organizing construct. While her choices had tracings of the prejudice of the time, it was more likely that Goldman strove for the universal, believing that all other positions reeked of nationalism and self-limitation. Even though her magazine honored her Russian Jewish readership, speckling its pages with Yiddish metaphors and translations, it also sought a following that shared Goldman's belief that anarchism in the United States had to move beyond the various ethnic enclaves within the immigrant left in order to gain wider acceptance.

Goldman was thrilled to be asked by the Boston *Globe* to enter its contest to write a new Declaration of Independence. Other radicals also rose to the challenge. Even though she won, the award check was issued and page proofs of her piece were on the editor's

92. See Observations and Comments, *Mother Earth* 11, no. 10 (December 1907): 426.
93. "Native Atavism," by Internationalist [pen name], *Mother Earth* 1, no. 1 (March 1906): 56.
94. In Goldman's time, "Jewish race" was the commonly used descriptor. Goldman, who felt connected to her secular Jewish roots, had strong aversion to those she believed exhibited narrow exclusivity in their political commitments, retaining what was considered a small-town "shtetl mentality."

desk, at the last minute the newspaper's owner reneged and ordered that her "damned anarchist declaration" be returned.[95] Goldman quickly incorporated her Declaration into the July 1909 issue of *Mother Earth*—proudly asserting, "We hold these truths to be self evident: that all human beings, irrespective of race, color, or sex, are born with the equal right to share at the table of life" (see "A New Declaration of Independence," Essay in *Mother Earth,* July 1909).

Goldman strove to be consistent in her attitude toward gender politics by choosing not to identify solely with women or with separatist women's organizations in any way. She later developed her ideas on the subject, producing nuanced essays on love and marriage, on birth control, and on sexuality. Although her thinking on the issue of race was more advanced than many of her contemporaries, she shared their prevalent inattention.

"NEGRO QUESTION MORE ACUTE THAN EVER"

However, in 1907 at the Anarchist Congress, she did include the horrors of racism in her description of America. She later published her scathing report in the October issue of *Mother Earth:* "Sad and deplorable in the extreme is the position of the American negro. Rivers of blood have been shed to free the black man from slavery; yet, after almost half a century of so-called freedom, the negro question is more acute than ever. The persecution, suffering and injustice to which this much-hated race is being constantly subjected can be compared only to the brutal treatment of the Jews in Russia. Hardly a day passes without a negro being lynched in some part of the country. . . . Nor are these terrible atrocities perpetrated in the South only. Though in a lesser degree, the North is guilty as well. Nowhere in the country does the negro enjoy equal opportunity with the white man—socially, politically or economically. . . . the negro is as much a slave now as in ante-bellum days, and even more ostracized socially and exploited economically."

She then pointed out that race hatred was not limited to African Americans, that it was a phenomenon that spread to other races and nationalities, most recently to Japanese immigrants. But instead of expounding and reiterating these issues of prejudice as a central concern, she introduced her readers to the issue of race—as a way of knowing America through the places that welcomed her and the places she dared not enter. When referring to the South, she countered her aversion to the "horrible pictures of little victims in the cotton fields, of bodies dangling from the trees, bodies mutilated to cinders and ashes" with an awareness of the horrors of sweatshops in the East, the race feuds in New York City, and the burning of blacks in Springfield, Illinois.[96] In El Paso, she addressed the plight of the thirty thousand Mexicans who were not permitted to hold public meetings in Spanish; in San Antonio she met with people but couldn't procure a hall.

Still, loyalty to the promise of her own "Mother Russia" occupied a substantial part of the coverage of international news and views in *Mother Earth*—of significance to all, but

---

95. For an account of this incident, see *LML,* p. 455.
96. Emma Goldman, "The Situation in America," *Mother Earth* (October 1907), p. 325.

especially to her Russian Jewish immigrant readership. The magazine tracked develop-ments in Russia as the revolution evolved, reporting on atrocities, pogroms, demonstra-tions, strikes, critical personalities, and individual acts of violence; it also raised funds for Russia by praising its Socialist Revolutionaries and Russian anarchists without revealing any specifics of her comrades' mostly clandestine financial support work.

In her magazine Goldman attempted to counter what she considered the politics and insularity of many of her Jewish comrades, even as she identified with their resilience. She even contrasted them to the very few "American comrades" who, she believed, "knew at least what anarchism means." She sometimes denigrated the Jewish anarchist with unflattering characterizations as people who "sell their anarchism in real estate, or in playing dominos in restaurants." She was critical intermittently of those associated with the Yiddish-language anarchist communist newspaper *Freie Arbeiter Stimme,* which, she complained, has "always opposed going into unions, has opposed every strike, every public event. Has acted cowardly, when courage was needed, as during the Union Square affaire. . . . Did you ever hear the American press or police make a fuss over that paper, or the Jewish propaganda, or [*Freie Arbeiter Stimme* editor] Mr Yanovsky? Certainly not. Why do they watch closely, everything, I do? Because I carry our ideas among the Americans, before thousands of people" (see Letter to Meyer Shapiro, 19 August 1908).

TENUOUS CITIZENSHIP

Although Goldman identified America as the locus of her life's work, the feeling was not mutual. Government officials had been trying to revoke her citizenship ever since she was first perceived as a threat. The process of gathering evidence against her, to carefully build their case, took many years, required research, the manipulation of facts, personal surveillance and an impeccable sense of when to strike. The year 1908 was a turning point in the government's efforts to establish Goldman's links to violence—links that would sustain the drive toward Goldman's ultimate deportation in 1919.

Although Goldman was profoundly aware of the growing legal consequences of any association with anarchist ideas and tactics, it wasn't until 1908 and 1909 that she fully appreciated the effect that the onslaught of anti-anarchist laws would have on her own life—especially because she believed that she had the safeguard of U.S. citizenship through her ex-husband (her comrade Alexander Berkman, on the other hand, had never been granted, nor had he desired, the privilege of citizenship).

The process of invalidating her citizenship, which she obtained years earlier through her former husband, as well as through her father, took place behind the scenes. As new anti-anarchist laws were steered through the legislature, it would become too risky for her to leave the country.[97] The right to get away, to choose one's geographic destiny, became

97. Goldman had been interrogated by immigration officials as she crossed back and forth through Canada, but enforcement of exclusion laws was still inconsistent. After she returned from the 1907 Anarchist Congress in Amsterdam, she risked no more trips out of the country.

a desire that hung like a yoke upon her neck, haunting her with ominous uncertainty and powerlessness that she abhorred.[98]

A federal warrant was issued for Goldman's arrest, but not until 1907. The government claimed that she was in violation of the February 1907 congressional act that amended the Immigration Act of 1903 with a provision to bar foreign-born anarchists from entering the United States (see Federal Warrant for the Arrest of Emma Goldman, 14 November 1907). The warrant coincided with her return from the 1907 International Anarchist Congress in Amsterdam, when she cleverly reentered the country through Canada and quietly sought to "get back to work."

To build the case against her, government agents attempted to follow Goldman everywhere. They were especially suspicious of the meetings dominated by immigrant radicals. Goldman, hoping to broaden her base, often did not address them in German, Yiddish, or Russian, which they might have preferred. A report from Boston noted that she spoke to "about 200 people . . . (about a dozen of them were women), all belonging to a foreign element . . . greatly disappointed . . . that the lecture was to be in English." The topics of her talk included the efficacy of direct action over the gradualism of trade union tactics that allowed bosses to prepare for strikes; the public schools of America that, unlike the Modern Schools of Europe, were engaged in "killing the individuality of the child, by teaching false history, submission to government"; her plea to "refrain from voting [by which] you . . . give the power into the hands of unscrupulous legislators, be they Republicans, Democrats or Social Democrats"; and her critique of the institution of marriage, whose sanctity most men easily disregarded but which women were compelled to honor. She also reminded women not to allow "any one to meddle in your love affairs. Neither priest, minister, Rabbi or Justice has anything to say in matter of such a private nature" (see Louis J. Domas to George B. Billings, 19 November 1907).

The field notes document one of the government's early unsuccessful attempts to find sufficient grounds for Goldman's deportation but signal the escalation of its concerted efforts to eventually cast her out of America: "To sum up,—If the only issue were whether or not she is an anarchist, I think there is no doubt whatever but that she is liable to deportation. The difficulty will turn on the question as to whether she is an alien within the meaning of the immigration act." Puzzling over her rights as a citizen, Oscar Straus, Secretary of Commerce and Labor, feared that the government's case against Goldman was too thin and might in fact be used against it. He articulated the fear that Goldman would "welcome arrest . . . it will not only advertise her and add to her prestige, but will be the means of bringing her in considerable sums in the way of contributions" (see Excerpt from Oscar S. Straus to Bureau of Immigration, 17 November 1907).

The disagreements on how to handle her case rippled. In February 1908, immigration

---

98. Anti-anarchist laws would be broadened in 1917, then further streamlined in 1918 as the country mobilized for war, and ultimately used to lay the legal groundwork for Goldman and Berkman's deportation in 1919.

authorities in Chicago intended to have her arrested upon her arrival in the city and to immediately begin the deportation process. In St. Louis, where Goldman was on tour, the chief of police announced "that he intended to run her out of town immediately, unless . . . action [was taken] under the Immigration Law." All awaited instruction from the Commissioner-General of Immigration in Washington, D.C., who was coordinating efforts to expel Goldman and who cautiously tempered zealous local officials intent on being the first to set the wheels of Goldman's deportation in motion (see James R. Dunn to F. P. Sargent, 28 February 1908 and Edwin W. Sims to Oscar S. Straus, 2 March 1908). With these internal pressures and intermittent disagreement within government ranks on strategies for containing this potentially dangerous anarchist, it is easy to see how such clashes built up and ultimately contributed to Goldman's harsh treatment and eventual deportation. In the meantime, until it could be determined whether or not Goldman's claim to citizenship was legitimate, Straus sent a telegram to the U.S. District Attorney in Chicago, advising that "No action should be taken. . . . Great care must be taken in such matters not to put Government in false position." In a follow-up letter, Straus explained that "The Bureau of Immigration, ever since Emma Goldman returned to the United States from her recent trip abroad, has through the United States Secret Service Division, been following up her movements and also taken stenographic notes of her addresses, which have been carefully examined by the Solicitor of this Department. Her addresses are very skillfully made, so as not to be open to the charge of anarchistic utterances" (see Oscar S. Straus to Edwin W. Sims, 9 March 1908). Straus's communiqué alerts the reader to the fact that all public talks and written essays during this time must be read with the awareness that Goldman was consciously attempting to avoid breaking the law that censored blatantly violent "anarchistic utterances" lest her speeches be used as incriminating evidence to expel her.

When the Ottawa Superintendent of Immigration caught wind of Goldman's intention to speak in Canada, he queried the Minister of the Interior about whether she might be prevented from entering the country "on the ground of insanity." Fortunately for Goldman, whose late November 1908 lectures in Winnipeg attracted over fifteen hundred listeners, the Canadian Minister of the Interior, upon reviewing the idea that anyone who believes in anarchism must be insane, curtly surmised, "I am afraid this is not sufficient warrant" to keep her from entering Canada (see W. D. Scott to Frank Oliver, 15 December 1908).

Although Goldman had received word that government agents in the United States were targeting her through her ex-husband, Jacob Kershner, she did not know that in 1909 a U.S. federal court in Buffalo, New York, canceled his citizenship[99] and in so doing,

99. See introduction, vol. 1, p. 6, and pp. 159n8, 175, 492–93, 537 for a brief discussion of the history of Goldman's marriage to and separation from Jacob Kershner, which was used to weaken her legal status in the mounting deportation case against her. Later in Europe, she would marry James Colton for the sole purpose of securing British citizenship (and the ability to travel freely) while she was in exile.

officially revoked Goldman's right of citizenship as well. The Secretary of Commerce and Labor's plan to revoke Kershner's citizenship first and then "deprive her of an asylum she now enjoys as the wife of an American citizen" was well under way (see Letter from Oscar S. Straus to Charles J. Bonaparte, 11 February 1909). Within the month Goldman found out and proclaimed herself a "Woman Without a Country," a harsh reality that nonetheless did not undermine the joy of *Mother Earth*'s May Day concert and dance, or Goldman's desire to celebrate perseverance and optimism in the face of adversity. Countering her genuine fears, in a commentary in *Mother Earth,* she addressed her aggressors: "Poor, poor United States government! Yours is, indeed, a difficult task. True. . . . You have Emma Goldman's citizenship. But she has the world, and her heritage is the kinship of brave spirits—not a bad bargain" (see "A Woman Without a Country," Essay in *Mother Earth,* May 1909).

IT BEGINS IN A WOMAN'S SOUL

"Her eyes are blue and her hair a light brown and fairly heavy. She carried a large, old-fashioned handbag full of newspaper clippings, letters, etc., and looked more like a farmer's wife on a shopping tour than a bomb thrower." Touching all the usual topics—the church, the state, violence, marriage, the military (especially the Buwalda case), Goldman dutifully and energetically replied to the journalist's queries. "No," she did not believe in marriage, and then launched into a critique of modern marriage arrangements, asserting that "we believe in the sanctity of marriage . . . through love, and not through form" (see "Goldman Traces Anarchy to 1776," Article in the *Spokesman-Review,* 31 May 1908).

Both the women and men who interviewed her highlighted Goldman's challenge to the suffrage movement, citing her charges that it lacked humor, was puritanical, and failed to attack the root cause of women's oppression. In a lengthy interview with Marguerite Martyn, writing for the *St. Louis Post-Dispatch* in November 1908, Goldman would boldly assert that "true emancipation begins neither in the courts nor at the polls. It begins with the woman's soul." Her suggestion that women must first demand respect and worship themselves with the meticulous attention they had hitherto given to men and that the more they receive from the world, the more they will be in a position to give, acted as a palliative to the frustration of the Every-Woman that Goldman hoped to reach.

With her fine-tuned aesthetic sensibility, Goldman counseled her young interviewer Martyn to notice that the attractiveness of the American Beauty roses on her desk came in part from the contrasting green of the foliage around them. With a firm belief in independence, she asserted that women needed to disengage from an exclusive involvement with a life devoted to domesticity. Although the workplace was far from perfect—often an exchange of "the narrowness and lack of freedom in her home to the narrowness and lack of freedom of office, department story or factory"—still worse was the situation of the woman "who confines herself to the four walls of a home" where she can never advance the world, and is in fact "an obstacle to her own and her children's progress" (see "Emma

Goldman Says Anarchism Will Mean Absolute Equality and Freedom for Women . . . ,"
Interview in the *St. Louis Post-Dispatch*, 1 November 1908).

Most women who wrote about Goldman were intrigued by her searing views on women's relationship to paid work and professional life, on free love and marriage, on family and children, on the issue of the public and the private, especially at a time when President Theodore Roosevelt linked patriotism with a campaign in favor of large families and traditional gender roles to insure that the "race" would perpetuate itself. The press responded with generous newspaper coverage of a topic Goldman considered "the most vital subject in the world—the sex problem." A small but growing number of women drawn to such ideas applauded Goldman's charge and her challenge. They appreciated the role of the left in hastening the process of change and awareness. Many moderates, on the other hand, including Alice Stone Blackwell and Jane Addams, who held onto a notion of respectability and conventional, circumspect sexuality, distanced themselves from Goldman's views (see "A Sentimental Journey—Police Protection," Essay in *Mother Earth*, April 1906). They considered Goldman a hindrance, a thorn in their side, and so much the ultra-sectarian anarchist that she couldn't see the ways in which the New Woman movement served all women, regardless of where they were on the political spectrum.

Without negating her own all-embracing espousal of the importance of confronting the political dimension of otherwise personal concerns, Goldman used the metaphor of childbirth as her way of describing the inescapable "pain and hardship" that would accompany the birth of a new society. Although she claimed to "by no means prefer riot and bloodshed and death," she also asserted that "anarchists are not passive spectators in the theater of social development," and as always, linked progress to "the spirit of rebellion." Reading backward, one can see that Goldman, even in an interview primarily devoted to what might conventionally be considered women's issues, remained true to an underlying message of the inevitability of the use of force against injustice, of striking back, as an integral and countervailing part of the same social vision in which she sincerely espoused her devotion to "love life . . . the big, human universe" (see "Emma Goldman Says Anarchism Will Mean Absolute Equality and Freedom for Women . . . ,"
Interview in the *St. Louis Post-Dispatch*, 1 November 1908).

While attendance at her lectures might vary wildly, due to circumstances beyond her control (including the public's preoccupation with electoral politics), Goldman relied on newspaper articles and interviews to spread the word. One of the most memorable articles was written by William Marion Reedy, the editor of the *St. Louis Mirror*, on election day in November 1908. In "Emma Goldman: The Daughter of the Dream," Reedy asserted that there was nothing wrong with Goldman's gospel except that she was "eight-thousand years ahead of her age." He assured his readers that newspapers never offer the correct ideas about their subjects and then proceeded to debunk the image of Goldman as "an ignorant, vulgar, shrieking harridan with a bomb in one hand and a bottle of vitriol in the other." Instead, he painted her as a woman "without trace of coarseness. . . . Her information is broad, her experience comprehensive, her reading in at least three languages almost limitless. . . . She is simple and not violent. She is positive without truculence . . . gentle and even at times tender . . . a woman who believes in her cause and feels it with a concentrated intensity." Reedy characterizes her desire as "Freedom—absolute, unconditioned, uninvasive freedom. That is anarchy." Commenting affirmatively on whether she posed a threat to society, he reported that "She threatens all society that is sham, all society that is slavery, all society that is a mask of greed and lust" and that she believed that "The spirits of Truth and Freedom" were "the pillars of society" from which to build "the power of human love having full play under limitless liberty." Goldman recognized that Reedy's tribute to her and her ideas was the best ever written by a nonanarchist and took it as a sign that, in spite of the dismal failure of this tour during election season, her ideas actually did resonate with some of the most influential among the educated American public—even though they might be unaware of the complexity of her political stance. Reedy did indeed hold a mirror to Goldman's beautiful ideal and the vibrancy of her personality, perhaps without realizing that the image of the harridan with a bomb that he so eloquently countered might have been a caricature of a shadow side equally bold. Although he reported that she despised violence, he also noted that if violence came, Goldman viewed it as "part of the working of the free human spirits." The violent underside of "The Daughter of a Dream" was especially difficult for a man to imagine in the company of a woman like Emma Goldman, who emanated erudition and grace.

In an interview with the *Chicago Inter Ocean*, Goldman focused her remarks on the relationship between anarchism and women's freedom to love in accordance with their hearts' desires rather than by the claims of the marriage vow. Reflecting on the roots of her anarchism, Goldman drew links between the Haymarket anarchists and pivotal experiences of her early childhood: the abuse of her father, her sympathy with the peasants and servants, her desire for an education to match that of her male counterparts, and the reading of leading philosophers about women that confirmed her own ideas and prompted her "to champion the cause of women and devote my life to their emancipation" (see "Emma Goldman Clashes with Police on Meeting," Interview in *Chicago Inter Ocean*, 8 March 1908).

With an astute sense of how to sidestep efforts to silence her, Goldman handed the *Chicago Daily Journal* interviewer the manuscript of her address, and the paper printed the text of the "forbidden speech" in full. In her attempt to prove her theories, she posited that "the individual instinct, standing for self-expression . . . [and] the social instinct, which inspires collective and social life . . . in their latent condition are never antagonistic to each other." Goldman asserted that "the first tendency of anarchism is to make good the dignity of the individual human being by freeing him from every kind of arbitrary restraint—economic, political, social. . . . Anarchism holds that the simplest human life, if given opportunity and scope, is infinitely more important to society than all the scientific regulation and adjusting of social arrangements" (see "Reds' Leader Flays Police," Article in the *Chicago Daily Journal*, 17 March 1908).

In 1908, the *New York World* arranged for Goldman to write a paid article on her beliefs as a featured article in the Sunday paper, because by this time Goldman had become "one of the most talked of women in the world" (see "What I Believe," Essay in the *New York World,* 19 July 1908).[100]

"MY GREATNESS ADDS NOTHING TO MY LIFE"

Still, Goldman rarely could predict when her meetings would be stopped by police. The thwarting of her efforts to reach the public through her lectures also limited her opportunities to attract subscribers and supporters to her magazine. Harassed on the lecture road, Goldman began to long for the intimacy of her past with Berkman, remembering their passion fourteen years before (see Letter to Alexander Berkman, 17 March 1907). The adulation of cheering crowds heightened her feeling of isolation: "My greatness adds nothing to my life. . . . If I am proud of anything, it is that I have learned . . . the power of love. Everything else means naught to me. 1200 people applauded . . . waved hats and handkerchieves, screamed and yelled last night . . . yet, I saw them not, I only saw one face, one soul, one being far away from me and yet so close, I could almost feel his warmth" (see Letter to Alexander Berkman, 19 March 1907). In a letter to her friend and anarchist historian Max Nettlau, even as she asserted the imperative for women's independence, she complained of her own personal and chronic dissatisfaction: "Yes, I am a woman indeed too much of it, that's my tragedy. The great Abyss between my woman nature and the nature of the relentless revolutionist is too great to allow much happiness in my life" (see Letter to Max Nettlau, 17 October 1907).

Her longing for intimacy began to permeate her life even more in 1908. After seventeen years in the public light, at the age of thirty-eight, the accolades of an audience could not fill her well of loneliness nor could her committed resolve to fight against injustice mitigate her desire for the closeness of a lover. Ed Brady, who had loved and protected her but could never fully compel her emotional loyalty, was dead. After fourteen hellish years in prison, Berkman, whom she would always love and protect, looked to a younger woman comrade—not to Goldman—for sensual intimacy.[101] Although she had other intermittent lovers among her circle of comrades, most, for all their avowal of free love, began pairing up, some even raising children, their activism often diminished by the rhythms of the reciprocity of maturing personal attachments.

Circumstance and desire coincided in Chicago in March 1908, when the young, dashing Ben Reitman entered Goldman's life. The city was on the alert; a man labeled an anarchist had just been accused of shooting Chicago's police chief. This coincided with a dramatic series of acts of terror that sent a fear of anarchism across the world—including the assassination of the king of Portugal on February 1 and the shooting of a priest in Denver while he was administering Holy Communion on February 23. Gold-

---

100. Grace Potter, who had contributed to *Mother Earth,* was the go-between for Goldman's July 1908 *New York World* article.
101. See *LML,* p. 412, for biographical detail about Edelsohn and her relationship with Berkman.

man was in Chicago during Lazarus Averbuch's alleged attempt on the Chicago police chief on March 2. Reinforcing the public's fears, on March 28 shortly after she left for her Midwest tour, a bomb exploded in New York City's Union Square as a demonstration for the unemployed dispersed. Hall keepers withdrew their booking agreements with Goldman, fearing criminal reprisal. She was stranded, with no venue for her scheduled talks. In this context, Reitman, known in Chicago as "The King of the Hobos," boldly offered Goldman, "The Queen of the Anarchists," a meeting place at the International Brotherhood Welfare Association.

Reitman was a flamboyant hero of the culture of self-education for itinerant laborers and was instrumental in the establishment of Chicago's "Hobo College"—a man who found brilliance and potential in the people of the streets though he also found them less inclined toward anarchism than he would have preferred. Goldman read with great interest about a beating Reitman endured at a recent demonstration of the unemployed and sensed a kindred spirit willing to live dangerously in the service of a cause.

Goldman was attracted at first sight by Reitman's earthy sensuality—though her more cerebral anarchist comrades could not see beyond his crassness. In her autobiography, she described Reitman's presence in her life, especially his love letters, as a narcotic that made her heart beat faster in ecstasy but put her mind to sleep.[102] Reitman, in addition to championing itinerant hobos, had a medical practice that included Chicago prostitutes; he later worked to eradicate venereal disease. His thorough familiarity with female sexuality was no doubt a source of his allure. In a love letter to Reitman, Goldman wrote that he "opened up the prison gates of my womanhood," releasing her dormant passions (see Letter to Ben Reitman, 27 September 1908). By 1909, Reitman, the most compelling and maddening love of her life—the wayward hobo ten years her junior—would become her traveling companion, road manager, and the office manager of *Mother Earth*.[103] Goldman's success on the lecture trail during these years was in part due to Reitman's incredible gift for public relations, his ability to work with city officials and with anarchist organizers, to prepare the groundwork—booking halls, arranging for advertising to gather an audience and newspaper coverage well beyond those who braved her lecture hall—to fan her colorful reputation. As her advance man, seller of literature and publicist extraordinaire, Reitman eventually would help Goldman withstand continued harassment and restrictions on free speech, enabling her voice to be heard more widely than ever before.

The troubled patterns of their interaction would be painfully evident throughout their ten-year relationship—plaguing the purity of their love with the shadow of jealousy. The same qualities that captivated her also swept other women under Reitman's spell. Determined to live out her principles of free love and to shed the demon of possessiveness,

---

102. *LML*, p. 523.
103. See Candace Falk, *Love, Anarchy, and Emma Goldman* (rev. ed., New Brunswick, N.J.: Rutgers University Press, 1990 and 1999).

Goldman struggled to beat back her outrage at her lover's rampant affairs. Their steamy love letters reveal the drama and passionate intensity of her struggle to reconcile political vision with personal life. Knowing that their worlds clashed, that his promiscuous behavior and her latent possessiveness and feelings of jealousy did not fit her beautiful ideal, nonetheless she was drawn to him like no other before (or after): she wrote him that she was "struggling, struggling the bitterest struggle of my life and if I succeeded, I fear I shall never be able to see you again. Yet, if I fail, I shall stand condemned before the bar of my own reason" (see Letter to Ben Reitman, ca. August 1908).

Linking her public and private lives, Goldman would fine-tune a lecture on the distinction between free love and promiscuity, ostensibly to educate the public, yet also surreptitiously to influence the obsessions of her "wayward boy." Later, when she worked through issues that seized her emotions, audiences loosely associated with the New Woman movement would gather to hear her address such concerns as "Variety or Monogamy, Which?" and "False Fundamentals of Free Love." Reitman, the man who shook the very foundation of her identity and her aspirations to political and personal consistency, also brought her closer to more contemporary, universal questions about love and marriage, thus widening her political audience. These concerns expanded the circle of people touched by her words at a transition stage in the history of gender and sexual relationships.

Together, Goldman and Reitman were a formidable team—and remarkably dramatic. In his broad-brimmed hat and elegant cape, Reitman often stood at the door, hawking her literature and drawing crowds to her talks. Goldman announced to her *Mother Earth* comrades that the "unfaltering optimism, the great zeal, and the cheerful bohemianism of our friend, Ben L. Reitman, helped to conquer many obstacles" (see "The End of the Odyssey," Article in *Mother Earth*, April 1909).

But their joy was not to last. Returning from a series of road trips, she realized that her relationship with Reitman was no longer a refuge, that it no longer renewed her energies or offered her hope and solace. Instead, she suffered from his "obsessions" (and her own) that pierced her soul. She began to experience his "moods" and "caprice" as a debasement of her dignity and love: "friends, my self-respect, my womanhood, my humanity had been outraged." Forlorn and depressed, Goldman lamented how entwined she had become with a man whose public-outreach work was wonderful but who was so utterly limited in his ability to maintain his personal attachment to one person, to one love: "It is too bad, we did not meet, when propaganda meant more to me than everything else in the World, when I had no personal interest in people or things, when I could use everything and everybody for the sake of the cause. That time is past much to the disadvantage of my own life." Noting that she no longer believed in the power of her love to teach Reitman the "greatness" of love, she despaired that "the joy of work with you is gone. I have no right to bring a message to people when there is no message in my soul. I have no right to speak of freedom when I myself, became an abject slave in my love" (see Letter to Ben Reitman, 13 December 1909). Reflecting on the contradiction between her public life as a "woman who has been treated with respect by friend and foe" but in her private life reduced to "crouch on [my] knees and beg and plead" with Ben, she felt unworthy of her message of love and freedom, declaring her marriage and love lecture "hateful to me, hateful because my faith in the power of love has been shattered. I used to think it can perform miracles, poor fool that I was" (see Letter to Ben Reitman, 18 December 1909).

The pages of *Mother Earth* often carried at least one feature article on the intersection between gender and politics, a topic closely woven into the fabric of Goldman's life and work. A complex tangle of sexual intimacies held the daily production work of the publication together. Reitman occupied an uneasy but necessary place at the magazine's office. The challenge of achieving consistency of intention, and love without possessiveness, would be tested and retested, and ultimately celebrated as a point of pride among anarchists.

"PERSEVERANCE AND EARNESTNESS OF THE FEW"

In *Mother Earth*, Goldman also counseled her readers about the discrepancy between federal law and local practice. Quoting the First Amendment to the Constitution, that Congress shall make no laws abridging the freedom of speech, Goldman asked "what has that to do with the police of the United States? They have 'evolved' their own laws, laws to suit their own purposes, and the most interesting thing about their laws is that they are almost always sustained in the courts, by the press, and public opinion." In the end, she asserted, it would be "the perseverance and earnestness of the few" upon which "the ultimate success of a truth depends." Goldman resolved not to be thwarted by police repression or exclusion laws: "they might as well attempt to direct the course of the stars as to direct the course of my life's work. They cannot do it; at least not while I live" (see "Our Friends, The Enemy," Article in *Mother Earth*, June 1909).

Among her great circumventions of police suppression, displaying her capacity to play a dual role among respectables as well as outcasts, came through her association with Alden Freeman, the radical scion of the Standard Oil family who had attended one of Goldman's New York Sunday morning lecture series on modern drama in May 1909 that was broken up by the city's anarchist squad, presumably on the charge of straying from the designated topic. Indignant, Freeman joined the campaign for free speech, first by inviting the radical lecturer surreptitiously to a luncheon at the exclusive Mayflower Society, convinced that he could dispel the aura of fear around his newfound friend (an act for which the outraged society proposed his expulsion or forced resignation). When Freeman proceeded to invite Goldman to his hometown of Orange, New Jersey, across the Hudson River, she experienced the same treatment by the police and was once again barred from speaking. He then opened his sprawling lawn and his barn to all who cared to hear her, knowing that the police, who had no authority to intrude upon his private property, could not silence her.

Because the noteworthy millionaire championed Emma Goldman's cause, journalists scrambled for exclusive stories on how the line between the rich and the poor had been crossed. As vividly reported in the *New York Times,* Freeman introduced Goldman to close to a thousand persons jammed tightly into his barn (with the local police chief "crowded right up against her chair"), on the anniversary of "Thomas Paine, who died 100 years ago yesterday." According to Freeman, Paine was "the most conspicuous agitator for freedom of thought and speech in America." The anarchist's host added that he was "glad that East Orange has this chance to observe that Miss Goldman has neither hoofs nor horns and does not ride on a broomstick." Freeman's remarks were followed by whistles and applause. After delivering her address, Goldman thanked the police and newspapers for their role in sparking independent thought (see "Miss Goldman Talks in Freeman's Barn," *New York Times,* 9 June 1909).

The groundswell of interest in Goldman as a kind of double-edged sweetheart of the movement for free speech in America was followed by another remarkable event in the city of Philadelphia, only a few months later. There, her lecture hall was lined with four hundred policemen determined to stop Goldman from speaking. But the authority's plan was subverted by the anarchist Voltairine de Cleyre, who read Goldman's talk aloud. A local newspaper later printed the full transcript of her appeal to the magistrate for an injunction against the police for barring her from speaking—a rare instance in which Goldman brought her own legal charges against a city goevernment. Other papers across the nation likewise reprinted portions of the Philadelphia court transcript. Characterizing the police as representing "an iron wall of physical power and ignorance worn with age," she cast herself as representing "a truth and a never-to-be destroyed longing for liberty." Goldman, a child of the Enlightenment, had endured frequent police harassment, believing that although "the club may be a mighty weapon . . . it sinks into insignificance before human reason and human integrity" (see Letter in the *Philadelphia Public Ledger,* 3 October 1909). Determined to speak not only in Philadelphia, but everywhere there was an open mind, Goldman welcomed her free speech challenge as an opportunity to articulate the profundity of her commitment to freedom of speech, freedom of assembly, and freedom of the press—aptly fought in the city of the Liberty Bell.

SHOWDOWN FOR FREE SPEECH

For Goldman and her circle, free speech was neither static nor secure. On the one hand, some anti-anarchist legislation enacted after the McKinley assassination threatened to drive the American anarchist movement underground. On the other hand, the absence of a systematically enforced body of laws or a national surveillance agency to restrict dissenters actually allowed Goldman considerable freedom. Even though the Comstock Act had been expanded in 1908 to include anarchism under the heading of obscenity (and thereby barring anarchist publications from the mails), Goldman continued to publish her magazine during this period with no interruption. At a time when the courts regarded the First Amendment as applying only to acts of the federal government, state and local authorities were free to provide as much as little protection as they chose. The inconsistent suppression of the spoken and printed word created an air of the Wild West in American law enforcement—a toned-down variation on the shoot-'em-up scenario, in this case in response to a challenging female newcomer who saunters into town, with both the anarchist lecturer and local authorities eager to defeat the other in a decisive showdown. But there was no final showdown. Rather, Goldman's defeats presaged her victories, and her victories would soon unravel in defeat.

Although anarchists never placed their trust in government as a fair arbiter of grievances, and liked to taunt the reformers for their faith in the capitalist system, many anarchists would inadvertently become not only the sacrificial champions but also among the most critical forces in establishing the First Amendment as the prime guarantor of free speech. The threat of success, however slight, of Goldman's ideas made government officials' hair stand on end as if a ghost of the dybbuk possessed them. The agents of law enforcement were accurate in their assessment that Goldman's fight for free speech was never without an angry charge against the state. Although not always visible to the untrained eye, the anarchist cause was indeed the political thread sewn through every pattern of freedom Goldman espoused. Avid First-Amendment absolutists—who may cringe at the anarchists' refusal to disavow the tactics of retaliatory violence—are still challenged to remain vigilant in their protection of free speech. They too must fight the winds, trust in the power of the people to serve the public good, and believe in the possibility of freedom, with the courage of Emma Goldman herself.

CODA: WAR OR PEACE?

Emma Goldman's political world encompassed the dark and the light, the violent and the peaceful, with no apparent sense of inherent contradiction. Her variation on the theme of patriotism was not loyalty to a country but rather to an ideal of justice. Akin to soldiers who sacrifice themselves in a war between nations, she supported those who chose to fight and were willing to die as martyrs for freedom in a social war. Extending her message beyond her circle of anarchists, she allied herself to the radical edge of liberal movements, especially of those who shared her belief that free speech was a central safeguard in a sane society. Goldman, though a staunch critic of liberalism and the limits of strategies of gradualist reform, nonetheless worked with advocates of civil liberties, worker's rights, and women's freedom—and prodded them to step further to the left. And, although in the United States the defense of free speech came primarily through the First Amendment to its constitution, she envisioned a social order that needed no law, no government, no external constraints, one in which freedom from coercion would ensure the flourishing of the individual and a positive future for all.

Goldman saw little or no difference between the morality of the violence the American patriot mustered in defense of the country and the violence to which anarchists resorted in their own fight for justice. Given the stories of Russian revolutionaries that swirled around her youth, including the widespread praise for the noble assassins of the Tsar, it is not surprising that in her adopted land, she gravitated toward the ideas of Thomas Jefferson, the nation's founding father, who believed that "The tree of liberty must be refreshed from time to time with the blood of patriots and tyrants." For Goldman, the violence she often claimed to abhor was as natural as the crashing waves on a stormy sea, and as inevitable. The destruction of the Old was the prerequisite for the creation of the New.

But, one wonders whether the fact that Goldman's activism was shaped during the earliest years of the twentieth century in a world so saturated in blood, limited her ability to imagine a truly peaceful alternative for realizing her vision, and to some extent allowed her enemy to define the parameters of her struggle. Miserable working conditions and rampant atrocities against organized labor in America belied strategies of gradual reform. Politicians, even those who espoused Progressive reforms, seemed beholden to the same forces of greed they campaigned against, and to measures intended to change the character of government that fell short of guaranteeing lasting and equitable change.

In her 1908 manifesto "What I Believe," Goldman distanced herself from those who considered her ideas impractical, extreme, and too threatening to serve the common good. She placed herself among others in the tradition of misunderstood and persecuted visionaries, proclaiming that "the history of progress is written in the blood of men and women who have dared to espouse an unpopular cause, as, for instance, the black man's right to his body, or woman's right to her soul. If, then, from time immemorial, the New has met with opposition and condemnation, why should my beliefs be exempt from a crown of thorns?" Goldman's self-identification as a likely martyr to her cause permeates her commitment to anarchism. On the subject of violence, Goldman carefully separated cause from action, ends from means, and consequence from intent—for herself, and for her comrades. By claiming to value "human life above all else," Goldman seemingly ignored the gravity of the paradox of committing violence to achieve peace: "I believe that anarchism is the only philosophy of peace, the only theory of a social relationship that values human life above all else . . . it is the terrible economic inequality and great political injustice that prompt[s] . . . acts [of violence], not anarchism" (see "What I Believe," Essay in the *New York World*, 19 July 1908).

Although the historical documents in *Making Speech Free, 1902–1909,* add texture to the history of anarchism, reveal new details, and memorialize a revolutionary who was well on her way to becoming one of the most formidable women of the twentieth century, the authentic Emma Goldman remains elusive. Although she never wavered in her empathy for the downtrodden and ill of spirit, the compassion Goldman claimed to feel for her enemies (even wishing she could have nursed the dying President McKinley after he had been shot in 1901),[104] seemed to recede into the background as the century of violence unfurled. In this context, it is difficult to determine where her motivational balance lay:

104. See Letter from Alexander Berkman, 20 December 1901, in vol. 1, pp. 484–88, esp. p. 485; also see introduction, vol. 1, pp. 83–84. Goldman's distinction between McKinley as the symbol of power and corruption of the state and McKinley as a wounded human being in need of care is yet another example of Goldman's political and personal bifurcation.

in the vision of a harmonious world or in righteous anger to overthrow the existing order by any means necessary. Goldman's political reach encompassed visionaries and rebels, progressive civil libertarians and militant anarchists. Because it was too dangerous for her to expose her views fully, she evaded government arrest by often encoding her ideas and, like most politicians, strategically calibrating her lectures to her audiences' ability to accept her message. As a crusader for anarchism, Goldman's strategy included an attempt to reach as many people as she could, even if this meant obfuscating aspects of her message or being disingenuous to those who might agree with some of her anarchist ideas but not with the movement's most extreme tactics. Only when speaking to like-minded anarchists (whether in Yiddish, German, or English) did she appear to speak without restraint—literally in a different tongue, in a different voice. Even here, however, it is quite possible that she felt compelled to tune her invectives to match the expectations of the militant comrades in her audience.

As a woman, an anarchist, and a Jew, Goldman knew how to maintain her identity in a world in which she was a political outsider, the exotic and feared Other. In the face of adversity, she called upon the remarkable resilience and survival instinct of her roots. Whether she herself was engaged directly in acts of retaliatory violence or simply played a supporting role to a covert movement, remains ambiguous.

For Goldman and the militants she defended, the underside of the country's glorious ideal of free expression was the silent but all too real mandate against openly debating, lecturing, speaking, or writing about the ongoing social and economic war in the workplace, on the streets, and in the home. Goldman's dedication to free speech was motivated first and foremost by her desire to combat injustice and create the conditions of social harmony through the contested concept and practice of anarchism.

Censorship is an attempt to eradicate unruly thoughts from crossing social, cultural, or national boundaries. Words—especially those tinged with whispers of violence—are labeled guilty provocateurs capable of toppling the social order and are to be banished without regard for the longing for justice they represent. Although she was ultimately deported from the United States, the impact of Emma Goldman's tireless work to make speech free, however, continues to ripple beyond the Left, keeping her place in historical memory as a grand expositor of freedom, a woman who spoke her truth to the powerful who would censor her and to the powerless who longed for the better world she articulated with such remarkable eloquence.

Perhaps the anarchists—often caricatured as bomb throwers, impractical dreamers, or self-defeating activists vulnerable to the superior power of the state—were in fact unsettling realists. Perhaps Emma Goldman, who looked straight into the fire surrounding her, accurately assessed that there may never be a totally peaceful solution to injustice, inequity, and greed, in a world already mired in violence. Perhaps only those who have never experienced direct oppression have the privilege to eschew violence, to bask in the radiance of pacifism. Goldman chose to embrace the dark as well as the light, to covertly support violent methods to reach her "beautiful ideal." In responding to the harshness of her own experience, Goldman channeled her fury, intellect, and sense of connectedness into the anarchist movement. Emma Goldman lived in a era permeated by violence, not only the government's use of force to suppress dissent and labor unrest, but also militant radicals' violent attempts to destroy a corrupt old order to allow a more equitable one to emerge. Could Goldman have found more peaceful ways to counter injustice and heal the wounds of a social war between the rich and poor, or did the brutality surrounding her limit her strategies for change? In the years to come, the challenges she faced would determine the ways she navigated those extremes. Remnants of these troubling questions lingered on for Goldman—and continue to plague our world today. Sadly, haunting contemporary parallels suggest that we, too, must find ways to transcend ingrained patterns of conflict if we are ever to break the accelerating cycle of violence.

CANDACE FALK, MARCH 2004
CHAMAKOME RANCH, CAZADERO
& THE EMMA GOLDMAN PAPERS,
UNIVERSITY OF CALIFORNIA, BERKELEY

SELECTION

The documents in *Making Speech Free, 1902–1909*, vol. 2 of *Emma Goldman: A Documentary History of the American Years,* are selected from the comprehensive microfilm edition of the *Emma Goldman Papers*, published 1991–1993. In addition, this volume contains documents discovered after, and in some cases as a result of, the publication of the microfilm collection. In selecting documents for this volume, which covers EG's career following the McKinley assassination through her launch of the anarchist magazine *Mother Earth* and her activities in a wider political sphere than she had inhabited in her earlier years (especially on the terrain of free speech), the editors have tried to select the most representative (and in some cases the only) documents to illustrate EG's life and career between 1902 and 1909. While correspondence from this period is greater than the period from 1890 to 1901, there is still not a large amount of extant correspondence. Consequently, approximately 50 percent of the extant correspondence from this period has been selected for this volume. Following the introduction of *Mother Earth*, EG's published essays and articles increased as she achieved growing prominence as a political writer, and the editors have also tried to represent this change in their selection. There is also a substantial collection of correspondence between EG and Ben Reitman following their meeting in 1908. Her emotional and sexual involvement with her road manager, Ben Reitman, prompted and necessitated frequent, sometimes daily, correspondence between them—thus leaving an unusual number of Goldman/Reitman letters. Roughly 10 percent of their correspondence between 1908 and 1909 has been selected for this volume. Also published in this volume are some of the only extant letters by EG to Alexander Berkman, who was in prison until 1906.

Documents fall into three general categories: personal correspondence, published writings, and government reports. The bulk of the published documents in vol. 2 are drawn from the radical and popular press. These documents are selected to show EG's activity within the anarchist community and include her articles on anarchism, free speech, women, and violence, as well as correspondence, travelogues, and articles published in the anarchist press, especially following the 1906 debut of EG's magazine *Mother Earth*. The documents selected illustrate her evolving public prominence both within the anarchist movement and in a wider political and cultural network in the United States. The documents surrounding the 1907 International Anarchist Congress in Amsterdam reflect her constantly growing stature as an important representative in the international anarchist community. Also included are lengthy newspaper accounts of her lectures and reporters' interviews with EG, selected as representative of mainstream media interest in EG, as well as offering alternative perspectives on EG's maturing political ideas and actions.

The government documents illustrate the fragile and adversarial relationship EG maintained with governments both in America and Europe. EG was recognized as a central figure in a movement offering a threat to the stability of the state, and thereby regarded as warranting surveillance. These official documents reveal the interplay between revolutionary activity and the structures of power opposing it. The selected documents also illustrate the emerging deportation battle being fought between EG and the U.S. government, early documents that help in understanding her eventual deportation in 1919.

FOREIGN-LANGUAGE DOCUMENTS
This volume includes three of EG's articles that were first published in the Italian-language anarchist paper *Cronaca Sovversiva*. Most likely these documents were written by EG in English and then translated into Italian for the paper. They have been translated back into English, as no extant English originals have been found. For historical accuracy, the particular style of writing prevalent in some Italian anarchist writings of this period has been retained in the English translations.

ARRANGEMENT
The documents are arranged chronologically, according to date of authorship or publication of text. Documents dated only by month and year are placed at the beginning of the month. Documents dated only by year are placed at the beginning of the year. Where possible, a place of authorship is also provided and added to the date line at the beginning of a document. For documents of the same date, EG's correspondence is placed first.

TEXT
Documents are presented in their entirety so that the reader may appreciate the full range and scope of each piece. In the case of Goldman's letters this is particularly important. The necessity of earning money as a traveling anarchist lecturer could make Goldman reflect poignantly on love or the execution of Francisco Ferrer while the next line could find her exercised about the price of admission to her talk or problems with the distribution of *Mother Earth* or an unsuitable travel itinerary.

FORMAT
Some features of all the documents have been standardized for this volume. All documents include a title line identifying them as correspondence, essays, articles, inter-

views, or government documents. A place and date line has also been standardized and immediately follows the document title. In the body of the documents, indentation of paragraphs has been consistently set, empty lines between paragraphs have been closed up, and in correspondence salutation and signature lines have also been consistently set. Following the text of the document an unnumbered endnote explains the original physical description of the document as well as the repository, archive, or institution where the original document may be found. This note also identifies and describes any irregularities not reproduced, information about any excised portions of text, alternate versions, publication history of the document, or accompanying matter such as photographs or illustrations.

TRANSCRIPTIONS

Goldman's correspondence from this period reflects her dramatic intellectual and linguistic development in the English language, from a seventeen-year-old immigrant whose primary languages were German and Russian with some command of Yiddish. She also gained some competence in French and Italian. With Goldman's correspondence we have rendered the transcriptions of the originals in a very literal form. All misspellings and grammatical errors are preserved. Words and characters struck out in the original, indicating an abandoned thought or construction, are transcribed when legible with a strike-out bar through them.

Spacing between words has been made regular. A single space is used between sentences. The editors have silently corrected minor punctuation errors. Often EG would demarcate the end of a sentence with a large space but no period, followed by a capital letter to mark the beginning of the next sentence. Periods have been silently added by the editors to standardize the text and increase readability. Apostrophes have been silently inserted in place of the thin spaces that EG often used to denote contractions or possessive constructions.

Interlineations and superscripts are brought down to the line. Long dashes at the end of a line or paragraph have been rendered with a dash of standard length. Hyphens at the end of a line in an original document are not preserved unless they are normally part of the word.

In printed texts a less literal transcription policy is used than for EG's own manuscript texts. Obvious typos are silently corrected, as are misspellings. Older or otherwise legitimate alternate spellings are preserved. This same practice applies to third-party government documents. Editorial insertions are rendered in italics and enclosed in square brackets, for example [*reminds*]. Conjectured words are also set in italics, followed by a question mark, for example [*comrade?*]; and illegible text is indicated by [*illegible*].

Readability, the convenience of the researcher, and a desire to prevent unnecessary confusion have informed the transcription policy. Certain elements in EG's correspondence that are less likely to be of interest to the student or historian have therefore been standardized.

ANNOTATION

Footnotes provide brief elucidation of specific persons, radical newspapers and organizations, and events mentioned or alluded to in the body of a document. Annotation is provided at the first substantive mention of the person, event, or periodical. Fuller contextual information is provided in the appendixes—the Chronology as well as in the three alphabetical directories of personal biographies, periodicals, and organizations. In addition to clarifying names, dates, and events and providing minimal cross-references to documents mentioned or cited in a given text, the footnotes alert the reader to vagaries in the original document not reproduced in this edition. Annotation also provides brief identification of important themes and ideas that informed the intellectual and philosophical development of EG.

Annotation also provides missing voices in a particular discussion or debate, or refers the reader to other sources in the microfilm edition or elsewhere that are directly related to a particular document. This has been done as thoroughly and consistently as possible, but the reader must be aware that the amount of material relevant in certain cases, even with respect to material contained in the microfilm edition, remains too vast to account for absolutely.

CHRONOLOGY

The Chronology provides both a broad overview of important events during the period from 1902 to 1909 as well as the day-by-day record of EG's activities and movements (as much as is possible from the historical record). The Chronology also traces EG's platform speaking, identifying where possible the date, location, and topic of her lectures.

DIRECTORIES

In addition to the annotations and the Chronology, the three directories help to contextualize the radical history of the period—the labor strikes, political events, social movements, and organizations and political figures, whether well known or obscure—that were integral to EG's world. Each volume is intended to stand alone, and the reader should be aware that the directories are time-bound primarily by the years covered in the volume. Thus, the entries may not cover the entire history of a person's life or an organization's trajectory.

INDIVIDUALS

The personal biographies in the Directory of Individuals add further detail to the short identifying footnotes accompanying the documents. The directory entry gives the individual's dates, nationality, and a short history of his or her political and social activities during the period of this volume. Where applicable, the entry also identifies the person's oeuvre, including periodicals contributed to as well as books and pamphlets published.

PERIODICALS

The Directory of Periodicals identifies the important radical, anarchist, and socialist newspapers and magazines that were part of the political world in which EG operated.

All periodicals in which EG's writings were published, as well as other contemporary periodicals that informed the political world in which EG lived, are listed. Each entry identifies publication dates and locations as well as editors and principal contributors. The periodical's political orientation is identified and, where possible, EG's participation in the life of the periodical or the view the periodical took toward EG's political career is described.

ORGANIZATIONS

The Directory of Organizations adds further documentation to the complex political world of which EG was a part. Entries identify important organizations mentioned or alluded to in the documents, giving contextual history to the period that helped to define the anarchist and radical movement in America.

BIBLIOGRAPHIES

In addition to the main Selected Bibliography, this volume also includes three detailed bibliographies of EG's published pamphlets as well as pamphlets published by the Mother Earth Publishing Association and the Free Speech League during this period. These titles are also cited in the Chronology, to locate the publications in response to the events of the period. The pamphlets were advertised for sale through *Mother Earth* and were also sold during EG's lecture tours. The pamphlets were both a way to raise funds and a way to increase the literature and understanding of anarchism for an American audience.

ABBREVIATIONS

DOCUMENT DESCRIPTIONS
FORM
A   autograph
P   printed
T   typed

TYPE
D   document (trial transcript, printed leaflet, etc.)
L   letter
Pc   postal card
W   wire or telegram

SEAL
f   fragment
I   initialed
S   signed
Sr   signed with signature representation
U   unsigned

EXAMPLES OF DOCUMENT DESCRIPTIONS
ALS   autograph letter signed
ALSf fragment of a signed autograph letter
API   autograph postcard initialed
PLSr printed letter with signature representation
TDS   typed document signed
TDSr typed document with signature representation
TLI   typed letter initialed
TLS   typed letter signed
TLSr typed letter with signature representation
TLU   typed letter unsigned
TWSr typed wire with signature representation

REPOSITORIES, ARCHIVES, AND INSTITUTIONS

CaOOA	Public Archives Library, Ottawa, Ontario, Canada
CBhSc	Scriptorium, Beverly Hills, Calif.
CtY-B	Beinecke Rare Book and Manuscript Library, Yale University, New Haven, Conn.
CU-B	Bancroft Library, University of California, Berkeley
DLC	Library of Congress, Washington, D.C.
DNA	National Archives, Washington, D.C.
GARF	Gosudarstvennyi arkhiv Rossiiskoi Federatsii (State Archive of the Russian Federation; formerly TsGAOR, Central State Archive of the October Revolution), Moscow
IEN	Northwestern University Library, Special Collections Department, Evanston, Ill.
IISH	International Institute of Social History, Amsterdam
IU-U	University of Illinois, Chicago
MCR	Schlesinger Library, Radcliffe College, Cambridge, Mass.
MH-H	Houghton Library, Harvard University, Cambridge, Mass.
MHi	Massachusetts Historical Society, Boston
MiU	Labadie Collection, Department of Rare Books and Special Collections, University of Michigan Library, Ann Arbor
MnHi	Minnesota Historical Society
NjP	Princeton Library, Princeton University, Princeton, N.J.
NN	Rare Books and Manuscripts Division, The New York Public Library, Astor, Lenox and Tilden Foundations, New York
NNC	Butler Library, Columbia University, New York
NNMA	New York City Municipal Archives
NNU	New York University Library, New York University, New York
PHi	Historical Society of Pennsylvania, Philadelphia
WHi	State Historical Society of Wisconsin, Madison

OTHER ABBREVIATIONS

PERSONS

AB	Alexander Berkman
BR	Ben Reitman
EG	Emma Goldman

PUBLICATIONS

EGP	Candace Falk et al., eds., *The Emma Goldman Papers: A Microfilm Edition*. Alexandria, Va.: Chadwyck-Healey, 1991–1993; reference is by reel number.
LML	Emma Goldman, *Living My Life*. New York: Alfred A. Knopf, 1931; reprint, New York: Dover Publications, 1970.

To *LA QUESTIONE SOCIALE*

New York, 5 July 1902

To the Strikers of Paterson

Since Wednesday, June 18,[1] when the police caused a riot by opening fire on a body of strikers whose offence only consisted of the attempt to induce those working in the mills to make common cause with them, the mouthpiece of the Weidmann, Auger and Simon[2] and the other upstarts in the silk trade, the *Paterson Guardian*, has exerted all its "Literary Genius" to spread fallacious and vindictive reports about the Wednesday outbreak and the strikers in general. Since that time it has employed every device to prejudice the public against the workers by maliciously holding up the foreign section of the strikers and the anarchists as the cause of the whole trouble.

As long as this worthy member of Capitalistic hirelings indulged in vile denunciations of Anarchists and Anarchism, we deemed it below our dignity to rectify any of its statements. We know too well that it requires intelligence to discuss anarchism and to do justice to its adherents, and to credit a yellow sensational and vicious journal like the *Guardian* with such cultured qualities, would even make the Gods laugh; but since it persists in holding us responsible for the general strike, we consider it highest time to speak.

We speak because we wish to have a heart to heart talk with you, the strikers. You men and women of the large masses, whose life is an endless chain of drudgery, of darkness and despair, to you we speak. In times gone by, when the workers dared to assert their rights, when driven to strike thru years of suffering and abuse, they have ever been misrepresented by the Capitalistic press. Their demands were stamped as unjust, and

1. A walkout on 23 April 1902 of Paterson silk dyers began a bitter strike that threw the textile industry of New Jersey into turmoil. Although the Paterson silk dyers worked together to sustain the strike, lack of support among other silk workers and the subcontracting of work to plants in Pennsylvania undermined it. By June the strike was on the verge of collapse. A rally in Belmont Park on 18 June nonetheless attracted thousands of workers. Among the first speakers was Luigi Galleani (editor at this time of *La Questione Sociale*), whose address in Italian calling for a general strike drew roars of approval; William MacQueen and Rudolph Grossmann also spoke. The excitement spilled over as the crowd dispersed: rioting broke out in Paterson's mill district and the police responded with gunfire. Galleani was shot in the face, but managed to escape, fleeing to Canada. Eventually martial law was declared, the National Guard called in to restore order, and the strike broken.
2. Actually two firms. In 1902 Jacob Weidmann, owner of the largest dye house in Paterson, led the opposition to collective bargaining. The National Silk Dyeing Company, the second biggest employer in Paterson, was founded and managed by Charles L. Auger and Charles Simon. The large manufacturers were the primary targets of the strike and it was the manufacturers' interests that the local newspaper, the *Paterson Guardian*, defended in its news columns. Many of the smaller firms had settled earlier with the strikers.

their brothers denounced as mobs and violators of Law and Order. In those days a whole machinery was employed to show, that the workers had no cause for discontent, that the conditions were good, and that each man could earn a comfortable living if he so desired. But those days are gone, and none but the intellect of the "Guardian Angel" can have the impudence to blow life, into the shadows of a past prejudice. Today every intelligent man from the Professor's chair down to the pulpit, from the literary genius down to the poorest scribbler, from the wealthy drawing room to the poorest hut, all have recognised this one great truth: that the condition of the workers is far from being good. That they are getting poorer, that 70,000,000 people in the U.S. not merely foreigners, but Americans also, are at the mercy of a small number of men, who have accumulated all the wealth of the Country, thereby widening the gulf between the rich and the poor.

Every one recognises, that these conditions render it impossible for the producer to rise out of a life of drudgery and dependence, a life of hopeless submission, while giving to the non-producer all opportunity for culture, development and affluence. That striker and conflicts between those who toil and those who live without work, are the most natural results of such conditions.

Every one knows that, and many there are who try their utmost to bring about a change for the better. To educate and elevate the laborer, to raise his self respect, and to awaken in him self consciousness. But the majority who could do much for the oppressed dare not speak, for they have sold their manhood for a mass of porridge, and their degraded occupation consists of making laws as a protection for a privileged few in their greedy rush for wealth. Or to shoot peaceful men and women, who dare, occasionally to ask for more than a mere crust. They are engaged in spinning cobwebs over the eyes of the public and inventing new excuses, new apologies and new lies as a cause of all labor trouble.

Now, it is the Anarchist, he, the outlaw is responsible for it. He, who believes in no master save his own intelligence, he, who insists, that no man, has a right to live at the expence of his fellow man, or to invade his freedom and to coerce him into submission. The anarchist who proves, that all government is based on force and violence and can only thrive on force and violence. He, who knows that the whole machinery of government breeds corruption, fraud and crime. Yes, the Anarchist is responsible for it. "Stamp him out! Imprison him! Hang him! until dead and a little longer".

Now, could the *Guardian* or any other yellow journal have raised a better cry as an excuse for strikes, than popular prejudice against Anarchists and Anarchism? Certainly not nothing excites the bull more, than the waving of a red cloth. However the thinking people among the strikers know better than to heed such sensational talk. They know that Anarchism means anything but crime and violence. That it is a philosophy dealing with all human life, based upon a deep longing for independence and a strong sympathy with the human family. Of course the "Guardian" cannot be expected to know anything of philosophies. Again we hear, it is the foreigner who is to blame, the Italian, the French, the German, etc. They are responsible. They, the strangers who come to our shores and have the audacity to speak a language we do not understand, because we hardly understand our own language. They, who came to America because they could not resist the treacherous charms of dame liberty, yet will not submit to the policeman's club. They, who will not starve silently while our own patriotic boys swallowed embalmed beef or died of fever without a murmur. Yes, the foreigner is responsible for the labor trouble. Another popular prejudice which may satisfy an ignorant populace but never those, who are united in a common cause, those, who have worked side by side in the time of peace and who, now strongly hold together, in the time of war.

How ridiculous, how illogical it is to hold any given idea or any set of men responsible for an evil that is deeply rooted in the very system of economic relations between millions of people, who produce all the wealth, yet are forced to live on a mere pittance, and a small minority, that not only owns all the products, but that can dictate terms according to a moment's caprice. A system that has given birth to a labor trouble because it has given birth to its enemy, capitalism. These two enemies can never under any circumstances be united, because the rise of one, means the fall of the other, the independence of one, the submission of the other, and when the submission has reached its limit, what then? Ah yes, what then? Then it breaks forth with all its pent up energies, all hopes, all dreams and aspirations and spreads like thunder and lightning all over the country in the form of strikes, conflicts and riots. And the militia, and the Mayor with the vigilance league might as well attempt to sweep back the rushing waves of the ocean with a broom, as to stop the current of discontent and long suffering.

Just such a strike is on in Paterson to-day and if the "Guardian Angel" together with the Weidmann, Auger & Simon, Geering etc. will continue, like the ostrich, to hide their heads beneath their feathers, you strikers of Paterson cannot and must not follow their example. You know yourselves that the cause of your strike is neither anarchists nor foreigners. You know as well, as one of your brothers who states in a N.Y. German evening paper, that the strike was brought about through your meager earnings, which made it impossible for you to exist. The writer, who, as the paper assures us, is a very conservative man and is opposed to both Anarchism and Socialism, explains the strikes as follows: The Mill owners who are mostly upstarts, that is to say, have recently risen to wealth, treat their workingmen in the roughest and rudest possible way. They have accumulated large fortunes and built magnificent mansions out of the sweat and blood of their employees. They live in luxury and abundance, while men with big families can hardly earn eight dollars per week, and this not all year around.

You see strikers that even the most conservative among you realize, that the men who have become rich through you, and who will, with the greatest ease squander thousands yet not grant your small demands, that they, who in their cowardice called for the militia to shoot you, and to protect their ill gotten wealth, that they and the system, that breeds them are responsible for the strike and no one else.

Mr. Weidmann and his companions claim, that they cannot pay the price demanded by the strikers. Perhaps they will change their minds when the whole industry of Paterson will be tied up. When all the textile workers, machinists and car drivers will join you in the general strike (the strike which is not composed merely of foreigners as the *Guardian* will have it but which has involved a large majority of American Workingmen) which to all appearance is but a question of a few days.

Commercialism has tried hard to crush human sympathy, but nature, in her all abounding love has come out victorious. She knows not of Italian, German, French or other nationalities; she knows, that all blood is red, and all tears are salt. She sees but her children with pale faces and bleeding limbs, and she faithfully leads them on to a victory, which they can only gain through a strong deep tie of sympathy and devotion in the battle for their rights.

EMMA GOLDMAN.

La Questione Sociale, 5 July 1902, p. 2; printed in English. Reprinted in *Free Society,* 20 July 1902, pp. 1–2.

To WALTER CHANNING

New York, 18 October 1902

Dear Sir

I am in receipt of your note of the 18th inst. and in reply would like to say this, I do not know whether Czolgogz[1] was an Anarchist, nor have I the right to say that he was not. I have not known him sufficiently to be acquainted with his political Views. In fact no one has, including Mr Isaak and Mr Shilling[2] and if they have expressed opinions either for or against his being an Anarchist they have done an injustice to the young man, who died such a brave death, ~~as you~~ and you, dear Sir will be guilty of the same offence if you attempt to prove that Czolgogz was not or was an Anarchist. No one can with certainty say, that the man was an Anarchist, since he was but little known, and since he has never ~~proff~~ made a public statement to that affect. Still less can one prove that he was not one; there is nothing in his act by which one can deny him the right of being an Anarchist. It is true, the Philosophy of Anarchy does not teach Invasion, but it does teach self defence, and Czolgogz's act was an act of self-defence and nothing else. You may question this, since Czolgogz was not personally attact by McKinley, quite true, but Czolgogz belonged to the Oppressed, to the Exploited and Disinherited Millions, who lead a life of darkness and despaire owing to those, of whom McKinley was one, therefore he was personally attacked by the ex President, or rather he was one of the Victims of the McKinley regime and those McKinley catered to. The act of Czolgogz may have been imprectical or inupportune, I will not argue this point now, but I insist it had nothing unanarchistic about it, since, as I said before Anarchism claims the right of Defence against Invasion and Aggression of every shape and form and no one, who has his eyes open will and can deny that those in Power are the Invaders, and McKinley certainly was one of them. I send you with this, 2 Articles[3]

---

1. Leon Czolgosz, who assassinated President McKinley at the world's fair in Buffalo in September 1901, was judged sane before his trial by three psychiatrists for the prosecution and two psychiatrists for the defense. Later, Tufts University Medical School psychiatrist Walter Channing assessed Czolgosz as mentally unstable, based strictly on the assassin's personal history, in a October 1902 article published in the *American Journal of Insanity.*
2. Cleveland anarchist Emil Schilling had been Czolgosz's first contact in the anarchist movement in May 1901, lending him reading materials and answering his questions. According to Schilling they were estranged even before Czolgosz's arrival in Chicago. Abe Isaak, editor of *Free Society,* introduced Czolgosz to EG in Chicago; Isaak found Czolgosz's behavior suspicious.
3. EG enclosed her essay "The Tragedy at Buffalo," published in the 6 October 1901 issue of *Free Society,* and her letter of 11 November 1901 to *Lucifer, the Lightbearer;* both documents are reprinted in vol. 1 pp. 471–78, 479–80.

in which I have stated my Views on the act of Sep 6th 1901 and I do not think I have anything to ad to it.

SINCERLY
EMMA GOLDMAN

ALS, Walter Channing III Papers, Channing Family Collection, MHi.

Free Speech in Chicago.

EDITOR *LUCIFER*:—

For the benefit of those of your readers who still believe that freedom of speech is a reality, and that America is the freest country on earth,[1] permit me to give you a few details of my experience with the Chicago police.

I came to this city to acquaint the American public with the conditions in Russia, and to raise funds for the unfortunate victims of the Russian knout, many of whom have been flogged to death, while others have been sent to long terms of imprisonment, simply because they dared to ask for bread for the suffering Russian peasants.

To my amazement I found two hundred policemen—some of them high officials, at my first meeting; men who came not out of sympathy with the starving Russian people but who were there to take me to the nearest police station should I not meet their own conception of what liberty means.[2]

O Liberty! poor outraged, degraded Liberty. Fallen indeed art thou from thy once lofty height when every petty policeman can soil thy pure form with his foul hands, and trample in the mire of Chicago's streets thy beauteous lineaments.

Since that first meeting the police have followed me from hall to hall, threatening me with arrest if I dared to say anything against the American government.[3] "Say what you please about Russia, but you must not attack our institutions," said Captain Campbell to me at a meeting on the West side.

Another little Tzar, Captain Wheeler, went his colleague one better: "I will not have

---

1. In the wake of President McKinley's assassination, repression of anarchists mounted. *Discontent* faced repeated suppression from postal authorities, and *Lucifer* and its editor Moses Harman led a movement to establish a organization to fight the growing suppression of free speech. As early as the 13 February 1902 issue of *Lucifer*, Harman encouraged the formation of a group to "create a public conscience that will be felt and heeded by our national lawmakers." Soon after, on 1 May 1902 the Free Speech League was loosely formed at a meeting of the Manhattan Liberal Club by E. B. Foote, E. C. Walker, and others; *Lucifer* continued to report on the free speech fights and support the cause and activities of the Free Speech League.
2. The article "Police Eyes on Anarchy," *Chicago Tribune*, 17 November 1902, *EGP* reel 47, also reported on the two hundred policemen present along with two patrol wagons.
3. On 23 November EG was barred by the police from speaking at Handel Hall, although later that day she spoke at the Trades Unions Hall on "The Radical and the Child."

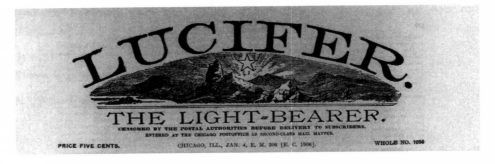

Masthead of *Lucifer, the Lightbearer* (used throughout the life of the paper), an anarchist journal promoting sex radicalism edited and published by Moses Harman with the help of his daughter, Lillian. The year "E.M. 306" is based on Harman's calendar for the "era of man," starting from the death of freethought martyr Giordano Bruno in 1600, instead of "E.C.," the era of Christianity, starting with the birth of Jesus. (By permission of the Kate Sharpley Library)

Miss Goldman speak in my district," and prohibited the meeting that was to take place at Aurora Turn Hall, corner of Ashland Ave. and Division street.[4]

Surely there must be something wrong with the American Institutions of today; something terribly black and corrupt, if they cannot stand the light of criticism; if they can thrive only when physical force is used to defend them against the light of free discussion.

This is not the first time that meetings for free discussion have been prohibited here; not the first time speakers have been shadowed from place to place. On previous occasions the Chicago authorities have had to give some excuse for such interference. They have had to plead either public excitement, too radical utterance on the part of the speaker, or some similar excuse as justification of their acts.

What excuse will they give now?

What excuse will the self-styled Jeffersonian-Democratic mayor of Chicago[5] give for the acts of his subordinates?

There is now no public excitement; no radical utterances made—at least not in reference to "our own sacred government."

What other conclusion can be reached, or inference drawn, than that America is fast being Russianized, and that unless the American people awake from the pleasant dream into which they have been lulled by the strains of "My Country 'tis of Thee," etc., we shall soon be obliged to meet in cellars, or in darkened back rooms with closed doors, and speak in whispers lest our next door neighbors should hear that free-born American

4. This event took place on 30 November.
5. Carter H. Harrison, Jr. (1860–1953), was mayor of Chicago from 1897 to 1905 and again from 1911 to 1915; after the McKinley assassination, Harrison prevented EG from speaking in Chicago. Harrison's father had been mayor of Chicago for five terms, one of which encompassed the Haymarket affair.

citizens dare not speak in the open; that they have sold their birthright to the Russian Tzar disguised by the coat of an American policeman?

Is it not time that something be done?

Is it not time that all advanced people unite in protesting against such brutal invasion? all, at least, who have enough Americanism left in them to maintain the right of freedom of speech, of press and of assembly?

Or, are they going to wait until the number of victims of suppression increase to legions—as in Russia today?

EMMA GOLDMAN.

Lucifer, the Lightbearer, 11 December 1902.

My dear Mr Traubel.

I feel awfully sorry that you should have been compelled to send one of your calls for aid to me also, when I should have paid you long ago. It is nothing else but hard times Mr Traubel that prevents me ~~from~~ to give to your paper all that it derserves, for it does deserve much very much indeed. I can say without flatery of all the paper in the English language I read, I enjoy the Conservator[1] most and it is really shameful that one can not do for one's favorite as much as one would like to. Enclosed please find $1. I know it does not half cover what I owe, but I can send no more for the present

Sincerly Yours.
Emma Goldman

ALS, Horace Traubel Papers, DLC. Note at top of manuscript, not in EG's hand, reads: "paid for Jan 1902–3."

1. *The Conservator* (1890–1919) was founded, published, and edited by Horace Traubel in Philadelphia, who was dedicated to preserving Walt Whitman's literary heritage.

Ai compagni e lettori della *Cronaca Sovversiva* del nostro nuovo ribelle giornale italiano saluti ed augurii di buona battaglia!

CARISSIMI COMPAGNI,

Era mio fermo proposito di testimoniare al nostro nuovo giornale i miei sentimenti di solidarietá col contributo affettuoso d'un articolo mio, vi avevo anzi promesso uno studio sul movimento anarchico degli Stati Uniti. Le non liete condizioni della mia salute, quelle piú gravi del mio penoso ufficio di infermiera mi hanno impedito di assolvere al mio voto di collaborare al primo numero del nostro giornale.

Non aggiungo inutili scuse. Voi assaporaste come me tutte le amarezze della lotta per l'esistenza e se voi anelate di dare alla causa della giustizia della veritá e della libertá eternamente soffocata dalla miseria, dal lavoro penoso, dalla disperazione tutte le vostre energie saprete comprendere e compatire se pur essendo con voi anima e cuore non posso darvi per ora che una fraterna parola di simpatia.

Parole d'incoraggiamento non vi abbisognano: di tutti i compagni che lottano in questo paese voi, figli della ridente Italia, siete stati sempre i piú tenaci, i piú ardenti, voi tra tutti quelli che i pericoli della propaganda affrontano su questo suolo sacro al dollaro onnipotente, alla ignobile forza che ha spento ogni scintilla d'entusiasmi, ogni fremito d'indignazione su questa terra in cui un pugno solido vale più che un cervello fosforescente, in cui Teddy il terribile vuole in ogni uomo uno schiavo sommesso, in ogni donna una femmina feconda.

E tutti quelli che conoscono i pericoli tremendi della propaganda in questo paese apprezzeranno i vostri assidui sforzi e l'abnegazione tenace che votate al trionfo del nostro ideale.

Avanti! Avanti! E all'opera vostra arrida luminoso il trionfo. Io intanto per non mancare alla mia promessa vi compiego due articoli. Il primo è di uno dei più sinceri e coraggiosi compagni nostri, John H. Cook, l'altro di W. Tharston Brown già ministro ed ora socialista rivoluzionario. Questi articoli vedranno la luce in uno dei prossimi numeri mentre ai valenti collaboratori mandiamo fin da ora sinceri e cordiali ringraziamenti vivissimi della Cronaca Sovversiva.

Egli ha abbandonato la sua posizione e la sua carica a quel mondo che tollera soltanto schiavi e padroni non mai una anima fiera ed è venuto, senza rimpianti, tra noi a cercarvi ambiente più puro e più nobile di libertà, d'indipendenza di solidarietà.

É uno dei nostri anche se non ha incondizionatamente aderito a tutte le nostre idee.

Che importa?

La libertà, madre, accarezza d'affetti generosi tutti i figli che armati d'integra onestà combattono contro l'oppressione e la tirannia per un avvenire in cui non saranno nè padroni nè servi, nè ricchi nè poveri nè oppressori nè oppressi; per l'avvenire che irradierà le fiamme delle sue aurore vermiglie sulle fanciulle felici, sui figli liberi perché avranno compreso che la libertà di ciascuno ha le sue radici nella libertà di tutti e che in questa libertà di tutti è la guarentigia della libertà, dello sviluppo, dell'autonomia, delle libere affermazioni di ciascuno.

Per questo ideale radioso il nostro collaboratore William Tharston Brown ha lasciato della vita le mollezze e gli agi tra cui la gente vana chiude i confini e le aspirazioni della felicità.

Per questo io lo tengo dei nostri e son certa che egli sarà contento di ridarvi all'occasione la sua collaborazione e tutto il suo appoggio per la Cronaca Sovversiva.

VOSTRA, EMMA GOLDMAN.

To the comrades and the readers of *Cronaca Sovversiva,* our new Italian rebel newspaper, greetings and may success crown your struggle![1]

DEAREST COMRADES,

It was my firm intention to declare to our new newspaper my feelings of solidarity with the affectionate contribution of an article of mine; I actually promised you a study of the anarchistic movement in the United States. My unfortunate state of health, as well as those even more insistent demands associated with my taxing employment as a nurse, prevented me from fulfilling my pledge to contribute to the first edition of our paper.

I will not offer any pointless apologies. You grapple, as I do, with all of the vexations of the struggle to survive, and if now you are eager to devote all your energies to the cause of justice, truth and liberty—a cause forever oppressed by misery, hard work and desperation—then you will find it in your hearts to forgive me and appreciate that, even though I am with you heart and soul, I have nothing to offer you at present save a fraternal word of fellow feelings.

Words of encouragement you do not need: of all the comrades fighting in this country you, sons of smiling Italy, have always been the most tenacious, the most passionate—you, out of all those who must brave the dangers implicit in propaganda in this, the sacred ground of the almighty dollar, that ignoble force that has extinguished every spark of enthusiasm, every tremor of outrage; in this land where a clenched fist counts for more than an enlightened mind, where Teddy the Terrible wants every man a craven slave, and every woman a brood mare.[2]

And all those who are familiar with the terrible dangers attendant upon propaganda in this country will appreciate your diligent efforts and the unyielding sacrifice that you make that our ideal may triumph.

Onward! Onward! May success smile bright upon your efforts. Meanwhile, not to break my promise, I offer you two articles. The first is by one of the most sincere and courageous

---

1. Luigi Galleani was involved in the Paterson silk workers' strike of June 1902 (see Letter to *La Questione Sociale,* 18 June 1902, above) and indicted for incitement to riot. He fled to Canada and in 1903 returned to the United States, settling under an assumed name in Barre, Vermont, a stronghold of Italian anarchists. On 6 June 1903 Galleani founded *Cronaca Sovversiva* (1903–1920), one of the most significant American anarchist publications.
2. Refers to Theodore Roosevelt's comment that the rising birthrate among immigrants and minorities, and the falling birthrate among Anglo-Saxons, was leading to "race suicide." The argument appeared in Roosevelt's introduction to Bessie McGinnis and Marie Van Vorst's *The Woman Who Toils (Experience of Two Ladies as Factory Girls)* (New York: Doubleday, Page, 1903).

Masthead of *Cronaca Sovversiva* (Subversive Chronicle), the leading Italian-language anarchist communist paper in the United States. Edited by Luigi Galleani, the weekly newspaper published Goldman's writings and regularly reported on her activities. (By permission of the Kate Sharpley Library)

of our comrades, John H. Cook; the other by W. Thurston Brown, a one time minister now a revolutionary socialist.[3]

He has left his calling and his office to the world that tolerates only slaves and masters and never a proud soul,[4] and he has joined us, without nary a regret, to seek a purer, nobler climate of freedom, independence, and solidarity.

He is one of our own, even if he has not unconditionally embraced all of our ideas.

What does that matter?

Mother liberty caresses with generous affections all the sons who, armed with the weapons of high-minded honesty, fight against oppression and tyranny for a future in which there will be neither masters nor slaves, neither rich nor poor, neither oppressors nor oppressed; for a future whose rosy fingered dawn will shine down upon girls carefree and sons free, because they will have grasped that the freedom of each is rooted in the freedom of all, and that in this universal freedom is the guarantee of liberty, self-development, autonomy, and free speech for each and everyone.

For the sake of this radiant ideal our collaborator William Thurston Brown has turned his back upon that life of petty comforts and conveniences wherein the vain would imprison the reach and the yearning for freedom.

3. Note in original reads: "These articles will see light in one of the next numbers, meanwhile to the valued correspondent we address in advance sincere and cordial thanks from *Cronaca Sovversiva*" (translated from Italian). An article by Providence, Rhode Island, anarchist John H. Cook entitled "Sull'autocratismo nelle Unioni di Mestiere" (Autocracy in the Trade Unions) appeared in the next issue, 13 June 1903; however, no article by William Thurston Brown was published in *Cronaca Sovversiva* in 1903.
4. Brown left the Congregational Church in 1902 after being expelled from two pulpits for his radical socialist politics.

For this reason I consider him one of our own and I am sure that he will be happy to collaborate with you again on any occasion and to offer his full support to *Cronaca Sovversiva.*

Yours
Emma Goldman.

Cronaca Sovversiva, 6 June 1903, p. 2. Translated from Italian.

From ALEXANDER BERKMAN

Western Penitentiary, Allegheny City, Pa., 20 July 1903

DEAR FRIEND MUSICK:—

I hope that this note, via Mo. [*Missouri*], will not reach you before the end of the month, so that it may find you back home. I am very much pleased to know that you have at last allowed yourself a short outing, you need it badly, I have no doubt.—Does it require, you think, a wonderful memory to remember anything with reference to a *liubimaia*.[1] Now, about Sol.,[2] I should think that a medical man, with a good clientelle, would find but little time for study, save to keep up with the progress of his particular science, besides, I do not understand in what sense S. is the "best-instructed man on the East Side". Of what earthly use is academic knowledge, except such which has direct bearing on human life & affairs; knowledge is good, but I think wisdom—the ability of practical application—is better. Or shall I understand that S. has become a lecturer, teacher etc—in what way is his "science" apparent. Not that I wish to detract from S.'s talents & parts, but there used to be, in my time, so much nonsense about "wissenschaftl. Social.",[3] that I have become sceptical & suspicious of the term.—The matter of "failed" and "neither party fraud" must be explained, but some other time. Is it not probable that the Sailor[4] is keeping in reserve a thought, which has no basis in fact.—By the way, can't we come to an understanding about that present—the gift for me—which was to be sent to you. You will think me thickheaded, but [*illegible*] not convinced. In the last letter you say that [*you*] had received *esseii*[5] from Tolst.'s brother, and I presume you mean the pretender who proved himself a fraud. Or am I wrong? Do you mean that you received last April a Kaleidoscopic view of various scenery, etc. Please explain which is which.—With your last letter I received two sermons—not three as you mention—by Brown: Soc & Church, and Estric. & Permeation.[6] Also a litogr. picture of Brown, who looks like a Puritan, with a mind capable of great concentration. The composite face of the type student. Observation & firmness prominent; a spark of the savage still extant. I enjoyed reading the two articles. He is clear,

---

1. AB writes the Russian word, transliterated here as *liubimaia* (beloved), in the Cyrillic alphabet.
2. AB refers to Hillel Solotaroff, M.D.; later in the letter he abbreviates Solotaroff's name as S.
3. The full German phrase is *wissenshaftlicher Sozialismus,* "scientific socialism."
4. "Sailor" or "Little Sailor" was one of AB's names for EG.
5. AB uses the Cyrillic alphabet to spell the Russian word, transliterated here as *esseii* (essay), although it is normally spelled *essé.*
6. "Socialism and the Church" by William Thurston Brown was published in the May 1902 issue of the socialist *Wilshire's Magazine,* with a photograph of the author; "Extrication or Permeation—Which?" was published by *Wilshire's* in the February 1902 issue. In July 1902, *Wilshire's* also published the letter Brown wrote when he resigned from Plymouth Church in Rochester, New York. Later in the letter, AB abbreviates Brown's name as Br.

very logical, with the rare gift of expressing his thoughts consecutively and plainly. But I can neither liken him to Ruskin,[7] as you did, nor do I see in his literary style the least approach to that of R. Reitzel.[8] Nota bene, I judge from these 2 sermons only. He may be a poet, like R., but there is not the least evidence of it in these 2 sermons. I find more poetry in his "benediction" at Herron's nuptials.[9] Ruskin was a grand past master of pure Engl. Br's style is rather faulty; I can cite passages, if necessary. Br's thoughts are grander than his style; the former are both beautiful & sometimes original; the latter lacks polish, occasionally even clearness. R.R. is unapprochable in point of Germ. style, in the poetic beauty & originality of expression. R's forte was the clothing of old & familiar thoughts into in such original dress that they seemed new. Br. uses old dresses for the new children of his mind. But send me more of his—he has an expansive mind.

Au revoir

Alex.

See about the information from the Blind Instit.[10]

ALS, Emma Goldman Archive, IISH. Addressed from "Ohioside"; Western Penitentiary was on the Ohio River.

7. AB refers to John Ruskin, the English art historian and social critic whose writings influenced many radicals.
8. AB refers to Robert Reitzel, editor of *Der arme Teufel;* his name also abbreviated as R.R.
9. William Thurston Brown presided at the wedding of Christian socialist George D. Herron (1862–1925) and Carrie Rand in a secular, unconventional ceremony on 25 May 1901, intended to dramatize the equitable, noncoercive nature of their union. See Leonard D. Abbott, *A Socialist Wedding* (New York: Knickerbocker Press, 1901).
10. Probably information for "Blind Charley." In *Prison Memoirs of an Anarchist,* AB writes of an inmate who was shot in the face, his optic nerves severed, and permanently blinded (pp. 425–26).

From ALEXANDER BERKMAN

Western Penitentiary, Allegheny City, Pa., 11 August 1903

My dear Friend:—

This via Mo. My letter to Our Farmer-Boy[1] was finished when the local mail-man handed me yours of the 9. inst. Your previous letter of over a week ago was also rec'd & my blind friend was greatly pleased with the information you sent.[2] He insists on my sending you his regards and thanks,—"to the party in N.Y. who takes such an active interest in me", to use his words. That Instit. for the Blind would be the proper place for my friend here, and the conditions—as printed—seem rather liberal; but whether the man will be able to take advantage of the offer, is rather doubtful.

Yes, I remember Dr. Girshdansky;[3] Certainly; I could draw his likeness this minute—if I could draw. He was studying medicine when I left N.Y. As to your queries—I arrived in N.Y. in Febr. 1888, a few months after the legal murders in Chi.[4] Arrested July 22. 1892.[5] Tried, convicted & sentenced—Sep. 19. 92—on 6 separate indictments. Received maximum penalty on all the charges, except one.

1. Felonious assault & battery, with intent to kill H. C. Frick, 7 years.
2. Ditto on J. L. Leishman (formerly of the Carnegie Co., now Minister to Turkey) 5 years.
3. Entering a building with intent to commit a felony.
4. Ditto.
5. Ditto.

3 years on each charge.

6. Carrying concealed weapons, 1 year.

A total of 22 years; 21 to be served in the Western Penitentiary of Pa. and One in the Allegheny County Workhouse.

---

1. By "Farmer-Boy," AB possibly refers to Sam Austin, who lived and farmed in Caplinger Mills, Missouri. His wife, Kate Austin, died in 1902.
2. See note 10 to Letter from Alexander Berkman, 20 July 1903, above.
3. Max Girzdansky was a New York anarchist, doctor, and member of the Pioneers of Liberty, the influential Jewish anarchist group of which AB had been a member. Girzdansky was also at the first conference of Jewish radicals organized by the Pioneers of Liberty and the Knights of Liberty in New York on 25 December 1890. The conference, overwhelmed by the breach between the socialists and anarchists, split into two groups—the anarchists founding *Freie Arbeiter Stimme* and the socialists, *Arbeiter-Zeitung.*
4. The Haymarket anarchists were executed on 11 November 1887.
5. In fact, July 23.

Now, old chum, by the time you are through with your present "Fifth Avenue" case—nearer Essex St., I presume—I shall be interested to hear something about your communion with the elves & the waves of the Atlantic. By the way, send the "Third" by Brown again,[6] per letter this or next week. If you find anything of interest in the magazine (that printed Br's picture)[7] send me the whole thing. Tell me more about Girsd. How is he doing & what are the data for.

Affect.

Alex.

ALS, Emma Goldman Archive, IISH. Addressed to E. Smith, 71–73 E. 100th St., N. Y. City. Addressed from "Castle on the Ohio," referring to Western Penitentiary's location on the Ohio River.

6. AB refers to articles by William Thurston Brown. See Letter from Alexander Berkman, 20 July 1903, above.
7. Perhaps AB refers to one of the socialist magazines to which Brown contributed, either *The Comrade* in May 1903 or *Wilshire's Magazine* in May 1902, both of which published photographs of the socialist and ex-Congregational minister. Brown also became a contributing editor to the *Socialist Spirit*, published in Chicago, and close politically to *Free Society*, shortly after he left the Congregational Church in 1902.

DEAR COMRADE METZKOW.

As you may gather from *Freiheit,* Comrade John Turner,[1] whom you no doubt know from England, is already in N.Y. His first meeting will take place on Friday Oct 23,[2] and a number of other meetings will follow on the heels of that.

Turner will speak on Sunday Nov. 1st in the Brooklyn Philosophical Association, in the Long Island business College. I will send you ~~various~~ tickets for distribution.

In addition I would like to ask you if you could arrange a larger meeting in Brooklyn for him, or perhaps if you could interest some organizations or societies in him. Perhaps you would like to speak to comrade Turner? He is staying with me and I would be delighted if you would visit us. He will be at home tomorrow until noon and on the other days until 3 in the afternoon.

I am enclosing a biographical sketch of Turner which you perhaps can use for agitation purposes.[3]

WITH REV. GREETINGS
EMMA GOLDMAN

Please address me with the name

E. G. Smith
1804 Madison Ave
New York.

ALS, Joseph Ishill Collection, MH-H. Translated from German.

1. The English anarchist and trade unionist John Turner was lecturing in the United States for the second time; his first lecture tour occurred in 1896. During that earlier tour Metzkow, who had been living in Buffalo at the time, helped organize Turner's local lectures.
2. The meeting took place at Murray Hill Lyceum in New York City. Turner spoke on "Trades Unionism and the General Strike." See EG's report, "The New Inquisition," Letter to Free Society, 23 October 1903, below, for more detail on this meeting.
3. See "A Glimpse of an Active Career," Essay in *Lucifer, the Lightbearer,* 22 October 1903, below, for EG's biographical sketch of Turner.

DEAR MR ELY.

I think you still remember me, so I take the Liberty to write to you.[1]

Our mutual friend Kropotkin writes me, that he has written you in behalf of one of our Comrades, now on a tour here, Mr John Turner.[2] In connection with this, I have been notyfied by Mr Bolton Hall,[3] a Gentleman, who is interested in Mr Turners tour, that he had written Mrs Sanders, asking her to if Mr Turner could be given a date in the League for Political Education[4] and that the lady had referred the matter to you.

I do not know whether or not you have received the matter regarding Turner. I am arranging Mr T tour and I inclose a card announcing the dates already fixed. Mr Turner remains in N.Y. until Dec 1st. Will you kindly let me know at your earliest convinience if you think Mr Turner could be given a date at your League?

I inclose a biographical sketch of the Man,[5] just to give you an Idea what he has done in the past.

YOURS TRULY

EMMA GOLDMAN

ALS, CBhSc. Addressed to Mr. Robert Ely, Sec. of League of Political Education, West 42nd St., City. Return address given as E. G. Smith, 1804 Madison Ave., City.

1. EG and Ely met during Peter Kropotkin's first U.S. tour in 1897, when Ely helped organize Kropotkin's lectures.
2. For details of the English anarchist John Turner's lecture tour, see Letter to Max Metzkow, 19 October 1903, above.
3. Bolton Hall, a lawyer, single-taxer, and Tolystoyan anarchist, was a loyal supporter of EG.
4. The League for Political Education, founded in 1894 by Eleanor Sanders and other New York suffragettes, sponsored nonsectarian, nonpartisan lectures and discussions on political, social, and cultural topics. Kropotkin lectured to the league in 1901. Robert Ely was the league's executive director from 1901 to 1937. Turner did not speak at any League meeting.
5. See EG's biographical sketch of Turner in "A Glimpse of an Active Career," Essay in *Lucifer, the Lightbearer*, 22 October 1903, below.

Essay in *LUCIFER, THE LIGHTBEARER*

22 October 1903

A Glimpse of an Active Career.

John Turner, chief organizer of the National Shop Assistants' Union of England and a member of the Executive Committee of the London Trades Council, is making a lecture tour of the United States. His first address will be at a mass meeting in Murray Hill Lyceum, New York, Friday evening, Oct. 23, on "Trades Unionism and the General Strike." The news of Mr. Turner's return to the United States will be quite pleasing to those who heard him during his visit here in 1896.

Mr. Turner is just under forty years of age and has been identified with various radical and revolutionary movements for twenty-two years, joining the National Secular Society of London before he was eighteen. At that time Charles Bradlaugh[1] was at the height of his popularity and was fighting to take his seat in the House of Commons. Three years later Mr. Turner joined the Socialist League, a revolutionary Socialist organization with William Morris[2] as its most active and militant personality, and in 1886 was a member of the Executive Board and financial secretary of the organization. From 1884 to 1892 was probably the most energetic period of the revolutionary Socialist movement in England, and during that time no one was more active or energetic than Turner.

The Chicago affair of 1886–7[3] made him an Anarchist, and during all these dark years no one has been more convinced of the justice of his cause or the ultimate triumph of those principles than John Turner, and few have been more active in spreading these ideas than he. He took an active part in the agitation for the pardon of the Chicago men in 1887, speaking at as many as eighteen meetings in one week.

In 1889 he was a delegate to the International Socialist Workers' Congress, held in Paris, where the now famous resolution calling on the workers of the world to throw down their tools on the first of May and demonstrate their solidarity was brought forth by a delegate from the Knights of Labor, and was carried.[4]

---

1. The English politician and freethinker Charles Bradlaugh co-founded the National Secular Society in 1866.
2. The Socialist League was founded in December 1884 by the libertarian socialist, poet, writer, and designer William Morris and others who left the Social Democratic Federation, eschewing political reform as a strategy for change. In 1890 Morris broke with the Socialist League over the growing influence of the anarchist faction.
3. Refers to the Haymarket affair.
4. A reference to the International Marxist Congress in Paris in 1889 (there was also a International "Possiblists" Congress in Paris that same year). At the congress, which was attended by English delegates from the Socialist League, a motion to support the first day of May as International Labor Day was

That year he set to work to organize into a trade union the shop assistants (retail clerks) of London. Several attempts had been made previously by others, but in vain; for, as is generally known in the labor world, the shop assistants are so steeped in middle-class prejudices that they are the most difficult of all men and women to organize. However, several of his colleagues having requested him to make the attempt, he decided to do so, and issued a call just after the historic dock strike.[5] The result of the call was the formation of the United Shop Assistants' Union, with himself as president, a post he held nine years, until 1898, when an amalgamation took place with the National Union of Shop Assistants, Warehousemen and Clerks, of which he is now chief organizer. During his first two years as organizer he brought into the union nearly 4,000 members. He was selected by his union to represent it at the International Congress of Shop Assistants held in Brussels last month.

He was connected with the *Commonweal,* the organ of the Socialist League, and in the early nineties, when Nicol and Mowbray were arrested for incitement to murder for protesting against the condemnation of Charles, Calles, Battola and Deakin,[6] Turner stepped in and wrote the leading article for the next issue of the paper, which had been confiscated, together with all the matter set up for that week. The paper was brought out only a day late, notwithstanding the police had the office under observation all the time and another raid was hourly expected.

He participated in the riots at Trafalgar Square on "Bloody Sunday,"[7] and was an active participant in the great dock strike.

His connection with the journal *Freedom* has been of many years' standing, and he is regarded as one of the ablest of the English Anarchists and one of the best-informed men in the labor movement.

In 1896 he made his first visit to America and undertook a lecturing tour under the auspices of the Anarchists. His tour lasted seven months, and embraced New York, Boston, Philadelphia, Brooklyn, Buffalo, Cleveland, Pittsburg, Indianapolis, Detroit, Chicago, St. Louis, Omaha, Denver and a score of smaller places. He delivered over a hundred lectures, the majority of which were before trade unions, Single Tax and Freethought societies. He was very cordially received by the great majority of the labor men he came in contact with, and addressed most of the central labor unions in the cities mentioned above. President

---

passed, recognizing that the idea of a May Day celebration by and for workers was first raised by the American Federation of Labor at their congress at St. Louis in 1888.

5. Refers to the London dock strike of 1889.
6. Refers to the Walsall anarchists, arrested in January 1892 in connection with the manufacture of bombs.
7. The events at Trafalgar Square took place on Sunday, 13 November 1887. Though banned beforehand by the police, a demonstration was called for that day to protest the arrest of the Irish Nationalist and member of Parliament William O'Brien, during a period of mounting unemployment in England, coupled with daily demonstrations and violent police suppression. On the day that came to be known as "Bloody Sunday," the demonstration was met by massive police aggression in and around the square, resulting in the deaths of three people and the arrests of more than a hundred.

Gompers of the American Federation of Labor took the chair at his meeting in Indianapolis and gave him a letter of introduction to the trade unionists of the country.[8]

Of late years his duties as organizer of the shop assistants have taken him somewhat from the Anarchist movement, but in spite of his many duties he can always be relied upon to speak or write for the cause whenever he can steal a moment's time.

When George Bedborough, the editor of the *Adult,* was prosecuted in 1898[9] Turner was on the defense committee and took an active part in raising funds to defend him.[10]

E. G.

Lucifer, the Lightbearer, 22 October 1903, p. 323.

8. See Samuel Gompers to John Lennon, 30 July 1896, in the *Samuel Gompers Papers,* 4:207–9. For Gompers's defense of Turner as a union organizer first and an anarchist second, see Gompers to George Perkins, 23 August 1896, ibid., 4:216–17.
9. George Bedborough was an English freethinker, sex reformer, editor of *The Adult,* and secretary of the free-love advocacy organization, the Legitimation League (1898). Arrested on 31 May 1898 with Lillian Harman on obscenity charges, he was indicted on eleven counts, including the sale to an undercover agent of a copy of *Sexual Inversion,* a volume of Havelock Ellis's *Studies in the Psychology of Sex,* as well as counts for selling a pamphlet by Legitimation League's founder Oswald Dawson entitled *The Outcome of Legitimation.* Nine counts were for articles appearing in *The Adult,* the official publication of the Legitimation League that Bedborough edited from 1897 to 1898, including Moses Harman's "A Free Man's Creed" and Lillian Harman's "Some Problems of Social Freedom."
10. A Free Press Defense Committee, which included such well-known radicals and reformers as Henry Seymour, Edward Carpenter, Frank Harris, and George Bernard Shaw, prepared to take the case to court as an infringement on the rights of free press. At the last minute Bedborough pled guilty to three counts. On learning of Bedborough's guilty plea the Free Press Defense Committee issued a manifesto denouncing Bedborough and publishing the details of the case, titled *The Bedborough Case* (London: Free Press Defense Committee, 1898).

To **FREE SOCIETY**

New York, 1 November 1903

The New Inquisition.

Of course we all know by this time that Comrade John Turner has been given a welcome reception by the authorities in this "free" land of ours. Undoubtedly few of us expected that a man would be driven from these so-called "hospitable, free shores," because he happens to hold opinions contrary to what this government prescribes and sanctions in her subjects.[1] But until we learn that governments are supreme in their power, we will all have to pay a heavy price.

Comrade J. Turner is not one of those sensational and bombastic reformers who choke their ideas down people's throats whether they like them or not. He is a mild man, and has by his very personality gained the love and admiration of all those who come into contact with him, conservative or radical. He is, however, unwilling to deny the fact that he believes in the necessity of human freedom and self-expression.

For his ideas he may be deported, unless we unite our efforts to fight a law, which was enacted at the moment when the American people, intoxicated by a sensational and vicious press, were hoodwinked into willing and submissive slaves. A law which would make the inaugurators of the American Revolution blush with shame, could they but know what the present lawmakers of this country have made of the institution which they so gladly died for.

Fortunately there are sufficient numbers of men and women left yet in this country who will not tamely permit this law to become a reality; who will not admit that authorities should have the right to deport any man, because of the school of thought to which he

---

1. On 23 October 1903, Immigration Bureau officers, Secret Service men, and New York policemen arrested Turner in the middle of his speech on "Trades Unionism and the General Strike" at the Murray Hill Lyceum. Turner was charged with violating section 38 of the Act to Regulate the Immigration of Aliens, passed on 3 March 1903, in the aftermath of the McKinley assassination (*United States Statutes at Large* 32 [1903]: 1213–1222). Of the several proposals before Congress in 1902 and 1903 to control anarchist activity in the United States, two sections specifically applicable to anarchists were written into law. Section 2 excluded anarchists from the country, categorizing them with criminals, the insane, the diseased, the mentally retarded, polygamists, and "paupers." Section 38 provided the conceptual language necessary for the enforcement of the law and defined an "anarchist" to include not only those who advocated the violent overthrow of the state but also any person "who disbelieves in or who is opposed to all organized government, or who is a member of or affiliated with any organization entertaining and teaching such disbelief in or opposition to all organized government. . . ." Based on this law, an initial hearing on 24 October 1904 resulted in an order for Turner's deportation. John Turner was the first to be arrested under the anti-anarchist provisions of the 1903 immigration act.

belongs or the system of philosophy he holds. And they are willing to begin an energetic and vigorous fight against this unjust and despotic law.

Let the Anarchists make the most of this opportunity for propaganda, and agitate.

E. G.

Free Society, 1 November 1903, p. 5.

Dear Miss Goldman:—

I have your favor of yesterday, and in answer will say that I have seen Mesrs. Jonas[1] Schlueter,[2] Peter Bores,[3] and L. Algernon Lee.[4] All of them consented to have their names on the committee,[5] and Mr. Schlueter, promised to publish an appeal of funds in the Volks-zeitung.[6] Mr. Lee, promised to write the appeal which I will have ready for the committee on Saturday night, and read it to you. I have collected yesterday $20.57, which makes it in all $40.67, outside of about $160.00 in the hands of the Forward[7] which money I will have ready for you to-morrow night to be handed over to Dr. Fult.[8]

There was a conference meeting held last night of the organization originally called by the Forward, and it was decided to make the existance of the conference indefinitely, and co-operate for the present with your committee. The opinion of the delegate of the

1. Alexander Jonas co-founded and edited the socialist daily *New Yorker Volks-Zeitung*.
2. Hermann Schlüter was active in both Europe and America as a journalist and editor for socialist publications.
3. Peter E. Burrowes was a socialist interested in the "Bible question" and a contributor to the socialist journal *The Comrade*. His many works include *Revolutionary Essays in Socialist Faith and Fancy* (New York: Comrade Publishing, 1903) and *Notes on the Class Struggle* (New York: The Collectivist Society, 1904).
4. Algernon Lee was on the executive committee of the Free Speech League in 1903–1904, along with Joseph Barondess, and for many years was the chief administrator of the Rand School of Social Science.
5. The Turner Defense Committee was established by the Free Speech League after English anarchist and trade unionist John Turner was arrested during his first lecture at the Murray Hill Lyceum in New York on 23 October 1903, at the beginning of his projected lecture tour (see "The New Inquisition," Letter to *Free Society*, 23 October 1903, above). The recently amended immigration act was designed to exclude alien anarchists from entry into the country (sections 2, 20, and 38, passed 3 March 1903). Turner was brought before Judge Lacombe of the U.S. Circuit Court for the Southern District of New York, who ruled the law constitutional and decreed that Turner should be deported. The case was then appealed to the U.S. Supreme Court. The Free Speech League, established in May 1902, became involved in the case in November 1903, and Edward Chamberlain, who had been involved in an earlier free speech organization, the National Defense Association, served as chairman of the Turner Defense Committee.
6. Refers to the socialist daily *New Yorker Volks-Zeitung* (New York People's News; 1878–1932), a major socialist daily edited by Alexander Jonas from 1878 to 1889, and Hermann Schlüter from 1891 to 1919. It was the official publication of the Socialist Labor Party (SLP) until 1901 when it associated itself instead with the newly formed Socialist Party of America. Its Sunday edition was published as *Vorwärts* (not to be confused with the Abraham Cahan's Yiddish paper of the same title). Appealing to a broad section of New York's German American working class (it boasted of having as subscribers the greatest number of organized German workers in the country), its circulation peaked at over 19,000 in the late 1890s.
7. The *Forward*, or *Forverts*, was the New York Yiddish daily paper edited by Abraham Cahan.
8. Barondess refers to Edward Bond Foote, Jr., who served as treasurer of the Turner Defense Committee.

conference was, that if we give the existance of the conference, we will not be able to collect any more money. The committee was also elected for the purpose of calling on the different organizations in order to collect money.

Your request for me to go to Philadelphia on Sunday, cannot be complied with by me for the reason that I feel very sick, and cannot possibly go. I have a lecture appointment, for the Socialist League of Philadelphia for Sunday next and I am not going to keep that for [*it is*] phy[s]ica[*lly*] [*impo*]ssible for me [*to*] [*kee*]p on talking all the time. I feel so tired, that I am compelled to disappoint the people with whom I have made the appointment for next Sunday. I am sorry that I cannot comply with your request, and I assure you that anything else that I can do in the Turner matter, I will do.

Fraternally yours,

TLU, Joseph Barondess Papers, NN. Addressed at top to Miss Emma Goldman, second page numbered and labeled with Goldman's initials.

Per la libertá

Avrei voluto prima d'ora intrattenervi nel caso Turner, ma mi impedirono fin qui l'incertezza della situazione, l'aver io dovuto dare a questa nuova battaglia per la libertá tutto il mio tempo, tutta l'opera mia.

Se ve ne scrivo oggi gli è che io posso dirvi quanto si è fatto, quanto si fará per lui, pel tionfo del nostro buon diritto.

Voi conoscete giá la sentenza del giudice Lacombe in forza della quale Turner dovrebbe, *perche' anarchico* essere deportato in Inghilterra, voi sapete la vanità dei nostri tentativi ad ottenergli la libertà sulla parola o sotto cauzione: non ci rimaneva quindi che una via, quella di ricorrere alla Suprema Corte Federale e non avremmo indugiato ad esperire anche quest'unico mezzo se il compagno John Turner non avesse dovuto attendere nelle carceri di Ellis Island durante tre o quattro mesi—che tanti ne occorrono alla Suprema Corte per decidere l'esito del ricorso. Abbiamo ritenuto miglior proposito rimetterci al compagno Turner stesso, al quale chiedemmo se preferiva starsene alla sentenza del giudice Lacombe o ricorrere alla Suprema Corte Federale. Dobbiamo aggiungere subito che la condotta del compagno nostro si é in questa circostanza come sempre ispirata unicamente al maggior vantaggio della nostra propaganda, lontana da ogni preoccupazione di vanatggi o di disagi personali. Egli ha eletto senza un indugio quattro lunghi mesi di prigionia nelle fetide sentine di Ellis Island sempre quando della nuova sopraffazione di cui é vittima sappiano i compagni trarre la ragione e la forza di una generosa battaglia contro la violenza reazionaria dei poteri costituiti, non perchè egli speri di veder rivocata dalla Suprema Corte la deportazione a cui é stato condannato ma perchè sente, come noi sentiamo, che un'energica ed intensa agitazione popolare potrebbe ammonire i pubblici poteri intorno ai pericoli che un replicato abuso delle leggi scellerate trarrebbe seco inevitabilmente.

Si é adunque interposto appello e si é dato il via ad un comitato *Pro Turner* il quale nel suo meeting del 4 novembre corrente ha non solo avvisato dei mezzi piú efficaci per impedire la deportazione del nostro compagno carissimo ma col proposito di combattere ogni sopraffazione alla libertà di pensiero, di riunione e di stampa ha dato vita con carattere permanente alla *lega della libera parola* la quale si propone di portare in ogni libero animo il convincimento che la legge antianarchica é inapplicabile e assurda.

Al comitato che ha con tanta energica efficacia iniziato i suoi lavori aderirono i signori E. N. Chamberlain, Dott. E. B. Foot junior, A. Pleydel (segretario, 175 Broadway), Benjamin Tuker, George Mac Donal, David Rousseau; E C. Nallen, Dr. J. B. Maryson, Herman

Schluter, Alexander Jonas del "Volkszeitung", Algernon Lee, P. Borowsky, Joseph Barondes, Bolton Hall, oltre a moltissimi altri che vi mandarono pure la loro adesione.

Clarence S. Darrou sarà il consulente di Turner, Hugh. O. Pentecost ne sarà l'avvocato. É stato intanto deciso un grande meeting pubblico di protesta che avrà luogo al Cooper Union Hall la sera del 3 Dicembre p.v. col concorso e con l'assistenza di notissimi personaggi tra cui mi basterà ricordarvi De Witt Warner, Ernest Crosby, Henry Frank ed altri moltissimi di ogni gradazione e partito. É di capitale importanza associare alla nostra protesta quanti, fuori dalle file libertarie, hanno sentimenti di giustizia e di umanità e mostrare loro che le leggi scellerate per cui Turner è arrestato, imprigionato e minacciato della deportazione sono un oltraggio alla tradizione liberale americana. Il meeting del 3 decembre provvederà aquesta urgenza, mentre più tardi, quando l'eco delle generali proteste avrà scosso anche la massa che vive lontana dalle nostre lotte, si penserà ad una serie di comizii libertari, si penserà, soprattutto, con una circolare in cui il caso di Turner sarà studiato dal punto di vista etico e legale, interessare i giornali operai e liberali dell'intiera nazione.

Deve pero' intendersi bene che Clarence S. Darrow non e' in caso di poter dare gratuitamente la sua assistenza, che meeting, manifesti, circolari importano spese continue e gravi al cui sopperimento occorrono denari che ciascuno quindi deve nel limite delle proprie forze sostenerci ed aiutarci. Dobbiamo intenderci sopra un altro punto: ne' Turner ne' quelli che con lui hanno ingaggiato questa battaglia si fanno illusioni sovverchiamente ottimiste introno al'esito della causa e aal decisione della Suprema Corte. Puo' essere benissimo che il magistrato confermi la deportazione comminata dal giudice Lacombe contro il compagno Turner ma i principii agitati durante questo febbrile periodo di battaglia riusciranno se non a vincere l'ostinatezza reazionaria dei mercanti di giustizia a convincere la parte sana del popolo che la liberta' e' qui uno storico lontano patrimonio del passato, che rinnegando la sua liberale tradizione repubblicana, l'America non ha piu' che un'ambizione, quella di contendere alla Russia il primato della violenza, della brutalita' e della tirannia.

Per questo ed anche perche' dobbiamo al compagno Turner ogni nostra piu' affettuosa e fraterna assistenza noi facciamo appello ai lettori della *Cronaca Sovversiva,* ai compagni di ogni lingua e d'ogni nazione perche' con ogni mezzo vogliano confortare l'opera nostra indirizzando adesioni e contributi il piu' sollecitamente possibile al *Dr. E. B. Foot junior, oppure a E. G. Smith, 180 Madison Ave, New York.*

IN QUEST'ATESA V'ABBRACCIA LA VOSTRA SEMPRE
EMMA GOLDMAN

To *CRONACA SOVVERSIVA*

New York, 29 November 1903

For Freedom

I should have liked to brief you on the Turner case[1] before now, but so far I have been prevented by the uncertainty of the situation, having had to devote all of my time to this new battle for freedom.

If I am able to write to you today about the matter, it is because I am in a position now to tell you how much has been done, how much has still to be done, on his behalf, if our just cause is to triumph.

You already know the judgment of Judge Lacombe under which Turner, *because he is an anarchist,* is to be deported to England. You know the lack of success of our efforts to secure his release on parole or on bail. The only course left for us was to appeal to the Federal Supreme Court and we would not have shrunk even from that forlorn chance, had comrade John Turner not been required to languish in prison on Ellis Island for three or four months—the period necessary for the Supreme Court to decide the result of the appeal. We thought it was a better idea to defer to comrade Turner himself, whom we asked whether he preferred to accept the decision of Judge Lacombe or to appeal it to the Federal Supreme Court. We should add at this point that, throughout, and as always, our comrade has, in this particular case, acted in the sole interest of our propaganda, rather than upon concern with personal advantages or hardships. He has chosen without hesitation to spend four long months imprisoned in the fetid dungeons of Ellis Island, confident that, from this new tyranny of which he is the victim, the comrades will be able to draw the inspiration and strength for a righteous battle against the reactionary violence of the established authorities. Not out of any expectation of repeal by the Supreme Court of the deportation order against him, but because he feels, as we do, that vigorous and intense popular agitation might furnish the State with a lesson in the dangers inevitably attendant upon repeated misuse of mischievous laws.

On that basis we filed an appeal and launched a *Turner Defense* committee[2] which, at its meeting on Nov. 4 last, not only discussed the most effective means of impeding the deportation of our beloved comrade but—for the purpose of resisting every encroachment

---

1. For further details of John Turner's case, see "The New Inquisition," Letter to *Free Society*, 23 October 1903, and Letter from Joseph Barondess, 20 November 1903, above.
2. Following the arrest of Turner, the Free Speech League became involved in the case. As their stationery read in December 1903, "the League has charge of the case of John Turner, now appealed to the Supreme Court of the United States." The Free Speech League formed an executive committee for Turner's defense.

upon freedom of speech, freedom of assembly, and freedom of the press—has founded a permanent Free Speech League[3] which has set itself the task of persuading every free spirit that the anti-anarchist law is unconstitutional and absurd.

The committee, which has embarked upon its task with great energy and effect, has the support of E. W. Chamberlain, Dr. E. B. Foote, Jr., A. Pleydell[4] (secretary 175 Broadway), Benjamin Tucker, George MacDonald,[5] David Rousseau,[6] N. F. Doll,[7] Moses Oppenheimer,[8] E. C. Nallen, Dr. J. A. Maryson,[9] Hermann Schlüter, Alexander Jonas of the *Volks-Zeitung*, Algernon Lee, P. Borowsky,[10] Joseph Barondess, Bolton Hall, along with many others who have sent messages of support.

Clarence S. Darrow is to be Turner's counsel[11] and Hugh O. Pentecost his advocate.[12] Meanwhile, we have planned a big public protest rally to be held at Cooper Union Hall on the evening of 3 December,[13] with the participation and solidarity of some very famous

3. The Free Speech League was actually organized by E. B. Foote, Jr., Edwin Cox Walker, and others at the Manhattan Liberal Club on 1 May 1902. The impetus for founding the League can be traced to the suppression in late 1901 of *Discontent*, the anarchist communist weekly newspaper published by the Home Colony in Washington state. The first activities of the League involved sponsoring a dinner for Ida Craddock, recently released from jail after being imprisoned under the Comstock Act for mailing an instructional booklet entitled *The Wedding Night*. Craddock was quickly rearrested and would, in 1903, take her own life after her continued persecution under the Comstock laws.
4. EG refers to Edward W. Chamberlain, Edward Bond Foote, Jr., and Arthur Pleydell.
5. George Macdonald (1857–1944) was an American freethinker who edited the San Francisco paper *Freethought* (1888–1890) with Samuel P. Putnam. He succeeded E. M. Macdonald as editor of the *Truth Seeker* in 1909, serving until 1937, and authored a history of the American freethought movement, *Fifty Years of Freethought* (New York: The Truth Seeker Co., 1929).
6. David Rousseau was a New York social reformer, populist, and state socialist. In 1894 he was on the New York State Committee of the People's Party. In his 29 March 1894 interview in the *Ossining Morning Advertiser*, later reprinted as a pamphlet, *A Nation of Fools, David Rousseau Gives His Views on the Social Problem* (Ossining, N.Y., 1894), Rousseau advocates the socialist ideas of Edward Bellamy.
7. William Frederick Doll was the author of *Money and Democracy* (Liberty, N.Y.: American Monetary Association, 1910) and president of the American Monetary Association in New York, a currency reform group which published the *Monthly Journal of the American Monetary Association* and believed that a "world commerce money" based not on corporate wealth, but on the wealth of the people, was the solution to the social problems of the day.
8. Moses Oppenheimer was a German-born socialist and the auditor of New York City. Oppenheimer was a proponent of the formation of the Proletarian Society, a school designed to educate workers. He delivered an address entitled "Jan Pouren and the Right of Political Asylum" before the Sunrise Club in New York City (1908). His writings include *Sozialismus in Acht und Bann: ein Ruckblick* (Chicago: Deutschen Sprachgruppe der Sozialistischen Partei, 1920) and *Outlawing Socialism* (Chicago: Socialist Party of the United States, 1920). He later became an editor of the socialist magazine *The New Review* (1913–1915).
9. Jacob Abraham Maryson was a Jewish American anarchist and physician who contributed to a number of Yiddish- and English-language anarchist papers, including *Freie Arbeiter Stimme*.
10. Identified at different times as Peter Bores or Peter E. Burrowes. See Letter from Joseph Barondess, 20 November 1903, above.
11. Attorneys Clarence Darrow and Edgar Lee Masters were hired through funds collected by the Free Speech League and argued Turner's case before the Supreme Court on 6–7 April 1904.
12. Hugh O. Pentecost unsuccessfully argued Turner's case in the United States Circuit Court before Judge Lacombe on 26 October 1903.
13. See to Letter to Abe Isaak, 4 December 1903, below, for further details about this meeting.

personalities, among whom I need only mention De Witt Warner,[14] Ernest Crosby,[15] Henry Frank,[16] and many another of every station and persuasion. It is a matter of capital importance that we should be joined in our protest by those outside of the libertarian ranks who are sensible to justice and humanity, and that we show them that the despotic laws under which Turner has been arrested, imprisoned, and threatened with deportation, are an affront to the American liberal tradition. The meeting on 3 December will fulfill this urgent requirement and later, once the echo of the general protest has stirred up the masses who stand aloof from our struggles, we shall organize a series of libertarian meetings; we shall, above all, seek, through a circular dealing with the ethical and legal implications of the Turner case, to capture the interest of the labor and liberal press across the entire nation.

Be it understood, however, that Clarence S. Darrow is not in a position to offer his services free of charge; that the meetings, posters and circulars will incur ongoing and sizeable expenditure that will have to be paid for, and everyone, therefore, must sustain and help us in so far as their resources allow. We must have agreement upon another point: neither Turner nor those who have joined him in this fight delude themselves with undue optimism as to the outcome of the case and the Supreme Court decision. It may very well be that the chief justice will confirm the deportation order imposed by Judge Lacombe upon comrade Turner, but the principles espoused during this period of frantic battle will, if not overcome the reactionary obstinacy of the traffickers in justice, then at least persuade reasonable people that liberty in these parts is an inheritance handed down over a long history, that by reneging upon its liberal, republican tradition, America's greatest ambition becomes that of competing with Russia for supremacy in violence, brutality, and tyranny.

For this reason, and also because we owe our comrade Turner all our most heartfelt and fraternal assistance, we appeal to the readers of *Cronaca Sovversiva,* to the comrades of every tongue and nation, insofar as we want every encouragement for our efforts, to address their support and contributions with the utmost haste to Dr. E. B. Foote, Jr., or to E. G. Smith, 180 Madison Ave., New York.

IN ANTICIPATION OF WHICH I EMBRACE YOU. YOURS ALWAYS,
EMMA GOLDMAN.

Cronaca Sovversiva, 5 December 1903, p. 1. Translated from Italian.

14. John DeWitt Warner (1851–1925) was a Democratic U.S. representative from New York. A congressman from 4 March 1891 to 3 March 1895, Warner resumed his law practice in 1895 and was president of both the Art Commission of New York City (1902–1905) and the American Free Trade League (1905–1909) and served on the commission to revise New York banking laws in 1913.
15. Ernest Crosby was a social reformer and the leading proponent of Tolstoyan anarchism in the United States.
16. Henry Frank was a reformer who authored books on rational Christianity.

Dear Isaak:

I intended to write a full report of our meeting in Cooper Union of Dec. 3rd,[1] but the daily press has brought such beautiful and good reports, that I deem it useless to repeat what it has already said.[2] I therefore enclose clippings from a number of papers which you may not have seen, and also a letter from our Comrade Turner sent to this meeting,[3] a copy of a letter written by a prominent man (which I think ought to be published in <u>Free Society</u>)[4] and a copy of the Resolutions passed at the meet-

---

1. On 3 December the Free Speech League sponsored a mass meeting held at Cooper Union to protest the arrest and deportation order of John Turner. (See "The New Inquisition," Letter to *Free Society*, 23 October 1903 and "For Freedom," Letter to *Cronaca Sovversiva*, 29 November 1903, above.) The meeting was presided over by John Sherwin Crosby, and the speakers included John DeWitt Warner, Congressman Robert Baker, Ernest H. Crosby, and Henry Frank. At the meeting letters of support were also read from William Lloyd Garrison, Jr., Edward M. Shepard, Alfred J. Boulton, Charles Sprague Smith, Rev. Thos. C. Hall, as well as Turner, who was then awaiting trial at Ellis Island.

2. According to E. C. Walker's report in *Lucifer* of 17 December 1903, the *New York Evening Post, New York Daily News*, and *Brooklyn Eagle* reported favorably on the meeting and included editorials "for fair play and better traditions of the republic." However, he also reported that the *New York Times, New York Tribune, New York Commercial Advertiser*, and *New York Mail and Express* ran editorials hostile to the meeting and its goals.

3. Turner's letter, dated 2 December and addressed to Arthur Pleydell, who was chairman of the meeting, appeared in *Free Society* on 13 December 1903 (pp. 6–7):

   I shall be grateful to you if you will convey to the Free Speech League, as also to all those who have in any way assisted, my high appreciation of their efforts on my behalf. But while I am quite unable to adequately express how I value their personal feeling of friendship, I am still more concerned that the whole force of public opinion shall be brought to bear, with a view to abrogating this law under which I was arrested and am now detained for deportation.

   That is the question of principle to keep steadily in sight, and my personality is only incidental to it. Whether I am deported or not makes very little difference, but the safe and permanent establishment of this measure means the beginning of an era of attempted suppression of opinion, which would soon menace every minority in the United States.

   What is there about America that can cause it to fear the ideal of one who in Great Britain and Ireland, France or Belgium remained unmolested? Is the new democracy more fearful of opinions than the older European countries? I hope for the credit of the United States honest opinion will not be permanently barred out by ill-conceived legislation, and that lovers of liberty will not rest till they have again placed America among those liberal countries which do not use political discrimination against the stranger at their gates.

   Very sincerely yours,
John Turner.

4. EG refers to a letter from William Lloyd Garrison, Jr., son of the abolitionist. Isaak reprinted Garrison's letter in the same issue as Turner's (*Free Society*, 13 December 1903, p. 7). Submitted to Chairman Pleydell and dated 28 November 1903, it read as follows:

   I desire to express my hearty sympathy with the object of your meeting. It is generous of Mr. Turner to suffer persecution voluntarily that citizens of the United States may test the constitutionality of the law against free speech and free thought as well. If the methods of Russia and Turkey are to prevail here, the sooner we know it authoritatively

---

ing.[5] How I should have liked you, dear comrade, and many of your readers to have been present at the meeting! If any of you doubt the advisability consistency and logic in taking up the Turner fight, the meeting last night, and the tone of todays papers, would surely have convinced you what a vast amount of propaganda was already done, and that more agitation must be the result, and that this was possible only because an appeal was made to the Supreme Court. No matter how much you may object to the legal side, or to the hiring of counsels, bear in mind that an appeal had to be made in order to Keep Turner on Ellis Island, which gives us time to make lots of propaganda, and that lawyers have to be retained in order to fight the case to an end. Those who have worked hard to make the meeting such a tremendous success (and they were few in number) feel a hundredfold rewarded; for the meeting was the grandest held in years, and some of the remarks—as glowing a tribute to Anarchism, and as fair an annalysis—as ever was made by conservative men. For you must not forget that although radicals arranged the meetings, the speakers (with the exception of Ernest Crosby) were Governmentalists.[6] Is that not in itself a wonderful result to have representatives of Government intelligently discuss Anarchism and denounce the Anti Anarchistic law[7] as despotic and barbarous? And is it not worth all the money we can raise, and all our efforts? Yes—I am convinced that the right step was taken by appealing to the Supreme Court, and that no matter what that body will decide, John Turner's detention on Ellis Island must unevitably result in great revival of our movement.

EMMA GOLDMAN

ALS, from the collection of Dr. William A. Peltz, De Paul University, Chicago, Ill., c/o Potsdam Archives, Germany. Marked *"Abschrift"* (copy) at top. Variously marked and stamped. Initialed "D." (for Dzinbanink) at bottom. Stamped received 17 December 1903. Addressed to *Free Society.* Not in EG's hand. The text of this letter is from a handwritten transcription of the original, no longer extant, which had been intercepted by a German police spy. The agent responsible for obtaining the letter, Eduard de Dzinbanink, was a close associate of Abe Isaak's daughter, Mary. A German translation of this letter appears in EG's German Police File, *EGP,* reel 67.

---

thru the Supreme Court the better. By this self-sacrifice we shall learn definitely whether or no we are to wear shackles extemporized for us by imperialism in a season of national hysteria.

Free expression is a danger to tyrants and stifling individual opinion is the first step from democracy to despotism. Against this manifest tendency let every lover of liberty protest.

"Now, while the padlocks for our lips are forging,
Silence is crime."

Yours for unfettered utterance,
Wm. Lloyd Garrison.

The concluding quotation in Garrison's letter is from "A Summons" by John Greenleaf Whittier.

5. For the resolutions passed at this meeting see Free Speech League, *Free Speech and the New Alien Law,* Press Bulletin No. 1 (New York, 1903).

6. The speakers were John DeWitt Warner, an ex-congressman and Democrat from New York; Henry Frank, a reformer; and Robert Baker, New York congressman.

7. The anti-anarchist law EG refers to is section 38 of the Immigration Act, amended 3 March 1903. The law forbid the entry of known anarchists into the United States. For further details of this law, see "The New Inquisition," Letter to *Free Society,* 23 October 1903, above.

DEAR EMMA:—

I have received a letter to-day from Algernon Lee, in which he says that he would like to have a copy of the appeal that he has written, which was originally intended for publication in the Worker.[1] He further says that if his name is among the members of the committee, that he should be invited to the meetings and should be made acquainted with what the committee is doing.[2]

I presume you have heard of the meeting that we had on 2nd Ave., where we made a collection of $100.00. You can see that my judgement was right, when I insisted on remaining in New York, otherwise, we would have lost $100.00 in the collection. Next time you will know that when it comes to collections, I ought to supervise it, for the very good reason that I know the "tricks of the profession" . . . I want to suggest to you a plan whereby we could make some money. You are probably aware that Jacob Gordon[3] has written a play in one act entitled, The Benefactors of the East Side.

We have played it for the Educational League, and I have taken the principal part.[4] It has been a success, and I am sure that if the same play could be produced in Yidish, at some down town big hall, that we would make a pile of money. If you like the plan, please let me know, and I will try to arrange it somehow with Mr. Gordon.[5]

SINCERELY YOURS,

JOS. BARONDESS

TLS, Joseph Barondess Papers, NN. Addressed to Miss Emma Goldman, 1804 Madison Ave., City.

1. Algernon Lee edited the New York socialist weekly *The Worker* from 1899 to 1909; the newspaper changed its name to *New York Socialist* in 1908.
2. The organizing meetings of the John Turner Defense Committee were held at the house of E. B. Foote, Jr.
3. Jacob Gordin (1853–1909) was a Russian-born Jewish playwright whose innovative, realistic style transformed New York's Yiddish theater. The son of a wealthy Ukrainian family, he worked as a farmer, journalist, actor, and laborer and founded the Spiritual Biblical Brotherhood, a reform Jewish organization, in Russia. He immigrated to New York in 1891. His work soon appeared in *Arbeiter-Zeitung* and by 1892 he was producing plays that paved the way for serious Yiddish drama, attracting a broad intellectual audience. He wrote a total of seventy plays, including *Siberia* (1892), *The Yiddish King Lear* (1892), *The Russian Pogrom* (1893), and *Mirele Efros* (1911) as well as founding the Yiddish Frei Folk's Buehne (Yiddish Free People's Theater).
4. The Educational League was founded in 1900 by Jacob Gordin and other Lower East Side Russian Jewish intellectuals as an alternative to the Educational Alliance, a philanthropic organization created in 1893. Gordin's play *The Benefactors of the East Side*, written in 1903, satirized the condescension and ignorance of the affluent German Jews who dominated the Alliance; the Educational League sponsored a performance of Gordin's play at a mass meeting in March 1903.
5. It was later decided that it would be impossible to produce Gordin's play; see Letter from Joseph Barondess, 29 December 1903, *EGP*, reel 1.

From PETER KROPOTKIN

Cambridge, England, 16 December 1903

My dear Emma

Harry[1] transmits me your request. Of all "well-to-do people" I saw in New York, & shook hands with, I know only one single man—who is not "well-to-do" at all, I am happy to say,—and he is Robert Ely,[2] whom you know as well. I spoke also a little to E. Crosby[3] whom I liked,—& who helps you already.

~~All~~ Altogether, I think that the agitation against the anti-Anarchist law[4] must be carried on by the Trade Unions & the American Radicals, who believe in political liberties under the present State. It is extremely kind of our dear Turner[5] to sit in prison, in order to lend support to this agitation; ~~But~~ this is really a <u>great</u> sacrifice of his. Are we not at war with the *bourgeois* society? If it takes against us drastic laws, like the <u>lois scélérates</u>[6] in France, all we can do is to fight that society albeit its laws.

As to repealing these laws, it is not our business to ask it. Let those who believe in legislation & "honest laws" do it. In France we leave it to the Radicals to the League of Human Rights &c.[7]

I really do not understand dearest Emma, what sort of letter could I write to support the agitation that is carried on by believers in the Constitutions.

It is evident that this letter <u>is not for print</u>. When men fight to repeal one of the disgusting laws—we must not <u>hinder</u> them,—the more so when Turner so generously undertakes to help in the fight.

---

1. Kropotkin refers to Henry May Kelly, a lifelong friend of EG's who helped her launch *Mother Earth*.
2. Robert Erskine Ely met Kropotkin during his 1897 American tour, and helped to arrange his lectures during his second tour in 1901.
3. Refers to Ernest Crosby.
4. The Immigration Act of May 1903 restricted foreign anarchists from entering the country.
5. Refers to John Turner, who agreed to wait out in prison on Ellis Island an appeal of his deportation order after his arrest under the terms of the 1903 anti-anarchist Immigration Act (see "The New Inquisition," Letter to *Free Society*, 23 October 1903, above).
6. The *lois scélérates*, or "villainous laws," were a series of acts passed by the French parliament in response to the periods of violent *attentats* in France (1891–1892 and 1893–1894) instigated by Ravachol, Auguste Vaillant, Émile Henry, and others. The first, an amendment to the press law of 1881, was passed on 12 December 1893; the second, concerning *associations de malfaiteurs* (associations of wrongdoers), on 18 December; and the third, *pour réprimer les menées anarchistes* (to quell anarchist schemes), on 28 July 1894. As a result of the laws, hundreds of workers, mainly anarchists, were sentenced to prison terms and deportation, and a great of number of radicals were driven into exile. The laws were rigorously applied for less than a year, but remained a permanent threat.
7. The League of Human Rights was founded in France in 1898 and grew out of the movement to defend Alfred Dreyfus. The members were radical socialists and pacifists, including Ferdinand-Edouard Buisson (1841–1932), who helped found the League.

The Radicals, the Trade Unionists accomplish their <u>duty</u> in fighting against such exceptional laws. But all I could say is, that the bourgeois Society is doing exactly what we expected it to do; throws its hypocritical liberties over-board, tears them to pieces,—as soon as it sees that people use these liberties for fighting that cursed Society.

Give Turner much love from me, and the same to you, dearest Emma, and all our good dear friends,

P Kropotkin

The "Resolution", with its Christian "nation", "violence" & "assassination" <u>whereases</u>, is just what one might have expected.[8]

As to the Cooper Union speeches—poor Turner, I am sure, will be wild on reading them. I should be.

[. . .] the agitation takes a very [*different?*] turn, as it tends to prove Turner is not the man whom the law means. Well, then, Angiolillo & Perovskaya[9] <u>ought to be</u> excluded ???!!!—

ALS, NNU, Tamiment Institute Library and Robert F. Wagner Archives.

8. For the complete resolutions passed at the 3 December Cooper Union meeting, see Free Speech League, *Free Speech and the New Alien Law*, Press Bulletin No. 1 (New York, 1903). The relevant passage is as follows:

Whereas, Russia, which excludes political opponents and represses free thought and free speech at home, has suffered more than any other Christian nation from violence and assassination, while England, which for sixty years has received and protected all kinds of political exiles, repealing or permitting to grow obsolete her own repressive laws, has alone maintained complete internal peace (except in the case of Ireland, where repression was used), and has been free from revolutionary agitation, and

Whereas, These examples demonstrate that repression tends to encourage and freedom prevents bloodshed and violence, therefore,

Resolved, That we, citizens of New York, protest against so much of the Immigration Law as authorizes the exclusion and deportation of an alien solely because of his opinions, believing that this provision of law is illiberal, unjust and contrary to the spirit of the Constitution, and that it tends to the creation and encouragement of the evils it is intended to prevent.

9. Michele Angiolillo, the Italian anarchist, and Sophia Perovskaya, the Russian revolutionary populist, were highly regarded by anarchists and some radicals.

DEAR FRIEND,

I really do not know how to begin my letter, nor am able to discribe to you what awful tortures I passed through the last two months between the Struggle of wanting to write you, yet being unable to do so. I know you will believe me when I tell you, that I simply could not write. I have not exactly been in the same state you discribed in your Nov. letter,[1] or like Faust on his return from dissipation,[2] I simply felt and still feel a mental and physical wearyness and fatigue, a state of mind and body that makes activity or concentration impossible and hateful especially when one is burdened and weighed down with work and worry and cursed by necessity to drag on one's weary limb although every step causes untold suffering. You therefor understand why I have not written. Tonight I was seized by an awful longing to see you to take you by the hand and look into your eyes, or at least to write to you, but I forget to take paper with me, so I am using these buletins, I hope you will be given the letter.[3] I am nursing a Phisician now, a Boston fr man, who has been a silent admirer of mine for many years. I met him at the house of Dr Foote[4] the teasurer of the Free Speech League a week ago last Sunday, just as he was about to start for Washington armed with some Resolution against Tur.s deportation and the suppression of <u>Lucifer</u> which took place several weeks ago.[5] He developed Pneumonia while there and was brought back Saturday, a very sick man. I must tell you a very interesting incident in conection with this case. <u>Dr Foote</u> I have for several years tried hard to get work with Dr Foote who has a very extensive practice, but never did succeed. Since the Turner Affaire I came in closer contact with Foote and when

1. For a letter illustrating AB's depression, see AB to EG, 23 November 1903, *EGP*, reel 1.
2. The best-known version of the story of the German magician Faust, who makes a deal with the devil, is the play *Faust* by Wolfgang von Goethe (first part written in 1808; second part, 1832).
3. The Free Speech League published a bulletin entitled *Free Speech and the New Alien Law*. Only two issues of the bulletin, No. 1 and No. 2, were published, both in December 1903. The bulletins reported on demonstrations and resolutions and reprinted editorials, in support of John Turner's case against deportation and the 1903 Immigration Act. Because the prison restricted AB's mail to sending and receiving personal letters only and forbade him from subscribing to any radical publications or receiving radical literature, EG was concerned that her letter written on the bulletin might not reach him.
4. EG refers to the physician and prominent free speech advocate E. B. Foote, Jr., who served as treasurer of the Free Speech League.
5. EG abbreviates John Turner's name as "Tur.s" and refers to the English anarchist's detention on Ellis Island awaiting the outcome of an appeal of his deportation order. During this period, Moses Harman's journal *Lucifer, the Lightbearer*, which had been deemed obscene by the post office for its frank discussion of sexual matters, sustained relentless harassment, including illegal seizures and the denial of its second-class mailing privileges, thus almost destroying it financially.

Dr Pfeiffer[6] was brought sick Foote sent for me. I have done very little work since the Turner Affaire, I was simply unable to do Justice to nursing and the Turner case and when I tell you that I raised allmost single handed 1600 D for the case, that we published and mailed about 20 000 copies of the bulletins and leaflettes and thereby forced the matter into public notice, you will realize what a mountain of work there had to be done and how little time I had for anything else. Of course, if it had goen according to our dear "Genossen"[7] Turner would have been deported long ago and not a voice raised against it. As it is we do not expect anything favorable from the Supreme Court, but we gained what we tried for, namely publicity and agitation. Oh yes consistancy, what a farce, the very people who shout the lowdest are usually does who are the most inconsistant every minute of their lives. Turner is faring fine, he gained 20 lb since he is on the Island, but then he is wonderfully evenly ballanced as easy going as only an Englishman can be. The Turner matter has also given birth to a general revival, we have been holding splendid meetings in our Club[8] and we are going to have FS ~~removed to N.Y.~~[9] Chicago is quite dead and the paper has been but Life and death ever since it has been removed to Chicago. N.Y is after all the Center of the Radical movement, thousands are being raised for the F Arb Stimme[10] and I have no doubt that F S would get along much better also. Yes time does change and so do we to some extent, only it seems we can not get rid of the old Adam alltogether. For instance I, never felt so weighted down, so tired, and worn out from and through people. I feel as if I were in a Swamp and try as much as I may I can not get out. Why can I not emancipate from them, why am I cursed with the inabity to say no although my whole being rebels against the ever lasting Yes, which people so easily abuse and misuse? Just say Yes, once and every body seems to have a mortgage on you. I am like the incurable drunkard, I have the best intentions to be reformed to get away from people, to take a small place and live alone or only with one friend, I know that I even have energy enough to carry it out, but will I have strength to keep it up? I fear not, I fear I am for ever doomed to remain public property and to have my life worn out through the care for the lives of others. Oh, my friend I can not say all I feel, but I only know I feel crowded out of my need for elbow space. I am tired, tired tired—I have

---

6. EG was nursing Dr. Immanuel Pfeiffer, a Boston physician and member of the Press Writers Association, a group dedicated to monitoring sensationalist portrayals of radicals and radical ideas and publishing letters to counteract misrepresentations in mainstream newspapers. Kate Austin and James F. Morton were also members of the association. In 1902 Pfeiffer offered the offices of *Our Home Rights*, a medical journal he edited in Boston, to be used as the headquarters of the Boston Press Writers Association. Dr. Pfeiffer appears to have had a history of illness; the 6 March 1902 *Lucifer* reported an earlier sickness, from which he was recovering.
7. German for "comrades."
8. The Radical Club began in December 1903, at Etris Hall, 198 West 23rd Street, a meeting place for lectures and discussions. EG spoke at their theater benefit for *Free Society* on 4 February 1904.
9. *Free Society* relocated, with editor Abe Isaak and family, from Chicago to New York in early 1904. The last Chicago issue was dated 21 February.
10. Abbreviation for the New York-based, Yiddish-language anarchist weekly *Freie Arbeiter Stimme*.

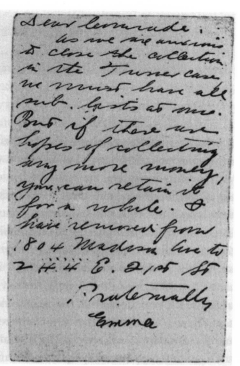

Front and back of postcard from Goldman to Max Metzkow, German-born anarchist and friend of Goldman and Berkman, mailed 9 February 1904, in which Goldman requested the receipt of money collected for legal fees to contest the deportation of English anarchist John Turner. (By permission of the Houghton Library, Harvard University)

been terribly necglegent towards you dear, have not even sent you Newyears greetings, but I have nevertheless been greatful that the newyear begain, as every day brings you nearer to me or rather nearer to the time when you will be quite close to me——

And you dearest, how are you, have you done anything in the line of preperotory work for your Medical course. Write me soon please and lots if you feel like it. I long to hear from you

WITH ALL THE DEVOTION THAT I AM CAPABLE TO
GIVE I REMAIN ALWAYS AND EVER YOUR FRIEND
M.[11]

ALI, Emma Goldman Archive, IISH. Written on the backs of the bulletin entitled *Free Speech and the New Alien Law,* published by the Free Speech League. Time of writing is noted as "12 am."

11. Perhaps meant phonetically to represent "Emma," or possibly short for "Musick," one of the code names ascribed to her in Berkman's *Prison Memoirs of an Anarchist.*

DEAR FRIEND:—

It is hardly necessary to assure you that the receipt of a letter from you is an event,—in my monotonous life; but that is no reason why you should torture yourself because of your inability—whatever the cause—to write often.[1] I don't wish for any letters, the writing of which costs you a struggle; it is true that we live—you and I—in entirely different worlds, as it were; yours is an ultra-strenuous life, while mine is that of the grave; still, I can in a certain measure realize the conditions of your inner life, and you may be assured there is no danger of my misunderstanding your occasionally protracted silence. And yet—such is the duality of our nature—when I fail to hear from you for a longer time than usual, I quickly decide to "revenge" myself by striking your name off my list of correspondents. Upon the heels of my decision comes—"like as not"—the long-expected letter from you,—and all my thoughts of dire revenge are quickly forgotten.—This [*reminds*] me of an incident of my corresp., now several y[*ears old.*] The late S. Patton[2] once requested me to write to our [*comrade?*] Havel,[3] informing me that H. took an interest in me & would be pleased to hear from me. The request seemed rather peculiar, (O Sancta Simplicitas![4] I exclaim <u>now</u>) & so I informed Susan that if H. wished to write to me, he could easily find out my address. A week or so later I heard from H. H., N.Y.,—well, you may imagine my surprise, for S's letter to me contained absolutely no hint as to the why & how.

It seems that many of our dear Genossen are not over-enthusiastic over the handling-methods in the T case.[5] "The money thus spent could be used to better advantage"; "it is not consistent with "pure" An." and one corresp. even tells me that "it is their, the Am., constit., let "them" fight for it, it does not concern "us"." Oh, the stupidity, the mental apathy & the idiotic self-sufficiency of these consistent imbeciles. I have no patience

1. See Letter to Alexander Berkman, 18 January 1904, above.
2. Susan Patton (ca. 1866–1901) was a Philadelphia anarchist and one of AB's regular correspondents while he was in prison. EG met her in Philadelphia in 1897. Patton contributed to *Free Society*, and EG presented a paper by her at the 1900 Paris anarchist congress. Patton died of pneumonia in 1901.
3. AB refers to Hippolyte Havel, EG's former companion whom she met during her 1899–1900 stay in London and Paris.
4. The Latin phrase *sancta simplicitas* means literally, "O holy simplicity." The phrase is used colloquially to describe someone who is innocent, humble and modest, or ignorant, credulous and naive.
5. AB refers to "comrades" *(Genossen)* who disagreed with anarchists' undertaking a free speech fight and hiring attorneys to defend John Turner, who was being deported under the 1903 Immigration Act, which was designed specifically to bar alien anarchists. See Letter to *Free Society*, 23 October 1903, above. Also see Letter to *Cronaca Sovversiva*, 29 November 1903, and Letter from Peter Kropotkin, 16 December 1903, above.

with their arguments, & when I receive such a letter from the Chi. crowd I go around looking for trouble to let out my accumulated bile. These intellectual pigmys want to reform the universe by their inane declamation of a few half-digested ideas; you and Abe[6] have both informed me of the present-time compar. great diversity of opinion on philos. subjects; but I am inclined to think that this independence of thought is limited to the very, very few; the mass of the Genossen seems now, as of yore, deeply rooted in the hard-beaten ruts of mental habit, a stagnation in the cranium of this collective jackass, requiring an earthquake within their ossified brains before a social upheaval could even be thought of. This being, however, even minus the chances of a lost hope, the best way is to amputate the rotten member. In fine, drop them, cut them out; their braying will continue, but 'tis unworthy of notice. It is time to reform the movemevent. The intelligent minority of the natives constitutes our real hope. It is among these that earnest and intelligent work is necessary; and it is this intelligent minority which, in the long run, stamps its mental character upon the national life at large. The movement in the T. case is of the right calibre; it is only by the character of such a mov. that we can ever reach the core of the social heart & mind.—But now a little about yourself. Poor little Soul, you remind me of my little first starling that used to beat so fiercely against the stout bars of his cage in a vain endeavor for that freedom which his instinct so incessantly craved. What if I was kind to him anticipated & supplied all his wants; with him, too, the complete & easy satisfaction of his physical wants could not for a moment quiet the crying necessity of his very existence; and so I let him go & I am sure that in all his former life he never uttered such a wild note of defiant joy as he did when I threw the cage-door open. And why should you not follow his example & [*discover?*] the "dangers of the undiscovered country" rather than "bear the ills we have". You mentioned your unspeakable [*illegible*] with your status quo; why not retire into the beneficial & mind-resting obscurity of a quiet private life, with one F[*rie*]nd, as you say,—why not try it? And what if you could not bear such a retired life "for ever", as I believe you could not; for a time you will enjoy it & benefit by the contrast—then you can always find your way to the city haunts.—You have inquired about my progress in my preparatory work etc. Since you have mentioned it, I shall say a few words upon the subject, though I fear it is like destroying another of your treasured hopes. Briefly, I think that this plan-making for the distant future is like building upon sand. And that future _is_ distant; I still have about 1 1/2 years of local life and then a change like unto from purgatory to hell, for the workhouse is incomparably nearer to the infernal regions than this abode,—and lately the previously unknown to me fear has entered my heart. I would rather not speak of these matters; I make an exception today, to you, to give you an adequate idea of my position, to enable you to understand my changed program. A decade or more of this life does not fail to leave its mark; today I am not the youth you knew, neither physically nor mentally. Entering with an almost iron constitution it required more than the usual time

6. AB refers to Abe Isaak, editor of _Free Society_.

to work those effects upon me which an imprisonment of 2 or 3 years usually produces on the average prisoner. And last year, especially, was hard on me. It seems as if each succeeding year the burden grows heavier, and [. . .](see extra "Supplement")[7]

ALf, Alexander Berkman Archives, IISH. Addressed to E. Smith, 1804 Madison Ave., New York, N.Y. Marked "#2" at top. Address given as "Direct to Box A-7."

7. Neither the "extra 'Supplement'" nor the rest of this document is extant.

MY DEAR DEAR FRIEND

The spirit moves me to night, so I will get a hold of this extraordinary event and answer yours of Jan 28th about time is it not? First let me set you right on one thing, it is not the writing to you that is a torture to me, it is writing in general. Only now and than I get a faint spell of by goen days energy ~~to write~~ when 15–20 letters per day were the easiest thing in the world—

Why not retire to a private life with one friend? Why, why? Can you always answer all whys? I can not. Not that I have not often longed to do so or that I do not long for it now. I never was so tired of people, I never felt so hedged in so pressed to the wall by my surroundings, yet I see no way of my getting out of this nerve destroying life of mine. I am tied economically hand and feet. I owe nearly 500 D some which <u>must</u> be paid. I am worn out from the fierce struggle of the last 3 years in building up a practice and I simply have not the energy and courage to drop whatever little ground I have gained here and go in search of a new field. To lead a private Life and live in N.Y. is no more possible than for a druncard to deal in Liquors and not to drink. I have lived to long here and people have acquired too much right to My Life for me to shake them off. This is just one feeble attempt to give you the reason why I can not retire. As your bird was lucky indeed to have you as its cage keeper, I am my own cage keeper. Our rather my publicity is ~~the~~ my cage and it is a strong hard and piercing cage at that. But what use is it to talk about it—

I am not surprised dear, that you dislike the Idear to enter College after 13–14 years imprisonement. I could not quite see the sense of it when you first wrote about it, but I cheerfully consented to it because I had hoped that whatever preperations you will have to make will help pass your time away. But since this is not the case I want to tell you that I am glad you have given up that Idea. I too would rather see you in the Country out West in Natures beauty than in a large City and in a new prison, an intellectual prison. Oh I have an Idea of your life and the Idea is so real, so vivid at times that I almost feel I shall go made being unable to do something, anything that would bring a change into your life, that would infuse new hopes to vitality. But I know of nothing except to beg and implore you to stretch your patience a little longer and not to let that fear you speak about get hold of you too much. I know it is not in your power and it is a folly to ask you to be more patient than you have been all these years, yet woman-like I am vain enough to believe that you could and that you will hold out for my sake for the sake of my devotion for the sake of meeting again. Do you think I have not suffered all these years, do you think I have not been on the verge of collaps oh so many times, but the vision of our meeting again of being able to take you by the hand to be close to you to help you rest up from ~~all~~ the horrible nightmare of all these past years, to bring you back to life through tender care and affection did not let me succumb and I know you will not either, I wont have it, I wont do you hear me *milyi, milyi, milyi!!!*[1]

I wrote you a postal soon after I wrote my letter asking you how you wish to have money sent, I have some for you from a friend in Calif. By the way, have you many articles of your manufactors, I think that same friend can dispose of them, let me know. Yes, I certainly think the right step was taken in the Turner case and a ~~wa~~ vast amount of aducational work was done by it. The Supreme Court has prosponed the hearing of his case until next Oct.[2] How do you like the Idea of punishing a man for having said or done nothing with a whole years imprisonement? Of course we are not going to let Turner remain on Ellis Island until Oct. Pentecost[3] is going to Washington to day, to make a motion for bail for T and see if we can continue with the case with T in England.[4] If not we have decided to drop the case for the present. We have achieved our Aim in calling general attention to the absurdity of the law and is we had no hope at all in a favorable decision of the higher courts, we do not care if we should have to drop the case. T has written a fine article in the N.Y. <u>World</u> on A.[5] I am so sorry you can not get it. ~~FS.~~ <u>Free Society</u> has been removed to N.Y. where it will be published from now on. It has been in a starved condition so long that it would have expired pretty soon. After all N.Y. is still a Gold mine for propaganda purposes, especially the Ghetto is simply remarkable. Thousands of Dollars are being raised yearly and now that <u>FS</u> is here it will get something of that lucre, which so far was swallowed up only by the <u>Freiheit</u> and <u>Freie Arb. Stimme</u>. Do you know that 2000 D. were raised for T.'s case in N.Y. and that nearly 1500 D I raised myself. This brings me to a plan I am maping out to raise a Fund for my beloved Rachmetoff.[6] Next Winter I want to set to work to raise not less than 2000 D for him and I already have the promis of Barondess, (you remember him do you not. He is a bit of a [*illegible*] *plut',*[7] but not a bad fellow at all) the <u>Freie Arb.</u>

1. EG writes the Russian word *milyi* (dearest) in the Cyrillic alphabet.
2. The case was actually argued before the Supreme Court on 6–7 April 1904, and the court decided to uphold Turner's deportation order on 16 May 1904. Turner, however, was never actually deported. He had returned to England on 30 April because his leave of absence from his union position had expired. When the Supreme Court delivered its opinion, Turner had been out of the country for two weeks (see Turner to EG, 10 April 1929, *EGP*, reel 21).
3. One of Turner's lawyers, Hugh O. Pentecost.
4. Turner was released on bail in March 1904. After his release he embarked on a short lecture tour, addressing a mass meeting at Cooper Union on 24 March, and speaking in Buffalo, Philadelphia, and Chicago, where, on 17 April, he spoke at a mass meeting organized by Harry Gordon, who had been secretary of the Berkman Defense Association. (For Turner's account of this tour, see Turner to EG, 22 April 1929, *EGP*, reel 21).
5. Turner's article on anarchism appeared in the *New York World*, 31 January 1904, p. 4.
6. Code for AB, who adopted the name Rahkmetov from the self-sacrificing revolutionary in Chernyshevsky's novel *What Is to Be Done?* to refer to himself in his prison correspondence; also, AB had signed in by that name at the hotel in Pittsburgh where he lodged before his attempt on Henry Clay Frick's life in 1892.
7. EG refers to Joseph Barondess by the Russian term *plut',* "rascal"; the Cyrillic word preceding *plut'* looks like *nisomr.*

<u>Stimme</u> and the <u>Vorwärts</u> and I know we will succeed. Tell me is there absolutely no possible way to get that hell house term off your back? Is there anything to be done or anything that you can suggest? I may be able to interest those people I have interested in the T case. I will leave nothing undone if you will only tell me what I can do. Helena M[8] is a common ordinary Woman, has not developed in the least. She has not left the pope but she has some affaire with an other beastly speciemen of the male sex,[9] although much younger than papa and phisically superior still a very inferior Man otherwise ein Kaffer und Waschweib[10] par Excellence. I am sorry to say, that all those of my sex we have known together have become ordinary Haustiere und Flatpflanzen.[11] Some have gained a college aducation to be true but have become even more narrow and limited than ever before and there is no excuse for it, because while there is not much of rebellious spirit in our ranks there is a very large intellectual jewish life on the East side. Literature, the Drama the Social Life have grown wonderfully, ~~but~~ so have some Men, but the Women have retrogressed to an amasing extent. It is sad, but true, will this always be so?

Well, Alex dear, I hope this letter will again do away with your dicision of revenge,[12] besides you ough to leave all such dicisions for a later day, when you will be able to really take revenge, by falling in love with another girl, for instance——

I hope to hear from you soon regarding the money. Write dear and tell me that you will cheer up a little bit for the little sailors sake please.

EVER AFFECTIONATELY

U INNIGER HEISSER LIEBE[13]

M.

PS. I forgot to tell you that I have moved to smaller quaters again to a 4 room Flat which is going to be turned into an old maids den <u>only</u> as soon as Stella[14] comes. I am making

---

8. EG refers to Helene Minkin, her sister Anna (who had a brief affair with AB), and AB's cousin Modest Stein, who had shared a household with EG and AB in New York and New Haven; later she became Johann Most's lover.

9. EG refers to Johann Most by the derogatory labels "pope" and "papa"; the "other beastly specimen" is Josef Jülich. By this time, AB had heard of Minkin's affair and Most's jealousy from Pittsburgh and Chicago anarchist Harry Gordon, to whom he responded: "The Pope?! I am not at all surprised; I have always thought that he lacked, by reason of his very character, a true understanding of the real spirit of liberty; and his chattel in danger of being stolen?! Well, well, it would have to be a blind burglar; I knew her well; neither inside or outside of her is there anything that would cause a man in his senses to think of—stealing? no—not even to take gratis, umsonst, free of charge, for nothing. I am pretty hard up myself, but I'd kick as a steer against 'that'!" (AB to Harry Gordon, 3 December 1903, Alexander Berkman Archives, IISH)

10. The German phrase *ein Kaffer und Waschweib* means "an idiot and a gossip."

11. *Haustiere und Flatpflanzen* literally means "pets and potted plants."

12. See Letter from AB, 28 January 1904, above.

13. EG closes her letter with the German for "and with deep passionate love."

14. EG refers to niece and friend Stella Comyn, who helped her with secretarial chores.

a bold attempt to get rid of stray and lost dogs. Meanwhile I have one room rented to a young Woman and Abe Isaak Jr[15] is with me until his folks come.

Emma Clausen was a Friend of Robert Reitzels and is a very dear friend of mine. She is typically German, but a dear soul, very lofty. ~~and~~ She has written some very good Poetry for Der AT and other papers and has also transalated much of Charlotte Perkins Stettson Poetry into German.[16] She is also a very brave girl, has cut loose from an obnoxious legal tie and taken her two small children along whom she has been supporting herself. She is now studying Medicine. I am glad she wrote to you and hope you will encourage her to write more.

Has Havel been[. . . .]

ALIf, Emma Goldman Archive, IISH. Fragment, last pages missing.

15. Abraham Isaak, Jr., the Russian-born son of Abraham and Mary Isaak, worked as co-publisher and editor of *Free Society* with his parents. At this time, the family was in the process of moving their editorial operations from Chicago to New York City.
16. Emma Clausen published ten German translations of the poetry of Charlotte Perkins Stetson (later Charlotte Perkins Gilman) in Robert Reitzel's *Der arme Teufel* between September 1899 and July 1900.

By note of this committee[1] Emma Goldman has been appointed, our agent to collect funds for the defense of Turner Case[2] and we ask all funds of this cause to aid her and us in providing means for prompt and energetic action.

E. B. FOOTE JR. TREAS.

ALS, Emma Goldman Archive, IISH. On stationery of the Free Speech League, Organized 1 May 1902. The stationery states the League's principles and goals, quotes Charles Bradlaugh, John Milton, J. William Lloyd, and M. D. Conway, as well as listing the officers and members of the executive committee.

1. The executive committee of the Free Speech League consisted of Edward Chamberlain, president, Arthur Pleydell, secretary, E. B. Foote, Jr., treasurer, as well as E. C. Walker, George MacDonald, Joseph Barondess, D. Rousseau, W. F. Doll, Alexander Jonas, Hermann Schlüter, J. A. Maryson, M.D., Moses Oppenheimer, H. Gaylord Wilshire, Charles Oberwager, William Graven, Charles B. Spahr, Algernon Lee, and Peter Burrowes.

2. For information on Turner's deportation appeal, see Letter from Joseph Barondess, 20 November 1903 and "For Freedom," Letter to *Cronaca Sovversiva*, 29 November 1903. During this time, the Free Speech League put all its resources into the Turner defense case.

E. B. Foote, Jr., in a 24 March 1904 memo written on letterhead of the Free Speech League, designated Goldman as a representative of the Free Speech League, authorized to collect funds on behalf of the League for the deportation case of English anarchist John Turner. (Emma Goldman Archive, International Institute for Social History)

DEAR MISS WALD.

The bearer of this note, Miss Lydia Landow,[1] is a friend of mine, who is making a brave fight, to gain an independent living for herself and her two children.

She has attempted several things without much success, owing to the fact, that she has no place where to leave her two little girls.

I have ~~addressed~~ advised her to see you, because I know of no one so competent to direct her, as to either a day nursery or home, where she can put the children, without great cost.

I know that you are very busy, and I really hate to bother you, but I would like the little woman to get on. And I hope you will be kind enough to give her whatever assistance you see fit

YOURS TRULY
EMMA GOLDMAN

ALS, Lillian Wald Papers, NN.

1. Lydia Landau was a Russian-born Jewish anarchist. She lived in Chicago until 1901 with Boris Sachatoff (1873–1952), who was a Tolstoyan anarchist, and had two daughters with him. She then moved with Harry Gordon to New York. Interested in experimental education, she enrolled her children in the Dyker Heights Children's Neighborhood Playhouse and Workshop, the experimental school organized by Alexis and Elizabeth Ferm, on the advice of Harry Kelly. She would later work as a janitor at New York's Ferrer school.

Dear old H M Kelly[1] has returned as vigerous and energetic a fighter as he left, though he was a hand packed husband for 7 years. After all marriage is not the the destructive factor in one's life. Is it? He looks, dead, poor chap. He has had a hard struggle. It is not likely he will have it easier in his own native Land. I have found the struggle here too bitter even for my tartar strength and have decided to go back to *Matuschka Rossia*[2] as soon as one is permitted to breath there. Meanwhile, gehe ich nicht fort, denn an Deinem Herzen ist der schönste Ort.[3] Tho your Herz[4] be far away, it is still quite near to me. I can not think of anything more sensible to day.

WITH LOVE,

M.

ALI, Alexander Berkman Archive, IISH. In Berkman, "*international.* August 1904," pp. 16–17, 20. EG's letter is not dated. It appears in a small booklet AB composed, a compilation of letters and clippings in the same format as his *Zuchthausblüthen* (Prison Blossoms). EG's entry is immediately preceded by one from Harry Kelly (also undated, but just after one dated 30 July 1904), and followed by an entry dated 10 August 1904.

1. EG refers to Harry Kelly, who returned from England in 1904, where he had been since 1898. Kelly was active in London anarchist circles, especially among the *Freedom* group.
2. "Little mother Russia."
3. "I will not go away, because next to your heart is the most beautiful place."
4. "Heart."

DEAR MISS WALD

The inclosed note I received to day, as a reply to my inquiry regarding advertisement rates in the "American Journal for Nurses."[1]

I do not quite understand, whether Miss Palmer[2] wants to know from what school of Nursing I graduated, or where I studied Scalp treatement.

I can not tell Miss Palmer that I could not graduate ~~from~~ as Nurse, because I was arrested[3] shortly before my graduation, nor can I tell her that trained under the name of E. G. and not Smith.

Do you trust me sufficiently Miss Wald, to give me a recommendation, to write a few lines for me to Miss Palmer?

I certainly think that the care of the Scalp and Face is a branch of nursing, since there are scientific courses for it, ~~both~~ in Vienna, Edinburgh and certain Cities in Sweden.

I studied Massage and Electro Therapeutics in Vienna, also Scalp and Face diseases and the treatment thereof under Prof. Gruly. Unfortunately, I am so situated, that I can not come out under my own name.[4]

I do not wish you to write to Miss Palmer, unless you feel you can do so with ease. I think you know me enough to trust me, at least I hope so.

SINCERELY

EMMA GOLDMAN

ALS, Lillian Wald Papers, NN. On stationery of E. G. Smith, Vienna Scalp and Face Specialist, 874 Broadway.

1. The publication was titled *American Journal of Nursing.*
2. Sophia French Palmer (1853–1920) was editor-in-chief of the *American Journal of Nursing,* the publication of the American Nurses' Association, from its inception in 1900 until her death. In 1893 she was a founder of the American Society of Superintendents of Training Schools for Nurses; and in 1903 she was the first chair of the New York State Board of Nurse Examiners.
3. In *LML,* EG described her medical education as culminating in diplomas in nursing and midwifery from the Allgemeines Krankenhaus in Vienna (see *LML,* p. 174), where presumably she trained under the name "Mrs. E. G. Brady." In this letter she seems to imply that she was also engaged in some course of training at the time of the McKinley assassination, which was interrupted by her arrest on 10 September 1901. No extant evidence has yet been found to document either claim.
4. Since EG's 1901 arrest, at times she had been living and working as E. G. Smith, camouflaging her identity by adopting one of the most common American Anglo-Saxon surnames.

Appeal in *LUCIFER, THE LIGHTBEARER*

Chicago, 8 December 1904

Voltairine de Cleyre.

Voltairine de Cleyre, the well-known radical poet, free thought and anarchist lecturer, is lying dangerously ill in Philadelphia, and in very straitened circumstances.[1] Her life and works are known to a great many readers of the *Lucifer* and to them we believe it unnecessary to do more than to mention this fact. To those to whom they are not, however, we would say that she has given seventeen years of her life with pen, voice and whatever way she could, to the cause of freedom and human progress. Possessed of ability, honesty and high moral courage, she never swerved from the hard and stony path which all idealists are compelled to travel. Devoting herself unceasingly to the uplifting and enlightening of the human family without hope or thought of reward, except that feeling of exhilaration that comes to the soldier of progress, it was inevitable that now in the hour of physical disability, she should find herself penniless and helpless. Her friends in Philadelphia have rallied to her assistance to the best of their ability and have placed her in a hospital where she is receiving medical attendance and the best of care. The expenses are considerable and as their means are limited, this appeal is issued in the hope that many friends till now not aware of her condition, may know it and render that assistance which is necessary and which we believe they will gladly give. Miss de Cleyre is too ill to be consulted in the matter, so the appeal is issued without her knowledge. The situation is so critical, however, that we have no alternative. She would be the last to say or imply that any obligation, moral or otherwise, rests upon anyone to assist her because of her devotion to the cause of freedom. We feel, however, that most of us have done far less than she and we must rally in the hour of need round a fighter who has fought so strenuously in that cause. Contributions can be sent to either E. G. Smith, 210 E. 13th St., New York City, or to N. Notkin,[2] 1332 S. 6th St., Philadelphia, Pa.

FRIENDS OF VOLTAIRINE DE CLEYRE.

Lucifer, the Lightbearer, 8 December 1904, p. 213.

1. De Cleyre was the victim of an assassination attempt by one of her former students, Herman Helcher, in 1902. She was seriously wounded but did recover. In 1903 she traveled to Europe and, upon her return, suffered a relapse and fell seriously ill in November 1904.
2. Natasha Notkin and others in Philadelphia organized the "Friends of Voltairine de Cleyre" to help pay for her medical expenses.

DEAR DARLING BABUSHKA,

I sent you 50 leaflets from the ones I had ordered, I hope that you received them, and that you managed to collect a lot of money.[1]

Dearest Babushka, my party last Thursday has already had a practical consequence. Stokes,[2] one of those from the Settlement, the tall one, perhaps you remember him, sent me 50D for you. If you want, I will send them to you, or else I can keep them until your arrival. I hope that your meeting as well as your trip as a whole will be successful, and that you will come back to us healthy and satisfied. Everyone in Philadelphia sends their respects.

If you have a free minute, write me how everything goes in Boston.[3]

I EMBRACE YOU WARMLY AND I KISS YOU, DEAR BABUSHKA,

YOUR EMMA—

Please pass on this note to Miss Dudley.[4]

ALS, Partiya Sotsialistov-Revoliutsienerov Collection, IISH. On stationery of E. G. Smith, Vienna Scalp and Face Specialist, 874 Broadway. Translated from Russian.

1. Catherine Breshkovskaya toured the United States in 1904 and 1905 to gain support for the Socialist Revolutionary Party in Russia. EG was among the organizers of Breshkovskaya's tour. Breshkovskaya was often addressed by her nickname, Babushka, which means "little grandmother." See Letter to Catherine Breshkovskaya, 28 December 1904, *EGP*, reel 1.
2. EG refers to J. G. Phelps Stokes, an American Socialist who worked with the settlement house movement.
3. On 14 December Breshkovskaya spoke, with Abraham Cahan serving as translator, to nearly three thousand people in Boston's Faneuil Hall. Also present were William Lloyd Garrison, Jr., Helena Dudley, Alice Stone Blackwell and her parents, Henry and Lucy Stone Blackwell, among other reformers. Breshkovskaya also appeared as the guest of Julia Ward Howe, prominent abolitionist, feminist and suffragist, at the 19 December meeting of the New England Women's Club, at Wellesley College, and at various private receptions. Although she was also scheduled to speak on 21 December, EG wrote to her in Russian on 14 December: "this is not possible, since we need to have you here at the minimum on Tuesday [20 December, two days prior to her scheduled speech on 22 December in New York City]. It is imperative that a certain reporter see you in order to give a good advertisement in the papers." At least one interview, in the *New York Times*, appeared the day before Breshkovskaya's 22 December meeting at New York's Cooper Union. See EG to Catherine Breshkovskaya, 14 December 1904, *EGP*, reel 1; *New York Times*, 21 December 1904, p. 8.
4. EG's handwritten note in English to Helen Dudley, with whom Breshkovskaya lodged at the Denison House in Boston during her lecture tour, reads as follows:

My dear Miss Dudley.

I hope, you will pardon me, that I have not written to you when Madame B is coming to Boston. I wrote to Miss

Catherine Breshkovskaya, known affectionately as "Ba-bushka" ("grandmother" of the Revolution), first toured the United States in the winter of 1904–1905 on behalf of the Russian Socialist Revolutionary Party, during which she met Goldman, initiating a friendship they would sustain all through the years leading up to the 1917 Russian Revolution. Note that although she signed her name informally as Catherine Breshkovsky, her full name was Yekaterina Konstontinova Breshko-Breshkovskaya. (Partija Socialistov-Revoljucienerov Collection, International Institute for Social History)

Blackwell asking her to notify you. I am so glad to know that my beloved friend is in your care, I know she will have the comfort she needs so badly. I hope too, that she may be successful in her effort to raise money for our sacred struggle in Russia and that you may be in a position to help her.

I am very anxious to have all the Newspaper reports of Madame Bs meetings and I would be very gratefyl to you indeed, if you would be good enough to send them to me. I will, of course, stand all expence.

Thanks you for all that you may do for our grand old lady.

Sincerely,
Emma Goldman

DEAREST BABUSHKA.

One of our friends from the Settlement[1] will come for you tomorrow between 6–7 o'clock in the evening to take you to Oscar Straus.[2] My dearest, if you have not yet written your speech for Monday then please write in French if it is at all possible write tomorrow. I will come by in the evening for the manuscript, leave it with Pasha.[3] It is imperative that you write in French, it will be easier to translate.

I EMBRACE YOU WARMLY DEAR BABUSHKA

EMMA.

ALS, Partiya Sotsialistov-Revoliutsienerov Collection, IISH. On stationery of E. G. Smith, Vienna Scalp and Face Specialist, 874 Broadway. Accompanying envelope addressed to Catherine Breshkovskaya, care of Clara Felberg. Translated from Russian.

1. Either the University Settlement house or the Henry Street Settlement, as Breshkovskaya had found sponsors at both.
2. Oscar Straus, an advisor to Theodore Roosevelt, member of the Permanent Court of Arbitration at The Hague since 1902, and Secretary of Commerce and Labor in 1906, does not mention meeting Breshkovskaya in his memoirs, *Under Four Administrations; From Cleveland to Taft* (1922). Straus was well known for his concern with Russian affairs, particularly the plight of the Russian Jews.
3. "Pasha" is the Russian diminutive for Pavel, or Paul.

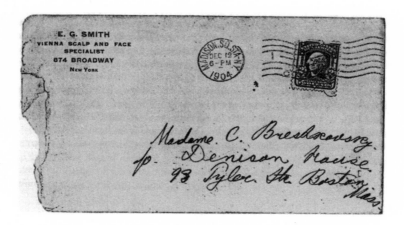

The return address on envelope of letter Goldman sent 12 December 1904 to Catherine Breshkovskaya during her stay at Denison House, a settlement house in Boston, is printed with the pseudonym—"E. G. Smith"—that Goldman used for her scalp and face massage business. (Partija Socialistov-Revoljucienerov Collection, International Institute for Social History)

DEAR MR ELY.

Madame Breshkovsky has decided to cut her tour short and to return to Europe by the 20th of this month.[1] We expect her in N.Y. about the 10th, so that we will have her with us only for every short time. The directing Committee of the Revolutionary Socialists of which I am a member,[2] have decided to arrange several Affaires for her before her departure, she is also to go to Philadelphia for one evening.[3] Do you not think, that the F.R.F.[4] of this City ought to have some farewell meeting or banquet for her? If you intend to have some such an Affaire, please write me at once. The Committee will meet next Saturday evening to make final arrangements, I would therefore wish to hear from you by that time, whether or not we are to leave a date open for the F.R.F.[5]

SINCERELY,

EMMA GOLDMAN

ALS, America's Town Meeting of the Air Records, NN. On stationery of E. G. Smith, Vienna Scalp and Face Specialist, 874 Broadway.

1. Although she did not actually leave until the middle of March, Catherine Breshkovskaya was drawn back to Russia in the wake of Bloody Sunday (9 January 1905), when government soldiers shot and killed workers and their families marching to petition the Tsar, and in the flurry around the failed assassination attempt on Minister of Justice Murav'ev on 19 January 1905 by the Combat Organization of the PSR, Breshkovskaya decided that she needed to return to Russia earlier than planned.
2. EG joined the local branch of the Socialist Revolutionary Party in New York in support of its actions in Russia, but without completely endorsing its ideology. See her letter to Marie Goldsmith, 14 April 1905 (below and *LML*, p. 359) for EG's reasons for supporting the Socialist Revolutionary Party.
3. Breshkovskaya spoke in Philadelphia on 5 March 1905.
4. EG refers to the Friends of Russian Freedom, which had dissipated after 1894; however, events in Russia and Breshkovskaya's 1904 tour sparked the formation of revitalized branches in New York, Boston, and Chicago. EG was instrumental in the formation of the New York branch, which was led by the Rev. Minot Savage (1861–1948) and in which Robert Erskine Ely was active.
5. A thousand guests attended the farewell banquet for Breshkovskaya on 9 March 1905.

DEAR BABUSHKA,

Finally you're closer to us in New York. When you were in Chicago,[1] it seemed like you were no longer in America. Dear, yesterday we were conspiring against you, that is, our Doctor,[2] Katz,[3] Pearlman, Stamm and I. Here is what the conspiracy is about. We want you to live at my place until your departure from America, do you want to, dear? At my place you can rest, write, see people or not see them, but you won't be bothering us, since we're gone from the house all day and besides, we have separate rooms. You have a lot of work to do here before you leave, there's a meeting almost every evening, and even twice a day sometimes, if you have no comfort or rest you won't be able to handle it all. Besides, I am such a big egoist, yes, yes, Babushka. You've been here so long and I haven't even been able to chat with you. I've wanted to talk to you about many things, but was never able to. That shouldn't be. Write, dear, if you'd like to stay with me, and also say when you're thinking of leaving Providence and when to expect you, what day and time.[4]

I EMBRACE YOU WARMLY, MY DEAR.

EMMA.

ALS, Partiya Sotsialistov-Revoliutsienerov Collection, IISH. Translated from Russian.

1. Catherine Breshkovskaya spoke at two large meetings in Chicago, on 20 January 1905, to an audience of Russian immigrants, and on 23 January in Russian and French through a translator, under the auspices of a hastily organized Chicago branch of the Friends of Russian Freedom. Jane Addams spoke at the latter meeting as well. Breshkovskaya also spoke at numerous smaller receptions in Chicago before leaving on 11 February for St. Louis and Cleveland.
2. Either Michael A. Cohn or Hillel Solotaroff, both physicians and part of the Russian Jewish anarchist community in New York.
3. EG refers to Moshe Katz, member of the New York City Pioneers of Liberty, editor of anarchist periodicals, and translator of anarchist books.
4. Before joining EG in New York, Breshkovskaya addressed the Rhode Island Women's Club at Brown University on the evening of 22 February 1905. Between 23 February and the first week of March, she spoke in and around Boston, returned briefly to New York, and then traveled to Philadelphia, where she spoke at the Casino on 5 March. After this meeting, she spent the remainder of her trip in New York before departing for Russia around 13 March.

From ALEXANDER BERKMAN

Western Penitentiary, Allegheny City, Pa., 12 March 1905

DEAREST GIRLIE:—

Let's have a talk now, little girl; it's Sunday, and the herd is at church, so we can talk quietly;—I just feel like talking to you,—if you are not too busy; be good, now!

Your last, via undergr., reached me yesterday. It was a surprise indeed; and as welcome & inspiring as to quantity as qualitatively; therefore you will understand and, understanding, "forgive" my replying with such unseemly haste.

Not intending the local Tsar's censor to bluepensil, figuratively speaking, this letter, I began to write to you this a.m., on unofficial paper, with pencil. But my supply ran short; at the "psychological moment" my paper contractor went on a strike; so here I am, using the sacred & carefully-guarded official paper for this most unofficial purpose. It's good to have friends at court; but oh! if the powers that be knew! . . .

Now, my dearie, why should you worry and fret because of your inability to write oftener?! No cause what ever; believe me, old chum, one good long letter, such as your last, repays me tenfold for all the days of waiting; and I always prefer one such to half a dozen brief notes. I am satisfied.

I was especially pleased that you wrote in German. From you, it somehow sounds more "sailor-like" to me than Engl. You know, you & I never conversed in Engl. outside—and when I read your letters it is like hearing you talk; for you are all there, in the letter; your whole self, the true one. Perhaps you too would prefer if I were to write Germ. or Russ. But both my R. & G. have become rusty, from lack of use; so you'll not mind my using Engl., I hope.

Now, let me take a breath & a puff. I am going to fill my pipe & then we will talk a little more.

With the pipe in my mouth, my eyes half-shut, I imagine I can see the outlines of "Old Salt's"[1] face in the clouds of smoke. My eyes dreamily follow the ringlets that hang suspended above my pipe-bowl;—soon they disappear, and others take their place; these in their turn disappear, like the first, swallowed by the all-embracing Nothingness, and again new smoke-ringlets take the place of the deserters,—still I see the face of Unchangeable Old Salt,—and the letter of Sat. is before me.

Ah, how this reminds me of the "Bewegung"![2] 'Tis like unto the smoke of my pipe. Do you remember old Tarass Bulba, of Gogol's tale,[3] returning from [*illegible*] of his

---

1. "Old Salt" is a continuation of the sailor imagery AB used to conjure EG while he was in prison.
2. *Bewegung*, "the movement," in German.
3. "Taras Bulba" is one of four stories in *Mirgorod* (1835) by the Russian writer Nikolai Vasilevich Gogol (1809–1852).

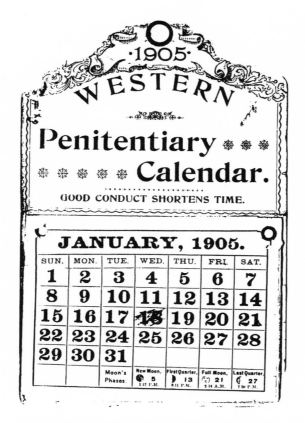

Alexander Berkman marked a personal calendar during his fourteen-year imprisonment at Western Penitentiary for the attempted assassination of Henry Clay Frick in July 1892. (Alexander Berkman Archive, International Institute for Social History)

Turkish raids & making inquiries as to the whereabouts of old chum [*6–8 words missing*] another died in a [*2–3 lines missing*] and glad that they died as they had lived, brave & unconquered. And your & my chums? Where are they? They too, have died, but died ingloriously, in heart & spirit, though they have saved their skins. Wish we could feel like Tarass Bulba.

Yes, die Bewegung! You did not "shock" me at all. I know that there is nothing doing, particularly in regard to propaganda among the natives. And ~~Fr Soc~~,[4] I hear, is dead, too. An inglorious death.

I ascribe the melancholy state of the movement to, chiefly, the following two causes. First, the lack of intelligent, Engl.-speaking public speakers. Second, misdirected efforts

4. *Free Society* had moved to New York in early March 1904, and ceased publication on 20 November 1904.

of propaganda. I think the first evil could be cured by organising an An. School for the younger & active element among the East Side Anarchists; the School is to combine the study of the Engl. language & literature with that of economics, the whole curriculum having as its main object the developing of the student's ability to express his thoughts & views, publicly, in a clear & concise way. In short, a school of oratory & sociology, combined, the Engl. l. to be the medium of expression. The critics might say to this suggestion that orators are born, not made. My reply is, we need no orators; but we do want good public speakers, and these can be trained.[5]

As to the second cause; by misdirected efforts of propaganda I mean the planless, sporadic disease, known as "touring the country". A useless disturbance, because merely temporary, of the sleeping zoo. "A tour" can have sense & results only when there is an organisation or group, here & there, which requires an occasional stimulus, encouragement, & help. The visiting speaker makes a stir in Rusticville; perhaps he succeeds in getting some local citizens interested in his ideas; but as soon as the speaker departs, if there be no permanent group in Rusticville to take advantage of the interest aroused, then the new-born, half-[*illegible*] interest quickly dies a natural death. Therefore it is evident that the work of organising An. groups must go hand in hand with "touring". Touring is a quite useless waste of money & effort, where there are no groups or where the latter are inactive; in such a case the tourist-speaker must also be organiser, for 'tis not at all sufficient to make a speech; after the speech, those interested must be organised into a group, where they can meet, study the questions at issue & further the propaganda.

Take a city like Pittsb., for instance. Say even a Kropotk.[6] visits the city & delivers a lecture. The "Genossen"[7] all present at the festive occasion, perhaps many outsiders, too; the speaker receives unstinted applause, and—departs; perhaps hastens on to Chi. to keep another like engagement. The Genossen go home and stay there till the next tourist-speaker is on the bill. Those outsiders who have perchance got in-[*2–3 lines missing*] twin cities—Pitt. & All.—and notwithstanding the compar. large number of "Genossen", there is not ~~here~~ a single group here which holds regular meetings or in any way tries to make propaganda. Evidently, Kropotk's visit to such a place would be a mere loss of time. Like P., like other places, with the exception, perhaps, of 4 or 5 cities in the whole U.S.

The Engl. propaganda, as it has been carried on so far, is thus systemless & planless, and, as a necessary result, lifeless. It is also misdirected in another, and entirely different, direction. But I have written at such unexpected length on the question of organisation,

---

5. An anarchist school was realized with the organization of the Ferrer Modern School in New York in 1911, and similar schools around the country were organized by the Francisco Ferrer Association. By this time AB and Harry Kelly had also been involved with a school for children, organized in association with the Arbeiter Ring. The earliest anarchist schools in the United States were those organized in Chicago in the 1880s in response to Johann Most's call in the 1883 Pittsburgh Manifesto for secular and scientific education on equal basis for both sexes.
6. AB refers to Peter Kropotkin.
7. *Genossen*, "Comrades."

that I must be brief now. I will merely say that, to make propaganda among the natives of any country, native speakers are a sine qua non. In other words, it is of far more immediate importance, and will prove of more real & lasting influence in the long run, to win for our ideas Americans of the intelligent middle class, rather than the masses. It is in this direction that our main efforts should be aimed. The ways are many; one of the most important of them is the higher class periodicals-route.[8]

It is evening now. I had intended mailing this letter on Monday, but I have been interrupted so often, I cannot finish the letter tonight.

I want to add a few remarks in regard to the movement, especially with reference to the remark in your letter that to the effect that the Am. people are not ready for An.

Well, my dear old-time chum, long years have passed since we have exchanged views orally. In the meantime both you & I have changed some opinions and perchance gone further; but whether [*illegible*] the same lines, that I do not know. To-day, I do not belong to any party; and I do not "share" views with anybody; and it goes without saying that I reserve to myself the right to think & act without the least "Rücksicht" auf[9] this or that party, movement or cause. In fine, I am for the absolute supremacy of the Individual.

But this is merely an aside. As to the readiness of the Am. people for An., I think that no people living are ready for it; in truth, I doubt very much if there be half a dozen An. in the U.S. who are themselves ready for An.—I mean the conditions, of course, and not the mere theory.

But Anarchism & Anarchy are two different things. By An-ism I mean the philosophy, while Anarchy, to me, means a social status. None of us are ready for Anarchy, though many are for Anarchism. Naturally, the acceptation of [*4–5 words missing*] ability to [pr]actise A[*narchy*] [*2–3 lines missing*] who are anything but An. in their actual daily lives. In fine, when we begin, as individuals, to live our An. ideas in our everyday lives, then—and no sooner—will the sun rise & shine on the first day of a germinating social Anarchy.

But though we are not ready for Anarchy, we—the people of quasi-civilisation—are ready to accept An. theories. But this readiness does not manifest itself in attending An. meetings etc. This readiness is called into being by the spirit of the times. Anarchism is not comprehended in a certain platform or set of theories; it is neither political, nor economical,—it is far more than that, far broader & deeper. Anarchism is a philosophy of social life, its ideals apply to all the phases of man's intellectual, physical and psychical life.

Opinions are propagated; but ideals grow; they must grow, very slowly, into the collective consciousness of society; they must take root in the social mind and, spreading

8. During this time EG began to work toward gaining a wider American audience for anarchist ideas through magazines, first by soliciting work from such mainstream magazines as *Metropolitan Magazine* (see Letter to *Metropolitan Magazine*, 4 December 1905, below), and later through the founding in 1906 of her own magazine, *Mother Earth*, dedicated to both social science and literature.

9. *Rücksicht auf*, "regard for," in German.

in their growth, they will choke off the weeds of outlived old ideas & old-time preconceptions & prejudices.

The struggle, then, is <u>not</u> between rich & poor, nor between the people & their government; these struggles are more apparent than real. The real struggle is far greater, far more important; it is the titanic struggle of an outlived barbarism against a new Civilisation; the struggle of two diametrically opposed "civilisations", I may say,—a life and death struggle between the New and the Old.

This struggle between the Real and the Ideal is like the turning of Night into Day. The darkness of a long night does not give way suddenly. Rays of far-off Light slowly penetrate the darkness & fight for the admission of more light. More & stronger rays follow and slowly "drive the darkness before them"; but the darkness does not really recede; there is no place for it to retire to, for the rays of light, once admitted, permeate the farthest nooks & corners. But the admission of the light tempers the darkness, as white paint mixed with black produces a grey,—and thus comes the dawn. But the rays of light keep on rushing additional forces, in ever stronger numbers, to the aid of their advance-guard; the black enemy, turned grey with the wrath of threatening defeat,—the dawn—makes a last stand, but is fiercely attacked at both flanks & center at once; it wavers and is swallowed up by the sudden inrush of the white warriors and—'tis daylight.

We live in the Night of social darkness; but the rays of the coming Day are already penetrating it; gradually the rays multiply and then comes the struggling dawn.

But Ideals are never realised; as we approach our ideal, it grows and expands and appears farther away; ~~but~~ it is a changed, a different ideal; but our approaching to the [5–6 *words missing*] essive march. [*1 line missing*] and realising [*1 line missing*]. . . .

ALf, Alexander Berkman Archive, IISH. Marked "#35" on first page. Addressed from "Hellonearth."

MY DEAR MISS WALD.

I did not reach home last night until very late.[1] I found your note only this morning too late to give our beloved Babushka[2] your message. However I provided some Champagne for her, as I knew it to be very good for sea sickness.

I am awfully sorry to have been out when you called. I wanted Babushka to have some comforts while she stayed with me, so I used to get away earlier, now I shall remain in the Office until 5 P.M. except next Thursday, when I want to see the Russian performance of the newly arrived Russian actors.[3] Have you met them? They came highly recommended by Kropotkin[4] and others.

I can not dine with you next Sunday much as I would love to, I am going out to the Ferms[5] for the day, but some other day, if you will let me, I will come with my niece.[6]

I will get Madame's Photo for you and bring it along. I am awfully sorry, I did not get home early yesterday, I went down town to meet Mme. B straight from the Office, from there I went to see FR[7] in Hamlet.

SINCERELY.

E. G.

P.S. I am certain Babushka will write you from London or Geneva. What is Miss Palmers[8] address [*in*] Rochester? I have forgotte[*n*]

ALI, Lillian Wald Papers, NN. "Nov? 1904?" at top.

1. EG wrote this letter between 13 March, when actor Johnston Forbes-Robertson's run in *Hamlet* began, and 23 March, when Pavel Orlenev's troupe opened in New York.
2. Catherine Breshkovskaya's nickname.
3. The Pavel Orlenev troupe (which anglicized their name as Paul Orleneff Lyceum, on stationery used during their American tour) made their New York debut on 23 March 1905, in *The Chosen People* at the Herald Square Theatre.
4. Peter Kropotkin had seen the troupe's production of *The Chosen People* in London in late January.
5. The radical educators Alexis (1870–1971) and Elizabeth Ferm (1857–1944) moved their experimental school, the Children's Neighborhood Playhouse and Workshop, which doubled as their residence, from New Rochelle to Dyker Heights, Brooklyn, in October 1902.
6. EG refers to her niece Stella Comyn.
7. Johnston Forbes-Robertson (1853–1937), primarily an English Shakespearean actor, was appearing that week in New York in three plays, including Ibsen's *When We Dead Awake,* as well as *Hamlet.*
8. For previous correspondence between EG and Wald on Sophia Palmer, who was editor of the *American Journal of Nursing,* see Letter to Lillian Wald, 12 November 1904, above.

DEAR COMRADE GOLDSMITH.

I dare say you will be surprised to hear from me, even as I would be, should I hear from you.[1] I suppose we do not write because we are both engaged in our work and do not have much leisure time. Still, it seems to me that Comrades ought to keep in closer touch with each other. For instance, if you, or the London Friends who are closer to Russia, would have kept in touch with us and kept us posted, as to the condition of our movement there, we would not have been instrumental in raising nearly 10,000 D for the R.S.[2] But as we did not know how urgently our assistance was needed and as we thought that after all the R.S. are the nearest we could help, we joined them in the work. Of course, you may say, that we ought to have judged by *Khleb i Volia*,[3] but to that I can reply, that the paper was in no way satisfactory, neither were the informations we received from some of the young people who arrived here from R. Only recently we began receiving more authentic news and that together with Kropotkins letter[4] has proven to a few of us, what we ought to do. Com. Solotaroff[5] for instance was never officially conected with the R.S. but he helped. I belonged to the group and also to the Committee[6] but I have resigned and will help Solotaroff in working out a plan of action, by which we can raise funds for our Russian Com. Unfortunately, there is very little activity in our ranks for the spread of Anarchism in America. F S[7] has stopped altogether and no paper has so far taken its place. A few of

1. Marie Goldsmith was a Russian anarchist living in France who was a close associate of Peter Kropotkin.
2. EG refers to the Socialist Revolutionary Party, a branch of which had been established in New York City by Russian émigrés and which EG joined for a short period.
3. *Khleb i Volia* (Bread and Liberty) was a short-lived Russian anarchist journal published in Geneva (1903–1905), edited by Georgii Goglia and his wife, L. V. Ikonnikova. Kropotkin, who had been instrumental in its founding, broke his association with the paper in 1904. In this letter, EG spells the journal's name in the Cyrillic alphabet.
4. Early in 1905 Peter Kropotkin wrote a letter to Hillel Solotaroff, intending it to be shared with other New York anarchists, stating that with regards to events in Russia, anarchists should concentrate on supporting the anarchists there rather than aiding the Socialist Revolutionaries. While this letter is no longer extant, other correspondence refers to it and reiterates its arguments. In another letter to Solotaroff and Saul Yanovsky, Kropotkin added that anarchists outside of Russia should aid the Russian revolution by agitating for revolution in their own countries. See Kropotkin to Saul Yanovsky, 3 March 1905, *P. A. Kropotkin i ego uchenie. Internatsional'nyi sbornik*, ed. G. P. Maksimov (Chicago, 1931), pp. 251–53; Kropotkin to Solotaroff and Yanovsky, 4 February 1905, ibid., p. 251; Kropotkin to Marie Goldsmith, 9 April 1905, Michael Confino, ed., *Anarchistes en exil* (Paris: Institut D'esstudes Slaves, 1995), pp. 164–65.
5. Hillel Solotaroff, M.D., was a prominent New York Russian Jewish anarchist.
6. See Letter to Robert Erskine Ely, 2 February 1905, above.
7. *Free Society* ceased publication on 20 November 1904.

us maintain the work still, but outside of the jewish Comrades, who are still very active, there is little ~~life~~ of what one would call an anarchistic movement, though there are many Anarchists.

How does our movement stand in France? I should be very glad to hear from you regarding our work in R. as well as France.

Do you ever see Dave[8] and will you tell me, how he is getting along?

I also want you to attend to a little affaire for me. Will you call on

Chas. ~~Carry~~ Carrington[9]

13 Faubourg Montmartre

and find out what became of the Manuscript "Mohammed" by Sadichici Hartman?[10] Hartman is a Comrade and very brilliant writer he has sent a Mss to Carrington over 18 months ago and has never received a reply. We would like to know if that work was ever published or what has become of it and we will appreciate it a great favor if you will gather some information about it.

What a wonderful Woman *Breshkovskaya*[11] is? She has captured everyone she came in contact with and has done a tremendious amount of work in the way of raising funds and awakening interest in Russia's Struggle for Freedom. Whatever my attitude towards her party may be, I shall always love and revere her, in fact we all shall.

Do write me soon, please

WITH KINDEST REGARDS TO YOUR MOTHER[12] AND YOURSELF.

EMMA GOLDMAN

The above is a safe address.

ALS, GARF, fond 5969, opis' 1, ed. khr. 1, listy 5–6. On stationery of Emma G. Smith, Vienna Scalp and Face Specialist, 874 Broadway.

8. EG refers to French anarchist Victor Dave, whom she first met in Paris in 1900.
9. Charles Carrington was a underground Paris publisher of both erotica and more mainstream literature.
10. Sadakichi Hartmann was a Japanese German anarchist and author. His play *Mohammed*, completed in 1896 but never published, was part of Hartmann's cycle of symbolist dramas that included *Christ* (for which he was prosecuted in Boston on obscenity charges), *Buddha*, and *Confucius*.
11. Breshkovskaya was a prominent member of the Socialist Revolutionaries. EG spells her last name in Cyrillic characters here.
12. Marie Goldsmith lived her whole life with her mother, Sofia Goldsmith (their apartment in Paris was a center of Russian exile radicalism). Marie committed suicide two days after her mother's death from old age in 1933.

DEAR BABUSHKA,

I received your letter on Monday, but could not respond earlier because I had to meet with M.[1] He is obviously ready to go but he doesn't have a cent, which is why I decided to speak with Raevsky.[2] I saw him yesterday and he promised to give me the needed sum in a few days. The thing is that M. will not be able to go any earlier than two weeks, because he has held various positions of responsibility in his Unions, and he cannot just abandon them. But in two weeks he will be through with all his affairs. My dear, I am still certain that a strictly organized method of work is necessary, but I am also certain that there are different methods, individual and collective, and that the individual is just as important and useful. I've received various news [sent] with R. that my comrades are working diligently and are asking for help. I thought for a long time and finally decided to help them to whatever extent I will be able to. I want to help you, that is, your party, as well, but not exclusively.[3] That is why I appeared with K.M. and the S.R.[4] group, and will also work independently. I hope, my darling, that you will understand that I love you and your work, but I must help those who are closer to me in principles and ideas.

Be well, dear Babushka. It is not you who should be thanking me, but I must thank you. You have given us so much that is good and useful and we will never forget you. If you ever have a minute, write to me.

I EMBRACE YOU WARMLY, AND WITH LOVE REMAIN

YOUR EMMA

ALS, Partiya Sotsialistov-Revoliutsienerov Collection, IISH. On stationery of Emma G. Smith, Vienna Scalp and Face Specialist, 874 Broadway. Translated from Russian.

1. Eric B. Morton, recommended to Breshkovskaya by EG, bought and smuggled arms to Russia for the Socialist Revolutionaries. He left for Russia in the early summer of 1905.
2. Chaim Rayevsky was a Russian-born Jewish socialist, doctor, and member of Am Olam. After the pogroms of the 1880s, the Ukraine was the birthplace of the Am Olam movement, which advocated settlement in the United States and the establishment of cooperatives or collectives. Am Olam was influenced indirectly by the Russian revolutionary movement, which called upon the intelligentsia to "go out to the people." Am Olam settlers established socialist Jewish agrarian communities in Oregon, Utah, North Dakota, New Jersey, Michigan, and Louisiana between 1881 and 1884. Rayevsky was co-founder, with Abraham Cahan, of the short-lived *Neie Zeit* (New Era; New York, 1886). From 1904 to 1905 he handled the American distribution of *Free Russia,* the official publication of the Society of American Friends of Russian Freedom from a Henry Street office on the Lower East Side.
3. See Letter to Marie Goldsmith, 14 April 1905, above, for EG's discussion of why she helped the Socialist Revolutionaries.
4. EG refers to Harry Kelly (K.), Johann Most (M.) and the Socialist Revolutionary Party; she spoke at a meeting with the two anarchists in New York on 11 September 1904.

My Dear Girl:

The last spring is here, and a song is in my heart. Only three more months, and I shall have settled accounts with Father Penn. There is the year in the workhouse, of course, and that prison, I am told, is even a worse hell than this one. But I feel strong with the suffering that is past, and perhaps even more so with the wonderful jewel I have found. The man I mentioned in former letters has proved a most beautiful soul and sincere friend.[1] In every possible way he has been trying to make my existence more endurable. With what little he may, he says, he wants to make amends for the injustice and brutality of society. He is a Socialist, with a broad outlook upon life. Our lengthy discussions (per notes) afford me many moments of pleasure and joy.

It is chiefly to his exertions that I shall owe my commutation time. The sentiment of the Inspectors was not favorable. I believe it was intended to deprive me of two years' good time. Think what it would mean to us! But my friend—my dear Chum, as I affectionately call him—has quietly but persistently been at work, with the result that the Inspectors have "seen the light." It is now definite that I shall be released in July. The date is still uncertain. I can barely realize that I am soon to leave this place. The anxiety and restlessness of the last month would be almost unbearable, but for the soothing presence of my devoted friend. I hope some day you will meet him,—perhaps even soon, for he is not of the quality that can long remain a helpless witness of the torture of men. He wants to work in the broader field, where he may join hands with those who strive to reconstruct the conditions that are bulwarked with prison bars.

But while necessity forces him to remain here, his character is in evidence. He devotes his time and means to lightening the burden of the prisoners. His generous interest kept my sick friend Harry alive, in the hope of a pardon. You will be saddened to hear that the Board refused to release him, on the ground that he was not "sufficiently ill." The poor boy, who had never been out of sight of a guard since he was a child of ten, died a week after the pardon was refused.[2]

But though my Chum could not give freedom to Harry, he was instrumental in saving another young life from the hands of the hangman. It was the case of young Paul, typical of prison as the nursery of crime. The youth was forced to work alongside of a man

---

1. John Martin was a "socialistically inclined" civilian instructor in the weaving shop at the Western Penitentiary who befriended AB in prison, helping him in various ways. Martin and AB corresponded after the latter's release.
2. AB later wrote about his friend Harry and his death in *Prison Memoirs of an Anarchist*, pp. 448–57.

who persecuted and abused him because he resented improper advances. Repeatedly Paul begged the Warden to transfer him to another department; but his appeals were ignored. The two prisoners worked in the bakery. Early one morning, left alone, the man attempted to violate the boy. In the struggle that followed the former was killed. The prison management was determined to hang the lad, "in the interests of discipline." The officers openly avowed they would "fix his clock." Permission for a collection, to engage an attorney for Paul, was refused. Prisoners who spoke in his behalf were severely punished; the boy was completely isolated preparatory to his trial. He stood absolutely helpless, alone. But the dear Chum came to the rescue of Paul. The work had to be done secretly, and it was a most difficult task to secure witnesses for the defence among the prisoners terrorized by the guards. But Chum threw himself into the work with heart and soul. Day and night he labored to give the boy a chance for his life. He almost broke down before the ordeal was over. But the boy was saved; the jury acquitted him on the ground of self-defence.

The proximity of release, if only to change cells, is nerve-racking in the extreme. But even the mere change will be a relief. Meanwhile my faithful friend does everything in his power to help me bear the strain. Besides ministering to my physical comforts, he generously supplies me with books and publications. It helps to while away the leaden-heeled days, and keeps me abreast of the world's work. The Chum is enthusiastic over the growing strength of Socialism, and we often discuss the subject with much vigor. It appears to me, however, that the Socialist anxiety for success is by degrees perverting essential principles. It is with much sorrow I have learned that political activity, formerly viewed merely as a means of spreading Socialist ideas, has gradually become an end in itself. Straining for political power weakens the fibres of character and ideals. Daily contact with authority has strengthened my conviction that control of the governmental power is an illusory remedy for social evils. Inevitable consequences of false conceptions are not to be legislated out of existence. It is not merely the conditions, but the fundamental ideas of present civilization, that are to be transvalued, to give place to new social and individual relations. The emancipation of labor is the necessary first step along the road of a regenerated humanity; but even that can be accomplished only through the awakened consciousness of the toilers, acting on their own initiative and strength.

On these and other points Chum differs with me, but his intense friendship knows no intellectual distinctions. He is to visit you during his August vacation. I know you will make him feel my gratitude, for I can never repay his boundless devotion.

Sasha.

Berkman, *Prison Memoirs of an Anarchist,* pp. 465–67. Address line includes the notation "On the Home-stretch, *Sub Rosa."*

From ALEXANDER BERKMAN

Western Penitentiary, Allegheny City, Pa., 19 July 1905

DEAREST GIRL:

It's Wednesday morning, the 19th, at last![1]

> Geh stiller meines Herzens Schlag
> Und schliesst euch alle meine alten Wunden,
> Denn dieses ist mein letzter Tag
> Und dies sind seine letzten Stunden.[2]

My last thoughts within these walls are of you, my dear, dear Sonya, the Immutable!

SASHA.

Berkman, *Prison Memoirs of an Anarchist,* p. 469. Also reprinted, with minor variations, in Goldman, *Living My Life,* p. 368.

1. The day AB was released from the Western Penitentiary and transferred to the workhouse.
2. Translated in *LML* as, "Go slower, beating heart of mine—and close, ye bleeding wounds—this is my final day—and these its waning hours" (p. 368).

DEAR FRIEND.

Mr Schumm[1] wrote last night telling me thad Mr Ryder has found the title in order and is now waiting to settle matters.

I can not tell you how happy I feel, that I will soon have a place all of my own[2] with no landlord or janitor to worry me. Of course, I still have a $500 debt before me, but I feel confident this will not weigh so heavy on me. My friends[3] are eagerly awaiting the moment, when they will be able to go out on the farm to do work and be useful. It is so hard to get along with a child in a large City, if one lacks the ability of adaptation. There are several things that will have to be bought for the farm right now, a large stove to keep the house warm, a few tools and Mr Schumms speaks of the necessity of buying manure as the place has been terribly necglected for over 2 years. I will need at least $50 for that, which I do not have, as my rent in the Office is due and I have so far been unable to get anything from the Russian theater.[4] Can you let me have that also? [. . .] position for the next 7 month and that, together with my earnings at the Office will enable me to pay off the largest part of the $500. You have been very beautiful in your interest in me and it is rather hard to ask you to do more, but if you can buy that farm for me, you will help me to a position of economic independence which is, as you know yourself, is the greatest Weapon in the hands of one who can not silently go by our present soul destroying Society. Should you, even for a moment doubt, that I may not be able to pay, buy the Farm on your own name, else, I would like to have it on my own name, that "terrible terrible name". I have forgotten the name of our radical Single Tax Lawyer in Ossening,

---

1. George "Otto" Schumm was an anarchist individualist, egoist, journalist, and brother-in-law of Max Baginski. Schumm and James L. Walker were the first to introduce Max Stirner's philosophical concepts to the anarchist individualists associated with Benjamin Tucker and his newspaper *Liberty*. "Libertas," a German-language edition of *Liberty* under the direction of Schumm was attempted and failed, running for eight issues between March and September 1888. Schumm translated works by Friedrich Nietzsche into English in *Liberty*, wrote a biography of Tucker entitled "Benj. R. Tucker—A Brief Sketch of His Life and Work" for *The Freethinkers' Magazine* (July 1893), and numerous articles for *Liberty*, including "For the Nature of the State" (14 April 1888), "Social Tendencies and Prospects" (5 October 1889), and "Our Obligations to the State" (13 September 1890).
2. Bolton Hall, a social reformer, lawyer, and Tolstoyan anarchist, was a loyal supporter of EG who helped her start her Vienna scalp and facial business in New York City and provided her with a farm to live at in Ossining, New York, early in 1905.
3. EG refers to Max Baginski and his companion Millie, who upon the birth of their child had recently moved from Chicago to New York. George Schumm was Millie's brother.
4. EG worked as a tour manager for Pavel Orlenev's theater troupe.

but when you will feel, that you can help me to the farm, we might have him transact the business for us.

Let me hear from you at your earliest convinience

DEVOTEDLY

E GOLDMAN

ALSf, Emma Goldman Archive, IISH. Pages 1 and 2 on stationery of the Paul Orleneff Lyceum, 15–17 East Third St., New York City; pages 3 and 4 on stationery of Emma G. Smith, Vienna Scalp and Face Specialist, 874 Broadway.

My dear Madam:

Dr. V. G. Simkovitch[1] asked us to mail to you the repertory for the coming week. It is as follows: tomorrow night, *Petty Persecution,* arranged by Mr. Orleneff in behalf of the victims of the recent Jewish massacres, Nov. 24th, Matinee Nov. 25th, Evening, Nov. 26, Nov. 27th, Orleneff in *Zwee Family,*[2] Evening Nov. 25th & 28th, Mme. Nasimoff in *Zaza,*[3] Sunday afternoon, Nov. 26th, Orleneff and Mme. Nasimoff in *Ghosts.*[4] Curtain rises at 2.30 and 8.30. Our repertory for the week will be published every Sunday in all the newspapers and every Saturday in the *Evening Post.* We are enclosing a circular we mailed last summer, in order to explain what our theater stands for. Tickets may be ordered in advance by telephoning 14 Orchard. Synopsises of untranslated plays will be on sale at the theater.

Truly yours,

Emma G. Smith

American Representative.[5]

TLS, IEN. On stationery of the Paul Orleneff Lyceum, 15–17 East Third St., New York City.

1. Vladimir Gregorievich Simkhovitch (1874–1959) was a Russian-born American political scientist and economist who became professor of economic history at Columbia University in 1904. His wife, Mary Kingsbury Simkhovitch, was a prominent social worker, a friend of Helena Dudley, and founder, in 1902, of the Greenwich House settlement in New York.
2. *The Family Tsvi* by David Pinsky (1903) was a drama about anti-Semitism and Jewish identity written in response to the Kishinev pogroms.
3. *Zaza, A Comedy in Four Acts* by Pierre Berton and Charles Simon was translated and adapted in English by David Belasco.
4. *Ghosts,* by Henrik Ibsen.
5. In March 1905 the St. Petersburg Players, headed by Pavel Orlenev, arrived in the United States, introducing American audiences to Russian naturalism seventeen years before the arrival of Constantin Stanislavsky's Moscow Art Theater. In addition to Orlenev, the troupe featured the actress Alla Nazimova and the works of August Strindberg, Henrik Ibsen, and Maksim Gorky, among others. It met with critical success in New York, despite the fact that many in the audience did not understand Russian. Financial hardship nevertheless stranded the company there in July 1905. Hearing of their plight, EG and friends invited the Russians to join them on nearby Hunter Island. EG soon became their interpreter and manager under the name Emma G. Smith, and thereby met some of the leading lights of the American theater. In late 1905 Russian Jews on the Lower East Side, the bulk of Orlenev's audience, boycotted the troupe in response to rumors, circulated in the wake of the repression following the Russian revolution, that some of the actors belonged to one of the notorious anti-Semitic organizations known as the Black Hundreds. Ironically, the troupe's first production in New York, *The Chosen People,* was an attack on state-sponsored anti-Semitism in Russia. Moreover, Nazimova (whose real name was Leventon) was herself Jewish. Plagued by financial woes, Orlenev returned to Russia in May 1906, but not before donating the proceeds of a performance to the launching of EG's *Mother Earth.*

My dear Mr. Huneker:

I received your *Visionaries*[1] and your card today, so I take it that you have returned to "our" shores[2] and were good enough to send me your book. I can not tell you how much I appreciate your kindness. I meant to buy as soon as it appeared, as I always have done in the past, but the Orleneff Lyceum has left me no time for anything else.[3] I am happy to know that you are with us again. Needless to say, I am very anxious to me[et] the man who thinks me "remarkable".

I am sending you a synopsis of a play that Mr. Orleneff will p[r]oduce for the first time tomorrow evening a play entitled *The Zwee Family* by David Pinsky. It will be repeated Sunday evening. Saturday evening Mme. Nasimoff will appear in her own interpretation of *Zaza*. I am very anxious to send you tickets for either of the performances. Will you let me know when you can come? No doubt you are very busy at present, but when you will have more leisure, I shall be glad to see you. My telephone number is 1560 Gramercy and please ask for Miss Smith, as I am known there by that name.

Most sincerely,

Emma Goldman

TLS, Dreer Collection, PHi. "E. G. Smith" handwritten at top, above return address of 874 Broadway.

1. James Gibbons Huneker (1857–1921) was an American critic who wrote on music (1900–1902), drama (1902–1906), and art (1906–1912) for the *New York Sun*. He was also a regular contributor to *Metropolitan Magazine* from 1904, and its drama critic by spring 1905. Huneker's story "A Sentimental Rebellion," in his recently published volume of short stories, *Visionaries* (New York: Charles Scribner's Sons, 1905), featured a portrait of EG as the anarchist heroine Yetta Silverman. Huneker was sympathetic to philosophical anarchism; a distinct individualism ran through his voluminous writings. A collection of essays, *Egoists: A Book of Supermen* (New York: Charles Scribner's Sons, 1909) featured an essay on Max Stirner. Huneker first met EG in Justus Schwab's saloon in the 1890s.
2. Huneker had returned in November to New York City after a sojourn in Italy.
3. For more on EG's involvement in Orlenev's theater troupe and their performances, see Letter to Unknown Recipient, 21 November 1905, above.

The Metropolitan Magazine

B. H. Russell, Publisher, New York

Contents for April, 1905

Price 15 Cents per Copy; $1.80 per Year.

Issued monthly by THE METROPOLITAN MAGAZINE COMPANY, 3, 5 & 7 West 29th Street, New York.

METROPOLITAN MAGAZINE.

Cover with table of contents for the April 1905 issue of *Metropolitan Magazine,* a New York literary magazine. Goldman, through her acquaintance with James Huneker, a frequent contributor to the magazine, tried unsuccessfully to interest the editor in publishing an article on modern drama as social commentary. (University of California, Berkeley).

GENTLEMEN:

I have been working in the field of literature for some time past under another name than my own, and now I wish to discard the pseudonym and take that which belongs to me, but which has in the past been associated with more strenuous work than writing and which therefore, at first thought, may not seem to you calculated to attract readers to your magazine.[1] It is my opinion, however, that the name of Emma Goldman in connection with a certain range of subjects will have positive value, both from your standpoint and from my own.

It is true that I have gained an unpleasant notoriety, which, however undeserved, may militate against me in a measure, but on the other hand my name stands for protest against the evil principles which underlie and are the cause of the very social ferment which is now agitating the minds of both the thinkers and the passive sufferers throughout the civilized world.

I have a great deal to say both in fiction and essay form on the sociological conditions as they exist either hidden or glaringly obvious, and I am writing this to ask you if you have room in your magazine for anything I, as Emma Goldman, may send you, providing always that it is presented in sufficiently good literary form[2] I beg to remind you, in this connection, that no one has or can have a more intimate knowledge than I of the conditions which exist in various parts of the civilized world, or of the near and remote causes of those conditions. Perhaps I should add that it is not my wish to write as an agitator, but only as a heart-sore actor and spectator.

HOPING FOR AN EARLY REPLY, I AM,

EMMA GOLDMAN

TLS, American Literature Collection, CtY-B. Addressed at top to "Editors of *Metropolitan Magazine*." Return address typed at top, 15–17 East Third Street.

1. EG first lectured on modern drama and literature within the anarchist movement and under her own name in 1904. In 1905 she acted as the Orlenev theater troupe's manager, often representing them under the assumed name Emma G. Smith; see, for example, Letter to Unknown Recipient, 21 November 1905, above. EG would continue to lecture on modern drama and literature and its connection to anarchism and revolution; her *Social Significance of the Modern Drama* was published in 1914.
2. No article written by EG ever appeared in *Metropolitan Magazine*.

My Dear Metzkow.

Enclosed find our circular that I spoke of yesterday. You will see from the content what we intend for our magazine. May I hope for your support? I also enclosed a few subscription blanks for you, perhaps you'll succeed in winning a few subscribers.

Sincerely,
Emma Goldman

ENCLOSURE

"The Open Road"

Comrades,—On March 15 will appear the first number of an Anarchistic monthly, "The Open Road."[1] This magazine will try to represent the center of all truly radical elements in the United States, who, tired of the loud dissonances of the present, and awakened in opposition thereto, see the only hope for struggling humanity in the reorganization of our social and economic life upon a basis of freedom and justice. Here and there are solitary individuals or groups of idealists who battle against external and internal tyrannies, against "Virtue," perched on her throne, self-satisfied, and against dull indifference.

What is badly wanted is an intellectual link that will bring these scattered elements together.

"The Open Road" will attempt to be that link. The contents will consist of articles, essays, and notes, treating of the development and growth of Anarchistic ideas, in various

---

1. In *Living My Life* (pp. 378–79), EG recollects the threat of a lawsuit by publishers of a Colorado paper named *The Open Road*. To date no record of a publication by this name has been found in Colorado. Other sources suggest another possible reason for the change of name to *Mother Earth*. Harry Kelly, a member of the original editorial group of *Mother Earth* (in his unpublished memoirs *Roll Back the Years: Odyssey of a Libertarian*, edited by John Nicholas Bethel, at New York University's Tamiment Institute Library), suggests that the name was changed simply because a journal by the name *Open Road* was already being published in Indiana. This journal, edited by Bruce Calvert, was also strongly influenced by Walt Whitman. Calvert was sympathetic to EG's fight for free speech and would later write a pamphlet in support of her activities, entitled *Emma Goldman and the Police* (Griffith, Ind.: The Open Road, 1910–1911). In a letter to Leon Malmed in February 1906, EG wrote that she was "compelled to change the name as there is a magazine by the name Open Road in existence," without any mention of a threat of legal action. See EG to Leon Malmed, February 1906, *EGP*, reel 2.

phases of human life; then too, it will bring international reports of the struggle of new ideas against the old, of the various movements of the oppressed against their oppressors, and the methods employed by them, such as the general strike, trade unionism, and the co-operative movement. Every endeavor at a higher, broader, and deeper life, literary, artistic, social, or economic, will be brought before the readers of "THE OPEN ROAD." "THE OPEN ROAD" proposes not only to deal with the serious side of life, but with its humorous, satirical and ironical phases as well.

In the certainty that many will agree with us, that in this country, where public opinion and sentiments are more successfully fabricated than abroad, such a publication is an absolute necessity, we ask for your co-operation and assistance. The magazine will be published monthly, and will be $1.00 a year, or 10 cents a copy.

Subscriptions and communications may be sent to the undersigned.

MAX BAGINSKI,
EMMA GOLDMAN.

PLSr, Joseph Ishill Collection, MH-H. The Open Road Solicitation included the return address: P.O. Box 217, Madison Square Station, New York, N.Y. On the reverse of the circular was EG's handwritten note, in German; translated. EG and Baginiski were co-editors of the anarchist monthly magazine that would be named *Mother Earth*.

To ALICE STONE BLACKWELL

New York, ca. February 1906

My dear Miss Blackwell.

I got back from Chicago late last night and found your letter.[1] All I can tell you about our beloved Babushka is, that she is still out of prison and doing good work.[2] I am hoping to hear more directly soon and will let you know.

I meant to write to you some time ago, dear Miss Blackwell and tell you, that I am about to publish a Magazine. The first number will be ready March 10th. I meant to bring a few stanzas of Gorki's Poem, that you have set into Verse. May I?[3] I want to advertise your book, of course and will take orders for it. Please write me soon regarding the Poem and if I may bring other Poems from your book.

I am going to write you a long letter soon, am too busy this morning

I hope you are well and active as ever.

Very Sincerely

Emma Goldman

PS. I am going to continue at my Office, of course. You can write to either address.

ALS, National American Women's Suffrage Association Collection, DLC. *Mother Earth* stamp on first page.

1. EG spent two weeks in Chicago with the Pavel Orlenev theater troupe before returning to New York City around the 25th of February.
2. Catherine Breshkovskaya met both EG and Blackwell while on a fund-raising tour in the United States in 1904 and 1905. By mid-March 1905 she had returned to Russia to take part in the 1905 revolution; she was arrested in December 1907. EG would reprint in the March 1916 issue of *Mother Earth* a number of letters Breshkovskaya sent to Blackwell describing her prison experiences in Russia.
3. EG included Blackwell's translation of Russian writer Maksim Gorky's "The Song of the Storm-Finch" in the first issue of *Mother Earth*. The poem originally appeared in Blackwell's translation of Gorky's *Songs of Russia* (Chicago, 1906). In the October 1906 *Mother Earth*, EG reprinted another poem Blackwell translated from the Russian, Ezekiel Leavitt's "The Streamlet," later published in his *Songs of Grief and Gladness* and *Deborah* with a foreword by Blackwell (St. Louis: Modern View, 1907).

MY DEAR SIS.[1]—

Yours of the 8th rec'd yesterday. It was certainly an unexpected pleasure. In the meantime I had sent you my New Year's letter, via St. L.

And so our [*illegible*] Chum[2] has told you that I was not competent to decide about the "operation." My, that I must be hopelessly out of date. The daft old hypocrite, he wanted to get your consent to something to which I would not consent. Why, I have told him half a dozen times that I want nothing done in the case. I warned him [*4 words illegible*] action without my sanction. Then he promised to consult me before doing anything and then straightway engaged a lawyer without saying a word to me about it.

He did so, because he is unspeakably anxious to have me out as soon as possible, and I don't know how much money he spent pulling wires since I am in this hole. I had informed him, in the beginning, that no gum-shoe policy would avail, and that the only possible way is per writ of habeas corpus, or rather, mandamus,[3] and I told him that I was not in favor of writ proceedings, not expecting any results.

But as to your queries, why, you should know. I have told you some months ago that the Febr. business was one of Chum's pipe-dreams—that's the exact words I used then; I repeat them. Do you think I have changed my mind in 2 or 3 months? Let me say it for the last time: I want nothing, absolutely nothing, to be done in my case. I hope this is plain enough, and it is final.[4]

Muchnic, of P, informs me that Chum's lawyer, on considering the merits of the case, decided that nothing could be done. I am glad of it, for I am sick & tired of this continual monkeying. Of course, I am entitled to 5 mos., but I will not get it, simply because it's "me". Consider this settled, dear friend, and don't bother about it. Say nothing to

---

1. AB employed a variety of nicknames for EG, at times to hide her identity from prison censors.
2. John Martin, a civilian instructor in the prison weaving shops, befriended AB and appealed to the pardon board to have AB's year in the workhouse set aside. See Letter from Alexander Berkman, 15 April 1905, above.
3. A mandamus is a writ issued by a superior court ordering a public official or body or lower court to perform a specific duty.
4. According to AB's *Prison Memoirs*, the Pennsylvania law stipulated five months' commutation for every year of a sentence, beginning with the ninth year, which meant AB would be entitled to parole in February. But the prison superintendent and board of directors granted AB only two months off his sentence, on the technicality that he was now serving a one-year sentence to the workhouse. AB's friend John Martin had attempted, without AB's knowledge, to engage a lawyer to ensure AB his full commutation, but the work was unsuccessful and AB served ten months in the workhouse, before being set free in May (*Prison Memoirs of an Anarchist*, pp. 478–84).

Chum, for he means it all for my benefit & his temperament is such that he would be miserable if he could not at least <u>try</u> to do something for me, no matter how hopeless the outlook.

You have no idea what a loyal friend he has been to me. A short time ago, failing to hear from me for some time & thinking something went wrong, he took matters into his own hand. He gave me quite a shock. Think of it; without any warning, I found him standing at my cell-door; actually in front of me; as if risen from the ground. I ought to turn Spiritualist; for that was certainly as good a spirit manifestation as ever produced at any séance, and it had, moreover, the merit of being real.

But my space is short. All this will be explained in person.

Yes, my dear, it's just 4 months plus a week or so.[5] It's hard to realize and harder still to bear, for these months are harder and slower than so many years.

But a little patience, which we have both learned, and a little courage, which we both have—and the goal will soon be reached.

So be of good cheer and don't imagine that I am coming out a wreck, for I hope you'll find my mind as active and my step as elastic as in the auld lang syne. And you, too, I know, are changed only, even as I was in having grown more mature and more—sympathetic.

Of R.[6] I shall not speak in this letter. It's too sad, and what's the use of words; I may take a notion to help build barricades—but don't let us peer into the future. And Solat. & Katz Turned Nationalists?![7] And how about Yanovski & Girshdanski?[8] By the way, did the latter wish some history or what. You remember getting data from me, for Girshd., about my case, about 2 years ago.[9] You might get the Freie Arb. Stimme[10] sent to me; it's not

5. AB was released on 18 May 1906.
6. "R." is AB's abbreviation for Russian, and probably refers to the abortive 1905 revolution.
7. Hillel Solotaroff and Moishe Katz were both prominent New York Jewish anarchists; Solotaroff was born in Russia. In his exclamation about their turning "Nationalists," AB is referring to the move toward Zionism on the part of some Jewish anarchists that was a response to the pogroms in Russia between 1903 and 1906. In the wake of an ongoing rebellion by many Russian intellectuals, including acts of terrorism, there was an increase in antisemitic agitation in the Russian press, which ultimately contributed to several anti-Jewish pogroms all over Russia. Although the attacks by the press targeted students and intelligentsia, Jews—against whom there was a long and deeply rooted prejudice—were the primary victims of the pogroms, numbering nearly 700, including a particularly violent pogrom in Zhitomir in 1905, openly supported by the police and the army. Jews were perceived as the principal agitators for a constitution during the 1905 revolution, which would lead to the disempowering of Tsar Nicholas II. Reactionaries and right-wing extremists violently defended the old order while the state government did nothing to stop the violence. Many Jewish people in Russia responded to the pogroms with an increased nationalist identification, forming Bund, Zionist, and Zionist-Socialist defense societies in nearly every town. This nationalism spread to the United States with the wave of Jewish immigration, and influenced many prominent secular Jewish anarchists, including Solotaroff and Katz.
8. AB refers to Saul Yanovsky and Max Girzdanksy, both New York Jewish anarchists.
9. See note 3, Letter from Alexander Berkman, 11 August 1903, above; AB reported to EG that Girzdanksky was studying medicine when AB left New York in 1892.
10. *Freie Arbeiter Stimme* was a New York Jewish anarchist communist paper with strong literary and cultural content.

being sent, for I'd get it if it were, as there is no literary quarantine here. The "overtones" I may get in a few days. Do you want it returned?

You say the massacres are the <u>only</u> cause you can assign for Sal's etc change of heart. So, my dear, the matter lies deeper. The massacres are but the immediate cause; the primary cause is to be found in the Lebens-Hunger[11] which must fill ~~the being of~~ every thinking An. For in the mere belief in & preaching of An. you can't find that satisfaction which the soul craves. Why? Because our preaching & our doctrines, as <u>not</u> practiced, are merely destructive; and yet the Soul demands most imperatively that satisfaction which can come only from ~~that you~~ the knowledge that you are building up, as well as tearing down. Da liegt der Hund begraben?.[12] By the very nature of things we, as An, can't build, we can only do the preparatory work of destruction—and that's the Why of our intell. hiatus, that gnawing feeling of inner dissatisfaction. ~~May-be~~ As Nationalists, Solat. etc can fill that heart's-void; they can feel now that they are doing some actual constructive work, building something, and that not the vague platforms for the dim future, but something tangible, handgreifliches,[13] for the present hour. Oh, there must be a grand satisfaction in such consciousness, and this satisfaction I envy Solat—for I know that such as he, Katz et are <u>sincere.</u> You & I do not possess that satisfaction of a full heart— and that must feel as good to the inner man as a full stomach is to the hungry physical man.—and still, I am sorry for Solat. etc; for, being sincere & also clear-thinking, they are bound to awaken soon to the realisation that, though their work is constructive, it is the wrong kind of architecture & essentially—in the long run—<u>de</u>structive & antagonistic to the world's progress. It is not segregation & nationalisation that is the need of the hour; rather the very opposite, for the brotherhood of man can never become reality until geograph., national and racial lines & prejudices are forgotten, overcome: Nationalism is a barrier, a barricade against International fellowship, a ditch which progress must fill & cover up not to speak of the impracticality of Nationalism, it is a false solution of the Jews' troubles. The only real salvation of the R. Jew lies in the Liberty of R.—It is allright to talk of government-incited riots etc. But you & I, who have lived in R. know that the hatred of Jews is a deep-set R. instinct; the instinct being given, it is easy to incite to pogroms. Could the governm. incite revolutionists to make pogroms? And it will take more than a mere constitution,[14] it will Take 2 or more generations of real enlightenment & education to eradicate the long-inbred racial prejudices of the R.moujik;[15] only Liberty can accomplish that. Till then there will be pogroms,—under Tsars as well as under a Russ. Constitution. Liberty, enlightenment is, after all, the only true cure for social & racial etc evils.

11. *Lebens-Hunger*, "zest for life," in German.
12. "That's what's causing it," in German.
13. "Tangible" or "obvious," in German.
14. In 1905 the tsar was compelled to grant a constitution to the people of Russia, sparking more anti-Jewish pogroms.
15. *Moujik*, or *Muzhik*, "peasant"; "R." is AB's abbreviation for "Russian."

But enough. We'll talk of this [*illegible*] may be the building of colonies, An, would supply to us the lacking satisfaction.

Would like to write more. No more paper. Just got Fr. Arb. Stimme. The first copy I saw here. Don't know who sent it, may be C.[16]—I don't know if I'll get another chance for underground, so I will say this. As to my plans for the future, it's like the chapter on snakes in Ireland. Made no plans, would be useless, anyhow. But I guess I'll pay a visit to my girls in N.Y. & to Chum. Will not be out until the latter part of May. Another thing—I want no fuss. And when I come, I hope I'll not find a houseful of friends. Only Sis & St.[17] and I'll not mind if there are a couple of little kids, say between 6–10 years of age. I like children of that age; but want no strangers, grown-ups. [*illegible*], my time must be short, indeed, when I am already giving "orders" of reception. Well, dear friend, Time to close. Don't know when this will reach you; send card as Sis, of receipt. Greetings to Orleneff[18] & Co., very good of him to give a performance for me. Remember me to St., has she quit writing? How is she doing.

GREETINGS TO ALL OF YOU, LOVE *SASHA*[19]

ALS, Alexander Berkman Archive, IISH. Addressed from "Allegheny Prison Workhouse."

16. AB may be referring to anarchist Dr. Michael Cohn.
17. AB refers to EG and Stella Comyn, EG's niece, who corresponded with AB while he was in prison.
18. AB is referring to Pavel Orlenev's theater troupe, for whom EG worked as tour manager from 1905 to 1906.
19. AB signs this letter with his Russian diminutive, Sasha, in Cyrillic characters.

Mother Earth

There was a time when men imagined the Earth as the center of the universe. The stars, large and small, they believed were created merely for their delectation. It was their vain conception that a supreme being, weary of solitude, had manufactured a giant toy and put them into possession of it.

When, however, the human mind was illumined by the torch-light of science, it came to understand that the Earth was but one of a myriad of stars floating in infinite space, a mere speck of dust.

Man issued from the womb of Mother Earth, but he knew it not, nor recognized her, to whom he owed his life. In his egotism he sought an explanation of himself in the infinite, and out of his efforts there arose the dreary doctrine that he was not related to the Earth, that she was but a temporary resting place for his scornful feet and that she held nothing for him but temptation to degrade himself. Interpreters and prophets of the infinite sprang into being, creating the "Great Beyond" and proclaiming Heaven and Hell, between which stood the poor, trembling human being, tormented by that priest-born monster, Conscience.

In this frightful scheme, gods and devils waged eternal war against each other with wretched man as the prize of victory; and the priest, self-constituted interpreter of the will of the gods, stood in front of the only refuge from harm and demanded as the price of entrance that ignorance, that asceticism, that self-abnegation which could but end in the complete subjugation of man to superstition. He was taught that Heaven, the refuge, was the very antithesis of Earth, which was the source of sin. To gain for himself a seat in Heaven, man devastated the Earth. Yet she renewed herself, the good mother, and came again each Spring, radiant with youthful beauty, beckoning her children to come to her bosom and partake of her bounty. But ever the air grew thick with mephitic darkness, ever a hollow voice was heard calling: "Touch not the beautiful form of the sorceress; she leads to sin!"

But if the priests decried the Earth, there were others who found in it a source of power and who took possession of it. Then it happened that the autocrats at the gates of Heaven joined forces with the powers that had taken possession of the Earth; and humanity began its aimless, monotonous march. But the good mother sees the bleeding feet of her children, she hears their moans, and she is ever calling to them that she is theirs.

To the contemporaries of George Washington, Thomas Paine and Thomas Jefferson, America appeared vast, boundless, full of promise. Mother Earth, with the sources of

Cover illustration of first issue of Goldman's magazine, *Mother Earth* (March 1906), by unknown artist. Note the broken shackles in the foreground. This illustration was repeated on subsequent covers of *Mother Earth* until September 1906. (By permission of the Kate Sharpley Library)

vast wealth hidden within the folds of her ample bosom, extended her inviting and hospitable arms to all those who came to her from arbitrary and despotic lands—Mother Earth ready to give herself alike to all her children. But soon she was seized by the few, stripped of her freedom, fenced in, a prey to those who were endowed with cunning and unscrupulous shrewdness. They, who had fought for independence from the British yoke, soon became dependent among themselves; dependent on possessions, on wealth, on power. Liberty escaped into the wilderness, and the old battle between the patrician and the plebeian broke out in the new world, with greater bitterness and vehemence. A period of but a hundred years had sufficed to turn a great republic, once gloriously established, into an arbitrary state which subdued a vast number of its people into material and intellectual slavery, while enabling the privileged few to monopolize every material and mental resource.

During the last few years, American journalists have had much to say about the terrible conditions in Russia and the supremacy of the Russian censor.[1] Have they forgotten the censor here? a censor far more powerful than him of Russia. Have they forgotten that every line they write is dictated by the political color of the paper they write for; by the advertising firms; by the money power; by the power of respectability; by Comstock?[2] Have they forgotten that the literary taste and critical judgment of the mass of the people have been successfully moulded to suit the will of these dictators, and to serve as a good business basis for shrewd literary speculators? The number of Rip Van Winkles in life, science, morality, art, and literature is very large. Innumerable ghosts, such as Ibsen saw when he analyzed the moral and social conditions of our life,[3] still keep the majority of the human race in awe.

Mother Earth will endeavor to attract and appeal to all those who oppose encroachment on public and individual life. It will appeal to those who strive for something higher, weary of the commonplace; to those who feel that stagnation is a deadweight on the firm and elastic step of progress; to those who breathe freely only in limitless space; to those who long for the tender shade of a new dawn for a humanity free from the dread of want, the dread of starvation in the face of mountains of riches. The Earth free for the free individual!

Emma Goldman,
Max Baginski.

Mother Earth 1 (March 1906): 1–4.

1. See, for example, "Censorship in Russia," *New York Times*, 16 April 1901; "The Coming Crash in Russia," *North American Review*, April 1905; "The Russian Chaos," *New York Times*, 17 December 1905; and "Chaos in Russia," *Collier's*, 23 December 1905.
2. Refers to Anthony Comstock, who since 1873 had pursued and suppressed radical publications as well as literature deemed obscene by terms of the congressional act bearing his name.
3. In his drama *Ghosts* (1881), Henrik Ibsen addresses issues of spousal abuse, venereal disease, and euthanasia, among other themes. EG often referred to this play in her lectures on modern drama, and included an in-depth analysis of its themes in her 1914 book *The Social Significance of the Modern Drama*, pp. 25–34.

Essay in *MOTHER EARTH*

March 1906

The Tragedy of Woman's Emancipation

I begin my article with an admission: Regardless of all political and economic theories, treating of the fundamental differences between the various groups within the human race, regardless of class and race distinctions, regardless of all artificial boundary lines between woman's rights and man's rights, I hold that there is a point where these differentiations may meet and grow into one perfect whole.

With this I do not mean to propose a peace treaty. The general social antagonism which has taken hold of our entire public life to-day, brought about through the force of opposing and contradictory interests, will crumble to pieces when the reorganization of our social life, based upon the principles of economic justice, shall have become a reality.

Peace and harmony between the sexes and individuals does not necessarily depend on a superficial equalization of human beings; nor does it call for the elimination of individual traits or peculiarities. The problem that confronts us to-day, and which the nearest future is to solve, is how to be oneself, and yet in oneness with others, to feel deeply with all human beings and still retain one's own innate qualities. This seems to me the basis upon which the mass and the individual, the true democrat and the true individuality, man and woman can meet without antagonism and opposition. The motto should not be forgive one another; it should be, understand one another. The oft-quoted sentence of Mme. de Stael: "To understand everything means to forgive everything,"[1] has never particularly appealed to me; it has the odor of the confessional; to forgive one's fellow being conveys the idea of pharisaical superiority. To understand one's fellow being suffices. This admission partly represents the fundamental aspect of my views on the emancipation of woman and its effect upon the entire sex.

Emancipation should make it possible for her to be human in the truest sense. Everything within her that craves assertion and activity should reach its fullest expression; and all artificial barriers should be broken and the road towards greater freedom cleared of every trace of centuries of submission and slavery.

This was the original aim of the movement for woman's emancipation. But the results

---

1. Mme de Stäel (1766–1817) was the pen name of Anne Louise Germaine Necker, Baronne de Stäel Holstein, a French author and intellectual. She ardently supported revolutionary republican ideals, yet was disillusioned by the violence and factionalism of the French Revolution. EG's reference is probably a minor misquotation of de Stäel's novel *Corinne* (1807), from part 5 of the chapter entitled "Le Sejour á Florence."

EMMA GOLDMAN

LA TRAGÉDIE

DE

L'ÉMANCIPATION FÉMININE

Traduction de E. ARMAND

Editions de *l'en dehors*

22, cité Saint-Joseph, Orléans

—

DEUXIÈME TIRAGE

Orléans. — Imp. Coop. La Laborieuse

20°C

Cover of the French translation of Goldman's 1906 essay "The Tragedy of Woman's Emancipation"—her first essay published in pamphlet form. The French edition was published ca. 1908 by the anarchist newspaper *L'en dehors (The Outsider)* and edited by the anarchist individualist E. Armand. Interest in her work in France reflected Goldman's growing international stature as a political theorist. (Center d'histoire du Travail, Nantes)

so far achieved have isolated woman and have robbed her of the fountain springs of that happiness which is so essential to her. Merely external emancipation has made of the modern woman an artificial being who reminds one of the products of French arboriculture with its arabesque trees and shrubs—pyramids, wheels and wreaths; anything except the forms which would be reached by the expression of their own inner qualities. Such artificially grown plants of the female sex are to be found in large numbers, especially in the so-called intellectual sphere of our life.

Liberty and equality for woman! What hopes and aspirations these words awakened when they were first uttered by some of the noblest and bravest souls of those days. The sun in all its light and glory was to rise upon a new world; in this world woman was to be free to direct her own destiny, an aim certainly worthy of the great enthusiasm, courage, perseverance and ceaseless effort of the tremendous host of pioneer men and women, who staked everything against a world of prejudice and ignorance.

My hopes also move towards that goal, but I insist that the emancipation of woman, as interpreted and practically applied to-day, has failed to reach that great end. Now, woman is confronted with the necessity of emancipating herself from emancipation, if she really desires to be free. This may sound paradoxical, but is, nevertheless, only too true.

What has she achieved through her emancipation? Equal suffrage in a few states.[2] Has that purified our political life, as many well-meaning advocates have predicted? Certainly not. Incidentally it is really time that persons with plain, sound judgment should cease to talk about corruption in politics in a boarding-school tone. Corruption of politics has nothing to do with the morals or the laxity of morals of various political personalities. Its cause is altogether a material one. Politics is the reflex of the business and industrial world, the mottoes of which are: "to take is more blessed than to give"; "buy cheap and sell dear"; "one soiled hand washes the other." There is no hope that even woman, with her right to vote, will ever purify politics.

Emancipation has brought woman economic equality with man; that is, she can choose her own profession and trade, but as her past and present physical training have not equipped her with the necessary strength to compete with man, she is often compelled to exhaust all her energy, use up her vitality and strain every nerve in order to reach the market value. Very few ever succeed, for it is a fact that women doctors, lawyers, architects and engineers are neither met with the same confidence, nor do they receive the same remuneration. And those that do reach that enticing equality generally do so at the expense of their physical and psychical well-being. As to the great mass of working girls and women, how much independence is gained if the narrowness and lack of freedom of the home is exchanged for the narrowness and lack of freedom of the factory, sweat-shop, department store, or office? In addition is the burden which is laid on many women of looking after a "home, sweet home"—cold, dreary, disorderly, uninviting—after a day's

2. By 1906, four states had granted women the vote: Wyoming (1869), Colorado (1893), Utah (1896), and Idaho (1896).

hard work. Glorious independence! No wonder that hundreds of girls are so willing to accept the first offer of marriage, sick and tired of their independence behind the counter, or at the sewing or typewriting machine. They are just as ready to marry as girls of middle class people who long to throw off the yoke of parental dependence. A so-called independence which leads only to earning the merest subsistence is not so enticing, not so ideal that one can expect woman to sacrifice everything for it. Our highly praised independence is, after all, but a slow process of dulling and stifling woman's nature, her love instinct and her mother instinct.

Nevertheless, the position of the working girl is far more natural and human than that of her seemingly more fortunate sister in the more cultured professional walk of life. Teachers, physicians, lawyers, engineers, etc., who have to make a dignified, straightened and proper appearance, while the inner life is growing empty and dead.

The narrowness of the existing conception of woman's independence and emancipation; the dread of love for a man who is not her social equal; the fear that love will rob her of her freedom and independence; the horror that love or the joy of motherhood will only hinder her in the full exercise of her profession—all these together make of the emancipated modern woman a compulsory vestal, before whom life, with its great clarifying sorrows and its deep, entrancing joys, rolls on without touching or gripping her soul.

Emancipation as understood by the majority of its adherents and exponents, is of too narrow a scope to permit the boundless joy and ecstasy contained in the deep emotion of the true woman, sweetheart, mother, in freedom.

The tragic fate of the self-supporting or economically free woman does not consist of too many, but of too few experiences. True, she surpasses her sister of past generations in knowledge of the world and human nature; and it is because of that that she feels deeply the lack of life's essence, which alone can enrich the human soul and without which the majority of women have become mere professional automatons.

That such a state of affairs was bound to come was foreseen by those who realized that in the domain of ethics, there still remained many decaying ruins of the time of the undisputed superiority of man; ruins that are still considered useful. And, which is more important, a goodly number of the emancipated are unable to get along without them. Every movement that aims at the destruction of existing institutions and the replacement thereof with such as are more advanced, more perfect, has followers, who in theory stand for the most extreme radical ideas, and who, nevertheless, in their every-day practice, are like the next best Philistine, feigning respectability and clamoring for the good opinion of their opponents. There are, for example, Socialists, and even Anarchists, who stand for the idea that property is robbery, yet who will grow indignant if anyone owe them the value of a half-dozen pins.

The same Philistine can be found in the movement for woman's emancipation. Yellow journalists and milk and water litterateurs have painted pictures of the emancipated woman that make the hair of the good citizen and his dull companion stand up on end. Every member of the women's rights movement was pictured as a George Sand in her absolute disregard of morality.[3] Nothing was sacred to her. She had no respect for the ideal relation between man and woman. In short, emancipation stood only for a reckless life of lust and sin; regardless of society, religion and morality. The exponents of woman's rights were highly indignant at such a misrepresentation, and, lacking in humor, they exerted all their energy to prove that they were not at all as bad as they were painted, but the very reverse. Of course, as long as woman was the slave of man, she could not be good and pure, but now that she was free and independent she would prove how good she could be and how her influence would have a purifying effect on all institutions in society. True, the movement for woman's rights has broken many old fetters, but it has also established new ones. The great movement of true emancipation has not met with a great race of women, who could look liberty in the face. Their narrow puritanical vision banished man as a disturber and doubtful character out of their emotional life. Man was not to be tolerated at any price, except perhaps as the father of a child, since a child could not very well come to life without a father. Fortunately, the most rigid puritanism never will be strong enough to kill the innate craving for motherhood. But woman's freedom is closely allied to man's freedom, and many of my so-called emancipated sisters seem to overlook the fact that a child born in freedom needs the love and devotion of each human being about him, man as well as woman. Unfortunately, it is this narrow conception of human relations that has brought about a great tragedy in the lives of the modern man and woman.

About fifteen years ago appeared a work from the pen of the brilliant Norwegian writer, Laura Marholm, called "Woman, a Character Study."[4] She was one of the first to call attention to the emptiness and narrowness of the existing conception of woman's emancipation and its tragic effect upon the inner life of woman. In her work she speaks of the fate of several gifted women of international fame: The genius, Eleanora Duse;[5] the great mathematician and writer, Sanja Kovalevskaja;[6] the artist and poet nature, Marie Bashkirzeff, who

3. George Sand (1804–1876) was the pseudonym for Amandine-Aurore-Lucie Dudevant (née Dupin), a controversial French author known for her outspoken and sometimes contradictory literary representations of gender roles. Her early works explored women's sexuality and encouraged the quest for emotional and sexual satisfaction and balance; her later works emphasized her Republican and socialist politics. Works include *Indiana* (1832), *Lelia* (1833), *Spiridon* (1838), *Un Hiver à Majorca* (1841), *Consuelo* (1842), and *Historie de ma Vie*, 4 vols. (1854–1855).

4. Laura Marholm-Hansson (1854–1928) was a Latvian author. Her work, *Modern Women* (1896), erroneously referred to by EG as *Woman, A Character Study*, explored the lives of six prominent women intellectuals (including Eleonora Duse, Sophia Kovalevskaya, and Marie Bashkirtseff) to illustrate the effective emptiness of unmarried women in the professions as compared to the inherent fulfillment of their sexuality in the maternal experience.

5. Eleanora Duse (1858–1924) was an Italian actress known for her portrayal of the torment in the everyday lives of contemporary women, most notably in the plays of Henrik Ibsen and Émile Zola. EG saw Duse perform in Vienna in 1895.

6. Sophia Kovalevskaya (1850–1891) was a prominent Russian mathematician, author, and pioneer of the early feminist movement. She fled to Germany in 1869 to escape the rigid gender norms of Russia, which impaired her ability to direct the course of both her career and her relationships; she was appointed professor of mathematics at Göttingen University in 1894. Her major works include *A Russian Childhood* (1890) and *Vera Branantzova (A Nihilist Girl*, 1895).

died so young.[7] Through each description of the lives of these women of such extraordinary mentality, runs a marked trail of unsatisfied craving for a full, rounded, complete and beautiful life, and the unrest and loneliness resulting from the lack of it. Through these masterly psychological sketches, one cannot help but see that the higher the mental development of woman, the less possible it is for her to meet a congenial mate, who will see in her, not only sex, but also the human being, the friend, comrade and strong individuality, who cannot and ought not lose a single trait of her character.

The average man with his self-sufficiency, his ridiculously superior airs of patronage towards the female sex, is an impossibility for woman, as depicted in the "Character Study" by Laura Marholm. Equally impossible for her is the man who can see in her nothing more than her mentality and genius, and who fails to awaken her woman nature.

A rich intellect and a fine soul are usually considered necessary attributes of a deep and beautiful personality. In the case of the modern woman, these attributes serve as a hindrance to the complete assertion of her being. For over a hundred years, the old form of marriage, based on the Bible, "till death us do part" has been denounced as an institution that stands for the sovereignty of the man over the woman, of her complete submission to his whims and commands and the absolute dependence upon his name and support. Time and again it has been conclusively proven that the old matrimonial relation restricted woman to the function of man's servant and the bearer of his children. And yet we find many emancipated women who prefer marriage with all its deficiencies to the narrowness of an unmarried life; narrow and unendurable because of the chains of moral and social prejudice that cramp and bind her nature.

The cause for such inconsistency on the part of many advanced women is to be found in the fact that they never truly understood the meaning of emancipation. They thought that all that was needed was independence from external tyrannies; the internal tyrants, far more harmful to life and growth, such as ethical and social conventions, were left to take care of themselves; and they have taken care of themselves. They seem to get along beautifully in the heads and hearts of the most active exponents of woman's emancipation, as in the heads and hearts of our grandmothers.

These internal tyrants, whether they be in the form of public opinion or what will mother say, or brother, father, aunt or relative of any sort; what will Mrs. Grundy,[8] Mr. Comstock,[9] the employer, the Board of Education say? All these busybodies, moral detec-

---

7. Marie Constantinova Bashkirtseff (1858–1884) was a Russian painter and diarist. Her posthumously published diaries, *I Am the Most Interesting Book of All* (1887), were cited by Laura Marholm-Hansson as representative of women's universally experienced "psychology of the unmarried state."
8. Mrs. Grundy is a fictional character who first appeared in Thomas Morton's 1798 play, *Speed the Plough*, as an arbiter of social etiquette. Later, her name came to signify prudishness, censorship, and the rigidity of social conventions.
9. EG refers to Anthony Comstock, author and enforcer of the 1873 Comstock Act (revised in 1876) prohibiting the use of the mails to distribute "obscene" material, which was broadly defined to include birth control information as well as radical treatises.

tives, jailers of the human spirit, what will they say? Until woman has learned to defy them all, to stand firmly on her own ground and to insist upon her own unrestricted freedom, to listen to the voice of her nature, whether it call for life's greatest treasure, love for a man, or her most glorious privilege, the right to give birth to a child, she cannot call herself emancipated. How many emancipated women are brave enough to acknowledge that the voice of love is calling, wildly beating against their breasts demanding to be heard, to be satisfied.

The French novelist, Jean Reibrach,[10] in one of his novels, "New Beauty," attempts to picture the ideal, beautiful, emancipated woman. This ideal is embodied in a young girl, a physician. She talks very clearly and wisely of how to feed infants, she is kind and administers medicines free to poor mothers. She converses with a young man of her acquaintance about the sanitary conditions of the future and how various bacilli and germs shall be exterminated by the use of stone walls and floors, and the doing away of rugs and hangings. She is, of course, very plainly and practically dressed, mostly in black. The young man, who, at their first meeting was overawed by the wisdom of his emancipated friend, gradually learns to understand her, and recognizes one fine day that he loves her. They are young and she is kind and beautiful, and though always in rigid attire, her appearance is softened by spotlessly clean white collar and cuffs. One would expect that he would tell her of his love, but he is not one to commit romantic absurdities. Poetry and the enthusiasm of love cover their blushing faces before the pure beauty of the lady. He silences the voice of his nature and remains correct. She, too, is always exact, always rational, always well behaved. I fear if they had formed a union, the young man would have risked freezing to death. I must confess that I can see nothing beautiful in this new beauty, who is as cold as the stone walls and floors she dreams of. Rather would I have the love songs of romantic ages, rather Don Juan and Madame Venus, rather an elopement by ladder and rope on a moonlight night, followed by a father's curse, mother's moans, and the moral comments of neighbors, than correctness and propriety measured by yardsticks. If love does not know how to give and take without restriction it is not love, but a transaction that never fails to lay stress on a plus and a minus.

The greatest shortcoming of the emancipation of the present day lies in its artificial stiffness and its narrow respectabilities which produce an emptiness in woman's soul that will not let her drink from the fountain of life. I once remarked that there seemed to be a deeper relationship between the old-fashioned mother and hostess, ever on the alert for the happiness of her little ones and the comfort of those she loved and the truly new woman, than between the latter and her average emancipated sister. The disciples of emancipation pure and simple declared me heathen, merely fit for the stake. Their blind

10. Jean Reibrach (ca. 1855–1927) was the pseudonym of Jean Chabrier, novelist and a captain in the French army, a position from which he resigned after the publication of his first novel, *La Gamelle* (1889), a negative portrayal of military life. Other works include *Aller et Retour* (1891), *Le Lendemain* (1892), and *La Nouvelle Beauté* (1903).

zeal did not let them see that my comparison between the old and the new was merely to prove that a goodly number of our grandmothers had more blood in their veins, far more humor and wit, and certainly a greater amount of naturalness, kind-heartedness and simplicity than the majority of our emancipated professional women who fill our colleges, halls of learning, and various offices. This does not mean a wish to return to the past, nor does it condemn woman to her old sphere, the kitchen and the nursery.

Salvation lies in an energetic march onward towards a brighter and clearer future. We are in need of unhampered growth out of old traditions and habits. The movement for woman's emancipation has so far made but the first step in that direction. It is to be hoped that it will gather strength to make another. The right to vote, equal civil rights, are all very good demands, but true emancipation begins neither at the polls nor in courts. It begins in woman's soul. History tells us that every oppressed class gained its true liberation from its masters through its own efforts. It is necessary that woman learn that lesson, that she realize that her freedom will reach as far as her power to achieve her freedom reaches. It is therefore far more important for her to begin with her inner regeneration, to cut loose from the weight of prejudices, traditions, and customs. The demand for various equal rights in every vocation in life is just and fair, but, after all, the most vital right is the right to love and be loved. Indeed if the partial emancipation is to become a complete and true emancipation of woman, it will have to do away with the ridiculous notion that to be loved, to be sweetheart and mother, is synonymous with being slave or subordinate. It will have to do away with the absurd notion of the dualism of the sexes, or that man and woman represent two antagonistic worlds.

Pettiness separates, breadth unites. Let us be broad and big. Let us not overlook vital things, because of the bulk of trifles confronting us. A true conception of the relation of the sexes will not admit of conqueror and conquered; it knows of but one great thing: to give of one's self boundlessly in order to find oneself richer, deeper, better. That alone can fill the emptiness and replace the tragedy of woman's emancipation with joy, limitless joy.

Mother Earth 1 (March 1906): 9–18. "The Tragedy of Woman's Emancipation" was reprinted in EG's *Anarchism and Other Essays* (New York: Mother Earth Publishing Association, 1911) with some minor differences.

Essay in *MOTHER EARTH*

April 1906

A Sentimental Journey.—Police Protection.

Chicago's pride are the stockyards, the Standard Oil University,[1] and Miss Jane Addams.[2] It is, therefore, perfectly natural that the sensibility of such a city would suffer as soon as it became known that an obscure person, by the common name of E. G. Smith, was none other than the awful Emma Goldman, and that she had not even presented herself to Mayor Dunne,[3] the platonic lover of Municipal Ownership. However, not much harm came of it.

The Chicago newspapers, who cherish the truth like a costly jewel, made the discovery that the shrewd Miss Smith compromised a number of Chicago's aristocracy and excellencies, among others also Baron von Schlippenbach, consul of the Russian Empire. We consider it our duty to defend this gentleman against such an awful accusation. Miss Smith never visited the house of the Baron, nor did she attend any of his banquets. We know her well and feel confident that she never would put her foot on the threshold of a representative of a government that crushes every free breath, every free word; that sends her very best and noblest sons and daughters to prison or the gallows; that has the children of the soil, the peasants, publicly flogged; and that is responsible for the barbarous slaughter of thousands of Jews.

Miss Jane Addams, too, is quite safe from Miss Smith. True, she invited her to be present at a reception, but, knowing the weak knees of the soup kitchen philanthropy from past experience, Miss Smith called her up on the 'phone and told her that E. G. S. was the dreaded Emma Goldman. It must have been quite a shock to the lady; after all,

---

1. The University of Chicago was founded in 1890 by John D. Rockefeller, president and founder of the Standard Oil Company.

2. Jane Addams was a prominent reformer and director of Hull House in Chicago, one of the first settlement houses in the United States. EG's relationship with the settlement house movement was rather ambivalent. In the February 1912 *Mother Earth*, EG published the article "The Reformers on the Wrong Track," which criticized Jane Addams and other reformers, who were recommending a state investigation of labor conditions in the wake of the 1910 explosion at the building of the *Los Angeles Times:* "Do the reformers really assume that the government would commit suicide for virtuous and moral considerations? Hardly. The State knows neither virtue not morality. Its sole aim is to strengthen and perpetuate its sway and prestige."

3. Edward F. Dunne (1853–1937) was an Illinois politician who served one term as mayor of Chicago (1905–1907) on a reform platform advocating municipal ownership of the transit system, a position blocked regularly by the city council. Dunne appointed Jane Addams chair of the School Management Committee and Louis F. Post to the school board. He was elected governor of Illinois in 1913.

one cannot afford to hurt the sensibilities of society, so long as one has political and public aspirations. Miss E. G. Smith, being a strong believer in the prevention of cruelty, preferred to leave the purity of the Hull House untouched. After her return to New York, E. G. Smith sent Smith about its business, and started on a lecture tour in her own right, as Emma Goldman.

CLEVELAND. Dear old friends and co-workers: The work you accomplished was splendid, also the comradely spirit of the young. But why spoil it by bad example of applying for protection from the city authorities? It does not behoove us, who neither believe in their right to prohibit free assembly, nor to permit it, to appeal to them. If the authorities choose to do either, they merely prove their autocracy. Those who love freedom must understand that it is even more distasteful to speak under police protection than it is to suffer under their persecution. However, the meetings were very encouraging and the feeling of solidarity sweet and refreshing.[4]

BUFFALO. The shadow of September 6 still haunts the police of that city.[5] Their only vision of an Anarchist is one who is forever lying in wait for human life, which is, of course, very stupid; but stupidity and authority always join forces. Capt. Ward, who, with a squad of police, came to save the innocent citizens of Buffalo, asked if we knew the law, and was quite surprised that that was not our trade; that we had not been employed to disentangle the chaos of the law,—that it was his affair to know the law. However, the Captain showed himself absolutely ignorant of the provisions of the American Constitution. Of course, his superiors knew what they were about when they set the Constitution aside, as old and antiquated, and, instead, enacted a law which gives the average officer a right to invade the head and heart of a man, as to what he thinks and feels. Capt. Ward added an amendment to the anti-Anarchist law. He declared any other language than English a felony, and, since Max Baginski could only avail himself of the German language, he was not permitted to speak. How is that for our law-abiding citizens? A man is brutally prevented from speaking, because he does not know the refined English language of the police force.

Emma Goldman delivered her address in English. It is not likely that Capt. Ward understood enough of that language. However, the audience did, and if the police of this country were not so barefaced, the saviour of Buffalo would have wished himself anywhere rather than to stand exposed as a clown before a large gathering of men and women.

The meeting the following evening was forcibly dispersed before the speakers had arrived. Ignorance is always brutal when it is backed by power.

TORONTO. King Edward Hotel, Queen Victoria Manicuring Parlor. It was only when we read these signs that we realized that we were on the soil of the British Empire.

---

4. The meetings were most likely organized by the philosophical anarchists Fred Schulder and Adeline Champney. Cleveland police closely monitored EG's lectures; two detectives were present at her 16 March lecture, "Anarchist-Communism," delivered in German to a full house.
5. A reference to the shooting of President McKinley on 6 September 1901 by Leon Czolgosz.

However, the monarchical authorities of Canada were more hospitable and much freer than those of our free Republic. Not a sign of an officer at any of these meetings.

The city? A gray sky, rain, storms. Altogether one was reminded of one of Heine's witty, drastic criticisms in reference to a well-known German university town. "Dogs in the street," Heine writes, "implore strangers to kick them, so that they may have some change from the awful monotony and dullness."

ROCHESTER. The neighborly influence of the Buffalo police seems to have had a bad effect upon the mental development of the Rochester authorities. The hall was packed with officers at both meetings. The government of Rochester, however, was not saved— the police kept themselves in good order. Some of them seem to have benefited by the lectures. That accounts for the familiarity of one of Rochester's "finest," who wanted to shake Emma Goldman's hand. E.G. had to decline. Baron von Schlippenback or an American representative of law and disorder—where is the difference?[6]

SYRACUSE. The city where the trains run through the streets. With Tolstoy, one feels that civilization is a crime and a mistake, when one sees nerve-wrecking machines running through the streets, poisoning the atmosphere with soft coal smoke.[7]

What! Anarchists within the walls of Syracuse? O horror! The newspapers reported of special session at City Hall, how to meet the terrible calamity.

Well, Syracuse still stands on its old site. The second meeting attended largely by "genuine" Americans, brought by curiosity perhaps, was successful. We were assured that the lecture made a splendid impression, which led us to think that we probably were guity of some foolishness as the Greek philosopher, when his lectures were applauded, would turn to his hearers and ask, "Gentlemen, have I committed some folly?"

Au revoir[8]

E.G. AND M.B.

Mother Earth 1 (April 1906): 43–45. "M.B." is anarchist Max Baginski, who edited *Mother Earth* with EG at this time.

6. Baron von Schlippenback was the Russian consul. In her autobiography EG explained that while working as Pavel Orlenev's tour manager, she had been invited, as E.G. Smith, along with Orlenev to meet von Schlippenback. EG refused, stating that he "represented the Russian imperial butcher" (*LML*, p. 375).
7. New York Central passenger trains ran along Washington Street in downtown Syracuse until 1936.
8. EG ended her lecture tour with stops in Rochester on 20–21 March, Syracuse on 22–23 March, and Toronto at the end of March, before returning to New York for the memorial celebration on 1 April commemorating Johann Most's life.

To LEON MALMED

New York, 7 April 1906

Dear Comrade Malmed.

Thank you so much for your kind note and your interest in my welbeing. It is very hard to take care of oneself, if one has so many things to attend to and many calls to satisfy. It is very hard for me to refuse young inthusiastic comrades, when they are eager to do work. I must help them, since there is no one else. We have not yet received Second class rights[1] but we are expecting to get a temporary permit Tuesday, the final discision will not come from Washington for a long time. I am glad, that my [*lecture?*] has had a good affect on the people who saw me.[2] After all, it is more important to do propaganda with ones personality, than with words. Yes, it is too bad, that we have so few speakers. However I would suggest, that you arrange an English meeting in a decent known Hall for me. The Comrades of the West,[3] are anxious, that I should go on a tour for Mother Earth. On my return, which would be about June 15th I could be in Albany.[4] It would be a good Idea to have a meeting in the afternoon and social in the evening. Let me know what you think of it. With affection for you and your companion[5] and greetings to our Comrades.

Emma Goldman

ALS, Leon Malmed Papers (Emma Goldman Microfilm), MCR. On stationery of Emma G. Smith, Vienna Scalp and Face Specialist, 874 Broadway.

1. Second-class mailing privileges for *Mother Earth* allowed the magazine to be sent at special low rates, vital to its circulation.
2. EG embarked on a national lecture tour in March 1906 with Max Baginski, associate editor of *Mother Earth*. She is probably referring to the lecture Malmed arranged for her in Albany, New York, delivered in German to a full house on 1 April at Engineer's Hall (Hudson Street), interrupted midway by a police raid.
3. On 12 May, EG began her lecture tour in Cleveland, continuing on to Detroit, Chicago, and St. Louis.
4. There is no record of a 15 June meeting.
5. EG refers to Millie Mott (b. 1882), Leon Malmed's wife. Partly in deference to this relationship, EG excluded from her autobiography the details of her love affair with Malmed (consummated while she was in exile in Canada, November 1926).

MY DEAR FRIEND.

I guess you will consider me a hopeless case, since I have kept you waiting for an answer to your welmeant letter. I hope tho that you are not angry. I thought of you daily and hoped I would get a chance to write to you. But mine is a very busy life, I can not always attended to my correspondents in a regular way, tho I always answer. By this time, you have already seen "Mother Earth". Whether you still think, I ought not to have started the publication I do not know. Of one thing I am certain, you surely will not say that Mother Earth, can be compared with The Demonstrator, Liberator or kindred papers.[1] What "Mother Earth" aims at, is not in existence in this country, a good literary radical Magazine and if it will be that, it will have a solid foundation.

The first number has been met with unusual success, 3000 having been disposed of in less than a week, so that another 1000 copies had to be printed. Since the March number appeared I received a considerable number of subscribers and an invitations from various cities to make a tour. You see dear friend, the prospects are not so very bad after all. If I decide on a tour, I will also strike Detroit, several friends have proposed my lecturing there.[2] Needless to say I shall be glad to come, if only to see you again

I have not written to the party, who's letter you sent me. Thank you for the kind suggestion to write him, but I do not like duty letters and since I felt no desire to write him, I just let it go. I do not consider myself at fault when people speak ill of me, nor do I think myself virtues, if they say kind things. In either case they are following their own desires, why should I then express thanks, or sorrow. Indeed it was awfully pleasent to meet you, so unexpectedly. I hope to see more of you tho, when I come to Detroit which might be some times in May.[3]

Write me, if you care.

SINCERELY

EMMA GOLDMAN

ALS, Joseph Labadie Papers, MiU.

1. *The Demonstrator* and *The Liberator* were anarchist weekly newspapers; *Mother Earth,* as a monthly magazine, published news items and longer articles as well as feature stories and literary works, including poetry.
2. On 12 May, EG began a lecture tour in Cleveland, continuing on to Detroit on the 18th, arriving in Chicago on the 22nd and Pittsburgh on 10 June.
3. EG arrived in Detroit on 18 May 1906, where she met AB, who had just been released from prison. They stayed with Carl Nold.

My DEAR, DEAR *Niunia.*

I can not tell you,[1] how happy your letter made me. I have had many encouraging words since the first number of Mother Earth appeared, but somehow your words touched the right spot in my sensitive soul. The April issue is even more beautiful I think, as far as the contents and the make up is concerned.

The only objection, I have is the cover, the wretched printer gave me blue instead of gray paper, without asking me whether, I would have that combination. It shall not happen again however. I sent you a dozen copies, I think, so that you can use them, as sample copies. I may go on a tour soon, but have decided not to speak in Pittsburg (tho I was asked,) as the release of Berkman is drawing very close and I fear, that my appearance in P at that time may injure him.[2] On my return trip from the West, I may stop off at P to see you and George and a few other friends

Orleneff—I am too miserable to tell you, all that man has suffered and what awful humiliations, that man has endured, all because he was unwilling to prostitute his Art. Our Russians in this City have acted most contamptibly towards him.[3] I was not in the City, if when he was arrested, else it might never have happened.[4] To make a long story short, I all the work that was about to establish a thorough footing for Orleneff was ruined by a few Russians. O is returning to Russia, as poor as he came, ill at heart and with great bitterness in his soul. He just called on me, he looks terrible. He intends to sail early in

1. EG addresses her Pittsburgh friend by her first name, Nunia, spelled in Cyrillic characters. Her husband, George Seldes, was a prominent Russian-born revolutionary utopian and anarchist. EG uses the same form of address in her 18 May 1906 letter to Nunia Seldes, below.
2. Alexander Berkman was to be released on 18 May, following his fourteen-year imprisonment in Allegheny City, Pennsylvania.
3. In late 1905 Russian Jews on New York's Lower East Side, a large part of Pavel Orlenev's audience, boycotted his theater troupe in response to rumors, circulated in the wake of the repression following the 1905 revolution, that some of the actors belonged to the notorious antisemitic organization "the Black Hundreds," despite his troupe's holding benefit performances for Jewish victims of pogroms (see Letter to Unknown Recipient, 21 November 1905, above).
4. Orlenev was arrested for grand larceny on 24 March 1906 and put in jail for two days after the troupe's treasurer complained to the police that he was owed three weeks' back pay. An article in the *New York Times* reporting on this event also suggested that the Chirikov Society, of which EG was a member, was also threatening to sue Orlenev, apparently because Orlenev had made a contract with a committee of influential New York liberals (including Ernest Crosby, and with backing by Andrew Carnegie and J. P. Morgan) for a limited season at the Berkeley Theater and a brief tour. According to the article, this would have been a breach of the contract he had made earlier with the Chirikov Society (*New York Times*, 25 March 1905). However, after his arrest for larceny the committee dropped the offer to arrange his tour.

Newspaper sketch from 18 June 1906 *New York World* of Goldman and Berkman kissing on the lecture stage shortly after his release from prison in May 1906. The meeting was chaired by Saul Yanovsky, editor of the Yiddish-language anarchist communist newspaper *Freie Arbeiter Stimme.* (University of California, Berkeley)

May and return next Nov. to play in order to pay his debts;[5] I know he means to, and wants to but. My belief is, that a sensitive being like O is bound to go down, no one wants to understand, it, or cares for it—He wishes to be remembered to you and George.

Good by dear, thank you for your assistance.

AFFECTIONATELY
EMMA.

Kiss George for me, if he will accept—

Write me to my P.O. address

ALS, Leon Malmed Papers (Emma Goldman Microfilm), MCR. On stationery of Emma G. Smith, Vienna Scalp and Face Specialist, 874 Broadway.

5. Plagued by financial woes, Orlenev left New York for Russia on 15 May 1906; he visited the United States once more in January 1912.

My dear *Niunia*.

I left your address in our address-book at home, so will send this through Muchnic.

I find, that I could conviniently come to Pittsburg for a few lectures, if you are willing to arrange the meetings, together with our other boys in P. Meitlin,[1] Mucchnic etc. I can come for June 10. 11. 12th.[2] What say you? Of course, I should prefer English meetings. I do not care for Jewish ones, especially since I do not speak Jargon[3] and they will understand English, about as well, as German and also because I want to interest the people all over the Country in our Mag. M. E and therefore want to appeal to an English speaking public. However, I have no objections to one Jewish meeting. You could therefore, have two English and one Jewish gathering. The themes, I wish to discuss, are; "The Constitution and the ~~Idaho in~~ Idaho Outrage,"[4] The General Strike. And "The false and true conception of Anarchism.

My trip this time, is not only to do propaganda, but also to raise a fund for M. E, so as to keep it ~~ali~~ going over the summer months, I would therefore suggest, that an admission be charged. I have not spoken in P. for a number of years and I feel confident, successful meetings could be arranged, if only properly organised and advertised. I also know, that you and George can do it well.

Let me hear from you at once dear, whether or not you will take up the work. I leave here for Chicago next Tuesday, my address there is General Post Office.

With lot of love to you and George.

Emma Goldman.

167. Hale Str until May 22nd.

ALS, MCR.

---

1. Harry and Becky Meitlin were Pittsburgh anarchists.
2. No confirmation that these proposed meetings took place has been found.
3. The word "jargon" was sometimes used by those who perceived Yiddish as a bastardized form of German.
4. See "To My Readers," Editorial in *Mother Earth*, December 1906, below.

Letters to the Editor in Prison

May you, our beloved convict,[1] soon join this circle of ex-convicts who rejoice in their honorable title. On the occasion of the resurrection from the dead of one of our number[2] we send you our deepest respect and love, and our hearts go out to the Nestor[3] of free expression, the many-time victim of governmental hypocrisy and persecution. May our love cast a ray of sunshine into the darkness of your nightmare.

AFFECTIONATELY,

ALEX. BERKMAN,

EMMA GOLDMAN,

CARL NOLD.

Lucifer, the Lightbearer, 27 September 1906, p. 590. Identified as one of a number of letters Moses Harman received during his year in prison. Harman was first incarcerated in Joliet, Illinois, and then moved to Leavenworth, in Kansas.

1. In June 1905 *Lucifer* editor Moses Harman was charged with obscenity and eventually sentenced to a year at hard labor in federal prison (at Joliet, Illinois) after publishing letters addressing the sexual health and rights of married women. Seventy-five years old at the time he entered Joliet in 1906, Harman's health was permanently ruined by prison conditions. Harman, whose editorial policy was to print without alteration letters from readers, had long been a target of government censors enforcing the Comstock Act of 1873 and consequently had suffered numerous legal attacks and imprisonments. In this latest entanglement he was aided by the Free Speech League, an organization he helped found in 1902. The letter to Harman from EG, AB, and Carl Nold was one of many sent by sympathetic public figures and reprinted in *Lucifer*.
2. A reference to AB's release on 18 May, following his fourteen-year imprisonment in Allegheny City, Pennsylvania.
3. Nestor in Greek literature was an elderly counselor to the Greeks at Troy; used here as a noun to describe a venerable and wise old man.

Emma G. Smith

Vienna Scalp and Face Specialist

---

874 Broadway, New York

As a graduated nurse of ten years' practice, and with a thorough knowledge of scalp, hair and face troubles, I guarantee absolutely reliable and scientific treatment, through a very thorough system of massage and electricity. I also have a special method of shampooing.

Prices moderate. Special terms to readers of the WOMAN'S JOURNAL.

Woman's Journal, 28 September, 1906, p. 309. The official publication of the American Woman Suffrage Association, *Woman's Journal* was edited by Alice Stone Blackwell.

Advertisement placed by Goldman under the name Emma G. Smith in the *Woman's Journal,* a suffrage paper. (University of California, Berkeley)

Notice in *MOTHER EARTH*

November 1906

To the Readers of Mother Earth.

Those of you who have been startled by the rumor of Comrade Alexander Berkman's disappearance and his supposed kidnapping I want to inform that there was little truth in the story.[1] People never realize that there are worse things in human life than merely external forces. But what made it impossible for our friend to continue his tour lies in the terrible contrast of solitary confinement, enforced silence and monotony and the rush and hurry of our daily lives. Few have stood the years of hell as bravely as Comrade Berkman, but the lack of idealism and enthusiasm in radical ranks and the pettiness and sordidness of our existence were too much for his sensitive nature. He hoped to regain interest in life through a tour, but before he was half through he realized that one can never find the strength to live outside of himself and that to find oneself at all, one needs absolute harmony and peace.

He has therefore decided to retire for a time and hopes those who have been disappointed will understand and appreciate.

Emma Goldman.

Mother Earth 1 (November 1906): 55.

1. EG had encouraged AB to embark on a lecture tour in conjunction with the publication of the October issue of *Mother Earth*, commemorating the fifth anniversary of Leon Czolgosz's death, hoping the activity would ease the depression that had troubled AB since his release from prison on 18 May 1906. Initially engaged by the idea of a tour, AB spoke at Albany, Syracuse, and Pittsburgh before his sudden disappearance in Cleveland. EG, having opposed AB's return to Pittsburgh so soon after his release, feared that he was either kidnapped by Pittsburgh authorities or that he had killed himself. AB, seriously considering suicide, had purchased a gun and wandered to Buffalo, seeking anonymity. After a day, he returned to New York City, where he spent two days wandering the city exhausted, ill, and, as EG recalled in *Living My Life*, "in constant terror of meeting anyone"(*LML*, p. 389). For a report denying AB's kidnapping, see *New York Tribune,* 27 October 1906, p. 8.

Essay in *MOTHER EARTH*

November 1906

Police Brutality.

Liberty by the grace of the police and the might of the club was again brought home to us in the most brutal and unspeakable manner. A club of young boys and girls, peaceably assembled Saturday night, October 27th, to listen to a discourse as to whether or not Leon Czolgosz was an Anarchist.[1] At the close of the meeting three of the speakers—Julius Edelson,[2] M. Moscow,[3] and M. Rubinstein—were arrested and placed under $1,000 bail each. Tuesday, October 30th, a meeting was called to protest against the arrest of these boys and the suppression of free speech. Mr. Bolton Hall, H. Kelly,[4] Max Baginski and myself were announced to speak. The meeting proceeded in absolute order, with Julius Edelson, who had meanwhile been released on bail through Mr. Bolton Hall, as the first speaker. He had spoken barely twenty minutes when several detectives jumped on the platform and placed him under arrest, while twenty-five police officers began to club the audience out of the hall. A young girl of eighteen, Pauline Slotnikoff, was pulled off a chair and brutally dragged across the floor of the hall, tearing her clothing and bruising her outrageously. Another girl, fourteen years of age, Rebecca Edelson,[5] was roughly handled and put under arrest, because she failed to leave the hall as quickly as ordered. The same was done to three other women—Annie Pastor, Rose Rogin,[6] and Lena Smitt—for no

1. The 27 October meeting was held at the Progressive Library, 106 Forsyth Street, New York City.
2. Julius Edelsohn was a New York anarchist and the older brother of Rebecca Edelsohn, whom EG took into her home when Rebecca was a teenager. Julius edited a short-lived Yiddish anarchist paper, *Leben un Kamf*, in New York in 1906, then moved to San Francisco where in 1909 he donated money to the San Francisco Free Speech League in support of EG. He also helped organized EG's May 1912 meetings in Los Angeles after the San Diego Free Speech Fight. He later started an anarchist colony in New York state's Catskill Mountains.
3. Max Moscow was a New York individualist anarchist who opposed violence. All three men—Edelsohn, Moscow, and Rubinstein—were charged with "criminal anarchy" under the New York state law (Penal Code, Section 468) passed in 1902, in the wake of the McKinley assassination, to prevent anarchist gatherings.
4. EG abbreviates Harry Kelly's name.
5. Rebecca Edelsohn was an anarchist militant who lived in EG's home as a teenager; she became AB's companion in late 1907.
6. Rose Rogin would later be active at the Ferrer Center. She became the companion of Louis Levine, and their son, Valentine Rogin-Levine (1907–1982), would attend the Modern School at Stelton, New Jersey.

Document from the City Magistrate's Court on the occasion of Goldman's 2 November 1906 arrest, noting questions that she "refused" to answer on "advice of Counsel," as explained in the handwritten note on the right side of the official form. (Municipal Archives, Department of Records and Information Services, City of New York)

other reason except that they were unable to reach the bottom of the stairs fast enough to suit the officers. I was about to leave when one of the officers struck me in the back, and put me under arrest.

Fortunately, Mr. Bolton Hall and H. Kelly could not be present at the meeting; they, too, might have been clubbed out of the hall.

Six women and four men were packed like sardines into a patrol-wagon and hustled off to the station house, where we were kept in vile air and subjected to vulgar and brutal annoyance by the police until the following morning; then we were brought before a magistrate and put under $1,000 bail each for *assault*. Fancy girls of fourteen and eighteen, of delicate physique, assaulting twenty-five two-hundred-and-fifty-pounders!

If we as a nation were not such unspeakable hypocrites, we should long since have placed a club instead of a torch in the hand of the Goddess of Liberty—the police mace is not merely the symbol, but the very essence of our "liberty and order."

Emma Goldman

Mother Earth 1 (November 1906): 2–3.

To JEAN E. SPIELMAN et al.

New York, 3 November 1906

DEAR COMRADE SPIELMAN & GROUP.

Troubles come upon Troubles. I was too ill to continue my tour; upon my return to N. Y. I find more trouble.

I suppose you have all read in the last Freie Arb. Stimme[1] & the daily papers about the arrest of our comrades, among them Emma Goldman. I do not at all agree with Yanovsky that the original meeting of the Progressive Library was a mistake.[2] We have a perfect right to discuss any questions we wish, and as last month was the 5th anniversary of Czolg's death, it was quite fitting to use the occasion to discuss the questions involved in the act of Czolgosz. I think Yanovsky & the Fr. A. Stimme are becoming entirely too "respectable", too anxious about "good public opinion". It is this fear of adverse public sentiment that created the principle "Religion is a private affair".[3] It is not important whether anybody knew Cz. or not; it is not important whether he was an An. or not. But it is important that we should have courage enough to discuss & explain the conditions that produce a Czolgosz. And the meeting was for that very purpose.

But whether we agree with the boys of the Progressive Library or not—our comrades are in trouble & it is our duty to come to their aid. The case is a good deal more serious than Yanovsky thinks, as he was not present at the last hearing in court, Friday 4 P.M. The Fr. A. Stimme was already in print then.

It stands now thus—The girls & boys under arrest may all come off with a heavy fine an a few months workhouse. Some of the girls could not possibly go to workhouse, they are of too delicate a physique to stand it. We'll need money to pay their fines. As to Ike Edelson[4] & E. Goldman, I am afraid that things look dark for them. They are held under the new N. Y. Criminal Anarchy Law[5] which makes almost every Anarchistic utterance a crime, punishable with $2000 fine & 10 years prison. Both Ike & Emma will be tried under this law, and the evidence against E. is the October number of Mother Earth—the Czolgosz number. We are going to make a hard fight, but we need money, much & at

---

1. The Yiddish-language anarchist paper *Fraye Arbeter Shtime,* edited by Saul Yanovsky from 1899 to 1919, was generally known by the transliteration of its title in German, *Freie Arbeiter Stimme.*
2. A reference to the 27 October meeting held at the Progressive Library in New York City (see "Police Brutality," Article in *Mother Earth,* November 1906, above) to discuss whether Leon Czolgosz, who assassinated President McKinley, was an anarchist.
3. A position adopted by Saul Yanovsky and other anarchists at the newspaper *Freie Arbeiter Stimme.*
4. AB refers to Julius Edelsohn.
5. The New York Criminal Anarchy Law (Penal Code, Section 468) was passed in 1902, in the wake of the assassination of President McKinley.

once. What money we had of "M. E." we used up for lawyers etc. We are broke now. We owe $238 to the printer, not counting the Nov. number. And we need money for the coming trial & present expenses relating to this case. We appeal to all comrades to do their utmost to aid us—both the existence of Mother Earth, the safety of our comrades & the right of Anarchists to speak & write in N. Y. are at stake. Come at once to our aid. Moneys to be sent to

> Defence Fund,
> Mother Earth,
> 217 Madison Sq. Sta. NY.

Wake up our comrades & the public. Inform us at once of your intentions; also whether you need more "Mother Earth's", as you may have a great demand for the October number; advertise it as containing the article for which E. G. is to be prosecuted.

Fraternally
Alex. Berkman
Emma Goldman

P.S. I regret very much that I was unable to come to Chicago. It was impossible—physically & mentally—to continue the tour. If it were not for this new trouble I should be resting up in retirement now. Greetings to all friends. Alex B.

ALS, Jean Spielman Papers, MnHi. In AB's handwriting.

Article in *MOTHER EARTH*

December 1906

As to "Crammers of Furnaces."

A Reply to E. C. Walker's Article in No. 46 "Truth Seeker."

It requires a very brave mind to be just to one's opponent. We are apt, only too often, to misstate facts in order to gain victory in an argument or discussion. But the really honest man, the truly broadminded, scorns such tactics; to him the triumph based on falsehood is bitter fruit.

This was the thought that persisted and kept obtruding itself at our perusal of Mr. E. C. Walker's article "Crammers of Furnaces and Sitters on Safety Valves."[1] Perhaps the article might have never been written had Mr. Walker realized that sincerity in literature and honesty towards opponents are as desirable as good weight and full measure in the matter of groceries. Or may be that, the opportunity being given, the temptation to lecture Anarchists on Anarchism was very, very strong and—Mr. Walker weak? Has he again succumbed to the passion for reiterating the claim—as ancient as it is stupid—that the Anarchist-Communists have no right to be called Anarchists.

Mr. Walker waxed eloquent over the "crime" of holding Czolgocz memorial meetings. As a matter of fact, no such memorial meetings took place and none were contemplated. The meeting in question was called for the purpose of discussing whether Czolgocz was an Anarchist or not.[2] We claim the right of discussing—even under the present iniquitous law—whatever subject interests us. If free speech and free press mean anything, they mean freedom of discussion. We, therefore, claim the right to discuss how it is and why it is that a native born American, in this—politically the most advanced—country, the "land of opportunity," enjoying universal adult suffrage, should wish to kill the President of the United States, elected as that official is by a majority of

---

1. Edwin Cox Walker's article "Crammers of Furnaces and Sitters on Safety Valves" was printed in the November 1906 issue of the *Truth Seeker* (no. 46), reprinted in the 22 November 1906 issue of *Lucifer, the Lightbearer,* and also reproduced as the pamphlet *Liberty vs. Assassination* (New York: Edwin C. Walker, 1907). In the name of fairness, *Lucifer* editor Lillian Harman appended to her reprint of the Walker article EG's account of the meeting (see "Police Brutality," Article in *Mother Earth,* November 1906, above). *The Truth Seeker,* the principal periodical of the freethought movement, was founded in 1873 in Paris, Illinois, by De Robigne Mortimer Bennett, a member of the National Liberal League (organized in 1876 and known after 1884 as the American Secular Union).

2. On 27 October 1906, New York City police arrested Julius Edelsohn, Max Moscow, and Max Rubenstein for speaking before a meeting at the Progressive Library (106 Forsyth Street). They were charged with "criminal anarchy" under the New York law (Penal Code, Section 468).

Goldman posing for a photograph for the *Chicago Daily News* in 1906. The photograph was probably taken during one of her two tours to the city that year, either in mid- to late February or in late May through late June. The book she is holding is *Towards Democracy* by Edward Carpenter. (Chicago Historical Society)

the voting population, in accordance with our political institutions. The Czolgocz act was an entirely new phenomenon on the horizon of our country,—neither sectional feeling nor personal interest played any part in the act. A social phenomenon of this character should, in our estimation, receive our most earnest attention; it should be intelligently discussed in order to help us arrive at a better understanding of causes, and at a solution, if possible, of effects.

An unpopular subject? Granted. Shall freedom of speech, then, mean the discussion of only such subjects as are popular? And is the sex question a popular subject? And yet Mr. Walker has been discussing that question for more years than some of us can boast of since our birth. And we venture to say that the sex question is more obnoxious to the great American public than the McKinley episode.

"When a minority drops the pen of reason," says Mr. Walker, "and draws the sword of physical force, does it expect still to be opposed by reason and waved back by olive branches?" Not at all, Mr. Walker. It is true Czolgocz drew the sword; he paid the penalty *without a murmur.* We, however, are using the pen of reason. On what grounds, then, should we be persecuted any more than the so-called philosophical Anarchists? And does not Mr. Walker know that eight out of the twelve arrested and held for criminal court were mere spectators,[3] and that one of the chief speakers at the alleged "memorial" Czolgocz meeting—Mr. Moscow—is a comrade of—Mr. E. C. Walker, an Individualist Anarchist absolutely opposed to violence.

We are open and avowed Revolutionists; but we defy any one to produce a single line from any English Anarchist paper or magazine published in this country within the last twenty-five years where assassination is advocated or even implied. And if this be true, can a just and honest man maintain that the followers of the Communist-Anarchist school of Thought should be treated as criminals?

Yes, literary honesty is a rare jewel, Mr. Walker. If you read in an article in "Mother Earth" that "Czolgocz was a soul in pain," you immediately declare the writer to be an apologist for Czolgocz. Is sympathy for an unfortunate man identical with justification of or apology for the man's act? As *real* Anarchists we neither condemn nor justify; our business is to try to understand, understand, understand, Mr. Walker. In view of this, is it not foolish to say, "Yes, the police have acted foolishly, badly; almost or quite as foolishly and badly as the Communist Czolgocz apologists?"

"To return to our examination of the policy of those who stand forth as apologists or quasi-apologists for political assassination in the United States: In the first place, as heretofore intimated"—thus spake Mr. Walker—"they are not Anarchists, for if Anarchism means one thing more than another, it means opposition to the government of man by man. To take a man's life without his consent is the last supreme step in governing him."

Let us see, Mr. Walker. Government is an invasive organization; it taxes people without their consent; it butchers Philippino men, women and children;[4] establishes bull pens

---

3. On 30 October EG and others held a meeting at the Manhattan Lyceum (66 East Fourth Street) to protest police suppression of the 27 October gathering. Billed as a key speaker with Bolton Hall, Max Baginski, and Harry Kelly, EG never had the opportunity to speak, but was arrested with ten others when police halted the proceedings midway through Julius Edelsohn's opening remarks. Edelsohn, out on $1,000 bail courtesy of Bolton Hall, was arrested along with EG, Rebecca Edelsohn, Lena Sweet (actually Lena Smitt or Smith, but named as Sweet on the arrest report), Annie Pastor, Pauline Schlechtinger (probably the Pauline Slotnikoff mentioned in EG's account of the incident in *Mother Earth*), Rose Rogin, Jacob Zitlen (elsewhere Jacob Veltin, Joseph Dillem, or Joseph Dillon), William Gordon, and Harry Lang. Most of those arrested and charged with "criminal anarchy" at the Manhattan Lyceum were young activists in their teens. In EG's case, this charge included articles printed in the October issue of *Mother Earth*, which were distributed at the meeting, commemorating the fifth anniversary of Leon Czolgosz's execution. EG, Julius Edelsohn, and Lena Smitt were further charged with inciting to riot, the rest with disorderly conduct. Bail was set at $1,000 each. The case, titled *People of New York v. William Gordon, et al.*, was dismissed by the grand jury on 9 January 1907. For more on this case, as well as the 6 January 1907 arrests of EG, AB, and John Coryell under the same criminal anarchy law, see the "Explanatory Note" in *EGP*, reel 56. For a transcript of the state's Criminal Anarchy Law, see *ME*, 1 (December 1906): 10–11.
4. A reference to the Philippine-American War (1899–1902). The Philippines, a colony of Spain for over 300 years, became an American colony after the naval defeat of Spain at Manila Bay on 1 May 1898,

at Idaho[5] and sends colored troops to inflame race prejudice, by allowing those troops to obtain liquor and then illtreat the people.[6] Government kidnaps men like Moyer and Haywood;[7] it violates its own laws and then delegates the secretary of war to give his official indorsement to the illegal acts.[8] In short, government and its representatives assassinate liberty at every step. At last a man arises who embodies in himself all the revolt of the people—he strikes down one of the invaders. According to Mr. Walker's logic he invades the invader. Is it not farcical to maintain that two persons can invade each other at the same time? Is this the celebrated "philosophic" logic?

We neither advocate nor advise acts of violence. But those who have come to realize that government is invasive of the liberty of the individual, can object to the assassination of tyrants on only two grounds—sentiment and expediency. Mr. Walker, who summons everything, except his own pet theories, to the bar of reason, would eliminate sentiment. Expediency is a matter of opinion and judgment.

As to that old, hoary chestnut about our not being Anarchists, do not permit it to worry

---

which ended the Spanish-American War. With President McKinley's "Benevolent Assimilation Proclamation" (21 December 1898), the United States declared its intention to annex the ceded Philippines, using military force if necessary. Encountering resistance from Filipino revolutionary forces led by Emilio Aguinaldo, the United States sent over 125,000 troops to the Philippines between 1899 and 1902. At least 34,000 Filipinos and 4,000 Americans died. Although President Theodore Roosevelt officially ended the Philippine-American War on 4 July 1902, the same proclamation also formally recognized a "second front" of the war—the resistance in the Mindanao Morolands—which would fuel the conflict between the United States military and Filipino nationalist forces until 1913.

5. A reference to the Coeur D'Alene, Idaho, strike by hardrock miners in 1899. Governor Frank Steunenberg declared martial law, which led to the suspension of the writ of habeus corpus and the calling of federal troops. Striking miners were arrested without warrants and held in small, dark cells known as "bull-pens."

6. A reference to the Brownsville Raid, which occurred on the night of 6 August 1906, when over 150 gunshots were fired on Elizabeth Street in Brownsville, Texas, killing a white bartender and injuring a police lieutenant. A group of African American soldiers from the Twenty-fifth infantry, which had arrived in Brownsville only two weeks earlier and had already encountered hostility from white civilians, was blamed for the "raid." In a highly controversial directive, President Theodore Roosevelt ordered the dishonorable discharge of 167 of the black soldiers. Although many observers attributed the incident to reckless drinking and carousing, the guilt of the accused remained a contested issue. It was suggested that white civilians staged the shootings, hoping to force the battalion out of town. In 1972 the Secretary of the Army reversed Roosevelt's order.

7. On 30 December 1905, former Idaho Governor Frank Steunenberg was killed by a bomb that exploded as he opened the front gate of his house. Incontrovertible evidence was found linking a drifter named Harry Orchard to the bombing. On 17 February 1906, Western Federation of Miners (WFM) leaders Charles Moyer, William (Big Bill) Haywood, and George Pettibone were arrested in Colorado without warrants on suspicion of conspiracy in the murder. Pinkerton Detective James McParland headed the investigation and apparently pressured Orchard to implicate the people whom Idaho officials referred to as the "inner circle" of the WFM, ignoring the fact that none of the accused were in Idaho at the time and that state and federal laws prohibited their extradition from Colorado. Amid widespread protest, Moyer, Haywood, and Pettibone were indicted on 6 March and remained in prison for the next year. In the end, Orchard's testimony was found to be insufficient to prove conspiracy.

8. Possibly a reference to Secretary of War Elihu Root's defensive response to criticism generated by U.S. military atrocities in the Philippines.

you, Mr. Walker. We shall continue our Communist-Anarchist education of the people, and for the rest, let posterity judge.

Emma Goldman,
Alexander Berkman,
H. Kelly.
Nov. 20, 1906.

(The "Truth Seeker" declined to print the above article on the ground that the "editor thought it best not to open up another discussion." Since it was Mr. Walker's article in the "Truth Seeker" that really opened up the discussion, we think it strange that a liberal paper should decline hearing the other side.—The Editor.)

Mother Earth 1 (December 1906): 21–24.

Editorial in **MOTHER EARTH**

December 1906

To My Readers.

The birth of "Mother Earth" was an eventful day for me. For years I longed to create a medium through which I might express myself in words more durable than oral language. The necessity was not merely subjective; conditions, too, called for the clarification of much-befogged ideas,—not merely from the narrow party standpoint, but on the broad basis of a better and nobler life.

The outlook for such a magazine seemed very favorable. An artist friend promised a theatrical performance, the proceeds of which were to establish a solid financial foundation for the undertaking. Alas, the conspiracy of circumstances! Owing to many unforeseen obstacles and difficulties, the performance was only a partial success,[1] and the greater part of the proceeds was swallowed up by the necessity of changing the original name, "Open Road," to that of "Mother Earth."[2]

Immediately on its appearance, however, the magazine enlisted the interest of a large circle of sympathizers and friends. All prospects pointed to success.

Then came the Summer, with its hot and sultry weather. Somebody has said that a Revolution would be impossible in July—"Mother Earth," too, suffered from the same cause, the revenue of the magazine largely depending on the sales at the various radical and liberal meetings, which are quite inactive during the Summer months.

Thanks to the active interest of a few friends, however, I was enabled to fertilize the soil, hoping that with cooler weather would come the harvest.

My expectations were amply justified. August, September and October brought a host of new subscribers and a great demand for single copies.

Then the Police Department got busy. What on earth is there for them to do, but to hound Anarchists?! Thus it happened that they raided two meetings, clubbed the audiences, arrested twelve persons and confiscated a considerable part of the October issue of "Mother Earth."[3]

---

1. In appreciation for EG's management of the Russian theater troupe bearing his name, Pavel Orlenev offered to stage a benefit performance of August Strindberg's *Miss Julie* to support EG's desire to publish an anarchist cultural and political magazine. Unfortunately, creditors soon arrested Orlenev and temporarily closed the theater, rendering Orlenev too distressed to rehearse the new material. His substitute performance of Ibsen's *Ghosts,* already familiar to the public, failed to draw sufficient crowds. This, combined with inclement weather on the performance night, rendered the benefit a financial disaster.
2. See "The Open Road," Appeal to Max Metzkow, 20 January 1906, above.
3. See two articles in *Mother Earth:* "Police Brutality," November 1906, and "As to 'Crammers of Furnaces,'" 20 November 1906, above.

Not satisfied with this arbitrary and highhanded proceeding, the police have since kept up their brutal persecution, closing radical meetings, terrorizing hallkeepers and audiences, and threatening them with arrest.

"Mother Earth" depends largely upon the sale of single copies, averaging monthly about eighty dollars; the action of the authorities has resulted in almost extinguishing that source of revenue. Some of our liberals, ever courageous in fighting dead gods, have been so frightened by the sight of a detective that they have entirely withdrawn "Mother Earth" from sale at their meetings. And yet the postal authorities continue to pass the magazine through the mails!

Through all this unwonted activity of the police can be plainly seen the determination to suppress the spreading of Anarchism, and particularly of "Mother Earth." Even our masquerade ball, a simple social affair, was invaded by the presence of uniformed Comstocks who left nothing undone to create a disturbance.[4] Fortunately, nothing happened; but the depressing effect made enjoyment impossible, resulting in financial loss.

All this, however, shall not influence in the least my determination to continue the magazine. Neither shall police persecution nor personal danger deter me from voicing my ideas. Are the readers and friends of "Mother Earth" willing to assist me?

A Sustaining Fund for the magazine has been suggested, and a number of friends have already contributed towards it. I should ask all those desirous to aid to come forward soon, that I may know what to expect.

At this writing I am unable to say what the charge against me will result in.[5] In case of my conviction and imprisonment, "Mother Earth" will continue. Comrades Alexander Berkman and John R. Coryell,[6] aided by Voltairine De Cleyre, Max Baginski and other able contributors[7] have consented to publish the magazine.

But whatever the future may bring, a Sustaining Fund is an immediate necessity.

EMMA GOLDMAN.

Mother Earth 1 (December 1906): 7–8.

4. The *Mother Earth* Masquerade Ball was held on 23 November 1906, at Webster Hall in New York City to raise money for the magazine and, according to an announcement in *Freiheit,* for the defense of EG and others arrested on 30 October. Police raided the ball, ordered people to leave, and forced the owner to close the hall.
5. EG was the only person arrested on 30 October who had been accused of "exhibiting anarchistic tendencies." She was held on two charges: one related to articles printed in *Mother Earth,* the other for inciting to riot. Judge Cornell, who presided at the indictment, had expressed his horror over the articles published in *Mother Earth,* and each person on trial faced a possible ten-year imprisonment.
6. John Russell Coryell was one of the small group EG convened to launch what would become *Mother Earth.*
7. Harry Kelly was also a principal contributor and member of the group that supported the launching of *Mother Earth.*

Interview in the *OHIO STATE JOURNAL*

Columbus, 8 March 1907

High Priestess of Anarchy Here

Emma Goldman Arrives to Give Three Lectures on Economic Conditions.

Says Conditions Are Worse in America Than in Europe— Not Anarchists' Head.

Emma Goldman, the anarchist, arrived in Columbus yesterday afternoon from Cleveland. In an interview she declared that conditions in America are worse than in Europe, and denied that she had ever advocated violence, explaining that it is contrary to the doctrines which she advocates. She ridiculed Columbus police and newspapers because she was refused the use of a hall in which to speak, saying that she was condemned without a hearing, and contrasting the course with that of Mayor Johnson in Cleveland.[1]

When Miss Goldman reached Columbus she was immediately taken in charge by representatives of the International Radical association, the local organization which has arranged for her to lecture here today, tomorrow and Sunday night. Use of the hall over H. M. Stone's saloon, 182 South Fourth street, it is said, was finally secured for her addresses. She is the guest of the local organization, which has engaged a room for her in the residence of Mrs. Rosie Baker, 446 South Eleventh street.

NO BELIEVER IN VIOLENCE.

"I never advocated violence," she said last evening. "It is contrary to the teachings of anarchism. Violence comes from a few individuals who cannot wait for the conditions for which we are working to come about in a natural way. The pressure and grinding of the authorities makes them wild for relief. They imagine that the removal of two or three persons will change conditions.

"I see the newspapers and police here have been making a lot of trouble," said the high priestess of anarchy, by way of greeting to the reporter. "That is where they always make fools of themselves. They must think I am dangerous. Why don't they wait and see what I have to say before they condemn me? They always imagine a lot of things. They adopt the surest method to draw a big crowd to my meetings. There will be no trouble and I will talk here three nights.

1. Tom Johnson (1854–1911) was a single-taxer and the Progressive mayor of Cleveland from 1901 to 1909. A millionaire utility magnate and steel mill owner, Johnson lobbied for equitable taxation and municipal ownership of street railroads and utilities in Cleveland.

"As I came here from Cleveland this afternoon they told me you have 3 1/2-cent car fare, largely through the efforts of Tom Johnson. It is a pity his influence does not extend to this city in other things. Since he has been mayor there never was a policeman at a meeting of anarchists in Cleveland. No meeting was ever stopped or broken up, either. I have spoken there for ten years and never had a particle of trouble.

"We have grown so rapidly that conditions here are worse than they are in Europe. There is more oppression and less freedom. With the possible exception of Russia, where things are abnormal just now, there is no country in the world that offers less opportunity for the individual. A few get all the money and spend in dissipation the earnings of the slaves who produce the wealth. I have traveled throughout Europe. Never, outside of this country, did a policeman in uniform attend our meetings. They stay on the outside and only enter if it is necessary to quell disturbance."

"If that is true, why does the flood of immigration continue to pour in?"

"They do not come with a hope of bettering their condition. Many of them have relatives. There are still lots of undeveloped natural resources here. Most of them have been so oppressed at home that they are restless. They want anything that is a change, hoping through that to secure relief. They are worse off here than at home."

"What has been the effect of the law against admitting anarchists to this country?"

"More have come here since the law was passed than ever before. When you attempt to tell people they can't do a thing, that is what they will want to do. The only result of the law is to compel people to lie. Instead of declaring truthfully, as they come in, that they are anarchists, they deny it. Nobody has been kept out.

"Frequently it is claimed that at the meeting of some society of anarchists, the death of one in authority has been decreed, and his assassin selected. What is back of those stories?"

"NO TRUTH IN THEM."

"Absolutely nothing except the systematic misrepresentation of anarchy. That never has been and never will be. It is contrary to our teachings. We believe in the individual. We are against all government. We think that this country is large enough, and has resources enough to satisfy all. The stories are false because to be true it would be necessary for one to tell another what to do. We do not believe in that."

It is generally said, and understood, that anarchists in this country, are largely composed of foreigners who have for generations been deprived of the opportunity to secure an education?

"That is as far from the truth as it could be. The doctrine of anarchy taught in this country was founded by Americans. It originated with men of the Concord school.[2] David Thoreau, Josiah Warren and Stephen Pearl Andrews[3] were anarchists. They were associates of Wil-

---

2. Throughout the nineteenth century, Concord, Massachusetts, was a gathering place for American intellectuals. Among its residents were Henry David Thoreau and Ralph Waldo Emerson, both American-born and prominent advocates of the rights of the individual taking precedence over the authority of the state. EG, following a tradition of nineteenth-century American anarchists, connected early Amer-

liam Lloyd Garrison, Wendell Phillips[4] and Emerson. Those men were anarchists, too. The first considered the economic side of the question, while the latter were more concerned with the political side. In my lecture tomorrow night I shall refer to Thoreau's book, "Civil Disobedience," which might be called the textbook of anarchy in this country.

"In Europe the recruits to anarchy come from the middle classes. They are the best educated and most intelligent. They are able to see the truth. They leave home, not because they have to, but because they can no longer stand the conditions and want to help educate the people. That is what our work is."

ABUSE OF NEW IDEAS.

"There never was an advanced theory that was not villified and abused. What men cannot understand they reject. It was so with abolition, and all the great movements of history. Before anarchism is adopted it will be necessary for the people to be in such a state of mind that they will dwell in peace, allowing each to live his own life, free from interference."

"How would crime be punished?"

"When you remove the conditions which create crime it will cease. We have policemen and armies now, but crime is on the increase. It is because all the time the producers are getting less of that to which they are entitled, and are driven to acts for which there would be no temptation if all had an equal opportunity."

"You have a big problem, if you expect to so elevate all the people that jealousies, enmities, violence and hate will disappear. It must be so vast that it is discouraging?"

"Not at all. On the contrary, I am greatly encouraged. The prospects are brighter each day. We believe that each country must work out its own salvation. That is why the foreign anarchists who come here work among their own people. They talk to those of their own language and customs about the conditions at home.

"Only Americans, or those who have become Americans, attempt to talk in English, or about our country. I was in this country ten years before I ever appeared in public. I have been here 22 years now. I know conditions here as they are, and I would like to know if I have not a right to talk to my fellow Americans."

NO PHOTOGRAPHS.

"I am sorry to refuse you, but I have none," she said when asked for a photograph. "I never gave a photograph to a newspaper. They have got them from the rogues' galleries

---

ican political thinkers with anarchist thought. See, for example, *The Famous Speeches of the Chicago Anarchists* (Chicago: Socialistic Publishing Society, 1886).

3. Josiah Warren, an American-born Midwesterner and an anarchist, founded several colonies based on his theory of labor exchange. Stephen Pearl Andrews, an American-born Texan and strong individualist driven out of Houston for his advocacy of abolition, co-founded an utopian colony with Warren in 1851 at Brentwood, Long Island.
4. William Lloyd Garrison and Wendell Phillips were prominent abolitionists, whose principled advocacy of the rights of the individual EG considered the essence of anarchist thought, especially because both Garrison and Phillips saw the Church and the State as barriers to individual freedom for slaves and freemen.

Sketch by C. W. Jefferys in the 14 March 1907 *Toronto Star* depicting Goldman speaking on "Misconceptions of Anarchism" at the Labor Temple in Toronto. (Reprinted with permission of Torstar Syndication Services)

in Chicago and New York," she explained with a laugh. "They do not look much like me, though. The pictures were not taken with my consent, and when the police have it in for a person they will lose no chance to misrepresent."

The woman, who is a native of Russia, and not far from 50 years old,[5] talks rapidly and aggressively. In her conversation she makes frequent reference to the purity of social conditions, falling back on that for justification of her theories. She makes a living as a professional nurse, but devotes much of her time to the publication of a magazine in New York, where she makes her headquarters. She explains that when "on tour" her expenses are paid by the local organizations where she appears, but she receives no pay.

"I am not the head of the anarchists in this country," she said deprecatingly. "I would hate to think that all the anarchists are depending on my brains. There is no head to anarchy. If there was, it would not be anarchy."

Ohio State Journal, 8 March 1907, p. 9.

---

5.   In fact, at this time EG was 38 years old.

Ernest Crosby

La sete di dovizie e di potere domina ed urge cosi' sciaguratamente ogni ora della vita nostra, turbandone e corrompendone le fonti vive, che noi la trascorriamo intera senza dedicare nè un minuto nè un pensiero al carattere, all'intelligenza, ai principii.

Freme in noi un'unica ossessione: arrivare, arrivare ad ogni costo! Se il successo si deve chiedere ad umani olocausti scellerati, se la fortuna deve ediñcarsi sullo strazio di tenace vite dilaniate nelle fabbriche, se la vittoria deve carpirsi tra l'ecatombe, non importa—purchè si arrivi.

Accade così che i cuori più nobili e le menti più elette passino inosservati ed ignorati fra la turba affannosa di cui hanno voluto elevare il tenore di vita, il sentimento della fierezza, il retaggio della libertà.

Così è accaduto di Ernest Crosby, uno dei più generosi figli che dal grembo di questa America cinica sieno nati, e che la morte ci rapì amaramente or sono sei settimane.

Oh, se egli fosse stato un armeggione della politica torbida, un arrivista senza scrupoli e senza pudore, un ladro avventurato del lavoro e del sudore degli umili, sarebbe dalle colonne del grandi quotidiani della pa lanca e della menzogna salito unanime tra gli incensi profusi e le lacrime bugiarde l'inno magnifico alle sue virtù!

Tacquero: nessuno mostrò accorgersi che una grande intelligenza ed un nobile cuore si erano spenti per sempre.

Gli è che Ernest Crosby era un innamorato del popolo, di cotesta immensa forza umana che lotta angosciata dalla tenebra e dal dolore, ed in mezzo alla quale egli procedeva agitando la fiaccola della speranza e della libertà.

"Ogni araldo d'emancipazione trovava un fratello in lui che si schierava con Tolstoi contro ogni ipotesi, contro ogni concezione dello Stato; che per la libertà del pensiero, del pensiero anarchico sopratutto, aveva combattuto e combatteva con un fervore e con un'energia che nessuno in questa nostra repubblica aveva osato per lo innanzi spiegare".

Così, parlando di lui, conchindeva recentemente un altro eletto spirito americano. Leonard Abbott: cosi noi che l'abbiamo intimamente conosciuto lamentiamo la perdita di Ernest Crosby come quella di uno dei più puri, dei più gagliardi campioni del nostro Ideale.

Perchè il Crosby fu anarchico piuttosto che socialista, e la sua predilezone non originava da dispetti, da capricci o da miserie ma da una ragione logica e da un esame coscienzioso delle due dottrine.

Uno studio accurato ed una diligente inchiesta aveva egli condotto sulla concezione socialista, e la sua ostilità al socialismo non si era che accentuata. Ciò spiega come egli alla conferenza tenutasi alla Stoke Mansion di Noroton, lo scorso anno, egli prendesse parte cogli individualisti piuttosto che coi socialisti; e come egli prendesse il suo posto di combattimento discutendo in contradditorio con Jack London l'ultima volta che questi parlò a New York.

L'ultimo articolo che egli mi mandò ribadiva i giudizii di Lafcadio Hearn che "il socialismo è una reversione a forme sociali superate"; e conchiudeva: "I socialisti hanno diritto a tutte le nostre simpatie in quanto lottano contro le iniquità presenti, ma essi seguono una diagnosi sbagliata quando coteste ingiustizie derivano dall'individualismo. A valle delle nostre sommità sociali noi abbiamo da parte del monopolio e del pregiudizio una vera negazione dell'individualismo, e, per me, unico efficace rimedio sta nel rendere l'individuo sempre più padrone di sè stesso, non nell'assoggettarlo schiavo di organizzaziuni dissepolte dagli ipogei della storia."

Ed ogni qualvolta io ho cercato di rimuovere il Crosby da questo sno atteggiamento convitandolo alle battaglie del socialismo libertario egli rispondeva che "simpatizzava colle idee nostre me giudicava il socialismo marxista una minaccia allo sviluppo dell'umanità e della libertà".

Mi scriveva nel corso di queste aminchevoli discussioni: "uno stato socialista richiederebbe in tutti i suoi citadini un'anima d'angeli che soltanto secoli e secoli possono maturare. In quest'attesa parmi che l'attingere un po' di giustizia sia campo abbastanza vasto al lavoro politico; all'infuori della politica noi non possiamo che fomentare una larga corrente di cooperazione. Certo è tentazione grande quella di lavorare ad un movimento internazionale, ma io non posso farlo: che pensereste di me se lavorassi a pro' della chiesa cattolica romana quando sapete che tutti i suoi dogmi ripugnano alla mia ragione? Mi conforta del resto l'essere in buona compagnia : nè Tolstoi nè Whitman. ne sono certo. si sarebbero mai ascritti ad un partito e neppure Carpenter, per quanto posso dai suci scritti giudicarne. Sarei lietissimo di associarmi all opera vostra tanto più che potrei portarvi un po della mia esperienza di vecchio repubblicano; la conscienza non vuole. Ma vi sarò grato se me vorete annoverare compagno in questa larga famiglia socialista in cui possono stare Edward Carpenter, Eugenio Debs, George Herron e Maxim Gorki.

Il ritratto di William Morris pendeva alle pareti del suo studio: di Carpenter aveva riassunto e volgarizzate le idee per gli americani. di Debs e di Herro fu amico sincero, e Massimo Gorki aveva repetutamente visitao a State Island e nelle vallate di Adirondacks.

Emma Goldman.

Obituary in *CRONACA SOVVERSIVA*

Barre, Vt., 16 March 1907

Ernest Crosby

Such is the calamitous hold of the lust for lucre and for power upon every last hour of our lives, miscarrying and corrupting their vital essence, that our entire lives are passed with not a minute, not a thought to spare for character, intellect, principles.

We have but a single obsession: success, success at any price! Should success require heinous sacrifice of human beings, should our fortune have to be built upon devastation of lives slowly shredded in factories, should the price of victory be mass slaughter, no matter—just as long as it comes.

So it comes to pass that the noblest hearts and choicest minds go unremarked and ignored amid the weary masses whose quality of life, sense of pride and allotment of freedom they sought to increase.

So it was with Ernest Crosby, one of the most selfless sons to have sprung from the loins of this cynical America and whom death so cruelly snatched from us six weeks ago now.

Oh, if he had been a puller of strings in the murky business of politics, an unscrupulous, bare-faced parvenu, a successful thief of the toil and sweat of the poor, the columns of the major newspapers of the lying, money press would have been unanimous in singing splendid paeans to his virtues, to an accompaniment of clouds of incense and crocodile tears!

They said nothing: no one seemed to have noticed that a great intellect and noble heart had been stilled forever.

The late Ernest Crosby was in love with the people, with that immense human power that bridles at darkness and pain and among whom he walked brandishing the torch of hope and liberty.

"Every harbinger of emancipation found in him a brother who would line up, with Tolstoy, against every theory and every conception of the State: who had fought and was fighting still for freedom of thought and above all for anarchist thought, with an ardor and a vigor that no one in this republic of ours had ever previously dared display."[1]

Such was the conclusion that another choice American mind, Leonard Abbott, reached concerning him recently: so we who knew him intimately lament the loss of Ernest Crosby as the loss of one of our ideal's purest and most courageous champions.

---

1. This quote is taken from Leonard Abbott's article, "Some Reminiscences of Ernest Crosby" (*Mother Earth*, February 1907), from which EG drew extensively in writing her own obituary of Crosby.

Because Crosby was an anarchist rather than a socialist, and his partiality derived, not from resentments, whims or wretchedness, but rather from reasoned argument and from conscientious examination of the two doctrines.

He had carried out a painstaking study and diligent investigation into socialist teaching, and his hostility to socialism simply grew and grew. Which accounts for why, at the conference held in Stokes Mansion in Noroton last year,[2] he sided with the individualists rather than the socialists: and how he came to enter the lists by debating against Jack London the last time that the latter spoke in New York.

The last article he sent me underlined Lafcadio Hearn's[3] view that "Socialism is a reversion to obsolete forms of society," and he concluded: "Socialists deserve our every sympathy insofar as they struggle against the iniquities of the present, but they follow a mistaken diagnosis when they allege that such injustices derive from individualism. In the valleys below the towering peaks of our society, we find monopoly and prejudice offering an outright negation of individualism and, as I see it, the only effective remedy is to make the individual more and more his own master, not render him slavishly subject to organizations exhumed from the high watermarks of history."

And any time that I attempted to budge Crosby from this stance of his by inviting him to join in the fight for libertarian communism, his answer was that "whilst he was sympathetic to our thinking, he reckoned that Marxist socialism represented a threat to the growth of humanity and freedom."

In the course of such friendly exchanges, he wrote me: "A socialist State would require all of its citizens to possess an angelic disposition that could only be incubated over centuries. In the interim, the securing of a little more freedom offers scope aplenty for political work: and outside of politics we can do nothing more than offer encouragement to a broad tendency towards cooperation. True, the temptation to work towards an international movement is great, but I cannot: what would your opinion of me be if I were to work on behalf of the Roman Catholic church when you know that my reason finds its every teaching repugnant? Moreover I have the solace of knowing myself in good company: neither Tolstoy nor Whitman[4]—of this much I am sure—would ever have joined a party, any more than Carpenter[5] would, insofar as I can judge from his writings. I would be

2. The conference, which was held 3–6 March 1906, took place at the Noroton, Connecticut, mansion of Anson Phelps Stokes. The organizer of the conference was his son-in-law, Robert Hunter (1847–1942), a radical settlement worker and socialist author. Attendees of the conference included Arthur Brisbane, Albert Brisbane, Charles E. Russell, Victor Berger, and John Spargo. This "talk-fest," as Morris Hillquit called it, brought a new group of wealthy activists into the Socialist Party, including Charles E. Russell, Robert Hunter, Helen Stokes, J. G. Phelps Stokes, and Rose Pastor Stokes.
3. Patrick Lafcadio Hearn (1850–1904) was a writer of Greek and Irish ancestry and a translator and teacher whose articles, essays, and editorials spanned various topics, including Jewish culture and social science. Hearn played a major role in introducing Japanese culture to Europe and the United States.
4. Crosby was the leading proponent of Tolstoyan anarchism in the United States. Walt Whitman's work was enormously influential in the freethought and radical movements.
5. Crosby refers to Edward Carpenter, the British poet and social reformer.

very glad to associate myself with your endeavors, especially as I might offer you a little of my experience as an old republican, but my conscience will not allow it. I will, though, be grateful if you will count me as a comrade in the broad socialist family that can accommodate Edward Carpenter, Eugene Debs, George Herron[6] and Maxim Gorky."

William Morris's[7] portrait hung upon his study walls: he had condensed and popularized Carpenter's writings for an American readership. He was genuinely friendly with Debs and Herron and he had visited Maxim Gorky time and again in Staten Island and in the valleys of the Adirondacks.

Emma Goldman.

Cronaca Sovversiva, 16 March 1907, p. 1. Translated from Italian. EG signed and dated her obituary of Crosby 27 February.

6. George D. Herron, a Congregational minister, in 1906 co-founded with his partner Carrie Rand a school for the advancement of socialism. Named for his partner's mother, who financed it, the Rand School lasted fifty years.
7. William Morris was an English libertarian socialist, poet, writer, and designer.

MY DARLING.

Detroit police too have "awakened" last nights meeting was stopped and there is a like-lyhood of to days meeting being interfered with.[1] I am quite discouraged, not so much because I have no chance to speak, as but because my tour will be a material failure if the police continue in their conspiracy.

I am quite determined to return home, should my meetings be stopped in Chicago. Partly I wish it would happen, I have such a longing for you, my own and for our home. I never imagined, that I would suffer homesickness, real genuine homesickness. Is it far to 210 E 13[2] do you think? Or the sunshine and love I have left there, my precious *dush'*?[3] Do you not think it disgraceful to be so completely in love at my age? Dearest, dearest, I am writing this in Huldas frontroom, the same room where we met one another alone, alone in 14 years, such terrible strangers to each other.[4] You do not know how my soul bled, when I realized that you had turned from me, that through my own fault, I had lost you, at least. it seemed to me at the time. It was awful, awful. This morning when I woke, I laid perfectly still and my mind wandered to the morning, our first morning. Do you know *dush'*, that my face burned with shame that I should have been so close to you a stranger, a perfect stranger. And yet I did not feel strange to you, my whole being was full with joy of your release. This and all that occurred during these last 10 months, every detail every incident came back to me this morning, a horrible picture until that moment when I met you near Schaeffels. *Dush'*, I think at that moment our love was born, not until then. Until that day evening, Oct 27th (that date is burned with letters of fire into my mind) we really were strangers. But at that moment when I held on to your arm and looked into your face, I knew some wonderful light had lifted the veil from both of us, so that we could look into each other.[5] *Sasha* dear, it was then, that I became part of you and you of me. Dearest, dearest how wonderfull it all. One almost believes

---

1. Detroit police prevented EG from lecturing on 16 and 17 March. During this lecture tour, EG spoke on a number of topics, including "The Revolutionary Spirit in the Modern Drama," "Misconceptions of Anarchism," "The Building of True Character," and "Direct Action versus Politics" (*Mother Earth*, February 1907).
2. In March 1907, the offices of *Mother Earth* were moved from 308 East 27th Street back to 210 East 13th Street, where EG had been living.
3. EG writes the Russian term of endearment, *dush'*, for "dearest" or "darling," in Cyrillic characters.
4. EG and AB spent their first night together after AB's 18 May release from prison at the Detroit home of Carl Nold.
5. EG writes the Russian diminutive for Alexander, "Sasha," in Cyrillic characters.

First page of 17 March 1907 letter from Goldman to Berkman, reporting on the continued attempts by the police to suppress her meetings, most recently in Detroit. (Emma Goldman Archive, International Institute for Social History)

in miracles, in some superhuman forces. Tell me *Sasha* dear, if you can, when was your love for me born, how did that mysterious force take possession of you? You never spoke of it my precious one.

Mir ist heilig zu Mute bei der Erinnerung der Auferstehung unserer Liebe.[6]

6. "When I remember how our love arose my feeling is one of sacredness" (in German).

Do not think mir[7] superstitious dear, but I really think it very very wonderful, all that has happened during these 10 months. I must wake up from my dream and get back to reality I might have to speak this afternoon. I shall write something as soon, as I reach Chicago, tho I do not know, how good it will be, but my precious editor will put it into shape.

Dearest, why not finish your translation of Nettlau's article "The developement of Anarchism".[8] It must be somewheres in the desk drawers. It is a good article and would not take long to finish it. I have written to Max asking him to send ~~the~~ Com. & Obs. as soon as possible. I hope he does, I could translate them in a day.[9] I have made arrangements with Labadie[10] to send you some of the old Twentieth Centuries,[11] containing McCready, and Pentecost's articles.[12] You will surely find something interesting Have[13] could look them over for you and mark whatever is good. The papers will have to be returned to Labadie unimpared so please be careful. I am also writing to Voltairine[14] to send article. I think you will have enough for April.

The inclosed clipping will show you, that you are with me, I wish it were true. I mean, I wish you were here sweetheart. The pamphlate is very neat thank you darling. Dearest, how big is "our Capital? If only the damned police would leave my meeting alone, I could raise a considerable amount of money, tho I hardly think, I will make many subscribers, but the meetings are well attended and a great many copies sold. The Oct numbers,[15] goes like hotcakes. Please see, how many Octs we still have and let me know. I am sending the Feb number I have left over to the house, we will need them, we have very few at home.

Please send Natasha[16] 100 tickets, ~~they~~ the Russian Tea party takes place March 22nd, she will have an excellent chance to sell the tickets. Write her a letter with it please.

---

7. "Me" (in German).
8. Max Nettlau first wrote "The Historical Development of Anarchism" for serial publication in *Freiheit* between April and May, 1890. AB's translation was not published in *Mother Earth*.
9. Max Baginski wrote a monthly feature in *Mother Earth*, in German, entitled "Observations and Comments"; the columns were then translated by EG.
10. EG refers to Joseph Labadie.
11. *The Twentieth Century* (1888–1898) was a single-tax periodical, published in New York and edited by Hugh O. Pentecost from 1888 to 1892 and Thomas L. McCready until his death in 1890.
12. Thomas L. McCready (d. 1890) was an American single-taxer associated with the religious wing of the movement. He was also leader of the Anti-Poverty Society and co-founder of the New York single-tax organization in 1887. He wrote for Henry George's *The Standard* until political differences between himself and George emerged in the late 1880s. During their conflict he began writing for *The Twentieth Century* and by 1890 had become its associate editor, along with Hugh Pentecost who, at various times in his life, expressed both socialist and anarchist allegiances.
13. EG abbreviates Hippolyte Havel's last name. Havel, who accompanied EG back to America after the 1900 Paris anarchist conference, was working as an editor for *Mother Earth* at this time.
14. EG refers to Voltairine de Cleyre, the Philadelphia-based anarchist and freethinker. Nothing by her was published in the April issue.
15. The October 1906 *Mother Earth* was the Leon Czolgosz memorial edition.
16. Philadelphia anarchist Natasha Notkin.

Will mail this later, so that I can tell you whether or not, our meeting has taken place Let me press you to my heart, that longs and aches for you.

Devotedly your
Em.

Please take Grotsky Detroit out of the cards. Do not send him any more. ~~The~~ He has paid what he owed. That is all the money, I have received here so far.

5 p.m.

Dearest, the meeting was not permitted, the police was at the Hall in full force and everybody was barred. I am feeling wretched over our inability to do anything.

I will see, how things will turn out in Chicago and probably return sooner than we expected. Do you want me *dush'*? I want you badly. Will write from Chicago.

Affectionately E

Emma Clausen, grüßt dich innig. Sie war sehr enttäuscht dich nicht zu sehen in Oct.[17]

ALS, Emma Goldman Archive, IISH. On *Mother Earth* stationery. Street address (308 East 27th Street, New York) is struck out.

17. "Emma Clausen sends you heartfelt greetings. She was very disappointed not to see you in Oct" (translated from German). Dr. Emma Clausen (b. 1867) was a German-born anarchist, living in Detroit.

DEARES PRECIOUS TREASURE MINE,

I developed a terrible headache from anxiety of waiting for a word from you[.] I know it is foolish to be so uneasy, but you can not imagine, how I suffer through our seperation and the anxiety about you. I know you hate your occupation and justly so, I know, you have no comforts, how then should I not worry about you. I have not spent a restful moment since I left and the night, oh the terrible nights. I can not sleep and when I finally dose off, I have such terrible dreams about you. Dearest, *Sasha*[1] darling mine, I implore you, do not despair again. You will, you must free yourself from your business[2] and then we will arrange our lives in harmony with ourselves. I am sure we can *Sashenka*.[3] We will give ourselves to M E and then you must write *dush'*,[4] your book, yes sweetheart your book, it must be written and I want to help you through my love, my devotion. I am sure dearest, you will be able to write now after you have come out so big, so beautiful, so true. Dearest, you should not curse the plan of your printing shop, bear in mind, that our plan did not include the business, as it is now, that our aim was something different. Besides it was a necessary experience[.] It helped you to clarify yourself, your own inclination. Really dear, there is nothing to regret. It is a pitty about that fellow who is with you,[5] but after all you did not lure him into the scheme, he knew what he was doing, nor can you sacrifise your soul for his sake. Therefore *dush'* you will have to get out, you will problably be forced to, as you lack means to carry on the business. Darling, I should have suffered greatly, were I to see, that the business satisfies you that you are consumed by it. But now there is no reason to despair or to regret. My darling has retained himself has remained true and beautiful. What joy, what happyness. How I wish, I were near you to embrace and

1. EG writes "Sasha," a Russian diminutive for the name Alexander, in Cyrillic characters.
2. Around January 1907, AB started a cooperative printing shop to serve the anarchist movement and to keep himself busy enough to escape the depression he experienced upon his 1906 release from prison.
3. "Sashenka," another Russian diminutive for Alexander, is written in Cyrillic characters .
4. EG uses the Russian term of endearment, *Dush'*, for "dearest" or "darling" (written in Cyrillic characters) several times in the remainder of her letter.
5. EG had "induced a good comrade" to lend AB the money he needed to set up his printing business and begin working as a self-employed compositor. By March 1907, however, AB announced, "The intense competition in the printing trade, however, plus union conditions, which do not permit the compositor to perform pressman's work, soon convinced me that my plan was not feasible." AB found that hiring an additional pressman at union wages "necessitated the enlargement of the business, involving the usual business methods, etc. In short, I stood before the alternative of sacrificing either my principles or my business. I quit the business. I feel as if I were released from prison again" (April 1907 issue of *Mother Earth* 2: 108).

kiss you to show you my great love for you and above all, my great admiration and ~~love~~ esteem. Dearest, you should go out more, especially now with the spring at our doors. You ought to go to the Park Sundays. My meeting last Sunday,[6] was a tremendous success, I should judge at least 1200 people present. It was a Commune celebration. I have to speak at another one to night the Bohemian Anarchists have one. I have a meeting for every night, while I am here, it is a great strain, but I do not care. I want to rush my tour to get back to my darling lover, who means life, joy happiness to me. The great E G. You make me laugh *dush'*. I am more of the little sailor to day, than I have been 15 years ago. My greatness adds nothing to my life or the wealth of my nature. If I am prowd of anything, it is, that I have learned to appreciate real true value in human nature that I have learned the power of love. Everything else means naught to me. 1200 people applauded, waved hats and handkerchieves, screamed and yelled last night, when I finished, yet, I saw them not, I only saw one face, one soul, one being far away from me and yet so close, I could almost feel his warmth. And my soul cried for that being, all night long. Do you know who it is, can you guess it?

Dearest, never mind about the money now, I will get some. I inclose check for $25 by the end of this week I hope to send you 75 or $100 so that you can give Goldman half of our debt. *Dush'*, I need not tell you, that you can use all you need, but do not put any more money in your business it is really useless. Have the reminders of renewals been sent out? How are the returns? Those who fail to renew must be taken off the list, we can not afford to supply M E to those, who have not interest enough to pay for it. Of course we must give the subscribers a little time, but if they fail to renew by April, take them off. Has anyone paid for outstanding tickets from our ball? We ought to have an article about Most,[7] but who is going to write it? I will ask Max,[8] I am willing to translate what he writes, but I could say nothing about the man myself. Tomorrow I will make an effort to write my traveling notes. *Dush'* you will have to see Buckley and have a talk with him.[9] He must have M E attended to more carefully. Fancy him sending Livshis[10] 150 copies of Feb instead of March. I have written Havel[11] yesterday to imidiately forward more copies of March, also Oct numbers, if we have any left. That is, we must leave ourselves about 100 for subscribers.

I will write again soon. Dearest darling mine; please please, write me often, if only a postal, only do not keep me in suspense.

---

6. Probably a reference to EG's 18 March meeting in Chicago to commemorate the 1871 Paris Commune; she spoke in Yiddish to an audience of 800 anarchists.
7. EG refers to Johann Most, who had died on 17 March.
8. EG refers to Max Baginski, who wrote a short piece on Most for the April issue.
9. Buckley and Wood Company was a New York City company employed by *Mother Earth* to bind and mail the magazine. Edwin C. Wood was president and treasurer of the company.
10. EG refers to Jake and Annie Livshis.
11. EG refers to Hippolyte Havel, who was working with EG, AB, and Max Baginski in New York on the publication of *Mother Earth*.

Let me nestle close, close to your and in your strong passionate embrace, let me drink the joy of life the ectasy of our love

VOZLINBLENNII,[12] I AM ALL YOURS.

E

ALI, Emma Goldman Archive, IISH. On *Mother Earth* stationery, with subtitle as *A Monthly Magazine Devoted to Social Science and Literature* and address as 210 East 13th Street.

12. EG finishes her letter with another Russian term of endearment, *Vozlinblennii,* "beloved," written in Cyrillic characters.

To PETER KROPOTKIN

En route from San Francisco to Portland, 31 May 1907

DEAR COMRADE.

I am ashamed really to have kept you waiting for a reply to your kind note of Oct 28th.[1] I have no other excuse to give save the one, <u>no time</u>. Your letter arrived when eleven Comrades and myself were in the hands of the authorities with 1000$ bail each to furnish or to stay in Jail until our "protectors of order will deign to take up the cases.[2] As there were children of 14–16 years among the arrested, we worked hard to get them bailed, which with our experience of Grossman and McQueen[3] and your experience of some fellow in London was a very hard task. However thanks to the generosity of Mr. Bolton Hall[4] an several others, bail was secured. Then came the care for those who had been under arrest, the anxiety about the condition of Com Berkman who had collapsed on a tour[5] and of course the entire care of M E. and the earning of a livelyhood. You can readily see dear Comrade there was not much time left for letters other than those directly conected with the propagand. I was just begining to recuperate from the weight of the various responsibilities when my second arrest came on,[6] which again upset all my plans and preparations of a prolonged tour, for we soon realized that M.E could not exist unless a fund were raised. Again every minute of my time was taken, especially since I also had a series of lectures to prepare. Finally on the 3rd of March, I started on my tour; among

---

1. Written to Peter Kropotkin in Bromley, England, where he lived in exile with his family.
2. EG and her associates were arrested on 30 October 1906, at a meeting to protest the suppression of free speech. See "As to 'Crammers of Furnaces,'" Article in *Mother Earth*, 20 November 1906, above.
3. Rudolf Grossmann and William MacQueen were convicted of "inciting to riot" and sentenced to five years of hard labor for their speeches at a demonstration during the 1902 Paterson silk dyers strike. Released on bail pending appeals, both initially fled the country (see Letter to *La Questione Sociale*, 5 July 1902, above).
4. Bolton Hall posted $1,000 bail for the release of Julius Edelsohn, arrested at the 30 October meeting.
5. After embarking on a lecture tour in October 1906, Berkman suffered a nervous breakdown and disappeared for three days. See Notice in *Mother Earth*, "To the Readers of *Mother Earth*," November 1906, above.
6. On 6 January 1907, New York City police detectives arrested Goldman at Clinton Hall, where she was speaking on "The Misconceptions of Anarchism" to the Brooklyn Philosophical Association. She was charged with making "inflammatory" statements and for allegedly asserting that "It is ridiculous to think that society cannot get along without government, and . . . we will say to the government: 'Give us what belongs to us in peace, and if you do not give it to us in peace, we will take it by force.' As long as I live and will be able to express myself I will be opposed to government, and as my brain dictates, will use force against the government." Cited in *People of the State of New York v. Goldman, Berkman and C[oryel]l*, transcript, 11 January 1907, City Magistrate's Court, First Division, Third District, *EGP*, reel 56. For a detailed account by the man who chaired the Clinton Hall meeting, see John Russell Coryell, "A New Crime," *Lucifer*, 31 January 1907, p. 1. The case was later dismissed.

Cover of *Mother Earth* used between September 1906 and July 1907. It was replaced by a monthly table of contents in an effort to reduce costs. (By permission of the Kate Sharpley Library)

other letters that needed answering, I took your letter along, but until this minute I could not attend to it. It takes 36 hours from San Francisco to Portland, thats why I have time to attend to a large bundle of letters, I do not know, whether or not you read M E. If you do, you surely have read my report in April and May of our work in various cities up to Denver.[7] My tour has proven tremendiously successful morally as well as finnancially. I raised over 1200$ from sale of M E, various literature and subscribers and as traveling is high in America I can safely say, that nearly 1700$ were raised. This is the first tour of any consequence I have made since 1898.[8] You can not begin to imagine the tremendious growth of interest in Anarchism since that time. Halls were packed in every City, too small

7. EG visited Cleveland, Columbus, Toledo, Toronto, Detroit, Winnipeg, Salt Lake City, Sacramento, San Francisco, Chicago, Cincinnati, St. Louis, and Minneapolis.
8. EG's first cross-country tour included ten states and sixty-six meetings between February and June, 1898. See vol. 1, Chronology.

to hold the people and while that may be taken as an indication of curiosity seeking the fact that 117$ literature was sold in 6 meetings in San Francisco, 65$ in four meetings in Los Angelos ect, completely disproves any Idea of curiosity. No doubt the sensational talk in some of the papers,[9] preceeding my arrival brings out many idle people, but in general I found that the audiences was eager to listen and to be informed. Three lectures have aroused the greatest interest and attandance the country over, Misconceptions of Anarchism, The Revolutionary Spirit in Modern Drama" and Direct Action versus Political Action.[10] I never would have thought it possible that Direct Action would receive so much recognition. At a Debate between a political Socialist and myself at Los Angelos last Sunday before an audience of 3000 my opponent after the second round of argument abandoned his field and openly declared that the argument for direct action could no more be disputed than twice time two being four and the Audience was completely with us. Naturally, the political Socialists felt terribly disgraced and will probably exclud Mr Riddle.[11] I ascribe this tremendous wave for Direct Action and the General Strike partly to the failure of the political Socialists to accomplish anything at all for labor, and but more so to the agitation in behalf of Moyer Haywood and Pettybone during the last year.[12] As to Anarchism, there is no doubt in my mind that Czolgosz[13] act is responcible for it. For never before was Anarchism so much before the public eye as it has been since 1901. Unfortunately our own Comrades have failed to utilize the great chance, most of them having lost courage and the few of us, who have not, could not reach out far enough. I was amused at your request, dear Comrade to send a few young able Americans, that's just what we need here. We have no workers, at least none for the English propaganda. Outside of Voltairine,[14] who can only work through her pen, Harry[15] who has neither strength nor time to lecture much, we have no one of consequence in this country, absolutely no one. I come to a City for 3–4 days, where enough work can be found to last for weeks. Not to lose too much time, so that I could be back to N.Y. and take care of M E, I lectured every

9. See for example, "Anarchy and Education," *Woman's National Daily*, 4 April 1907; "Miss Emma Goldman Says Religions Are Curse to Humanity," *San Francisco Call*, 17 May 1907, p. 14, *EGP*, reel 47.

10. See summary of "Direct Action as the Logical Tactic of Anarchism," and lecture drafts of "The Revolutionary Spirit in Modern Drama" and "Misconceptions about Anarchism," 19 November, 14 December, and 24 December 1907, *EGP*, reel 47. Other lectures Goldman delivered during this period included "The Corrupting Influence of Religion" (in German), "The Building of True Character," and "Crimes of Parents and Educators."

11. The debate, preceded by a series of three well-attended lectures, was sponsored by the Los Angeles branch of the Socialist Party. EG's opponent, physician Claude Riddle, evidently faced no immediate sanctions for his admission of defeat in the debate. He was suspended from the Socialist Party, however, after becoming a public supporter of EG. Riddle eventually denounced the party and proclaimed himself an anarchist.

12. After their indictment in March 1906 for conspiracy to assassinate ex-Idaho Governor Frank Steunenberg, Charles Moyer, William (Big Bill) Haywood, and George Pettibone spent a year in prison awaiting their trial. Their case attracted nationwide publicity.

13. Leon Czolgosz assassinated President McKinley in September 1901.

14. EG refers to Voltairine de Cleyre.

15. Harry Kelly helped edit *Mother Earth*, and was also a regular contributor of articles to the magazine.

night since March 3rd and yet I have not begun to satisfy the demand. Colorado and Calif being the best States for radical Ideas I have only given 4 weeks where 4 months would not suffice. You see our predicament, we have no workers. We have plenty of good boys and girls, interested ready to help, but none to take the iniative. The reason why some of them rather go to Russia than do anything here, seems to me to lie in the fact that there they merely follow orders, here they have to develope iniative.

You have probably also read, that the Comrades of Chicago and Winnepeg want me to go to the Congress at Amsterdam,[16] I think there will be more groups to cooperate. I have not yet decided that I shall go. I have a horror of going an at the expence of the Comrades, have avoided that all these years, still I might do it after all. The Comrades here sadly need an infusion of revolutionary blood from Europe. Will you be present at Amsterdam?

I have made a few subscribers for The Voice of L[17] and could have done much more, if I had been supplied with copies. But I had none in fact, I have not seen a copy since April. I have tried to locate a copy of Drapers biography,[18] but found nothing. Maisel[19] too has tried but unless he succeeded recently, he did not get one. How are things in Russia? Poor bleeding suffering *Matushka*?[20] Outside of the daily papers, I know little about Russia, as I do not see our exchanges. By the way, I have tried so hard to get "*Listki, Khleb i Volia*,[21] to exchange. We send M E, have written to B. Wess[22] but no reply. We would so much like to keep the American public posted on Russian affaires, can you suggest some reliable source? I have gathered a lot of material about the condition in Mexico which seems to be worse than Russia. Do you know anything about it? Some of the Mexicans who have been sentenced to be shot, have to live here in seclusion or the U.S. Governement would turned them over to Mexico. They are all intellectual people, they tell me, that all the intellectuals in Mexico, are revolutionary and many of them Anarchist. One of them

16. The International Anarchist Congress was to be held in Amsterdam, 24–31 August 1907.

17. The London-based anarchist paper *The Voice of Labour*, supported by Peter Kropotkin and edited by Alfred Marsh and Tom Keell, began publication on 3 November 1906.

18. Probably George F. Barker's *Memoir of John William Draper, 1811–1882* (1886). Draper was an important figure in the nineteenth-century American scientific community. A professor of chemistry and head of the medical school at New York University, he was also a historian of science, best known for his *History of the Conflict between Religion and Science* (1874).

19. Max N. Maisel (1872–1959) was the owner of a bookshop at 424 Grand Street in the Manhattan borough of New York City; he published and sold works on the left, European literature, and Yiddish translations as well as anarchist periodicals. Maisel was also a New York agent for *Free Society* and *Mother Earth*, and sold tickets for EG's lectures. He was a founding member of the Kropotkin Literary Society (1912).

20. EG uses the Russian term *Matushka* for "Mother," meaning here the homeland or "Mother Russia"; written in Cyrillic characters.

21. EG was looking for the replacement to the Russian anarchist journal *Khleb i Volia*, titled *Listki, Khleb i Volia* (Leaflets of Bread and Liberty).

22. Probably William (Woolf) Wess (1861–1946), a Lithuanian-born, London labor organizer, orator, and anarchist.

a highly cultured man, ex judge and distinguished lawyer of Mexico,[23] told me that all your works are quite known to the revolutionists. It is my intention to start a movement in behalf of Mexico here, for that purpose, I have asked several Refugees who live here to prepare authentic statements as to the present situation especially among the workers of Mexico and by next Fall we may work out a plan to arouse the radical American element. The train is shaking terribly and I am tired, have not slept for two nights and I have still another night to travel. How are you, dear Comrade,? How is your health and Sophie[24] and *Sasha*,[25] how are they? We are all very eager to know how you are and would feel very happy indeed to have an occasional line from you in M E. I know you must be over burdened with work, but an occasional letter to M E would be a great incentive to our young folks here I can assure you.

I expect to be in N Y again about June 25th. As I have seen neither H. K[26] nor dear Alex B. since the 3rd of March, I do not know how they are, except that Alex is doing a great deal of work for M E and H K is writing regularly. With love to Sophie, *Sasha* and yourself

EMMA

PS I forgot to tell you, that we have quite a Japanese Anarchistic movement on the Coast.[27] I addressed several hundred Japanese, and found them very intelligent and beautiful in Spirit, they are intense admirers of yours, great student of everything written on Anarchism.

ALS, GARF, fond 1129, opis' 2, delo 978, listy 14–22.

23. Probably either Ricardo or Enrique Flores Magón, both of whom had gone to law school.
24. Refers to Peter Kropotkin's wife, Sophia Kropotkin.
25. *Sasha,* which is the Russian diminutive for Alexandra (as well as Alexander), was the name of Kropotkin's daughter (1887–1966). EG writes the name in Cyrillic characters here and in the closing line of her letter.
26. EG refers to Harry Kelly.
27. In May, *Mother Earth* published the proclamation of the newly formed Social Revolutionary Party of Japanese in America, which called for equal rights, the abolition of the "industrial, economic competitive system," and "racial prejudice" (*Mother Earth*, May 1907). The group was active for a short time, primarily encouraging other Japanese not to work as scabs during an IWW longshoremen's strike, but soon disintegrated. In April 1908 EG would lecture again in San Francisco to audiences that included Japanese anarchists.

DEAR COMRADE

In a hurry a few lines. Com. Baginski and I are going to the Congress.[1] I do not know whether or not you will be there, but we want to see you. We intend to run over to London after the Amsterdam affaire. Are you going to be home or will you be away in Sep?[2] Please drop me a line. c/o Jah J. Ladewijek Amsterdam Carn. Anthgnystrasse 49, and tell me when it will be most convient for you to receive me, or rather us as I am certain Com. Baginski will want to see you.[3]

Everything else personally you no doubt have received my letter en route.[4]

SINCERELY

EMMA GOLDMAN

Love to Sophie and *Sasha*

ALS, GARF, fond 1129, opis' 2, delo 978, listy 14–22.

1. EG and Max Baginski attended the International Anarchist Congress in Amsterdam, held 24–31 August 1907, as the representatives from the United States. Peter Kropotkin did not attend.
2. EG and Baginski met with Victor Dave and Kropotkin in France in September 1907. While in France they also met the artist Jules-Félix Grandjouan and solicited artwork for the cover of *Mother Earth;* visited "La Ruche," Sebastien Faure's experimental and "rational school"; and enjoyed extended visits with Max Nettlau.
3. EG wrote a similar note to Max Nettlau. See Letter to Max Nettlau, 25 July 1907, *EGP*, reel 2.
4. EG refers to her 31 May 1907 letter to Kropotkin (see above).

As soon as they learned of the result of the Haywood trial our comrades of Mother Earth sent the following telegram:

President Roosevelt, Oyster Bay, N.Y.: Undesirable citizens victorious.[1] Rejoice!

EMMA GOLDMAN,

ALEXANDER BERKMAN,

HIPPOLYTE HAVEL.

The Demonstrator 5 (21 August 1907): 6.

1. The phrase "undesirable citizens" appeared in a private letter by President Roosevelt, which was released to the press. In the letter Roosevelt describes railroad magnate E. H. Harriman as a liar and "at least as undesirable a citizen as Debs or Moyer or Haywood." The phrase became a rallying cry for the defense of Charles Moyer and William (Big Bill) Haywood, whom Roosevelt had publicly denounced following the Harriman scandal. EG later explained that the telegram to Roosevelt "was an expression of our contempt for the man who, though President of the United States, had joined the pack of hounds" (*LML*, pp. 429–30).

New York, September 23rd, 1907.

Hon. Joseph Murray,
    Acting Commissioner,
        Department of Commerce and Labor,
           Ellis Island, N. Y.

S i r :

        Your letter of September 21st to Commissioner
Bingham has been referred to me. The criminal record
of Emma Goldman is as follows according to our records.

        She was arrested September 9th, 1893, and
on October 16th, 1893, was sentenced to one year in the
penitenary for inciting to riot and unlawful assemblage.
She has been arrested in Philadelphia, but the date I
do not know; also in Chicago on September 10th, 1901,
and in Providence, R. I., on September 11th, 1897. In
each of these three instances, however, she was discharged.

        As to her nationality and whether she has
obtained citizenship we have no information.

            Respectfully yours,

            Arthur Woods

            Fourth Deputy Commissioner.

C.

Letter dated 23 September 1907 from Arthur Woods, Fourth Deputy Commissioner of the New York City Police Department, in response to a request from Joseph Murray, Acting Commissioner of the Department of Commerce and Labor (the executive office that oversaw immigration), for information on the Goldman's arrest record and the status of her citizenship, perhaps in anticipation of creating a case for her deportation. The black-crayoned "over" was added later. (Department of Commerce and Labor, National Archives and Records Administration)

No. 51694/2.

September 24, 1907.

STRICTLY CONFIDENTIAL.

Commissioner of Immigration,

Bos. N.Y. Phil. Balto

Sir:

The Bureau is confidentially advised that Emma Goldman, the notorious anarchist, is now out of the United States, but intends to return very shortly to resume her propaganda in this country. She may be accompanied by one Max Baginski.

It is desired that either or both of these persons who may arrive at your port should be detained and rigidly examined; any claims of American citizenship to be fully verified before being accepted as correct.

The Secretary of Commerce and Labor especially directs that no publicity be given to this matter in any way whatsoever, and you should take especial pains to that end.

Respectfully,

(Signed) F. P. Sargent;

Commissioner-General.

JEB

Confidential memo dated 24 September 1907, alerting the Commissioner of Immigration that Goldman and Max Baginski were currently out of the country (attending the International Anarchist Congress in Amsterdam), and requesting that upon their return, they be detained without publicity and their citizenship status fully verified before allowed reentry. (Department of Commerce and Labor, National Archives and Records Administration)

Article in **_MOTHER EARTH_**

October 1907

The International Anarchist Congress

Reported by Emma Goldman

An International Congress! The suspicious mind will at once conjure up horrors of majority rule, of politicians and platforms—platforms carefully devised to appeal to the stupid, and politicians who will make it appear that the stupid themselves have chosen their programs. The majority has but to be made to believe that it enjoys sovereignty and the power of decision, and it will cheerfully seal its own degradation.

However, the International Anarchist Congress at Amsterdam had none of that.[1] The eighty delegates who had come from monarchies and republics did not assemble to get up a catechism. Their purpose was to crystallize—out of the contrast of temperaments, theories and opinions—harmonious and concerted action. Of such contrasts there were many, occasionally bursting out at one another like bomb-shells, the Latin temperament readily bubbling over, often threatening to destroy the dearly cherished German sense of "order." But after the delegates had come into comradely touch with one another, a quieter atmosphere made itself felt, uniting all in a sincere desire to co-operate in every way possible to make the Congress a success.

Enrico Malatesta,[2] the senior of the Congress, full of youthful spirit, his eyes glowing with the divine fire for the revolutionizing of mind and body, was one of the most interesting figures. His enthusiasm for the cause, together with his sweet personality, produce an exquisitely harmonious character, the influence of which is both soothing and inspiring.

Pierre Monatte,[3] a representative of the "Confédération du Travail"[4] (Revolutionary

---

1. The congress was held 24–31 August 1907 in Amsterdam. Approximately eighty delegates came from France, Belgium, Russia, Italy, England, the United States, Poland, Bulgaria, Serbia, Sweden, Rumania and Holland; delegates from China and Spain were expected but failed to arrive. The central issues discussed were the relation of anarchism and organization, the formation of an Anarchist International, and the relevance of syndicalism to the anarchist movement. This was the fourth in a series of congresses. The anarchists considered the other three to have been the two congresses of the Second International—the first in Zurich in 1893, at which the anarchists had constituted a caucus; the second in London in 1896, at which the anarchists were formally excluded—and the anarchist congress scheduled in Paris for September 1900, which was canceled at the last minute by the French Council of Ministers, and which EG had expected to attend.
2. EG misspelled Italian anarchist Errico Malatesta's first name.
3. Pierre Monatte (1881–1960) was a central figure of the French anarcho-syndicalist movement and was influenced by Émile Pouget. Monatte played a central role in the 1907 International Anarchist

Trade Unions of France), an agitator of great force, thoroughly versed in the literature of the economic and anti-militarist movements, simple and unassuming, full of the spirit of solidarity and true comradeship. Together with such men as Pouget,[5] Delesalle,[6] Greffulheus,[7] he is building up a tremendous economic force, the "Confédération Générale du Travail," of which *Mother Earth* will have more to say in a later issue.

R. De Marmande,[8] *revolutionaire* and true *bohême,* jovial, full of esprit, with a keen sense of humor. He refuses to see in the Mother of Freedom—Revolution—a black-robed nun, walking about in penitence and despair over the sins of mankind. Revolution, to him, is the great liberator, the joy-bearer.

Henri Feiss-Amoré, the Belgian, was one of the most typical Frenchmen at the Congress: impatient, hot-headed and impulsive, yet polite and chivalrous; he necessarily proved a failure in everything that required system and self-control.

Broutchoux,[9] a power in the mining regions of France, belongs to the type of working-man who has helped to make revolutionary history,—intelligent, daring and uncompromising. He is beloved by his fellow-workers and hated by all authoritarian parties.

Congress in Amsterdam, where he argued for syndicalism as the primary means of achieving revolutionary change. He fled to Switzerland in 1908 to escape arrest for his involvement in the strike at Villeneuve-Saint-Georges. He returned to Paris and worked as a librarian for the Confédération Générale du Travail. In 1909 Monatte founded the magazine *La Vie Ouvière,* which ceased publication in 1914. Although opposed to the war, Monatte was drafted for military service and fought in the trenches during the First World War.

4. The Confédération Générale du Travail (General Confederation of Labor; CGT) was founded in 1895. In 1906 the CGT approved the Charter of Amiens, a manifesto of trade-union autonomy, self-reliance, and revolutionary syndicalism, which rejected electoral change as a tactic for trade unions.

5. Émile Pouget was a French anarchist syndicalist, author, and editor.

6. Maurice Paul Delesalle (1870–1948) was an anarchist and revolutionary syndicalist militant who served as assistant secretary of the Fédération des Bourses du Travail and of the Bourses section of the CGT from 1897 to 1908. A precision toolmaker by trade, Delesalle was instrumental in drafting the Charter of Amiens in 1906. He was a regular contributor to, and briefly worked for, Jean Grave's *Temps Nouveaux,* and also contributed to *La Voix du Peuple.* He was arrested in 1907 for his protest against the government's use of troops in the Midi. He opened a bookstore and left the CGT in 1908. Delesalle was author of many pamphlets, including *La Confédération générale du Travail* (1907) and *Syndicate et syndicalisme* (ca. 1909). See also "Syndicalism: Its Theory and Practice," Article in *Mother Earth,* January 1913, vol. 3.

7. Victor Griffuelhes (1874–1922) was an influential French syndicalist and shoemaker by trade. He was secretary of the CGT from 1901 to 1909 and co-author, with Delesalle, of the Charter of Amiens in 1906, which argued for keeping party politics out of union matters. Griffuelhes was administrator and manager of *La Bataille Syndicaliste* after 1911.

8. René de Marmande (Constant Emmanuel Gilbert Le Vicompte de Rorthays de Saint-Hilaire Marie; b. 1875) was an anarchist and a journalist who contributed to *Les Temps Nouveaux* and *La Guerre Sociale* and played an active role in the libertarian and syndicalist movements before the First World War. In 1917 Marmande launched a pacifist magazine, *Les Nations.*

9. Benoît Broutchoux (1879–1944) was a miner and militant anarcho-syndicalist.

Dunois,[10] from Switzerland, and Chapelier,[11] a Belgian, furnished much human document—the former too democratic to appreciate the real value of the individual; the latter, too sectarian for a universal movement. Chapelier's internationalism lies in Esperanto.[12] No doubt, much could have been gained at the Congress had all the delegates known Esperanto, as the interpretations from the French, Dutch and German consumed a tremendous amount of time. But to believe that an arbitrary, mechanical language can ever replace anything that has grown out of the soil, the life and the customs of a people, is to be sectarian indeed.

Another of the delegates was Luigi Fabri,[13] from Italy, well known through his writings on Anarchism and his affiliation with Mollinari's *L'Università Popolare*.

Dr. Friedeberg,[14] the German delegate, is an ex-member of the Social Democratic Party, which he represented as Alderman in the city of Berlin. In that capacity he has had ample opportunity to learn the uselessness of parliamentarism, which induced him to turn to Anarchism. Dr. Friedeberg is now one of the foremost champions of the General Strike, direct action and anti-militarism. Though he is indicted for high treason—a very serious offense in the land of the Kaiser—he was completely wrapped up in the work of the Congress, unconcerned as to what the future may bring him.

Two Bohemian comrades, Vohryzek[15] and Knotek, were very interesting delegates. Vohryzek, alert and ever ready with suggestions and resolutions, is a fanatical admirer of the achievements of his country, without the slightest sense of relative proportion. His friend, Knotek, was quite a contrast. He never spoke once during the entire session, yet one could not fail to perceive the artistic, dreamy and refined temperament. I regret that time did not permit me to see more of Comrade Knotek.

10. Amédée Dunois (1878–1945) was a revolutionary syndicalist who joined *Les Temps Nouveaux* in 1906 and contributed to *La Bataille Syndicaliste* from 1908 to 1912. In 1912 he joined the French Section of the Workers' International and began writing for its paper, *L'Humanité*. Dunois was a critic of the First World War and published Romain Rolland's anti-war protest, *Au-dessus de la mêlée*.

11. Émile Chapelier was a Belgian anarchist who was a founding member of the Libertaire Communist Colony and "The Experiment," in Stockel, Belgium. He published the pamphlet *Les Libertaires et l'Esperanto*.

12. A language constructed by "Ludovic" Lazar Markovitch Zamenhof (1859–1917), who went by the name of Dr. Esperanto. The artificial language was of interest to many radicals and anarchists as a means of facilitating international communication and breaking down national identities.

13. Luigi Fabbri (1877–1935) was an Italian anarchist and writer who, along with Pietro Gori, founded *Il Pensiero* (1903–1913), one of the most important Italian anarchist periodicals. Fabbri also contributed to *Volontà*, edited it from 1913 to 1915, and refounded the periodical after the end of the First World War. His publications include *Workers' Organisation and Anarchy* (1906) and *Lettere a un socialista* (1914).

14. Dr. Raphael Friedeberg (1863–1940) was a German physician, anarchist, and friend of EG. A Social Democratic city council member of Berlin, he was expelled from Sozialdemokratische Partei Deutschlands in 1907. In Ascona he opened a sanatorium, which became a meeting place for European revolutionaries. Friedeberg was the friend and doctor of Peter Kropotkin, Errico Malatesta, and Max Nettlau.

15. Karel Vohryzek was a Czech delegate who assisted in the production of the Austrian paper *Dampforgan des Proletariats* from December 1904 to March 1905.

Then there was R. Rocker,[16] editor of the *Workers' Friend* and *Germinal,* Jewish papers published in London. German by birth, he has acquired the Yiddish language, and through his able pen he is doing much to bring light and hope into the gloomy existence of the Jewish proletariat in England. He has acted as an impetus to the idealism, the earnestness and studiousness of the young Yiddish element, both in England and America. But one of his greatest merits is that he has made accessible to the Jewish reading public the revolutionary literature of the world.

There were many other delegates, who, for lack of space, cannot be discussed here; but they added much interesting material on the growth of our ideas in their respective countries.

After a few preliminaries, the Congress began its real work Monday afternoon, August 26th. Reports were read from France, Italy, Switzerland, Belgium, Germany, Austria, Bohemia, Russia, Serbia, Bulgaria, Holland, England and the United States. The report on the American situation our readers will be able to follow in *Mother Earth*. A résumé of the other reports will appear later.

The first subject for the consideration of the Congress was "Anarchism and Organization," with Dunois as speaker. The constant misrepresentation of Anarchism by its opponents has resulted in the widespread notion that Anarchism is merely destructive. That it is also constructive, our enemies carefully avoid stating.

In his opening remarks Dunois regrets that so little attention has hitherto been paid to the necessity of organization. "The individualistic notion, as expressed by Dr. Stockman[17] in Ibsen's 'Enemy of the People,' that the strongest is he who stands alone, has been very detrimental to the Anarchist movement. This statement has no relation to Anarchism, since Stockman merely voiced the egoistic notion of the bourgeoisie." After a lengthy discourse on similar lines the speaker proposed the following resolution to the Congress: "Anarchism and organization are not antagonistic; on the contrary, the common material interests of the workers as well as the mutual interests in ideas necessitate federated organizations."

In opposition to Dunois' conception, the Dutch comrade Croiset spoke of the individualistic phase of Anarchism—not in the sense, however, of private property, mutual banking, contracts and a voluntary police force—but of the importance of the individual in society. He is not opposed to organization, on principle. But, believing egoism the

---

16. Rudolph Rocker was a German anarchist active in the Jewish trade union movement in London's East End; he edited the Yiddish-language anarchist paper *Arbeiter Freint.*

17. Dr. Stockman is the public-minded and idealistic leading character of Henrik Ibsen's play *An Enemy of the People.* Dr. Stockman discovers that the water supply to the public baths is contaminated, causing illness to bath patrons. In his efforts to clean the water supply, he is met with obstacles from all directions. His idealism is shunned, and he is publicly labeled an enemy of the people and ostracized. Some anarchists considered the Dr. Stockman character, who voices the sentiment "the strongest man is he who stands alone," to epitomize individual resistance to the state.

main-spring of all our desires and actions, he holds that organization can be founded only on purely individual interests. "Egoists may combine to more successfully carry out some mutual project. But organization, not based on individual interests, is in danger of developing into an arbitrary and authoritarian factor."

Max Baginski[18] and myself spoke in favor of organization, laying stress on the fact that it is always the self-conscious, free individualities which decide the character and influence of an organization. We further illustrated our point by the following paper on "The Relation of Anarchism to Organization," read by Max Baginski:

"The charge that Anarchism is destructive rather than constructive, and that, therefore, Anarchism is opposed to organization, is one of the many falsehoods spread by our opponents. They confound our present social institutions with organization; therefore they fail to understand how we can oppose the former and yet favor the latter. The fact, however, is that the two are not identical.

"The STATE is commonly regarded as the highest form of organization. But is it in reality a true organization? Is it not rather an arbitrary institution, cunningly imposed upon the masses?

"INDUSTRY, too, is called an organization; yet nothing is farther from the truth. Industry is the ceaseless piracy of the rich against the poor.

"We are asked to believe that the ARMY is an organization, but a close investigation will show that it is nothing else than a cruel instrument of blind force.

"The PUBLIC SCHOOL! The colleges and other institutions of learning, are they not models of organization, offering the people fine opportunities for instruction? Far from it. The school, more than any other institution, is a veritable barrack, where the human mind is drilled and manipulated into submission to various social and moral spooks, and thus fitted to continue our system of exploitation and oppression.

"Organization, as *we* understand it, however, is a different thing. It is based, primarily, on freedom. It is the natural and voluntary grouping of energies for the achievement of results beneficial to humanity; results which should endow life with meaning, worth and beauty.

"It is the harmony of organic growth which produces variety of color and form, the complete whole we admire in the flower. Analogously will the organized activity of free human beings, endowed with the spirit of solidarity, result in the perfection of social harmony, which we call Anarchism. In fact, Anarchism alone makes non-authoritarian organization of common interests possible, since it abolishes the existing antagonism between individuals and classes.

"Under present conditions the antagonism of economic and social interests results in relentless war among the social units, and creates an insurmountable obstacle in the way of a co-operative commonwealth.

18. German American anarchist Max Baginski, who edited *Mother Earth* with EG, also traveled to the 1907 Amsterdam congress with her in mid-August.

"There is a mistaken notion that organization does not foster individual freedom; that, on the contrary, it means the decay of individuality. In reality, however, the true function of organization is to aid the development and growth of the personality.

"Just as the animal cells, by mutual co-operation, express their latent powers in the formation of the complete organism, so does the individuality, by co-operative effort with other individualities, attain its highest form of development.

"An organization, in the true sense, cannot result from the combination of mere non-entities. It must be composed of self-conscious, intelligent individualities. Indeed, the total of the possibilities and activities of an organization is represented in the expression of individual energies.

"It therefore logically follows that the greater the number of strong, self-conscious personalities in an organization, the less danger of stagnation and the more intense its life-element.

"Anarchism asserts the possibility of an organization without discipline, fear or punishment, and without the pressure of poverty: a new social organism, which will make an end to the terrible struggle for the means of existence,—the savage struggle which undermines the finest qualities in man and ever widens the social abyss. In short, Anarchism strives towards a social organization which will establish well-being for all.

"The germ of such an organization can be found in that form of trades unionism which has done away with centralization, bureaucracy and discipline, and which favors independent and direct action on the part of its members."

Malatesta, discussing the various attitudes towards organization, finds the difference not so much in principle as in the method of expression. "One is apt to lay too great stress on some particular pet phase, whereas in reality all the speakers are agreed as to the necessity of organization. I, too, can see little in the position of Dr. Stockman. Were he a worker in some factory, at the mercy of poverty and exploitation, he would soon descend from his lofty pedestal."

Baginski and myself opposed the opinion expressed by Dunois and Malatesta, that Ibsen represented, in his art, the attitude of the egoistic bourgeoisie. Anarchism does not mean Kropotkin *or* Ibsen: it embraces both. While Kropotkin has explained the social conditions which lead to a collective revolution, Ibsen has portrayed, in a masterly manner, the psychological effects which culminate in the revolt of the human soul,—the revolt of the individuality. Nothing would prove more disastrous to our ideas, were we unable to unite the external, the physical, and the internal, the psychological, motives of rebellion against the existing institutions.

Vohryzek agreed with us, adding: "Stirner[19] is not opposed to organization; on the

---

19. In his *The Ego and Its Own* (trans. Steven T. Byington; New York: Benjamin Tucker, 1907), the German philosopher Max Stirner proclaimed enlightened self-interest as the only valid motive for human conduct.

contrary, a close study of 'The Ego and his Own' will show that Stirner saw in the organization of free individuals a lofty aim of human endeavor."

Cornelissen,[20] of Holland, took exception to the views of the American delegates. "Individual liberty is desirable, yet a limit must be set as to how far it is admissible; it must not be allowed to become injurious to the movement, as a whole."

After several others had spoken, Dunois consented to accept my amendment[21] to his resolution, to the effect that collective activity in no way denies individual action; that, on the contrary, they complete each other. In this form the resolution was accepted by the Congress.

The evening sessions, lasting until midnight, were turned into public meetings wherein reports of the day's work and some of the speeches were interpreted into the Dutch language.

Wednesday afternoon's session was of a private nature, to which the press was not admitted. Incidentally, I wish to say a few words in regard to the Amsterdam press. Coming from the land of yellow journals, it was refreshing to read Dutch papers. All the important publications, even those of the most extreme conservative type, had correct and honest reports; not a word of misrepresentation or sensationalism. When I think of what our New York papers would have made of the Congress, I am grateful to Fate that in "free" America, with its "free" immigration laws, an Anarchistic Congress is out of the question. That the New York papers would bring some sensational and blood-curdling news was to be expected; thus they reported, for instance, that Malatesta and I had advised a "reign of terror."[22] Poor, dull brain of our penny-a-liners that must forever invent a "story"!

The formation of an Anarchist International Federation was thoroughly discussed and finally agreed upon. The International is to be composed of groups and federations, as well as of individual comrades who wish to join. The groups, federations and individual members are to retain their full autonomy. A Bureau of Correspondence, consisting of five members,[23] has been chosen, the purpose of which is to bring about closer communication and greater solidarity between the groups of various countries; also to keep them posted on the current events of the movement. Individual comrades, desiring to become members of the International, must be identified by their organization, the Bureau, or some comrade known to the Bureau. The expenses of the Bureau are to be defrayed by contributions of the groups and comrades belonging to the International.

20. Christiaan Cornelissen was a Dutch syndicalist organizer.
21. EG amended the resolution "that individual action, however important it may be, could not be sufficient without common action" with the following clause: "just as common action could not be sufficient without individual action".
22. *New York Times,* 17 August 1907, p. 3.
23. Members of the International Correspondence Bureau were Alexander Schapiro, Jean Wilquet, Rudolph Rocker, John Turner (who was unable to attend the conference), and Errico Malatesta.

Various views were expressed as to the merits of a Bureau, some of the delegates being apprehensive of the resurrection of the General Council of the International—an authoritarian clique, full of national and international intrigue and gossip. The fact that such irreproachable characters as Malatesta, Rocker, etc., have been chosen as members is safe guarantee, however, that the new Bureau will have a different character. The American delegates were in favor of a Bulletin, which should furnish all countries with data on the growth of our ideas.[24] However, those who preferred the Bureau hope that such a Bulletin may be issued as soon as money will be forthcoming.

Syndicalism was discussed by Pierre Monatte, from whose paper I quote a few paragraphs: "Syndicalism is the arena where the proletariat can gather for the battle, whose final object is the overthrow of the present economic and social institutions. There are various means, of course, but the most effective ones have proven to be *sabotage* (the despoiling of property and material), direct action and the General Strike. All these means, in contradistinction to the old authoritarian and political methods, have already caused a great deal of consternation among the enemy. It is to be regretted that many Anarchists still cling to the tradition of the old political revolution. No wonder they often despair of the means of realizing their ideals. Syndicalism, however, organizes the proletariat into a revolutionary phalanx giving the workingman confidence in himself, in his own power. Syndicalism, imbued with the true spirit of Internationalism, also propagates anti-militarism, anti-political and anti-parliamentary action, seeing in all these dangerous obstacles in the way of human liberation."

These remarks, followed by an interesting discussion, left the impression that the keeping aloof, in the past, from the trade union movement has been a mistake. The destructive, as well as the constructive, forces for a new life come from the working people. It, therefore, behooves us to keep in close contact with the latter. There was little diversity of opinion on this point. The various speakers merely considered whether syndicalism is to be looked upon as an aim or as a means. Malatesta was particularly brilliant in his remarks anent this question. "I, too, regret that most of the comrades isolated themselves from the trades union movement; but there would be still more cause for regret were they to go to the other extreme and dissolve in the present syndicalist agitation. To regenerate society, more is required than the battle on the economic field. Direct action and the general Strike are to be hailed as glorious weapons in the present struggle; but to assume that they will bring about a Social Revolution, as we conceive the latter, is to be guilty of great *naïvité*. Such a revolution goes far beyond every class interest, its aim is the liberation of man in all phases of life. Therefore, our methods must never become one-sided. It may be impossible and, in fact, inadvisable for *all* workingmen to join the General Strike—railroad men, sailors, carmen and others, holding the means of transportation

24. EG spoke against the creation of a formal International Bureau, preferring that each national movement publish the addresses of two of its members instead.

in their hands, may serve the cause of labor infinitely more by carrying the necessities of life to their striking brothers. Statistics prove that a city like London has provisions only for three months. What would become of the strikers after three months, if the railroad employees, too, were to join them?"

Malatesta has in view, particularly, periods of a great uprising or an insurrection. So far as ordinary strikes, however, are concerned he will probably agree with me that, if those employed in transportation were to join the strikers, the question at issue could be settled long before the supply of any large city would give out.

The subject closed with two propositions. One, signed by Monatte, Nacht,[25] Dunois and Marmande, was to the effect that they see in syndicalism and in the material interests of the proletariat the principal basis of revolutionary activity.

The second, signed by Malatesta, myself and others,[26] explained that revolutionary trade unionism and the General Strike are only means and can in no way replace the Social Revolution. It also expressed the conviction that the capitalistic régime can be abolished only through an insurrection and expropriation, and that our battle must be directed against all authoritarian forces.

As the first resolution was merely an addition to the second, both were accepted by the Congress. So also was the following declaration as the "Individual and Collective Terror," signed by Max Baginski and myself:

"We recommend that the International Anarchist Congress declare itself in favor of the right of rebellion on the part of the individual, as well as on that of the masses.

"We hold that most terroristic acts, especially those directed against representatives of the State and the plutocracy, must be considered from a psychological viewpoint. They are results of the profound impression made upon the psychology of the individual by the terrible pressure of our social injustice.

"As a rule, only the noblest, most sensitive and tender spirits are subject to such deep impressions, which manifest themselves in internal and external revolt. Thus viewed, terroristic acts can justly be characterized as the socio-psychological consequences of an unbearable system; as such, these acts, together with their causes and motives, must be understood, rather than praised or condemned.

"During revolutionary periods, such as the present one in Russia, for instance, terrorism—apart from its psychological character—serves a twofold purpose: it undermines the very foundation of tyranny, and kindles in the timid the divine fire of revolt. Especially is this the case when terroristic activity is directed against the most brutal and hated agents of despotism.

25. Siegfried Nacht (1878–1956) was an Austrian anarchist and journalist who published under pen name Arnold Roller; he edited *L'Espagne Inquistoriale* and wrote the highly influential pamphlet *The Social General Strike* (Chicago: Debating Club No. 1, 1905), which was translated into Japanese and published in mimeograph form in 1907 by Kōtoku Shūsui.

26. Signatories included Christiaan Cornelissen, Karel Vohyrzek, Jean Wilquet, René de Marmande, Nikolai Rogdaev, and the Bohemian anarchist Knotek.

"The Congress, endorsing this resolution, manifests its understanding for the act of the individual rebel, as well as its solidaric feeling with collective insurrection."

The paper on "The General Strike and the Political Strike," by Dr. Friedeberg, was an able critique of the Social Democratic notions in regard to the merely political General Strike. The speaker stated that the latter was being advised merely to infuse new life into the anemic condition of the political activity of that party. A résumé of Dr. Friedeberg's resolution follows:

"The class struggle and the economical liberation of the proletariat are not identical with the ideas and aims of Anarchism. The latter extend beyond the class aims and stand for the complete material and psychological regeneration of human individuality. Anarchism sees in the abolition of class régime and economic dependence the first step towards a free society. It cannot, however, employ those means of combat which are contradictory to itself and its purposes. Anarchism, therefore, refuses to recognize parliamentary action, conservative trade unionism and the right of the majority to dictate to or coerce the minority."

"Anarchism and Anti-Militarism" was referred to the anti-militaristic Congress that had been arranged by comrade Domela Nieuwenhuis.[27] The opening session, Friday afternoon, August 29th, was attended by all the delegates of the International Anarchist Congress. Interesting reports were read as to the growth of anti-militarism in various countries. Switzerland furnished the most gratifying results, seventy men having refused military service. The delegates expressed their solidarity with all those imprisoned for such heroism. Pierre Ramus[28] and R. De Marmande spoke on "Anarchism and Anti-Militarism." All agreed on the necessity of a vigorous agitation among soldiers and militiamen, urging them to refuse obedience when ordered to shoot strikers. Also to impress upon the workingman the necessity of abstaining, as much as possible, from the manufacture of all articles of wholesale slaughter. A letter of greeting from Dutch soldiers, also one of sympathy from Ferrer[29]—recently rescued from the clutches of the Spanish authorities—were read.

Saturday, August 30th, the last day of our own Congress,[30] was taken up by a paper on co-operative societies in Holland, by comrade Samson; a paper on co-education, by Leon

---

27. Ferdinand Domela Nieuwenhuis was a Dutch anarchist and freethinker, and editor of *De Vrije Socialist* (The Free Socialist).
28. Rudolf Grossmann (pseudonym Pierre Ramus) was an Austrian anarchist who had fled the United States after he was arrested in 1902 with William MacQueen and Luigi Galleani in Paterson, New Jersey, for inciting to riot. At this time he was editing two anarchist papers in Vienna.
29. Francisco Ferrer was a Spanish anarchist and Modern School educator. In 1907 he helped launch *Solidaridad Obrera*. He would be executed by the Spanish government in 1909 for being "author and chief of the rebellion" in the July 1909 General Strike in Barcelona.
30. EG chaired the closing day of the congress.

Clement,[31] read by Marmande; an exposition of Esperanto, by Emile Chapelier, and a paper on Alcoholism, by a Christian Anarchist.[32] As time was limited and the delegates worn out, the subjects were not discussed. A letter of greeting was received from comrade Yvetôt,[33] Marck, Levy, Bousquet, Corton, Loubot, Berthet, Clementine Delmotte and Gabrielle Petit (who are now in prison).[34] At the same time we express our sympathy and solidarity with all the champions of liberty, suffering under the capitalistic régime. We urge that the International Bureau consider it one of its first steps to defend and assist all these."

A resolution in behalf of Russia, signed by Rogdaeff,[35] Zabregneff,[36] Cornelissen, Baginski, Munjitsch, Fabri, Malatesta and myself, was enthusiastically accepted by the Congress. It follows:

"Considering that with the development of the people of Russia the proletariat of the cities and country will never be satisfied with mere political liberties, it is their aim to free themselves from economical as well as political bondage, and to employ in their struggle such means as have been propagated by the Anarchists for a considerable time. They can not expect anything from above, and they must, therefore, conquer their rights by direct action.

31. Leon Clement (b. 1880) was a building technician and the treasurer of the national construction workers' federation from 1907 until 1912. He attended the fifth, fifteenth, and seventeenth CGT congresses.

32. The paper was presented by J. van Rees.

33. Georges Louis François Yvetôt (1868–1942) was a French typesetter, anarchist, anti-militarist, and militant syndicalist. Born in the Minimes barracks, he was brought up by the Christian Brothers and the Orphan Apprentices of Auteuli charity. He learned the typesetting trade between 1880 and 1887. Yvetôt became an anarchist under the influence of Fernand Pelloutier (see vol. 1, p. 550), and when Pelloutier died, he became secretary of the Bourses federation and was reappointed to that position at every congress until the First World War. In December 1902 he launched the Antimilitarist League (Ligue Antimilitariste) with other anarchists, which became a branch of the International Antimilitarist Association (Association Internationale Antimilitariste). His works include *Vers la grève générale* (1902), *ABC syndicaliste* (1908), and the *Nouveau manuel du soldat* (1908), a pamphlet which attacked patriotism and urged soldiers not to fire upon their fellow workers.

34. The Anarchist Congress passed the following resolution: "[The Congress] Sends his fraternal greetings to comrades Yvetôt, Marck, Lévy, Bosquet, Corton, Lorulot, Berthet, Clementine Delmott, Gabrielle Petit; to the twelve antimilitarists now detained in Paris and to all Comrades who are in the Republican jails." Georges Yvetôt was imprisoned in 1906, along with Louis Grandidier and Gustave Hervé (an anti-militarist and revolutionary socialist), for anti-militarist activities. André Lorulot (1885–1963) was imprisoned for "provoking soldiers to disobey" in his pamphlet *Idole patrie et ses conséquences*. Gabrielle Petit (b. 1860), a feminist and socialist militant, was sentenced on 21 November 1907 to a six-month prison term for inciting soldiers to disobey orders.

35. Nikolai Ignatievich Rogdaev (alias Muzil; d. 1932) was an anarchist communist who fought behind the barricades in the December 1905 Moscow uprising. He was editor with Maksim Raevskii of the Paris-based *Burevestnik* (The Stormy Petrel). Rogdaev was placed in charge of Soviet propaganda in Turkestan during the Civil War and died in Tashkent after completing a long prison sentence.

36. Vladimir Ivanovich Zabrezhnev (alias Federov; d. 1920) was the leader of the first Moscow anarchist circle, Svoboda (Freedom). A contributor to *Golos Truda* (Voice of Labor), he was arrested and imprisoned following the 1905 revolution. He escaped and found his way to Kropotkin's London circle. Zabrezhnev joined the Communist Party, became secretary of *Izvestiia* in Moscow during the Russian Civil War, and died in Moscow.

"The Russian revolution is not only of local or national importance, but the near future of the international proletariat depends on it. The bourgeoisie of the new and the old worlds co-operate to defend their privileges and to postpone the abolition of their régime. They furnish moral and material support to the government of the Tsar, even supplying it with ammunition for the destruction of the Russian people.

"We therefore urge that the proletariat of all countries should inaugurate an energetic activity, opposing capitalist, monarchical, republican, democratic and constitutional government. It is in the interest of all workingmen to refuse any compromise in their attitude toward the Russian Revolution. Never, under any circumstances, ought they to be willing to assist any foreign power in its attempt to crush the revolt. If during a strike in Russia a General Strike cannot be declared in the corresponding industries in other countries, the proletariat should resort to such means which would spoil or injure the material sent to the Russian government, refusing to carry arms or other sinews of war into Russia.

"The Congress recommends to all comrades the necessity of furthering Anarchism in Russia and the Russian Revolution."

Two Christian Anarchists, who seemed to think that the régime of the Tsar can be met with Bible texts, refused to vote.

The Congress closed with a few warm and expressive remarks by Malatesta, and the singing of the "Internationale."

The delegates were in no way molested by the authorities at Amsterdam, except for a few Dutch detectives, who were occasionally following some of us.

I may mention that on the 2d of September, the day when Queen Wilhelmina came to Amsterdam, Baginski and I were supposed to have been watched very carefully. As if Anarchists were engaged in the slaughter of geese!

Whatever may come of the work or the resolutions of the Congress, it has undoubtedly brought about a closer international feeling and proven to the world that the Anarchist movement can no longer be treated as the "pastime of a few cranks," but that it is a widespread, earnest endeavor to wage war against all power and oppression.

Mother Earth 2 (October 1907): 307–19.

In Favor of an Anarchistic Weekly.

Comrade Alexander Berkman requests us to reproduce the following appeal which we do with pleasure. We are in hearty sympathy with the proposition:

Friends: We are living at a time of great social unrest. The simple democracy of former days has been changed by capitalism into a despotic imperialism. The people feel their bondage growing daily more unendurable, but fail as yet to understand the cause or the cure.

Social quacks and professional politicians are busy exploiting popular dissatisfaction for their personal aggrandizement; they seek to pacify the people by palliatives, in order to continue safely riding on their backs.

Dissatisfaction with existing conditions is finding its strongest expression among the working class. The man of toil begins to understand that there is no hope for a radical change under the capitalist regime. He is gradually realizing that the methods heretofore employed by labor are ineffectual and not designed to improve his economic position. He is embittered by the regularity of his defeats. He is fast losing confidence in his so-called leaders, in whom he is beginning to see the friends of labor's enemies.

Comrades! Let us not fail to properly appreciate this crucial period in the history of American labor, and let us prove our appreciation actively. We have an all-important work before us. It is for us, as Anarchists to point out to the workingman the real cause of his dissatisfaction, misery and oppression; to impress upon him the inefficiency of trades unionism, pure and simple; to convince him of the dangerous uselessness of parliamentary methods. We must discover to him his natural weapons and the powerful means at hand to make himself free; we must point out to him the methods so successfully being used by his European brothers: the revolutionary tactics whose final destiny it is to free labor from all exploitation and oppression, and usher in a free society; the modern efficient weapons of direct action and general strike.

The best medium for introducing these battle methods to the workingman is a weekly revolutionary paper. Our magazine, Mother Earth, is doing excellent work. But it is a monthly, and, as such, it must deal with the various manifestations of our social life; it can not devote itself exclusively to one particular phase. The projected weekly, however, is to deal entirely with labor, its battles, hopes and aspirations.

To Mother Earth whose work is theoretical, literary and educational, must be added a practical weekly, a fighting champion of revolutionary labor. We must carry our ideas to the men that toil.

Therefore we appeal to you, comrades. If you have the cause of Anarchism seriously at heart; if you want the workingmen to learn our ideas; if you realize how all important is the propaganda of direct action and the general strike, then come to our aid by financing the project of a weekly revolutionary paper.

Comrades! It is for you to decide whether we, as Anarchists, should take our stand in the midst of throbbing life or remain on the philosophic byways.

Voltairine de Cleyre.

Alexander Berkman.

Hippolyte Havel.

Emma Goldman.

George Bauer.

Harry Kelly.

P.S.—The comrades are urgently requested to act without delay. For obvious reasons it were desirable to begin the publication of the weekly paper on the 11th of November. All communications and contributions for this purpose should be addressed to Alexander Berkman[1] Box 47, Station D, New York.

The Demonstrator 5 (2 October 1907): 7. Originally published in *Mother Earth* 2 (September 1907): 292–93.

---

1. AB was, in fact, the principal author of this appeal. In her autobiography, EG explains that AB, who was still in the process of readjusting to life after his fourteen years in prison, had been dissatisfied with his editorial work on *Mother Earth* and wanted to produce a weekly addressed specifically to workers. "He had already discussed the project with Voltairine de Cleyre, Harry Kelly, and other friends. They had agreed with him that such a paper was needed and had promised to sign an appeal for the necessary funds. They had worried, however, that I might misunderstand, that I might consider the new publication a competitor of *Mother Earth*. 'What a ridiculous notion,' I protested; 'I claim no monopoly of the movement. By all means try to get out a weekly paper. I will add my name to the call'" (*LML*, pp. 399–400). The idea of an anarchist weekly would eventually materialize a decade later when *The Blast* was launched and edited by AB in San Francisco in January 1916, and *Revolt* was launched by Hippolyte Havel in New York at the same time. *Revolt*'s publishing run was three months, *The Blast*'s, two years (see vol. 3). Another signer to this appeal was George Bauer, a German-born anarchist who was the manager of *Freiheit* in New York City during the time that Max Baginski was the editor (1906–1910).

SIR:–

I attended the meeting in Holborn Town Hall,[1] "Gray's Inn Road," London, W.C. where Emma Goldman spoke to a small audience on The labor struggle in America," The meeting was not enthusiastic.[2] She discussed the case of Moyer, Haywood and Pettibone,[3] and remarked: "The trial of Haywood has failed because the Western miners know how to handle dynamite.[4] It is dangerous for a judge to secure condemnation of such a man as Haywood. The labor struggle of America is going to be the fiercest that has ever occurred, when the two forces of organized labor and capital clash it will be no joke, but the workers will win." John Turner said that Emma Goldman intends to lecture in the provinces, and that it is uncertain when she will return to America, as she also intends to visit some comrades in Italy. The confiscation of the October number of "Mother Earth" by the American Government was also discussed by the Anarchists. While I was engaged in some work for the Bureau of Immigration in Antwerp, I got acquainted with a Scotland Yard detective, who seemed to be fairly well acquainted with the European Anarchist movements, and I came to the conclusion that Scotland Yard could probably be of some assistance to me. I met Mr. Quinn, Superintendent of the Criminal Investigation Department, who promised to assist the American Government in the matter, and will notify the American Ambassador, #123 Victoria Street, London, S.W. in case he receives any reliable information about the proposed sailing for America of Emma Goldman and Max Baginsky. The

1. Maurits Hymans was a spy for the U.S. government who trailed EG in Amsterdam and London. After this 7 October lecture, EG became aware that she was being trailed by Scotland Yard detectives. She had been scheduled to speak in London and elsewhere in England, as well as in Scotland, but, as she reported in *Mother Earth*, the magazine and "other matters" (rumors that her re-entry to the United States would not be allowed) forced her to cut her visit short.
2. Another report stated that "for about an hour she held her audience interested" and that she was well received. See also "Emma Goldman's Lecture," Article in *Freedom*, November 1907, below.
3. Charles Moyer, William (Big Bill) Haywood, and George Pettibone, leaders in the Western Federation of Miners, were indicted in February 1906 and held in prison for a year before being acquitted on the charge of conspiracy in the killing of the governor of Idaho. See "As to 'Crammers of Furnaces,'" Article in *Mother Earth*, 20 November 1906, above.
4. At the turn of the century, the Western Federation of Miners (WFM) was known for its militancy. In 1899 the WFM dynamited the Bunker Hill Company mill in Idaho, and during the 1901 gold and silver strike at Telluride, Colorado, WFM strikers engaged in a fierce shoot-out with scabs. Other violent WFM strikes erupted in Cripple Creek in 1894 and 1904, Coeur d'Alene in 1899, and Colorado City in 1903.

American Ambassador will then cable this information to Washington. In the mean time I will keep in touch with the Anarchists in Europe. We have engaged passage on the "S.S. Nieuw Amsterdam," which leaves Rotterdam, Netherlands, November 9, 1907.

Yours respectfully,
Maurits Hymans.

TLU, file #51,694/2, Immigration and Naturalization Service, RG 85, DNA. Addressed to "Mr. John E. Wilkie, Chief of the Secret Service Division, Washington, D.C."; Hyman's street address given as "Krugerlaan 873."

DEAR COMRADE.

You see, I have not kept my promis after all to write you while in London. I did not get the time, had so much to do and to rush off in a hurry. Since I have received your letter, I have been kept busy solving the riddle as to the terrible influence of the Press on even the most unbiased mind. We all know that the papers lie, yet we believe every line of it. The story about my not being admitted in America originated in a London paper, was republished by all others including those of America. The latter with the exception of one of the yellowest sheets the World,[1] stated that the Immigration authorities knew nothing about and I am sure they do not still such hypnotic power have the papers, that I have been receiving numerous letters expressing great anxiety about me. And what is more I have begun to worry tho I know it is stupid. The authorities will never venture to extradict me, once I am there. I have taken great precautions to get in and I think everything will pass safely. However it has spoiled my voyage considerably. I hate uncertainty and I hate to get possessed of something, that I know to have no foundation.

You were right about Europe being 50 years ahead of America, but you forget that in one respect it is far behind it. The economic struggle is after all not so terribly tense, especially for women, in America. When I think, that I should have to earn my living in England or France, I shudder. As I said, before nothing will happen, but if it does, I am going to tour through Canada and then go to Australia, but it won't come to that——

I can not tell you, how much I regret missing you. Aside from my desire to see you, I wanted to talk to you about Mother Earth. I wanted to ask you to assist me, I mean to write for it, I feel sure it has a future, but the lack of contributors is really exasperating. We have so few in America and none at all from Europe. You can not imagine how much you would aid me and at the same time help our efforts in America. Anything will do, International Notes, biographical articles, articles on any subject you may chose, or translations, once in two three months if you can not write more often.[2] I am glad you mentioned your trouble at Dieppe I spoke to Dave[3] about it just two days before we left

---

1. EG refers to the *New York World*.
2. Between 1896 and 1914, and again after 1919, Nettlau was a regular contributor to *Freedom*. His sole contribution to *Mother Earth* after 1907, in 1914, reflected his perennial concern with "the useless and disastrous character of sectional exclusiveness among Anarchists." See "Anarchism: Communist or Individualist?—Both," *Mother Earth* (July 1914): 170–76.
3. EG refers to Victor Dave, the Belgian-born anarchist writer and editor living in London who EG first met in Paris in 1900.

Paris and it was very fortunate. We did not know what might happen to us, as we intended going 3rd class. Of course we went 2nd and had no trouble at all.

No Dave had not spoken to me about your loss, he is too discret, but he told me after your letter came.[4] I loath the words, I am sorry, they sound idle, still I must say that I was deeply moved to learn, that your happyness had been brief. I wish I could have been able to compensate you in a small measure through my friendship, but even that was not to be—

It is not really important, whether you said that I belong zu dem Zwischen-geschlecht.[5] But really it was you, else I would not have remembered it. You see, you impressed me more than you imagined, or more than I was willing to admit, I therefore remember everything! Yes, I am a woman indeed too much of it, thats my tragedy. The great Abyss between my woman nature and the nature of the relentless revolutionist is too great to allow much happyness in my life. But then, who can boast of happyness.

I hope you will write me soon and help me with M E. It means so much to me.

Affectionately

E. G.

ALI, Max Nettlau Archive, IISH. Address given as "On board the Steamer."

4. Nettlau's companion, Thérèse Bognar, died in 1907. Although he had known her since 1900, only a few close friends were aware of their relationship.
5. German for "to the middle-gender" or "third sex," a term EG and Nettlau used privately to describe feminists or advocates of women's liberation. See Letter to Max Nettlau, 4 January 1900, in vol. 1, pp. 374–76.

Article in **FREEDOM**

November 1907

Emma Goldman's Lecture

An eager, expectant audience filled the Holborn Town Hall on October 7 to hear our comrade Emma Goldman lecture on "The Labour Struggle in America." A charge of sixpence for admission did not deter them. The gallery, which was free, was filled some time before the lecture was to begin. At the Press table quite a crowd of reporters were waiting. Prompt as the clock chimed 8:30 the chairman, John Turner,[1] led the way on to the platform, followed by our comrade. A word or two of introduction, in which it was pointed out that few people were better qualified to speak on the subject of the American Labour Movement than our comrade, as she had just completed a tour of the States before leaving for the Anarchist Congress at Amsterdam,[2] and the lecturer was on her feet. For about an hour she held her audience interested. Starting by saying that America no longer attracted the emigrants from Europe who desired political freedom, but almost entirely those who went there for material gain, she pointed out that almost the entire outlook was a sordid one. The only exception was the Russian refugee fleeing from the Black Hundreds, the pogroms, and all the tortures of the cowardly and bloody Czardom.

The growth of the American Federation of Labour was dealt with, and the recent unholy alliance of it with the Trust bosses, through the Civic Federation, touched on.[3] Then the more robust spirit of the Western States was pointed out, and the revolutionary attitude of the Western Federation of Miners portrayed. The explanation of the recent acquittal of Haywood[4] was forcible and startling. "It was not," she said, "that the State authorities had not got the human creatures ready to carry out the wishes of the mining and other capitalists of that part of America. They had the judges, the lawyers, the policemen,

1. The British anarchist John Turner was at this time nominal publisher of *Freedom*. During 1903 and 1904 his deportation from the United States as an anarchist under the 1903 immigration law was the reason for EG's first involvement with the Free Speech League.
2. See "The International Anarchist Congress," Essay in *Mother Earth*, October 1907, above.
3. American Federation of Labor leaders Samuel Gompers and John Mitchell were charter members of the National Civic Federation (founded in 1900), an organization with representatives for wage earners, corporate employers, and the general public. Although the NCF's purpose was to ease relations between labor and big business, the Advisory Council was weighted with representatives known for their anti-union policies—influencing the character of the NCF in some people's eyes. From 1901 on, at every convention of the American Federation of Labor, a resolution calling for the declaration of non-confidence in the NCF was introduced and rejected.
4. William (Big Bill) Haywood, along with Charles Moyer and George Pettibone, his fellow leaders in the Western Federation of Miners, was acquitted on 28 July 1907 of the charge of conspiracy to commit murder, in the killing of ex-Idaho governor Frank Steunenberg.

the gaolers, the executioners, all ready to do their bidding, just as they did it in Chicago in 1887.[5] The reason Haywood was acquitted was that the jury knew right well that the Western Miners thoroughly understood how to handle and use dynamite."

The American workers, who were very quick, were beginning to show dissatisfaction with the tactics of Gompers and Mitchell. If the Industrial Workers of the World had kept out of politics, it might have become a powerful body. Any new organisation to succeed must certainly do so. Once the real solidarity of Labour was understood, and the General Strike made a principle of economic warfare, the Labour Struggle in America would sweep everything before it.

At the close of the lecture a large number of questions were asked, and splendidly answered by our comrade. It is very satisfactory to report that there was a surplus after paying all expenses.

As it was announced that other lectures would probably be given by Emma Goldman in London and the provinces, a word of explanation is necessary to the many applicants for her services. It seems that the publication of *Mother Earth,* and other matters in America, made it imperative for her to return after a few days' rest. This was not known till the receipt of the U.S. mail. Disappointment at this is tempered by the pleasure at the success of the Amsterdam Congress, and the anticipation of the revival of Anarchist propaganda.

Freedom (London) (November 1907): 68.

5. A reference to the Haymarket incident. After a clash between strikers, scabs, and police, during which some strikers were killed, at the McCormick Reaper Works in Chicago on 3 May 1887, a meeting was called for the following evening at Haymarket Square to protest the deaths of the strikers. As the meeting began to disperse, a bomb was thrown at the police, who retaliated by firing into the crowd. Seven officers died, sixty were injured, and four civilians were killed. In the days after the bombing, leading militants were arrested, all of whom were prominent anarchist and labor activists in Chicago and some of whom were not even at the demonstration. Albert Parsons, who surrendered himself on the day of the trial, and August Spies, Louis Lingg, Samuel Fielden, Michael Schwab, Adolf Fischer, and George Engel were sentenced to death. Oscar Neebe was sentenced to a fifteen-year prison term. The sentences for Fielden and Schwab were later commuted to life imprisonment. On 10 November 1887, the night before the planned execution, Louis Lingg killed himself by biting on a dynamite cartridge, probably smuggled in to him by Dyer D. Lum. The remaining four, who were executed as scheduled, became martyrs of the left. Their executions were instrumental in the politicization of EG, AB, Voltairine de Cleyre, William (Big Bill) Haywood, and countless others.

To ROBERT WATCHORN, COMMISSIONER OF IMMIGRATION, ELLIS ISLAND, N. Y. H. OR TO ANY IMMIGRANT INSPECTOR IN THE SERVICE OF THE UNITED STATES.

WHEREAS, from evidence submitted to me, it appears that EMMA GOLDMAN, alien, who landed at ~~the~~ a port ~~of~~ unknown, on or subsequent to the 1st day of July, 1907,[1] has been found in the United States in violation of the Act of Congress approved February 20, 1907, to wit:

That said alien is an Anarchist, or one who believes in or advocates the overthrow by force or violence of the Government of the United States, or of all government, or of all forms of law, or one who disbelieves in or who is opposed to all organized government, or one who is a member of or affiliated with an organization entertaining and teaching such belief in or opposition to all organized government, and by reason of such belief, disbelief, or opposition, is specifically excluded from this country under the provisions of Sections 2 and 38 of the Act above-named.

also That said alien entered the United States without inspection, contrary to the terms of Section 38 of the Act mentioned above.[2]

I, OSCAR S. STRAUS, Secretary of Commerce and Labor, by virtue of the power and authority vested in me by the laws of the United States, do hereby command you to take into custody the said alien, and convey her before a Board of Special Inquiry, at Ellis Island, to enable her to show cause why she should not be deported in conformity with law.

The expenses of execution, conveyance to Ellis Island, and detention pending the disposition of warrant proceedings are authorized, payable from the appropriation "Expenses of Regulating Immigration."

For so doing, this shall be your sufficient warrant. Witness my hand and seal this 14th day of November, 1907.

OSCAR S. STRAUS
SECRETARY OF COMMERCE AND LABOR.

TDS, file #52,410–43, Immigration and Naturalization Service, RG 85, DNA. On Department of Commerce and Labor stationery.

1. The Immigration Act of 1907 was passed on 20 February 1907 and took effect on 1 July 1907; it amended the 1903 immigration law, which had barred foreign-born anarchists from entering the United States. The language regarding anarchists was not changed in the 1907 act; however, the act did streamline the methods for prosecuting and deporting excludable aliens.
2. Criteria for government inspection of entering immigrants were not outlined in Section 38, but rather in Section 16, which mandated an initial inspection of immigrants by immigration officers, and Section 17, which required a medical examination of immigrants at the port of entry.

UNITED STATES OF AMERICA
Department of Commerce and Labor
Washington

No. 51694/2

To   ROBERT WATCHORN, Commissioner of Immigration, Ellis Island, N. Y. H.
   Or to any Immigrant Inspector in the service of the United States.

WHEREAS, from evidence submitted to me, it appears that

EMMA GOLDMAN,

alien, who landed at this port of unknown,

or subsequent to
on the   1st   day of July, 1907, has been found in the United States

in violation of the Act of Congress approved February 20, 1907, to wit:
That said alien is an Anarchist, or one who believes in or advocates the overthrow by force or violence of the Government of the United States, or of all government, or of all forms of law, or one who disbelieves in or who is opposed to all organized government, or one who is a member of or affiliated with an organization entertaining and teaching such belief in or opposition to all organized government, and
by reason of such belief, disbelief, or opposition, is specifically excluded from this
country under the provisions of Sections 2 and 38 of the Act above named.
And that said alien entered the United States without inspection, contrary to the
terms of Section 36 of the Act mentioned above.
   I, OSCAR S. STRAUS,   Secretary of Commerce and Labor,

by virtue of the power and authority vested in me by the laws of

the United States, do hereby command you to take into custody the

said alien, and convey her before a Board of Special Inquiry, at Ellis Island,

to enable her to show cause why she should not be deported in

conformity with law.
   The expenses of execution, conveyance to Ellis Island, and detention pending
the disposition of warrant proceedings are authorized, payable from the appropriation
"Expenses of Regulating Immigration."

   For so doing, this shall be your sufficient warrant.

   Witness my hand and seal this 14th   day of November, 1907.

                                    Oscar S. Straus
                        Secretary of Commerce and Labor.

11—1190

Warrant dated 14 November 1907 from Oscar Straus, Secretary of Commerce and Labor, to Robert Watchorn, Commissioner of Immigration authorizing immigration authorities to take custody of Goldman under the 1903 Immigration Act that excluded alien anarchists. On her return in mid October from the 1907 anarchist congress in Amsterdam, Goldman evaded arrest by traveling straight to Canada. (Department of Commerce and Labor, National Archives and Records Administration)

MEMORANDUM FOR SECRETARY:

IN RE ILLEGAL ENTRY OF *EMMA GOLDMAN.*

[. . . .]To sum up,—If the only issue were whether or not she is an anarchist, I think there is no doubt whatever but that she is liable to deportation.[1] The difficulty will turn on the question as to whether she is an alien within the meaning of the immigration act.[2] If she is a citizen, as seems to be barely possible, the question is settled in her favor. But even if she is not a citizen, her long continued residence in this country—22 years—may be held to give her a status which would take her out of the class denominated aliens, in the immigration law, when returning from a temporary absence abroad. There is a direct conflict in the decisions of the lower federal courts on this question; the Supreme Court has never passed on it. A further matter which will have to be carefully considered, is the question as to what country she should be deported to. It is not known what is the "trans-Atlantic port from which she embarked for this country" on the occasion of her last arrival; and in returning a character of this sort to the "country whence she came," care must be taken that the right country is selected, especially in the case of a person so long a resident in the United States.

The general opinion of the officers who have been following her up is that she will welcome arrest; that it will not only advertise her and add to her prestige, but will be the means of bringing her in considerable sums in the way of contributions. Nevertheless, I think she ought to be arrested, if only to vindicate the administration of the immigration law. She entered the country surreptitiously, and while it may be difficult to deport her

1. The Bureau of Immigration was first created by the Immigration Act of 1891, under the jurisdiction of the Treasury Department. The Immigration Act of 1903 transferred jurisdiction over immigration to the newly created Department of Commerce and Labor. The Naturalization Act of 1906 combined the federal government's immigration and naturalization functions in the Bureau of Immigration and Naturalization.

2. In the Immigration Act of 1903, the term "alien immigrant," which had been used in preceding acts, was replaced by the term "alien" (though the latter term was not defined until the 1917 act). "Alien immigrant" had been defined as a person who was entering the United States for the first time with the intention of establishing residency (and not a native-born or naturalized citizen); the new term "alien" included any non-citizen. The change in language proved to be a point of contention, as the broader term "alien" was open to conflicting interpretations in the courts. See *United States v. Aultman,* 143 Fed. 922, where the court upheld that the 1903 immigration act did not apply to a resident alien (one who had established a domicile) returning after a temporary absence; *Rodgers v. United States,* 152 Fed. 346, where the same was held; and *Taylor v. United States,* 153 Fed. 1, where the court held that the 1903 act applied to all aliens (reversed on appeal).

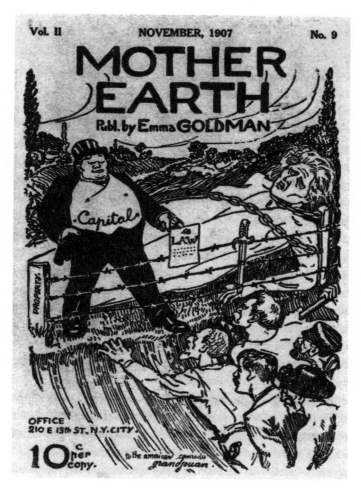

Cover of November 1907 *Mother Earth,* inscribed "to the American comrades, Grand-jouan." The French artist Jules-Félix Grandjouan met Goldman in Paris following the Amsterdam International Anarchist Congress. (By permission of the Kate Sharpley Library)

on this ground, if she entered in the regular way, and only made false statements, she should be made to undergo the examination required by law to determine her right to admission, and to determine further whether she has committed perjury.[. . .]

TDU, file #51,692/2, Immigration and Naturalization Service, RG 85, DNA.

> # LOUIS J. DOMAS to GEORGE B. BILLINGS
>
> *Boston, 19 November 1907*

SIR:

Pursuant to your verbal instructions I proceeded last night to Paine Memorial Hall on Appleton St. to listen to a lecture Delivered by Emma Goldman. The lecture was announced to take place at 7.30, but it did not commence until 8.40. There was no one on the platform to introduce the speaker. Miss Emma Goldman stepped on the platform at 8.40 and promptly began by saying that she was well enough known to the audience to need any introductions.

There was a murmur of disappointment in the Hall when it was found that she was to lecture in English, as at least one third of the people assembled could not understand the English language.

There were about 200 people in the Hall (about a dozen of them were women), all belonging to the foreign element. A young Russian who was sitting next to me told me that he was only six months in this country, and felt confident that Miss Goldman would not speak in English, from fear of the Police. He was therefore greatly disappointed when he found that the lecture was to be in English.

Shortly before the lecture began a young man distributed a leaflet entitled "The Assassination of McKinley from an Anarchistic stand point"[1] (appended to this report as Ex. A.) and a card announcing the Annual Anarchistic Ball, known as the "Baueren Ball" (The Peasants Ball), which is to take place on the 3rd of January.[2] (Ex. B).

Not having a note-book with me I did not take notes, but will try to give a digest of the lecture last night.

The lecturer after making the statement mentioned before, that introductions were superfluous in her case, went right on to say that the subject for her lecture would be "Direct Action as the logical tactic of Anarchism". Christianity—she said—, as well as the Government of the United States, have failed by employing methods which were not in harmony with the underlying principles or ideas. Anarchism in order to succeed must work out its policy by direct action and not to prepare and delay thereby the achievement aimed at. We cannot expect to accomplish to-morrow, what we don't begin to do to-day.

She then went on to criticise the tactics of the trade unionism in this country. "They—

---

1. Voltairine de Cleyre, *McKinley's Assassination from the Anarchist Standpoint* (New York: Mother Earth Publishing Association, 1907). This essay first appeared in *Mother Earth* 2, no. 8 (October 1907).
2. Bouren Ball (the Peasant's Ball) was an annual fundraiser for the Anarchist Red Cross, which was an organization formed in America in 1907 to aid imprisoned anarchists and other radicals who were not receiving aid from other established revolutionary groups in Russia.

she said—delay matters by preparing for a strike and negotiating with their masters; by putting it up to arbitration; giving the employers time to prepare themselves for a strike, instead of employing direct action, and that is to strike at once without waiting for to-morrow. The trade unions in France have accomplished more in a few days than the trade unions have in this country for last 20 years. The strike of the Electricians in Paris was won in 24 hours, because they resorted to direct action.[3] They didn't say to their employers: "We are going to strike six months hence. Prepare yourselves", but enveloped the entire city in darkness striking at once."

She then scored the Public School system in this country. She said, that the children here are taught old and worn out and decayed ideas; taught to bow down to authority, to be law abiding; they are killing the individuality of the child, by teaching false history; submission to government, etc. She related the most modern school as introduced by a well known French Anarchist, Sebastian Faure, where children don't have to go through the humdrum methods of discipline, where the child's mind is allowed to be developed into normality.[4] She said, that this new system is being greatly propagated through the European countries.

She then took up the matter of voting and abjured all those who are radically inclined from going to vote. She said "Refrain from voting. By going to vote you acknowledge yourself to be a weakling unable to manage you own affairs; you give the power into the hands of unscrupulous legislators, be they Republicans, Democrats or Social Democrats, to get the best of you. Try and train the people to shun the Army, or militarism in any form. Let them see that when they are increasing the Army and Navy in this country, it is not for the purpose, as given out, to fight for your country; but for the purpose of shooting your poor and down trodden brethren down in case of a strike. It is to protect Capital and nothing else. It is not to fight the External Enemy, but to crush down the Internal Enemy. Enlistment in the Army is not compulsory in this country, still there are enough fools here who voluntarily allow themselves to be trained as murderers.

Some of the startling statements she made were:

"A Revolution in this country is bound to come and not in the very remote future".

"Law abiding citizens, who believe in Government, Law and Order, are as a rule men with very little brains".

"It is not wrong for people in time of a strike to destroy their own products".

Outside of these statements, one could easily perceive that great precaution was used by her in couching her statements. While it was easily understood what she meant by "Direct Action", it was left to the public to conjecture, as to the real meaning of it. When

3. Without warning, Parisian electricians went on strike on 8 March 1907, leaving the city in darkness for two nights before the electric companies yielded to the workers' demands for better pensions, wages, and hours. This event was reported in the 20 March 1907 *Demonstrator*.

4. After the 1907 International Anarchist Conference in Amsterdam, EG visited Sebastian Faure's libertarian school, La Ruche (The Beehive), near Paris, and wrote about her experiences in the November 1907 *Mother Earth*.

MASSMEETING

to commemorate

The Twentieth Anniversary

of the

11th of November

will take place at the

MANHATTAN LYCEUM

66-68 E. 4th St., New York

Monday, November 11th, 1907, 8 P. M.

The following speakers will address the audience:

VOLTAIRINE DE CLEYRE, of Phila.   MAX BAGINSKI

EMMA GOLDMAN   L. CAMINITA

ALEXANDER BERKMAN   V. REJSEK

HARRY KELLY   L. ELSTEIN, and others.

Appropriate Musical Program.

Card advertising mass meeting to commemorate the twentieth anniversary of the execution of the Haymarket anarchists. The range and stature within anarchist circles of its speakers underscore the importance of the meeting. (Emma Goldman Papers)

after the meeting was over she invited the audience to ask questions and the question was put to her, as to what she meant by direct action, she gave an evasive answer.

She wound up her lecture by taking up the Institution of marriage, and ridiculed the idea of having the State or Church anything to do with such private affairs. "I have yet— she said—to find a man who really believes in the sanctity of marriage; but man expects woman to believe in the sanctity of married life. Do not allow any one to meddle in your love affairs. Neither priest, minister, Rabbi or Justice has anything to say in matters of such a private nature."

Among those who participated in the debate at the close of the lecture was a Russian Leth; an Armenian; a Russian Jew and one who spoke with a strong English accent.

I tried very hard to find out as to how Miss Goldman gained entrance to this country, but there was no one who could throw any light upon it.

I may add, that contrary to expectations, the meeting was of an extremely orderly nature. There seemed to be even a damped air of apathy, but that may be due to the fact that as I said, at least a third of the audience could not follow the lecture in English.

The meeting closed at 10.30 with the announcement by Miss Goldman that copies of the November issue of "Mother Earth", could be procured at the door, at 10 cents a copy. Mother Earth is an Anarchistic magazine (Monthly) published by Emma Goldman. I procured a copy of it, but had no time as yet to peruse it.

RESPECTFULLY,
LOUIS J. DOMAS
INTERPRETER.

TDS, file #51,694/2, Immigration and Naturalization Service, RG 85, DNA. Addressed to Commissioner of Immigration, Boston, Mass.

MY DEAR COMRADE.

Your letter and article received.[1] I delayed answering you as I had to go to Boston[2] for several lectures and on my return I was busy with the M E Concert. Of course we shall bring your article in M E, it will appear in the Dec issue, the rest will appear in Jan. I hope, that you may become a regular contributor, as I feel sure that our readers would be interested in anything you have to say. Yes, I have reached America safely, but my staying here is not quite so safe. The N.Y. police is especially desirous to shut me up. Since last winter they have stopped every meeting, I was announced to address. This years 11th of Nov Anniversary[3] was again interfered with by the police no one was admitted into the Hall. To the great anger of "our protectors, the audience went to the hall of the Bohemian Anarchists, who were holding an Anniversary of their own and Vol. de Cleyre, Berkman Baginski[4] and myself spoke under the very noses of the uniformed brutes. At the M E Concert 40 officers were present trying by every possible device to cause a disturbance. They did not succeed, so out of anger they arrested a young Comrade towards morning.[5] Of course he was let go the next day, only the annoyence impudence and brutality of the N.Y. police are getting beyond endurence. I am sure I shall not be able to control myself the next time I am present at a meeting where the police act worse than Russian Cossaks.

I shall write again, when I get more time, hoping to hear from you meanwhile.

SINCERELY

EMMA GOLDMAN.

Comrade Berkman sends his greetings as he does not know you personally.

ALS, Max Nettlau Archive, IISH.

1. Nettlau's letter was dated 5 November 1907; his article, "Are There New Fields for Anarchist Activity?" was published in its entirety in the December 1907 issue of *Mother Earth*, signed with Nettlau's initials.
2. On 18 November 1907, EG spoke on "Direct Action as the Logical Tactic of Anarchism" to a crowd of about 200 at Paine Memorial Hall in Boston. She was also scheduled to speak in nearby Lynn, Massachusetts, on 17 November.
3. The anniversary commemorated the deaths of the Haymarket martyrs, Albert Parsons, August Spies, George Engel, and Adolph Fischer, hung on 11 November 1887.
4. EG refers to Voltairine de Cleyre, AB, and Max Baginski.
5. The concert and ball were held on 22 November 1907, at Everett Hall as a semi-annual *Mother Earth* reunion. Julius Edelsohn was clubbed without provocation upon leaving the event at 2 a.m., according to *Mother Earth*, and arrested along with a young woman who protested the beating. Both were fined.

DEAR MR. ANDREWS:—

The attitude of Anarchism towards Competition? Do you mean Individualist (Tucker) Anarchism, or Anarchist Communism.

The latter philosophy, based on the brotherhood of man, and solidarity of interests, recognizes no commercial or industrial competition. Disbelieving in private owner-ship, we recognize in competition for material well being the greatest enemy to human progress.

We look upon competition—and the spirit it has created & fostered—as a result of the institution of private property. The Anarchist authors who have written on this Subject, have mostly confined themselves to an examination of the source of most social evils—property—rather than to its particular manifestation in the form of competition.

The position of Individualists Anarchists is an entirely different one on this subject. For an expression of their views I can refer you to "Instead of a Book", or to its author, Benj. R. Tucker,[1] Box 1312, N.Y.

SINCERELY,

EMMA GOLDMAN.

TLSr, John R. Commons Papers, WHi. Addressed at top to John B. Andrews. "Anarchism" and "Emma Gold-man" typed and underscored at top of page.

1. Benjamin Tucker, *Instead of a Book* (New York: Benjamin Tucker, 1893).

Sir:

Pursuant to your instructions I proceeded to Lowell, Mass., last night and attended a lecture given by Emma Goldman at the Odd Fellows Hall, #84 Middlesex St. The lecture was given in English and the subject was "Trade Unionism". In many respects it was a repetition of the lecture she gave here in Boston at Paine's Memorial Hall several weeks ago, a report of which I submitted to you at the time. "Direct Action by Trade Unions" was mainly what she advocated

I shall attempt to give the substance of her lecture in brief.

"Conservative trade unionism, the way it is carried on in this country, consists of a body of certain workingmen of a certain trade getting together and organizing for the purpose of getting a few minutes less labor and a few pennies more pay. They will get together and discuss the advisability of a strike and then confer with their employers. They will give their employers sufficient time to prepare for the strike, while they themselves remain entirely unprepared for it.

Just take the Printers Strike for instance in New York.[1] The printers in the different publishing houses in New York gave their employers notice that within four months they have decided to go out on a strike. The publishers at once proceeded to inform their contributors and urged them to send material four months in advance and the most ardent among the printers, who got up the strike, worked overtime to get the stuff out and thereby preparing their employers for the strike, and naturally killed all prospects of ever winning that strike.

"I had the good fortune to be present in San Francisco when the Carmen strike broke out.[2] For a month before they struck the employers were informed that on a certain day at a certain time they would go out on a strike if their grievances were not adjusted. The employers at once sent for enough blacklegs or scabs, who were quietly stored away to be used on the occasion. Then on one morning at two o'clock when every body was in

---

1. Typographical Union No. 6 called a general strike, which began on 2 January 1906. One thousand printers struck for an eight-hour work day and a closed shop. A court injunction prevented the strikers from intimidating or using force against Butterick Publishing Company employees or customers. Several of the large printing firms hired non-union men and were largely unaffected by the strike, which ended in March 1906.

2. The Carmen's Union strike began in San Francisco on 5 May 1907. Violence soon broke out as the United Railroads union president kept cars running by employing strikebreakers. The strike, ending in defeat for the Carmen's Union, was officially called off in March 1908.

bed and street cars were not needed, the workmen took the cars to the sheds, left them in proper order and good shape, and then the strike was declared on. The following morning the cars were out as usual and manned by the scabs who were brought over by the Company for the emergency. In addition to that when it was found that these scabs were not thorough in their work, and one of the cars was stuck in middle of the street thereby blockading traffic, the president of the Carmen's Union,[3] who had not done any work himself for over five years and was receiving a good salary, paid by the hard earned money of the poor carmen, boarded that car and took it to the station. How could they win the strike this way?—Just think how easily they could have won, if instead the carmen decided to strike on the spur of the moment, at a busy time of the day, left the cars on the tracks, and refused to move them a step further unless they were granted their just demands the employers would have to come to terms".

"The Electricians strike in Paris illustrates the wisdom of direct action ~~of a str~~ in a strike.[4] They struck at a time when the streets of Paris were gay with all sorts of festivities; when the fashionable ladies were out in their automobiles; when all the fashionable restaurants were brilliantly lighted; when the theatres were filled to the doors. All of a sudden the entire city was enveloped in darkness, and naturally the strike had to be settled at once, without any more ado. It also showed these gay and fashionable people, who take everything as their due that back of these Electric Lights there is a force they never dreamt of, and never took the trouble to consider.

"Another great error of the Trade Unions nowadays, in this country, is that every branch of trade looks out for its own interests only. There should be no such thing as the Union of the Textile Workers; the Shoemakers Union; The Bakers Union. There should be an international brotherhood of workingmen, and when they are to strike they should strike all at once and together. Just imagine two millions and a half of the American Federation of Labor going out on strike, without any notice to employers, how quickly a settlement would be reached at, as it is not so easy to replace two millions and a half of workingmen all at once.

"Mind you, that in my personal opinion, even if you bring the eight hour law, around and get a few more pennies for your labor, that is far from bringing around the millennium, as long as there is somebody to direct you to work, even four hours a day or even four ~~months~~ minutes a day. But I am speaking to-night from a trade unionists point of view, and I will simply tell you that conservative trade unionism has had its day and served its purpose. A new method of action must be adopted to vanquish capital.

"Conservative Trade Unionism believed that there is a relationship existing between capital and labor, in spite of the fact that big brother "Capital" tramples under feet poor

---

3. The Carmen's Union president was Richard Cornelius (ca. 1864–1914).
4. See note 3, Letter from Louis J. Domas to George B. Billings, 19 November 1907, above.

weak sister "Labor". They therefore tried to get their demands settled in a lawful way and their managers were law abiding citizens and desirable citizens,[5] who were dined and "wined" at the White House, and declared by Teddy to be in every respect desirable citizens,[6] who look for peace and quiet. I tell you friends, the law is the friend of the capitalist and never had any friendly feeling for the poor downtrodden laborer. An eminent Lawyer of New York once said that there are more laws on the Statute Books then one could observe even in a life lasting three hundred years. But laws are not made for the purpose of being observed. They are made to be held out as scarecrows to the poor in case they get restless and cease to be law abiding citizens. At the point of the bayonet and supported by law the poor are quickly hushed and everything assumes a peaceful mien.

"You are being taught in your Sunday Schools that there is a Supreme Being, who supervises everything on earth, and that there must be rich and poor; that it is in the order of things to have and employer and an employee. Voltaire very wisely said: "If there is a supreme being and could not manage any better than he did in these many years, it is high time that he be deposed from his throne of rule". The Church is always with the rich and the successful. They preach to you about loyalty to your country. Whose country? The Country of the Rockefellers, the Morgans, the Astors and the Vanderbilts?[7] It is about time you woke up and see the absurdity of all these myths. We are civilized and losing our sense of hearing and seeing. The savage indian put his ear to the earth and can hear

5. A reference to President Roosevelt's statement that Charles Moyer and William (Big Bill) Haywood were "undesirable citizens." See letter to Theodore Roosevelt, 21 August 1907, above.

6. In March 1906 Samuel Gompers met with President Roosevelt, who rejected his Bill of Grievances as unnecessary and impossible.

7. EG names four of the richest families in the United States. John D. Rockefeller (1839–1937) was an industrialist and founder of Standard Oil. In 1859, with $1,000 he had saved and another $1,000 borrowed from his father, Rockefeller started his career in Cleveland. In 1870, Rockefeller organized the Standard Oil Company, and by 1879 he was on the list of the world's twenty wealthiest people. In 1882 he merged all his properties into the Standard Oil Trust, which then controlled 95 percent of the oil refining business in America as well as interests in iron ore mines, lumber tracts, manufacturing plants, and transportation. The patriarch of the Morgan financial family, Julius Spencer Morgan (1813–1890), was made rich by his son, banker John Pierpont Morgan (1837–1913). J. P. Morgan formed United States Steel, General Electric, and International Harvester, as well as reorganizing and integrating railroad and coal interests; when J. P. Morgan died, his estate was worth over $70,000,000. The Astor family was founded by John Jacobs Astor (1763–1848), whose fur trading company was the first American business monopoly. His grandson John Jacob Astor III (1822–1890) was the largest private owner of real estate in New York City. John Jacob Astor IV (1862–1912) built four of the largest hotels in New York and several large office buildings and apartments. During the Spanish American War he organized and equipped an artillery battery that served in the Cuban campaign. When John Jacob Astor IV died, his estate was worth $87,218,000. The Vanderbilt family fortune was established through shipping, both steamship and railway lines. Cornelius Vanderbilt (1794–1877) and his son William Henry Vanderbilt (1821–1885) controlled much of the eastern railroad lines, including the route from New York to Chicago, and both served as president of the Lake Shore and Michigan Southern, the Canada Southern, and the Michigan Central railways. The Vanderbilt wealth was estimated at around $100,000,000.

the hoofs, and the sound of his enemy coming on miles distant but you hear not nor do you see beyond your noses.

"Another essential thing for the Trade Unionists is to organize the body of "unemployed", as they are doing now abroad. Get them together and greet them as your brothers and promise to share with them while they are out of work, so that they could not be used by your enemies the capitalists as scabs in case of a strike.

"Why should the workmen be under the moral obligations to notify his employer when he wants to strike? Does your mill owner ever think of notifying you when he intends to lock you out for an indefinite period?

"There is a panic to take place, although our authorities the tools of the rich are trying to hush it up, even appealing to the Church to appease the people. But is bound to come. Now, let me tell you , no man, woman or child has any right to go hungry or go without shelter as long as there are mansions and house enough shelter all of us, and the warehouses are full.

"I know this is high treason you will say. It is criminal to lay hands on private property. But whose property is it? Does it belong the man who produced it or to the one who appropriates what others have produced? Who ix the thief, you who are demanding what is yours, or the one who takes away from you what belongs to you? I am not telling you to steal, I am merely telling you to help yourselves to what by every right belongs to you.

"I will sum up my lecture by these three points:

a) There must be an international union of workmen and act in harmony.
b) Direct Action in case of a strike without notice to employers.
c) Organization of the unemployed with the motto: "No body will starve while the warehouses are full, of all earthly goods.

"If trade unions adopt this method they will bring around a salvation, not the salvation into heaven, but the salvation of mankind on earth."

There were about two hundred people present at the lecture and as all of them understood English, there was a great deal of enthusiasm displayed by the audience, which was evidenced by the frequent ~~enthusiasm~~ applause. As at her lecture in Boston, the lecturer was very cautious in coaching her sentiments. When she mentioned the word "undesirable citizens", which she did frequently it was with great emphasis, and the audience seemed to understand whom she was referring to. She made brief mention of the Haymarket affair, saying that their idea of trade unionism was the same as outlined by her.

At the close of the lecture she announced that she had several copies of the "Mother Earth", which could be had for ten cents a copy, or a dollar a year by subscription. She called special attention to the frontispiece on the cover of the magazine, a drawing by some great French Artist, representing mother earth chained and fettered and kept guard over by Capital with a revolver in one hand and law in the other thus driving the people, the children of the earth from their "mother earth".[8]

RESPECTFULLY,
LOUIS J. DOMAS
INTERPRETER.

TLS, Immigration and Naturalization Service. From the Commissioner of Immigration, Boston, Mass.

8. Jules-Félix Grandjouan (1875–1968) was a French artist who, after leaving law school to pursue a career in art, became a prominent cartoonist for some of the most influential satirical and anarchist journals, including *Les Temps Nouveaux, Le Rire, Le Sourire, Le Canard Sauvage,* and *L'Assiette au Beurre,* was the cover artist for the November 1907 *Mother Earth.* His drawings depicted a wide range of social and political issues, including Algerian independence, foreign spies, and labor laws.

SIR:

Following your instruction, I proceeded last night to #15 Leverett St., to listen to a lecture given by Emma Goldman at that place. At about 8.45 the speaker was introduced by a man, whose name I learned is Shub, a member of the "Group of Anarchists" of this city. The speaker then apologized for her inability to lecture in Yiddish, as her Yiddish was not fluent enough for that but that she would endeavor to use a plain German so that she could be understood by the audience.

The subject for last night's lecture was "The Revolutionary Spirit in the Modern Drama".

"It is commonly thought—she said—that the Revolution as pirit pervades only through the masses of laborers, factory hands, prisoners of Siberia, or those who suffer oppression at the hands of the tyrannic autocrats. Very few stop to realize that the modern drama and our higher literature are full of the spirit of rebellion. The short time allotted to me to-night will not allow me to enumerate all the different plays of that nature, but I will try to depict a few.

"Gorki's play "Na-Dnie" (At the bottom), presents two grand characters.[1] that of old Luka,—a grand old man, who is a friend of all who suffer, all who are downtrodden; who sympathizes with the degraded prostitute and petty criminal, fully understanding that they are the victims of the foul systems of the present Society. Then, there is the character of Nastasia, an ignorant girl, who is mistreated by her brother, brought up amidst vice and immorality,—inspite of all that she comes out pure and honest; instead of being bitter and vengeful she is sympathetic and compassionate with all suferers of mankind, and in her own cruel way she understands that there is something wrong in the present state of affairs, and her spirit cries out: Rebellion against society.

"There is another play, "The Jews", by Chirikov.[2] Nachman, the hero of the play, rebels against Russian Tyranny, not because he is himself oppressed but because his nation is trampled under the feet of the autocratic Czar. He is told that the Jew must wait until there

---

1. Maksim Gorky's controversial and heavily censored play, *The Night's Lodging* (1902, also known as *The Lower Depths* and *At the Bottom*), portrays the destitute lives of people living on the streets of Moscow. EG discusses this play in her 1914 book, *The Social Significance of the Modern Drama*, pp. 294–301.
2. Evgenii Nikolaevich Chirikov (1864–1932) was a Russian playwright. *Die Juden, Shaupiel in 4 Aufzügen* was translated by Georg Polonsk (München: Marchlewski, 1904). Pavel Orlenev opened his U.S. tour with a production of Chirikov's play *The Chosen People* or *The Jew*. EG was a member of the Chirikov Society, a group of Russian immigrants who supported Orlenev's theater troupe.

is a universal emancipation. Nachman ridicules that idea. He says the Jew has suffered long enough; he has been beaten and maltreated and he must get up and rebel, even with weapons in his hands demand justice.

"Tchikov is another one of the Russian playwrights, who endowed his plays with the spirit of rebellion. Tchicov is termed in Russia "The Modern Turgeniev". In his play "Tchaika" he takes up a new field. He does not deal with the poor peasant but with the so-called "Middle Class".[3]

"The principal characters of that play are a Journalist and Poet, an Idealist. The Journalist discovered that this is not an age of ideals; that in order to make use of his pen for remunerative purposes he must strip himself bare of any ideal, and suit the taste of the publisher and the editor, who cater to the Men in Power. The Poet, made the same discovery, but unlike the Journalist, chose to remain loyal to his conscience and his ideals. In spite of the protestations of his friend the Journalist that he is lacking in experience in practical life, he refuses to give up his ideals and prostitute himself by selling out to the Reigning Power. He struggled on and when he found that he could not win out he ended his life with a bullet through his brains.

"Some people ridicule this idea; they say if you beat your head against a thick wall, you are bound to crush your head without affecting the wall any. But, I say, every head crushed against the wall counts, and the time will come when these heads crushed against the wall, and the precious blood besprinkling it, will crash down that thick wall of darkness; the thick wall of tyranny, the thick wall of dspotism. People say what did this fool gain by ending his own life. Nay, my friends, it only proves that in the foul atmosphere of the present corrupt Society it is impossible for a man of pure and idealistic tendencies to live.

"We will now enter the Scandinavian Drama.

"It was said that Ibsen threw more bombs into the present system of social life, than a hundred men could have done.

"Nora of the "Dolls House",[4] after living with her husband eight years and bringing him three children, wakes up one day and leaves him. Not because she was ill-treated; not because she was beaten. She was provided with every luxury by her husband; elegant dresses beautiful home, etc. She leaves her husband because she woke up to the realization of the fact that she lived with her husband for eight years and found that she was living with a stranger. That their ideas were far apart; that her husband loved her not as a companion; not as a fellow associate, but for material reasons,—pleasures of the flesh, and nothing higher than that. She was his puppet, his plaything. She rebelled against it and refused to live any more with a man who was a perfect stranger to her.

---

3. Either EG's interpretation of Anton Chekhov's play *Chaika* (The Seagull) or the interpreter's account of EG's speech is mistaken, as the play's content and structure differ somewhat from this description. EG discusses it again in her *Social Significance of the Modern Drama*, pp. 283–89.
4. Henrik Ibsen's domestic tragedy, *A Doll's House* (1879), addresses the inner conflicts of the nineteenth-century married woman, and her desire for autonomy and freedom. EG discusses this play in *Social Significance of the Modern Drama*, pp. 18–24.

"In the "Ghosts",[5] Ibsen portrays a woman who had the misfortune to marry a man who is afflicted with loathsome diseases, and being afraid that her offspring might suffer by it, goes to Pastor Mondes. She pleads with him, and shows him how distasteful her life would be with the man whom the Law and Church bound her to. The Pastor, what cares he for the suffering of humanity; he is devoid of any feeling for a tortured fellow being, he knows his duty towards GOD, and points out to her her duty to her husband, no matter what her feelings are. She rebels against it but finally submits to the moralizing of the "spiritual adviser", and is recompensed for her years of martyrdom, finding after long years of agony and torture, that the sins of the father are visited on her beloved son, in spite of all precautions she took.

"In the modern German Drama, Gerhard Happtman, in his strong play the "Weavers",[6] describes the sufferings of the poor proletariat, the starved and under paid weavers, and when a spirit of discontent began to pervade among them, the bombastic employer, surrounded by all kinds of comfort and luxury; smoking expensive cigars, laughed to scorn these poor ignorant "animals". But he finally found that it was a matter of more gravity than he ever thought and ultimately found it expedient to submit to the just demands of the poor weavers.

"Of the American Dream I will just mention "Mrs. Warren's Profession", by Bernard M. Shaw.[7]

"Mrs. Warren who conducted several houses of ill fame, reared her daughter, surrounding her with everything she desired, giving her the best of education, and the best of moral training, but she was brought up in absolute ignorance of the mode of life led by her mother and the source of her income. When she discovered that she became very despondent and ran away from home, refusing to benefit by money made through prostitution. A friend of hers, when told by her the reason for her desertion of her mother's home, said to her: "Your mother's money is not any more tainted than all the money there is in the world. There is a mill owner employing six hundred girls paying them $3 a week. Do you mean to say that these girls are able to live on this miserly salar? They are forced to prostitution. The owner of the Department Stores is doing the same. Carnegie with all his libraries he gave to the people who have not the time to read the books in those libraries, produced more prostitution than your mother did. And finally, whose money was it that enriched your mother, and paid or your education? Your mothers numerous

5. In his drama *Ghosts* (1881), Henrik Ibsen addresses issues of spousal abuse, venereal disease, and euthanasia, among other themes. EG analyzes the play in *Social Significance of the Modern Drama*, pp. 25–33.
6. Gerhardt Hauptmann's play *The Weavers* (1892) was a tragic perspective on the lives of the working class. In Germany Max Baginski had helped Hauptmann with his research for the play, and in New York City, Johann Most produced, directed, and acted in it regularly. EG discusses *The Weavers* in her *Social Significance of Modern Drama*, pp. 98–107.
7. George Bernard Shaw's play *Mrs. Warren's Profession* (written 1893, produced 1902) criticizes Victorian attitudes about prostitution. In 1906, in New York City, the police interrupted the play and stopped its performance. EG discusses Shaw's play in her *Social Significance of Modern Drama*, pp. 175–85.

establishments were patronized by cannons of the Church, by Pillars of Society, by representatives of the Army and by representatives of every walk in the life.["]

The Hall was crowded to the doors by Yiddish speaking people, but owing to the fact that the lecture was given in German, instead of Yiddish, as it was announced, there was a spirit of discontent, and I heard murmurs of regret by many people there, saying that they could not follow her.

At the end of the lecture Miss Goldman invited the audience to ask her questions and that she would endeavor to answer them. But save for a few very silly questions asked by a couple of young men, who it could be easily perceived could not follow the trend of her lecture, none cared to ask any questions. She scored the women present for the lack of interest displayed by them, by not coming forward and debate with her upon questions paramount to their own welfare, but after waiting a considerable length of time, for answers which failed to come forth, the meeting was closed.

RESPECTFULLY,
LOUIS J. DOMAS
INTERPRETER

ALS, Immigration and Naturalization Service.

Sir:

I have the honor to report that pursuant to your verbal instructions, I proceeded to Paterson, N. J., on the 7:21 p.m. train from Rutherford, December 23, 1907, arriving at the first-named place at 7:57 p.m. A police officer at the Station directed me to the Paterson Police Headquarters on Washington Street, where I presented your letter. The police stated that they had no knowledge of an anarchist meeting at 184 Main Street. The Chief of Police was not there, but the Acting Captain promptly detailed two plain clothes men to accompany me to the place indicated. The hall was on the top floor of the building over The New York Dental Parlors. To avoid attracting attention, I went up ahead and had the officers follow a little while afterward. I found about five hundred men, women and children in the hall, Hebrews predominating. A number of Italians were also present. Two men seated at a table near the door were collecting money from members, but no admission fee was charged.

Emma Goldman began her address about 8:30 o'clock p.m., and spoke continuously until 9:45. She stated the subject of her ad [*2-3 words illegible*]

"Anarchism does not stand for what the newspapers tell you it stands for, namely, bomb throwing, and the free use of dynamite and daggers. Such a conception of anarchism arose and exists only in the shallow brains of newspaper editors. Anarchism does *not* aim at the destruction of life and property. I stand here to-night to advocate no such practices. I advocate the same principles that Thoreau, Emerson, Stuart Mills,[1] and many other great thinkers advocated. The majority of people who denounce anarchism and the anarchists have never taken the trouble to investigate what these terms really mean. It is fashionable to be against the anarchists, so they condemn them without a hearing. Now what does anarchism really stand for? It stands for the universal brotherhood of man, for the emancipation and complete freedom of the individual. As we look at the present state of society, we cannot help but notice that something is radically wrong. Why? Because we notice unwholesome and distressing abnormalities. On the one hand we notice people like John D. Rockefeller, with his uncounted millions, gained by the defraudation of his

---

1. EG, following the tradition of the Haymarket anarchists, often refers to Henry David Thoreau's and Ralph Waldo Emerson's philosophies as expressing anarchist ideals. John Stuart Mill (1806–1973), the English philosopher and economist best known for his adherence to utilitarian political theories, envisioned a liberal democratic government, efficient and responsive enough to benefit the widest possible range of citizens. The influence of John Mill (Mill's father) and Jeremy Bentham (the originator of utilitarianism) can be seen in Mill's works, including *A System of Logic* (1843), *Principles of Political Economy* (1848), and *Utilitarianism* (1863).

fellow men and the relentless crushing of every competitor. On the other hand we see men like Tschaikowsky,[2] who is even now in the hands of the Czar's minions, because he dared to speak and to act in the interests of the common people. These two men are types of the two extremes in society as it is constituted at the present day. Rockefeller has amassed great wealth by reaping the profits of the hard labor of others. He represents the individualistic principle carried to excess. He is a man who thinks first, last and always of himself. Tschaikowsky on the other hand lives his life to bettering the condition of his fellow men. He teaches them what is their right, teaches them how to help themselves and each other, and in this way works for the betterment of society in his own country and the world at large.

["]Some people will tell you that the anarchists want to destroy all property rights and divide up everything equally. Nothing was ever more erroneous than this. I myself do not want any such division. You do not want it either. What we anarchists demand is this: Each man is entitled to, and should be protected in the enjoyment of the fruits of his own individual labors—no more, and no less. If one man by his greater ability accumulates greater possessions than another—well and good,—there is nothing objectionable in that to the anarchists. But when a man reaches out his hand in greed to grasp the profits and earnings of his fellow men, and appropriates to his own use the results of the labor another, or of ten, or fifteen, or a hundred, or of thousands of others, and thereby causes them to lose their share of this world's legitimate pleasures, the anarchist is aroused to action. Just what that action will be depends upon his personal disposition and character entirely.

["]The claim is made that anarchists are opposed to all forms of government. That may be true or it may not be true. If government really does the people good, by all means let us have government. But does the government really do all that is claimed for it? It is claimed that the government protects our property. Does it? What the government really protects is the property of the rich. It does not protect your property, because you have great riches. When there is a great strike, does the Government protect the workingmen? No, indeed. The Government in such a case sends out its militia or its regular army to protect the very people who are responsible for the strike through their selfishness. Was not this what happened in the mining districts of Nevada?[3] They tell us we cannot get along without laws. But who knows all the laws? A noted lawyer said not so long ago that at the present time there were so many laws on the statute books that no man could possibly live long enough to learn them all. And all these laws were not made for your protection, mind you.

2. Nikolai Chaikovsky (1851–1926) was a prominent member of the Russian Socialist Revolutionaries and a proponent of terrorism and guerrilla warfare against the regime of Tsar Nicholas II.
3. During the miners' strike at Goldfield, Nevada (1906–1908), Governor John Sparks, having no state militia, requested federal troops from President Roosevelt. Despite the lack of evidence of violence on the part of the strikers, Roosevelt sent troops to Goldfield. With federal protection and the state legislature's passage of a police bill establishing a state militia, owners of the mines defeated the WFM and IWW, cementing open-shop policy by early 1908.

They were made for the protection of the fellow that robs you. We are told that these laws guarantee to us our freedom and our equality. That is the same old lullaby that has been repeated over and over again to us. Every Fourth of July something like this is sung to us, and to the unthinking masses it is a lullaby that puts them to sleep for the rest of the year. We are told that America is the most civilized country in the world, while Russia is uncivilized and barbarian. Is this really so? Can any of you who have watched events in this country, I will not say for the past twenty-five, or twenty, or ten years,—let us say for the past five years only,—can you truthfully say that America, with its laws favoring the rich and persecuting the poor is really so far advanced? I tell you Russia has done more during the past five years to advance the world in science, literature and art, and general civilization that America has in twenty-five.

["]It is said that the Government educates our children. Does it? What is education? True education is a training that leads to self-knowledge and gives the individual the power to help himself and others. Your children are not given this kind of an education. When they are taught history, for instance, they are told about a few emperors, kings and presidents who waged war on neighboring or distant countries, and they are taught that the greatest of these is the one who holds the record for the largest number of deaths through the wanton slaughtering of so-called Christian warfare. Does such instruction instill good principles and build up pure character? It is as Carlyle says regarding two rulers, too cowardly to do their own fighting, who force a lot of young men into uniforms, stick guns into their hands and then turn them upon each other like so many savage beasts.[4] And this they label patriotism! There are the principles the Government instills into the minds of your children. They are taught to allow themselves to be led like sheep to the slaughter, simply because some official orders it. President Roosevelt has a big stick and a little brains, very little brains, but then—he has a big stick. As long as people will not make use of their own brains, they will always be easy marks for men with big sticks. The idea that we need the Government to preserve order has been repeated so often that the unthinking accept it as absolutely true; and even when they reach the point where they believe that they themselves can get along without the policeman and his club, they still cling to the idea that the other fellow needs such restraining power. In this same class are the majority of reformers. Such people will do many things for their fellow men: They will give them soup-kitchens, free lectures and libraries, sewing and much more, but there is one thing they will not do, and that is, get off the other fellow's back and give him a chance to plan and work out his own life. They want to exercise control in return for their gifts. You know the old fable in the Bible about Adam and Eve. How God placed them in a garden and told them not to eat of the tree of knowledge, and when they did, he kicked them out of heaven. This is exactly what our Governments do. As soon as we

---

4. In an address given by EG in London on 20 February 1900, she similarly alluded to Carlyle's *Sartor Resartus: The Life and Opinions of Herr Teufelsdröckh* (bk. 2, chap. 8; see "The Effect of War on the Workers," Transcript of address in *Freedom*, 20 February 1900, in vol. 1).

strive after real knowledge, the kind that is not taught in their schools, they will kick us out too. The Government strives to suppress crime by imprisonment and execution. Do you know that it taxes you over a million dollars a year for the maintenance of prisons? And yet these prisons contain only people who have been foolish enough to steal small sums of money or articles of little value. Most of these prisoners have been forced by the existing economic conditions to commit the offences for which they have been arrested. The real thieves, the men who do their stealing on a large scale, under the mantle of business operations, they go free; and not only do they go free, but the laws actually protect and legalize their robberies. I think the man who steals my pocketbook is a harmless person compared to the man who steals my chances of employment and ruins the possibilities of my making a living for myself and my family.

["]Anarchism has no set rules. Its precepts and its methods vary according to the age, the temperament and the surroundings of its followers, but there is one principle it teaches which is fundamental, and that is the imperative duty of direct action of the individual. For instance, take the matter of eighty cent gas. . . . [*1 line illegible*]

["]But it is one of those problems which can only be solved by the direct action of each individual consumer. The law will not help you. That has been proven by the fact that the Supreme Court has declared the eighty cent law unconstitutional. How can you achieve the desired end? Very easily. When the collector comes with his bill made out at the one dollar rate, pay him only eighty cents, and if he protests, politely throw him downstairs. If all of you did that the gas company would soon come to the conclusion that eighty cents is all it can expect. The real trouble is that you think you cannot get along without the gas company, when the fact is, the gas company cannot get along without you. You have convinced your mind that the company is really very kind because it does not ask $1.25, and is letting you off easy at a dollar. The same principle holds true in regard to carfare. If you all boarded street cars and when the conductor came around for the fare paid him only two or three cents, he would have to accept that or nothing; and you would be justified in doing this, because you know that the company would be making great profit even at the lower fare. Just so, in every department of life, direct action by the individual will solve all the problems that come up. I believe with Nietzsche[5] that the time has come for a trans-valuation of things. In the past we have been taught to regard many worthless and harmful things as necessary and beneficent. I tell you friends, the time has come for a trans-valuation, that is, for a re-consideration of the value of things, and to this end each of you must do his share by his individual, direct action. Here it is where anarchism will help you. You will know that you have comrades striving for the same results as yourself, helping you by their example, but not interfering with your personal efforts. Some people say the world is not ready for anarchism, that it must first pass through many preparatory stages, but I tell you, if the principle is right at all, it is as right now as it ever was, or ever

---

5. Works by the German philosopher Friedrich Nietzsche, including *The Will to Power; an Attempted Transvaluation of All Values*, influenced EG and other anarchists.

will be. Study these great principles and apply them in your own lives—<u>now.</u> That is all, friends. I thank you for your attention."

Miss Goldman was the only speaker of the evening. After her speech the persons in the hall gathered in groups to discuss her remarks. As I was about to leave the hall I found that two more plain clothes men had been detailed for my protection. The Paterson police were prompt and courteous in taking up this matter, which was unexpectedly brought to their attention.

One of the two men first detailed accompanied me to within two blocks of the railroad depot. I boarded the 10:14 train for Rutherford.

RESPECTFULLY SUBMITTED,

F. W. C. MAASCH.

CLERK-STENOGRAPHER.

TDS, file #51,694/2, Immigration and Naturalization Service, DNA. Addressed to Hon. Robert Watchorn, Commissioner of Immigration, Ellis Island, N.Y.H. [New York Harbor]. On stationery of the Office of the Commissioner.

SIR:

Yesterday morning I was requested by Chief of Police Creecy,[1] of this City, to call upon him for a "confidential discussion of an important matter," and when I reached his office he showed me an unsigned message from Chicago stating that the Immigration authorities and United States Attorney there had stated that when Emma Goldman, the Anarchist lecturer, appeared in that City she would be arrested, as the Immigration Bureau desired to bring about her deportation, she "having lost her right of citizenship by departing from the country last year". This message was palpably garbled and erroneous, but the main point appeared plausible, and Chief Creecy announced that the Goldman woman was now in St. Louis, at a given address,[2] and that he intended to run her out of town immediately, unless I chose to take action under the Immigration law.[3] He promised to withhold action until the afternoon upon my agreement to obtain instructions at the earliest possible moment, whereupon I communicated with you by telegraph, receiving your reply very promptly, for which I beg to thank you.

I enclose a clipping from the St. Louis "Times", February 28,[4] which was shown me shortly before I received your reply, and was a matter of surprise, for the reason that no one in this office except myself and stenographer knew of the case,[5] and Chief Creecy had enjoined strict secrecy, which I supposed would be observed by the police authorities as well.

1. Edmund P. Creecy (1847–1913) was chief of police in St. Louis. Creecy had worked as a civil engineer, joined the St. Louis Police Department as a patrolman in 1877, was promoted to sergeant in 1895, captain in 1899, and chief on 19 September 1906. Creecy was tried and found guilty of indiscretion concerning embezzlement of money from the police relief fund by the fund's secretary; he was dismissed on 9 April 1910.
2. EG was staying at 1530 Walsh St., St. Louis.
3. Under the Immigration Act of 1907, anarchists could be excluded from immigrating to the United States. Although EG's citizenship status was in question at this time, the government did not have sufficient grounds to deport her under the terms of the act.
4. The 28 February 1908 article in the *St. Louis Times,* titled "Would Banish Emma Goldman," stated that Chief Creecy was considering whether to arrest her, having had a conference with Immigration Inspector Dunn. The article also stated that both the U.S. district attorney's office and the Labor and Commerce Department were working together "cleaning out the anarchists" under the 1907 Immigration law.
5. EG claimed citizenship through both her father (a naturalized citizen) and her marriage to Jacob Kershner (also a naturalized citizen). The government, however, was compiling a case to revoke Kershner's citizenship, and EG's claim to citizenship through her father was tenuous, given that she was not a minor at the time of his naturalization.

No action was taken by me in this matter with the exception of conferring with Chief Creecy at his request, telegraphing you for instructions.

RESPECTFULLY,

JAMES R. DUNN

INSPECTOR IN CHARGE.

TDS, file #51,694/2, Immigration and Naturalization Service, DNA. Addressed to Hon. F. P. Sargent,[6] Commissioner-General of Immigration, Washington, D.C. On stationery of the Office of Inspector in Charge.

6. Frank P. Sargent (1854–1908) was appointed to the U.S. Industrial Commission in 1898 and became U.S. Commissioner General of Immigration in 1902, where he worked to restrict immigration and was especially critical of the increased immigration from southern and eastern Europe. Sargent had been a railroad worker and grand master of the Brotherhood of Locomotive Fireman from 1885 to 1902. He was a member of the National Civic Federation and a confidant of Samuel Gompers and John Mitchell and acted as counsel for their conferences with President Theodore Roosevelt during the anthracite coal strike of 1902.

City authorities very much worked up over activity of Chicago anarchists Emma Goldman, noted anarchist, scheduled to speak here Friday evening, March sixth. Am informed she is not a citizen, that she departed from Port of New York for Europe sometime ago, and that she reentered this country within last few months. Have you any record as to her citizenship and whether her re-entry was lawful. If not a citizen and her re-entry unlawful and surreptitious request warrant by wire for her arrest and deportation. Suggest warrant be directed to Inspector Seraphio, who is here. City authorities will cooperate.

Sims,
U.S. Attorney.

W, file #51,694/2, Immigration and Naturalization Service, RG 85, DNA.

Sims sent his telegram on the same day that the Chicago police chief's life was apparently threatened by an alleged anarchist. (Department of Justice, National Archives and Records Administration)

Appeal
Chicago, 6 March 1908

A Letter to The Public of Chicago

By the Anarchist Federation

Monday morning a shooting episode took place at the house of Chief of Police Shippy, an episode both brutal and tragic.[1] A few hours later the papers of the city came out in large, sensational headlines stating that the boy who had been shot and killed by Chief Shippy was an anarchist, that he had come with the intention to kill the chief of police, that the boy had been chosen by lot to commit this act in an anarchist conspiracy in this city.[2]

This was said even before Lazarus Averbuch had been identified. As a consequence the anarchists of this city as well as anarchists at large were hounded, maligned, and misrepresented in the grossest manner. Their clubrooms were closed, their libraries confiscated in true Russian autocratic manner. Not a paper was willing to hear "the other side," an old cherished American custom.

The victim of Monday's tragedy being dead, no one is in a position to say what his intention might have been in calling upon the chief, nor has he left a written statement as to his belief or disbelief in organized government. The police have certainly tried their utmost to do that and to connect him with anarchy. That they have failed shamefully no one but the most foolish will deny. However, that is not of importance at present. What is of importance are the facts connected with the mystery at the chief's house.

First, according to Chief Shippy's own statement,[3] he grabbed Lazarus Averbuch by the wrist as soon as he handed him the "famous letter," while the chief's wife searched the boy's pockets—which means she found a revolver and a knife and, no doubt, she had the good sense to take these weapons from him. How, then, could Averbuch shoot the chief?

---

1. On 2 March 1908 Lazarus Averbuch, a young Russian Jewish immigrant, went to the home of Police Chief George Shippy. What happened next remains unclear. The newspapers reported Averbuch coming into the police chief's house on the attack. However, Averbuch was shot six times and killed, Shippy was left with minor wounds, his son Harry Shippy was hospitalized from gunshot wounds, and their driver James Foley was also wounded.
2. This statement was printed in the *Chicago Daily Journal* on 2 March 1908. The incident was front-page news in the 3 March 1908 *Chicago Inter Ocean*, with statements by Shippy's family, and a description of Averbuch as "born and bred a nihilist, and fresh from the horrors of Kishenev."
3. Shippy released a statement that appeared in the afternoon papers, including the 2 March 1908 *Chicago Daily Journal*.

Second, according to Chief Shippy's second statement, the boy succeeded in tearing away from him, which in itself is absurd, with the chief as an expert official at handling all sorts of desperadoes holding with an iron grip the wrists of a half starved Jewish boy. But taking it for granted that the boy did tear away from that human handcuff, which in itself disqualifies Chief Shippy from further holding of office for protecting law and order, we, the anarchists of Chicago, ask what did Averbuch shoot the chief's son with after Mrs. Shippy had ransacked his pockets?

3. Will the chief produce the bullet taken from the body of his son? He owes it to the public and to himself, since the general rumor about town will have it that this bullet belonged to a 38-caliber revolver, while Averbuch's weapon was supposed to have been a 32.

4. Why did Chief Shippy shoot Averbuch seven times after he had struck the boy down with the first shot, and when he could have put him on the floor with one knockout blow?

We ask these questions out of common humanity to the dead boy in the potter's field and in justice to the anarchists of this country, who, notwithstanding all misrepresentations, stand for an ideal of human regeneration, which, according to the Century Dictionary, denotes "a state of society based upon the union of order of man by man"—in short, individual liberty and human brotherhood.

We further wish to know whether the police department of this city have taken it upon themselves to interpret the constitutional rights of the American people, to whom free speech and a free assembly still seem the most important bulwark of this country.

The anarchists of this city, federated into one body and affiliated with the anarchist federation of New York and of Massachusetts, also with the international body organized at the anarchist congress at Amsterdam August, 1907,[4] have carried on an educational work through lecture and literature. They have invited me to deliver a series of lectures. For that purpose they have engaged halls under written agreement. In doing so they merely assumed what Chief Schuettler admitted today,[5] namely, "Emma Goldman and her people have constitutional rights which we cannot stop." Yet Mr. Schuettler, who is suffering from anarchia-mania (he is hysterical for his supposed rooting out of anarchism and discovering of anarchist plots), aided by the police department, has taken it upon himself to rob me of my constitutional rights, to throttle free speech and free assemblage by intimidating hallkeepers on the grounds that their beer licenses would be taken from them.[6]

I do not know the sentiments of the intelligent public of this city as to the sacred rights

---

4. EG attended the International Anarchist Congress in Amsterdam in 1907, where the idea for an international federation of affiliated anarchists groups was proposed. The first American Anarchist Federation was organized in late 1907 and early 1908 by AB. See also "The International Anarchist Congress," Essay in *Mother Earth*, October 1907, above.

5. Chief Herman Schuettler was well known to EG. As a young detective on the Chicago police force, he had captured Louis Lingg after the Haymarket riot and, in 1901, he had interrogated EG after the assassination of President McKinley.

6. Police did not allow EG to give any lectures while she was in Chicago. From her 5 March arrival until 20 March when she departed, she was barred from all public speaking engagements.

of free speech. I know, however, that police persecution, brutality and misrepresentation are not the methods that will ever stop the truth. I therefore wish to inform those who are still eager to maintain their freedom that neither the anarchist federation of Chicago nor I will be silenced; that we shall be heard even at the expense of personal liberty.

We believe, with the great American anarchist, David D. Thoreau, and in his drastic reply to his friend, Ralph Waldo Emerson, American anarchist.

Thoreau had been imprisoned for refusing to pay taxes. Emerson, the other great American anarchist visited his friend and asked, "David, what are you doing here? Ralph, what are you doing outside, when honest men are in prison"!

Emma Goldman.

TDU, Emma Goldman Archive, IISH. The letter was drafted by EG on 6 March at the home of William Daltich and was approved by the Anarchist Federation of Chicago. According to the 7 March *Chicago Inter Ocean,* William Nathanson, Miriam Yamplosky, and Lucy Parsons were all present. Fifty thousand copies of the document were mailed to Chicago residents.

Interview in the *CHICAGO INTER OCEAN*

Chicago, 8 March 1908

Emma Goldman Clashes with Police on Meeting

Queen of "Reds" Flings Down Challenge to Officials, Declaring that She Will Address Gathering Today Despite Opposition.

Today it is Emma Goldman, queen of the anarchists, against the police.

The high priestess of anarchy says she will speak at a hall in the Masonic temple today. The police say she will not. What will come out of the clash of wills time alone will tell.

Last night the leader of the reds gave detectives a merry chase around the city, following her statement that she had been engaged to address half a hundred wealthy Chicagoans at a mansion on the Lake Shore drive. Miss Goldman made the statement that she would speak in a residence on the drive, without reservation, in the afternoon. But she accompanied it with the assertion that no one would follow her, as she would "give them the slip."

Consequently, a body of six or more men haunted the vicinity of the Winchester avenue house last night in the effort to shadow the leader of the reds. When a score or more persons emerged from the house and boarded a street car they were permitted to depart in peace.

A few minutes later, when a short, nervous woman emerged from the house and boarded a car the detectives were fast on the scent.

"Shh! Emma sure!" said the leader of the sleuths.

The trail was a devious one. It led from the West Side to the North Side, then to the loop, and thence south on Wabash avenue to the Coliseum Annex, where the annual ball of the Garment Workers was in progress. As soon as the diminutive woman entered the hall she whipped out a black silk domino, and plunged into the vortex of masked dancers. The sleuths sought and sought until unmasking time. And then the figure could not be found.

TEACHES FREE LOVE CULT.

Emma Goldman, leading exponent of anarchy in America, is in Chicago to encourage the establishment of a free love colony and to urge among women, with reference to marriage, adoption of the only practice recognized in anarchist propaganda.

"This Shippy case is a very small matter. My visit to Chicago was arranged long before the killing of the Averbuch boy,"[1] said Miss Goldman.

---

1. EG refers to Chicago Police Chief George Shippy and his alleged "assassin" Lazarus Averbuch (see "Appeal to The Public of Chicago," 6 March 1908, above).

As she did the day before, Miss Goldman spent yesterday indoors. She is at the home of William Daltich, 970 North Winchester avenue. During the morning and afternoon she received a long string of visitors.

"The new thing in anarchistic educational work is connected with women," she continued. "Elevation of women to a plane of equality is not a whit less important to us than the dissolution of government. Spasms of the police all over this land have served to give greater prominence to our anti-government beliefs. But we really are just now vitally interested in the emancipation of woman.

"Work to this end has been pushed, particularly since the international conference of anarchists in Amsterdam.[2] Then it was determined that work for the freedom of woman should go hand in hand with efforts toward the abolition of government.

"We believe in free love. Such a relation as that of husband and wife should only be constituted when a man and a woman love each other. When they cease to love that relationship should end. Women anarchists all over the country practice that theory now. I am here in Chicago for the purpose of encouraging the practice."

Anarchists of Chicago, who have been seeking to secure a hall in which Emma Goldman may speak, reported complete failure last night.

Miss Goldman said: "It is impossible to secure a hall. We have approached the managers of dozens of halls and theaters in Chicago. Men who have the halls told us that the police had threatened to revoke their liquor licenses if they rented their places to us. The managers of the down town theaters, to whom we offered any sum they saw fit to ask, told us that since the Iroquois fire the police had exercised such arbitrary supervision that they did not dare do anything contrary to the desires of the department.[3]

"During the day four or five vacant lots were found where a tent could be erected, but water stood on all of them, so I refused to have any of them rented. I don't want typhoid and pneumonia to follow my lecture."

WILL SPEAK THIS AFTERNOON.

"No meetings will be held tomorrow, except in the rooms of the Social Science club on the fourteenth floor of the Masonic Temple building. The place will accommodate 300, I think. The club has been meeting there regularly for four years. I shall leave the house at 7 o'clock and will go in a cab to the Masonic temple. If the police stop me I'll come back home. If they don't I'll talk at the meeting. I will speak about local conditions, of course.

"Tonight, late, I am going to a conference of leading anarchists of Chicago. I cannot say where. The family is prominent and wealthy. Fifty more like them in Chicago are anarchists, but by reason of their business and social relationships cannot afford just now

---

2. The International Anarchist Congress took place in Amsterdam from 24 to 31 August 1907.
3. On 30 December 1903, between 550 and 600 people were killed in a fire at the Iroquois Theater in Chicago.

to let their position be known. You can say that the house is on the North Side, on the Lake Shore drive. Invitations to fifty or fifty-five have been sent out."

"What further has been done, Miss Goldman, with reference to investigating the shooting at the home of Chief of Police Shippy?"

SIFTING AVERBUCH DEATH.

"We secured information today that young Averbuch had been trying to get on the fire department, and that the letter he had in his hand when he went to Shippy's home was from some political friend recommending him to the chief. Of course we have no proof of that yet. Anarchists of Chicago are now at work collecting a fund which will aggregate several thousand dollars with which to push this investigation.

"Wealthy Jews of the city, who wish to wipe from their race the stain attaching when a murderer rises among them, have contributed generously to this fund. The matter will be taken up next week, and the best attorney Chicago affords will be engaged to do the work.

"I am determined to speak in Chicago. We have decided to rent a store building. If necessary to secure one we will rent it for a year. I shall be in Chicago only until the 19th of this month. On the 20th I speak in Milwaukee. I go from there directly to Minneapolis, New Ulm, and Winnipeg, then to Omaha, Denver, and the coast."

Speaking of her life Miss Goldman said she was born in St. Petersburg and that she was educated there and at Konigsburg, Prussia.[4]

"As a child I resented any authority. My father was severe. He used to beat me whenever he caught me talking to the servants. We had three. I used to try and see that they had good things to eat, and whenever father caught me saving a dainty morsel for them he would whip me.

"I suppose I have always been an anarchist, but the Haymarket riots in Chicago, and the action of the brutal police on that occasion, determined me to become an avowed anarchist, and to devote my life to the cause. Though the police killed a few members of the Chicago society then, they have not killed anarchy in America.

"While I was a young girl my parents decided that I should have a limited education. I rebelled. I did not understand why a girl should not know just as much as a boy. So I got hold of all the forbidden books I could and I devoured them all. My sister helped to get them to me by one source and another."

BECOMES WOMAN'S CHAMPION.

"I used to read what the leading philosophers wrote about women. That's what led me to champion the cause of women and devote my life to their emancipation. I shall strive until I die to break the shackles that make them the chattels of men. My whole life shall be a plea for their freedom.

4. EG was actually born in the Russian city of Kovno, in modern Lithuania.

"I remember when I was a little child robbing a bank. I was 8 years old. In the village where I lived a beautiful young peasant girl had been deceived in love. The people of the village were talking about her and she was crushed under the shame. I resented the fingers that were pointed at her. I knew she was suffering and I sorrowed with her. So I took the money from another little girl's bank and told the deceived girl to use it getting out of the country.

"Years afterward, when I read Hawthorne's 'The Scarlet Letter,'[5] it reminded me of that peasant girl."

Chicago Inter Ocean, 8 March 1908, pp. 1, 3.

5. Nathaniel Hawthorne's *The Scarlet Letter* (Boston: Ticknor, Reed and Field, 1850) is about a woman's stigmatization for love outside the norms of the community; Hester is punished for her adultery with the wearing of the scarlet letter "A".

Dear Sir:

Your telegram of March 2d, regarding Emma Goldman, was received in due course. Immediately upon its receipt I sent you the following telegram:

> "No action should be taken until we have the facts whether the person referred to in your telegram of yesterday is citizen or not. We are having investigations made. Should person be citizen, effect of arrest will be the very opposite what is desired. Great care must be taken in such matters not to put Government in false position. Forward any information you have, in accordance with requirements of immigration law."

The Bureau of Immigration, ever since Emma Goldman returned to the United States from her recent trip abroad, has, through the United States Secret Service Division, been following up her movements, and also taken stenographic notes of her addresses, which have been carefully examined by the Solicitor of this Department. Her addresses are very skillfully made, so as not to be open to the charge of anarchistic utterances. Besides the foregoing, and this is of most importance, the Bureau of Immigration has been unable to ascertain whether Emma Goldman is or is not an American citizen. Such information as was obtained would indicate that she is an American citizen, having become such while a minor through the naturalization of her father.[1]

The entire subject has had my careful attention and I feel convinced that any precipitate action, which might be vacated by the courts upon habeas corpus,[2] would defeat the purposes of the Government, and in the eyes of the masses make a martyr of Emma Goldman. This, upon deliberate consideration, is precisely what I wish to avoid, and therefore I deem it highly inadvisable to take any action that might have such an effect as above indicated.

Could you perhaps ascertain whether Emma Goldman is or is not an American citizen, and if she claims naturalization through her father, whether that claim is well founded. You are familiar with the immigration laws, and therefore know what facts are necessary

---

1. The status of citizenship by "naturalization" was based upon strict criteria: an immigrant had to reside continuously in the United States for at least five years prior to filing a petition for citizenship and through the granting of citizenship, as well as for six months within the state in which the immigrant was petitioning. The petitioner also had to be a person of "good, moral" character, willing to abide by and uphold the principles of the U.S. Constitution *(54 Stat. 1142)*.
2. Habeas corpus literally means (in Latin) "that you have the body," referring to a writ issued by a court demanding that a person held in custody be brought before the court to determine whether the detention is lawful. Habeas corpus ensures that a prisoner is accorded due process of law; it is not a determinant of guilt or innocence.

in order to issue an order of arrest, and to bring about deportation. Up to the present time the Department has not been able to get any information upon these points.

To arrest her in order to ascertain these facts would, in my judgment after careful consideration, be very unwise, unless an order of deportation could certainly follow.

RESPECTFULLY,

TDU, file #51,694/2, Immigration and Naturalization Service, RG 85, DNA. Addressed to Mr. Edwin W. Sims, United States District Attorney, Chicago, Illinois. Carbon copy of this letter ends with the typed word "[signatory]".

Article in the *CHICAGO DAILY JOURNAL*

Chicago, 17 March 1908

Reds' Leader Flays Police

Emma Goldman Explains Anarchy in Written Address
Shippy Refuses to Let Her Deliver

Bitterness of Chicago's anarchist colony was centered today upon Capt. John J. Mahoney and the policemen under him for alleged brutality toward the chosen leader of the "reds," Emma Goldman.[1]

It was asserted the big police captain with fifty men at his back struck Miss Goldman in the face before he dragged her from Workingmen's hall, West Twelfth and Waller streets, and broke up the anarchist meeting which she was trying to address.

Charges that free speech is being suppressed were renewed, following the incident, and it was intimated that appeal to that which anarchists most abhor—the courts—would be the outcome.[2]

Announcement by the police that they will seek means to deport the "Queen of the Reds" from Chicago led her to cancel engagements that would have caused her to leave the city voluntarily Thursday.

"When the police could no longer resort to subterfuge in closing halls for noncompliance with building regulations in order to silence us they did not hesitate to use violence," said Miss Goldman.

"I was struck in the face and dragged like a sack of flour through the hall, in addition to being sworn at and subjected to a tirade of language of the gutter.

"Capt. Mahoney said to me, 'I will break every bone in your body.' I told him I knew he could, but that he could not break my spirit.

"I had said nothing unlawful, nor did I contemplate such a thing."

1. On 17 March, Assistant Police Chief Herman Schuettler criticized Captain John J. Mahoney for acting "contrary to orders" by preventing Goldman from speaking.
2. Ben Reitman, Chicago physician and hobo who would become EG's lover and tour manager, sought an injunction against police interference in anticipation of EG's talk at a North Side hall, a strategy in which EG chose not to participate. No hall was secured. In response to the infringement of free speech at the 16 March meeting, protest "letters to the editor" were written by some of Chicago's leading citizens. Rabbi Hirsch, leader of the Chicago Sinai Congregation, delivered a sermon in support of EG's right to speak.

TEXT OF FORBIDDEN SPEECH

In support of her contention Miss Goldman handed the interviewer the manuscript of her address.[3] The complete text follows:

"To the popular mind anarchism stands for destruction; to the more enlightened it stands for an ideal—a beautiful but thoroughly impracticable ideal. Anarchism does stand for the destruction of the institutions that have been and are keeping the human mind in bondage and that are robbing mankind of the right to the use of the necessities of life.

"Viewed from the standpoint of cents and dollars, anarchism is truly impracticable, and those whose aim in life is wealth and power will do well to keep out of the anarchist movement. But measured by true value, namely, human character, integrity and real usefulness to society, anarchism is the most practical of all theories—a proposition which I shall attempt to prove.

"Anarchism is a theory of human development which lays no less stress than socialism upon the economic or materialistic aspect of social relations; but while granting that the cause of the immediate evil is an economic one we believe that the solution of the social question confronting us today must be wrought out from the equal consideration of the whole of our experience.

"To understand society as a whole it behooves the social student to analyze the separate atoms of society—namely, the individual and the motives that prompt every individual and every collective act. What are these motives?

"First, the individual instinct, standing for self-expression; second, the social instinct, which inspires collective and social life. These instincts in their latent condition are never antagonistic to each other.

"On the contrary, they are dependent upon one another for their complete and normal development. Unfortunately, the organization of society is such that these instincts are being brought into constant antagonism.

"Indeed, the history of our experience in thought and action is the record of this strife within each individual and its reflection within each society.

"To better illustrate my point, let me give you two cases, representing the extreme development of individual and social instinct. Take Russell Sage,[4] for instance, a man

3. "Anarchy and What It Really Stands For" was later published in pamphlet form under the title *A Beautiful Ideal,* with the subheading, "The lecture which Emma Goldman was to have read before the Edelstadt Social, March 17th, 1908, at Workingmens' Hall, 12th & Waller Streets, Chicago. But was prevented by Captain Mahoney of Maxwell Street Station with a squad of about fifty police" (Chicago: J. C. Hart, 1908). See *EGP,* reel 47. A reworked version of "Anarchism: What It Really Stands For" is published in *Anarchism and Other Essays* (1910). The title is revisited again by EG in the late 1920s. See *EGP,* reel 51.

4. Russell Sage (1816–1906) was a New York City financier, railroad magnate, Whig representative in Congress (1853–1857), and business partner of Jay Gould. EG wrote a short piece on his life in the August 1906 *Mother Earth.* At the time of his death he was one of the nation's wealthiest individuals. After his death, his widow, Margaret Olivia Sage, donated millions of dollars to charity, reframing the negative cast on the Sage legacy.

whose individual instincts knew no bounds, a man who, to use a common proverb, did not even observe the ordinary honesty existing among thieves."

SAYS SAGE CRUSHED OUT LIFE

"I mean that his methods of accomplishing his aim, the accumulation of wealth, were so obscure, so unscrupulous, that even his own colleagues in the rogue business had little regard for him.

"Indeed, it is safe to say that the instinct that prompted the actions of Russell Sage were so antisocial that every one of his steps resulted in crushing out human life and in bringing untold misery and poverty upon those whom his iron heel did not actually crush.

"Such a type of a man is possible only in a society based upon inequality, a society that is held together not by natural bonds, but by artificial and arbitrary methods.

"Again, let us take a type of human being with the social instinct developed to the extreme—Louise Michel, the world-renowned anarchist, "Mother Louise," as she was called by every child of the gutter. Her love for man and beast knew no bounds.

"It mattered not whether it was a forlorn kitten or a homeless dog, or a shelter less human being—she gave to all, even the last crust of bread."

BELIEVE CONDITIONS WRONG

"Yet to satisfy her great soul she was compelled to deny her individual instinct to the extent of living in great and constant poverty, of exposing herself to many dangers, to imprisonment, and to the heat of New Caledonia, whither she had been sent with many other political prisoners after the Paris Commune of '71.

"Anarchists insist that conditions must be radically wrong if human instincts develop to such extremes at the expense of each other.

"Anarchism in its scientific and philosophic calculations represents that force in human life which can harmonize and bring into unity the individual and social instincts of the individual and society.

"The greatest obstacle in the way of such harmonious blending are property, or the monopoly of things—the denial of the right of others to their use, and authority—the government of man by man, embodied in majority rule, or the absolute disregard of individual life in the organization that for want of a better name stands for society.

"Therefore the first tendency of anarchism is to make good the dignity of the individual human being by freeing him from every kind of arbitrary restraint—economic, political, social."

WHAT CREED PROPOSES

"In so doing anarchism proposes to make apparent in their true force the social bands which always have and always will knit men together and which are the actual basis of a real normal and sane society. The means of doing this rests with each man's latent qualities and his opportunities.

"I have already spoken of the coercive and arbitrary tendency of centralization in either the industrial or political life of a people, and I now wish to say a few words of what seems to the anarchist the most dangerous side of centralization.

"Man has been degraded into a mere part of a machine and all that makes for spontaneity, for originality, for the power of initiative, has been either dulled or completely killed in him until he is but a living corpse dragging out an aimless, spiritless and idealess existence.

"Man is here to be sacrificed upon the altar of things, heaps and heaps of things, that are as gray and dull as the human machines that have produced them.

"Yet how can we talk of social wealth when the production of that wealth can be attained only at the expense of human lives, thousands and thousands of human lives? And what are these lives worth without the power of initiative, of spontaneity?

"Anarchism holds that the simplest human life, if given opportunity and scope, is infinitely more important to society than all the scientific regulation and adjusting of social arrangements."

STRIKE AT "MONOPOLY"

"For in proportion as that simple life grows into a conscious, intelligent, well-rounded factor, recognizing its true relation to its fellow, regulations and forms will take care of themselves.

"Anarchists believe that organized authority, or the state, is necessary only in the interest of monopoly. They fail to see that it has at any time in the history of man promoted human welfare or aided in any way in the building of human character or human possibilities. Anarchism, therefore, aims at the simultaneous overthrow of monopoly and government.

"It is well to distinguish here between government as organized authority, whose purposes are realized at all times through the exercise of brute force—police clubs, state militias, the armies, and the navies of the world—and government in the sense of a spontaneously arising social order and happiness, whose immediate appearance among men awaits only the disappearance of the world-enslaving and world-slaughtering forces of monopoly.

"The centralized method of production has necessitated a centralized form of government that is constantly increasing its power and forever prying into the minutest detail of human life.

"In fact, it is safe to say that man's whole life from the cradle to the grave is under constant surveillance of authority. I think that America illustrates this point perfectly."

SAYS GROWTH HURT NATION

"So long as this country was young, its people battling with the elements and striving for life, liberty and the pursuit of happiness, every man counted for something.

"People were more closely related to each other and the sense of comradeship and brotherhood was keener and deeper.

"But in the proportion as America grew in wealth its method of governing became more centralized, more far-reaching, more contrary to the life and rights of man, until today he is suffered to drag along his wretched existence, not by the 'grace of God,' but by the grave of a network of laws which he knows nothing about and which are absolutely foreign to his natural growth and development.

"With this in view anarchism stands for voluntary productive and distributive associations, using a common capital and loosely federated into communities, eventually developing into communism in production and consumption, recognizing at all times, however, the right of the individual or a number of individuals to arrange their mode of work in harmony with their taste or inclination."

HITS POLICE METHODS

"As to crimes and criminals, anarchists know only too well that they are naught else but symptoms of an artificial social arrangement, enforced by authority. They will disappear to a large extent with the destruction of their creators, namely, capitalism and government.

"Crime, resultant from a defective brain, can surely not be cured by brute force. But certainly modern medical methods and an increased sense of fraternity, aided by improved education, can accomplish more than prison bars, handcuffs, locksteps, or chains.

"The American methods proposed or employed to hound down anarchists have been practiced by European powers for nearly one hundred years and have been given up in despair.

"The truth can not be silenced by constant discoveries of 'anarchist plots,' or by designating every demented being as an anarchist, nor even by burning anarchist literature or establishing a system of espionage which invades the sanctity of individual privacy and makes the life of its victims an intolerable evil.

"There are thousands of people in this country who see in such methods the last desperate efforts of a dying age. The new, strong in thought and ideals, strong in human sympathy and fellowship is fast approaching, and when it arrives the present will be remembered as a nightmare that humanity dreamed rather than as an awful reality it actually lived."

Chicago Daily Journal, 17 March 1908, pp. 1, 3.

I have tried so hard, oh so very hard to sleep, to forget that awful scene at the Restaurant,[1] but I can not, I can not! My head feels, if fire had been set to it, and my heart, my heart is convulsed in agony over the abyss between our lives. The fact, that you knew of no theories or philosophies, that you had neither aim nor ideal to live or suffer for, has not even for one moment in the last two weeks, disturbed me. It was your great daring, your simplicity, your beauty of soul in spite of your past that, appealed to me so forcibly, that made me so oblivious to all considerations, as to whether you could or could not enter my life. When you first mentioned that you wanted to follow me, I did not credit it, in fact it had no meaning to me. It is only since Sunday and especially the atmosphere that hovered over us yesterday last night that awakened an intense desire to have you go with me, regardless of all obstacles. And then the terrible happened and my castle fell with me, hurled me right into the gutter. Now that I have gethered up my bruised soul, I looked into the Abyss, ~~into~~ of our lives, widely seperated through our past, our view points, our espirations, and try as I may, I can not see the bridge that leads across it

You said, you can not hate those people, why should you? But I do hate them, with an intense and uncomprimising hate, that never, never can make peace. That the man, who cares for me, or lives in my World, should want to make peace with a World I so detest is something, I could never overcome, or reconcile myself to.

I shall never be able to tell you, how much, how very much you have grown to mean to me. How much, I appreciated the love and devotion you showed me. But it would be playing you false, if I refrained from letting you know, that to nights incident has made it clear to me, that our roads can, and do not lead in the same direction. Do not think me hard, dear Ben, or unkind. Goodness only knows, I do not want to Scold you. But, all the love in the World could not induce me to deny my principles, my work, my self respect—Believe me it is best for you, to keep away from my World, for it is a World of war, bitter relentless war, ever, lasting strife and battle until death——

Thank you, dear for your great devotion and esteeme. For your courage and assistance. It has meant so much, so very, very much to me, to have met you, to have been taken by

---

1. Shortly after the incident at Workingmen's Hall (see note 1, "Reds' Leader Flays Police," Article in *Chicago Daily Journal*, 17 March 1908, above), EG and BR spotted Assistant Police Chief Schuettler at a restaurant, where EG was horrified to witness Reitman and Schuettler's friendly exchange, which she considered guilt by association in spite of Schuettler's comparatively lenient and liberal bent (see *LML*, pp. 421–22).

Ben Reitman, standing at middle rear, proposing a toast at a meeting of the Chicago branch of the International Brotherhood Welfare Association, also known as the Hobo College, on 20 May 1907. (Ben L. Reitman Papers, BLR neg. 5, Special Collections, University Library, University of Illinois at Chicago)

you into a land of dreams, of flowers and beauty, but in the words of my brave comrades in Paris, that I have quoted, "I have no little business there—

Good night, good by

E

ALI, MCR.

Article in the *CHICAGO TRIBUNE*

Chicago, 29 March 1908

Emma Goldman Blames Police.

Queen of Reds Says the Union Square Tragedy Is Bluecoat Plot.

To Injure Anarchists.

Doesn't Know Silverstein and Never Wrote Letters to Him,
She Declares.

Minneapolis, Minn., March 28.—(Special.)—Emma Goldman, after her lecture here tonight, discussed the bomb tragedy in Union square, New York.[1]

"Union square, New York City, where the bomb was exploded this afternoon and two men were killed," she said, "is the identical spot where I have lectured for the last fourteen years and was arrested and made to serve one year in the government prison on Blackwell's Island."[2]

"I did not know Selig Silverstein,"[3] replied Miss Goldman to a question concerning the man who now lies in the Bellevue hospital in New York and is accused by the police of having thrown the bomb.

"I did not know the dead man Irwin Bassky. I have never heard of either of them. The report that letters from me to Silverstein were found in his room is absolutely false as well, I think I know my correspondents."[4]

POLICE TO BLAME, SHE SAYS.

"You want to know who I think was at the bottom of the whole riot? The police.

"They do it to show their authority. Such affairs as occurred this afternoon in New

---

1. On 28 March 1908, an abortive attempt to throw a bomb at the police took place near the end of a demonstration of the unemployed called by the unemployed conference of the Socialist Party. The bomb killed a bystander and fatally wounded the thrower, Selig Silverstein.
2. EG was imprisoned for a year at Blackwell's Island in 1893 for incitement to riot. She served ten months of her sentence. (For further discussion, see vol. 1, pp. 144–47).
3. Selig Silverstein (1889–1908), also identified as Selig Cohen, was a Russian-born Jewish New York anarchist and member of the Anarchist Federation of America. The bomb he was responsible for was intended for the police, but a miscalculation caused it to explode in his hand. One bystander was killed and Silverstein died of injuries two weeks later.
4. In fact, some mimeographed fund-raising letters and Selig's membership card from the Anarchist Federation, signed by AB as treasurer, were all that the police found in Silverstein's apartment.

The sensationalist headline in the 5 April 1908 *Chicago Sunday Tribune Magazine* referred to the bloody month of March 1908 when several incidents of violence involving alleged anarchists took place across the country. The sketch of the bomber was intended to be anarchist Selig Silverstein, who died after a bomb exploded in his hand at a demonstration of the unemployed in New York City's Union Square on 28 March 1908. Portraits of anarchists Errico Malatesta, Berkman, and Goldman and a facsimile of Selig Silverstein's Anarchist Federation membership card accentuate the article's political intent. (Reprinted with permission of *Chicago Sunday Tribune*)

York have been traced in many instances to the police, who grasp the opportunity to lay all blame on anarchists.

"Who knows that Silverstein threw the bomb? Did any newspaper men see him do it? Why do you come to me for enlightenment? Am I supposed to know every anarchist any more than President Roosevelt is supposed to know every republican?

"As soon as there is a riot, a bomb explosion, an assassination, or an uprising the police immediately try to attach the affair to me. And that is why I say that they even go so far as to instigate these plots themselves for the purpose of incriminating us and heaping praise on themselves. I don't believe a workingman threw the bomb, as it would not have been to his advantage. The logical conclusion in my mind is that the police are in some way behind the whole matter."

ROASTS CHICAGO POLICE.

"Some years ago in Chicago a quantity of dynamite was 'discovered' by the police in one of the downtown tunnels under the city. I have absolute proof that the explosive was placed there by the police who later 'discovered' it and lauded themselves to the skies in the newspapers for their ingenuity in preventing a catastrophe. Those are police methods which are known only to anarchists.

"The injured men who are now held in New York may have heard me in my many lectures in that city and at that place.

"I have only communicated recently with two people in New York City. They are Alexander Berkman and the business of my magazine, Mother Earth. I am writing to Mr. Berkman tonight for particulars concerning the affair and will be better informed on the subject Sunday morning."[5]

Chicago Tribune, 29 March 1908, p. 2.

5. After a membership card signed by AB as treasurer of the Anarchist Federation of America was found in Silverstein's apartment, AB was arrested on 30 March in connection with the bombing. However, on 3 April he was released for lack of evidence. Socialist Meyer London acted as AB's attorney during his arrest.

En Route

DEAR READERS OF MOTHER EARTH:

I had hoped to be able to give you in this issue an account of the truly "American chivalry and hospitality" extended me by the Chicago Police Department.[1] I know you would enjoy it almost as well as I did. But such an important account can not be properly treated en route, in a shaking train. It requires more time and leisure than I have now. I shall, therefore, ask you to content yourself meanwhile with the information that I am seriously considering to send a vote of thanks to the Chicago protectors of law and disorder for their tremendous interest in the spread of our ideas and in my welfare. Appreciating the fact that I had lectured every night, holding tremendously large meetings in St. Louis and other cities, until I reached Chicago, the police immediately issued strict orders that no halls should be rented us, that I might not be tempted to speak, in order that my throat may rest up. Also mindful of the fact that the truth speaks loudest when an attempt to silence it is made, the Department had a special squad at large to suppress free speech and assembly at all costs. Of course, all that was done from paternal motives and especially to supply the reporters with material to write about. They meant no harm, I am sure, not even when one of them tenderly lifted me off the platform. Who said the age of chivalry is gone? No, indeed, not so long as the Chicago police and captains are in existence. The police evidently thought that it is time Emma Goldman be heard by a large number of people, instead of a mere hallful. That is why they gave me an opportunity to have my undelivered lecture printed in a Chicago daily, having a circulation of more than 50,000;[2] also another article in a morning paper of large circulation. Don't you think they deserve thanks? As to the amount of good their action has done in other cities, that could not be fully estimated. Thousands came to the meetings in Minneapolis; thousands were turned away, as our halls were not large enough to hold such unexpected multitudes. The same will no doubt be true in all the other cities along the line of my route. Just think of how much other speakers would pay to get such splendid advertising, and all without any efforts on my part, at that.

1. For details on how Chicago police thwarted every attempt to obtain a hall for EG's planned lectures, see "Emma Goldman Clashes with Police on Meeting," Interview in *Chicago Inter Ocean*, 8 March 1908, above.
2. For transcript of address EG was prevented from delivering, see "Reds' Leader Flays Police," Article in the *Chicago Daily Journal*, 17 March 1908, above.

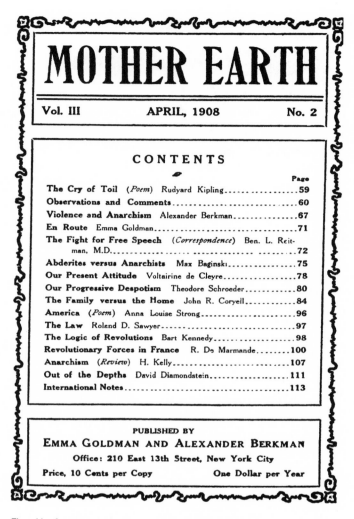

MOTHER EARTH

Vol. III   APRIL, 1908   No. 2

CONTENTS

PUBLISHED BY

EMMA GOLDMAN AND ALEXANDER BERKMAN

Office: 210 East 13th Street, New York City

Price, 10 Cents per Copy   One Dollar per Year

The table of contents on the cover of the April 1908 issue of *Mother Earth,* by this time published by both Goldman and Berkman, displays the magazine's editorial mixture of literature and politics. (By permission of the Kate Sharpley Library)

True, one who is not used to such "kind handling and such flattering attention," as I have received, might have felt somewhat annoyed; but as I have enjoyed similar honors on several previous occasions, I can probably stand it the better. At any rate, I assure you, dear friends, I am hale and hearty and more than ever determined to go on. Of course, I am a little tired, but that is not the fault of the authorities. Not at all. Lack of privacy, constant visitors, lectures every night, a large correspondence, two bodyguards closely on my heels,

Who watch him when he tries to weep,
And when he tries to pray;
Who watch him lest himself should rob
The prison of its prey,[3]—

would make anybody tired.

Friends, the American sky looks black and sinister; the sun has hidden in shame, unwilling to witness the growing brutality and despotism on the part of those who have taken it upon themselves to outrage every sense of liberty and justice. One can not afford to be tired these days, when brave souls are needed for the battle. Yes, brave souls and clear heads, who will help to free the earth from the chains of ignorance, brutality, and cowardice.

EMMA GOLDMAN

Mother Earth 3 (April 1908): 71–72.

3. Oscar Wilde, *The Ballad of Reading Gaol* (London, 1898), 1.63–66.

To BEN REITMAN

Winnipeg, Manitoba, Canada, 1 April 1908

My beautiful tramp sweetheart

This is fools day, and I appear foolish to myself in my intense longing for you. Not, that you are undeserving of affection, indeed ~~you dearie~~ you are dearie. Only it seems so foolishly strange, that anyone should get such hold of my affection just now, with the entire force of police both in America and here after me, and the repeated outbreaks against Anarchy. Don't you think it foolish to be infatuated at such a moment, when one needs as much fighting spirit, as one can muster up? And yet, dear precious tramp, its my affection for you, that is the only bright star in these gloomy days. You came into my life, like a star, bursting suddenly through a black cloud. Truly dear, you have helped me more, than you imagine to keep bitterness out of my soul.

Mail delivery is awfully slow here, nothing was delivered this morning. I am sure you have written, shall I be disappointed. I am waiting to get your letter by the 4 o'clock delivery. It seems such a long time, since I have heard your deep melodious voice and looked into your eyes, God, what eyes! they thrill me so. The meeting was a success, of course. The papers advertised me during two weeks why should it not be a success? The inclosed clipping will show you that your "history has reached W— as well.[1] How strange, that I should feel hurt, over anything said about you? I never care what they say of me— somehow it hurts me, when I read disagreeable things about you. How are you dear and where are you? Are you as "happy and contented" as you were without me in Chicago?

What are your plans? I want to see you very much Ben, but I really would not like you come here. It is an awful place, besides, we could not be alone a minute. I can not afford to be dragged before the public now. You know, why do you not? If you go out of town let me know. If you do not want to see me anymore, let me know. I should not blame you dear though I must admit, it would hurt, oh! how it would hurt! For your sake, I wish you would emancipate yourself from your true blue.

Write soon, and tell me how you are, what you are doing. Put yourself into the letter dear, with all your tenderness and all your brutality,

Affectionately

E

ALI, IU-U.

---

1. The 31 March 1908 *Winnipeg Telegram* carried a front-page article announcing EG's anticipated tour in Winnipeg and mentioned BR as a leader in an unsuccessful march of the unemployed in Chicago.

MY DEAR, DEAR FRIENDS.

I do not know what you will think of me, having kept you waiting so long. I can not tell you how much your letter of March has touched me. It came at a moment of the greatest excitement, worry anxiety and heartache. You wrote your letter on the day, when our meeting in Chicago took place.[1] I was dragged off the platform by brutal force that same night. Yet, all the trouble I went through in Chicago with the authorities, was nothing compared with my disappointments over the comrades. Just when energy, judgement courage, were needed, there was no one on hand, or at least very, very few. It was a great blow to me, I assure you. Of course that only helped to increase my own energy. I needed all could muster up to meet so much brutal and ignorence, that confronted me in Chicago. Well, dear friends, I have accomplished my aim. I have brought Anarchy before 150.000 people through articles in the Chicago daily papers, which brought out much opposition to the police and sympathy for our ideas and what is more important. It has helped to defeat the authorities, to make them absolutely ridiculous and to advertise me all over the country, as I have never been before. As a result my meetings in Milwaukee, Minneapolis and here have been tremendous, thousands of people crowding the Halls and just as many being turned away, because of lack of space.

Of course all that required a great deal of strength and nerve supply. While the reports, that I broke down were not true, I feel pretty worn out and tired, terribly tired. I must go on however, now more than ever because of the terrible reaction against our ideas. The news from N Y and especially the arrest of Comrade Berkman[2] have truly been terrible to me. B. has been released, I am glad to say, so I can go on with my tour, which from every standpoint is very vital at present. Yes, dear friend, the simplest truth is indeed the greater truth. Thats why you were so impressed by my expression that it is best to live one day true to oneself, than life-time true to others. I never felt so intensely about it, as I did these last few weeks. Had I listened to the "good advise of our comrades in Chicago, who sent special letter and telegrams, I should not come to Chicago, because it is dangerous, I would have acted a lie and undone the work of 18 years of my activity in the movement. I had to be true to myself, I had to go, even if it were straight to the gallows. And it was best all around. My coming and presence in Chicago helped to dispell the "anarchist plot.

---

1. EG attempted to speak on 16 March 1908, at the Workingmen's Hall. See "Reds' Leader Flays Police," Article in the *Chicago Daily Journal*, 17 March 1908, above.
2. AB had been arrested and briefly detained after the bomb explosion at Union Square on 28 March 1908. See "Emma Goldman Blames Police," Article in the *Chicago Tribune*, 29 March 1908, above.

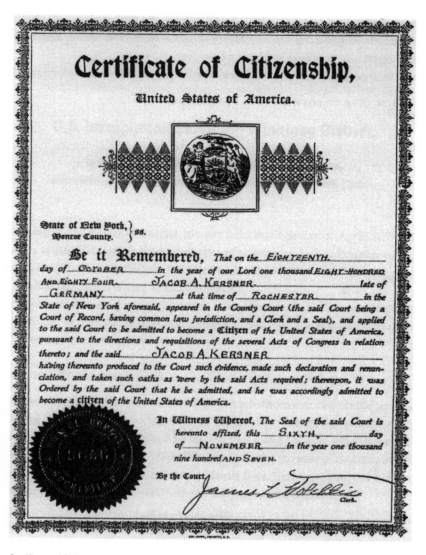

Certificate of Citizenship,

United States of America.

State of New York, } ss.
Monroe County.

Be it Remembered, That on the *EIGHTEENTH*
day of *OCTOBER* in the year of our Lord one thousand *EIGHT-HUNDRED*
AND EIGHTY FOUR *JACOB A. KERSNER* late of
GERMANY at that time of *ROCHESTER* in the
State of New York aforesaid, appeared in the County Court (the said Court being a
Court of Record, having common law jurisdiction, and a Clerk and a Seal), and applied
to the said Court to be admitted to become a Citizen of the United States of America,
pursuant to the directions and requisitions of the several Acts of Congress in relation
thereto; and the said *JACOB A KERSNER*
having thereunto produced to the Court such evidence, made such declaration and renunciation, and taken such oaths as were by the said Acts required; thereupon, it was
Ordered by the said Court that he be admitted, and he was accordingly admitted to
become a citizen of the United States of America.

In Witness Whereof, The Seal of the said Court is
hereunto affixed, this *SIXTH* day
of *NOVEMBER* in the year one thousand
nine hundred *AND SEVEN.*

By the Court,
James L. Holden
Clerk.

Certificate of Citizenship for Jacob Kershner, Goldman's husband, dated to 1884, had been Goldman's legal basis for U.S. citizenship. In April 1909 government authorities revoked Kershner's citizenship, thus surreptitiously invalidating Goldman's claim of citizenship. (National Archives and Records Administration)

---

it helped to rescue Anar of the accusation of cowardice and what is most important I do not have to blush before myself. As to the prise paid—Well, the truth is rather expensive. Everything beautiful costs a lot, and truth is the most beautiful of all arts—

Well, dear friends, I wanted to write much, but have been having callers constantly, so I will have to give it up now. Last nights meeting here, the first, was very successfull. We expect to have more like it. In fact, outside of Chicago I had success allover and in Chicago, the moral result was simply marvelous.

I leave here next Tuesday, you may write me here, the letters will be forwarded

WITH MUCH LOVE TO BOTH OF YOU. YOUR FRIEND
E

ALI, IU-U.

U.S. Immigration Service—Winnipeg District.

In the matter of the application of Emma Goldman, alias Mrs. Jacob A. Kersner, for admission to the United States.

At a meeting of the Board of Special Inquiry held this 6th day of April, A. D. 1908, at 10:00 P.M., at the Village of Noyes, in the States of Minnesota, U.S.A. Present:—Inspectors Walter E. Carr (Chairman), Person A. Robbins, and Shirley D. Smith. Meeting conducted in the English language. Walter E. Carr, Secretary.

The above mentioned Emma Goldman, alias Mrs. Jacob A. Kersner,[1] appearing before said Board of Special Inquiry and making application for admission to the United States, upon examination testified as follows:—

EXAMINATION BY CHAIRMAN CARR.

Q. You have already been informed by the Inspector whom you saw on the train coming from Winnipeg, that it is suspected that you are an alien, that is, that you are a citizen of some country other than the United States and that being the case it becomes necessary that you be examined at this time before this Board, for the purpose of ascertaining whether or not you are admissible to this country under its laws. Before we proceed further it will be necessary that you swear to tell the truth during this examination.

A. Being an atheist, I will only affirm, not swear.

Q. Do you consider an affirmation binding both legally and morally?

A. I certainly do. It is just like giving my word of honor, and I would stick to it.

Q. Do you affirm that such statements as you shall make to this Board in connection with your examination for admission to the United States shall be the truth, the whole truth, and nothing but the truth?

A. I do.

Q. What is your name?

---

1. EG married Jacob A. Kershner in February 1887. Although divorced in late 1887, they later remarried and never officially divorced when EG left him in 1888.

A. Mrs. Jacob Kersner.

Q. What was your maiden name?

A. Well, I am Emma Goldman. I don't go by the name of my husband, I always have my own name, and use it.

Q. How old are you?

A. 38 years.

Q. Are you married or single?

A. I am married.

Q. Can you read and write?

A. Yes, certainly.

Q. What is your occupation?

A. Well, at the present time I am a lecturer, but I am also a trained nurse.

Q. Where were you born?

A. I was born in Germany, Konigsberg, Province of Prussia.[2]

Q. When and where did you land in this country when you first came?

A. I landed at New York in January, 1885.[3]

Q. On what steamer?

A. I really don't remember, it was so long ago. I was a mere girl.[. . .]

Q. Do you remember the name of the Justice before whom you were married?

A. I do not, in fact I don't remember much of the details of that affair, I was young. I remember that my parents insisted that we have a religious ceremony. They are of the Jewish faith, and insisted that we have a religious ceremony after the other one and so we submitted and were also married by the Rabbi. I was therefore married in a legal way.

By Inspector Robbins:—

Q. The Rabbi, in the Jewish faith, must keep a record of the marriages he performs, must he not, and record them, the same as any other minister?

A. I think so. Besides the man who married me is still alive and he will testify to it.

Q. You mean the Rabbi?

A. Yes.

---

2. EG was born in 1869 in the Russian city of Kovno in modern Lithuania. Her family moved to Königsberg when she was a young girl.
3. EG arrived in the United States with her sister, Helena, on 29 December 1885.

Q. Do you know whether the Justice, or the civil officer before whom you were married is still alive?

A. I don't know.

Q. Were there any witnesses to the marriage?

A. Yes. I don't remember the witnesses. I was very young and it was so many years ago, and I don't really recollect them, but that can all be verified. In fact, when my sister sent these papers she made an investigation as to the existence of the whole thing, and the records are still there. I got a letter from her some little time ago saying that an inspector was there, a secret service man, who interviewed all the members of the family and looked up the records, so the Government knows it if you don't.

By Chairman Carr:—

Q. What is the name of the Rabbi who married you, performed the ceremony?

A. I don't know. It may seem strange to you that I don't remember all these things, but I have lived away from there so long that I have forgotten many things.

Q. Why do you travel under the name of Kersner at times and as Emma Goldman at others?

A. I never travel under my own name, just to avoid annoyance. When I am asked seriously, I give my own name, Emma Goldman.

Q. Why did you inform the officer on the train to-night that you were born in the United States?

A. Because I thought that would avoid trouble and satisfy him.

Q. Why did you change your plans so suddenly and give up your western trip as announced from the platform in Winnipeg, and jump your engagement to speak in Winnipeg to-night?

A. Well, I intended going to Calgary and from there to Vancouver and Victoria, then to San Francisco. They failed to make the necessary arrangements in Calgary and the jump from Winnipeg to the coast is too long and too expensive to make all at once, so I arranged to go to San Francisco by way of Salt Lake City and Minneapolis, and in order to get there on time I had to leave at once.

Q. Was that the only reason?

A. Yes, I guess I will miss it now anyway.

Q. As an anarchist, I understand that you believe in no Government? Is that correct?

A. Exactly. I believe in man governing himself. Each man.

Q. Do you also believe in the overthrow of existing governments by force or violence or otherwise?

A. I believe in the method laid down by the Constitution of the United States, that when the Government becomes despotic and irksome the people have the right to overthrow. You will have to hold the Government of the United States responsible for that. The Government of the United States was formed by the people uprising to crush a despotic power.

Q. You refer to the Declaration of Independence rather than to the Constitution do you not?

A. It is in the Declaration of Independence instead of the Constitution but the Constitution provides for it too.[4]

Q. Do you believe that the Government of the United States has reached such a stage as you describe now?

A. Well, the people haven't reached the stage of overthrowing it, and therefore I suppose they are satisfied.

Q. That hardly answers my question. You only evaded it. I asked you whether, in your opinion, or belief, the Government of the United States had reached that stage where it should be overthrown by force or otherwise?

A. I believe that if America goes on very much farther it will reach that point. It is on the way.

Q. Now Miss Goldman, the question is, do you or do you not believe that the Government of the United States has reached such a stage at the present time as would warrant its overthrow by force or violence or otherwise. It is only delaying matters when you insist upon evasive answers.

A. I would much rather not express an opinion or a belief on that matter at all. It hasn't much farther to go. I think it is fast on the way, that is certain.[. . .]

By Chairman Carr:—

Are there any more questions? (No reply) Then Miss Goldman is entitled to an immediate decision. It is the desire that this case be handled with a great deal of care and judgment and therefore, before passing final judgment as to the merits of this case, I would like to hear an expression of opinion from the members of this Board as to their view of the case is it now stands.

By Inspector Smith:—

A claim has been made by Miss Goldman that she is a United States Citizen, having ac-

4. The Constitution does not recognize the right to overthrow government; rather, it establishes the right of citizens to "petition the government for a redress of grievances" (First Amendment). This sentiment is, however, expressed in the Declaration of Independence: "That whenever any Form of Government becomes destructive of these ends [to secure the rights of the people], it is the Right of the People to alter or to abolish it. . . . [W]hen a long train of abuses and usurpation . . . evinces a design to reduce them under absolute Despotism, it is their right, it is their duty, to throw off such Government. . . ."

quired citizenship through an alleged marriage to Jacob A. Kersner. While she presents a certificate as to the citizenship of Mr. Kersner, there is nothing in the evidence, other than her statement to that effect, to show that she was married to this man, and I should think it might be well to defer decision in this case until such time as we could be in receipt of evidence as to said marriage, say the marriage certificate.

By Inspector Robbins:—

From the general attitude of Miss Goldman before the Board, and her evident willingness to answer questions, and her manner of answering those questions, I am inclined to the belief that she is telling the truth. Her answers appear to me to have been straightforward and honest. As I understand it we should handle this case in the same manner as other cases and I feel sure that upon the evidence submitted in this case, were it not for the notoriety of the person before the Board, there would be no hesitancy shown on the part of any member of the Board in reaching a decision to admit.

By Chairman Carr:—

In view of the claim made by Miss Goldman that she is a United States Citizen, the first question for this Board to decide is not whether she is admissible or inadmissible under the Immigration Laws proper, for before we can consider that question, we must of necessity determine whether or not she is an alien,[5] as the United States Immigration Laws refer to aliens only. Even though she has admitted that she is an anarchist and believes in no Government, and therefore would, if an alien, be a member of one of the excluded classes, the question of citizenship must first be decided. If we decide that she has sufficiently proven her status as a United States citizen then we can only admit, and on the contrary should we decide that she is not a citizen of the United States, then we must take up the question of her standing under the Immigration Laws. She makes claim to citizenship on two separate counts, that is, through the naturalization of her father, and through marriage to a United States Citizen.[6] As to her claim that her father was a naturalized American Citizen, she has also admitted that at the time of the naturalization of her father she was the wife of Mr. Kersner, but in any event we are dependent upon her statement of the facts in the case, and she has given us sufficient information upon which to base an investigation should the Department so desire. As to the citizenship of her alleged husband, she produces a court certificate which appears to be correct in every detail, to the effect that Mr. Jacob A. Kersner was admitted as a Citizen of the United States on the 18th day of October, 1884, which certificate, as I said before, appears to be correct in every detail, and I think there should be no doubt in the mind of any member

5. "Alien" refers to a person who is not a citizen, whether native-born or naturalized.
6. According to the Naturalization and Citizenship statutes of the Revised Statutes of 1874, a woman who marries a U.S. citizen and who is also eligible for naturalization automatically becomes a citizen. Any child under the age of 21 whose parent becomes a naturalized citizen is also considered a citizen (Section 1994 of Citizenship statutes; Section 2172 of Naturalization statutes).

of this Board as to the citizenship of Mr. Kersner. We have no evidence as to the marriage other than the statement of Miss Goldman to that effect, but even though we were in possession of absolute evidence establishing beyond a shadow of a doubt the truth of her statement as to her marriage, there would still remain a question as to whether she is still his wife. She states that she lived with him but two years and that she has never had a divorce, she also states that she has never resided abroad for a long enough period to effect her expatriation even under the strictest interpretation of the naturalization laws.[7] In case we deferred this case for further evidence, we could not hope to secure such evidence as would absolutely prove each and every question incident to this case, and would still be dependent upon the statements of Miss Goldman to a large extent. Should we defer decision for such evidence as would satisfactorily establish her claims to United States Citizenship, such decision would in effect be one of debarment, or would at least cause such delay as would, in the event of her claim being substantiated, work considerable hardship. On the other hand a decision of admission could not in any way injure the position of the United States Government, nor would it deprive it of any legal remedy. Rule 31, clause (a), gives as one class of aliens who may be deported, "Aliens who, at the time of entry, belonged to any of the classes of persons enumerated and defined in section 2 of the Immigration Act————." Should her claim to United States Citizenship be proven fraudulent, she should therefore be deported at any time within three years from today. Should it be proven upon investigation that Miss Goldman has made fraudulent use of the papers which she has presented before the Board, and made claim to citizenship which she is not entitled to, she would, under the provision of Section 16 of the Naturalization Act of June 29th, 1906, be deemed guilty of a felony and subject to punishment therefor. However you should vote as you think the evidence warrants. Are there any motions?

By Inspector Smith:—

I move to admit.

By Inspector Robbins:—

I second the motion.

By Chairman Carr:—

The motion is made unanimous. Miss Goldman, you are informed that this Board of Special Inquiry has decided to permit you to proceed to your destination at your own convenience. Inspector Smith will attend to the matter of getting your tickets extended, if necessary.

(Before————

---

7. Residing abroad for longer than six months, under the Naturalization statutes, results in a loss of citizenship eligibility for aliens.

BOARD OF SPECIAL INQUIRY.
[SIGNED] WALTER E. CARR, CHAIRMAN.
[SIGNED] PERSON A. ROBBINS, INSPECTOR.
[SIGNED] SHIRLEY D. SMITH, INSPECTOR.
[SIGNED] WALTER E. CARR, SECRETARY.

This is to certify that the above is a verbatim report of the proceedings of the Board of Special Inquiry, held at Noyes, Minn., on the 6th day of April, 1908, in the case of Emma Goldman (alias Mrs. Jacob A. Kersner), same having been taken by me in shorthand notes and by me subscribed.

Dated April 8th, 1908.
Winnipeg, Manitoba.

[SIGNED] WALTER E. CARR,
IMMIGRANT INSPECTOR.

TDS, file #51,694/2, Immigration and Naturalization Service, RG 85, DNA.

To *MOTHER EARTH*

Los Angeles, 30 April 1908

En Route

It is quite "angelic" here, indeed, and as angels never do anything but sit at God's throne playing the harp, my friends will have to forbear with me if I, too, am influenced by the local atmosphere.

With Mother Earth so rich, so beautiful and abundant in southern California, one is inclined to forget, at least for a while, the bareness and dreariness of life at large, with its eternal strife and unnecessary struggle.

Even my angel guardians, the police, seem to be imbued with the spirit of restfulness and peace that emanates from nature in this city. At any rate, they have so far let me go my own way, a treat which only he can fully appreciate who has felt their presence as long and persistently as I have.

I stated in my last review[1] that the Chicago "finest" deserve a vote of thanks for the tremendous advertising which their stupidity has given Anarchism and that "most disreputable of all Anarchists, Emma Goldman."

Since I have come to California and have been "entertained" by the San Francisco police, I have decided that our thanks will have to be voted to the authorities of that city instead of to Chicago.[2] As an exhibition of monumental stupidity and absurdity the San Francisco police are deserving of the first prize. True, in Chicago free speech was prohibited, but such action is perfectly consistent with the functions of authority, a fact which many of our lukewarm radicals have yet to learn. All their talk of free speech and their great indignation against the suppression thereof are to my mind nothing but sentimentality. If they truly believed in free speech they could not at the same time stand for the continuance of government. Free speech means either the unlimited right of expression, or nothing at all. The moment any man or set of men can limit speech, it is no longer free. The Russian Tsar stands for free speech, which means *his right* to say what he pleases. So do also the American Tsars: they have *their rights* of free speech. But the moment you or I claim the same right, law and authority become indignant at such Anarchist impudence. Let all reformers and radicals realize, once for all, that to love liberty means to become lawless, since freedom and law can never harmonize.

---

1. EG refers to her letter "En Route," written on her way by train to Winnipeg from Chicago and published in *Mother Earth*, April 1908.
2. See Alexander Horr's account of EG's treatment by the police in San Francisco, entitled "In 'Frisco," *Mother Earth* (May 1908): 135–38.

There was at least some consistency in the actions of the Chicago authorities, even though they helped our propaganda tremendously. The meetings in Milwaukee, Minneapolis, Winnepeg, Salt Lake City,[3] etc., would never have been attended by such vast crowds had it not been for that consistency. The San Francisco authorities, however, can claim neither consistency nor ordinary common sense.

No potentate was ever received with greater deference or hospitality. The Chief[4] himself was there, with his staff, in a large automobile, ready to see me safely to the palace of the Police Department; but as I preferred a hotel, the Chief submitted to the caprice of the sovereign and escorted me to the hotel, placing four detectives at my disposal, who had strict instructions to be close, very close at my side during my stay at San Francisco.

When I changed quarters and went to stop with friends, the Chief placed an additional force at my disposal, two mounted officers, to watch the cottage and neighborhood. However, all this care and devotion could not satisfy the zeal of a true subject like Chief Biggey. His heart craved greater manifestations of loyalty; therefore he spent forty-eight hours preparing a parade in honor of the distinguished visitor, probably hoping that the sovereign would review her "faithfuls." One hundred and fifty officers on horseback, in automobiles, on foot, "police to the right of her, police to the left of her, in back of her, and in front of her"; a light brigade heavy in body and mind, but "ready to charge, ready to risk their lives for duty's sake."[5] They protected every meeting, always watchful lest some harm should befall her majesty. What if these devotees exposed themselves to scorn and ridicule, what if they had to listen, listen for the first time, to a voice so strange, foreign, and jarring to their delicate ears, and hear the truth, the truth, that hateful thing, that will not be silenced or awed, even by the presence of such a force. They stood their ground, these one hundred and fifty, firmly, unflinchingly, unto the very end.

Deeds of love, of kindness,—great, heroic deeds may go down into oblivion in the history of this country, but the deeds of Chief Biggey and his one hundred and fifty men,—never! In years to come a young and free generation will read the story of how Chief Biggey and his hundred and fifty brave souls helped to spread the ideas which paved the way for a free society.

Life's struggles either kill or strengthen the power of human endurance. I hope I will not appear boastful if I say that the difficulties and obstacles and annoyances of the last ten weeks have not diminished my endurance. I am still on deck. The storm is now raging

---

3. EG spoke to large crowds in Milwaukee on 22 March, in Minneapolis 25–28 March, in Winnipeg 31 March through 5 April, and in Salt Lake City sometime in early April before arriving in California on 16 April.

4. William J. Biggy (d. 1908) was San Francisco police chief during EG's 1908 visit and arrest. Biggy told the *San Francisco Call* (1 April 1908) that he had explicit instructions from the state department in Washington, D.C., to "keep a close guard on Emma Goldman." On 31 November 1908, Biggy, who had been involved in the notorious San Francisco graft trials, fell overboard from a police launch in the San Francisco Bay and drowned.

5. A play upon "Charge of the Light Brigade," by Alfred, Lord Tennyson.

more fiercely than ever and the waves are competing with each other in their mad rush, but our colors are flying as proud and unyielding as ever.

Friends, we have all reason to rejoice that ignorance, brutality, and viciousness have conspired against the spirit of liberty. They have left nothing undone to break her proud neck. They have hounded us, annoyed us, driven us almost to desperation. In their kindness of heart they have even decided that this is not a safe place for us to live; therefore they are going to deport some of us or keep those out who will venture to these hospitable shores. Yet all their attempts have failed, failed miserably. The voice of truth rings more sonorous, more voluminous than ever; it sounds like an approaching thunder, strong, commanding, threatening. Do you see the convulsive efforts of ignorance and brutality? In vain, in vain! The truth, the truth has conquered!

EMMA GOLDMAN

Mother Earth 3 (May 1908): 132–34. EG's dateline was "Angel City."

Article in **COMMON SENSE**

Los Angeles, 16 May 1908

Goldman-Bauer Debate

On Anarchism Versus Socialism—"Artful Dodger" Caught By the Wing and Skillfully Carved. By the Wife of Our Managing Editor

That socialism and anarchy as theories of social life are as far apart as the two poles, was the one point upon which both principals were agreed, in the debate Saturday night, May 2d, at Howell hall on the question of Anarchy vs. Socialism, between Emma Goldman and Kaspar Bauer.[1]

Adherents of these two doctrines chiefly made up the audience, and from the applause which greeted the remarks of the two speakers it was apparent that sentiment was pretty evenly divided.

Though more skillful and vastly more experienced in debate, Miss Goldman was unable to defend her purely idealistic position from the onslaughts of her opponent's scientific argument.

Miss Goldman opened the debate, and from that time to the close Comrade Bauer put her on the defensive and kept the fight wholly within her territory.

The chairman of the evening, Mr. Sprading,[2] an anarchist, had referred to the two principals as two different kinds of socialists, or of belonging to two different schools of socialism. Miss Goldman, as the first speaker, set him right on this by stating that socialism and anarchy are as far apart as the poles.

Those acquainted in advance with the temperaments of the two contestants had no reason to expect a tame performance, and in this they were far from disappointed.

Miss Goldman's first point was that humanity is suffering from two evils: first, capitalism, and organized government, which protects capitalism in its robbery of the rights of the individual.

In their desire to abolish capitalism, said the speaker, anarchy and socialism stand on common ground, but that the latter stands for and advocates government and centralization, while anarchy stands for "liberty" and "voluntarism."

Miss Goldman made use of a common trick of the debater who cannot face the is-

---

1. Kasper Bauer was a Southern Californian socialist and editor of the Los Angeles–based Socialist paper *Common Sense* from 1904 to 1909. Bauer went on to become treasurer of the California Free Speech League in 1912 (see vol. 3).
2. Charles T. Sprading was a Los Angeles–based libertarian and freethinker.

sue squarely by attempting to construct straw men for the purpose of knocking them down.

The first bugaboo was the "state" and she went to such eminent authority as Marx and Engels themselves to substantiate her in her contention that the socialists believe in the "state." If, however, she had been minded to give the audience the benefit of her fuller knowledge on the subject she would have read farther to convince them it was not the class state such as that of capitalism that socialists advocate, and as the manifesto makes plain, and that the manifesto also points out that the "state" according to the present conception, would disappear.[3]

She quoted from Karl Kautsky[4] in his reference to the impracticability of an absolutely equal wage for all work.[5] She also stated that monopoly was only possible because of the force of organized government behind it.

In his first reply Comrade Bauer explained that not ALL of humanity is suffering from capitalism, but the WORKING class. He ridiculed the phrase "anarchist communist," showing how the individualism of the anarchist and the social instinct of communism were incompatible.

Referring to the quotation from the Manifesto, he said that when the movement was young it carried a long string of immediate demands, like the tail of a kite, but that in the process of evolution we had found that we could shorten the tail of the kite and it would fly just as well, even better. He said the state, as the socialist literature referred to it, was not understood by the anarchists—that the class state of the present time was one of oppression but that working man's state would be an entirely different thing.

The liberty of the working man depends upon his ownership of the means of production. He must study these means of production and treat the machine according to its nature in order to get the greatest possible liberty for the individual.

3. Presumably a reference to the Marxist idea of the withering away of the state and a line from the *Communist Manifesto:* "In place of the old bourgeois society, with its classes and class antagonisms, we shall have an association in which the free development of each is the condition for the free development of all."

4. Karl Kautsky (1854–1938) was a Marxist theoretician of the German Social Democratic Party. His works included *The Class Struggle* (1892), *On the Agrarian Question* (1899), and *Foundations of Christianity* (1908).

5. This is a reference to a passage in Kautsky's work *The Class Struggle;* his proposal, known as Das Erfurter Programm, was adopted by the German Social Democratic Party in 1891 and later published in 1892. Kautsky was responding to an imagined argument against those who assumed that a socialist agenda for an equal wage would have undesirable effects. Kautsky refuted this by arguing that socialism and equal wages were not necessarily linked, and that "should socialist society ever decide to decree equality of incomes, and should the effect of such a measure threaten to be the dire one prophesized, the natural result would be, not that socialist production, but that the principle of equality of incomes, would be thrown overboard." Goldman, for the sake of argument, underscored her point perhaps too strongly by suggesting that Kautsky thought an equal wage impractical; Kautsky had clarified and elaborated his position by suggesting that "it does not, however, follow . . . that the principle of equality of incomes not necessarily identical with their uniformity will play no part in socialist society."

As to an equal wage the socialist stands for an equal opportunity, which is far more important.

As to government causing monopoly the exact reverse is true. It is the present economic system, resulting in monopoly, which creates the present form of government.

The anarchists deny the necessity for organization, which means discipline. The anarchists make a hue and cry against the invasion of individual "rights." If the anarchists refuse to attack the capitalist, how is he going to pry him loose? Will he come and say "Please abdicate in my favor, Mr. Capitalist?"

How could a small group of "voluntary associates" operate the modern machinery of production and thereby produce a living?

We believe it is better to count noses than to break heads. When we find by counting our ballots that we have a majority we will simply take over the means of production and free ourselves. If, of course, the capitalists then refuse to abdicate, it will be up to the majority, the working class, whose duty it is to organize also industrially, to employ whatever other means that may be necessary to accomplish their will.

Miss Goldman returned to the charge full of fire. She said that not only the working class but also the capitalist class is suffering today, to which Comrade Bauer later retorted, "Ask the capitalist how much he is suffering. Let him tell about his own misery."

Instead of showing how the anarchists propose to oust the capitalist, Miss Goldman confined herself to explaining that the capitalists were the first invaders and that all they, the revolutionists, would be doing would be to defend themselves against invasion. She quoted Liebknecht[6] in saying that socialists propose to indemnify the capitalists, whenever such a course would be for the good of the people. To which Bauer retorted that, for that matter, it will not be found to be for the good of the people to indemnify many capitalists when the working class is in power.

Not many new points were brought out in the last speeches. Miss Goldman dwelt mostly on the terrible oppression it would be for the individual to be obliged to work in the time and place dictated by the majority. She seemed to think that it was practicable for each person to dictate for himself when and how he should earn his living. To which Bauer showed how in his own former trade, if the killers and skinners and cleaners, etc., had all come in and worked just when they felt like it, chaos would result. She said so long as we were only changing one despotism for another where was the good in making the change at all. We were exchanging the whip of the Republicans or Democratic boss for that of Mr. Bauer, for instance. Bauer answered easily by reminding her how harshly the Republicans crack the whip over themselves, the Democrats likewise, and suggesting that the same principle would certainly hold good when the people, the workers, themselves held the whip.

---

6. Wilhelm Liebknecht (1826–1900) was a German theorist of social democracy as well as co-founder and a leader of the German Social Democratic Party. He participated in the 1848 revolution and was a member of the German Reichstag from 1874 to 1900.

Bauer showed that there would be more than a slight difference between the conditions of the workers under capitalism and under a system which would compel from all a few hours of work under pleasant conditions in order to give as much time as possible to each individual to spend exactly as he pleased, much more liberty than he could possibly have under any other method of getting his livelihood.

For instance, he said the wild Indian would be cited by the idealists or anarchists as an example of noble freedom, while as a matter of fact he was the absolute slave to his necessity for just as long a time as it took him to catch his buffalo, after which he was free only so long as his buffalo meat held out. He said that Miss Goldman absolutely denied the materialistic conception of history, and that he had her written statement of ten years ago to bear him out in that, to which Miss Goldman retorted that the statement was absolutely false, as she never denied the "material aspect of life." That was a fair example of the manner in which she eluded points, rather than met them.

It is to be hoped that the many socialists who have been flirting with anarchy, believing it to be a condition to which we will grow when we get good enough, heard this debate in which Miss Goldman showed herself either unconscious of modern economic development or else chose to ignore it and evade it at every turn until her listeners felt inclined to designate her as "the artful dodger."

E. E. B.

Common Sense, 16 May 1908, pp. 1, 3.

Article in the _PORTLAND MORNING OREGONIAN_

Portland, 27 May 1908

Too Large an Army Now

Emma Goldman Talks on "Patriotism."

Arraigns General Funston and Army Officials
for Court-Martialing Man Who Shakes Her Hand.

The spacious hall in the Merrill building was fairly well filled last night by a crowd of curious ones who assembled to hear Emma Goldman deliver her widely-heralded address on "Patriotism." Many who expected a fierce tirade against the Government were only partially satisfied, for the remarks of the "high priestess of anarchy" were quite moderate.

In the course of her address she took occasion to berate the United States Army and the Government officials roundly for having tried and sentenced an enlisted man at San Francisco to five years in a military prison for having, as she termed it, "merely shaken hands with me" at the conclusion of one of her lectures at San Francisco.[1] According to Miss Goldman, the United States Government is to be compared with the tyranny of Russia in this instance. "The citizens of this United States of America can no longer point the finger of shame at Russia, Germany and other European governments propped up by aggressive militarism," said the woman advocate of anarchism.

Continuing along this line Miss Goldman said: "This man, mind you, an enlisted man in the service of the United States Army, and who had put in 15 years of his life in the service, was condemned by court-martial to serve five years for having shaken hands with me after one of my lectures. He did not state that he believed in the doctrines I advocate, but merely did as many of you here in Portland have done—congratulated me on presenting my line of argument in favor of the doctrine of anarchism. Yet for this act he was sentenced to serve five years in prison. General Funston has commuted this to three years, and no doubt General Funston is a good, upright, honest American citizen.[2] He probably goes to church every Sunday, and while there studies out new plans for killing people on Monday, Tuesday and Wednesday. I tell you, brothers and sisters, we have too

---

1. A reference to the case of William Buwalda, who faced a court martial on 14 May 1908 for violating the 62nd Article of War (for the act of shaking EG's hand while in uniform, implying military approval by association). See Judge Advocate George B. Davis to William Howard Taft, 19 June 1908, below.
2. Frederick Funston was appointed brigadier general of the U.S. Army in 1901; his military actions against the insurgents in the Philippines between 1898 and 1901 were criticized by, among many others, both Mark Twain and EG.

much militarism in this country today, and the time is coming when the cry for a standing army will be overwhelmingly rejected. We have too large an Army and Navy now, and do not want any more soldiers for the Government to repeat the scenes enacted under General Bell[3] and his troops in Colorado."

During her remarks Miss Goldman was frequently interrupted by applause, which came principally from a few of her fellow anarchists scattered throughout the audience. In conclusion she stated that patriotism was a mistaken idea as prevalent in this country today, and that anarchism taught the only genuine style of patriotism extant.

Tonight Miss Goldman will deliver her farewell address in this city at Alisky Hall.

Portland Morning Oregonian, 27 May 1908, p. 9.

3. Sherman M. Bell (ca. 1870–1942) was adjutant-general and commander of the Colorado state militia, by order of Governor Peabody, for the duration of the Colorado coal miners' strike in 1903 and 1904. He had previously been a detective for Wells Fargo, served in the Roosevelt company of Rough Riders in the Cuban campaign (1st U.S. Volunteer Cavalry), and was a mining superintendent in the Cripple Creek district. See also note 21, p. 380.

Article in the **SPOKESMAN-REVIEW**

Spokane, Wash., 31 May 1908

Goldman Traces Anarchy to 1776

Bases Her Right to Rebel on Declaration of Independence.

In Spokane to Speak Today

Woman Terrorist Denies Her Followers Are Bombthrowers
and Advocates Free Love.

"We claim the right of rebellion when government becomes tyrannical, according to that portion of the Declaration of Independence which reads, 'When a long train of abuses and usurpations, pursuing invariably the same object, evinces a design to reduce them under absolute despotism, it is their right, it is their duty, to throw off such government," said Emma Goldman, high priestess of anarchy, as she sat in the parlor of the Victoria hotel last night.

Miss Goldman was not able to quote the passage, but was able to designate it as embodying her sentiments. "Our attitude is that the philosophy of anarchism does not advocate violence, but regards all human rights so long as they do not conflict with others' rights," she said.

Miss Goldman, accompanied by her manager, Ben L. Reitman, who calls himself "professor" and boasts of having led the "hobo parade" in Chicago in March[1] and of having been beaten by police billies, arrived from Seattle yesterday noon. Miss Goldman is a small woman, of the type termed "shapeless," who dresses in a manner not calculated to impart charm, and whose face has the glow of health, although extremely plain. Her eyes are blue and her hair a light brown and fairly heavy. She carried a large, old-fashioned handbag full of newspaper clippings, letters, etc., and looked more like a farmer's wife on a shopping tour than a bombthrower.

Regarding bombs, Miss Goldman responded vigorously to the question whether she believed in such a method.

---

1. As organizer of the Chicago branch of the International Brotherhood Welfare Association, BR led a march of the unemployed on 23 January 1908. The demonstration was stopped by Police Chief Shippy and BR beaten and arrested.

DENIES COERCION IS ANARCHISM.

"No! By the very nature of anarchism that could not be a tenet of ours. We believe in every person living his own life in his own way and not in coercing others to follow any one's dictation; we could not advocate such coercion and be anarchists."

"How do you account for the fact that so many have perpetrated violence at your meetings or as a result of them, if that is the case?" was asked.

"There has never been a case on record where any one of these persons has been inspired by anarchists' lectures; and not one such has ever been proven to have any connection with us," replied Miss Goldman, warming instantly to her subject, and losing the mild appearance she at first conveyed.

She relapsed into calm again for a few minutes while she continued:

"People have the right to think—that is one of the rights guaranteed by our government. If it does not give us that liberty, it gives us nothing. There are many people who think that the American government is drifting into tyranny such as that of Russia, and it is the purpose of anarchists only to teach that people are free to think as they please. You must make a distinction between the people who advocate the throwing of bombs and anarchists. They are terrorists, and their home is in Russia. They comprise people of many political parties, socialists as well as others, entirely regardless of anarchy. There are none of them in this country, as has been reported sometimes. There is not any circle of people here organized to destroy government, and no anarchist has ever been found among them."

When asked about Czolgosz, who killed McKinley, the man who killed the priest in Denver recently,[2] etc., Miss Goldman had several explanations, the essence of which was that these were persons who had individual grievances and could not be credited to anarchists.

ANARCHISM MISUNDERSTOOD.

"Anarchism is misunderstood just as early Christianity was misunderstood," she continued. "When Christians first began to organize, they were persecuted by those who did not know of their beliefs, and that continued for centuries. Anarchists are martyrs in the same way. People are willing to accept what others say about anarchists, but will not try to understand them.

"We are absolutely opposed to churchism—the word Tolstoi uses to express the power

---

2. On 23 February 1908, Father Leo Heinrichs was shot and killed at St. Elizabeth's Church in Denver while administering holy communion. Heinrichs's assassin, Guiseppe Alia, an Italian immigrant who had been in America for three months, made contradictory statements about his motives, some of which suggested he had acted as an anarchist. At his trial, however, no evidence was offered to indicate that he was an anarchist. Together with the killing of Lazarus Averbuch on 2 March in Chicago and the Union Square explosion on 28 March in New York, Heinrichs's murder alarmed the government, spurring retaliatory "loyalty" programs and a vicious press campaign against anarchists in which EG was a prime target.

and influence of the church.[3] We are opposed because the modern church no longer follows out the teachings of Christ, and has abandoned his doctrine of love. The modern church we believe is undermining human thought, and I agree with the great Tolstoi that the church no longer serves the oppressed, but serves the golden calf. There are some exceptions among churchmen, such as Edward Everett Hale,[4] a beautiful and lovable person, and Mr. Duncan of Butte,[5] but on the whole they serve capitalism."

ADVOCATES FREE LOVE.

"The church of course was good at one time, but it came to say, 'Give to Caesar what is Caesar's'; it conceded the right of kings and governors to take from the people what they had earned, and became in fact tyrannical and was merged in the Roman empire. Churchism never has adapted itself to progress, and the expulsion of Dr. Crapsey,[6] the noted Episcopalian rector, and some of his associates, is but another evidence of it."

"Do you believe in the institution of marriage?" Miss Goldman was asked. Contrary to what one might think, Miss Goldman blushed like a girl, cast down her eyes, and then recovering said firmly, "No."

ADVOCATES FREE LOVE.

"We believe the state has no right to interfere between the private feelings of individuals. So long as a man and woman love each other there can be no right to separate them. It is degrading for man and woman to live together after they no longer love—it is immoral. Love is the one and only right test for marriage, and so long as they love they are doing right to live together. But as soon as this is over they would be committing sin to live together.

3. Leo Tolstoy, though an advocate of spiritual brotherhood, which he saw as at the core of Christian philosophy, opposed institutionalized religion.
4. Edward Everett Hale (1822–1909) was an American author, social reformer, Unitarian minister, and chaplain of the U.S. Senate from 1903 to 1909. He was editor of the magazine *The Christian Examiner* (1857–1861). Best known for his short story *The Man Without a Country* (Boston: Ticknor and Fields, 1865, first published in *The Atlantic Monthly*, December, 1863), his novels include *Ten Times One Is Ten: The Possible Reformation* (Boston: Roberts Brothers, 1871) and *In His Name: A Christmas Story* (Boston: Old and New, 1873).
5. Lewis Duncan (1857–1936) was a socialist and Unitarian pastor in Butte, Montana. He resigned from his post in 1910 and became secretary of the Montana Socialist party. Elected mayor of Butte in 1911, he was re-elected in 1913, then defeated in 1915. In 1911 he edited both the *Butte Socialist* and the *Montana Socialist*.
6. Algernon Sidney Crapsey (1847–1927) was a Rochester, New York, Episcopalian minister known for his application of Christian gospel to social issues. He published a volume of his lectures, entitled *Religion and Politics* (New York: T. Wittaker, 1905). In 1906 Crapsey was charged with heresy by the Rev. William David Walker, the bishop of western New York, for denying doctrines of the virgin birth and the divinity of Jesus, and was eventually deposed and forced to resign from his church. He wrote a favorable review of AB's *Prison Memoirs of an Anarchist* in the January 1913 issue of *Survey*. His other writings include a second volume of lectures, *The Re-birth of Religion* (New York: John Lane, 1907), and an analytical work, *The Rise of the Working-Class* (New York: Century, 1914).

"Modern marriage is based upon only superficial purposes. Women marry for a home, and men to perpetuate their names. The state has taken up a surveillance of marriage because it yields revenue. Enormous sums are brought into the public coffers, and have been so brought in for centuries, through fees charged for marriage. When it comes to dissolving the tie that binds a man and woman, the state partially recognizes this right, but only because it also derives a fee for the divorce.

"What do people actually do, even under the marriage laws? If a man is rich he marries a wife to keep up his house, and has half a dozen mistresses. If he is not rich, he has the wife and not the mistresses. Every one knows that these things are true, and yet some will say it is immoral to live together without the sanction of the state, and all right if the state approves. We believe in the sanctity of marriage, but the sanctity of marriage through love, and not through form."

Miss Goldman when shown a copy of The Spokesman-Review bearing a dispatch from Butte saying that the Rev. Mr. Duncan, pastor of the Congregational church there, would be dynamited if he allowed her to speak in his church, penned the following telegram, which was later sent to Mr. Duncan:

BOLSTER DR. DUNCAN BY WIRE.

"I congratulate you upon your libertarian and determined stand. America needs more men like you. Will see you Tuesday. EMMA GOLDMAN."

"Who will blow up the church if you speak there?" was asked.

"Some of the law-abiding citizens, I presume," she replied quickly. Miss Goldman then told of a theater manager at Astoria, who requested her to come there and speak, which she says she did. Relative to William Buwalda,[7] the soldier who at San Francisco shook hands with her and was sentenced by General Funston to three years in prison, she said:

"Buwalda merely shook hands with me and said, 'I thank you for the treat you have given me this week,' and expressed no sympathy with my views. He had no time to, for the crowd of those who shake hands with platform speakers was about him. I do not know whether he is an anarchist or not. But we are going to organize a national fund, the movement having been set on foot at Portland already, to provide money for him when he gets out and to keep him for awhile until he gets work afterward. He had served 18 years in the American army. I am not interested in his case for any religious or political reason. It is nothing to me whether he is a Protestant or Catholic, socialist, anarchist or democrat; I am interested merely because it is a matter of human freedom. Such action is unprecedented in the American army.

"Erskine Wood,[8] an attorney there and ex-Senator of Oregon, will try to get his release

---

7. Details of the Buwalda case are given in "Too Large an Army Now," Article in the *Portland Morning Oregonian,* 27 May 1908, above.
8. EG refers to Charles Erskine Scott Wood, a Portland lawyer who often chaired her meetings in that city and described himself as a philosophical anarchist.

by appeal directly to the president, and if not, by indignation meetings throughout the country. He says he is interested merely on grounds of personal freedom of speech. Mr. Wood is not an anarchist."

MISS GOLDMAN SPEAKS TWICE TODAY.

Miss Goldman will speak in the Spokane theater at 2 o'clock and 8 o'clock this afternoon and will charge an admission fee. Permission was secured by Charles Muehlman, manager of the theater, to sell anarchist literature in the theater, and this will be done.

A number of persons who casually dropped into the parlor while Miss Goldman was speaking made hasty exits, casting fearful glances behind them, as she expanded upon her views of marriage or let drop some telltale word that revealed her true significance. No less than a dozen persons came in, but one and all they hurried out again, often whispering in awed tones as they gained the corridor.

Miss Goldman will go to Butte Tuesday and will then lecture in several Montana cities, spending a week or more in that section, with Butte as her headquarters.

The Spokesman-Review, 31 May 1908, p. 9. Copyright 1908. Reprinted with permission of the Spokesman Review.

S IR:

I have the honor to submit a report[1] upon the record of trial in the case of First-class Private William Buwalda, Company A, 1st Battalion of Engineers, who was tried at the Presidio of San Francisco on May 14, 1908, under the following charge and specification:

"CHARGE: Violation of the 62nd Article of War."[2]

"Specification: In that First-class Private William Buwalda, Company A, 1st Battalion of Engineers, U.S. Army, being present in his uniform at an address delivered by one Emma Goldman at Walton's Pavilion, San Francisco, California, on April 26, 1908, which said address was an attack and criticism on government and especially an attack and criticism on the Government of the United States and the Army and Navy thereof, did frequently and repeatedly applaud the said address and did on its conclusion declare to the said Emma Goldman his sympathy with her and his approval of her remarks.

"This at San Francisco, California, on or about April 26, 1908."

To the foregoing the accused pleaded "Not Guilty."

The facts charged in the specification were fully established by the testimony of reliable witnesses. The incident attracted the attention of Captain Henry Gleeson, Police Department of San Francisco (record, p. 3), who was present at the meeting, and who testified as follows as to the character of the address (record, p. 5):

"The address under the title of 'Patriotism' was an attack on the army and navy system of this country, in which the speaker took particular occasion to brand the system of armies and navies, particularly of this country, under the title of 'legalized murder.' She took occasion to mention that she had visited the Presidio and had noticed the difference between the quarters for the enlisted men and the quarters for the officers, and drew from that a picture which she claimed was an object lesson that soldiers and citizens alike should take care to notice and should resent, and that citizens in particular should not enlist in any part of the army or navy, to become the tools for officers, to be told to shoot

---

1. The author of this report, George Breckenridge Davis (1847–1914), was a lawyer, military officer, and professor at West Point, who had been appointed judge advocate in 1888 and judge advocate general in 1901. Davis was a delegate to the second peace conference at The Hague in 1907 and wrote on both international and military law, including *Elements of International Law* (1887). The recipient of this report, William Howard Taft (1857–1930), was serving as secretary of war (1904–1908) under President Roosevelt, who favored him as his successor. Taft became the twenty-seventh U.S. president (1909–1913). He had also served as governor of the Philippines (1900–1901) under President McKinley.

2. The 62nd Article of War allowed for a soldier to be arrested and court-martialed on non-capital crimes, disorders, and neglects that are not specifically mentioned in any other of the Articles of War.

down and kill men of other nations at the command of an officer. The whole lecture was, to my mind, an attack on the entire system of army and navy of this country, intended to reflect discredit on the United States.

"Q. Did her remarks contain any reference to the Government of the United States apart from the Army and Navy thereof?

"A. Yes, sir; the system of governments she attacked, claiming that there should not be any government of any kind, though I looked upon those remarks as not particularly confined to the Government of the United States, except that when she mentioned the system of obtaining men under the Government to join the army of this country and to be used by this country in shooting down friends, perhaps, when called upon."[3]

When asked by the Court:

"Q. Did all the remarks she made in this address tend to attack the Government of the United States, and more particularly the Army and Navy?"

the witness replied:

"A. Not all of them, sir; no, sir, not all of them; not all confined to this country alone. A portion of her remarks was relating to other countries, to happenings that had taken place in other countries when her doctrine had become strong enough to be put into execution, giving the impression to everyone who listened to her that revolution was the ultimate end of her doctrine."

"Q. Did she make any remarks which a loyal citizen of the United States or loyal soldier could applaud properly, in your opinion?

"A. Not in my opinion, sir. I don't recollect any part of her speech that could have been properly applauded.

"Q. Did you feel any inclination yourself to applaud any time during the address?

"A. No, sir, my inclinations were in a different way."

This witness also testified (record, p. 9) that the conduct of the accused was such that the attention of the audience was attracted to it; that the accused was in the uniform of his grade in the Army while in attendance at the meeting.

Police Captain Gleeson's testimony was corroborated by that of Officer McPhee (record, p. 9), who testified that the accused attended several meetings which were addressed by Miss Goldman. He also overheard the remark made by the accused to the speaker, which was—"My sympathies are entirely with you, Miss Goldman" (record, p. 11). His testimony was also corroborated by that of Officer Cornelius (record, p. 12), and by Officer Boyle

3. Selective service, or the drafting of men into military service in times of war by the U.S. president, was first enacted in 1863. Eligible men were native-born and naturalized citizens, and those who had declared an intent to become a citizen.

(record, p. 14). The latter took notes of the address delivered at the meeting of April 26, which are appended to the record as Exhibit "A."

Private Buwalda testified as a witness (record, p. 19), his story being that he was learning stenography and attended the meeting for the purpose of becoming proficient in the taking of shorthand notes. He admitted wearing his uniform, but stated that he attached no importance to that fact at the time of the meeting, but realized the impropriety of his act in the light of subsequent events. He denied applauding the remarks of the speaker, and said that the disarrangement of chairs, incident to the breaking up of the meeting, was such as to make it his easiest way of exit to cross the platform to the stage door, as other persons in the audience did. He testified that (record, p. 20), as he passed the speaker, she smiled and extended her hand, which he took and said—"How do you do, Miss Goldman?" He denied making the remark to which the police officer testified.

The police officers were recalled, and adhered to their original testimony. They said that the accused had a single piece of paper about half covered with notes, and were positive that he frequently applauded the speaker.

The accused called a number of enlisted men of Company A, First Battalion of Engineers, several of them noncommissioned officers, who testified to his excellent character as a soldier. Their testimony is uniform and positive in that regard.

The accused at the time of his trial was serving in his fifth enlistment. His first and second discharges were from the Fourth Cavalry, the first with character "Very Good," the second with character "Excellent," and with the notation that he served during the Spanish-American War in 1898. His third discharge from the First Cavalry has an "Excellent" character and the remark that he served in the Philippine Islands, being engaged in mountain attacks in the Island of Mindanao.[4] His fourth discharge, from the same regiment, was with character "Excellent." His enlistment in Company A, 1st Battalion of Engineers, in which he was serving at the time of his discharge by sentence of the general court-martial in his case, began on May 25, 1905.

The accused was convicted of the charge and specification, and was sentenced—

"To be dishonorably discharged the service of the United States, forfeiting all pay and allowances due him, and to be confined at hard labor at such place as the reviewing authority may direct for five years."

The following was the action of the convening authority in giving execution to the sentence imposed by the court:

"Headquarters Department of California, San Francisco, California, May 22, 1908.

"In the foregoing case of First-class Private William Buwalda, Company A, 1st Battalion of Engineers, the sentence is approved. In view of the fifteen years of excellent service the accused has rendered his Government, during which time he appears to have been loyal, it is thought that the disgraceful acts of which he has been convicted were the result, not of

---

4. The Philippine American War was waged from 1899 to 1902, although the United States continued to occupy the Philippines until 1913. For more details on the conflict, see note 4 in "As to 'Crammers of Furnaces,'" Article in *Mother Earth*, 20 November 1906, above.

opinions deliberately formed, but of a mind temporarily thrown off its balance by the words of an anarchist orator. The period of confinement imposed in the sentence is therefore reduced to three years, and as thus modified the sentence will be duly executed. The Pacific Branch of the United States Military Prison, Alcatraz Island, California, is designated as the place of confinement, where the prisoner will be sent under suitable guard.

"FREDERICK FUNSTON,
BRIGADIER GENERAL,
COMMANDING."

It seems hardly conceivable that an enlisted man of the long service and excellent standing of Private Buwalda should so far forget his duty as to attend, in the uniform of his grade in the Army, a public meeting called for the purpose of setting at defiance the Government of the United States, to which he had sworn to bear true faith and allegiance, and which he had solemnly undertaken to serve against all their enemies and opposers whomsoever. It is apparent from the testimony adduced at the trial, including his own story, that while an excellent soldier he had some peculiarities of manner and disposition, and was lacking in judgment or discernment as to what constituted a proper rule of conduct when separated from the command and military control under which his duties were habitually performed. Many old soldiers are peculiarly helpless when confronted with temptations to which they are not habitually exposed, in the routine performance of their duties in the companies or commands in which they are rendering service in the operation of their contracts of enlistment.

As the matter now stands, the accused has been tried by a competent tribunal, the sentence imposed upon conviction has been approved by the legal convening officer, and there is no authority in any military superior, save by an exercise of the pardoning power, to review or revise the conclusions reached by the court and approved by the proper convening authority.

The Commanding General of the Department, in the exercise of the discretion vested in him by the 72nd Article of War,[5] has reached the conclusion that the case is one justifying a resort to disciplinary measures. The action taken in this case is important chiefly by reason of its deterrent effect upon other enlisted men. With a view to obtain the benefit of the example afforded by the punishment in this case, it is recommended that the conviction stand, and that there be no present exercise of clemency or of the pardoning power.

VERY RESPECTFULLY,
GEO. B. DAVIS
JUDGE-ADVOCATE GENERAL.

TDS, file #48,140, Records of the Adjutant General's Office, RG 94, DNA. Addressed "To the Honorable, The Secretary of War." On stationery of the War Department, Office of the Judge Advocate General, Washington. Endorsed with stamp of Chief Clerk, War Dept., 20 June 1908.

5. The 72nd Article of War allowed for the appointment of a general court-martial.

DEAR MR WOOD

Your letter in The Public reporting my visit there, contains a few errors, which I would very much like to correct. Please do not misunderstanding as implying that you have misquoted me, you probably do not remember, but I am quite certain that, I have never said, "violence as tactics would be folly, it only entrenches more firmly the ones assailed. Individual force against individual officials is worse than useless."[1] I have not argued these question in the first place, nor do I look upon them in this light. I do not propagate violence, but not because, I am particularly sentimental about the life of an tyrant, as because I do not believe in inducing a man to act under influence of any other power, save his own reason and the dictum of his own soul. Besides, so long, as I am not to pay the penalty of the act, I do not feel justified in inducing another person to do it.

That is my only reason for not propagating violence. I am therefore quite sure that I have not said the things, as you quote them any more, than I said that the men, who have committed violent act ~~are~~ were "unballanced, or that they are insane."[2] The fact of the matter is that I called our friend from the Oregonian[3] to account for saying these things.

I fear, that in your great zeal to render me a service, you have put your ideas into my mouth. Needless to say, I appreciate your kindness very much. But, I would rather stand misrepresented by my enemies, than my friends. Much rather, do I want the press to say, that I preach violence, than to join in the general lack of understanding for those, who merely give back to organized society that, which society has given these individuall, when ~~she~~ it has closed the door of every chance and fellow feeling into their faces.

---

1. Wood, a Portland lawyer, philosophical anarchist, and free-speech advocate who often chaired EG's meetings when she was in town, published "Emma Goldman in Oregon" in the 26 June 1908 issue of *The Public*. The full quote that EG makes reference to was, "I have never advocated violence in my life. Anarchism expressly condemns force against peaceable men. And besides, violence as tactics would be folly. It only entrenches more firmly the ones assailed. Individual force against individual officials is worse than useless. It is not the official who is to blame; it is the institution; and the only way to destroy the institution is to make it obnoxious to the human mind. An act of violence obscures the whole issue; creates sympathy for the one attacked, fear for the peace of society, and discredits the sanity of the cause."
2. EG is paraphrasing Wood's 26 June account of EG's words. The published quote reads: "poor, excited, unbalanced individuals do brood over the wrongs done in the name of the government, and rush off to kill. They are insane; they have my pity."
3. EG implies that the statements Wood attributed to her were actually made by a reporter from the *Oregonian*.

I remember, that when we walked to the meeting from Mrs Beck[4] house, you expressed your ideas on violence and I argued against. I have always refused to look upon this phase from a utilitarian standpoint. The psychologic cause is most important to me.[5] That great power that will induce one human soul to act against our social crimes while others will barely lisp their indignation against it. I can not and never have believed that the cause was insanity, rather has it been a great sensitiveness to the meaness and coarseness of life. How, then should I condemn these souls. At any rate, I hope you will write Mr. Post[6] and have him correct some of the statements,[7] truly, I can not let them stand.

You will see by the inclosed that, whatever little work in the B case[8] we have already done is telling. Probably the judge-advocate general could be prevailed upon to reconsider the sentence. How could we reach him? Let me know.

Sincerely

Emma Goldman

PS. So sorry, we mixed up your initials. It won't happen again, if you would only send something soon.[9]

ALS, Charles Erskine Scott Wood Papers, CU-B. On top center of first page, a third party wrote "Goldman."

4. Kathryn (Kitty) Seaman Beck (d. 1922) was hired by Wood in 1897 as his personal secretary. Over the years Kitty (as he called her) was Wood's confidant and intermittent lover. EG stayed with Beck when in Portland and the two corresponded throughout the rest of Beck's life. Kitty suffered through three disastrous marriages: the first to a Seattle pioneer, the second to Lloyd Irving in 1911, and the third to George W. Vanderveer in 1922. Miserable and increasingly an alcoholic, she committed suicide on 31 October 1922 by suffocating herself.

5. See vol. 1 for EG's essay "The Tragedy at Buffalo" (*Free Society*, 6 October 1901; reprinted in *Mother Earth*, October 1906) and her pamphlet *The Psychology of Political Violence* (New York: Mother Earth Publishing Association, 1911) for further discussion of EG's views on political violence.

6. Louis F. Post was the editor of *The Public*.

7. Wood published a correction in *The Public* which appeared in the 24 July 1908 issue. In the original Wood misquotes EG as having said that "violence as tactics would be folly," and that those who engage in violence are "poor, excited, unbalanced individuals . . . They are insane." The correctional letter affirms that EG never made these statements and clarifies her position on violence as follows: "she does not propagate violence and never has done so; but not because she is particularly sentimental about life, so much as that she does not believe in inducing any one to act under the influence of any power save his own reason and the dictum of his own soul."

8. EG refers to the William Buwalda court-martial case, which Wood took an interest in (for details, see George B. Davis to William Howard Taft, 19 June 1908, above).

9. In EG's June 1908 *Mother Earth* article entitled "En Route," which included a report on her visit in Portland, she wrote, "The great and generous efforts of Mr. E. C. S. Wood, the most liberal and unique figure on the Coast." Also published in the June issue was Wood's introduction to EG's Portland lecture, "In Portland (Verbatim Report of the Introductory Address by former Senator C. E. S. Wood." Wood's next contribution to *Mother Earth* was the poem "In Memory of Francisco Ferrer" (November 1909).

Hoboo, treasure hoboo

Now, that I have tasted the invigorating breeze of your primitive, untramled nature, I feel the narrowness of family even more. I never could stand it, indeed my own family made me hate, such narrow, enslaving and degrading confines. I feel them more to day probably because I still have you near me, oh so closely, darling mine. I came here for my sisters sake, but I wish I had stayed another day with you and then gone to N Y. Its over soon, this ordeal of seeing people, with whom, one has naught in common. My own trampie, I am so eager to hear from you, I hope a may have a line, when I arrive tomorrow and you will always tell me, how you are, won't you sweetheart. Joy or sorrow, delight or pain, I want to share everything with my precious boy, may I not? I hope to be in a more rational mood soon, when I shall suggest a few things for your consideration dearie. If you and I are to pass the next three months gracefully, we must at least busy ourselves with <u>our future</u> but of that later. I am too restless to reason now. Not too restless to love you, love you intensely and passionately.

Write soon, tell me how you are, how things impress you now. Have you seen Post?[1] And what result? And Steinhauser? Above all, write me, if you love me, as much as ever. You are with me dearest, at least your spirit is so close to me, in <u>me</u>.

Affectionately

Momie

P.S. Leave for N Y to night.

ALS, IU-U.

---

1. EG refers to Louis Post, a liberal Chicago lawyer and founder and editor of *The Public*, which reported sympathetically on EG.

SIR:

I have the honor to transmit herewith a letter from Captain F. A. Pope, Corps of Engineers, commanding officer at Fort Mason, California, relative to the case of Military Convict Wm. Buwalda, whose sentence was published in General Orders, No. 84, these headquarters, May 22, 1908.[1]

Captain Pope's letter was written at my suggestion after I had been informed by him as to the correct attitude of this man regarding his trial and conviction, he having assured that officer before being transferred to the Pacific Branch of the U.S. Military prison that his punishment was deserved, that he was deeply penitent and was grateful for the clemency that had been extended by the reviewing authority in remitting two years of the sentence of imprisonment imposed by the court martial before which he had been tried. Buwalda further stated to Captain Pope that he does not now and never has held anarchistic or disloyal views, but that he was swept off his feet by the eloquence of Miss Goldman and the applause of her audience.

In view of these facts, as well as in consideration of the man's long and faithful service, and believing that the ends of discipline have already been subserved in his case, I desire to recommend an Executive pardon,[2] coupled with specific authority from the War Department to re-enlist if he should desire to do so.

In making this recommendation, I am not moved to the slightest degree by the certain amount of ill informed clamor that has arisen regarding the case, but have considered it entirely apart from such influences.

In case my recommendation for a pardon be approved, I suggest that, owing to the deep public interest in the case, and for fear an act of clemency be misunderstood, it be specifically stated by the War Department that this act is not to be considered as a precedent but is Executive clemency pure and simple; or that this letter be made public, thus showing the reasons for the action taken.

In my opinion, Buwalda is too good a man to have his life ruined, and having had this experience, it is safe to say that it will be many a year before he or any other soldier

---

1. William Buwalda was found guilty, dishonorably discharged, and sentenced to five years hard labor, later commuted to three years. Upon his release on 31 December 1908, Buwalda wrote a letter thanking President Roosevelt for his recommendation of a shortened sentence, but Buwalda asserted that he was in fact guilty of no crime. Later he also returned the medal he had received for service in the Philippines.
2. An executive pardon is a release of guilt or remission of punishment by the chief executive officer of the state. As Commander-in-Chief of all armed services for the United States, the President could pardon a military convict by commuting his sentence.

participates in an anarchist meeting or applauds abuse of the government to which he had sworn allegiance.

VERY RESPECTFULLY,
FREDERICK FUNSTON
BRIGADIER GENERAL,
COMMANDING.

ALS, DNA, RG 94, on letterhead of Headquarters Department of California. Addressed to Frederick Crayton Ainsworth (1852–1934), who was adjutant general of the U.S. Army from 1907 to 1912. Ainsworth initiated the central archiving of army records for soldiers in all American wars up to the time of his generalship; his records were incorporated into the National Archives.

THE WHITE HOUSE
WASHINGTON

Oyster Bay, N.Y.,
June 24, 1908.

To the Judge Advocate General of the Army:

I am in receipt of the Department's letter of the 22d instant concerning William Buwalda, and return the enclosures herewith. I do not wish to disturb this sentence at present; but it is perfectly clear to me that the case is one deserving of punishment; that the man should be dishonorably discharged and suffer some term of imprisonment; but it seems to me that the amount is altogether too severe. What is your opinion as to whether six months' imprisonment would not be sufficient? The officers and men of the army should hold an offense like this in peculiar horror; but for that very reason I do not wish, by having too heavy a penalty imposed, to change their feeling into one of sympathy for the offender.

Theodore Roosevelt

Enclosure.

Letter from President Theodore Roosevelt to the Judge Advocate General of the Army, dated 24 June 1908, in which Roosevelt affirmed his belief that William Buwalda's crime of shaking Goldman's hand in uniform "is one deserving of punishment" and a "peculiar horror" but suggested that perhaps the sentence of five years of hard labor on Alcatraz Island was too severe and might evoke sympathy for Buwalda's plight. (National Archives and Records Administration)

THE WHITE HOUSE
WASHINGTON

Oyster Bay, N.Y.,
July 7, 1908.

My dear Mr. Secretary:

I return herewith the Judge Advocate General's memorandum and other papers in the case of William Buwalda. The President has signed the order granting clemency to Buwalda, and approves of the recommendation of the Judge Advocate General that the clemency which is proposed to be shown be not published until the date for its execution approaches, and that applicants for clemency in the meantime be advised that the case is undergoing careful consideration.

Very truly yours,

Secretary to the President.

Hon. Robert Shaw Oliver,
Acting Secretary of War.

Enclosures

Confidential letter dated 7 July 1908, from the White House presidential secretary to Robert Shaw Oliver, Acting Secretary of War, confirming President Roosevelt's order granting clemency to William Buwalda. (National Archives and Records Administration)

Essay in the **NEW YORK WORLD**

New York, 19 July 1908

"What I Believe"—By Emma Goldman

**The Leader of the Anarchists, One of the Most Talked of Women
in the World, Declares that She Has Been Persistently Misrepresented,
and Writes of Her Creed, Caustically Arraigning Existing Social
Conditions—"I Do Not Believe that Acts of Violence Can Bring About
the Social Reconstruction"—"As a Promoter of Individual Liberty
Government Stands Condemned"—"Ninety Per Cent. of All Crimes Are
Property Crimes, Which Have Their Root in Our Economic Iniquities"—
"Anarchists Are the Only True Advocates of Peace"—
"Marriage and Love Are Not Synonymous."**

Emma Goldman, the recognized leader of Anarchists
in this country and one of the most talked of women in the world,
who herself says that her name is used to frighten children and that
she has been persistently misrepresented, here makes her own statement
of her creed. Her creed will both shock and astonish, for her document is
as remarkable for what the writer says she does not believe as for what
it says she does believe. It will afford to readers of the Sunday World an
opportunity for the first time to estimate the radical beliefs of this
singular woman and of the scattered and rebellious social
elements which she represents.

"What I believe" has many times been the target of hack writers. Such blood-curdling and incoherent stories have been circulated about me, it is no wonder that the average human being has palpitation of the heart at the very mention of the name Emma Goldman. It is too bad that we no longer live in the times when witches were burned at the stake or tortured to drive the evil spirit out of them. For, indeed, Emma Goldman is a witch! True, she does not eat little children, but she does many worse things. She manufactures bombs and gambles in crowned heads. B-r-r-r!

Such is the impression the public has of myself and my beliefs. It is therefore very much to the credit of The World that it gives its readers at least an opportunity to learn what my beliefs really are.

The student of the history of progressive thought is well aware that every idea in its early stages has been misrepresented and the adherents of such ideas have been maligned and persecuted. One need not go back two thousand years to the time when those who believed in the gospel of Jesus were thrown into the arena or hunted into dungeons to realize how little great beliefs or earnest believers are understood. The history of progress is written in the blood of men and women who have dared to espouse an unpopular cause, as, for instance, the black man's right to his body, or woman's right to her soul. If, then, from time immemorial, the New has met with opposition and condemnation, why should my beliefs be exempt from a crown of thorns?

"What I believe" is a process rather than a finality. Finalities are for gods and governments, not for the human intellect. While it may be true that Herbert Spencer's formulation of liberty is the most important on the subject, as a political basis of society, yet life is something more than formulas. In the battle for freedom, as Ibsen has so well pointed out, it is the struggle for, not so much the attainment of, liberty, that develops all that is strongest, sturdiest and finest in human character.[1]

Anarchism is not only a process, however, that marches on with "sombre steps," coloring all that is positive and constructive in organic development. It is a conspicuous protest of the most militant type. It is so absolutely uncompromising, insisting and permeating a force as to overcome the most stubborn assault and to withstand the criticism of those who really constitute the last trumpets of a decaying age.

Anarchists are by no means passive spectators in the theatre of social development; on the contrary, they have some very positive notions as regards aims and methods.

That I may make myself as clear as possible without using too much space, permit me to adopt the topical mode of treatment of "What I Believe:"

I. AS TO PROPERTY.

"Property" means dominion over things and the denial to others of the use of those things. So long as production was not equal to the normal demand, institutional property may have had some raison d'être. One has only to consult economics, however, to know that the productivity of labor within the last few decades has increased so tremendously as to exceed normal demand a hundred-fold, and to make property not only a hindrance to human well-being, but an obstacle, a deadly barrier, to all progress. It is the private dominion over things that condemns millions of people to be mere nonentities, living corpses without originality or power of initiative, human machines of flesh and blood, who pile up mountains of wealth for others and pay for it with a gray, dull and wretched existence for themselves. I believe that there can be no real wealth, social wealth, so long as it rests on human lives—young lives, old lives and lives in the making.

It is conceded by all radical thinkers that the fundamental cause of this terrible state

---

1. Henrik Ibsen, in a letter to Georg Brandes, wrote: "He who possesses liberty otherwise than as a thing to be striven for, possesses it dead and soulless. So that a man who stops in the midst of the struggle and says, 'Now I have it,'—thereby shows that he has lost it."

of affairs is (1) that man must sell his labor; (2) that his inclination and judgment are subordinated to the will of a master.

Anarchism is the only philosophy that can and will do away with this humiliating and degrading situation. It differs from all other theories inasmuch as it points out that man's development, his physical well-being, his latent qualities and innate disposition alone must determine the character and conditions of his work. Similarly will one's physical and mental appreciations and his soul cravings decide how much he shall consume. To make this a reality will, I believe, be possible only in a society based on voluntary co-operation of productive groups, communities and societies loosely federated together, eventually developing into a free communism, actuated by a solidarity of interests. There can be no freedom in the large sense of the word, no harmonious development, so long as mercenary and commercial considerations play an important part in the determination of personal conduct.

II. AS TO GOVERNMENT.

I believe Government, organized authority, or the State, is necessary *only* to maintain or protect property and monopoly. It has proven efficient in that function only. As a promoter of individual liberty, human well-being and social harmony, which alone constitute real order, government stands condemned by all the great men of the world.

I therefore believe, with my fellow-Anarchists, that the statutory regulations, legislative enactments, constitutional provisions, are invasive. They never yet induced man to do anything he could and would not do by virtue of his intellect and temperament, nor prevented anything that man was impelled to do by the same dictates. Millet's pictorial description of "The Man with the Hoe,"[2] Meunier's masterpieces of the miners that have aided in lifting labor from its degrading position,[3] Gorki's descriptions of the underworld,[4] Ibsen's psychological analysis of human life, could never have been induced by government any more than the spirit which impels a man to save a drowning child or a crippled woman from a burning building has ever been called into operation by statutory regulations or the policeman's club. I believe—indeed, I know—that whatever is fine and beautiful in the human, expresses and asserts itself in spite of government, and not because of it.

The Anarchists are therefore justified in assuming that anarchism—the absence of

---

2. Jean-Francois Millet (1814–1875) was a French painter whose *The Man With a Hoe* (1863) was among several depicting peasants at work; the painting influenced Edwin Markham's famous 1899 poem of the same name.

3. Constantin Meunier (1831–1905) was a Belgian sculptor and painter, many of whose works were visual depictions of labor, including *The Mine*, a three-part painting, and *Monument to Labor*, a series of bronze and stone statues and reliefs.

4. Maksim Gorky's controversial play, heavily censored by the Russian government, *The Night's Lodging* (1902, also known as *The Lower Depths* and *At the Bottom*), portrays the destitution of life in the streets of Moscow. EG discussed Gorky's play in her *The Social Significance of the Modern Drama*, pp. 294–301.

government—will insure the widest and greatest scope for unhampered human development, the cornerstone of true social progress and harmony.

As to the stereotyped argument that government acts as a check on crime and vice, even the makers of law no longer believe it. This country spends millions of dollars for the maintenance of her "criminals" behind prison bars, yet crime is on the increase. Surely this state of affairs is not owing to an insufficiency of laws! Ninety per cent. of all crimes are property crimes, which have their root in our economic iniquities. So long as these latter continue to exist we might convert every lamppost into a gibbet without having the least effect on the crime in our midst. Crimes resulting from heredity can certainly never be cured by law. Surely we are learning even today that such crimes can effectively be treated only by the best modern medical methods at our command, and, above all, by the spirit of a deeper sense of fellowship, kindness and understanding.

III. AS TO MILITARISM.

I should not treat of this subject separately, since it belongs to the paraphernalia of government, if it were not for the fact that those who are most vigorously opposed to my beliefs on the ground that the latter stand for force are the advocates of militarism.

The fact is that Anarchists are the only true advocates of peace, the only people who call a halt to the growing tendency of militarism, which is fast making of this erstwhile free country an imperialistic and despotic power.

The military spirit is the most merciless, heartless and brutal in existence. It fosters an institution for which there is not even a pretense for justification. The soldier, to quote Tolstoi, is a professional man-killer.[5] He does not kill for the love of it, like a savage, or in a passion, like a homicide. He is a cold-blooded, mechanical, obedient tool of his military superiors. He is ready to cut throats or scuttle a ship at the command of his ranking officer, without knowing or, perhaps, caring how, why or wherefore. I am supported in this contention by no less a military light than Gen. Funston. I quote from the latter's communication to the New York Evening Post of June 30, dealing with the case of Private William Buwalda, which caused such a stir all through the Northwest. "The first duty of an officer or enlisted man," says our noble warrior, "is unquestioning obedience and loyalty to the Government to which he has sworn allegiance; it makes no difference whether he approves of that Government or not."

How can we harmonize the principle of "unquestioning obedience" with the principle of "life, liberty and the pursuit of happiness?" The deadly power of militarism has never before been so effectually demonstrated in this country as in the recent condemnation by court-martial of William Buwalda, of San Francisco, Company A, Engineers, to five years in military prison. Here was a man who had a record of fifteen years of continuous service. "His character and conduct were unimpeachable," we are told by Gen. Funston,

5. Leo Tolstoy, "Thou Shalt Not Kill" (*Freedom*, December 1900).

who, in consideration of it, reduced Buwalda's sentence to three years.[6] Yet the man is thrown suddenly out of the army, dishonored, robbed of his chances of a pension and sent to prison. What was his crime? Just listen, ye free-born Americans! William Buwalda attended a public meeting, and after the lecture he shook hands with the speaker. Gen. Funston, in his letter to the Post, to which I have already referred above, asserts that Buwalda's action was a "great military offense, infinitely worse than desertion." In another public statement, which the General made in Portland, Ore., he said that "Buwalda's was a serious crime, equal to treason."

It is quite true that the meeting had been arranged by Anarchists. Had the Socialists issued the call, Gen. Funston informs us, there would have been no objection to Buwalda's presence. Indeed, the General says, "I would not have the slightest hesitancy about attending a Socialist meeting myself."[7] But to attend an Anarchist meeting with Emma Goldman as speaker—could there be anything more "treasonable?"

For this horrible crime a man, a free-born American citizen, who has given this country the best fifteen years of his life, and whose character and conduct during that time were "unimpeachable," is now languishing in a prison, dishonored, disgraced and robbed of a livelihood.

Can there be anything more destructive of the true genius of liberty than the spirit that made Buwalda's sentence possible—the spirit of unquestioning obedience? Is it for this that the American people have in the last few years sacrificed four hundred million dollars and their hearts' blood?

I believe that militarism—a standing army and navy in any country—is indicative of the decay of liberty and the destruction of all that is best and finest in our nation. The steadily growing clamor for more battleships and an increased army on the ground that these guarantee us peace is as absurd as the argument that the peaceful man is he who goes well armed.

The same lack of consistency is displayed by those peace pretenders who oppose anarchism because it supposedly teaches violence, and who would yet be delighted over the possibility of the American nation soon being able to hurl dynamite bombs upon defenseless enemies from flying machines.

I believe that militarism will cease when the liberty-loving spirits of the world say to their masters: "Go and do your own killing. We have sacrificed ourselves and our loved ones long enough fighting your battles. In return you have made parasites and criminals of us in times of peace and brutalized us in times of war. You have separated us from our brothers and have made of the world a human slaughterhouse. No, we will not do

---

6. On 14 May 1908, William Buwalda was court-martialed for violating the 62nd Article of War (for the act of shaking EG's hand while in uniform). Found guilty and sentenced to five years hard labor, he was eventually dishonorably discharged. On 22 May General Funston commuted his sentence to three years in light of Buwalda's fifteen years of excellent military service.
7. "Gen. Funston on the Buwalda Case," *New York Evening Post,* 30 June 1908.

your killing or fight for the country that you have stolen from us." Oh, I believe with all my heart that human brotherhood and solidarity will clear the horizon from the terrible red streak of war and destruction.

IV. AS TO FREE SPEECH AND PRESS.

The Buwalda case is only one phase of the larger question of free speech, free press and the right of free assembly.

Many good people imagine that the principles of free speech or press can be exercised properly and with safety within the limits of constitutional guarantees. That is the only excuse, it seems to me, for the terrible apathy and indifference to the onslaught upon free speech and press that we have witnessed in this country within the last few months.[8]

I believe that free press and speech mean that I may say and write what I please. This right, when regulated by constitutional provisions, legislative enactments, almighty decisions of the Postmaster-General or the policeman's club, becomes a farce. I am well aware that I will be warned of consequences if we remove the chains from speech and press. I believe, however, that the cure of consequences resulting from the unlimited exercise of expression is to allow more expression.

Mental shackles have never yet stemmed the tide of progress, whereas premature social explosions have only too often been brought about through a wave of repression.

Will our governors never learn that countries like England, Holland, Norway, Sweden and Denmark, with the largest freedom of expression, have been freest from "consequences?" Whereas Russia, Spain, Italy, France and, alas!—even America have raised these "consequences" to the most pressing political factor. Ours is supposed to be a country ruled by the majority, yet every policeman who is not vested with power by the majority can break up a meeting, drag the lecturer off the platform and club the audience out of the hall in true Russian fashion. The Postmaster-General, who is not an elective officer, has the power to suppress publications and confiscate mail. From his decision there is no more appeal than from that of the Russian Czar. Truly, I believe we need a new Declaration of Independence. Is there no modern Jefferson or Adams?

V. AS TO THE CHURCH.

At the recent convention of the political remnants of a once revolutionary idea it was voted that religion and vote getting have nothing to do with each other.[9] Why should they? So

---

8. A reference to mounting police suppression of free speech in 1908, most notably in Chicago where EG's meetings were suppressed, and Philadelphia where anarchists, including Voltairine de Cleyre, were arrested and charged with "inciting to riot" at a 20 February 1908 meeting of Jewish and Italian anarchists.

9. At the 1908 National Convention of the Socialist Party held in Chicago (10–17 May), the following declaration was made regarding the Party's stance on religion: "The Socialist Party represents primarily an economic and political movement. It is not concerned with matters of religious belief . . . Our aim is a definite, material transformation of society, a different regulation of labor, the substitution of the

long as man is willing to delegate to the devil the care of his soul, he might with the same consistency delegate to the politician the care of his rights. That religion is a private affair has long been settled by the Bis-Marxian Socialists of Germany. Our American Marxians, poor of blood and originality, must need go to Germany for their wisdom. That wisdom has served as a capital whip to lash the several millions of people into the well disciplined army of Socialism. It might do the same here. For goodness' sake, let's not offend respectability, let's not hurt the religious feelings of the people.

Religion is a superstition that originated in man's mental inability to solve natural phenomena. The Church is an organized institution that has always been a stumbling block to progress.

Organized churchism has stripped religion of its naiveté and primitiveness. It has turned religion into a nightmare that oppresses the human soul and holds the mind in bondage. "The Dominion of Darkness," as the last true Christian, Leo Tolstoi, calls the Church, has been a foe of human development and free thought, and as such it has no place in the life of a truly free people.[10]

VI. AS TO MARRIAGE AND LOVE.

I believe these are probably the most tabooed subjects in this country. It is almost impossible to talk about them without scandalizing the cherished propriety of a lot of good folk. No wonder so much ignorance prevails relative to these questions. Nothing short of an open, frank and intelligent discussion will purify the air from the hysterical, sentimental rubbish that is shrouding these vital subjects, vital to individual as well as social well being.

Marriage and love are not synonymous; on the contrary, they are often antagonistic to each other. I am aware of the fact that some marriages are actuated by love, but the narrow, material confines of marriage, as it is, speedily crush the tender flower of affection.

Marriage is an institution which furnishes the State and Church with a tremendous revenue and the means of prying into that phase of life which refined people have long considered their own, their very own most sacred affair. Love is that most powerful factor of human relationship which from time immemorial has defied all man-made laws and broken through the iron bars of conventions in church and morality. Marriage is often an economic arrangement purely, furnishing the woman with a life long insurance policy and the man with a perpetuator of his kind or a pretty toy. That is, marriage, or the training thereto, prepares the woman for the life of a parasite, a

---

Socialist mode of production for the capitalist system. Nothing else. Anybody who wants to cooperate with us for the attainment of this aim is welcome as a comrade-at-arms, regardless of his philosophic, religious or other personal views. Our aims bear no relation to religion—they move in entirely different spheres."

10. Tolstoy's drama *The Dominion of Darkness* (written in 1886; also known as *The Power of Darkness*) is a tragedy about a group of church-going Russian peasants whose lives are permeated with misery and ignorance.

dependent, helpless servant, while it furnishes to man the right of a chattel mortgage over a human life.

How can such a condition of affairs have anything in common with love?—with the element that would forego all the wealth of money and power and live in its own world of untrammelled human expression? But this is not the age of romanticism, of Romeo and Juliet, Faust and Marguerite, of moonlight ecstasies, of flowers and songs. Ours is a practical age. Our first consideration is an income. So much the worse for us if we have reached the era when the soul's highest flights are to be checked. No race can develop without the love element.

But if two people are to worship at the shrine of love, what is to become of the golden calf, marriage? "It is the only security for the woman, for the child, the family, the State." But it is no security to love; and without love no true home can or does exist. Without love no child should be born; without love no true woman can be related to a man. The fear that love is not sufficient material safety for the child is out of date. I believe when woman signs her own emancipation, her first declaration of independence will consist in admiring and loving a man for the qualities of his heart and mind and not for the quantities in his pocket. The second declaration will be that she has the right to follow that love without let or hindrance from the outside world. The third and most important declaration will be the absolute right to free motherhood.

In such a mother and in an equally free father rests the safety of the child. They have the strength, the sturdiness, the harmony to create an atmosphere wherein alone the human plant can grow into an exquisite flower.

VII. AS TO ACTS OF VIOLENCE.

And now I have come to that point in my beliefs about which the greatest misunderstanding prevails in the minds of the American public. "Well, come, now, don't you propagate violence, the killing of crowned heads and Presidents?" Who says that I do? Have you heard me, has any one heard me? Has any one seen it printed in our literature? No, but the papers say so, everybody says so; consequently it must be so. Oh, for the accuracy and logic of the dear public!

I believe that anarchism is the only philosophy of peace, the only theory of a social relationship that values human life above everything else. I know that some Anarchists have committed acts of violence, but it is the terrible economic inequality and great political injustice that prompt such acts, not anarchism. Every institution to-day rests on violence, our very atmosphere is saturated with it. So long as such a state exists we might as well strive to stop the rush of Niagara as hope to do away with violence. I have already stated that countries with some measure of freedom of expression have had few or no acts of violence. What is the moral? Simply this: No act committed by an Anarchist has been for personal gain, aggrandizement or profit, but rather a conscious protest against some repressive, arbitrary, tyrannical measure from above.

President Carnot of France was killed by Caserio in response to Carnot's refusal to commute the death sentence of Vaillant, for whose life the entire literary, scientific and humanitarian world of France had pleaded.[11]

Bresci went to Italy on his own money earned in the silk weaving mills at Paterson to call King Humbert[12] to the bar of justice for his order to shoot defenseless women and children during a bread riot. Angelino executed Prime Minister Canovas for the latter's resurrection of the Spanish inquisition at Montjuich Prison.[13] Alexander Berkman attempted the life of Henry C. Frick[14] during the Homestead strike only because of his intense sympathy for the eleven strikers killed by Pinkertons and for the widows and orphans evicted by Frick from their wretched little homes that were owned by Mr. Carnegie.[15]

Every one of these men not only made their reasons known to the world in spoken or written statements, showing the causes that led to their acts, proving that the unbearable economic and political pressure, the suffering and despair of their fellowmen, women and children prompted their acts, and not the philosophy of Anarchism.[16] They came openly, frankly and ready to stand the consequences, ready to give their own lives.

In diagnosing the true nature of our social disease I cannot condemn those who through no fault of their own are suffering from a widespread malady.

I do not believe that these acts can or ever have been intended to bring about the social reconstruction. That can only be done, first, by a broad and wide education as to man's place in society and his proper relation to his fellows; and, second, through example. By example I mean the actual living of a truth once recognized, not the mere theorising of its life element. Lastly, and the most powerful weapon, is the conscious, intelligent, organized, economic protest of the masses through direct action and the general strike.

It is the harmony of organic growth which produces variety of color and form—the complete whole we admire in the flower. Analogously will the organized activity of free human beings endowed with the spirit of solidarity result in the perfection of social harmony—which is anarchism. Indeed, only anarchism makes non-authoritarian

11. In 1894 French President Marie François-Sadi Carnot was stabbed to death by Italian anarchist Sante Caserio, in retaliation for the 1894 execution of Auguste Vaillant (for further discussion, see also vol. 1, p. 522).
12. In 1900 Gaetano Bresci assassinated Italian king Umberto.
13. In 1897 Michele Angiolillo shot and killed Spanish prime minister Antonio Cánovas del Castillo.
14. AB attempted to kill Henry C. Frick in 1892.
15. Andrew Carnegie (1835–1919) was an American industrialist who, along with his business partner Henry C. Frick, began acquiring steel factories in 1873, consolidating them into the Carnegie Steel Company; in 1901, Carnegie was bought out by the U.S. Steel Corporation. Following the tenets set forth in his essay "The Gospel of Wealth" (1889), Carnegie established a foundation in 1911 to administer his fortune for philanthropic purposes.
16. See, for examples, Caserio's trial speech printed in Freedom Pamphlet No. 9, "Anarchy on Trial" (1896); and Vaillant's trial speech in *Liberty* 9, no. 47 (24 February 1894; whole issue no. 281).

organization a reality, since it abolishes the existing antagonism between individuals and classes.

Emma Goldman

New York World, 19 July 1908, p. 3M. Facsimile of EG's signature appeared at end of essay. Later reprinted as a pamphlet, entitled *What I Believe* (New York: Mother Earth Publishing Association, 1908).

DEAR MR WOOD

Your very kind and interesting letter received last week, also copy of letter to Mr. Post.[1] Thank you for both.

I can not tell you how much I enjoyed your letter. Sincerity is what I love more, than anything else. And when that is coupled with beauty of style and expression, I easily fall a prey to it. Still I have to disagree with you, dear Mr Wood.

It seems to me that you are very much under the sway of Lombroso[2] in his contention that Genius and Insanity, are one. For that I am sorry as I never considered Lombroso anything, but a Charlatan a man, who caters to popular passions. Whether you take Lombroso as an authority on the subject or not, I never can agree that Genius means insanity. Why I could name, a host of truly great genius that were as sane and normal as all intellectual people. Turgeneff,[3] Zola,[4] Meunier,[5] Millet,[6] Wagner[7] etc

The fact, that Maupassant[8] happened to be insane, had no more to do with his genius, than if your next door neighbor should suddenly turn maniac. The same holds good, of

1. EG had asked Wood to write a letter of correction to Louis F. Post, editor of *The Public,* which had published in its 26 June issue Wood's mostly sympathetic report on EG's lecture tour in Portland (see Letter to C. E. S. Wood, after 26 June 1908, above).
2. Cesare Lombroso (1836–1909) was an Italian phrenologist and criminologist noted for two controversial theories. The first maintains that genius is closely related to insanity. The second asserts that criminality has a biological basis; criminals are born with an innate potential for anti-social behavior. Lombroso held that criminals were identifiable by what he considered primitive and degenerate physical characteristics.
3. Refers to Ivan Turgenev.
4. Refers to Émile Zola.
5. EG cites the Belgian sculptor and painter Constantin Meunier as an example of an artist dignifying laborers (see "What I Believe," Essay in *New York World,* 19 July 1908, above).
6. The French painter Jean-François Millet is cited by EG for his paintings of peasants at work (see "What I Believe," Essay in *New York World,* 19 July 1908, above).
7. Richard Wilhelm Wagner (1813–1883), the noted German composer and theorist, was known for developing a new form of operatic stage production referred to as "musical dramas," exemplified by his tetralogy *The Ring* based on his epic poem *Der Ring des Nibelungen* (The Ring of the Nibelung, 1852). Wagner was also an associate of anarchist Michael Bakunin and took part with Bakunin in the 3 May 1849 uprising in Dresden.
8. Henri-René-Albert-Guy de Maupassant (1850–1893), a French naturalist author and disciple of Gustave Flaubert, Émile Zola, and Ivan Turgenev, first gained recognition for his short story "Boule de Suif," published by Zola in *Les Soirées de Medan* (1880). Maupassant went on to capture both peasant and bourgeois life in over 300 short stories, six novels, three plays, three travel books, and one book of verse, *Des Vers* (1880). Suffering from syphilis throughout most of his adult life, in his last years, the illness caused Maupassant to grow increasingly deranged; he was confined to a mental institution.

those, who have committed acts of violence, not one of them, and I have known many has been insane, or even abnormal. Their violence was incidental to their nature and might never have asserted itself, had not the conditions brought it out.

I speak from personal knowledge of these people, while you make the mistake in estimating their mental status, by your own standard of sanity and insinaty. I do not think, that is a correct estimate. People, who believe that genius and insanity are inseparable, may, by your method of reasoning declare <u>you</u> insane. Yet I have met few people who are so sane, as you. Your modesty may not permit you to acknowledge yourself a genius. But you are one nevertheless. It seems to me, that there is little logic in such onesided judgement. One, may consider an act impractical, imprudent, useless, but that does not make the perpetrator of that act insane. If I can find time, I shall hunt of the speeches of Etievant and Vaillant to French anarchists who have committed acts of violence.[9] I am confident, you would never think these men insane, after you read their ideas. I am sure, you would think them perfectly sane and logic, especially if you would read their speeches and not know, that these men have used violence.

I really think, that very few of us can be so objective, as to disassociate our own ideas from the action of other people. Thats why we are apt to call a man insane because his act does not quite harmonize with our idea of logic or sanity.

Yes, I could mention quite a number of acts that had an imediate bearing on a lot of reforms and changes in arbitrary laws. For instance the killing of the Schipiogin Minister of Interierer, by the young Russian Balmasheff[10] has brought about, tremendous changes in Russia, the same is true of the killing of Van Plevhe[11] and Sergi-

---

9. George Etiévant (1865–ca.1900) was a French anarchist sentenced in 1892 to five years of hard labor in prison, charged with stealing dynamite cartridges. His speech "Reward and Punishment" was delivered before the court in Paris and published in *Anarchy on Trial* (London: Freedom Office, 1896). Also included in this pamphlet are Jean Grave's "Defense of Anarchism" and Sante Caserio's "Why He Killed Carnot." Auguste Vaillant threw a homemade bomb into France's Chamber of Deputies on 9 December 1893, injuring about eighty people but killing no one. He was executed on 6 February 1894. In Vaillant's argument in defense of his act, he stated that "a society in which one sees such social inequities as we see all around us, in which we see every day suicides caused by poverty, prostitution flaring at every street-corner, a society whose principal monuments are barracks and prisons,—such a society must be transformed as soon as possible, on pain of being eliminated, and that speedily, from the human race. Hail to him who labors by no matter what means for this transformation! It is this idea that has guided me in my duel with authority, but as in this duel I have only wounded my adversary, it is now its turn to strike me." His speech was widely circulated in pamphlet form and reprinted by Benjamin Tucker in *Liberty*, 24 February 1894.
10. Stepan Valerianovich Balmashev (1882–1902) was a member of the Russian Party of Socialist Revolutionaries (PSR). Balmashev was also a member of the Combat Organization, a separate unit designated specifically to carry out terrorist activity. In April 1902, Balmashev assassinated Minister of the Interior Dmitrii Sipiagin.
11. Vyacheslav Konstantinovich Plehve (1846–1904) was the successor to Sipiagin as minister of the interior. Following the assassination of Sipiagin, Plehve called for harsh suppression of radical elements in Russia. He also aggressively pursued Russification policies particularly among Armenians, Finns, and Jews. This resulted in a violent pogrom in April 1903 in Kishinev and made Plehve

ues.[12] The fact, that Russia is now again reactionary is not due to these acts but to the naiveté of the Revolutionists, who begain with parlamentarism and the Duma, when acts were needed.

The act, that has been truly epoch making was the killing of Prime Minister Canovas of Spain, by Angelina.[13] Canovas was responcible for the horrors of the Inquisition in the Montjuich prison. The entire World was opposed to him, but not until Angelina fired his heroic shot, was the Inquisition abolished. However that is not really at the bottom of acts. As I have already stated not one of the men, I have known ever flattered himself that his act is going to bring about great changes, or that a liberal ruler will take the place of the one taken off the throne. What these men aimed at, was the calling attention to a grave wrong which undermines our lives and no one seems to see. And in that, they have certainly succeeded. Just as the lightening succeeded in shining in indicating the right path, which we have lost in the dark, so does an act illuminate the horizon of our social life, which is usually so thickly covered with clouds of ignorence, so that everybody stumbles along in the dark, unable to see the wrong or injustice at his very door.

How strange, you reason Mr. Wood. You say "I can conceive killing of an official to save your own life, or in revenge." May not the human and fellow instinct of an Alexander Berkman have been so strange, that any wrong committed on his fellows would smart, even more, than if committed on himself. Why then should he not evenged that wrong with the same justification, as you in saving your own life?

But enough, if I keep on, even you will begin to think me a blood thirsty creature.

Have you read Tolstoys letter in The Sunday Times July 19th?[14] You will see that even this great, wonderful man, who while abhoring violence, insists, that there is no man,

a prime target for revolutionary hatred. On 15 July 1904 Plehve was assassinated when Egor Sazonov (also known as Abel or Avel in Russian), a member of the PSR's Combat Organization, launched a bomb into Plehve's carriage. Sazonov was sentenced to hard labor in prison and committed suicide on 27 November 1910 in protest against penal repression. Envo Azev (1869–1918), an agent provocateur, was later exposed in January 1909 by the Socialist Revolutionaries, as playing an initiating part in this and other events of the Combat Organization, including the assassination of Dmitrii Sipiagin.

12. Grand Duke Sergei Aleksandrovich (1857–1905) was governor-general of Moscow as well as uncle to Nicholas II and one of the Tsar's closest advisors. He was extremely conservative and pressed on the Tsar his concern about growing social unrest and the need for action against revolutionary activity. On 4 February 1905 Aleksandrovich was assassinated by a homemade bomb thrown by Ivan Kaliaev, a member of the PSR's Combat Organization. This assassination was the organization's first successful attack on the Imperial family.

13. Antonio Cánovas del Castillo, prime minister of Spain, was assassinated on 8 August 1897 by Italian anarchist Michele Angiolillo, in retribution for the tortures and deaths of prisoners held at Montjuich prison in Spain.

14. EG is referring to a full-page article written by Leo Tolstoy entitled "I Cannot Be Silent" that appeared in The New York Times on 19 July 1908. In the article Tolstoy spoke against State executions, making the argument that State violence breeds depravity "as fire spreads amid dry straws." He asserted that violent revolutionaries are the "disciples," "products," and "children" of State violence and that "If you did not exist, neither would they."

who has the right to justify his illdoings, on the grounds that he is ~~carrying out he is~~ "only executing a law which popular opinion upholds." Popular opinion upholds electricution, by what right does the executioner claim his title to the sovereignity of his life, when he thrives of the deaths of others? No, no, everyone who helps to maintain our system, is reponsible for it and therefore must stand consequences———

Tolstoy does not approve of violence, to be sure, but he realizes, that the governors are responcible for the acts of the revolutionists, since their very breath brings disaster, death and distruction, wherever they come.

I hope, you will succeed in getting the exact facts in the Buwalda[15] case. I am anxious for them myself. You will let me know when you hear something definite, will you not?

SINCERELY
EMMA GOLDMAN

ALS, Charles Erskine Scott Wood Papers, CU-B.

15. EG refers to the court-martial of William Buwalda in San Francisco. Wood, a lawyer, was acquainted with President Roosevelt.

I want so to tell you how I feel, to send you a soothing word, to pass my hand over your forehead, to look into your eyes with kindness. But I can not. All is blank before me, all is dark and dreary, nothing is left behind. Oh, Ben, Ben! Fate is hard and cruel—38 1/2 year a walked through life with a burning and insatiable longing in my heart for the Unknown. I could reason then, or so clearly on all human subjects, on every secret string of the human heart. The miracle came, in a most radiant glorious color. It envelopes me, took possession of me, crept into my soul and body and robbed me of all reason. Its but 24 hours ago, the miracle lifted me to a dazzling hight, with the World all puny and insignificant at my feet. Now all is dark, I can not see, nothing is left alife. Oh, Ben Ben, Ben. I am so chilled and pained. I am struggling, struggling the bitterest struggle of my life and if I succeeded, I fear I shall never be able to see you again. Yet, if I fail, I shall stand condamned before the bar of my own reason—

I am not in a fit condition to write, I can not find the right expressions and I do not want to say anything that will hurt—

I should not come to the City until my souls battle is over, but I have something to attend to tomorrow. I will be in the flat about 7 P M tomorrow, if the day is not too hot. Else I shall have to walk later, I am too wretched to risk the long tramp in the heat. If you care, you might meet me at the station. I will arrive either 6.57 or 8.50. You will have to inquire whether the train gets in on the Lexington Ave side or not. Or better wait in the ~~depot~~ waiting room of the Madison Ave & 42st side. I will look for you there.

Have I ever told you the legend of a mothers love. A man had a cruel heartless mistress, who would forever tease him, with her lack of faith in his love. He wanted her to believe in him so he said one day, "Is there anything I can do to prove my love? Yes, go and bring me your mothers heart. The man adored his mother,

Ben Reitman in Chicago in 1908, around the time Goldman first met him. (Chicago Historical Society, *Chicago Daily News* collection)

she had always been so kind and good to him. But his passion was great, so he killed his mother tore out her heart and rushed with it to his mistress. On the way he stumbled and fell. And his mothers heart said to him, "My precious child, have you hurt yourself?" Its that side of my nature, Ben dear, that stretches out to you, that would like to embrace you and sooth you. The mother calls to you, my boy, my precious boy!!!

But the woman, the woman that lie asleep for 38 1/2 years and that you have awakened into frantic savage hungry life, recoils from you, feels outraged because you have thrust her aside from a moments fancy, because you have outraged her sacred shrine, that tent, oh god where passion held its glorious madning feasts. Oh, it is horrible, horrible!

But what is the use of grievin when the mother that bore you, knew it all before me—

Good by—

E

ALI, IU-U. Dated "Wednesday 4, AM."

To MEYER SHAPIRO

New York, 12 August 1908

DEAR COMRADE.

Your letter lacked the usual kind and friendly tone[1] it therefore appeared cold to me. Of course, you were disatisfied because I did not write, when I promised to do so, on my postal from Sacramento. But do you think, that is quite fair on you part? Can you not imagine that some things must have happened, which made my writing impossible.

You live a settled and to some extent secure life, but I am like the vessel and the waves of the Ocean, never sure of a safe whend. Tossed about, hurled against the rocks, bruised and beaten ever alone. Can you not understand, that under such circumstances, one is unable to keep promises, even though one may like to?

That your letter contained some bitterness, I could best see, when you write that a woman in the hallway, looked like Emma, who did not want to recognize you. I can not possibly think, you are serious in saying that. E G has never yet denied a friend, especially one, whos hospitality she has enjoyed. Will you kindly remember that. I can not tell you, how sorry I am, that you did not write me, when you are coming. I should have been so happy, so very happy indeed to entertain you, to have you at my home. Why did you not write me in advance? You say, you were in N Y the end of May. But I did not return until June 27th. Miss Edelsohn[2] was in the country, when I arrived, that may be the reason, why she has not told me, that you have called. At any rate, I knew nothing about it, until you wrote me. As to the article in the World.[3] It was not a question, how many will understand it, if the general public, or only a few intellegent people. The idea was, to write the article in such a manner, as to get it accepted at all. Besides, I could not have published the July M E, if I did not get 150 $ for my article. I receive literally no support from the Comrades. The magazine exists only through my lectures. Of course, I raise a great deal during the winter. But even during that time, I have to cover a monthly dificit of more than 110 $. During the Summer months it is even more, as barely enough for stamp is coming in after 4 1/2 months hard work, I am having a desperate struggle to keep M E alife now. I have been informed by the printer, that unless I give him 200 $ in account by the first of Sept, he will not print the Sep issue.

I know my next tour promises to be even a greater success, than the last. I know, I could return a loan, if only I could make one. But there is no one among the Comrades here whom I could approach. Those, who have money, cling to it too much. Besides I

1. Meyer Shapiro was a friend and financial supporter of EG from London, Ontario, Canada.
2. Rebecca Edelsohn was a New York City anarchist militant who lived with EG.
3. EG refers to "What I Believe," Essay in the *New York World*, 19 July 1908, above.

have never had much in common with them. And so here, I am wearing my very life away, when I ought to be resting and gaining strength for the Winter.

I could not give up M E, it would be like killing my own child, yet I am really in despair about it. I wonder, dear Comrade, if you could help me out of my present dilemma. I do not want any donation. But, if you could, I should be very grateful for a loan of 150, or 200 $. I can not pledge myself to a certain month, when I would pay it back. But I feel certain, that I will pay it sometimes next year, by Feb, or March. I hope, you will let me know soon.

Indeed, I should like to come on a visit to you, but I fear, it will be impossible. I do not know in what Cities, I will speak, but it is very doubtful, whether I will be anywhere near London. We will see, however.

I hope you and Sophie as well as the son are well and that you are enjoying your Summer. If you can, do not be too angry with me, for my long silence.

Sincerely, as ever
Emma Goldman

Love to your best girl and boy.

ALS, IU-U.

To MEYER SHAPIRO

Ossining, N.Y., 19 August 1908

DEAR, DEAR FRIEND.

I meant to write you a long letter in reply to your two letters, but I broke my glasses and my eyes hurt without them. Besides, dear Sophia[1] was with me two nights and a day. She left awhile ago, Berkman took her to the station. She will tell you that I simply misunderstood your first letter. I thought you were angry and that you doubted my friendship. But its alright now. If my letter seemed harsh, please forgive me.[2]

I can not tell you, how glad I was to have Sophia out here in Natures beauty. She is such a beautiful soul, so motherly and tender. I really fell in love with her. How, I wish you too had been here. I know you would also have enjoyed the place. It is a very ideal spot, where one can feel really free. Thank you so much, dear friend for the loan, you consent to let me have. I know, that you would have given me the amount I asked, if you could. I shall have to try hard to get 100 $ somewhere else, as I must have 200 $ by the 1st of Sept. At any rate what you will send me, will be a great help. And now as to the letter in the F Arb Stimme.[3] The people who write for that paper live either on the East side all their lives, or in small town or village, where they never come in contact with Americans. With few exceptions, they do not read anything else except the daily papers. How then can the writer of that article have the impudence to insinuate that the American report to the Congress was incorect, or that there are no American Anarchists? His only aim can be a malicious misrepresentation a narrowmindedness, that is the character of the F Arb Stimme, its editor and the entire clique.

All you have to do is to read the M E, who writers for it, outside of Berk and myself, if not American Comrades? Who helps my tours, who is interested in English agitation, if not American Comrades? Of course, they are not so numerous, as one would desire, but that is only, because just such people as the writer of the F Arb Stimme, as Yanovsky etc, have always opposed English agitation, because outside of Isaak[4] and myself nobody, ever did anything for the English movement. The same is true regarding the Unions—nothing

1. EG refers to Meyer Shapiro's wife, whose name was spelled "Sophie."
2. EG refers to her letter to Meyer Shapiro, dated 12 August 1908, above.
3. *Freie Arbeiter Stimme,* the Yiddish-language anarchist weekly, was edited from 1899 to 1919 by Saul Yanovsky. The 4 May 1908 issue contained an editorial criticizing the idea of sending an American delegate to the International Anarchist Congress and characterized the report on the American anarchist movement (in the September, October, and November 1907 issues of *Mother Earth*) as concerned only with free love and commemorating Leon Czolgosz, concluding that American anarchists had no influence on American society or the labor movement.
4. Abe Isaak was publisher and editor of *Free Society* from 1897 to 1904.

was ever done for the Unions. On the contrary, the F Ar S always opposed going into the unions, has opposed every strike, every public event. Has acted cowardly, when courage was needed, as during the Union Square affaire, a few months ago.[5] True there are not many American Comrades, but the few, know at least, what Anarchism means. They do not sell their Anarchism in real estate, or in playing domino in restaurants. They live Anarchism and thereby they are having a moral influence, of greater more lasting value, than 10 years publication of a F Ar St. Did you ever hear the American press or police make a fuss over that paper, or the Jewish propaganda, or Mr Yanovsky? Certainly not. Why do they watch closely, everything, I do? Because I carry our ideas among the Americans, before thousands of people. The fact, that I sold 800 $ literature on my last tour, particularly in cities where there are but few foreigners, shows that there are Americans interested in Anarchism people who read and that is more, than can be said of the F Arb St gang. But enough, you can rest assured, that neither Baginski[6] nor I, would be so foolish, to say anything in a report to an international Congress, that is not true, even, if we were really dishonest. And now, dear friend, I must close, my eyes are very tired

AFFECTIONATELY

E G

ALI, IU-U. Addressed from "On the farm."

5. EG is referring to the Union Square bomb that killed Anarchist Federation member Selig Silverstein (for EG's denial of any knowledge or influence on Silverstein, see "Emma Goldman Blames Police," Article in the *Chicago Tribune,* 29 March 1908, above).
6. Max Baginski co-founded and edited *Mother Earth* with EG and was also a frequent contributor to the magazine.

DEAR FRIEND:—

If I weren't so goodnatured, and if I did not remember all the pleasant and beautiful hours we spent together in gay Paris, I should be angry and never write you.[1] But you know I belong to the weak sex, that has not only always been the cause, o all temptation, but itself never had the strength to resist evils—so here I am with my private secretary (Stella),[2] making writing such a pleasure, sending you these few lines.

Besides I want to combine the pleasant with the practical. I am preparing a series of essays to begin in Mother Earth with November possibly, treating of Anarchism in relation to various phases of life. It is our intention to turn these articles into pamphlets, and eventually to combine them all in one volume. We are very poor in literature in this country, and while we esteem and honor all that our great old man Peter[3] has written, we nevertheless feel that a new and more modern medium of propaganda is absolutely essential for the growth of our ideas in America. We have already the colaboration of a number of people, who have undertaken to write on Anarchism and Science, History, Literature, etc. I address myself to you with the request to contribute an essay on Anarchism and Philosophy. I know that you are the man best equipped for it. I do not, of course, wish to ascribe any particular theme to you or limit you to space, but the size of Mother Earth (by the way, will be issued in 64 pages soon) compels me to have a certain scope for each contribution from ten to fifteen pages of the magazine. Please do not give me a whole lot of excuses. You know you promised to write for Mother Earth, and if you like the magazine half as well as you like the publisher, you will surely not refuse my request, especially so since it is really very important to us here.

Hoping to hear from you at once[4]

AFFECTIONATELY

EMMA GOLDMAN

1. EG first met Victor Dave, a Belgium-born anarchist writer and editor based in London, in 1900 in Paris during preparations for the aborted anarchist congress.
2. EG refers to her niece, Stella Comyn, who helped her with secretarial work.
3. EG refers to Peter Kropotkin.
4. No article from Dave appeared in *Mother Earth*.

DEAR MARIE:[5]

You know that our dear bebe Victor is very irresponsible and indeed I do not know what would have become of him, if it had not been for you and your thoughtful spirit hovering over him, as behooves notre chere mere, Sainte Marie. Please let this spirit be instrumental in inducing our friend to set to work at once, and to carry out the scheme of establishing a useful and educational literature in America.

LOVINGLY
EMMA.

TLS, Alexander Berkman Archive, IISH. "Affectionately" and "Lovingly" are handwritten.

5.   Marie was Dave's companion.

| To **PETER KROPOTKIN** |
| *New York, 27 August 1908* |

Dear Comrade:—

During my last tour, which lasted nearly five months and covered a great deal of territory, I realised more than ever the great lack in adequate literature for propaganda purposes, especially in the English language. Of course, we have your pamphlets and books,[1] and it will no doubt interest you to learn that I disposed of more than three thousand copies of the penny pamphlets, and a great many of the larger books, but nevertheless we are very poor in literature that would represent Anarchism in its relation to various phases of human life to the American public. To meet, that crying need, we have decided upon a scheme, which I hope will meet with your approval. We intend to begin a series of essays, treating with the above subject, in the November issue of Mother Earth.[2] The space ascribed to each article is from six to fifteen pages, or a few more, if need be. Comrade Solotaroff, Voltairine de Cleyre, James, Berkman,[3] and others are to collaborate on the work. I know that you are very busy, and I have heard to my great regret that your health is not as we all desire it to be, but I nevertheless venture to ask you for a contribution. Of course you can take any theme you like, but the most interesting to the American public, and the most instructive and educational, I think would be—Anarchism and Education.[4] I need not assure you that all the comrades would enjoy some such essay from you, but particularly so would you thereby serve the general propaganda and aid Mother Earth tremendously.

1. In 1908 *Mother Earth* advertised a large selection of Kropotkin's books and pamphlets, including *Anarchism, Fields Factories and Workshops, Memoirs of a Revolutionist, Ideals of Russian Literature, The State, The Wage System, An Appeal to the Young, Anarchism Communism, War*, and *Law and Authority*, as well as publishing a new edition of *Modern Science and Anarchism*.
2. The November 1908 *Mother Earth* issued an announcement, "Are You Interested in Anarchism?" in which EG explained that the magazine would begin a series of articles on various theoretical aspects of anarchism for the English-speaking American audience. The announcement also included the names of various authors and the subjects on which these articles would be published in the coming months.
3. Voltairine de Cleyre's "Anarchism and American Traditions" was published in the December 1908 and January 1909 issues of *Mother Earth,* and later as a Mother Earth Publishing Association pamphlet in 1909. Hillel Solatoroff's article on "Scientific Aspects of Anarchism" was announced in the November 1908 *Mother Earth* but was never published. C. L. James's "Anarchism and the Malthusian Theory" was serialized in the April through August 1909 issues of *Mother Earth* and then published as a Mother Earth pamphlet entitled *Anarchism and Malthus* in 1910. The November 1908 announcement suggested AB would contribute an article, but none appeared. Others announced included John R. Coryell, Max Baginski, Hippolyte Havel, Harry Kelly, and John Turner; contributions were expected from Max Nettlau, Victor Dave, EG, and Russian anarchist Varlaam Cherkesov.
4. The November 1908 announcement in *Mother Earth* suggested that they expected a contribution by Peter Kropotkin on anarchism and education, but none was ever published.

All through last Spring we have suffered a siege of extreme police brutality and press misrepresentation, but it has worked out for the best of the propaganda after all.[5] It has aided my tour tremendously, and it has brought our ideas before the thoughtful public more than anything else within years. I am sending you a copy of a brochure reprinted from the N.Y. World of July 19th, for which the paper paid $150.[6] I say this, not to boast of my so-called popularity but to substantiate that there is a tremendous growth of Anarchism in this country. May I hope to hear from you very soon? Kindly remember me to Sophie. Comrades Berkman, Baginski and others send their greetings,

AFFECTIONATELY,
EMMA GOLDMAN

P.S. Please do not think, that you must write only 15 pages. You can write, as many as you please. We will bring your contribution in several issues.

TLS, GARF, fond 1129, opis' 2, delo 978, listy 14–22. On *Mother Earth* stationery. Handwritten postscript by EG. A similar letter, also written on 27 August 1908, was sent to Victor Dave; it immediately precedes this one.

5. Throughout the spring of 1908 police and local authorities kept EG and other anarchists from speaking in public on a number of occasions. In Philadelphia Voltairine de Cleyre and others were arrested and charged with "inciting to riot" at a 20 February 1908 meeting of Jewish and Italian anarchists, and EG was kept from speaking in Chicago in March 1908 (see "Emma Goldman Clashes with Police on Meeting," Article in the *Chicago Inter Ocean*, 8 March 1908). The suppression would continue through the rest of 1908 and into 1909. For details of suppression in New York, see "The Latest Police Outrage," Article in *Mother Earth*, September 1908; for police suppression and arrests in San Francisco, see "On Trial," To *Mother Earth*, 2 February 1909; and for sustained police suppression on the East Coast in 1909, see "Our Friends, the Enemy," Article in *Mother Earth*, June 1909.
6. EG's essay "What I Believe" was published in the 19 July 1908 issue of the *New York World* and was later reprinted as a pamphlet by the Mother Earth Publishing Association. For the text, see "What I Believe," Essay in the *New York World*, 19 July 1908, above.

Article in **MOTHER EARTH**

September 1908

The Latest Police Outrage

Police brutality and outrage against Anarchists have become such an every-day occurrence, that one no longer feels inclined to refer to them.

However, the latest "bravery" is so flagrant, so unspeakably brutal, that we can not possibly keep silent.

Comrade Alex. Berkman and a young girl friend, Miss E.,[1] were arrested, at a meeting of the unemployed, at Cooper Union, on Labor Day without the slightest provocation.[2] They were brutally hustled out of the hall and fairly dragged to the station house. There they were received by a wild, raging, foaming human beast, Lieutenant Brenner, with the "kind and Christian" remark, "Yous ought to be brought here on a stretcher."

This disgraceful member of the human family must have waited for such a golden opportunity to show his heroic devotion to his trade of bullying people. At any rate, when Comrade H. Havel[3] called at the station house to see Berkman, and asked on what charge he was being kept, the uniformed bully fairly yelled in his face, "We'll land him this time," and he kept his promise.

Until midnight Attorney Meyer London and H. Havel waited in the station to assist our arrested friends, when they will be taken before the night court. But they were assured that the hearing will not take place until morning.

No sooner had the lawyer and Havel departed, when Miss E. and Berkman were hustled over to court and tried without a chance of hearing or counsel. Comrade Berkman was railroaded to the workhouse for five days and Miss E. fined $10. Fortunately, dear staunch friend Bolton Hall had rushed to the scene and paid her fine, else she too would have had to go to the Island.

The charge against her was vagrancy, as she refused to give her address, not wishing to annoy the people she was living with. Berkman was tried on disorderly conduct.

The morning press was full of bloodcurdling accounts of the "intentions and doings" of the Anarchists, and how the prompt action of the police prevented a "riot."

The newspaper flunkeys, about as coarse and vulgar as their uniformed brothers, glory in the fact that the officers landed one boy a blow in the jaw and knocked another one down.

---

1. EG refers to Rebecca Edelsohn, a young, militant anarchist who lived in EG's home as a teenager and who became AB's companion in late 1907.
2. For an explanation of the circumstances surrounding AB and Edelsohn's arrest, see note 1 to "Labor Day," Address in *Mother Earth*, September 1908, below.
3. EG refers to Hippolyte Havel.

Wonderful spirit of liberty and human decency, is it not?

Now, what are the real facts about the whole matter?

The Brotherhood Welfare Association of New York held a parade and meeting of the unemployed, at Cooper Union.

Dr. Ben. L. Reitman, Chicago organizer of that Association, had been invited, as one of the speakers. Unfortunately he caught a severe cold, and, unable to concentrate on what he had intended to say at the meeting, he asked me to prepare a paper, which he would read. The Doctor probably thought that most of the speakers were either unfamiliar with the conditions of the unemployed, or too weakkneed to treat it in a radical manner.

That Dr. Reitman is well known and liked by society outcasts was very apparent by the ovation he was given when he began to read the manuscript, his voice hardly being audible. But the enthusiasm reached high tide when our Hobo friend announced, in his usual frank manner, that the paper was prepared by Miss Emma Goldman. (The readers will find the speech on another page.)[4]

Naturally a commotion followed, especially among the "Gentlemen" speakers, who felt compromised. A certain Oberwager,[5] well known as the worst lickspittle and yellow dog in trade union ranks, launched into the Doctor and Anarchism, in a most ferocious manner boasting of his great feat in having just knocked down a boy for distributing the anarchistic panic pamphlets.

Comrade Berkman quietly rose and called the speaker's attention to the fact that Dr. Reitman was no longer in the hall, and that it was unfair, to say the least, to attack a man who could not reply.

Thereupon several detectives fairly jumped on Berkman and Miss E., pulling, kicking and dragging them out of the hall.

The audience protested, but American audiences have too terrible an awe for the sacredness of authority to show a really vigorous and manly protest which would teach the uniformed bullies a lesson, once for all.

In no country, Russia not exempt, would the police dare to exercise such brutal power over the lives of men and women.

In no country would the people stand for such beastliness and vulgarity. Nor do I know of any people who have so little regard for their own manhood and self-respect as the average American citizen, with all his boasted independence.

Poor outraged, abused Goddess of Liberty, no foreign land has so little place for you as your own native soil.

Mother Earth 3 (September 1908): 273–75.

---

4. The text of the address written by EG and read by BR appears immediately following (see "Labor Day," Address in *Mother Earth*, September 1908).
5. EG may be referring to Charles Oberwager, who was a member of the Free Speech League in 1904.

Address

September 1908

Labor Day

**A paper prepared for the meeting of the unemployed
at Cooper Institute, Sept. 7th.**

Labor Day![1] What a deep and significant meaning that term implies! Labor, the creator of wealth, the nourisher of the human race, the harbinger of peace and happiness,—Labor having its day, Labor arisen from the abyss, from out of the mines and mills and shops, from out of its pale, trembling, cringing condition, Labor, the mighty giant, conscious of its power, celebrating its great day of regeneration. What a wonderfully sublime and inspiring vista!

Such it might be, nay, will be some day. But to-day, what is it to-day? A ghastly lie, a caricature, a mocking, fiendish monster, sapping the very life element from its slaves, that its masters may become more powerful, more exacting. Yes, look at the thousands of workers who are marching to-day, I mean those whom the fiend labor holds in its clutches, what has labor done for them? True, it has given them bread for the moment, a cover over their heads, and possibly an extra coat, but what has it not taken in return, oh! what has it not taken from its ever yielding victims? It has taken their souls, their dignity, their self-respect, it has condemned them to carry the burdens of the world, a hard, cruel, merciless world, wherein they have no place, no rights, no chances. It has stolen their liberty that others may better enslave them.

And you, army of unemployed, you men and women of the road and the street, you countless numbers, who carry the banner, month after month, week after week, you, with empty stomachs and dull, heavy heads, with hunger and despair lurking in your eyes, what has labor done for you?

---

1. This speech was written by EG but delivered by BR, who as a member had been invited by the Brotherhood Welfare Association of New York to participate in a Labor Day meeting of the unemployed at Cooper Union. In the audience were EG, AB, Rebecca Edelsohn, and Hippolyte Havel. When Reitman finished, he revealed the author of the speech, which announcement caused an uproar. Berkman rose in defense of the speech and was arrested along with Edelsohn, who gave her name alternately as Mary Smith and Helen Edwards. The two were sped through court before they could be represented by socialist attorney Meyer London. Edelsohn's $10 fine for vagrancy was paid by Bolton Hall. Berkman, who acted as his own counsel and carefully interrogated the arresting patrolmen, spent five days on Blackwell's Island for disorderly conduct. See EG's account of this affair in "The Latest Police Outrage," Article in *Mother Earth*, September 1908, above.

Hundred thousand men out of work in the city of New York[2]—homeless, shelterless, clothless, foodless, in this city of wealth and affluence. Who dares speak of Labor Day in the face of this awful spectacle?

The "Evening Post" of September 5th in discussing the significance of Labor Day says: "It is a well-established tradition of American business affairs that Labor Day marks the end of holiday and idleness. On the morning of the Tuesday following the first Monday in September, the average American, metaphorically speaking, throws his coat off and gets to work." What wonderful wisdom our newspapers feed their readers on.

A well-established tradition, indeed; we Americans are full of traditions, but whoever lives up to them? We also boast of well-established tradition of free speech, press and assembly, yet we could not have marched without the grace of the police commissioner, yet we could not express ourselves, if the club should decree against it, yet men and women are dragged off the platforms and imprisoned, if they dare exercise that "well established tradition." Ah, we have loads of traditions, we Americans, *on paper*.

"Labor Day marks the end of holiday and idleness." You men have had a holiday and have been idle, not by choice, but by grim, iron necessity. Have you enjoyed either? Have you been merry-making with your wives and children? Have you feasted on nature's gifts? Have you strengthened your body in the invigorating embrace of the ocean? Or has not the street, the alleys, the gutter, the filthy quarters of tenth-rate saloons, the road, the box cars, been your holiday places?

To-day is to mark the end of idleness, and you, average Americans, are to throw off your coats and begin work?

Is there any one here who is not ready for it? But where, where is that all powerful, omnipotent God—Labor—that will give you a chance?

The end of idleness, yes, some day, when Society will have embraced the human family into a great brotherhood,—the end of idleness only when man realizes that labor has the power of his Liberation and not his damnation. When you and I will become conscious, that you and I must make labor subservient to us, to our needs, our happiness, our joy, and that *we* must stop being subservient to labor. Not until then will the end of idleness come.

But what now? What is to be done with the great host who are only too ready to throw off their coats—tatters would be a more appropriate term—and to set to work:

First and foremost to organize, to organize the unemployed from the Atlantic to the

---

2. The United States was in the midst of an economic depression, which began with a bank panic in the fall of 1907. Bank panics had become a commonplace fixture in the United States since the Civil War, in part because banks were controlled at the local and state level with no central authority to govern and provide protection. In March 1907, a sharp drop in the stock market precipitated such a panic. By the end of November, beginning with the Knickerbocker Trust Company, several banks failed. A national recession followed the March 1907 panic and lasted well into 1908. Congress later passed the Aldrich-Vreeland Currency Act, establishing a commission to examine the banking system. As a result, the Federal Reserve Bank was established in 1913.

Pacific into a great body of men, not cringing slaves, who are satisfied with a chunk of bread and a cup of coffee, men, who want food, and who will demand it as loud as their stomach dictates. Men, who will demand that some of the money, that city officials appropriate for themselves, should be used in building homes, where the unemployed shall find rest during the day and sleep at night, men who will insist that kindergartens and playhouses shall be erected, where the children of that vast army will be looked after. Who will demand that the cities shall have fewer churches, and fewer policemen, and that the money spent in keeping these breeders of superstition and crime shall be used in building large dining-halls for the unemployed.

I realize that these demands are but palliative, that they can not eradicate the unemployed question, but there is nothing that can eradicate that awful problem, except organized stalwart, brave, daring demands.

When we have learned to demand these immediate reliefs, we will also have learned to demand labor's true day—the day that will feast the dawn of human brotherhood and social well-being.

E. G.

Mother Earth 3 (September 1908): 297–99.

DEAREST HOBO.

Again the agony of sleeplessness. I walked 40 blocks yesterday, worked on a translation 4 hours, yet I can not sleep, I don't know what's become of me.

Dearest Ben, don't you suppose I know you do not understand me. Don't you suppose that I feel this as the black spot of upon the golden horizon of our love? You never will know the agony, that shook my body when I stood before you all aglow with a devine fire trying to make you see beauty and fairness. When I wanted to awaken in you a feeling of consideration for the lives and feelings of others or when I wanted to show you the uglyness of and the dishonesty of yellow journal sensationialism and my greate and bitter disappointement, when you could see nothing understand nothing. Don't you suppose I have realized that more, than once? Oh, Ben, ~~your lov~~ our love has already given me great, wonderful joy. I feel that it has much more in store for me, but I also feel that it has great tragedies in store for me. Oh, I know, you love me. In fact, I feel that no man has loved me, as you do. I know the ecstasy, the inexpressible delight your love can give, but I also know that while my body and soul will feast on the nectar of life, my mind will sit at the palace of your lover, famished for the want of understanding and it will receive nothing. Oh, I know it, I know it only too well. And yet with all that life without you seems an utter impossibility seems absolutely barren, dead. Ben, Ben, you are intelligent, can you not try to realize that one may have intellectual struggles, and yet love. That one may undertake self analysis and disections and yet cling with every fiber to ones love? Can you not understand that one may be impressed by a book, as I have been by 9009,[1] all wrecked by it, ~~without~~ and that that has nothing to do with ones love? So you think that I really used a subterfuge? ~~I~~ That I do not really want to go to Australia,[2] that I do not need you or love you? That I only pretended or cheated myself. Do you really think that? No doubt my last few letters will convince you even more that you are right. Why, if I say, that we may not have enough money, or whether I have the right to go to extra expences, you conclude that I do not love you any longer. You foolish, foolish boy. Thats the way, you reasoned, when I spoke to you of how little was left from my tour. Like a child you imidiately took it, that I blaime you—now, baby hobo mine, let me tell you

---

1. AB reviewed the book *9009*, by James B. Hopper and Frederick R. Bechdolt (New York: The McClure Company, 1908), asserting that the authors "deserve unstinted praise for the courage of telling the unvarnished truth about prison conditions" (*Mother Earth*, November 1909).
2. EG planned to tour Australia in January 1909 at the invitation of Australian anarchist J. W. (Chummy) Fleming. Fears concerning her citizenship status, among other things, prompted EG to cancel the tour at the last minute.

this. Of course I love Alex,[3] of course ~~the~~ our past has a strong hold on me, but I would go away now even to Australia, if you had not come into my life 1) Mother Earth necessitates my going, 2) my physical welbeing necessitates my going. 3) Alex full expression of his love for B[4] necessitates my going. That I want to go with you, more than I know how to express, has nothing to do with these 3 reasons. That's because I love you, deeply, intensely madly. Because I need you more than anyone else. You have opened up the prison gates of my womanhood. And all the passion, that was fettered and unsatisfied in me for so many years, leaped into a wild reckless storm boundless, as the sea. Can you then imagine that I could stay away from you? What is love, family ties, the power of association to the wanderer in the desert. His mind is bent on the spring that will quench his thirst. And when he reaches that spring, is that not the greatest passion of his life? You are that spring to me, I am famished, do you hear the woman in me is famished, what else is there for me to do or where to hide, but to follow the call of the wild, the savage, the master lover? Of course lifes yearning would be almost too great to endure were I to find in you, not only invigorating nectar for my soul and body, but also for my mind. I mean understanding, Yet, if I were asked to choose between a world of understanding and the spring that fills my body with fire, I should have to chose the spring. It is life, sunshine, musik, untold of ecstasy. The spring, oh ye Gods, that have tortured my body all these years. I will give you my soul, only let me drink, drink drink from the spring of my master lover. There, you have the confession of a starved, tortured human being, my Ben I hope if ever you doubt me again, you will remember this cry I am sending across to you. Please also remember that I have no choice in staying away from you. I have got to go with you, if it were to take me straight into the Abyss. After this can you ask if I love you no more, or if I am weary of you? Can you dare you ask? Ben, Ben all the agony of your lack of understanding for my mental depression are as naught compared with the despair life without you has in store for me. Good night. I am weary, but my love is strong. My hobo, my hobo—

M

ALS, IU-U. On *Mother Earth* stationery. Time of writing is noted as "2 A.M."

3. EG refers to Alexander Berkman.
4. EG refers to Rebecca Edelsohn, who was known by her nickname, Becky.

So the Obsession has come, the "obsession that was to take you away from me" as you once wrote me. It must have been a terrible obsession Ben dear, if you could send me that telegram. I only hope with all my heart that the sending of it has not caused you the agony it has brought me, oh, I hope not, it would be too terrible. I have tried hard, so very hard to ask myself "why this to me?" Have I deserved such a shock from Ben? Have I not given him my love my hearts&nbhy;blood, my thoughts everything, everything? Why then this awful shock? But I can find no answer, there is no answer for obsessions is there? As far as my own sorrow or suffering is concerned, I have long made up my mind that your obsession will bring me more than one human being can endure. Yet, my love was strong enough to endure even that. But as far as my work is concerned, I can not and will not let your impulses stand in the way. I am undertaking a collossal task, a tour for nearly a year into distant lands and I can not run the risk of one of your obsessions to come along and fustrate every thing. You have just thrown everything overboard, you have refused to act in the capacity you have yourself chosen and gladly so. A letter, a word, an opinion of mine was enough for you to do such a thing. Now supposing this happens, when we are in Australia when I am helpless what then? Now Ben dear, I can not risk that really not. I therefore ask you, as tenderly yet dicesively, as I can put on paper to reason before you act. Impulses are beautiful dear, but when it is a vital question, a cause one has had at heart for 20 years one can not allow an impulse to destroy it at all. It's all right for an impulse to pierce a human heart, to make it bleed and twitch as your impulses have done more than once. Thats what the heart is here for, Momies heart is here for. But ideas are more important dear. Don't you think so?

I do not accept your telegram as final Ben. I know you are not strong and that you have surely acted on the spur of the moment. I shall therefore wait a few days, until you have had time to consider. Then write me definitely, as I shall have to change my route and dates. Please, please dear do not consider me, nor even the tour. Consider only, if you can work with me no matter what differences may came up between us. If you can work and if you feel yourself strong enough to carry out what you undertake until the last. I would rather except a ~~no~~ decisive no, at this moment, than a meek yes, that you will break, when the obsession comes, in the middle of the tour or when we are in Australia.

You are right dear, why should you reform? Really no reason for it. Axcept possibly the power of love, which you have told me, has changed your entire life. No other reason, I am sure.

It would be absurd for me to assure you of my love now. If I have not shown it to you a thousend times, if I have not made you feel it in a thousend little things, what's the use talking about it?

I have received a letter from Fleming,[1] very inthusiastic. He promises great results. I will send it to you when I know what your difinite answer is.

If the past 7 months have given you nothing, at least night that should have strengthen your character or made your life worth while. They have given me, a whole World. A beautiful World of all the exquisitness that a great love can give. I thank you for it, Ben dear. I shall always carry it with me and when the moment comes, that I shall have to forfeit my life for my ideas, the World of the last 7 moments will illuminate my soul and I shall feel, I have not lived in vain, no, I have not lived in vain!

YOUR MOMIE.

ALS, IU-U. On *Mother Earth* stationery.

1. J. W. (Chummy) Fleming was organizing EG's tour in Australia.

Pamphlet

October 1908

Patriotism: A Menace to Liberty

What is Patriotism? Is it the love of one's birthplace, the place of childhood's recollections and hopes, dreams and aspirations? Is it the place where, in childlike naïveté, we would watch the fleeting clouds and wonder why we, too, could not run so swiftly? The place where we would count the milliard glittering stars, terror-stricken lest each one "an eye should be," piercing the very depths of our little souls? Is it the place where we would listen to the music of the birds, and long to have wings to fly, even like they, to distant lands? Or the place where we would sit at mother's knee, enraptured by wonderful tales of great deeds and conquests? In short, is it love for the spot, every inch representing dear and precious recollections of a happy, joyous, and playful childhood?

If that were Patriotism, few American men of to-day could be called upon to be patriotic, since the place of play has been turned into factory, mill, and mine, while deafening sounds of machinery have replaced the music of the birds. Nor can we longer hear the tales of great deeds, for the stories our mothers tell to-day are but those of sorrow, tears, and grief.

What, then is Patriotism? "Patriotism, sir, is the last resort of scoundrels," said Dr. Johnson.[1] Leo Tolstoy, the greatest living anti-patriot, defines Patriotism as the principle that will justify the training of wholesale murderers; a trade that requires better equipment for the exercise of man-killing than the making of such necessities of life as shoes, clothing, and houses; a trade that guarantees better returns and greater glory than that of the average workingman.[2]

Gustave Hervé,[3] another great anti-patriot, justly calls Patriotism a superstition,—one far more injurious, brutal, and inhumane than religion. The superstition of religion origi-

---

1. Samuel Johnson (1709–1784), English writer and lexicographer, reportedly spoke these words at a tavern in April 1775; the statement does not appear in Johnson's published works. James Boswell, in his book *The Life of Samuel Johnson, LL.D.* (1791), writes, "Patriotism having become one of our topics, Johnson suddenly uttered, in a strong, determined tone, an apophthegm, at which many will start: 'Patriotism is the last resort of a scoundrel.' But let it be considered that he did not mean a real and generous love of our country, but that pretended patriotism which so many, in all ages and countries, have made a cloak for self-interest."
2. Leo Tolstoy (1828–1910) directly addressed the topic of patriotism in several pieces: *Patriotism and Government* (1900); *Patriotism and Peace* (1895); and *Christianity and Patriotism* (1894).
3. Gustave Hervé (1871–1944), French socialist and anti-militarist, founded the socialist newspaper *La Guerre Sociale*.

nated in man's inability to explain natural phenomena. That is, when primitive man heard thunder or saw the lightning he could not account for either, and therefore concluded that back of them must be a force greater than himself. Equally so, he saw a supernatural force in the rain, or in the various other changes in nature. Patriotism, on the other hand, is a superstition artificially created and maintained through a network of lies and falsehoods; a superstition that robs man of his self-respect and dignity, and increases his arrogance and conceit.

Indeed, conceit, arrogance, and egotism are the essentials of Patriotism. Let me illustrate. Patriotism assumes that our globe is divided into little specks, each one surrounded by an iron gate. Those who have had the fortune of being born on some particular speck, consider themselves better, nobler, grander, more intelligent than the living beings inhabiting any other speck. It is, therefore, the duty of everyone living on the chosen spot to fight, kill, and die in the attempt to impose his superiority upon all the others.

The inhabitants of the other specks reason in like manner, of course, with the result that, from early infancy, the mind of the child is poisoned with blood-curdling stories about the Germans, the French, the Italians, Russians, etc. When the child has reached manhood, he is thoroughly saturated with the belief that he is chosen by the Lord himself to defend *his* country against the attack or invasion of any foreigner. It is for that purpose that we are clamoring for a greater army and navy, more battleships and ammunition. It is for that purpose that America has within a short time spent four hundred million dollars. Just think of it—four hundred million dollars taken from the produce of *the people*. For surely it is not the rich who contribute to Patriotism. They are cosmopolitans, perfectly at home in every land. We in America know well about the truth of this. Are not our rich Americans Frenchmen in France, Germans in Germany, or Englishmen in England? And do they not squander with cosmopolitan grace fortunes coined by American factory children and cotton slaves? Yes, theirs is the Patriotism that will make it possible to send messages of condolence to a despot like the Russian Tsar, when any mishap befalls him, as President Roosevelt did in the name of *his* people, when Sergius[4] was punished by the Russian Revolutionists.

It is a Patriotism that will assist the arch-murderer, Diaz,[5] in destroying thousands of lives in Mexico, or that will even aid in arresting Mexican revolutionists on American soil and keep them incarcerated in American prisons, without the slightest cause or reason.

---

4. In February 1905 Russian Socialist Revolutionary Ivan Kaliaev assassinated Grand Duke Sergei Aleksandrovich, an uncle of the tsar, by throwing a bomb into his carriage, killing the driver as well. Kaliaev's act was regarded as an ethical revolutionary act by radicals, as Kaliaev avoided excessive casualties by intentionally striking the Grand Duke alone.
5. José de la Cruz Porfirio Díaz (1830–1915) was a military general and president of Mexico, whose elected regime functioned like a dictatorship.

But, then, Patriotism is not for those who represent wealth and power. It is good enough for the people. It reminds one of the historic wisdom of Frederick the Great, the bosom friend of Voltaire, who said, "Religion is a fraud, but it must be maintained for the masses."[6]

That Patriotism is rather a costly institution, no one will doubt after reading the following statistics:[7]

The progressive increase of the expenditures for the leading armies and navies of the world during the last quarter of a century is a fact of such gravity as to startle every thoughtful student of economic problems. It may be briefly indicated by dividing the time from 1881 to 1905 into five-year periods, and noting the disbursements of several great nations for army and navy purposes during the first and last of those periods. From the first to the last of the periods noted the expenditures of Great Britain increased from $2,101,848,936 to $4,143,226,885, those of France from $3,324,500,000 to $3,455,109,900, those of Germany from $725,000,200 to $2,700,375,600, those of the United States from $1,275,500,750 to $2,650,900,450, those of Russia from $1,900,975,500 to $5,250,445,100, those of Italy from $1,600,975,750 to $1,755,500,100, and those of Japan from $182,900,500 to $700,925,475.

The military expenditures of each of the nations mentioned increased in each of the five-year periods under review. During the entire interval from 1881 to 1905 Great Britain's outlay for her army increased fourfold, that of the United States was tripled, Russia's was doubled, that of Germany increased 35 per cent., that of France about 15 per cent., and that of Japan nearly 500 per cent. If we compare the expenditures of these nations upon their armies with their total expenditures for all the twenty-five years ending with 1905, the proportion rose as follows:

In Great Britain from 20 per cent. to 37; in the United States from 15 to 23; in France from 16 to 18; in Italy from 12 to 15; in Japan from 12 to 14. On the other hand, it is interesting to note that the proportion in Germany decreased from about 58 per cent. to 25, the decrease being due to the enormous increase in the imperial expenditures for other purposes, the fact being that the army expenditures for the period of 1901–5 were higher than for any five-year period preceding. Statistics show that the countries in which army expenditures are greatest in proportion to the total national revenues are Great Britain, the United States, Japan, France, and Italy, in the order named.

6. Frederick II "the Great" of Prussia commented on religion in his *Political Testament* (1752): "All religions, if one examines them, are founded on superstitious systems, more or less absurd. It is impossible for a man of good sense, who dissects their contents, not to see their error; but these prejudices, these errors and mysteries were made for men, and one must know enough to respect the public and not outrage its faith, whatever religion might be involved."

7. All of the following figures regarding military expenditures were originally printed in a newspaper article ("The World's Military Burdens; Enormous Increase in Cost in Last Two Decades Used in Argument Against Militarism," *New York Times*, 31 May 1908). The following six-paragraph section, beginning with the sentence "The progressive increase of the expenditures for the leading armies and navies of the world," and concluding with the sentence "In other words, a continuation of the increased demands of militarism," is a verbatim duplication of the bulk of the *New York Times* article.

The showing as to the cost of great navies is equally impressive. During the twenty-five years ended with 1905 naval expenditures increased approximately as follows: Great Britain, 300 per cent.; France, 60 per cent.; Germany, 600 per cent.; the United States, 525 per cent.; Russia, 300 per cent.; Italy, 250 per cent., and Japan, 700 per cent. With the exception of Great Britain, the United States spends more for naval purposes than any other nation, and this expenditure bears also a larger proportion to the entire national disbursements than that of any other power. In the period 1881–5, the expenditure for the United States Navy was $6.20 out of each $100 appropriated for all national purposes; the amount rose to $6.60 for the next five-year period, to $8.10 for the next, to $11.70 for the next, and to $16.40 for 1901–5. It is morally certain that the outlay for the current period of five years will show a still further increase.

The rising cost of militarism may be still further illustrated by computing it as a per capita tax on population. From the first to the last of the five-year periods taken as the basis for the comparisons here given it has risen as follows: In Great Britain, from $18.47 to $52.50; in France, from $19.66 to $23.62; in Germany, from $10.17 to $15.51; in the United States, from $5.62 to $13.64; in Russia, from $6.14 to $8.37; in Italy, from $9.59 to $11.24, and in Japan from 86 cents to $3.11.

It is in connection with this rough estimate of cost per capita that the economic burden of militarism is most appreciable. The irresistible conclusion from available data is that the increase of expenditure for army and navy purposes is rapidly surpassing the growth of population in each of the countries considered in the present calculation. In other words, a continuation of the increased demands of militarism threatens each of those nations with a progressive exhaustion both of men and resources.

The awful waste that Patriotism necessitates ought to be sufficient to cure the man of even average intelligence from this disease. Yet Patriotism demands still more. The people are urged to be patriotic and for that luxury they pay, not only by supporting their "defenders," but even by sacrificing their own children. Patriotism requires allegiance to the flag, which means obedience and readiness to kill father, mother, brother, sister.

The usual contention is that we need a standing army to protect the country from foreign invasion. Every intelligent man and woman knows, however, that this is a myth maintained to frighten and coërce the foolish. The governments of the world, knowing each other's interests, do not invade each other. They have learned that they can gain much more by international arbitration of disputes than by war and conquest. Indeed, as Carlyle said, "War is a quarrel between two thieves, too cowardly to fight their own battle; therefore they take boys from one village and another village, stick them into uniforms, equip them with guns, and let them loose like wild beasts against each other."[8]

---

8. The preceding is not an exact quotation but rather is EG's paraphrase of a passage on the subject of war in Thomas Carlyle's *Sartor Resartus: The Life and Opinions of Herr Teufelsdrockh in three books* (1838). EG initially referred to the passage in her address "The Effect of War on the Workers" (20 February 1900; see vol. 1, p. 384), wherein she quoted the passage entirely.

It does not require much wisdom to trace every war back to a similar cause. Let us take our own Spanish-American war, supposedly a great and patriotic event in the history of the United States. How our hearts burned with indignation against the atrocious Spaniards! True, our indignation did not flare up spontaneously. It was nurtured by months of newspaper agitation,[9] and long after Butcher Weyler[10] had killed off many noble Cubans and outraged many Cuban women. Still, in justice to the American nation be it said, it did grow indignant and was willing to fight, and that it fought bravely. But when the smoke was over, the wounded buried, and the cost of the war came back to the people in an increase of the price of commodities and rent,—that is, when we sobered up from our patriotic spree, it suddenly dawned on us that the cause of the Spanish-American war was the consideration of the price of sugar; or, to be more explicit, that the lives, blood, and money of the American capitalists which were threatened by the Spanish government. That this is not an exaggeration, but is based on absolute facts and figures, is best proved by the attitude of the American government to Cuban labor. When Cuba was firmly in the clutches of the United States, the very soldiers sent to liberate Cuba were ordered to shoot Cuban workingmen during the great cigarmakers' strike, which took place shortly after the war.[11]

Nor do we stand alone in waging war for such causes. The curtain is beginning to be lifted on the motives of the terrible Russo-Japanese war, which cost so much blood and tears.[12] And we see again that back of the fierce Moloch of war stands the still fiercer god of Commercialism. Kuropatkin, the Russian Minister of War during the Russo-Japanese struggle, has revealed the true secret behind the latter.[13] The Tsar and his Grand Dukes, having invested money in Corean concessions, the war was forced for the sole reason of speedily accumulating large fortunes.

The contention that a standing army and navy are the best security of peace is about as logical as the claim that the most peaceful citizen is he who goes about heavily armed.

---

9. The "yellow journalism" newspaper coverage of and leading up to the Spanish-American War was led by Joseph Pulitzer's *New York World* and William Randolph Hearst's *New York Journal*. The reportage was widely regarded as biased and sensationalized, intended to inflame public opinion and promote newspaper sales.

10. Valeriano Weyler y Nicolau (1838–1930), Spanish army general and governor of Cuba, was referred to as "Butcher" Weyler for his wartime establishment of concentration camps in Cuba, intended to keep civilians safe during the war but which instead led to the deaths of thousands of Cubans due to starvation and disease.

11. A general strike of Cuban labor, declared through a manifesto drafted by the Circulo de Trabajadores, began in Havana on 20 September 1899 and ended by 3 October 1899. Cuban cigarmakers joined the strike several days after it began.

12. The Russo-Japanese War took place from February 1904 to September 1905, fought over conflicting interests in Korea and Manchuria. Both Russia and Japan sustained heavy losses throughout the conflict, with Russia's total casualties estimated at well more than 100,000.

13. Alexei Kuropatkin (1848–1925), Russian military commander, opposed the course of action that precipitated the Russo-Japanese War but served as commander of troops in Manchuria once the conflict broke out. Kuropatkin's *The Russian Army and the Japanese War* (London: J. Murray, 1909) was an account of the conditions leading up to and resulting from the conflict.

The experience of every-day life fully proves that the armed individual is invariably anxious to try his strength. The same is historically true of governments. Really peaceful countries do not waste life and energy in war preparations, with the result that peace is maintained.

However, the clamor for an increased army and navy is not due to any foreign danger. It is owing to the dread of the growing discontent of the masses and of the international spirit among the workers. It is to meet the internal enemy that the Powers of various countries are preparing themselves; an enemy, who, once awakened to consciousness, will prove more dangerous than any foreign invader.

The Powers that have for centuries been engaged in enslaving the masses have made a thorough study of their psychology. They know that the people at large are like children whose despair, sorrow, and tears can be turned into joy with a little toy. And the more gorgeously the toy is dressed, the louder the colors, the more it will appeal to the million-headed child.

An army and navy represent the people's toys. To make them more attractive and acceptable, hundreds of thousands of dollars are being spent for the display of these toys. That was the purpose of the American government in equipping a fleet and sending it along to the Pacific Coast, that every American citizen should be made to feel the pride and glory of the United States.[14] The city of San Francisco spent one hundred thousand dollars for the entertainment of the fleet; Los Angeles, sixty thousand; Seattle and Tacoma, about one hundred thousand. To entertain the fleet, did I say? To dine and wine a few superior officers, while the "brave boys" had to mutiny to get sufficient food. Yes, two hundred and sixty-thousand dollars were spent on fireworks, theater parties, and revelries at a time when men, women, and children were starving in the streets; when thousands of unemployed were ready to sell their labor at any price.

Two hundred and sixty thousand dollars! What could not have been accomplished with such an enormous sum? But instead of bread and shelter, the children of those cities were taken to see the fleet, that it may remain, as one of the newspapers said, "a lasting memory for the child."

A wonderful thing to remember, is it not? The implements of civilized slaughter. If the mind of the child is to be poisoned with such memories, what hope is there for a true realization of human brotherhood?

We Americans claim to be a peace-loving people. We hate bloodshed; we are opposed to violence. Yet we go into spasms of joy over the possibility of projecting dynamite bombs from flying machines upon helpless citizens. We are ready to hang, electrocute, or lynch any one, who, from economic necessity, will risk his own life in the attempt upon that of some industrial magnate. Yet our hearts swell with pride at the thought that America

14. From 16 December 1907 to 22 February 1909 the U.S. battle fleet (the "Great White Fleet," with ships painted white during peacetime) circumnavigated the globe, stopping in many ports along the way.

is becoming the most powerful nation on earth, and that it will eventually plant her iron foot on the necks of all other nations.

Such is the logic of Patriotism.

With all the evil results that Patriotism is fraught with for the average man, it is as nothing compared with the insult and injury that Patriotism heaps upon the soldier himself,—that poor, deluded victim of superstition and ignorance. He, the savior of his country, the protector of his nation,—what has Patriotism in store for him? A life of slavish submission, vice, and perversion during peace; a life of danger, exposure, and death during the war.

While on my late lecture tour in San Francisco, I visited the Presidio, the most beautiful spot overlooking the Bay and Golden Gate Park.[15] Its purpose should have been playgrounds for children, gardens and music for the recreation of the weary. Instead it is made ugly, dull, and gray by barracks,—barracks, wherein the rich would not allow their dogs to dwell. In these miserable shanties soldiers are herded like cattle; here they waste their young days, polishing the boots and brass buttons of their superior officers. Here, too, I saw the distinction of classes: sturdy sons of a free republic, drawn up in line like convicts, saluting every passing shrimp of a lieutenant. American equality, degrading manhood and elevating the uniform.

Barrack life further tends to develop tendencies of sexual perversion. It is gradually producing along this line results similar to European military conditions. Havelock Ellis, the noted writer on sex psychology, has made a thorough study of the subject.[16] I quote: "Some of the barracks are great centers of male prostitution. . . . The number of soldiers who prostitute themselves is greater than we are willing to believe. It is no exaggeration to say that in certain regiments the presumption is in favor of the venality of the major of the men. . . . On summer evenings, Hyde Park and the neighborhood of Albert Gate, are full of guardsmen and others plying a lively trade and with little disguise, in uniform or out. . . . In most cases the proceeds form a comfortable addition to Tommy Atkins' pocket money."[17]

---

15. The Presidio served as a U.S. military post from 1848 until 1994, when it became part of the Golden Gate National Recreation Area, managed by the National Park Service.

16. Henry Havelock Ellis (1859–1939), English psychologist, physician, socialist, sex reformer, and author, conducted pioneering studies in the varieties of sexual behavior. EG refers to Ellis and his work frequently in *Anarchism and Other Essays* (1910).

17. EG quotes correspondence published in Havelock Ellis's introduction to *Sexual Inversion,* his study of homosexuality in Britain. The section quoted by EG has been rearranged from its original order in Ellis's text, the middle section appearing last in the original. The quoted sentences appear with punctuation variations and with some word differences from the original text. The first sentence appears in the original as "Some of the barracks (notably Knightsbridge) are great centres." The fourth sentence appears as "On summer evenings Hyde Park and the neighborhood of Albert Gate is full of guardsmen and others plying a lively trade, and with little disguise, in uniform or out." The final quoted sentence originally reads "In any case it means a covetable addition to Tommy Atkins's [the name is a Briticism for an enlisted man] pocket money."

To what extent this perversion has eaten its way into the army and navy can best be judged from the fact that special houses exist for this form of prostitution. The practice is not limited to England; it is universal. "Soldiers are no less sought after in France than in England or in Germany, and special houses for military prostitution exist both in Paris and the garrison towns."[18]

Had Mr. Havelock Ellis included America in his investigations of sex perversion, he would have found that the same conditions prevail in our army and navy as in those of other countries. The growth of the standing army inevitably adds to the spread of sex perversion; the barracks are the incubators.

Aside from the sexual effects of barrack life, it also tends to unfit the soldier for useful labor after leaving the army. Men, skilled in a trade, seldom enter the army or navy, but even they, after a military experience, find themselves totally unfitted for their former occupations. Having acquired habits of idleness and a taste for excitement and adventure, no peaceful pursuit can content them. Released from the army, they can turn to no useful work. But it is usually the social riffraff, discharged prisoners and the like, whom either the struggle for life or their own inclination drives into the ranks. These, their military term over, again turn to their former life of crime, more brutalized and degraded than before. It is a well-known fact that in our prisons there is a goodly number of ex-soldiers; while on the other hand, the army and navy are to a great extent supplied with ex-convicts. Of all the evil results I have just described, it seems to me none so detrimental to human integrity as the spirit Patriotism has produced in the case of Private William Buwalda,[19] now serving a term of three years in military prison. Because he foolishly believed that one can be a soldier and exercise his rights as a man at the same time, the military authorities punished him severely. True, he had served his country fifteen years, during which time his record was unimpeachable. According to Gen. Funston, who reduced Buwalda's sentence to three years, "the first duty of an officer or an enlisted man is unquestioned obedience and loyalty to the government, and it makes no difference whether he approves of that government or not."[20] Thus Funston stamps the true character of allegiance. According to him, entrance into the army abrogates the principles of the Declaration of Independence.

What a strange development of Patriotism that turns a thinking being into a loyal machine!

In justification of this most outrageous sentence of Buwalda, Gen. Funston tells the American people that the soldier's action was "a serious crime equal to treason." Now,

18. The original text reads, "Soldiers are no less sought after in France than in England or in Germany, and special houses exist for military prostitution both in Paris and the garrison-towns."
19. On 14 May 1908 William Buwalda, U.S. Army private, was court-martialled for violating the 62nd Article of War (attending EG's 26 April speech, applauding repeatedly, and shaking EG's hand while in uniform). Buwalda was found guilty, sentenced to five years hard labor, and dishonorably discharged. Buwalda's sentence was later reduced, and he was granted clemency by Theodore Roosevelt.
20. See article in the *New York Evening Post*, "Gen. Funston on the Buwalda Case," 30 June 1908.

what did this "terrible crime" really consist of? Simply in this: Wm. Buwalda was one of fifteen hundred people who attended a public meeting in San Francisco; and, oh, horrors, he shook hands with the speaker, Emma Goldman. A terrible crime, indeed, which the General calls "a great military offense, infinitely worse than desertion."

Can there be a greater indictment against Patriotism than the one that will brand a man a criminal, throw him into prison, and rob him of the results of fifteen years of faithful service?

Buwalda has given to his country the best years of his life and his very manhood. But all that was as nothing. Patriotism is inexorable and, like all insatiable monsters, demands all or nothing. It does not admit that a soldier is also a human being, who has a right to his own feelings and opinions, his own inclinations and ideas. No, Patriotism can not admit of that. That is the lesson which Buwalda was made to learn; made to learn at a rather costly, though not a useless, price. When he returns to freedom, he will have lost his position in the army, but he will have regained his self-respect. After all, that is worth three years of imprisonment.

A writer on the military conditions of America, in a recent article, commented on the power of the military man over the civilian in Germany. He said, among other things, that if our Republic had no other meaning than to guarantee all citizens equal rights, it would have just cause for existence. I am convinced that the writer was not in Colorado during the patriotic régime of General Bell.[21] He probably would have changed his mind had he seen how, in the name of Patriotism and the Republic, men were thrown into bull-pens, dragged about, driven across the border, and subjected to all kinds of indignities. Nor is that Colorado incident the only one in the growth of military power in the United States. There is hardly a strike where troops and militia do not come to the rescue of those in power, and where they do not act as arrogantly and brutally as do the men wearing the Kaiser's uniform. Then, too, we have the Dick military law.[22] Has the writer forgotten that?

A great misfortune with most of our writers is that they are absolutely ignorant on

21. Sherman M. Bell (ca. 1870–1942) was adjutant-general and commander of the Colorado State Militia, by order of Governor Peabody, for the duration of the Colorado coal miners' strike in 1903 and 1904. He had previously been a detective for Wells Fargo, served in the Roosevelt company of Rough Riders in the Cuban campaign (1st U.S. Volunteer Cavalry), and was a mining superintendent in the Cripple Creek district. Bell established martial law and with the Citizen's Alliance, a vigilante organization, shipped 560 union men out of the state. He was quoted as saying "the soldiers never will be taken out of here until we have rid the country of the cut-throats, murders, socialists, thieves, loafers, agitators and the like who make up the membership of the Western Federation of Miners. We don't care what the Supreme Court, the newspapers or anybody or anything else does. The soldiers are going to stay there, regardless of court decision; and if there is any more monkey business there is going to be some much-needed shooting."
22. The Dick Act, sponsored by Ohio senator Charles W. F. Dick, was passed in January 1903, and amendments to the act were passed in 1908. The law provided increased military funding and led to the establishment of the National Guard.

current events, or that, lacking honesty, they will not speak on these matters. And so it has come to pass that the Dick military law was rushed through Congress with little discussion and still less publicity,—a law which gives that President the power to turn a peaceful citizen into a bloodthirsty mankiller, supposedly for the defense of the country, in reality for the protection of the interests of that particular party whose mouthpiece the President happens to be.

Our writer claims that militarism can never become such a power in America as abroad, since it is voluntary with us, while it is compulsory in the Old World. Two very important facts, however, the gentleman forgets to consider. First, that conscription has created in Europe a deep-seated hatred of militarism among all class of society. Thousands of young recruits enlist under protest and, once in the army, will use every possible means to desert. Second, that it is the compulsory feature of militarism which has created a tremendous anti-militarist movement, feared by European Powers far more than anything else. After all, the greatest bulwark of capitalism is militarism. The very moment the latter is undermined, capitalism would totter. True, we have no conscription; that is, men are not usually forced to enlist in the army, but we have developed a far more exacting and rigid force—necessity. Is it not a fact that during industrial depressions there is a tremendous increase in the number of enlistments? The trade of militarism may not be either lucrative or honorable, but it is better than tramping the country in search of work, standing in bread line, or sleeping in municipal lodging houses. After all, it means thirteen dollars per month, three meals a day, and a place to sleep. Yet even necessity is not sufficiently strong a factor to bring into the army an element of character and manhood. No wonder our military authorities complain of the "poor material" enlisting in the army and navy. This admission is a very encouraging sign. It proves that there is still enough of the spirit of independence and love of liberty left in the average American to risk starvation rather than don the uniform.

Thinking men and women the world over are beginning to realize that Patriotism is too narrow and limited a conception to meet the necessities of our time. The centralization of power has brought into being an international feeling of solidarity among the oppressed nations of the world; a solidarity which represents a greater harmony of interests between the workingmen of America and his brothers abroad than between the American miner and his exploiting compatriot; a solidarity which fears not foreign invasion, because it is bringing all the workers to the point when they will say to their masters, "Go and do your own killing. We have done it long enough for you."[23]

This solidarity is awakening the consciousness of even the soldiers, they, too, being flesh of the flesh of the great human family. A solidarity that has proven infallible more than once during past struggles, and which has been the impetus inducing the Parisian

---

23. Compare EG's discussion of militarism in "What I Believe" (see Essay in the *New York World*, 19 July 1908, above).

soldiers, during the Commune of 1871, to refuse to obey when ordered to shoot their brothers.[24] It has given courage to the men who mutinied on Russian warships during recent years.[25] It will eventually bring about the uprising of all the oppressed and down-trodden against their international exploiters.

The proletariat of Europe has realized the great force of that solidarity and has, as a result, inaugurated a war against Patriotism and its bloody spectre, militarism. Thousands of men full the prisons of France, Germany, Russia, and the Scandinavian countries, because they dared to defy the ancient superstition. Nor is the movement limited to the working class; it has embraced representatives in all stations of life, its chief exponents being men and women prominent in art, science, and letter.

America will have to follow suit. The spirit of militarism has already permeated all walks of life. Indeed, I am convinced that militarism is growing a greater danger here than anywhere else, because of the many bribes capitalism holds out to those whom it wishes to destroy.

The beginning has already been made in the schools. Evidently the government holds to the Jesuitical conception, "Give me the childish mind, and I will mould the man." Children are trained in military tactics, the glory of military achievements extolled in the curriculum, and the youthful minds perverted to suit the government. Further, the youth of the country is appealed to in glaring posters to join the army and navy. "A fine chance to see the world!" cries the government huckster. Thus innocent boys are mor-ally shanghaied into Patriotism, and the military Moloch strides conquering through the nation.

The American workingman has suffered so much at the hands of the soldier, State and Federal, that he is quite justified in his disgust with, and his opposition to, the uniformed parasite. However, mere denunciation will not solve this great problem. What we need is a propaganda of education for the soldier: anti-patriotic literature that will enlighten him as to the real horrors of his trade; one that will awaken his consciousness to his true relation to the man to whose labor he owes his very existence.

It is precisely this that the authorities fear most. It is already high treason for a soldier to attend a radical meeting. No doubt, they will also stamp it high treason for a soldier to read a radical pamphlet. But, then, has not authority from time immemorial stamped

24. The Paris Commune occurred between 18 March and 28 May 1871.
25. In 1905 three separate instances of mutiny occurred in Russian ports or on naval ships. On 14 June 1905 sailors on the *Potemkin*, some of whom were active members of revolutionary groups, instigated mutiny when the sailors' spokesman was shot after complaining about substandard food and condi-tions on the ship. Following the release of the October Manifesto, sailors and soldiers in the city of Kronstadt initiated mutiny on 26–27 October. The demands of the mutineers concerned the status and rights of sailors, including pay and terms of service, as well as cursory demands for universal suffrage. An additional instance of mutiny occurred in the naval base of Sevastopol in the Crimea. Led by naval lieutenant P. P. Schmidt, the mutineers intended to block the entry of troops into the Crimean peninsula, sent a telegram to the tsar, and threatened all officers who opposed Schmidt's authority with hanging.

every step of progress as treasonable? Those, however, who earnestly strive for social reconstruction can well afford to face all that; for it is probably even more important to carry the truth into the barracks than into the factory. When we have undermined the patriotic lie, we shall have cleared the path for that great structure wherein all nationalities shall be united into a universal brotherhood,—a truly FREE SOCIETY.

Mother Earth Publishing Association, 1908. First advertised for sale in *Mother Earth* 3, no. 8 (October 1908).

Interview in the *ST. LOUIS POST-DISPATCH*

St. Louis, 1 November 1908

Emma Goldman Says Anarchism Will Mean Absolute Equality and Freedom For Women With No Dual Moral Code

She Tells Marguerite Martyn That When Perfection is Achieved Men and Women Will Be Equal.

Weaker Sex Will Achieve Glorious Equality
by Demanding the Worship They Have Always Been Given.

Emma Goldman, leader of anarchy, whose speech and actions have shown nothing but defiance and hatred of what we term law, she who has been called the red-mouthed enemy of law, has more laws in her own heart than Blackstone ever recognized,[1] and she obeys the laws she knows as proudly and willing as all "respectable" people obey our man-made laws.

She is by no means a lawless woman, as you might think, for she acknowledges all the laws of nature.

"Nature spells harmony. Even the dullest, the least impressionable of us is affected and influenced by the calmness and grandeur of nature when we come in contact with the great out-of-doors," she said.

We agree with her. Then why are we not all of Emma Goldman's belief? And why has she been pictured and written of as an implacable enemy of law?

These questions I was left to ponder upon after a talk with her. O, she is most convincing.

"THE DEVIL EXONERATED."

She is staying with her anarchist friend, Mrs. E. I. Adams[2] of 1327 Franklin avenue, and is giving four lectures at Druid's Hall,[3] Ninth and Market streets, before her departure on Monday for Australia.[4]

1. A reference to *Blackstone's Commentaries on the Laws of England* (first published in 1765), the standard legal dictionary and guide for England and its colonies, later adopted (and adapted) in the United States.
2. Refers to Edith Adams.
3. EG spoke at Druid's Hall on Sunday, 1 November. She argued that the Devil is a force of creativity, passion, and rebellion. In a review of her lecture, which appeared the following day, the *St. Louis Post-Dispatch* characterized her argument, attributing EG with the quote, "The Devil is the greatest benefactor the world has ever had."
4. EG cancelled her tour of Australia.

"The Devil Exonerated," Sunday, at 3 p.m., at which meeting Mr. Marion Reedy will preside, is built upon the recent dramatic craze, "The Devil," and it is expected to attract the attention of many professional men.[5]

She is a vividly impressive personality. One must have a good deal of imagination to

5. Probably a reference to George Bernard Shaw's play *The Devil's Disciple* (1897). Set during the American Revolution, the play focuses on the eldest son in a Protestant family who becomes so disillusioned with Christianity—in particular with the way religious piety is used in his family to justify selfish and cruel acts—that he starts to support the Devil. Although an outcast in his community, by the final scenes he is recognized for his bravery and selflessness. In her notes on the play, EG writes "what [Shaw] really teaches in this play is that our so-called bad people, people brutalized by conditions almost out of human semblance, are often capable of the highest deeds, in fact much more so than our smug and pious brethren and sistern" ("Plays by George Bernard Shaw—Discussion of His Works, notes," *EGP,* reel 54).

fancy Joan of Arc as a more potent power in leading a revolution. And yet with all her railing against existing conditions, she has as yet led no armies to violence.

I asked her if it is her opinion that the wholesale murder of oppressors will be necessary and inevitable.

"The signs of the times are more and more reassuring," she replied. "Books, the drama and many of our most influential forces are preaching anarchy. But you know the pain and hardship it costs a mother to bring one little child into the world. I do not see how this complicated child, Society, is to be brought into a new being without pain and hardship.

"I love life," she continued. "The big, human universe. I by no means prefer riot and bloodshed and death. But anarchists are not passive spectators in the theater of social development. And through all ages the spirit of rebellion has been the spirit of progress."

THE GREATEST PROBLEM.

Then, while I made a line drawing of her, I asked her to draw a word picture of what woman's position will be when the theories of anarchism prevail.

"You touch upon what I should consider the most vital subject in the world—the sex problem—if society were not so complex as to make it impossible to decide just what is the most important force.

"Woman's position should mean woman's freedom—her total emancipation; absolute sex equality. When perfection is achieved there will be no more of this absurd idea of the dualism of sex. Man will possess enough of the womanly quality of gentleness—woman will possess enough of the manly quality of strength.

"The equalization of the forces of gentleness and strength will eliminate the undesirable forces of weakness and brutality—men and women will be perfect companions and the most enduring love is founded upon comradeship."

"WOMEN NOT GEORGE SANDS."

"Woman has achieved some civil rights. Equal suffrage, gained in some localities, was a good demand.[6] But the emancipated woman has been so misrepresented by yellow journalists and milk-and-water literateurs that the exponent of woman's rights rebelled, and, lacking a sense of humor, has exerted her energy to prove that they are not as bad as they are painted; that they are not George Sands,[7] with absolute disregard of morality.[8]

"This narrow, puritanical vision has banished man as the disturber from their life.

"Man was not to be tolerated at any price, except, perhaps as the father of a child, since a child could not very well come to life without a father.

---

6. By 1908 four states allowed women the right to vote: Wyoming, Idaho, Colorado, and Utah.
7. The French novelist George Sand's early works explored women's sexuality, encouraging a quest for emotional satisfaction. Her later works reflected Sand's Republican and socialist sympathies.
8. EG makes an identical reference to George Sand in her 1906 essay, "The Tragedy of Women's Emancipation," Essay in *Mother Earth*, March 1906, above.

"We have seen also the tragedy of the economic emancipation of woman, since she can choose her own trade or profession. We have seen her exchange the narrow walls and lack of freedom in her home to the narrowness and lack of freedom of office, department store or factory. We have seen her attempt to compete with men in business and professions prove futile under existing conditions.

"Nevertheless, the position of the working girl is far more natural and human than her seemingly more fortunate sister. You will say that with leisure and wealth a woman may have more opportunity for freedom. True, but what freedom of thought or action she allows herself must be hidden behind closed doors at the peril of losing her position. And her cage is no less irksome for being a gilded one."

WHERE EMANCIPATION BEGINS.

"Not until woman possesses some attraction besides her sex will she have a mental or moral footing to stand upon. And the true emancipation begins neither in the courts nor at the polls. It begins with the woman's soul. Women are to achieve this glorious sex equality by demanding the respect, the worship for themselves that they have hitherto given the opposite sex. So much as woman demands, so much shall she receive. The more she receives from the world, the more she is in a position to give.

"There is no reason why she should always be merely a means to an end. So long as she makes a doormat of herself, so long will she be treated as such.

"She is no more responsible for the perpetuation of the race than are men, although she has shouldered the whole responsibility always. Anarchists do not believe with Socialists that so much as you produce so much should you consume.

"We do not talk of quantity, but of quality. The quality of woman's contribution to society would be equal to man's under proper conditions."

WOMEN'S HIGHEST SPHERE.

"The highest sphere of woman lies in developing her individuality, and she needs the whole world as a setting when she can shine resplendent.

"Those roses," and she alluded to a tall stalk of American Beauties which stood at her side, "would lose their effect without the green foliage to set them off. Just so does woman need her complimentary colors and environment. No woman who confines herself to the four walls of a home can advance with the world, so she is an obstacle to her own and her children's progress."

FINDS PURITY IN FREE LOVE.

"But you have no idea how many couples are living quietly and beautifully in what you call free love. The higher the mental development the more difficult to find a suitable mate—but the flower of such a union is the more perfect.

"I have in mind a man and his sweetheart who are too well known to mention, who, with their child, are examples of its exaltation. I know another radical couple who have lived side by side until now their sons are entering Yale and have proven the efficacy of the theory."

"But why don't we hear of them, since they have the courage of their convictions?" I asked.

"Because refined people consider that phase of life their own, their very most sacred affair. No church or state has the right to the means of prying into it; no president has the right to dictate it, as Theodore Roosevelt has the impertinence to do. He would not have the right, if he were the father of all the large families he so approves of, much less from his altitude of patriarch.[9]

"Your love affairs are no more the business of your neighbor than how many times you have clean linen."

"What do you think of the novel, 'Three Weeks,' as a declaration of independence?" I now asked, without trepidation.

HER IDEA OF "THREE WEEKS."

"As a literary work I do not consider it, and at first I was inclined not to read it, as it had been misrepresented to me. I had been given the impression that the heroine used her fine passion only as a means to an end, which would have been wholly wrong. But as the love story developed it was magnificent—a masterpiece.

"No, I do not believe Elinor Glyn is an anarchist.[10] I rather think she relies upon her strong social position in defying conventions, and the people of her class humor her, as an amusing freak."

I asked her if she had dictated the numerous descriptions I have read of her as having fierce black eyes, dark, somber hair and masculine physique.

"No," she replied, "I have no desire to make myself felt in that way even for the sake of the strength such an appearance might imply. I think you can see that I resort to no artificialities. And yet I love a naughty, sparkling black eye."

Her eyes are blue, her skin fair and soft and colorful. Her hair is very light brown, almost blonde, and it waves gracefully back from her smooth brow. Her waist is uncorseted, but none the less womanly. She wears the comfortable but not unpicturesque costume of the Russian women students.

9. A reference to Theodore Roosevelt's support of marriage and his campaign in favor of very large families and distinct traditional gender roles within families. In his *Autobiography*, he claimed, "The married woman able to have children must on average have four or the race will not perpetuate itself . . . normally the woman must remain the housemother, the homekeeper. . . ." (New York: MacMillan, 1913).

10. Elinor Glyn (1864–1943) was a Canadian-born English novelist of sensational and romantic fiction, whose novels were typically filled with exotic characters and passionate (though improbable) relationships. *Three Weeks* (1907) was the most popular and scandalous of her works, in which an Englishman and a woman from a Balkan royal family share three weeks of uninterrupted lovemaking. In 1908 a bookseller in Boston who sold the novel was convicted of selling obscene literature. Glyn's other novels include *It* (1927) and *Did She?* (1934).

"I do not try to afford pretty clothes for myself," she said, "but I admire any amount of adornment which is artistic upon another woman. I saw a woman in a sheathe gown on the stage the other night, who was a thing of infinite beauty."

As I departed she gave me one of the burning red roses. Was it symbolic? There are those who tell of the psychic message of flowers. I only know that it reminded me that a picture of Emma Goldman in warm, living, glowing colors would be far more adequate than an attempt to reproduce her personally in plain black and white.

St. Louis Post-Dispatch, 1 November 1908, p. 1. Copyright 1908. Reprinted with permission of the St. Louis Post-Dispatch. The interviewer, Marguerite Martyn Kenamore (d. 1948), was a popular St. Louis author.

MY DEAR, DEAR FRIENDS

I can not tell you, how guilty, I feel not having written you so long. But I hated to send a letter and not inclose something on account of my debt. Oh, I know that you would rather have had the letter. But you will understand, that it was hard, for me, not to be able to keep my promise. You know to some extent I have been getting along I reported it in M E of Nov and when this reaches you, you will no doubt also have the Dec issue. If I were religious, I should believe that an evil spirit is following me for I have certainly gone through tortures of the damned since I left N Y. The first obstacle was the campaign time, when it was even impossible to get people to attend a lecture. Then came police interference in Indinapolis. After that the stupidity of our comrades who, though years in the movement, have not yet been able to learn the simpliest ways of arranging meetings. They either get the dirtiest most obscure halls and don't advertise at all. Or they spent 100$ in getting up three meetings. You can imagine that my tour has not been very flourishing under the circumstances. I am two months on the road and all I could do is to keep M E going and invest about 100$ in literature which was sent to Australia. The inclosed express order for 25$ is the first towards the payment of my debts, which amounts to about 500$, outside of our printer. Of course, the Pacific Coast in always the best place for propaganda, morally and materially. Last spring, I raised 1100$ on the Coast in one month. This time, I have a few new places, so I may do even better. I must have quite a lot of money, because I can sail for Australia. The trip alone will swallow a furtune I want to pay my debts before I go and leave enough to keep M E alife for 2–3 months. Altogether about 1500$ If I can not raise that until Jan, I will until Feb. But, oh! the patience and power of endurance one must have.

How are you and Sophie and the boy?

I am sending you a clipping that will give you great pleasure. It was written by the editor of the St. Louis "Mirror"[1]

Well dear friend, forgive my silence and write me soon to Portland will be there from the 18–26th of this month

WITH MUCH LOVE AS EVER YOUR FRIEND

EMMA

ALS, IU-U. On Hotel Butler stationery.

1. William Marion Reedy was editor of the *St. Louis Mirror* from 1893 to 1920 and introduced EG to many influential people in St. Louis during her visits in 1908, 1909, and 1911.

<u>THE HON. FRANK OLIVER.</u>

I have received a message as follows from W. J. Corbett, Border Inspector at Blaine, Wash.

> "Emma Goldman anarchist intends speaking in Canada shall I keep her out, immediate answer necessary."

About six months ago the Mayor of Winnipeg[1] wrote enquiring whether the law could not be amended in such a way as to keep such persons out. I referred the matter to the Department of Justice and had a reply stating that none of the sections of the Immigration Act dealing with deportation appearsed to cover the case.

We might perhaps debar her on the ground of insanity if she attempts to come across the boundary. What do you think of this plan?

W. D. SCOTT

SUPERINTENDENT OF IMMIGRATION.

TDS, reel C-10612, file #800111, vol. 513, RG 76, Immigration Bureau, CaOOA. On stationery of the Department of the Interior, Canada. Handwritten note by Frank Oliver in upper left-hand corner reads, "I am afraid this is not sufficient warrant. F.O." Frank Oliver (b. 1853) was a Canadian journalist and member of Parliament. As minister of the interior from 1905 to 1911, he dramatically altered Canadian immigration policies, making immigration more selective and encouraging only those of English origin to immigrate.

1. James Henry Ashdown was mayor of Winnipeg from 1907 to 1908.

Emma Goldman Says Everett Ought to Be Annexed to Russia

Last evening Emma Goldman shook the mud of Everett from her indignant feet and with her business agent, Dr. Reitman, departed for Bellingham, where the doctor has several college mates who have promised to hold a little reunion and the police have promised to arrest the belligerent Emma if she shall attempt to publicly proclaim her seditious doctrine.

In the absence of Mayor Jones[1] the members of the police and fire commission yesterday afternoon conferred on the matter of allowing the apostle of anarchy to speak here, and it was decided that it was for the best interests of the city that she be denied this privilege. Chief Marshall accordingly notified Miss Goldman that he would arrest her if she tried to speak in public, and she promised that she would leave the city without making any demonstration.

Miss Goldman has found few opportunities of addressing audiences in this state on her present tour. Spokane refused to allow her to talk, and in Seattle Sunday evening she was headed off at the door of the hall which a crowd of about 200 sympathizers had broken into, and was taken to police headquarters where she was allowed her liberty on promise to leave the city and on payment of $1.50 to replace the broken lock. The landlord claimed no arrangements had been made to lease the hall.

As one of the leading anarchists of the world Miss Goldman is an interesting personage. She is of short and rather pudgy figure, and not at all prepossessing. She dresses plainly but well as to quality of her apparel. In conversation one is impressed with her pugnacity, which is evidenced whenever the subject of interference with her liberty to speak is mentioned. Great muscles stand out on her neck when she grows indignant, and one can easily imagine her at the head of a mob or inciting her followers to violence. It is evident she is sincere in her crusade. She is a woman of education and has written much anarchistic literature. After she had been notified that she would not be allowed to speak here she came to the Tribune office to leave a parting protest.

---

1. Newton Jones (1866–1922) was the pro-management mayor of Everett, Washington, from 1907 to 1909. Prior to his election, Jones was superintendent for the Clough and Hartley Mill, whose proprietor, former Minnesota governor David Clough (1846–1924), was known as one of the nation's shrewdest timber capitalists. Roland Hartley (1864–1952), Clough's son-in-law and mill co-owner, succeeded Jones as Everett's mayor, intensifying the city's pro-management atmosphere.

"I am surprised," she said, "to find Russian methods in Everett. I offer your good people this:

"Resolved, that the city of Everett, in the state of Washington, should be taken off the American map and turned over to the dominion of the Russian czar.

"Free speech! Free assembly! What a glorious principle! We alone, the children of a free country, can lay claim to it. Indeed, we give it to our children with their mother's milk; we give it to them in the schools. How it makes their hearts kindly and bosoms swell with that great refrain: Free speech, free press, free assembly! And yet, and yet, a handful of men, in a stuffy room in the city hall of Everett, decided on this day of the Lord, Dec. 14, 1908, that freedom of speech may be all right for America but it's all wrong for Everett. Their decision being backed by the power of the club, and might being right, free speech was grabbed by the throat and choked to death. 'My country 'tis of thee, sweet land of liberty.'

"Friday, Dec. 12, Dr. Ben L. Reitman, acting as my manager, secured Fraternal hall for a meeting to take place this evening. A deposit was paid after a contract was signed turning over Fraternal hall to Emma Goldman. No doubt the gentlemen of that hall are law-abiding citizens. The law provides that a contract is binding. Yet these very law and order people are the first ones to break the thing they believe in and demand. They refuse the hall, but forget that they have made themselves liable to damage.

"Another hall is secured, but the chief of police, who also believes in law, the law which guarantees free speech and assembly, this great patriot breaks his allegiance to American liberty and orders that Emma Goldman shall not speak. The city fathers, who certainly believe in law, aid and abet the conspiracy to throttle free speech.

"And so it has come to pass that American officials should Russianize an American city and that henceforth Columbia shall blush with shame over the treachery of her child Everett.

"Yes, but Emma Goldman is an anarchist. Oh, horrors! But what is anarchy? How are we to know if Emma Goldman is stopped from expression of her views or telling us what anarchism means? That's just it. Not Emma Goldman but free speech was stopped. As to anarchy, after all I do not blame the chief of police or the city fathers. Anarchism is a theory of human development, is therefore opposed to stagnation. Anarchism stands for freedom and non-interference, and is therefore opposed to the club. Anarchism stands for righteousness, and is therefore opposed to our social and economic inequities; to crime and criminals. In short, anarchism believes in fellowship and brotherhood. Don't you see why it is offensive to a chief of police and city fathers?"

Everett Morning Tribune, 15 December 1908, p. 4.

The following is a portion of a letter sent by Emma Goldman to a confidential anarchist in this city.

"At first I took this case of the U.S. Authorities of taking my papers away as a joke but now it turns out serious; altogether too serious. The U.S. Authorities are planning to take us by surprise. We, a few of us, had a meeting and decided to be prepared. Now what I ask of you is very important and you should attend to it at once. Go to his brother and find out how long since Jac. K.,[1] left Rochester, how long since he last heard from him and if he is alive. If he is dead that alters my case. I am worried to death over it and hope that you will do your share to relieve me from it."

TD, file #52,410–43, Immigration and Naturalization Service, DNA. On stationery of Herman F. Schuettler, Assistant General Superintendent.

1. EG refers to Jacob Kershner, whom she married at age seventeen, in 1887.

SIR:

I herewith forward to you a photographic copy of the letter referred to in my confidential communication of January 2, 1909, No. 1002/1, relative to which you instruct me in your communication 51694/2-c, January 5, 1909.[1]

I am now at liberty to state the reason for the condition imposed. The party who secured this letter is in the employ of the City Secret Service, and is further in the inner circle of the anarchic society—Group Edelsdald.[2] There is no opposition to this copy being used in the Department. It was intended that it could be used in the Bureau or the Department, but not taken into court for fear it might injure the future usefulness of the above mentioned party. He holds the office of Secretary of the Group, he is in the way of securing valuable information, all of which he turns over for the inspection of the city anarchistic secret service.[3]

In this letter are used the initials "J.K.". This means the supposed husband of Emma Goldman. "D" refers to a brother of the above mentioned supposed husband.[4] The signature at the end "A" is that of Alexander Berkman, and it is addressed to Dr. Miriam Yamplosky, who is the President of the above mentioned group.

RESPECTFULLY,

DANIEL D. DAVIES

IMMIGRANT INSPECTOR IN CHARGE

TLS, file #10,02/1, Immigration and Naturalization Service, RG 85, DNA. Marked "Confidential" on stationery of the Department of Commerce and Labor Immigration Service. Addressed to Commissioner-General of Immigration, Washington, D.C.

1. Daniel Joseph Keefe (1852–1929) was a labor leader, industrial arbitrator, and U.S. Commissioner-General of Immigration (1909–1913; appointed by President Roosevelt). He spent much of his career working for organized labor, including serving as president of the National Longshoremen's Association (1893–1908, except for three years) and as a member of the executive council of the American Federation of Labor (1903–1908). After leaving the office of Commissioner-General of Immigration, Keefe worked as a conciliation commissioner for the U.S. Department of Labor (1913–1925).
2. The Edelstadt Group, inspired by the Yiddish anarchist and poet David Edelstadt, was founded by his brother, Abe.
3. Harry Goldstein was the secretary of the Edelstadt Group.
4. David Kershner was Jacob's brother.

Interview in the *SAN FRANCISCO BULLETIN*

16 January 1909

Priestess of Anarchism Becomes Dramatic Seer

Ben Reichtmann, anarchist, and manager for Emma Goldman, called upon me at the office and presented a letter of introduction. He wanted me to talk to his principal on the drama and asserted as a recommendation that she was the best-informed person in America on the subject. I knew her only from newspaper and police report as an inflammatory agitator, a Red radical and a menace to society in general, so I naturally smiled at Reichtmann's extravagance.

He also smiled—a superior sort of smile. "Oh, well," he said, "come up and meet her, anyway. Then you can decide for yourself." The following article not only explains why I ceased to smile at the notion that Emma Goldman, anarchist, knew anything about the theater, but is also offered to the public as evidence on which to decide whether or not her manager was right.

Our meeting had all the atmosphere of Stevenson's "The Dynamiters."[1] I went, as directed, to a little anarchist bookshop on Golden Gate Avenue,[2] and, coming out of the dreary drizzle of the street into the low-ceilinged and dimly lit room, with its tables full of crimson literature, found myself at once in another world—an under world of obscure strivings and strange hopes. Figures passed in and out—anarchists, I suppose. I heard one fair-haired, rosy-cheeked boy murmur to a dark Arab of a man, "We had a great Red meeting in San Jose last night." There seemed to be a rustle of suppressed activity through the crowded headquarters of the annihilators.

A little group stood near the door, and I approached this, announcing: "I'm looking for Emma Goldman!" Perhaps I resembled an immigration officer (which I find hard to believe) or some other hated hireling of an oppressive body politic, for I seemed to sense a double note of suspicion and defiance in the answer of a small, swart woman who stepped forward and replied:

"I am Miss Goldman!"

Queer. I had expected to find some one quite different—I cannot say just how, though possibly I had pictured an older woman, one with harsher features. The leader of Ameri-

---

1. The novels of Robert Louis Balfour Stevenson (1850–1894), Scottish novelist and essayist, include *Treasure Island* and *Dr. Jekyll and Mr. Hyde*. His novel *The Dynamiter* (1885), co-written with his wife, Fanny, paints a conspiratorial and sensationalist portrait of anarchists and anarchism.
2. The Liberty Bookstore, 1260 Golden Gate Avenue, San Francisco, California, was operated by independent socialist William McDevitt and anarchist Alexander Horr.

can anarchists is not physically impressive, though she is not entirely unattractive. Her costume answered the requirements of decency and warmth, but scorned any weak impulse toward adornment. Back of her glasses, however, glitters the light of an acute intelligence and there is a distinct personal magnetism about her as she frames her thoughts in quick and highly expressive words.

As soon as I outlined my mission the faint air of hostility disappeared from her manner, a smile flickered on her lips and she motioned me to a seat.

"Oh, yes, sit down," she invited. "Dr. Heichtmann told me about you. I'm glad there's one newspaperman who isn't afraid to come and talk to me."

I hastened to stipulate that it was not anarchism I wished to discuss, but the drama, on which I had heard she was an expert.

"Well," she began, plunging at once into her subject, "I look on the drama as the most powerful disseminator of radical ideas that exists, so all my life I have made more or less of a study of it.

"Perhaps I can explain what I mean by telling you something of the progress in Germany. There the Socialists worked for years trying to extend their ideas with but indifferent success. They were only able to reach the working people, and even these only to a slight extent. But when the galaxy of great dramatists began to consider social conditions and exploit pressing problems on the stage every one was interested, no matter how reluctantly. The highest classes were forced to listen by the sheer power of art.

"The first of the radical plays was written about 1880 or 1881 by Arno Holtz and caused a tremendous sensation.[3] Before this the stage had been devoted almost entirely to the sentimental, the romantic and the mildly philosophical. But Holtz' play, "The Family Zelica," undertook to present the question of utter, absolute poverty. It pictured the life of a family of alley-dwellers, who fished their daily necessities out of the garbage barrel.

"This was soon followed by Herman Sudermann's "Ehre," or "Honor," directed against the silly, pernicious and crazy custom of duelling.[4] Of course Bertha Von Suttner,[5] an aristocrat, had voiced the first protest against the practice, but in essay form. The military Germans had come to imagine from success in the field that they were 'it,' as we say.

---

3. Arno Holz (1863–1919), a German journalist and editor of the journal *Freie Bühne,* was also a dramatist, identified with the Naturalist movement. EG cites his plays in her 1914 work, *The Social Significance of the Modern Drama,* especially *Die Familie Selicke* (The Family Zelicka, 1890), a portrayal of the abject poverty of life in the streets; other plays by Holz include *Traumulus* (with O. Jerschke; 1904), *Frei!* (with O. Jerschke; 1907), and *Ignorabimus* (1913).

4. Hermann Sudermann (1857–1928) was a German dramatist and novelist and author of realist plays including *Honor* (1889) and *The Fall of Sodom* (1891). He was a contributor to the magazine *International.* EG included Sudermann's play *Magda* (1893) in her *Social Significance of Modern Drama* (pp. 69–86) and describes him as the first German dramatist to seriously address social topics.

5. Bertha von Suttner (1843–1914) was an Austrian writer and the first woman to win the Nobel Peace Prize for her tireless activism against German militarism. In 1891, she helped form a Venetian peace group, initiated the Austrian Peace Society, and initiated a fund to establish the Bern Peace Bureau. Her best-selling novel *Die Waffen Nieder!* (Lay Down Your Arms!), published in 1889, won her international acclaim. Her essay on dueling was most likely from her anthology *Age of Machines.*

'Ehre' showed that there could be no definite, stable idea of honor, which depended strictly upon the conditions under which the notion was fostered. Sudermann exhibited honor upside down, so to speak, by picturing a savage tribe whose idea of the fitness of things was absolutely outraged because a guest among them left their women alone when he had been generously left in a tent among them.

"Then came Gerhard Hauptman, who is at once the greatest dramatist, the greatest poet and the greatest revolutionist living in Germany today.[6] His first play, 'Before Sunrise,' was considered so extreme that he was unable to get it produced at any of the 'respectable' theaters and had to put it on under most trying circumstances in a little place back of a beer garden. The play treats the Agrarian question and the corrupting influence of money on the peasantry, as well as the gloomy fact that poor people, who are least able to care for their children, always have the greatest number. Hauptman was audacious enough to imagine a woman in labor just off the stage and her groans are heard by the audience.

"The play created an impression that almost amounted to a social upheaval. Everyone flocked to see it and opinion as to its merits was fiercely divided. On one occasion a physician leaped up in the midst of the performance and waiving a pair of surgical forceps over his head shouted, 'Here! Look at this! Just see what we've brought into our theaters and put on our stage!' He made his rumpus, was thrown out and forgotten." The speaker smiled a little twisted smile and added, "but Gerhard Hauptman wasn't forgotten."

"I have a friend," she went on, "who was with Hauptman when he collected the material for 'The Weavers,' his most socialistic play. They lived together in the weaving district and learned thoroughly the lives of these unhappy people. 'Hanelle,' his dream play, also resulted from this expedition. In fact, the original of the girl Hanelle, was the little girl of the house in which they lived. She was the daughter of a drunken father, who beat her and made her life an aching misery. Hauptman used to take the child in his lap and pet her, and as she gradually came to understand his tenderness, something absolutely new to her, her shyness disappeared and her character expanded and expressed itself much as it does in the play. Hauptman has developed and flowered in somewhat the same way, slipping unconsciously from material studies into the realm of the ideal, where he is seen with perfect artistry in that most wonderful of plays, 'The Sunken Bell.'

"Two other German dramatists ought to be mentioned. One of them is Max Halbers,[7] whose 'Youth' deals with the development of love in the adolescent heart and the stupidity of society in meeting the new demand. Wedekind is the other, and he treated the same

6. Gerhardt Hauptmann (1862–1946), a Silesian (now Poland) writer and playwright, was the recipient of the Nobel Prize for literature in 1912. EG included his plays in her *Social Significance of the Modern Drama*, including *The Weavers* (1892), a devastating portrayal of poverty caused by industrialization, *Before Sunrise* (1889), and *Hannele* (1893). The "friend" EG mentions is Max Baginski.

7. Max Halbe (1865–1944) was a German playwright and novelist whose play *Youth* was published in 1893.

problem in 'Spring's Awakening.'[8] In this play a boy gets a girl of fourteen into trouble without in the least understanding the consequences of his act. The girl's mother kills her with quack medicines, trying to conceal the truth, while the boy is sent to the reformatory to expiate a sin which he utterly fails to comprehend and about which no one takes the trouble to tell him."

Miss Goldman paused in the perfect geyser of speech with which she had favored me only to adjust her glasses and continue.

"The same process can be traced in all other countries and is even beginning to be felt in America," she expounded. "After the immense efflorescence such as that apparent in Germany, sometimes comes the reaction and the schism. For instance, when the Socialist party reached its zenith it naturally became limited and no longer free in its theories. Paradoxically enough, one of the great Socialist leaders found himself ranged against Hauptman, whom he found it necessary to denounce as a degenerate. Sudermann, on the other hand, has recanted his early radicalism and conformed, so that he is now referred to as the boarding-school dramatist.

"Scandinavia illustrates the tendency of which I speak, as well as Germany. Ibsen,[9] of course, has been popularized to a certain extent in America, but really he was not the first in the field in his native land. Bjornsen preceded him, and after attacking various abuses for years in essays and fiction wrote his great play, 'The Downfall,' which was an illuminating discussion of commercialism.[10] Yet it was Ibsen, standing alone in his loneliness, who stamped the intellect of Norway. But there are others as tall as Ibsen in Northern literature—Strinberg, for example, who appears to be entirely unknown in the United States. He is a Swede, a colossal figure, whom Ibsen himself admitted was the greatest of them all. His two best plays are 'The Countess Julia' and "The Father."[11] Strinberg, like Ibsen, is a strict individualist, though perhaps not so consistent. He has devoted himself largely to exposing the deficiencies of the woman's suffrage movement and has attacked it so bitterly that, by many he is classed as a woman-hater, which he really isn't. For a long time he was looked on as the most prominent opponent of Christianity, but in recent years underwent a change, was received by the Pope and became a Catholic. His frequent shifts of position have led to the charge that he is a weather-cock, but his is such a versatile nature that his many-sidedness is scarcely inconsistency."

The priestess of anarchy had many interesting reminiscences of the now famous com-

---

8. Frank Wedekind (1864–1918) was a German dramatist and poet whose play *Frühlings Erwachen* (The Awakening of Spring, trans. 1909) was first performed in Berlin in 1906. Wedekind's plays often explored sexual themes.

9. EG often cites Henrik Ibsen and the social significance of his work; she discusses several of his plays, including *Hedda Gabler, A Doll's House, Ghosts,* and *An Enemy of the Society* (sometimes produced under the title *An Enemy of the People*) in her 1914 *Social Significance of the Modern Drama* (pp. 11–42).

10. Bjørnstjerne Bjørnson (1832–1910) wrote *En fallit* (The Downfall, 1875; also published as *A Bankruptcy* in 1914).

11. EG discusses several plays by August Strindberg (1849–1912), Swedish teacher and dramatist, including *The Father* (1887) and *Countess Julia* (1888), in her 1914 book on modern drama (pp. 43–68).

pany of Russian players who visited New York some time ago, and from whose ranks Alla Nazimova was drafted.[12] It was she, indeed, who managed them when they first reached this country and (says she) it was largely through her efforts that the money was raised to build the Bowery theater in which Henry Miller found them performing and first saw Nazimova, whom he persuaded to star under his management.

"Not one of them spoke English, so I acted as interpreter and American manager," she explained. "Orleneff was the great artist among them. Indeed, he is the greatest living artist on any stage. The most wonderful thing about the company was its ensemble work, for nearly every one was of equal ability with Nazimova. Orleneff had picked up peasants, trained them, inspired them with his fire and finally turned out finished artists. In their own country they had a tremendous influence, especially with Checkhov's 'The Chosen People,' an appeal for more liberal treatment of the Jews.[13] In fact, it was that play which really brought them to America as a sort of missionary crusade. All the company were hot with the missionary spirit, which is rather curious, considering that they were all Gentiles except Nazimova; she is a Jewess.

Recollections of the Russian players brought her around to a consideration of the Slavic drama.

"In Russia," she said, "the process I spoke to you about has been a little different. The abyss between the intellectual and artistic life of the people and the governmental regime is so great that it did not remain for the drama to excite radical ideas. The government did that. The drama there—at least the vital drama, for the older plays had little to do with the life of the people—is still very young and the interest in the notions and theories about which it revolves are mostly excited by Turgenev[14] and Tostoi,[15] both in fiction and plays.

"The most famous of the modern dramatists was Tcheckof, who died two years ago of tuberculosis.[16] His greatest play was 'The Seagull,' which was largely autobiographical. He had a fearfully hard life, though, unlike Gorky, he was a university man and highly cultured. 'The Seagull' deals with the literary prostitution to which so many authors are forced by want, and Tcheckof finds that the solution in this particular case is suicide.

---

12. EG worked as tour manager in the fall of 1905 for the St. Petersburg theater troupe headed by Pavel Orlenev. The troupe's leading actress, Alla Nazimova, stayed on in the United States after the Russian group's departure in 1906. Henry Miller (1860–1926) was a New York producer and theater owner.

13. *The Chosen People; A Play in Three Acts* (New York: Frank V. Strauss, 1905), by Evgenii Nikolaevich Chirikov (1864–1932), was performed in New York by Pavel Orlenev's theater company on 23 March 1905.

14. Ivan Turgenev (1818–1883) was a Russian author and dramatist who turned to writing novels as a retreat from tsarist censorship of the performances of his plays. The main character in his novel *Rudin* (1855) was based on Russian anarchist Michael Bakunin. Other works include *A Sportsman's Sketches* (1852), *A Nest of Gentlefolk* (1859), *On the Eve* (1860), and *Fathers and Sons* (1862), a novel that reflected nihilistic ideas. Turgenev's short stories appeared in *Mother Earth*, including "The Reporter" (July 1906) and "The Beggar" (August 1906).

15. EG refers to Leo Tolstoy, the Russian author and Christian pacifist, whose opposition to militarism and organized religion led to his association with aspects of anarchism.

16. Anton Pavlovich Chekhov's major plays included *The Seagull* (1895), *Uncle Vanya* (1900), *Three Sisters* (1901), and *The Cherry Orchard* (1904). EG lectured on his works regularly and analyzed *The Seagull* and *The Cherry Orchard* in her *Social Significance of the Modern Drama* (pp. 283–93).

However, this conclusion does not produce the effect of pessimism, as so much of Ibsen's work does, but elaborates the idea that it is best for certain superior material voluntarily to go out of society rather than submit to mediocre standards. Other plays of his which are greatly loved in his own country are 'The Three Sisters' and 'Uncle Vanaya.'

"Gorky probably ranks next to him.[17] His play 'The Abyss,' or, as it is called in the translation, 'At the Bottom,' was not appreciated when it was produced here because America doesn't understand her tramp problem. Its theme is lost existences—the tramp, the prostitute and the criminal, who is not congenital but is persuaded to crime by conditions. Gorky's most valuable plea is that crime is not only the effect of conditions but also of the inability of the individual to conform to conventional standards, which are infinitely more rigid than the statutes. He denies the effect of heredity, or at least asserts that it is not the most important formative influence, in that the soil of the soul, no matter what the seeds of heredity may be, is either fertile or barren.

"Another great genius among the Russians is Andriev,[18] whose mostly widely known play is 'The Dim Distance.' This contrasts the contending forces of conservatism and radicalism as seen in the home. A son who has been broadly educated returns to his home to find the same old mediocrity operating in the same old rut that he knew in his youth and outgrew in his manhood. There is mutual love between himself and his family, but the conflict of thought is too grinding, and he finally goes out, seeking for hope in 'the dim distance.'"

Miss Goldman also talked in the same thorough fashion of the Italian drama, with D'Annunzio,[19] the artist-individualist, towering above the rest, and of the French drama, with Mirabeau's[20] "Business Is Business" and Hervieu's[21] and Bernstein's[22] later plays.

17. Maksim Gorky (1868–1936) was a Russian novelist whose works portrayed the life of the Russian lower classes; he is acknowledged as a conceptual founder of socialist realism.
18. Leonid Nikolayevitch Andreyev (1871–1919) was a Russian novelist and playwright whose works were frequently cited by EG.
19. Gabriel D'Annunzio (1864–1918) was an Italian poet, dramatist, author, and soldier. His dramas include *The Dream of a Spring Morning* (tr. 1902) and *The Dream of an Autumn Sunset* (tr. 1904), both written during his love affair with Eleanora Duse.
20. Octave Henri Marie Mirbeau (1848–1917) was a French playwright, novelist, and anarchist. His play *Business Is Business* was published in France in 1903 and first performed in New York in 1904. His novel *The Torture Garden* (1899) was a savage attack on government. Known as a leading anarchist "man of letters," he wrote more than 1,200 short stories and articles, including three autobiographical novels laced with anarchist themes: *Le Calvaire* (1886), *Sebastien Roche* (1890), and especially *L'Abbe Jules* (1888). In 1901, anarchist Benjamin Tucker translated Mirbeau's *A Chambermaid's Diary* into English, after which it was confiscated by the U.S. Postmaster under the Comstock Act.
21. Paul Hervieu (1857–1915) was a French lawyer, writer, and playwright, whose plays were often included in the repertory of the Comédie Française, and cited in EG's lectures on modern drama. Major works include *Le Dedale* (The Labyrinth, 1905); *LeReveil* (1905), *Connais-Toi* (Know Thyself, 1909), *Bagatelle* (1912).
22. Following the Dreyfus Affair, the French dramatist Henry Bernstein (1876–1953) wrote two plays exploring issues of anti-Semitism: *Samson* (1907) and *Israel* (1908). His other works include *Le detour* (The Detour, 1902), *Le bercail* (The Fold, 1904), *La rafale* (The Whirlwind, 1905), *Le voleur* (The Thief,

She was anxious to rid herself of the Hungarians and Spaniards when I inveigled her back to America, with whose infant drama she seemed to be on equal terms of intimacy.

"What you call pessimism and consider morbidity in the foreigners," she said, "will gradually impregnate the drama of America, for those who think deeply cannot evade the tragic contrasts and misadjustments of life. But this tendency will never be so pronounced here as it is abroad. The lines will be less delicate and fine, for America is, above all things, massive. And there is a reason for superior optimism in America, because you have accomplished in a century what it has taken Europe thousands of years, with immeasurable conflict and bloodshed, to reach. Europe is old. America is young. That difference will appear in the native drama, which will display the youthful spirit."

"I would like to ask you, Miss Goldman," said I, "why your inclinations towards the socialist dramatists seem to be quite as friendly and respectful as toward those who preach anarchism."

"Because I am an anarchist," she replied. "I look on all art as the mirror of human life, so I cannot confine myself in that regard to the principles of any party. The merit and virtue of true drama is that it shows life as it is. The only remedy for conditions must come from an understanding of human character and needs. There is no cut-and-dried political cure which has any value. I hold, with Neitzsche, that we are staggering along with the corpse of dead ages on our backs. Theories do not create life. Life must make its own theories. We have not understood that in our evolution. We cannot mold life to our notions. Life must teach us. We may learn it from the stage. Moreover," she added, "Europe is not socialist in its drama in a party sense—in the sense of getting control of the government. Even Sudermann, who is the most generally recognized as a political socialist, is quite comfortable and bourgeois in his later plays. The rest of them object to being called Socialists at all."

Emma Goldman gave me considerable more subversive doctrine, unrelated to the drama, which I refrain from using because I do not care to advertise a cause which I believe is fundamentally wrong and am positive is immediately dangerous. But I left her with a very active impression that on the drama, at least, she knows what she is talking about.

R. E. R.

San Francisco Bulletin, 16 January 1909, p. 9.

1906), *La griffe* (The Claw, 1906), *Apres moi!* (After Me! 1911), *L'assaut* (The Assault, 1912), and *Le secret* (The Secret, 1913).

DEAR FRIEND:

You have no doubt heard of the latest police outrage on free speech and our comrades Emma Goldman, Dr. Ben L. Reitman and others. Without the shadow of an excuse, and after our first meeting was inadvertently permitted to take place unmolested, Emma Goldman and Dr. Ben L. Reitman were arrested and charged with conspiracy to incite to riot, etc., on eight separate counts each, and placed under $16,000 bail in cash (or double that in property).[1] The object, seemingly, of placing their bail at such an exorbitant figure was to crush our comrades by the mere magnitude of the threat involved. As a matter of fact, it did succeed in keeping our comrades in prison and did break up our meetings, with the resultant financial loss to all concerned, and most of all to the injury of Mother Earth.

The police department was evidently under the impression that they had only to deal with the handful of obscure comrades within easy reach, for when the country promptly responded to the occasion their bail was reduced to $2800, then their bail waived on the eight charges and they were put on trial on a new charge of attempting to hold an unlawful assembly for the purpose of opposing all government and the advocacy of Anarchism, (this, presumably, is due to the fertility of the District Attorney's office, in order to make good on the novelty of the charge as against the malicious imbecility of San Francisco's "Finest"), and were released on $500 bail—quite a drop, from $16,000 to $500.

These tactics in open court is equivalent to a confession of culpability on the one hand and on the other hand it indicates a well-defined purpose to prosecute to the limit. Emma Goldman has been arrested times without number; this, however, is the first time that the authorities have actually put her on trial;[2] and, judging by the venom, cunning and brutality that characterized the arrest of our comrades, the breaking up of our meetings, the clubbing of our friends and the general handling of the situation, there seems to be a determined effort on the part of the prosecution to convict at any cost, and it is up to

1. During EG's first meeting, held on 13 January 1909, it was announced that eight other meetings would take place in San Francisco. The police considered each planned meeting an individual act of conspiracy and consequently issued warrants for the arrest of EG and BR on eight counts of conspiracy to incite a riot. On the evening of 14 January, they were arrested upon arriving at the Victory theater meeting. Bail was set at $1,000 for each offense (for each person), for a total of $16,000, and then, in default of bail, they were taken to prison. William Buwalda, who had been released from military prison two weeks earlier, on 31 December, was arrested with them for protesting EG's arrest. Supporters were initially stunned by the exorbitant bail, but in the next several days about $8,500 was raised, with more funds forthcoming. In the following week, bail was reduced and, soon after, all charges were dropped.
2. EG had in fact been placed on trial and found guilty for her speech at an 1893 meeting of the unemployed, in New York City's Union Square.

us, who are on the ragged edge of this battle-field, to see that these malignant plans shall fail, if a thorough and well-conducted defense can make it fail. For this purpose we need a defense fund to supplement the slender means supplied by local comrades, and you are asked to contribute according to your means, at once, and to constitute yourself a committee of one to get others to contribute.

If, in spite of all our efforts, these comrades of ours should be convicted, they will go to jail, for they scorn to appeal from one grade of tyranny to another; and some of the rest of us will also go to jail, and we hope that others will make it their business (whether Anarchists or not) to go to jail in such numbers that the public conscience may be roused to a realization of the infamy of attempting the suppression of free speech, _for mark this_: _if Emma Goldman and Ben L. Reitman are railroaded to prison on this police-made excuse for a statute it will be impossible for them or any other Anarchists to speak anywhere in California, that the precedent will be followed up by other States with lively enthusiasm, and this will effectively check the Anarchistic propaganda in this country. This is not all. If the attempted suppression of the legal right of Anarchists to freely express their opinions and freely assemble for the discussion of their views, plans and purposes will succeed, it will be considered a mere wedge that Tyranny will hammer in the armor of Free Speech, and the next victims will be the Socialists, the Single-Taxers, the Mormons, the Prohibitionists and any and all minority movements that may stand in the way of plutocracy and respectable vice_, and so we call on all liberty-loving people, without regard to differences on other matters, to join us in this fight with the common enemy. Piece-meal the enemy can cut us into mince-meat, but working together we are invincible. In the words of the elder Adams: "If we don't hang together we'll hang separately."[3]

Note:—We are deeply involved in the defense and expense accounts, and we must have funds immediately to meet pressing obligations.

Address all communications to EMMA GOLDMAN, care of Alex. Horr, 1260 Golden Gate Avenue, San Francisco, Cal.

EMMA GOLDMAN,
DR. BEN L. REITMAN,
ALEX HORR,
CASSIUS V. COOK,
COMMITTEE

PLSr, Lillian Wald Papers, NN. Also hand-signed by Ben L. Reitman, Emma Goldman, and Cassius V. Cook.

3. To Benjamin Franklin, at the signing of the Declaration of Independence, is attributed the saying, "We must indeed all hang together, or assuredly we shall hang separately."

To **MOTHER EARTH**

San Francisco, 2 February 1909

On Trial

DEAR FRIENDS:

Police brutality and outrages have become such everyday affairs, no one pays the slightest attention to them. We are a novelty-loving people. We like variety: The news of a lynching, one day; an earthquake, the next; a big fire, the third; some sensational murder, the fourth; a prize fight, the fifth; the deportation of an Anarchist, the sixth, and so on, and so forth. Only not one and the same thing two days in succession; that would never satisfy our sensational tastes. Besides, brutality to Anarchists is but true American spirit. "Them foreigners have no business here, anyway; why don't they leave this country?"

However, the police outrage in San Francisco, while common enough, was really unusual in its extraordinary stupidity. It is for this reason that we have taken the trouble to record it at all.

We were charged with "Conspiracy and riot, making unlawful threats to use force and violence, and disturbing the public peace," etc., charges so "grave," indeed, that the Judge felt $16,000 bail for each defendant was but a trifle. But suddenly, four days after our arrest, these "grave charges" were set aside, and a new charge concocted, that of "unlawful assemblage, denouncing, as unnecessary, all organized government, and preaching Anarchist doctrines." O horrors! On this "wise and dangerous" charge I was put on trial, Dr. Reitman to follow, after I shall have been given a vacation at the expense of the City of the Golden Gate.

I wish I were gifted with the power to describe the performance. The gravity of the Judge; the important air of the District Attorney; the mysteriousness of the detective witnesses for the State; the scared faces of the men called to serve on the jury. Each one anxiously watching the other fellow, lest he might be an Anarchist, which means dynamite and bombs. It was a spectacle for the gods. And then our lawyer, Mr. Ernest E. Kirk,[1] a young and vivacious Californian, with the true Celtic spirit of humor and mischief. How he sweated every venire-man! How he made him sit up and listen. Listen and hear, for the first time in his life, things as they really are, and not what a prostituted press has fed its readers on for years. "What do you know about Anarchism?" "The papers say, it teaches bombs and dynamite." "What do you know about the defendant?" "The papers

---

1. Ernest E. Kirk (1872–1950) was a San Francisco attorney and a socialist, who acted as both EG's and BR's personal lawyer.

say, she induces people to kill." The papers, the papers! The only source of information, of knowledge, of the American people. The poisoners of the mind, the corrupters of the human soul. The villifiers and misrepresenters of the truth, America's greatest scourge and pest, the arch-enemies of all that is big and fine and true. If ever the day of judgement should arrive, not in heaven, but here on earth; if ever the forces for and against human regeneration shall meet in open battle, the men of the newspaper profession will be the first ones to face the wrath of an outraged, cheated, defrauded people. It has always been my opinion that the police department is recruited from the most contemptible human material; but my experience in San Francisco has taught me that, compared with the human species which is polluting American journalism, the police are as white and virtuous as the proverbial angels.

It required almost superhuman patience to clear the superstition and rubbish from the minds of a hundred and twenty men, before twelve could be selected as jurors capable at least of a semblance of fairness. However, it was our good fortune to find in Mr. Kirk not only an earnest and sincere man, but a mental athlete with the tenacity of a bull-dog. Once in his grip, no man escaped until every vestige of cobweb was torn, and he made to see that Anarchism resembled the newspapers stories about as much as the average penny-a-liner resembles the cherubim. We knew, of course, that the evidence gathered by the prosecution was so flimsy and absurd, that even the densest jury would acquit. "Denouncing, as unnecessary, all organized government, and preaching Anarchist doctrines." We pleaded guilty, not only to that, but even to more. We insisted that all government is criminal, destructive of liberty and well-being, and that it must be abolished by every method at our command. But, while the police and the court of this country have gone beyond the limit in suppressing free speech and press, they could not, by the widest stretch of the imagination (which, by the way, they sorely lack), make it a crime to denounce anything as "unnecessary." Of course, no one can tell to what contemptible measures detectives and prosecuting attorneys would stoop. Because of that, Mr. Kirk's method of examination, of sifting and selecting the jurors, was an admirable one. Besides, our trial was not only for the purpose of vindicating free speech, but also to propagate Anarchism, which, while an alleged crime in a hall, was perfectly legal in the court room, you see. And we did preach Anarchism, every phase of it, more thoroughly and effectively than I could have done in a dozen meetings. This was particularly apparent from the change of attitude of the Judge.

Police Judge Deasy is but two months on the bench. He is therefore still humane, when dealing with the victims of a cold and cruel world. I have watched for four days, when poor, hungry, shivering, body and soul broken humanity was brought before him. Not once did I hear an unkind word, or even a reproach. "What is a man to do, your Honor, when he can find no work, and is hungry? He must beg or steal." "Yes, yes, I know, I do not blame you. I do not think you a criminal. You are only unfortunate." No, dear Judge, it is not even that. It's our damnable economic and social iniquities, our mad world of greed and money and power; the heartless, bloody mill of commercialism that grinds the dignity and self-respect out of these unfortunates; the system you believe in and maintain, Judge Deasy, is responsible for the horrible panorama that passes you daily. You are a party to it, like the rest of your class, like everyone who is indifferent to the terrible life about him. Fat, self-satisfied, contented, narrow minded, and narrow hearted Philistines.

But the Judge was kind, so he quite won my heart. I should not have cared, were he to send me to prison. He was humane with the victims of an inhuman society.

Of course, when Anarchists were brought before Deasy, he turned to stone, becoming cold and rigid and stern. He, too, had been poisoned by the newspapers. He, too, had read that Anarchists were human beasts, forever thirsting blood and plotting murder. Little wonder that he should be prepared to use his authority to send them where they would no longer disturb the "peace" of the community.

We do not flatter ourselves to have turned Judge Deasy into an Anarchist. That would mean to make him see the criminality of his position. But we did succeed in bring a little light into his head. Light which will make him realize that the Anarchists are, indeed, dangerous; not because of their dynamite and bombs, but because they threaten every vested interest. Because they do not compromise, because they have declared war on every institution of to-day, based on hypocrisy, sham, and the destruction of life and happiness. Yes, Judge Deasy became humane even to the Anarchists. He was really fair, as fair as any one can be in the capacity of a Judge.

And the evidence? A detective who had listened to my lecture for over two hours, and could only remember me saying, "The judiciary and police take your money, that's all they do for you." Pretty good for the memory of a detective, is it not? Further, that the audience was orderly and applauded good-naturedly. That nothing violent or boisterous occurred, and so forth. "Is that all?" asked the Judge.

The prosecuting attorney, the most amusing clown in the circus, became confused, fidgety, and nervous. He finally mastered spunk enough to say, "Your Honor, I want to show that the Industrial Workers of the World is an Anarchist organization, that the members wear red shirts and neckties." Everybody in the court room leaned forward to look at the jury box. Three jurors wore red neckties. Were they too, I.W.W. members? "But what have red shirts and the I.W.W. organization to do with the defendant Emma Goldman?" asked the Judge. Nobody knew, least of all the poor little District Attorney. He sat down in despair, large drops of perspiration running down his dear little, fat pig's cheeks.

We were disgusted. Here we had prepared ourselves to meet a gladiator, but alas, it turned out a louse.

There was nothing left to do, but to instruct the jury to render a verdict of not guilty. Mr. Cameron King,[2] the partner of Mr. Kirk, delivered a beautiful address, which we hope to publish in the next issue of MOTHER EARTH. His address was intended for the Judge

---

2. Cameron Haight King (1877–1947) was a San Francisco attorney and partner of E. E. Kirk. King was chairman of the Socialist Party in California from 1918 to 1924 and editor of *Labor World,* a socialist weekly. No address or article by King was published in *Mother Earth.*

and the jury, but the logic of the law will have it that the twelve men, who have the power to rob one of his freedom, may listen to the prosecution, but must not hear the defence. Can there be more striking proof of the law's stupidity? The jurors were ordered to leave the court room, like little boys and girls are ordered out of the room, when grown-ups are talking about things which good little children must not hear.

Judge Deasy listened attentively, and seemed quite impressed by Mr. King's address. When the latter had finished, the jury was recalled, and the Judge instructed them to render a verdict of not guilty. Within a few minutes the farce was over, the clowns retired, and the circus was cleared. Of course, all other charges against Dr. Reitman and myself were dismissed.

Poor, stupid police. It was not their intention to help the cause of Anarchism to such a victory. But they did it, just the same. In appreciation thereof I suggest that we club together and buy a little dog's collar with red ribbons, for Detective Sergeant Bunner and District Attorney Ward.

Dogs are not so stupid, did you say? Quite right. Only in this case it was really a stroke of genius to arrest us, break up our meeting, club the people out of the hall. For three reasons. First, my meetings would have been a failure, because of the heavy downpour of rain. (God, in his goodness, seemed to feel that Frisco's corruption, filth, and rottenness needed a bath. It has been raining for three weeks, and if that won't wash this city clean of its sins, she is doomed to perish). Second, nothing awakens public interest so much as persecution of an idea. Third, our trial furnished us the grandest opportunity to expose the lies and rascality of the American press in general, and the San Francisco newspapers in particular; the latter positively the most rotten in the country. A victory almost worth going to prison for. However, the Anarchists are a discontented sort. That's our greatest forte. There yet remained the reinstatement of free speech, which the police attempted to throttle with the club.

Within two days the largest hall in the city was hired, and a meeting advertised: "Emma Goldman Not Guilty, Monster Reception," etc. Sunday evening, January 31st, two thousand people streamed into the hall, and Emma Goldman spoke with her soul in her mouth.

The police were there, of course; so were our attorney and stenographer, and our dear, energetic bondsman, Cassius V. Cook,[3] all ready to meet the "gentlemen of the force." But whether they had enough of the Anarchists, or whether they did not dare to act, I do not know, nor do I care. I only know that the meeting sealed our victory, and that the police must have felt like whipped curs.

Of course, I am not yet through with the Golden Gate City. I have inflicted myself on her "great hospitality" for the next four weeks. During that time I will deliver the series of lectures which the uniformed ruffians prevented two weeks ago. They have caused us a loss in actual expenses of two hundred dollars, not to mention the regular receipts.

---

3. Cassius V. Cook became secretary of the San Francisco Free Speech League, formed after EG's and BR's arrests in the city.

Some comrades have suggested that the city be sued. I know they mean well; but they seem to overlook that fact that Satan takes care of his ilk. That it would therefore be a loss of time and money on our part; besides, it were inconsistent to ask the help of the very institution we abhor more than any other—government.

The experience was, of course, costly and trying, but it was worth while, at least to me. It demonstrated the spirit of solidarity on the part of the Anarchists in this city. No matter what their differences, they all acted as one. It proved the generosity of our Los Angeles comrades, C. J. Sprading[4] and the Foresters,[5] who promptly sent the necessary bail. And, indeed, the solidarity of our comrades and friends all over the country. But the greatest joy to me during the last trouble was the staunchness of a few, who are still very young in our movement. Wm. Buwalda[6] came out of prison December 31st. When he was arrested in connection with our meetings, he was asked why he persisted in associating with such bad people as the Anarchists, or Emma Goldman. Staunch Buwalda, who had faced fire more than once in the service of that insatiable monster, Uncle Sam, waved his jailers aside and proudly declared his right to associate with whomever he pleased. I shall soon acquaint out readers with Buwalda, the man and his character. Meanwhile I ask our friends to join me in a vote of thanks to the military authorities. They have annihilated the soldier, but have given birth to a *man*. Buwalda's "case" was dismissed.

Then there is Dr. Reitman. He has been locked up many times for vagrancy. But so long as a man is not an Anarchist, he is still considered respectable. It is the Doctor's first experience to be arrested for such an awful crime as "denouncing, as unnecessary, all organized government." But he stood his ground handsomely. He is rather disappointed that he missed the chance to swing between two thieves.

Thus Anarchists came out with flying colors, and the police look as stupid as ever, and a little more.

Emma Goldman.

Mother Earth 3 (February 1909): 411–17.

4. Charles T. Sprading, Los Angeles–based libertarian and freethinker, would later edit *Liberty and The Great Libertarians,* which contained extracts of EG's *Syndicalism* (1913).
5. Perhaps Louise B. or May S. Forrester, who both lived in Los Angeles and were subscribers to *Mother Earth.* May S. Forrester's poem "War's Winecup" was published in the April 1915 issue of the magazine. Or possibly Matilda Reuben Forrester, also of Los Angeles, who in 1916, at EG's urging, helped pay the bond releasing Ricardo Flores Magón from prison while his case was on appeal.
6. William Buwalda, U.S. Army soldier, was dishonorably discharged and served time in military prison in 1908 on charges relating to his attendance at EG's lecture in San Francisco on 26 April 1908.

SIR:

I have the honor to acknowledge receipt of your letter of the 8th instant, file No. 133149–5, WRH, asking for an expression of the view of this Department as to the advisability of making Emma Goldman a party to the proceedings instituted by the Government to secure the cancelation of the certificate of naturalization which was granted Jacob Kersner, her husband.

I have noted the two memoranda accompanying your letter, but do not understand that you ask for my opinion upon the merits of the position taken in these memoranda, respectively, but simply upon the question of policy involved of making Emma Goldman a party to the said proceedings. After a consideration of the subject I doubt seriously the wisdom of taking that course. It would too obviously indicate that the ultimate design of the proceedings is not to vindicate the naturalization law, but to reach an individual, and deprive her of an asylum she now enjoys as the wife of an American citizen.

It therefore seems to me that whatever steps may ultimately be taken, as a consequence of the action of the court in this case, the wise course is to direct the activities of the Government toward the revocation of the unlawfully acquired citizenship of Jacob Kersner, solely.[1] As requested, the inclosures with your letter are herewith returned.

I HAVE THE HONOR TO BE, SIR,

YOUR OBEDIENT SERVANT,

OSCAR S. STRAUS

SECRETARY.

TDS, file #13,3149, Department of Justice, RG 60, DNA. Addressed to Hon. Charles J. Bonaparte, Attorney General. On stationery of the Department of Commerce and Labor, Office of the Secretary, Washington, D.C. A personal friend of Theodore Roosevelt, Bonaparte served as the president's attorney general from 1907 to 1909. Bonaparte advocated the death penalty for any anarchist who sought, directly or indirectly, to take a life, and whipping and imprisonment for less serious offenses, including "seditious" speeches.

1. Revocation of Jacob Kershner's citizenship could be achieved by cancellation of his certificate of citizenship, obtained at the time of his naturalization.

My dear, dear Friend.

Your letter of the 10th and check for 2.50 $ to hand. Will credit the amount, with the rest, in the March M E. I wish, I could write as inthusiastically, as I did in my last letter. But, I can not. Every little gleem of hope is covered with a black sky of disappointement and dispair, so that life seems a perfect mockery to me, at times.

I wrote you in my last, that we have gained a victory over the police, and so we have.[1] But it is beyond human power to combat the elements. It has been pouring here for weeks, with the result, that every meeting has been a complete failure. You might ask, why we did not discontinue? Did you ever observe the psychology of a gambler? He knows, he is losing, that if he goes on, it means complete distruction. But he is driven on by an ir-ristible force, until he has lost his last shirt. I am such a gambler. My tour was a failure from the beginning. But instead of returning to NY, I kept on gambling and hoping, until I have gambled away all my energy together with some of my heartsblood. I knew all along, it was insanity, I will not win out, but on I went. Every bit of hope raised my inthusiasm to the highest zenyth, when suddenly something would come along to shatter my whole system. Just think of it, after 4 months, struggle, almost superhuman struggle and suffering, I have not enough to go to NY with. Still, I have not let go, I can not let go. I have urged the comrades on to a last supreme effort, three debates for the 27 & 28th of this month. What will come of that, I do not know, not much I suppose. Well, I shall at least have the satisfaction, that I have not given up easily, a poor satisfaction when I will come to NY to burry M E, the child of blood and tears.

Life is a terrible mockery, dear friend—And yet, there is one bright spot, in all the black-ness. The consciousness of having gained, a few friends, who understand and feel with you. You are such friend, dear Meyer. When I think, I might never have gone to London Ontario and might never have met you, something grips my heart. I have not met many friends on this tour, I think, that is why, I feel so poor. This week, I have read a book, a masterpiece, that has shown me the futility of fighting single handed against a World of falsehoods and lies. The book deals with the Haymarket event, our comrades and the entire tragedy of 1887. It is the simplest, clearest, truest and most humane document, on the matter. In fact, it is greater than anything, that has been said or written about it.

---

1. On 31 January 1909, EG spoke in San Francisco to an audience estimated at 2,000 by the *San Francisco Call*. Because EG and BR had just been acquitted of charges against them from an earlier attempt to speak in the city, the San Francisco police were rendered powerless to intervene. Shapiro had written to EG and collected money from friends for her defense.

It's called the "Bomb" by Frank Harris.[2] You must read it, dear friend, write to Berkman for it, I suppose it is 1.50 $ or thereabout.

Well, I must close, I am very tired. I leave here for Los Angeles March first and will be there until the 10th,

> c/o Claude Riddle
> 622. S Broadway

after that, I do not know

Affectionately to Sophie Frederick and yourself

E

ALI, IU-U.

---

2. James Thomas (Frank) Harris (1856–1931) was an English writer, freethinker, and socialist. His novel *The Bomb* (New York: Mitchell Kennerley, 1909) claimed to present "all the facts just as they occurred" about the Haymarket explosion, although it erroneously identified Rudolph Schnaubelt as the bombthrower. Reviewed favorably by AB in the March 1909 *Mother Earth*, the novel was bitterly criticized by Lucy Parsons in later years, for its portrayal of events. Harris edited *The Fortnightly Review*, a mainstream English periodical, from 1886 to 1894 and was publisher and editor of the popular *Saturday Review* from 1894 to 1898. He claimed that in 1909 EG, after reading *The Bomb*, solicited his friendship. From 1914 on he edited *Pearson's Magazine* and supported EG's antiwar work.

DEAR MR BARRY.

I hope you have not considered me ungrateful, not having heard from me in reply to your kind letter.[1] I was terribly pressed for time before I left Frisco

I thank you very much indeed for your generosity in giving me the two weeks ad, in your paper gratis. It helped me some. You see, I have received no redress from our uniformed invaders save my right to the freedom of speech.[2] But the material loss was so great, that I literally left poorer than when I reached SF.

"Bitter against the people, who are loyal to the cause of free speech"? How should I be? Each one gives what he thinks is advisable. I only regret, that most loyal friends of freedom consider advisability before the cause itself. I am not a utilitarian, you see, the cause of free speech is more important to me than all other considerations. But, we do not all think alike, therefore can not act alike. Speaking of my ideas, which you have referred to several times. I am curious to know, if you have ever heard me expound anarchism. Or if you are conversant with anarchism. You must be, or you could not possibly say, you disapprove of E G ideas

I want to thank you also for having gone to the trouble of giving me an estimate of the cost of M E. I can not see my way of moving the magazine to the Coast. At least now the loss at SF has been too great. But if I ever do, I shall ad my little fighter to your list of publications.[3]

---

1. James H. Barry (1855–1927) was a prominent San Francisco progressive publisher and editor. His publishing house, James H. Barry Company Publishers, founded in 1878, issued many works, including Charlotte Perkins Gilman's *In This Our World, and Other Poems* (1895), *The Pacific Coast Council of Trades and Labor Federation* (1893), *The Plan of Organization of the Democratic Party in This City (San Francisco)* (1892), *The Charter of the City and County of San Francisco* (1900), and *The Missions and Missionaries of California*, 4 vols. (1908–1915). He was the founder and editor of the *San Francisco Star* (1887–1921), an influential weekly newspaper.

2. For details on EG's San Francisco free speech fight, see "Circular Letter," 26 January 1909; "On Trial," Letter to *Mother Earth*, 2 February 1909; and Letter to Meyer Shapiro, 20 February 1909, above.

3. Presumably Barry had offered to publish *Mother Earth* for EG, from San Francisco.

Mail addressed c/o. Claude Riddle

620 S. Broadway
Los Angeles Calif

will be forwarded to me.

SINCERELY

EMMA GOLDMAN

ALS,CU-B. On stationery of Arlington Hotel and Annex. Addressed "Mr James H Barry Editor. The Star San Francisco Calif".

Article in **_MOTHER EARTH_**

April 1909

The End of the Odyssey

"Perseverance and postage stamps will get any article published"—is a favorite slogan of a friend of mine.

On several occasions, when I have sent contributions to some of the leading magazines, they were returned. Indeed, it would have been nothing short of a miracle had my articles been accepted. "Progressive ideas are all right, if presented in moderate form and by respectable writers. But Emma Goldman, who is neither . . . Dear me! How can we compromise our good standing." And so I stopped wasting Perseverance and postage stamps.

However, I can bear my friend out in the truth of his claim. Perseverance is indeed a wonderful factor in helping to overcome difficulties, especially when combined with postage stamps of their equivalent.

He who travels on the wings of imagination travels far—sometimes. At least I thought so last October, when I took leave of my few but faithful friends to begin my tour around the world.

Ere I had gone very far I had occasion to verify my friend's opinion as to Perseverance and postage stamps.

In India the people are often overtaken by famine epidemics, bringing great disaster to that John Bull ridden country.[1] But how insignificant is the harm wrought by such awful outbreaks when compared to our national pest—election. Its poisonous effects are being felt at all times, but at no time does it assume such monstrous form as during a presidential campaign.[2] Electiomania, America's greatest malady, far worse and more destructive than cholera. Will medical science never invent some serum to relieve us from its ravages? Just fancy talking reason or ideas to a feverish, delirious brain.

Perseverance and postage stamps suggested that cold compresses of reason have often broken the most stubborn fever. So for a month I diligently applied the cold-cure method. By the latter part of November my methods were crowned with success. The audiences

---

1. A reference to English colonial rule, personified in the character John Bull. The figure of John Bull was introduced in eighteenth-century political pamphlets by John Arbuthnot as a satire of Whig war policy (1712) and came to represent and caricature England or the typical Englishman.
2. The 1908 presidential campaign pitted Republican candidate William Howard Taft (1857–1930) against the twice-defeated Democratic presidential candidate William Jennings Bryan (1860–1925) and the Socialist candidate Eugene Debs. Taft won the election with 51.6 percent of the popular vote and became president in 1909.

United States District Court,

Western District of New York.

The United States of America,   :

                    Complainant.   :

         vs.   :   IN EQUITY.

Jacob A. Kersner,   defendant.   :

                                 :

          The above entitled suit coming on regularly to
be heard on default of the defendant before the Court on
the 8th day of April, 1909, and the Court having heard
the proofs of allegations on the part of the complainant
and having heard the testimony of Abraham Kersner and
Simon Goldstein, on due deliberation having made and
filed its Conclusions therein, whereby the Court finds
and decides as Conclusion of Law that the complainant,
the United States of America, is entitled to judgment
setting aside and annulling the citizenship of Jacob A.
Kersner, and cancelling the certificate of citizenship
heretofore issued to Jacob A. Kersner, the said defendant,
by the County Court of Monroe County, on the 18th day of
October, 1884, on the ground that the said citizenship
and certificate of citizenship were illegally procured,
and having ordered judgment accordingly,

    IT IS ORDERED, ADJUDGED AND DECREED, that the citi-
zenship in the United States, and the certificate of citizenship heretofore issued to Jacob A. Kersner, the defendant herein, by the County Court of Monroe County,
on the 18th day of October, 1884, be, and the same is,
hereby set aside, annulled and cancelled on the ground
that the said citizenship and certificate of citizenship

U.S. District Court document, dated 8 April 1909, authorizing the annulment of citizenship of Jacob Kershner, whom Goldman had not officially divorced. The action was taken as part of an official strategy to revoke Goldman's claim to U.S. citizenship. (Department of Justice, National Archives and Records Administration)

WOMAN ANARCHIST MAY BE DEPORTED

Naturalization of Emma Goldman's Husband Illegal and Both Face Banishment

Local Manager Says Queen of the Reds Will Not Be Be Sent Away

Emma Goldman May Be Banished From Country

[*Special Dispatch to The Call*]

BUFFALO, N. Y., April 8.—Judge Hazel in the United States court this morning granted an order canceling the citizenship papers of Jacob A. Kersner. Through this order all rights of citizenship also are taken from Kersner's wife, who is Emma Goldman, the well known woman leader, so called, of the anarchists in this country, whose fiery teachings, it is charged, incited Leon Czolgosz to the assassination of President McKinley.

The order was granted upon motion of Special United States Attorney P. S. Chambers of Pittsburg, and the evidence upon which it was based was presented principally by Kersner's own father, who was subpenaed from his home in Rochester.

Kersner, it appeared, secured his citizenship documents in 1884, when the statutes governing such procedure were quite lax compared to the present law. He was two years under age at the time, being only 19 years old, and had been in this country only two years, instead of having lived here for five years, as is required by law.

Three years later he married Emma Goldman. She was a foreigner herself, but by virtue of her marriage to a citizen she was clothed with the rights of citizenship. Emma was only a girl then and had barely begun upon the career that later connected her so closely with the "reds." No defense was made to the proceedings before Judge Hazel.

The elder Kersner said that his son disappeared three years ago. Emma Goldman is believed to be in California with her supposed husband, Alexander Berkman. Attorney Chambers denied that the action was taken with a view of deporting Emma Goldman, although such is believed to be the fact.

EMMA GOLDMAN

ALEXANDER BERKMAN

Article in the 9 April 1909 *San Francisco Call,* reporting on the possibility of Goldman's deportation and suggesting that she was in California with her "supposed husband" and co-editor Alexander Berkman. They were, however, in New York at this time. (University of California, Berkeley)

began to show signs of normal temperature and an appetite for wholesome food. High-spirited and light-hearted, I swiftly moved along the route of success for MOTHER EARTH, nearing to the Pacific ocean and Australia.

But a new spectre appeared now on the firmament, black and sinister, challenging the utmost vigilance and perseverance—Christmas. What? The month of glad tidings—of peace on earth and good will to all—a spectre? yes, a hideous, black, deceiving spectre, that has held the human mind in bondage for almost two thousand years. The legend of the birth of the Redeemer, like all legends, is based on a lie. It has gone on perpetuating itself, until to-day it serves but as an excuse for commercialism, greed, and petty specula-tion. Christmas—a howling, pushing, scrambling, obsessed bargain huntress; with no interest or time for anything, least of all for Christ himself, were he to chance into the madhouse at Christmas time.

Hopes were low, and postage stamps few. But Perseverance shook his mane and cried, Onward! Nor did he relax his grasp when confronted with police brutality and persecution.

In January I reached Los Angeles, very much depressed and weary. But the balmy clime of the sunny South, coupled with the devotion and thoughtfulness of friends, rejuvenated my spirit. Comrade Claude Riddle's skillful management of my meetings did the rest. I left the Angel City relieved from a heavy burden in the form of a considerable debt, with a hundred and fifty dollars for MOTHER EARTH's friend, the enemy—our printer. But all that was as nothing compared to the hope and strength that were mine, thanks to the love and kindness of my Los Angeles friends.

San Francisco was to be my last battlefield, the date of my departure for Australia having been set for January 23rd. The comrades of that city, with Alexander Horr as prime mover, left nothing undone to insure success; but the treacherous Conspiracy of Circumstances assassinated our efforts.

The Conspiracy of Circumstances! Who does not know its power, its quiet, persistent, merciless power. Unlike a foe of flesh and blood, one cannot meet it in open battle, or even escape it. It is always with you. Never in my experience did I feel its blind, relentless fury as during my stay in San Francisco. It was this inanimate, dumb, blind force that was ever at our heels, using a thousand conceivable tricks to frustrate our every plan. More than once the Conspiracy of Circumstance was near succeeding. But Perseverance was no easy mark; especially the combined tenacity of sturdy warriors who met the enemy with unsheathed sword.

It was a desperate battle, with Perseverance as victor, the Conspiracy of Circumstance eloping with all the postage stamps. No equivalent at hand to pay transportation to Aus-tralia, there was nothing left to do but to steer back to the little home of MOTHER EARTH. But Perseverance would not yield. The South, the South! it urged. Why not?

In all my travels I had never visited the South. Somehow the very thought of it conjured up horrible pictures—pictures of little victims in the cotton fields, of bodies dangling from the trees, bodies mutilated to cinders and ashes. But when the idea of going to Texas was suggested to me, I recollected the wise saying, "He that is without sin among you, let him cast the first stone." Remembering the sweatshops of the East with its countless victims, how could I condemn the South? Mindful of the race feuds in New York City,[3] the burning of negroes in Springfield, Illinois,[4] how could I cast stones?

After visiting Los Angeles, where I had two good meetings and a debate, I proceeded to Texas. It was indeed a rich experience—though not in postage stamps.

My first stop was El Paso, a city containing, among other nationalities, thirty thousand Mexicans, whom an American administration subservient to that monster Diaz,[5] would not permit to hold public meetings addressed in Spanish. Perchance these poor victims might tell the horrors of their country, the terrible despotism, the appalling poverty, more terrible than in the domain of the Bloody Tsar.

The press of El Paso, with the exception of the *News*, thrives on the Judas Iscariot gold pieces, ground out of the Mexican peons. No wonder it was so venomous in its denunciation of Anarchism. But with all that we had one meeting in El Paso and disposed of some literature. The principle good, however, was done by the intelligent and fair editorial of the *News*, which of course would never have been written had I not visited the South.

San Antonio, the most southern city of Texas, with its lazy, quiet, and easy-going exterior, with its old market place where slaves were bought and sold (selling and buying still continues with less cost to the modern master and with the consciousness of the slave that he is now *free* to sell himself). No hall could be procured in this city, except at a very high rent, and as the outlook was not promising, we decided to hold no meeting. But some propaganda was accomplished by several decent accounts in the local newspapers of interviews.

Houston looks like the average American city, but unlike others, it can boast of a miracle: the Chief of Police and Mayor[6] offering the city Hall for a lecture by Emma Gold-

---

3. During this period in New York City, tensions between blacks, recent Italian immigrants, and whites sporadically erupted in the form of physical conflict broken up by the police and characterized by the *New York Times* as race feuds.

4. In Springfield, Illinois (home of Abraham Lincoln), in the summer of 1908, racial tensions, already high, reached a boiling point after two black men were arrested for the alleged rapes of white women. On Friday, 14 August 1908, a crowd formed outside the jail demanding that the two accused men be turned over to the lynch mob. When the men were shipped out of town for safety, a riot ensued lasting three days. Two black men were killed, including William Donnegan, a longtime Springfield resident, known to have been Abraham Lincoln's friend and cobbler. The "Badlands," Springfield's African-American neighborhood, was burned to the ground and its residents forced to flee the city. The National Guard was called in and order restored by Monday, 17 August. In the aftermath newspapers published many stories of liberal protest against the brutal riot, including the 3 September 1908 article in *The Independent* by William English Walling, entitled "Race War in the North," in which he asks "who realizes the seriousness of the situation, and what large and powerful body of citizens is ready to come to their aid?" Walling's article was instrumental in the formation of the National Association for the Advancement of Colored People (NAACP), whose founding members included Jane Addams, Louis Post, Lincoln Steffens, Lillian Wald, J. G. Phelps Stokes, William Lloyd Garrison, and W. E. B. DuBois, among others.

5. EG refers to Porfirio Díaz (1830–1915), who was president of Mexico from 1877 to 1880 and again from 1884 to 1911.

6. H. Baldwin Rice was mayor of Houston in 1896, and again in 1905 and 1912.

man. Who can say that the twentieth century lacks wonders? Having enjoyed the hospitality of the police so often without my consent, I could not accept their offer voluntarily. We secured a hall from some Catholic order, but when it became known that I would speak, the brethren thought Satan broke loose. Terror-stricken, they sent a committee to pay all our expenses and begged to be released from their contract. Who ever heard of a Catholic bargain with Hell?

For a time it looked as if Houston, too, would remain in darkness as to the real meaning of Anarchism. But, thanks to a few brave Houstonians, that city has now some excuse for being on the map. A group of Single Taxers came to our rescue in the freest and kindest spirit. The Single Tax "Log Cabin," donated by one of their comrades, Mr. J. J. Pastoriza,[7] an extraordinary man in many respects, was turned over to our use. The Cabin is on the outskirts of the city, crude and rugged, with a romantic air about it, to satisfy the most poetic imagination. With lamps dimly lighting the place, and the men and women closely pressed together, it was nevertheless the most inspiring meeting of my entire tour. When I looked into the earnest faces, so near that I could almost touch them, I forgot the hardships of the past and the disappointments of the future—all I felt was the warm pulse of humanity, a rich, great, beautiful possibility of human brotherhood.

Man is greater than all theory. It is therefore of little moment whether Single Tax, economically, is but a petty reform and that, politically, it is hanging on the coat-tails of the Democratic party. As men I have found them the bravest and staunchest champions of liberty in the widest sense. And that is a great deal more than can be said of the party which has a mortgage on "scientific" Socialism, with a premium on the densest kind of stupidity. Its cowardice of authority and intolerance of everything not baptized in the holy church of Marxian-Engels rites, are really sickening. Of course, there are exceptions, but they merely prove the rule. The few Socialists of independent mind and spirit are not very long tolerated by the Holy Synod.

With two meetings in Fort Worth I closed the tour of Golgotha, and reached New York nailed to the cross of necessity.

Reviewing the struggle of the last six months, I can say that but for Perseverance it would have been impossible. But it was not that alone. My friends and comrades have a big share in the accomplished feat. Especially is this true of the San Francisco and Los Angeles comrades, whose efforts were truly heroic. By that I do not mean to undervalue the assistance of comrades in other cities. Indeed not. Everyone helped in his own way. The way may not always have been the right one, but that is only because most of our comrades make up in idealism what they lack in practical judgment.

However, more than anything else, the unfaltering optimism, the great zeal, and the cheerful bohemianism of our friend, Ben L. Reitman, helped to conquer many obstacles.

---

7. Single-taxer J. J. Pastoriza served as Houston's city finance and tax commissioner and as mayor of Houston in 1917. He introduced the Houston Plan of Taxation, a limited application of the single tax. He was also wrote *Souvenir of the Galveston Storm* (Houston: J. J. Pastoriza Printing, 1900).

My tour to Australia is not abandoned; only postponed[8]—until I can discover the eloped postage stamps. That I do not lack Perseverance our readers know. Meanwhile I shall deliver a series of lectures in New York, the first to take place Sunday, April 11, 11 a. m., at Lyric Hall, Sixth avenue, near Forty-second street.

The subject of my first lecture will be: "The Psychology of Violence."[9]

The series will be continued during April and May, the lectures to take place Sunday mornings at Fraternity Hall, 100 West 116th street, corner of Lenox avenue, New York.

Mother Earth 3 (April 1909): 47–51.

8. EG may have canceled her Australia tour for lack of funds or because of the threat to her citizenship due to the government's decision to revoke Jacob Kershner's citizenship.
9. Presumably this speech was a version of EG's "The Psychology of Political Violence," later published in *Anarchism and Other Essays* (1910).

LOVER MINE.

Your short note of the 12th and Special of the 13th came together, this morning.

I suppose my letter was delayed because you moved. It should have reached you early yesterday. I hope you got it. I am writing you every day, dear and the day I pass by, I make up by sending the letter Special. I know the agony of waiting how then, would I cause my treasure agony?

If ever I reach the stage that your "moods" I call them stunts, won't make me unhappy, you dearest will be the last person on Earth to rejoice over it. It will only be, when I no longer care for you, or have grown indifferent. Would you want such a moment to come? As long as I love you and care for you hobo, I will suffer over many things you do. I do not believe in the story, that love is blind. I hold that a truly great love sees with a thousand eyes. At any rate, my love watches, and when it detects a speck on the beautiful sky of its aspiration it weeps, tears of blood. Yes, I shall always endure great tortures over some of your traits. I am not foolish to believe or belie myself, that you and I can or will live a harmonious and unruffled lifes—But with all that, I want you, lover dear. A It is a week love indeed that lives, only because it has nothing to content against, when everything is smooth and nice and comfortable. 9 such loves out of ten are of that kind. They die an easy death, at the slightest obstacle. Would you be satisfied with such a love dear, would you? If not, then do not expect Momy to be happy, when her boy has obsessions that pierce her soul. No doubt you can not help your moods, nor can I help my aversion to some of them. I know dearest, you want to make me happy. Dear, if you would so completely satisfy my mind or tastes as you do the t b[1]—I think one could not live—besides the love and passion you gave me dearest consumes me so. I do not care for anything else. Sweetheart, I do not expect you to be conventional, I am too much opposed to that. But you confound estheticism with conventions. Something maybe repulsive to me, not because it lacks conventionality, but because it lacks grace or cleanelyness. You see the difference, dearie? Why should you keep away from the unemployed meetings. Personally, I can not see, how you can work together with Howe,[2] when you have realized, that

---

1. In her letters to Ben Reitman, EG referred to her vagina as "treasure box" or "t b."
2. James Eads How (1874–1930) was an American socialist known as the "hobo millionaire." How founded the International Brotherhood Welfare Association, a union for migratory workers, with local branches known as hobo colleges. The colleges served both as an employment service and a free educational forum, where men could learn about labor, economics, political systems, industrial law, and hear lectures on socialism and anarchism. In 1907, How asked BR to start a local chapter of the association

he is only hurting instead of helping the unemployed. You yourself criticise him for his silly reforms, you no longer believe in them, or do you still? However once you have accepted the delegations, I want you to attend their meetings. You can come to the M E Ball late, as it is an all night affaire.[3] One thing, if the Chicag organization elected you dearest it ought to pay your fare.[4] How is that force practiced sweetheart—

Ben dear, do not worry as to what other say or think about you being dependent on me and M E. They give nothing to the magazine and even less to me, so why should we worry.

The only thing that worrys me dear, is that we will probably have very little to live on. Literally nothing comes in for M E. My only hope lies in the meetings. If they too fail, we will have a hard Summer. But if I have your love and devotion, we will pull through, I am sure. I would rather eat one meal a day with you than Champaign feasts without you. Besides, do not imagine, I am going to keep you near me long enough to tire of me. I am planing a short lecture tour through Massachusettes and Connecticut between the middle of May and June.[5] Of course, I want you to do advance work there, will you? Also, you will have work to do for my meetings here. Yesterday, I have been asked to debate either with Hanford[6] or Hilquit.[7] I have consented making 50.00 my condition. A girls Union is arranging it. As soon as they get the Hall, they will let me know.[8] So you see, there is work awaiting you not only love—I too wish, you could get something to do outside of my meetings, not for my sake, or because you are a burden to me. Oh dear no, for your own sake precious hobo mine, it would make you feel better. Dearest, if you could earn your fare to NY I would rather keep the money I had intended for it, for a suit for you and the fixing up of our room. Please dear, do not misunderstand your Momy, just tell me, if you can earn or get your fare. This will reach you Friday, you might wire me, if you can not get it. If you can, you need not wire, only be sure to let me know the exact day of your arrival. You will arrange to come next Wednesday won't you dearest. I am sorry that I can not come to stay with you in Chicago, now that you have an office. But since I can not lecture there, with be sure to starve until you work up a practice wouldn't we. And your mother will she not be up to a higher rent now?

in Chicago. How published the official organ of the International Brotherhood Welfare Association, *The Hoboes Jungle Scout* (1913–1915), later renamed *Hobo News* (1915–1923).

3. The Mother Earth Ball was held on 1 May 1909, at the Terrace Lyceum in New York. EG was scheduled to speak and Sadakichi Hartmann and others were scheduled to perform.
4. EG refers to the Chicago branch of the International Brotherhood Welfare Association.
5. On 14 May 1909, in New Haven, Connecticut, the police allowed EG into the hall but denied admittance to her audience. In late August and early September, she toured parts of Massachusetts.
6. Benjamin Hanford (1861–1910) was a New York–based socialist printer and Socialist candidate for vice president of the United States with presidential candidate Eugene Debs in 1904 and 1908, as well as a member of the 1909 Free Speech Committee. His works include *Railroading in the United States* (New York: Socialist Co-operative Publishing Association, 1901), *The Labor War in Colorado* (New York: Socialist Co-operative Publishing Association, 1904), and *Fight for Your Life* (New York: Wilshire, 1909).
7. Morris Hillquit was a founding member of the Socialist Party of America.
8. There is no record of this debate.

Do the m— miss you? Wait until you see them and you will know. Why they are famished— They do not want deamons and trinkets, they want your touch, your magic maddning touch—

The t b refuses to be petted gently or by me — Don't you know, what she craves, and crys for, don't you? We haven't the means of the lovers in Three Weeks but we have even a great love, so why care[9]

Is hobo waiting for t b—really, has he? Oh, she will reward him a thousand fold, a million times. Hobo, my hobo, I am ready to have you right now, but I have not a place yet and I can not get one this week. It is no easy task to wait my own, every day, I catch myself wanting to wire you, to call you. I want you terribly. But you must keep you date with the Edelstadt people[10] and it is no use to come Sunday, as I speak three times on that day. Also, I know you have wanted to see Hapgood[11]—I will be patient until next Wednesday, but no longer, dear. Monday I will look for a room where I can hide with hobo in a new beautiful World—

I may get an order from The World for an article. I hope so. Grace[12] came to tell me, but I was out, will see her in the morning—

Just a week from today and I shall have my hobo, my own, my all, I love so madly.

MOMMY

ALS, IU-U. On *Mother Earth* stationery.

9. A reference to Elinor Glyn's novel *Three Weeks* (New York: Macaulay, 1907), in which an Englishman and a woman from a Balkan royal family share three weeks of uninterrupted lovemaking; see also note 10, p. 388 above.
10. EG refers to the Edelstadt Group, in Chicago.
11. Hutchins Hapgood was an author, journalist, and social critic who occasionally contributed to *Mother Earth*.
12. Probably a reference to Grace Potter, a New York social worker, and, later, Freudian psychoanalyst, as well as a staff journalist of the *New York World* during this period. She was secretary of the 1909 Free Speech Committee, member of the Free Speech League, and participated in the first New York protest meeting against the death sentence for Kōtoku Shūsui and other Japanese anarchists and socialists on 12 December 1910. Potter was married to Ernest Holcombe, president of the Liberal Club on MacDougal Street in Greenwich Village, and she was a member of the Heterodoxy Club. She contributed articles to the *New York Call* in support of the striking shirtwaist makers in 1909, as well as to *Everyman, Physical Culture,* and *Mother Earth,* including its inaugural issue (March 1906). Her article *What We Did to Bernard Carlin* (Hillacre, Riverside, Conn.: Private Print, 1912), a polemic against capital punishment, was first published in *Mother Earth* (June 1909).

Essay in *MOTHER EARTH*

May 1909

A Woman Without a Country

The United States government in a mad chase after Emma Goldman.

What a significant title for a funny story. What rich material for a cartoon!

By the decision of the Federal government,[1] Emma Goldman, the terrible, may now be deported. Well, serves her right. What on earth made her select our dear country, anyway? It's different with us Americans. We are here through no fault of ours. But for her to come voluntarily, to live here twenty-five years, and to go on as if she were at home—that is strong, indeed!

What didn't our government do to get rid of her?! For seventeen years the police have camped on her trail; her meetings were broken up; her audiences clubbed innumerable times, but that didn't seem to help. Then she was arrested again and again—not for what she said, but for what she was going to say. Why, she was actually sentenced to Blackwell's Island penitentiary once, for inciting to riot which didn't take place, but which might have taken place.[2] Well, what happened? When she came out, she was worse than ever. In 1901 she was held under twenty thousand dollars bail,[3] while our poor government spent thirty thousand dollars to connect her with McKinley's death.[4] In short, every conceivable method was used to relieve the anxiety of the United States government. But that woman simply sticks and sticks. However, if there is anything Uncle Sam cannot do, we should like to know it. Hasn't he men in the secret service patriotic enough to do any kind of a dirty job for money? Well, we sent some of them to a city called Rochester, where, many years ago, a man had the misfortune to marry that there Emma Goldman. He was a good man, you know; for no American citizen can be a very bad man. But that marriage was a blotch on his citizenship. So, out of Christian kindness and American loyalty, his naturalization papers were annulled.[5] Wasn't that a clever idea? Of course, it cost quite

---

1. A reference to the revocation of Jacob A. Kershner's citizenship on 8 April 1909 (see note 5, below).
2. EG was arrested on 31 August 1893, on charges of incitement to riot, found guilty, and sentenced to one year at the penitentiary on Blackwell's Island. For the details of EG's arrest and imprisonment, see vol. 1, "The Law's Limit," Article in the *New York World*, 17 October 1893.
3. The amount of EG's bail was reported in *New York Times*, 19 September 1901.
4. EG was accused of "inspiring" Leon Czolgosz's assassination of President McKinley and arrested on 10 September 1901. For details of government and press efforts to tie her to the assassination, see vol. 1, "Assassin's Trail of Crime from Chicago to Pacific Coast," Article in the *San Francisco Chronicle*, 8 September 1901.
5. On 8 April 1909, the citizenship of EG's husband, Jacob A. Kershner, was annulled, with no conclusive evidence to support the grounds that at the time of his application for citizenship he was not yet

Department of Justice.

Office of
Assistant United States Attorney,
Federal Building,
Pittsburg, Pa.

226-30

April 22, 1909.

The Attorney General,

Washington, D. C.

Sir:

I have the honor to report that judgment was given for the
United States on April 8th in the case of United States vs.
Jacob Kersner, No. 133149-1. This is the suit which was
entered for the purpose of depriving Emma Goldman of her
rights of citizenship, she being the wife of Kersner. By
some oversight I neglected to send in this report earlier.

Respectfully,

P. Chambers,

Assistant United States Attorney.

Letter dated 22 April 1909 to the U.S. Attorney General from the assistant U.S. attorney in Pittsburgh, Pennsylvania, reported that Jacob Kershner's citizenship had been revoked. The letter explicitly acknowledged that this action was undertaken by the U.S. government for the "purpose of depriving Emma Goldman of her rights of citizenship." (Department of Justice, National Archives and Records Administration)

a lot. Some people in Rochester had to be cajoled, intimidated, threatened, frightened, and possibly bribed. But it was done all right, and the country might now breathe easy if—but there is Emma Goldman, still enjoying *our* air, looking at *our* sky, counting *our* stars, basking in *our* sun, and dreaming un-American dreams,—can there be a greater indictment against any human being? Not enough of that, she actually disbelieves in our or any government, and insists that they are only here to divide human interests. She attacks the entire system; she will have it that it is a life-and-soul-destroying mechanism, and that it strips man of the finest and best in him.

Did anyone ever hear of such treason?

Were she an American citizen, we might some day hang or electrocute her. But an alien—what's left for us to do but to deport her. The trouble is, where, oh where can we send her?

Poor, poor United States government! Yours is, indeed, a difficult task. True, your hard, persistent labors have been crowned with some success. You have Emma Goldman's citizenship. But she has the world, and her heritage is the kinship of brave spirits—not a bad bargain.

EMMA GOLDMAN.

Mother Earth 4 (May 1909): 81–82.

---

twenty-one and had not been in the United States for five years as he had claimed. Kershner was targeted for denaturalization to make EG, his former wife, vulnerable to deportation. *United States v. Jacob A. Kersner:* Bill of Complaint, 24 Sept. 1908; *United States v. Jacob A. Kersner:* Findings, 8 April 1909, Palmer S. Chambers to Charles J. Bonaparte, 22 April 1909, *EGP*, reel 56.

MY DEAR LABADIE.

Baginski[1] tells me that you have a letter from Henry George. I am now having a controversy with a single taxer anent Georges action in the case of our Chicago boys.[2] As that was before I entered the movement I relied principally on Tuckers reference to George.[3] Now, that I have heard of the letter in your possession, I am anxious to know its nature. Can you not send me a copy? You will greatly oblige me and help clear up some of my doubts.

The police all over the country are pressing closer on my work. Last week my lectures were stopped in New Haven.[4] In NY the hallkeepers have been terrorized to the extent of refusing me their premises. Yet, free speech is suppod to exist.

Let me hear from you soon

SINCERELY. E GOLDMAN

ALS, Joseph A. Labadie Papers, MiU.

1. EG refers to Max Baginski, her co-founder of *Mother Earth*.
2. One month before the election for secretary of state in New York, candidate Henry George wrote an editorial for the *Standard* (a New York weekly he had established in January 1887) in which he claimed that the Illinois Supreme Court's conviction of the Haymarket anarchists was valid. George, who had previously defended the anarchists, was labeled a traitor by those who sympathized with the Haymarket defendants, including EG. According to the New York *Leader,* George, if he had chosen to, could have taken this opportunity to publicly redeem the memory of the anarchists as martyrs. Critics suspected that his retraction of support was motivated solely by pressures to gain Catholic and middle-class votes.
3. In the 5 January 1889 issue of *Liberty*, Benjamin Tucker denounced George for changing his position regarding the Haymarket anarchists: "It is too late in the day, Mr. George, for you to pose as a champion of freedom of speech. You once had a chance to vindicate that cause such as comes to a man but once in a lifetime, and in the trial hour you not only failed the cause, but betrayed it. . . . We have known you, Henry George, in the past, and we know you for the future. The lamp holds out to burn, but for no such vile sinner as yourself."
4. On 14 May 1909, EG was scheduled to speak in New Haven but the police, while allowing her admission to the building, barred the audience from entering.

To CHARLES ERSKINE SCOTT WOOD

New York, 19 May 1909

MY DEAR MR WOOD

I have your letter of the 6th, also a short note received to day. I am being so terribly har-rassed and pressed, by the authorities, that I have not much time left, to think or write. Within a few days my lectures were stopped in New Haven Conn, in New York city several times.[1] Evidently the police are determined to drive me to more <u>drastic methods</u> and if they keep on they may succeed.————————

I am inclosing a clipping from the New Haven Union, the only paper that had decency enough to sencure the Chief for his arbitrary interference. But, even that did no good. Not a soul came forward to offer assistance and as the expenses of arranging the meetings came to over 45$, I could not invest another sou in starting a legal fight. In NY, the police have kept up the chase for 3 years, intimidating one hall owner after another. One man, stood by us, but even he, had to submit to the inexorable. They threatened to arrest the man and send him away for 5 years. So great is the ~~police~~ power of headquarters, that when we asked the owner to sign an affidavit, that he was threatened, he refused, saying "Miss G that would mean ruin to me." Under the circumstances we could not apply for an injunction, as we had intended. If I am to be chased into silence in this country, I see no use fighting deportation. After all, I would have more Freedom anywhere in the World, don't you think so?

The most painful side of this percecution, is, the indifference of the liberal element in America. Nobody seems to care, just so they are not bothered.

I thought you knew, that the Federal authorities expatriated my husband.[2] They worked on that two years and succeeded, of course. They claim Kersner got citizenship fraudulently,[3] but that of course, is nonsense. First, of all the various states were not so particular 25 years ago, citizenship could be obtained easily. 2) The Federal authorities

---

1. EG was scheduled to speak in New Haven, Connecticut, on 14 May 1909, on "Anarchy: What It Stands For." She was admitted into the hall by the police, who then refused to allow anyone else to enter. She was also barred from speaking in New York on 23 May when police stopped a morning lecture, arguing that she had strayed from the announced topic. When she returned in the afternoon to speak, the police barred all access to the hall. These and other events during the spring of 1909 led to the formation of the Free Speech Committee.

2. Jacob Kershner, EG's first husband. Russian-born, he settled in Rochester, N.Y., and worked as a tailor. He and EG were married in 1887; they divorced and then remarried in 1888.

3. In 1884, based on the belief that Kershner was born on 1 April 1863 and that he had lived in the country since 1879, the U.S. government granted him citizenship. In 1908, the government initiated an inquiry regarding the legitimacy of Kershner's naturalization, "for the purpose of depriving Emma Goldman of her rights of citizenship." Although Kershner never appeared in court to defend himself and the evidence does not offer a consistent date of birth or emigration, Judge John R. Hazel concluded that

must have been aware of Kersners rights, why did they wait so long? 3) Why did it take them 2 years to reverse his papers? Simply, they had to get someone willing to swear to Kersners fraudulancy, which they did, in his parents——

If the man himself could be located, it might not be hard to prove the conspiracy. But we have no idea where he is. I have heard nothing from him for 16 years. No one else seems to know so here we are, simply helpless. I hear that my case is in the hands of the Attorney General. He is to decide, whether or not, my visit to Canada constitutes legal grounds for my deportation.[4] If it does not, I will probably not be bothered, as long as I remain in America. Should I go out, I could not return, that is certain. If any attempt to deport me is made, I shall fight it of course, not so much because I am eager to remain in this "blessed land—I will keep you posted. As, I have said, I would very much like you to represent me before the higher courts, should it be necessary. But, ~~of course~~ I do not want to inconvinience you in any way. ~~But~~ We can see about that later.

It will probably surprise you to know, that I have considered your suggestion long before you made it. In fact, I have collected the necessary data, as to what state one can obtain a divorce, easiest. You see, I have to go through that stupid formality, before I can undertake the other. I never have been divorced—

I can assure you, it is not an easy step for me. I have attacked that infernal institution all my life, since I begain independ thinking. To make such a concession now is very painful to me. But would not fighting deportation also be a concession? Well, I have considered divorce and remarriage. But here comes the difficulty. I can issue a call for financial assistance to fight deportation, but I can not ask the radical public to help me to a divorce, can I? I must go to some State where 6 months residents is necessary. I must keep quiet and in the background during that time. That means to withdraw all support from ME. It means, that I must save 4- 500$ to live and cover legal expenses. Where am I to get them? As you see, Mr Wood, one's life may sometimes reach the point to make an honorable death preferable. Have I gotten there? I don't know, I only know I am pretty desperate.

I am glad you enjoyed my review of the "Easiest Way"[5] I wish I could do more in that line. I am very fond of the drama. But who would take anything from E G?

Sincerely

Emma Goldman

ALS, Charles Erskine Scott Wood Papers, CU-B. On *Mother Earth* stationery. With enclosure addressed to "Kittie." The enclosure to Kathyrn Beck, Wood's secretary, summarized the letter sent to Wood.

Kershner was born in 1865, emigrated to the United States in 1882, and was therefore underage and had lived in this country less than the required five years when he was granted citizenship. On 9 April 1908, Jacob Kershner's citizenship was revoked, thereby nullifying EG's citizenship as well. This ruling would become a central issue in EG's deportation in 1919. See also *EGP*, reels 56 and 62.

4. See the government's questioning of EG at the Canadian border, "Excerpts from Examination of Emma Goldman before Board of Special Inquiry," 8 April 1908, above.

5. *The Easiest Way*, a drama by Eugene Walter, premiered in New York City on 19 January 1909. EG's review appeared in the May 1909 issue of *Mother Earth;* she called the play "the first American work of real dramatic art."

Interview in the *NEW YORK TIMES*

New York, 30 May 1909

An Interview with Emma Goldman

Character Study by One Who Had Never Seen or Heard Her Before.

What She is Like and What She Believes.

Ibsen and Hauptmann Used in Her Lectures.

By Charles Willis Thompson.

"And that," said the lecturer, who had been talking about five minutes, "is the impression which any one will get by either reading or hearing a drama by Hauptmann, let us say, or Sudermann."

The alert sleuth in citizen's clothes, who had been sent to the meeting to repress the first utterance that tended to provoke a breach of the peace, nudged his neighbor.[1]

"Say," he asked in a whisper, "who's them—Hauptmann and Sudermann?"

"Oh, some of them Anarchists," was the reply.[2]

"I'll give her another chance," muttered the Sherlock Holmes who had been assigned to prevent Emma Goldman from starting a revolution. "I'm here to quell a riot, but I don't want to be unfair. If she makes another break like that though, out she goes." And he composed himself to listen.

"And as for Ibsen,"[3] Miss Goldman was saying. That was enough. Central Office Detective Rafsky—for it was he—strode to the front, quelled Miss Goldman, and chased the crowd into the street. Some of them said they had paid money to hear the lecture, and had only had a chance to hear about ten sentences, and wanted their money back. Central Office Detective Rafsky summoned the reserves, and the next morning the newspapers announced that the dangerous Anarchist and riot inciter, Emma Goldman, had been suppressed in the nick of time by the fidelity and courage of Old Sleuth Rafsky.

---

1. On 23 May EG was scheduled to speak on "Modern Drama: The Strongest Disseminator of Radical Thought" at Lexington Hall in New York City but, according to police, did not stick to the subject, giving them the right to break up the meeting of 200 persons, dispersing 1,000 people outside of the hall. Becky Edelsohn and Leopold Bergman were arrested and charged with disorderly conduct. EG returned in the afternoon and attempted to deliver her lecture, but the police denied all access to the hall and cleared the street with their clubs.

2. Gerhardt Hauptmann (1862–1946) was a Silesian (now Poland) writer and playwright. Hermann Sudermann (1857–1928) was a German dramatist and novelist.

3. EG refers to popular and controversial Norwegian playwright Henrik Ibsen.

To the average newspaper reader Emma Goldman is a red spectre, a wild-eyed inciter of violence, shrieking madly against government, and getting weak-minded folks to kill Kings. The real Emma Goldman is a well-read, intellectual woman with a theory of society not very different from that entertained by a lot of college professors who can talk without danger of police interference, and her way of preaching it is serious, sensible, and quiet.

What sort of a woman is Emma Goldman?

The interview with her, given in this article, will serve in large measure to answer the question.

Some of the stories that have been printed about her call her a "little woman." She is short, but not "little" as women go. They describe her with unnecessary emphasis as a "Russian Jewess."[4] She is that, but there is so little of either the Russian or the Jewess about her looks that if he was introduced to you as a descendant of John Alden or Miles Standish,[5] you would not be able to detect the fraud. A high, broad brow, clear, earnest eyes, a frank and honest face, a firm mouth that has elements of sweetness and nobility in it, and a manner that is fascinating without trying to be—that is the physical and exterior make-up of Emma Goldman.

As for the rest of it—what does she teach? What are these deadly doctrines for the preaching of which the police have to intervene and protect the audience?

A reporter of *The New York Times* asked Miss Goldman that question. "Do you know William Marion Reedy?" she asked.

The reporter confessed that he did.

"Well," she said, "here is what he said about me in *The St. Louis Mirror*. I am willing to stand by that."

Here is what Mr. Reedy wrote about Miss Goldman's beliefs:

"Law is nothing but the tryanny of a King here, an Emperor there, a Parliament in another place, a majority everywhere. No man has a right to prescribe for another, or to proscribe another. No one has a right to punish another. No one will injure another in the time to be when laws and institutions, being removed, shall cease to distort the mind and abort the spirit. Parties are a superstition.

"This is Emma Goldman's gospel. Is it ugly or brutal or ignorant or vicious? It is not. It is an aspiration toward and an effort for the perfection of humanity.

There is nothing wrong with Miss Goldman's gospel that I can see, except this: she is about 8,000 years ahead of her age. Her vision is the vision of every truly great-minded man or woman who has ever lived."[6]

---

4. There is no extant evidence to show that newspapers in 1909 placed an inordinate amount of emphasis on EG's ethnicity. William Marion Reedy affectionately described EG as a "Russian Jewess" in his article "Emma Goldman: The Daughter of the Dream," first published in the *St. Louis Mirror* on 5 November 1908. EG quotes Reedy's remarks about her later in this interview.

5. John Alden (ca. 1599–1687) and Myles Standish (ca. 1584–1656) were both *Mayflower* pilgrims and Plymouth Colony founders.

6. This extract is from Reedy's favorable 1908 article about EG. In the original article, Reedy described EG's vision as that of every truly "great-souled" man or woman, not "great-minded."

"What were you saying when Rafsky stopped you?" she was asked.

"The subject of my lecture," she said, "had to do with the drama as a disseminator of advanced thought. I intended to show that the drama, more than any other vehicle of human expression, sows the seeds of radicalism.[7] To prove that contention I had a number of illustrations ready, showing how new ideas had been propagated through the playhouse. I was trying to show—or would have tried to show, if I had had a chance—that persons who had never been interested in radicalism, who had believed, as unfortunately most persons do in this country, that such ideas are entertained only by the discontented and the hungry, received their first hints of the real importance of social studies from the writings of such dramatists, let us say, as Hauptmann and Sudermann, or from such plays as 'Ghosts' and 'A Doll's House.'[8]

"At the moment that Rafsky thought I was disturbing the peace and interrupted me I was discussing an article written by Wakeley,[9] arguing that in course of time the drama would disappear altogether, because it was impossible to depict the experiences of a lifetime in a performance of two hours. On the subject I was saying that the drama was bound to be the best possible expositor of an idea because an idea expressed through it has a double expression—first, the intellectual, that made manifest through the mind of the dramatist, and, secondly, the psychological, that through the interpreter, the actor—and I was illustrating it by references to Ibsen when Mr. Rafsky decided that I was inciting to riot."

Miss Goldman has a sense of humor. Every time she referred to Rafsky a quiet smile stirred her face. But there was no resentment, no ill-humor.

"What are the titles of your lectures?"

"'The Easiest Way,' 'Minorities Versus Majorities,' and 'Anarchism and What It Really Is,'" she answered. "The first deals with Eugene Walter's play and seems to be the most popular.[10] My first lecture in New York this season was delivered April 11. I must say that the police of that precinct were very decent, but the Headquarters police were there, and they notified the proprietor of the hall that I must not be allowed to speak again.[11]

"After that we had more trouble with the police, but when I made my contract for

---

7. EG's lecture series on modern drama were published as *The Social Significance of the Modern Drama* (Boston: Badger, 1914).

8. EG refers to Ibsen's plays *Ghosts* (1881) and *A Doll's House* (1879).

9. EG refers to an article by the London *Times* theater critic Arthur Bingham Walkley (1855–1926), later published in his book *Drama and Life* (London: Methuen, 1907 and New York: Brentano's, 1908).

10. *The Easiest Way,* by the American playwright Eugene Walter (1874–1941), described the relationship between a chorus girl and her producer, who maintained her career in return for sexual favors. On a trip the woman falls in love with a young reporter who promises to marry her when he has made his fortune but asks that she promise to end her relationship with her producer. She agrees but in the end returns to the producer and his wealth. The play opened on Broadway in January 1909. EG's speeches "Minorities versus Majorities" and "Anarchism and What It Really Is" (reworked as "Anarchism: What It Really Stands For") appeared in her 1910 book *Anarchism and Other Essays,* published by Mother Earth Publishing Association.

11. EG delivered the first lecture of her Sunday lecture series on "The Psychology of Violence" at Lyric Hall (Sixth Avenue, near 42nd Street) in New York City on 11 April. The following Sunday she moved her lecture to Fraternity Hall (100 West 116th Street, on the corner of Lenox Avenue).

lectures in Lexington Hall the police and the proprietor were perfectly well aware of who I was and what lectures I was going to delivers. Not less than 12,000 circulars advertising the lectures had been distributed and the police had no excuse for not knowing the circumstances.

"The police never addressed themselves to me, but they went to Wasserman, the owner of the hall, and threatened him with the criminal Anarchy law of this State, which makes it an offense for a hall keeper to rent it to any one who will propagate 'criminal Anarchy.'

"What is 'criminal Anarchy?'" she was asked.

"It has never been defined," she said with a smile.[12] "It never will be defined, because there is no such thing in existence. No Anarchist gets up on the platform and propagates assassination, and if he doesn't the idea of such a law is an absurdity. However, the thing is even more ridiculous than that, for in order to know whether or not one is going to advocate assassination you must first let him speak. If you are a hall keeper, you can't reasonably refuse to let a speaker have your hall to advocate 'criminal Anarchy,' because you can't tell whether he is advocating it or not until after you have heard him speak.

"At any rate, I had not talked more than five minutes before Rafsky came up to me and told me that the proprietor of the hall didn't want me to talk any longer. I replied that I and not the proprietor was entitled to the use of the hall, because I had paid for it. Rafsky went out and came back with some policeman from Headquarters, and cleared the hall in five minutes. The audience didn't want to go—it was not a Jewish audience, but an American audience, and knew its rights. It had to, though. I expected an arrest, and remained on the platform after the audience went out, but they didn't arrest me." She said that in a matter-of-fact sort of way, as though an arrest for talking about Ibsen were an every-day matter with her. It isn't though. She has only been imprisoned once in America, though the popular impression is that prison fare is her daily bread. She served time in 1893 but that was the only occasion.[13]

It is difficult to give an idea of the impression made by hearing an intelligent, ladylike, womanly woman of Emma Goldman's sort talk in such a tranquil way about arrest and imprisonment, as if it were an ordinary and expected incident of daily life. It is just about as it would be if some lady of your acquaintance started that topic at a progressive euchre party.[14]

"Did you ever advocate violence!" she was asked.

12. The Criminal Anarchy Act was passed in New York on 3 April 1902, following the McKinley assassination. One section made it a felony for owners and managers of halls to allow their premises to be used for assemblages of anarchists. The offense was punishable by up to two years imprisonment, or by a fine not exceeding two thousand dollars, or both. The Criminal Anarchy Act defined criminal anarchy as "the doctrine that organized government should be overthrown by force or violence, or by assassination of the executive head or of any of the executive officials of government, or by any unlawful means. The advocacy of such a doctrine either by word of mouth or writing is a felony."

13. EG served ten months of a one-year sentence at Blackwell's Island prison from October 1893 to August 1894, having been found guilty of "inciting to riot" after speaking at an unemployment meeting in August 1893.

14. Euchre is a card game.

"No," she said, but in the same matter-of-fact way—no one can doubt that if Emma Goldman advocated violence she would announce it and accept the responsibility for it, for there is not an atom of sham in her make-up.[15] "One of the first lectures I delivered was on 'The Psychology of Violence,' because I wanted to show that acts of violence had very little to do with any philosophy of life."[16]

Just imagine Rafsky hearing that sentence and trying to figure out what it meant. Why, he'd arrest her in a minute.

"I wanted to show," she went on, "that such acts proceed from several conditions. First, of course, is the psychology of the individual himself, as shown, for instance, in abnormal sensitiveness to a great wrong. Secondly, there is the great pressure, economic or social, and thirdly—which I consider the most important factor—the feeling resulting from the bitter opposition which every new idea meets."

"But is Anarchism, as you teach it, a thing which has to do with violence?" she was asked.

"Violence," Miss Goldman said, "has nothing whatever to do with the philosophy of Anarchism."

And she went on to illustrate, to say that if a man threw a bomb because he believed in prohibition, or civil service reform, or the Emmanuel movement,[17] it would not be charged against the principle that the man believed in; but that every time a man who happened to believe in Anarchism threw a bomb or fired a pistol, that was charged up against the thing he happened to believe in. Lots of us think that Anarchism is a philosophy, and bomb throwing is just such an incident as might happen to any doctrine, from Methodism to Kneipp cure;[18] anyway, it has nothing to do with the doctrine.

"What did you serve time for?" Miss Goldman was asked.

"For quoting Cardinal Manning," she said, laughing. "He said, 'Necessity knows no law,' and I quoted it."[19]

---

15. In October 1895 the London anarchist newspaper *Liberty* reported on a speech made by EG where she advocated violence and praised AB's assassination attempt on Henry Clay Frick. The newspaper quoted EG as saying, "The acts of Berkmann, Caserio, Henry, Vaillant, Pallás, and other brave heroes were but the heralds of the coming Social Revolution." Sante Caserio, Émile Henry, Auguste Vaillant and Paulino Pallás were all anarchists executed for committing *attentats* or causing explosions. However, while she celebrated the lives of *attentaters* and would never denounce them, she did not herself ever specifically call for violence. See vol. 1, pp. 221–27, for full transcript of the 1895 *Liberty* article.

16. EG is referring to the first lecture in her Sunday lecture series, delivered on 11 April 1909. "The Psychology of Political Violence" was first published in EG's 1910 book *Anarchism and Other Essays*, and then published as a separate pamphlet in 1911 by Mother Earth Publishing Association.

17. The Emmanuel movement was founded by Elwood Worcester, a clergyman of the Emmanuel Episcopal Church in Boston, Massachusetts. Worcester believed that psychotherapy and spiritual methods could be used to cure physical ailing.

18. Sebastian Kneipp was a German priest who advocated natural healing processes. His popular book, *My Water Cure* (Edinburgh: W. Blackwood, 1891), earned him a mass following.

19. In response to the Trafalgar Square "Bloody Sunday" deaths on 13 November 1887, Cardinal Henry Edward Manning wrote: "Necessity has no law, and a starving man has a natural right to his neighbour's

"I have read," said the Inquirer, "that after you were closed up at Lexington Hall you were allowed to speak at the Sunrise Club without being arrested. Did you moderate your views at all?"[20]

Miss Goldman smiled gently. "No," she said, "and I don't moderate them anywhere. I try to show everywhere that Anarchism does not stand for what it is supposed to represent—assassination, violence, murder; that Anarchism is really a world concept that is closely related to every aspiration toward a better world since the beginning of time.

"But I have never advocated assassination in the whole course of my career. I did say once that whenever despotism is flagrant violence is the inevitable result. I take that view to-day, and neither do I condemn the men who commit such deeds. I have never condemned, and I never intend to condemn, a man who commits a crime of violence. The reason is that if organized society does not recognize the individual the individual will and must feel himself an alien to society and will therefore retaliate."

"If you do not preach violence, how do you account for the activity of the police against you?"

"Because the police are very ignorant and don't understand what they hear. Personally, though, I believe the yellow journals are more responsible than the police. They have surrounded my name with such a cloud of falsehood that you can hardly blame a not over-educated policeman for thinking Emma Goldman is a very dangerous person."

"Did you ever know Czolgosz, the murderer of President McKinley?" she was asked.

"I met him twice," she said, with a straight look that had nothing behind it except honesty. "I knew him just about as much as I know you, and that's all. I never knew who he was until after the death of McKinley. The first time I saw him was at a meeting in Cleveland—I didn't know his name then. I had just finished my lecture and he came up and asked me if I had any literature to distribute.

"I said I did and pointed out to him the place where radical pamphlets were being sold. The second time I saw Czolgosz was when I was going to the Rock Island station on July 12, just before McKinley was shot. Czolgosz rang the bell just as I was getting ready to start, and I came to the door and asked what he wanted. He said he wanted to meet some of the radical leaders and I said: 'I am going to the station now, and if you will come along I will talk to you on the way.'[21]

bread" ("Distress in London: A Note on Outdoor Relief," *Fortnightly Review* 49, January–June, 1888). Voltairine de Cleyre, in her 1894 essay "In Defense of Emma Goldmann and the Right of Expropriation," attributes EG's 1893 unemployment speeches to Cardinal Manning, as does EG later. However, there is no evidence that EG actually quoted Manning in her 1893 speech.

20. EG spoke on "The Hypocrisy of Puritanism" at the Sunrise Club in New York City on 24 May. The Sunrise Club discussion group was started by E. C. Walker and ran from 1890 to 1931. The club met fortnightly at the Cafe Boulevard at Tenth Street and Second Avenue, where EG was a regular speaker.

21. On 5 May 1901, EG lectured on "The Modern Phase of Anarchy" before the Liberty Association of the Franklin Liberal Club in Cleveland, Ohio. Leon Czolgosz was in attendance, approached her at the intermission, and asked her recommendation of books to read. On 12 July 1901, Czolgosz at-

"So we walked along. I didn't ask him his name, and I never knew who he was until, a couple of months later, I saw his picture in the papers as the slayer of President McKinley."

"If your acquaintance was so short, how did you know him by casual newspaper picture?"

"Czolgosz," said Miss Goldman, "had a very remarkable face. Having once seen him you could not forget him. You must have remarked that yourself, by seeing his picture in the papers—didn't you?"

Emma Goldman is not a beautiful woman. She is, however, one of those rather rare women with whom a certain brilliancy of the intellect takes the place of mere prettiness. That is to say, her face is so attractive and charming that it produces all the effect of beauty. Her features are regular, and her eyes, which are large and fine, have the curious combination of brilliancy and softness—rare, that, in eyes of blue and gray; and Miss Goldman's eyes have both those colors, according as she changes from one emotion to another.

But she would not like to have her looks made the subject of even a paragraph in a newspaper article; she is too much an advocate to let the sex question enter in for a moment. To call her "pretty"—though she really is a woman of charm—would be as much out of place as it would be to call Daniel Webster[22] handsome, instead of intellectual or brilliant. It is hard to avoid such a characterization in speaking of a woman.

But then Emma Goldman is not a woman. She is a force.

New York Times Sunday Magazine, 30 May 1909, p. 7. Charles Willis Thompson (1871–1946) was a New York journalist, chief of the Washington Bureau of the *New York Times* during the Theodore Roosevelt presidency, and a prominent reporter during the First World War. Thompson again interviewed EG about the Ferrer Modern School for the 29 March 1914 edition of the *New York Times Sunday Magazine.*

---

tempted to visit the office of the anarchist communist newspaper *Free Society* in Chicago. He came back later the same day and introduced himself as Mr. Nieman from Cleveland. Hippolyte Havel, Max Baginski and others from the office were leaving for the train station to see EG off to Buffalo and Rochester. Czolgosz joined them. After EG left Chicago, her comrades became suspicious of Nieman's repeated references to acts of violence. A letter later arrived at the *Free Society* office from Cleveland warning Nieman was an assumed name and that he was probably a spy. For more on Czolgosz's assassination of President McKinley, and the reaction against EG and other anarchists, see vol. I, especially pp. 460–88.

22. U.S. Supreme Court lawyer and politician Daniel Webster (1782–1852) served variously as a congressman, senator, and secretary of state between 1813 and 1852. He is known for his advocacy of business interests during the period of Jacksonian agrarianism.

MY DEAR DEAR BEN.

I wish I could make you understand, just how I feel, while writing this. You would know then, dear, that I do not mean to scold or hurt you. You would know, that deep sorrow, and pain, dictates these lines.

I fear we have come to our journey's end, my boy. It was a hard and thorny journey, but so long as we had faith in our love, we stood the hardship. But faith is gone, Ben, my faith in your love for me, and faith in my love for you. I know, I have failed with my love failed miserably, so what is the use in dragging it on?

Our first trip together, brought us many unpleasent moments, but I had infinite faith in you and in the power of my love to urge you on and out of the old.

I received my first shock, when you could not hold out in Chicago, that first time, though you were so sure you would work and get on ~~you~~ your feet. For one, who has never known, weakness, it was a shock indeed. But my love said, "Ben loves you and can not be away from you, that is why he has made no attempt in Chicago". And I listened to loves voice, for it is so good to be loved, you know

Then you came to NY and you gave me new faith in the power of my love. You were active, you did try to do things, ~~an~~ to write to work to be on your own feet. When you left me, my love was jubilant, for a time. When I left you, on that memorable day, last March I believed in your determination, to practice. Alas, that believe was soon shattered. Your inertia, your lethargy, your absolute indifference since you are in NY has gradually undermined my faith, that my love must be an impetus, must give you strength and energy. I hope with all my heart you will not insinuate, as you have last year, that I care for the money you might earn. You know it isn't that. Only I wanted, I hoped I longed, with all my heart, that my love will pull you out of the old. It has not it has not and that's why my faith is gone.

And then there is that other thing, the thing ~~to be~~ so abhorant, so utterly impossible to endure—your irresponcible unscrupelous attitude towards women—your lack of honesty with them, with yourself, with myself. Oh, I know you will ascribe it to jealoucy. But it is not. I have told you over and over again, if you really care for a woman, if you love her, no matter how ~~I~~ much that may grieve me, I should have strength enough to face it. Or if you were honest in your dealings with women, openly and plainly telling them, "I want you for a sex embrace and no more". That too, I could stand. But your complete lack of justice of common humanity, of consideration for the rights of another is simply killing me. You deny leading on these women, but I know that that not one of them, certainly not, Grace,[1]

---

1. Possibly Grace Potter; see note 12, Letter to Ben Reitman, 14 April 1909, above.

or Lioness[2] or Lilly, or this latest fancy of yours, would consent to be used as a toy, not one of them. Even a prostitute wants to be loved wants one man, at least, to have her because of love and passion and not as a toy. Cann't you realize that Ben?

You say, I do not understand your psychology. But you are mistaken I understand it only too well, else I should not have endured it for a year. But, do you think I must inthuse myself with a psychology, that drains the lifes blood out of victims and then thrusts them aside? I can not do that, Ben, everything in me rebells against it.

However your toys in the past, were at least women, who can take care of themselves, but what about the latest victim? You tell me you do not lead her on, what do you call, phoning to the shop, making appointments spending hours at the time with her, except leading her on? Must she not think, and justly so, that if you have singled her out, of all others, you must care for her? She can not be so stupid as to imagine, it is because of your intellectual or spiritual communion with her that you are out with her seeking her. You tell me she is impressionable, more reasons for her to assume, that you care for her—But you say she is only a child, and you play with her. Oh Ben, where is your sense of justice, of fairness that you should play with a human being, no matter of how little importance. Has my love, our love meant so little that you have not learned developed a spark of consideration and honesty? Why not tell the girl, "I only play with you, you amuse me, you are nothing to me"? That would be honest at least. But no, you would not tell her that, for you know, that you she would refuse to be your play thing. She believes in you, because she imagines that the man who is loved by E G can be trusted, must be big and honest, do you realize that? No, you do not you can not, you never have. Can you see, why I have lost faith in your love and in my love?[. . .][3]

Good night.

Momie

ALS, IU-U. On *Mother Earth* stationery. Dated "Afternoon."

2. The Lioness is Margaret Eleanor Fitzgerald, so named for her red mane of hair; Fitzgerald served as office manager for *Mother Earth* and was a lifelong friend of both EG and BR, and future companion to AB.

3. The letter continues for eight more pages; the next section is dated 1 June, 2 A.M. See *EGP*, reel 3.

My lover, my Ben.

What mysterious power eminates from you, that has such a terrible hold over my life. A power that can at once take me to a World of the greatest bliss and deepest sorrow. Tell me dearest, what is it?

You often ask me, if I would be happier without you. Do you know my beloved, that the very though of our possible seperation gives the shiver. Yet, I often feel, as if some great blow will seperate us—As I told you in my last letter, I can not reconcile my established belief in the power of love, (a belief much deeper in my system, than even the belief in freedom) with the realization of how little love has done for you. I do not feel that way, when we are together sublimly together, as last night, or this morning. At such a moment, it seems if you were million miles away from the old hurts, as if you were completely at one with me. But at other moments, oh, the agony, the grief. I wonder if you know and understand dearest. You see, my Ben, you say yourself, you have never loved, before. The woman you love has completely abandoned herself to you. But, can you imagine how you would feel, if this woman were carried away by every insignificant man, men who give her disgust only for a moments gratification. Can you imagine how you would feel? I doubt, if you can, now, that you are so very sure of your Momie. Else, you would understand my great grief—Dearest it is beyond my power of endurence, sometimes and if ever we are torn apart, that will be the cause for it. Somehow, I feel that if you had activity, something of interest to do either in our propaganda or your profession and Momie could be near you to love and inspire her boy things would be different. Don't you think so? You see, how I want to believe in you dear, how I cling to possibilities

I wish I had gone with you lover. Nothing accomplished through Hall[1] and I feel so lonely and my soul is so full of doubts and fears. Lover, precious lover, if only we could go away together. Hall was told at headquarters that their orders came from Bingham. You see the corruption and how little, we can hope to gain in that way. Besides what we need is an established right, not a favor to be withdrawn any moment.

I am expecting Stella[2] soon, so will know just what Abbott[3] has done. Had a letter from

1. Bolton Hall was a single-tax lawyer and an official of the 1909 Free Speech Committee.
2. Stella Comyn, EG's niece, who often acted as her secretary.
3. Anarchist Leonard Abbott was chairman of the 1909 Free Speech Committee and was trying to secure EG's right to lecture in public without police suppression.

First page of handwritten love letter from Goldman to Reitman, dated 28 August 1909, typical of many she wrote to him during this period. She addressed him as her "Hobo" while referring to herself as his "Mommy." (Special Collections, University Library, University of Illinois at Chicago)

Freeman telling me he is better and that he is preparing for "our meeting next Tuesday."[4] He wants the manuscript of my drama lecture. Foxy cuss, he wants to assure himself that

4. Alden Freeman invited EG to lecture at the centennial celebration of Thomas Paine's death in East Orange, New Jersey, on 8 June. Freeman was scheduled to introduce EG; however, the police refused all entrance to the hall, and the event was moved to a barn on Freeman's private property. Protected from

all is correct. I told him, I had only notes, but that he need have no worry as to trouble. I asked him, if he has cards ordered and if he wants you to distribute them.

I also had a beautiful letter from Fleming. Not an unkind word about the disappointement and the work, we caused him.[5] We will try to raise money for my fare. When will I be able to go, I wonder. I want this to go with the 6 post, so must hasten. I sent you a Call, at 4 o'clock. I hope my boy feels good away from Mommy, what is so hard to please The Mommy what loves Hobo so intensely and madly, what wants him so, every minute always.

I hope you can finish all there is to do and come back tomorrow evening. You have spoiled the m—and t—They want you terribly much and Mommy wants her boy, her irresponcible beautiful boy. Really dear, I am so silly about you. The t b embraces you tightly she informs me, that it is cruel to leave her after such a feast, especially to make her sleep alone.

Dear, dear Hobo lover I love you awfully much.

ALWAYS YOUR MOMMY

ALS, IU-U.

---

police interference, EG delivered the lecture, "Modern Drama, the Strongest Disseminator of Radical Thought." This incident led to the formation of the 1909 Free Speech Committee and the compilation of the pamphlet *The Suppression of Free Speech in New York and New Jersey* (New York: Alden Freeman, 1909). The 8 June meeting was among several suppressed meetings (see note 1 to "Our Friends, the Enemy," Article in *Mother Earth*, June 1909, immediately following).

5. J. W. (Chummy) Fleming, an Australian anarchist who had been planning a lecture tour for EG in Australia that never materialized. For further discussion of the Australian tour, see Letter to Meyer Shapiro, 20 February 1909, above.

Article in **MOTHER EARTH**

June 1909

Our Friends, the Enemy

Suppression of Anarchist meetings and clubbing of their audiences have become such an ordinary affair, one hates to waste space in writing about it.

After all, what are police for, if not to suppress the Anarchists? No one attacks the machinery of government, the corruption of politics, the brutality of the police, the sham of our existing society, so persistently as do the Anarchists. Therefore they must be silenced. Therefore they must be suppressed.

Realizing this, I should have not the least objection to the attitude of those in power towards myself and my comrades. What I do object to is the contemptible, cowardly, sneaking methods they employ.

Within the last month, the police of New Haven, Brooklyn, Yonkers, East Orange, and New York have suppressed eleven meetings that I was to address.[1] Was it done openly? No. Detectives sneaked behind the hall owners, bullying and threatening them with arrest and ruin, until they had to yield. That is the curse of this country. Everyone imagines himself free and independent, and yet nearly everyone is mortally afraid of the police. It is because they know that the average officer on his beat is omnipotent. No matter in what trade, business, or profession one is engaged, the success or failure thereof will depend on the grace of the police. Therein lies the secret of the absolute indifference on the part of the general public to the daily and hourly criminality of those who are here to "protect the lives and the liberties of the people."

But, "the Constitution of the United States declares that Congress shall make no laws abridging the freedom of speech."[2] That is all well and good for Congress, but what has that to do with the police of the United States? They have "evolved" their own laws, laws to suit their own purposes, and the most interesting thing about their laws is that they are almost always sustained in the courts, by the press, and public opinion; else how is it

---

1. To date, nine suppressed meetings have been verified. On 14 May EG was scheduled to speak in New Haven, Connecticut, on "Anarchy: What It Stands For." She was admitted into the hall by the police, but the audience was denied admission. Two meetings scheduled for 15 May in New Haven were also, presumably, stopped. On 23 May at Lexington Hall in New York, EG's two attempts to speak on "The Modern Drama" were blocked by the police. A meeting at Yonkers, New Jersey, was also suppressed in late May. A 28 May meeting at Liederkranz Hall in Brooklyn on "The True Significance of Anarchism" was also stopped. On 30 May EG again attempted to deliver her lecture of "The Modern Drama" at Lexington Hall. On 8 June the police attempted to suppress a meeting commemorating Thomas Paine, at which EG was scheduled to speak (see note 4 to Letter to Ben Reitman, ca. June 1909, above).
2. Included in the Bill of Rights, First Amendment, Article 3.

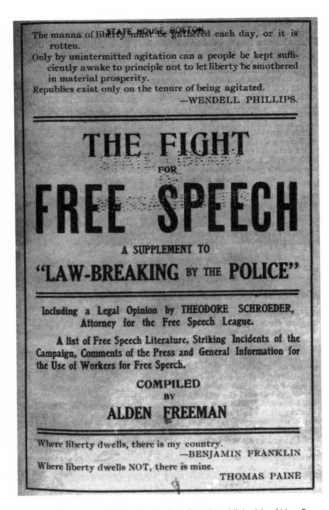

The manna of liberty STATE HOUSE BOSTON each day, or it is
  rotten.
Only by unintermitted agitation can a people be kept sufficiently awake to principle not to let liberty be smothered
  in material prosperity.
Republics exist only on the tenure of being agitated.
                                    —WENDELL PHILLIPS.

THE FIGHT

FOR

FREE SPEECH

A SUPPLEMENT TO

"LAW-BREAKING BY THE POLICE"

Including a Legal Opinion by THEODORE SCHROEDER,
Attorney for the Free Speech League.

A list of Free Speech Literature, Striking Incidents of the
Campaign, Comments of the Press and General Information for
the Use of Workers for Free Speech.

COMPILED
BY
ALDEN FREEMAN

Where liberty dwells, there is my country.
                        —BENJAMIN FRANKLIN
Where liberty dwells NOT, there is mine.
                                    THOMAS PAINE

Cover of the pamphlet *The Fight for Free Speech,* published by Alden Freeman in 1909, a compilation of protest letters and articles written in support
of Goldman's right to speak in public. The systematic suppression of her
lectures throughout the northeastern United States in the summer and fall
of 1909 prompted the creation of a Free Speech Committee. Alden Freeman's
firsthand experience of police breaking up an 8 June 1909 Goldman meeting
in East Orange, New Jersey, sparked his interest in anarchism and support of
Goldman's political activities, as well as his offer of financial aid to the New
York Modern School. (By permission of the Kate Sharpley Library)

possible that the Chief of New Haven, assisted by a few officers, can prevent five thousand people from entering a hall? Is it that these people do not know their rights as guaranteed by the Constitution, or is it because they have been police-ridden so long that they have lost the manhood to sustain their rights? Or how are we to explain the 275 American citizens dining at the Sunrise Club[3] in New York City under police surveillance, without the slightest protest? Did they, too, not know their rights?

I am being assured that most people approve of the suppression of Anarchists, or of myself, because their minds have been poisoned by gross misrepresentation of Anarchy. Possibly; but in that case there is even less excuse for their slavish submission, since the interference with the right of expression means also the interference with the right of hearing or listening to anything that might dispel misrepresentation. In short, it is impossible to get away from the fact that the authorities of this country are so arbitrary, so outrageously brutal because they rely on the ignorance and cowardice of the people.

Fortunately, I have learned long ago that the ultimate success of a truth depends not on the many, but on the perseverance and earnestness of the few. Too bad that the police never learn anything; else they would know that their action during the last month tends only to strengthen the zeal, devotion, and faith in a great cause. This, too, they would know: that while they have suppressed eleven meetings, thereby causing MOTHER EARTH a great material loss, they have planted the seed of discontent and hatred in many hearts. Already there exists great bitterness among those who feel, and great opposition among those who think. As to myself, I hate to hurt the sensibilities of my friends, the police; but they might as well attempt to direct the course of the stars as to direct the course of my life's work. They can not do it; at least not while I live.

Mother Earth 4 (June 1909): 110–11.

---

3. The Sunrise Club was a New York discussion group started by E. C. Walker that ran from 1890 to 1931; other anarchist members included John Coryell and his wife, Abby. The club met fortnightly at the Cafe Boulevard at Tenth Street and Second Avenue, where EG was a regular speaker.

Article in the *NEW YORK TIMES*

New York, 9 June 1909

Miss Goldman Talks in Freeman's Barn

Police Keep Her from Public Hall and Stand Beside Her in the Stable.

Curious Throng Present.

Big Audience in and Outside the Barn—
She Raps the Police and Says We're Getting Russianized.

Emma Goldman, although she was thwarted by the police of East Orange, N. J., under the leadership of Mayor Cardwell and a delegation of leading citizens and Police Chief Bell from speaking in English's Hall last night, had a triumph nonetheless.[1] With a band of distinguished adherents, including Ferdinand P. ("Affinity") Earle,[2] she drove to the stable of Alden Freeman and there by the light of oil lamps, standing on a chair, she delivered the address on the modern drama which New York police had suppressed, and that, too, right in the most fashionable section of East Orange.

Close upon 1,000 persons must have listened to her, for the stable was so jammed with people that Chief of Police Bell was crowded right up against her chair. The yard of Mr. Freeman's place outside was black with people, and evidently there were well-known citizens among them, for in the road behind the house many automobiles were parked.

In the course of her speech she said many bitter things against the police, "useless ornaments of society," as she called them; she lauded high as a great drama—as the greatest American drama—"The Easiest Way,"[3] and when some one derisively asked her

---

1. EG had been scheduled to speak at English's Hall in East Orange, New Jersey, at a meeting held to commemorate the 100th anniversary of Thomas Paine's death. When police prevented EG and the waiting audience from entering the hall, Alden Freeman, who had been scheduled to introduce EG, invited the meeting to regroup at a barn on his nearby private property. Freeman had organized and served as secretary of the reform Citizens Union of East Orange, New Jersey; he became acquainted with EG in 1909 when he attended a meeting at which EG was to lecture on Ibsen that was broken up by the police.
2. Ferdinand P. Earle (1878–1951) was an artist, editor, and publisher, who in 1912 edited a collection of poetry, *The Lyric Year*, in which Edna St. Vincent Millay's poetry was first published.
3. *The Easiest Way*, a play written by Eugene Walter dealing with the exploitative relationships between an actress and the men who finance her career, premiered on Broadway in 1909.

"How about 'Uncle Tom's Cabin?'"[4] she cited the words of Justice Dugro[5] to the effect that a negro could not be entitled to as much damage for injured feelings as a white man, by way of showing that the book had not yet served its purpose.

When Miss Goldman decided to give her address, "The Drama as the Strongest Disseminator of Radical Thought," she engaged English's Hall, in East Orange, and gave him $5 to seal the bargain. Then the Mayor brought pressure to bear, and Mr. English tried to withdraw. Miss Goldman wouldn't take back her $5 and said she would see about it. She said it in such a way as to put the police on their mettle.

Fifteen of them, with the chief and Mayor Cardwell, were on hand early last night in English's restaurant, to be ready for a surprise.

So when Mr. Freeman, meeting the Anarchist at the station, arrived at the hall with Mr. Earle, Alexander Berkman, Leonard Abbott,[6] Manager Reitman, and others, at the same time that Miss Goldman drew up in front of it in Mr. Freeman's carriage, the place was well defended.[7]

Miss Goldman made one sally. She pushed through the little crowd, followed by the men of her party, and advanced directly against the chests of the police force. The chief and his men stood like a stone wall. Mr. Freeman then announced that the lecture would be given in his barn, and that all were welcome. All moved thither, including the police force.

When Miss Goldman pushed into the stable, she could only find room to stand by making the people crowd closer together. There was not even an extra inch, so far as any one could see by the light of the oil lamps on the empty wagon inside and outside the stable, and hundreds crowded about the doors, scores about the windows. Every one cheered and whistled, and some without cried: "Come to the door so's we can see you." Then Mr. Abbott got to the chair, and read a manifesto on the constitutionality of free speech, which he said many distinguished people had signed.[8]

Then Mr. Freeman, amid considerable whistling and applause, read by the dim oil lamp-

4. *Uncle Tom's Cabin*, a play based on the novel by Harriet Beecher Stowe, premiered on Broadway in 1852 and was performed again in New York City in 1907, in its third revival.
5. Philip Henry Dugro (1855–1920) served as associate justice of the New York Superior Court from 1896 until his death.
6. Leonard Dalton Abbott was the president of the Free Speech League after 1907, and chairman of the Free Speech Committee in 1909. He occasionally contributed articles to *Mother Earth* and was associate editor of *Current Literature* for over twenty-five years.
7. EG describes the incident in East Orange in a brief, metaphorical anecdote in "Observations and Comments" in the June 1909 issue of *Mother Earth*.
8. "A Demand for Free Speech," written and distributed by the Free Speech Committee, was published in the June 1909 issue of *Mother Earth*. The document was originally signed by Bolton Hall, Leonard Abbott, Meyer London, Alexander Irvine, and Grace Potter; in the June 1909 issue of *Mother Earth*, additional names were appended to the document, including Rose Pastor Stokes, William Marion Reedy, Ferdinand Earle, Daniel Kiefer, C. E. S. Wood, Alden Freeman, and Anna Strunsky Walling, among others.

light an eulogy of Thomas Paine,[9] who died 100 years ago yesterday, and after it introduced Emma Goldman as:

"The most conspicuous agitator for freedom of thought and speech in America—and I am glad that East Orange has this chance to observe that Miss Goldman has neither hoofs nor horns, and does not ride on a broomstick."

Loud cheers and laughter followed this, and the cheers mingled with loud whistles from without as Miss Goldman took the chair.

"As I drove here," she said in a piercing voice, "it came to me that those Russians battling for freedom could not have believed possible what happened in your town tonight. They think this country is the cradle of liberty—they do not believe such things happen here at all. But America is gradually coming to Russian conditions—she is nearing them faster all the time."

Here there came more cheers and whistles, and Miss Goldman entered on the subject, and the people without the dim-lit barn pressed forward, and Chief Bell took his place by Miss Goldman's chair.

But here the noise from without so increased that one of the audience got to his feet and said sententiously: "I for one would be very glad if the people who don't want to hear would disperse; the police are here—they might disperse them."

"Not the police," said Miss Goldman; "they would make more confusion in one minute than they could stop in five years." More cheers and laughter, followed by comparative silence, which enabled Miss Goldman to point out how all the most radical plays she could think of had wakened up "the sleepy brains of the people" to thought.

New York Times, 9 June 1909, p. 2.

---

9. Thomas Paine (1737–1809), English-born writer, freethinker, and humanitarian, was influential in the American Revolution and an active participant in the French Revolution. EG and many anarchists identified with Paine's hostility to established religion, to the sentiment behind his assertion that government is a necessary evil, and to his interest in a government that is as small as possible. EG, like the earlier Chicago Haymarket anarchists, often evoked the name of Thomas Paine, along with Thomas Jefferson, Wendell Phillips, and John Brown, to demonstrate an American anti-statist tradition.

Circular Letter

New York, 20 June 1909

To the Friends of *Mother Earth*

DEAR FRIEND:

When I returned from my last tour, in March, I promised myself that if I had to tax the friends of MOTHER EARTH again this summer, I would give up the magazine. With that in view I immediately arranged for a series of meetings in New York and vicinity, though I was then by no means fit to continue lecturing.

How my plans have been frustrated by the police you will learn from the account of recent events, in the June issue of MOTHER EARTH.

With all my meetings systematically prevented by the authorities, and the sole source of the magazine's revenue thus cut off, I face the alternative of either again calling on you for financial aid or suspending MOTHER EARTH.

You will no doubt agree with me that the latter course, especially at the present moment, were a tremendous victory for the enemy, and a miserable defeat for us.

Will you, then, come to the rescue of MOTHER EARTH, as you have done so generously on previous occasions?

SINCERELY,

EMMA GOLDMAN

We make an especial appeal to our more recent subscribers to come to the aid of our cause.

TLS, NN.

A New Declaration of Independence

When, in the course of human development, existing institutions prove inadequate to the needs of man, when they serve merely to enslave, rob, and oppress mankind, the people have the eternal right to rebel against, and overthrow, these institutions.

The mere fact that these forces—inimical to life, liberty, and the pursuit of happiness—are legalized by statute laws, sanctified by divine rights, and enforced by political power, in no way justifies their continued existence.

We hold these truths to be self-evident: that all human beings, irrespective of race, color, or sex, are born with the equal right to share at the table of life; that to secure this right, there must be established among men economic, social, and political freedom; we hold further that government exists but to maintain special[1] privilege and property rights; that it coerces man into submission and therefore robs him of dignity, self-respect, and life.

The history of the American kings of capital and authority is the history of repeated crimes, injustice, oppression, outrage, and abuse, all aiming at the suppression of individual liberties and the exploitation of the people. A vast country, rich enough to supply all her children with all possible comforts, and insure well-being to all, is in the hands of a few, while the nameless millions are at the mercy of ruthless wealth gatherers, unscrupulous lawmakers, and corrupt politicians. Sturdy sons of America are forced to tramp the country in a fruitless search for bread, and many of her daughters are driven into the street, while thousands of tender children are daily sacrificed on the altar of Mammon. The reign of these kings is holding mankind in slavery, perpetuating poverty and disease, maintaining crime and corruption; it is fettering the spirit of liberty, throttling the voice of justice, and degrading and oppressing humanity. It is engaged in continual war and slaughter, devastating the country and destroying the best and finest qualities of man; it nurtures superstition and ignorance, sows prejudice and strife, and turns the human family into a camp of Ishmaelites.

We, therefore, the liberty-loving men and women, realizing the great injustice and brutality of this state of affairs, earnestly and boldly do hereby declare, That each and every individual is and ought to be free to own himself and to enjoy the full fruit of his labor; that man is absolved from all allegiance to the kings of authority and capital; that he has, by the very fact of his being, free access to the land and all means of production, and

---

1. The word "special" was replaced by "social" in the 1910 reprint of this essay in pamphlet form.

entire liberty of disposing of the fruits of his efforts; that each and every individual has the unquestionable and unabridgeable right of free and voluntary association with other equally sovereign individuals for economic, political, social, and all other purposes, and that to achieve this end man must emancipate himself from the sacredness of property, the respect for man-made law, the fear of the Church, the cowardice of public opinion, the stupid arrogance of national, racial,[2] religious, and sex superiority, and from the narrow puritanical conception of human life. And for the support of this Declaration, and with a firm reliance on the harmonious blending of man's social and individual tendencies, the lovers of liberty joyfully consecrate their uncompromising devotion, their energy and intelligence, their solidarity and their lives.

Mother Earth 4 (July 1909): 137–38. A footnote to this essay reads: "This 'Declaration' was written at the request of a certain newspaper, which subsequently refused to publish it, though the article was already in composition." In *Living My Life,* Goldman claims that her essay won a contest sponsored by the *Boston Globe* (p. 455). The essay was later published as a pamphlet, entitled *A New Declaration of Independence* (New York: Mother Earth Publishing Association, 1910). The pamphlet contained two significant changes to the text of the essay as it appeared in *Mother Earth* (see nn. 1, 2).

2. The word "racial" was replaced by "social" in the 1910 pamphlet.

MY DEAR MR ROGER

Your letter of the 7th was forwarded to me, as I have been touring Massachusetts, Vermont & Road Island during the last month.

Your subscription has been credited to you and our magazine forwarded regularly.

I contemplate being in St Louis some time in November.[1] Do you think, I could get the Hall of the Self-Culture[2] society? I mean would it be rented to me for a series of lectures? If yes, will you let me know soon its seating capacity and price?

VERY TRULY

EMMA GOLDMAN

I shall be in NY Tuesday next.

ALS, American Civil Liberties Archive, NjP. Addressed to Mr. Roger N. Baldwin, St. Louis, Mo. On stationery of Narragansett Hotel, Providence, R.I.

1. EG did not speak in St. Louis in November 1909.
2. The Self-Culture Hall was a St. Louis settlement house where Roger Baldwin lived and worked.

My dear Miss Goldman:—

Thanks for your kind letter of Sept. 10th. I am glad to hear that you are to be in St. Louis in November. I note your request for the use of Self-Culture Hall[1] and beg to say that we are slaves to public opinion and the good-will of our subscribers. I hardly think the Board would consent to its use for such subjects as you would desire to speak on, altho many of us personally are very much interested.

A number of persons active in social work are anxious to meet you privately when you come and I should be obliged to you if you will let me know in advance.

With best wishes, I am,

Very truly yours,

TLU, ACLU Archives, NjP. Addressed to Miss Goldman, 310 E. 13th St., New York. At bottom left: RNB/CP.

1. EG had requested use of the hall for a lecture tour later in the fall (see Letter to Roger Baldwin, 10 September 1909, above).

To the Editor of Public Ledger:

Sir—I take the liberty to ask the hospitality of your paper, because I found you exceedingly fair and impartial during the recent police outrages on free speech.[1] During the court hearing on my appeal for injunction it developed that the police department of this city stopped my lecture on September 28 for the following reasons.[2]

First. That my police record proved my utterances always lead to disturbances.

Second. That I am a convicted anarchist.

It requires neither Solomonic wisdom nor a deep sense of justice to see that such reasons are poor grounds for the suppression of an old-established tradition—that of free speech and assemblage.

Evidently the forefathers of this country realized that police records are not always very accurate, else they would not have provided "that Congress even shall make no law abridging the freedom of speech or press or the right of assemblage";[3] much less did they delegate that right to the police department of Philadelphia.

As to what my record may or may not be has nothing to do with the present struggle. But for the benefit of your readers I wish to say this:

I have been in the lecture field for 18 years; have spoken in inumerable cities, including Philadelphia, and have never had a single disturbance. The only disturbers were the police, when they attempted to stop meetings and suppress free speech. I may also state

1. The police broke up a Philadelphia meeting of the unemployed, organized by Jewish and Italian anarchist groups and attracting over 2,000 people, on 20 February 1908. Voltairine de Cleyre, who was scheduled to speak at the meeting, was arrested along with several others. The *Philadelphia Public Ledger* and the *Philadelphia Evening Bulletin* printed the transcript of de Cleyre's speech on 21 February.

2. On 28 September 1909, EG was scheduled to lecture at Odd Fellow's Temple. Henry Clay, Philadelphia's Director of Public Safety, demanded to see an advance copy of the text of EG's address. When she refused, EG was prohibited from speaking. During the next two months, backed by the Free Speech League and prominent individuals including single-taxer G. Frank Stephens, anarchist George Brown, former congressman Robert Baker, socialist Rose Pastor Stokes, and St. Louis editor and publisher William Marion Reedy, EG fought for the right to speak, unsuccessfully (and, apparently, reluctantly) contesting the matter in court. Clay, according to EG, was later driven from office by allegations of bribery and graft.

3. The First Amendment of the U.S. Constitution guarantees several rights, including freedom of speech and the press: "Congress shall make no law respecting an establishment of religion, or prohibiting the free exercise thereof; or abridging the freedom of speech, or of the press; or the right of the people peaceably to assemble, and to petition the government for a redress of grievances."

that in all these years I have been held for trial but once—1893—and not because of any riot,[4] but for quoting Cardinal Manning, to wit, "Necessity knows no law."[5]

My lectures have been published in my magazine, Mother Earth, the latter being entered in the United States second class mail. Yet it remained for the police of Philadelphia to suppress me even before I was heard.

Does it not seem as if this city has come to a very lamentable state of affairs if the right of free speech is made to depend on the grace and whim of the police department?

A convicted anarchist? Though not an authority on jurisprudence, I know that there is no such law in the statutes that can make such a discrimination. Just as well discriminate against a convicted Christian, Jew, Buddhist or Mohammedan.

Besides, to say whether or not an anarchist may speak the officals must make themselves conversant with the philosophy of anarchism. Far be it from me to reflect on the intelligence of the Philadelphia police; but I do not wish to say that they know as much about anarchism as they know about anything that requires the capacity of reasoning and reflection.

Were the authorities to know but the history of their own country they would know that some of the greatest anarchists have raised their voice for human justice and liberty right here in America. David Thoreau, the author of "Walden," was an anarchist, for it was he who in his famous tract, "Evil Disobedience," proclaimed the human truth to wit, "I am at all times called upon to do only what I think is right and not what the State thinks is right."[6] Thoreau went to prison for refusing to pay taxes.

Ralph Waldo Emerson was an anarchist, and with his essay on "Self-reliance"[7] has contributed to the wealth of anarchistic literature that champions individual freedom. John Brown,[8] Wendell Phillips, Lloyd Garrison[9] and scores of others were anarchists, in-

---

4. In 1893 EG was tried and sentenced to one year in prison for incitement to riot.
5. In response to the Trafalgar Square "Bloody Sunday" deaths on 13 November 1887, Cardinal Henry Edward Manning wrote: "Necessity has no law, and a starving man has a natural right to his neighbour's bread" ("Distress in London: A Note on Outdoor Relief," *Fortnightly Review*, vol. 49, 1 January to 1 June, 1888; London: Chapman and Hall). Voltairine de Cleyre, in her 1894 essay "In Defence of Emma Goldmann and the Right of Expropriation" (Philadelphia, 1894) also paraphrases Cardinal Manning.
6. A reference to Henry David Thoreau's essay "Civil Disobedience," in which he states, "It is not desirable to cultivate a respect for the law, so much as for the right. The only obligation which I have a right to assume, is to do at any time what I think right."
7. First published in Ralph Waldo Emerson's *Essays* (London: James Fraser, 1841).
8. John Brown (1800–1859) was an American abolitionist and leader of the raid on Harper's Ferry in 1859 who was tried for murder, slave insurrection, and treason to the state of Virginia, and hanged on 2 December 1859. Brown was seen by EG as exemplary of an American tradition of standing in opposition to the abuse of power by the state.
9. Both William Lloyd Garrison (1805–1879) and Wendell Phillips (1811–1884) were American abolitionists, orators, and advocates of labor and women's rights, whom EG identified as part of an American anti-statist tradition.

עמא גאלדמאן די גראנגערסע און פרייע רעדע אין אמעריקא.

Caption to this cartoon in the November 1909 issue of the Yiddish-language newspaper *Die Grosse Kundes* (The Big Stick), published in New York, reads "Emma Goldman, the noisemaker, and free speech in America." Lack of free speech in America is illustrated with a padlock on Goldman's mouth, satirizing police suppression of Goldman's public lectures. (Stanford University)

asmuch as they opposed the abuse of power. Yes, they were dreamers of a state of society wherein each man shall have the greatest scope and opportunity for self-development; a society wherein the individual shall learn to appreciate his relation to his fellows and the value of mutual assistance and voluntary co-operation.

A dangerous theory? Yes, but dangerous to those who would fetter the human mind and gag the human voice; dangerous to those who always have opposed every truth for social progress and individual well-being.

As to myself, I came here not to enter into a fist fight with the police. I came here to get forth my ideas, and I absolutely deny the right of any official to stop me from speaking. True, the police represent an iron wall of physical power and ignorance worn with age, but then I represent a truth and a never-to-be-destroyed longing for liberty.

The club may be a mighty weapon, but it sinks into insignificance before human reason and human integrity.

Therefore I shall speak in Philadelphia.

EMMA GOLDMAN.

Philadelphia Public Ledger, 3 October 1909, p. 2.

To the *PHILADELPHIA PUBLIC LEDGER*

Philadelphia, 7 October 1909

Emma Goldman and M'Kinley's Death

A Caustic Denial That She Was in Any Way Implicated, and a Vigorous Retort.

TO THE EDITOR OF PUBLIC LEDGER:

Sir—In the issue of your paper of the 6th instant, there appeared the following letter:

> "Sir—The fact that the assassin of William McKinley, under oath, swore that he attributed his act of crime to the utterances of Emma Goldman is ground enough for preventing her speaking here. T. T. H."

Among decent people it is customary to ignore any printed accusation that is not signed in full.

However, I ask the courtesy of your paper, not for my defense, but for the benefit of your readers, who, I take it, believe in hearing both sides.

T. T. H. states that the "assassin of William McKinley swore under oath that he attributes his act of crime to the utterances of Emma Goldman." It requires but little logic to see that T. T. H. speaks from hearsay and not from knowledge.

If the "assassin" had given any such sworn testimony would not the authorities have confronted him with me, and would that not have been sufficient evidence, especially at that moment of popular frenzy, to hold me for trial, yea, even to send me to prison?

For the enlightenment of T. T. H. permit me to say that the State of New York employed 200 detectives and spent $30,000 to connect me with the "assassin." Evidently they were leaving nothing undone to get sufficient evidence. Is it reasonable, then, to assume that sworn testimony, such as referred to in the letter of T. T. H., would have been allowed to pass?

In justice to that victim of economic inequity and social ignorance, Leon Czolgosz, I wish to state once for all, that he made no such statement under oath, or otherwise, nor had he ever claimed to be an anarchist.

Leon Czolgosz made one statement, however, when he was placed in the electric chair. "Good Christian brothers," "in their great Christian love," attempted to draw a confession from their helpless victim.

They told him that Emma Goldman had denounced him as a worthless beggar, or something to that effect. "It makes no difference what she says, she knew nothing of the act," was the "assassin's" reply.

As to what else that boy may or may not have said, only his warders and the prison walls know.

Warders, in the sublime words of Oscar Wilde,

Must set a lock upon their lips, and make their face a mask.[1]

And again.

Every prison that men build for men is built with bricks of shame,
And bound with bars, lest Christ should see
How men their brothers maim[2]

No, the "assassin" made no statements, nor could there be found even circumstantial evidence to connect me in any way.

Besides, I absolutely deny that utterances, no matter how incendiary, have ever induced any one to violence. Two conditions are necessary for such acts: One is a great social wrong that is undermining the liberties of a people. Secondly, a deep, sensitive social or individual psychology incapable of enduring that wrong. Where these factors are lacking one might preach violence from every housestop, without the slightest result. On the other hand, where social conditions outrage every sense of justice violent acts are then natural results.

This brings me to the most vital point. Not anarchism, the philosophy of social peace and harmony, not Emma Goldman's speeches are responsible for the act of the "assassin" of William McKinley, but people like T. T. H., like those who are the supporters and maintainers of a system which, as Thomas Paine said, "Sends old age to the workhouse and youth to the gallows."[3]

No doubt if T. T. H. means well, but he has much to learn. I suggest that he attend the free speech meeting Friday night at Labor Lyceum.[4] He might learn there what liberty really means.

Emma Goldman.

Philadelphia Public Ledger, 8 October 1909, p. 8. Reprinted in Alden Freeman, ed., *The Fight for Free Speech: A Supplement to "Law-Breaking by the Police"* (New York, 1909); and *Mother Earth* 4 (October 1909): 239–41.

1. Oscar Wilde, *The Ballad of Reading Gaol,* canto 3, st. 5.
2. Ibid., canto 5, st. 3.
3. From part 2 of Thomas Paine's *Rights of Man* (1791): "When, in countries that are called civilized, we see age going to the workhouse and youth to the gallows, something must be wrong in the system of government."
4. The meeting was chaired by Leonard Abbott. On 8 April 1909, EG's citizenship was revoked as a result of the denaturalization of her first husband, through whom she had obtained citizenship. EG, still awaiting the court's decision on whether aliens had a right to receive the protection of U.S. law, did not attend, but participated by sending a message to be read at the meeting.

Ferre has been murdered. What a terrible indictment against the revolutionary labor movement of Europe.[1]

I am arranging a Ferrer meeting for Sunday,[2] though my being here will be kept quiet. It will be announced, that I came from Phil. to speak. Could you hustle up the Radical Library[3] boys to arrange a Ferrer meeting and you do the press work? I think Nelson[4] would get them the Labor Lyceum[5] for $30 maybe and it ought not to be difficult, to have men like Earle White & Jackson[6] speak. Such a meeting is more important than Voltairine[7] on anarchism. She could speak a week later. I have also written to James F Morton, asking if he would go to Phil to speak.

Through the terrible show of Ferrers death, I have forgotten my own useless battle, my own heart wretched.

I came here 5 A M to day, after the most frightfully agonized journey of my life. When

1. Francisco Ferrer was executed by the Spanish government on 13 October 1909, at Montjuich, Barcelona's military prison, for his alleged part in the July 1909 general strike in Barcelona called by Solidaridad Obrera (Workers Federation). The organization's newspaper, also called *Solidaridad Obrera*, was heavily influenced by anarchists, with Ferrer as one of its founders and subsidizers in 1907. He was not actually in Barcelona during what would later be known as the "Tragic Week."
2. A meeting protesting the execution of Ferrer, at which EG was the primary speaker, was held in New York City on the evening of 17 October at Clinton Hall (on Manhattan's Lower East Side), attended by over 1,000 people.
3. The Radical Library was initially affiliated with the Ladies' Liberal League of Philadelphia, when the League joined the Radical Library around 1895. Guided by Voltairine de Cleyre and her friends, the Radical Library worked to "repair a deficit in the public libraries by furnishing radical works upon all subjects at convenient hours for working men and accessible to all at only a slight expense." In 1905, after the Ladies' Liberal League disbanded, Philadelphia anarchist Natasha Notkin, who had been the caretaker of the library, passed the books on to Joseph Cohen, a former student of de Cleyre's. Cohen started a new group, which settled at 424 Pine Street. The newly reconfigured Radical Library, led by Cohen, became an established center of Philadelphia anarchism. In 1906 the Radical Library and the Social Science Club sponsored a Paris Commune commemoration, at which Voltairine de Cleyre, George Brown, Frank Stephens, Chaim Weinberg as well as French and Italian anarchists spoke.
4. Henry Nelson was the lawyer representing EG in the 1909 free speech case in Philadelphia.
5. BR and Voltairine de Cleyre held an afternoon memorial meeting for Ferrer in Philadelphia on 17 October. The evening meeting at Industrial Hall (Broad and Wood Streets) was disrupted by police, relocated to 424 Pine Street, and disrupted again.
6. W. E. Jackson and Thomas Earle White were both sympathetic to anarchism. Jackson contributed to the Philadelphia Free Speech Fund in 1909 and to the Kotoku Defense Committee Fund in 1911. White, a lawyer from a prominent Philadelphia family, had been a member of an anarchist study group in the early 1890s organized by, among others, Voltairine de Cleyre. He contributed to the Philadelphia Free Speech Fund and to the *Mother Earth* Free Speech Fund in 1909. After a fire destroyed Benjamin Tucker's compositing room on 10 January 1908, White offered him $600 to replace his equipment.
7. EG refers to Voltairine de Cleyre.

I too, shall walk the path of Ferrer it will be no new experience. Last night, I tasted its horrors.

I am broken in spirit and body. I feel weary, just weary. My struggle never seemed more useless, a lone voice, against a multitude. My effort to keep our relation on a high plane too has failed. Our relation is has grown common place and is being dragged through the myre. Yes, yes, I know its my fault. I forgot that habit is stronger than love. Yet it is terrible to contemplate, that it should be so.

I do not reproach you, really not, I am only indiscribly sad and weary—

I hope the map has reached you. Alex[8] got your letter too late last night to send the map special. He meant to do it this morning, but my physical and mental condition, when I got here upset him so, he forgot all about the map. I woke up at three PM and hastened Alex to the PO. I hope it did reach you in time and that you did well.

Are the watchdogs about? Anything new? I fear, I am not made for rest, nor am I quite fit for everlasting war. I feel completely shipwrecked. I am writing Voltairine about the Ferrer meeting.

If no such meeting can be arranged, Voltairines ought to be made a success

I expect to return late Sunday night.

E. THE CRASY ONE

ALI, IU-U. On *Mother Earth* stationery.

8. EG refers to Alexander Berkman.

Essay in *MOTHER EARTH*
November 1909

Francisco Ferrer

Never before in the history of the world has one man's death so thoroughly united struggling mankind.

Never before has one man's death called forth such a universal cry of indignation.

Never before has one man's death so completely torn the veil from the sinister face of the hydra-headed monster, the Catholic Church.

Never before in the history of the world has one man's death so shaken the thrones of the golden calf, and spread ghastly fear among its worshippers.

One solitary death, yet more powerful than a million cringing lives. More powerful even than that black spectre which, for almost two thousand years, has tortured man's soul and poisoned his mind.

Francisco Ferrer stretched in the ditch at Montjuich, his tender, all-too-loving heart silenced by twelve bullets[1]—yet speaking, speaking in a voice so loud, so clear, so deep. . . . Wherein lies the secret of this wonderful phenomenon?

Francisco Ferrer, the Anarchist and teacher? Yes, but there were other Anarchists and teachers: Louise Michel[2] and Elisée Reclus,[3] for instance, beloved by many. Yet why has their death not proved such a tremendous force?

Francisco Ferrer, the founder of the Modern School?[4] But, then, the Modern School did not originate with Francisco Ferrer, though it was he who carried it to Spain. The father of the Modern School is Paul Robin,[5] the latter-day Dr. Pascal,—old in years, with the spirit of Spring, tender and loving, he taught modern methods of education long before Ferrer. He organized the first Modern School at Cempuis, near Paris, wherein children found a home, a warm, beautiful atmosphere.

---

1. Francisco Ferrer, executed by the Spanish government on 13 October 1909.
2. Louise Michel (1830–1905) was a French anarchist and teacher whom EG met in London in 1895.
3. Élisée Reclus was a French geographer and leading theorist of anarchist communism.
4. Ferrer's Modern School (Escuela Moderna), founded in Barcelona in 1901, established a curriculum based on moral rationalism, free from all religious doctrine. The co-educational school countered the common atmosphere of competition by suspending all grading and testing and emphasized the unity of mind and body. It was, in Ferrer's words, a "school of emancipation."
5. Paul Robin (1837–1912) was a French anarchist educator and neo-Malthusian. As director of a French orphanage in Cempuis, he experimented with a teaching program tailored to the individual child, informed by observation, and driven by a desire to nurture creativity. He was a great influence on both Ferrer and Sebastian Faure. EG met Robin in Paris during 1900.

"FRANCISCO FERRER, HIS LIFE AND WORK"

On this interesting subject

EMMA GOLDMAN

will lecture

Sunday, November 28th, 8 P. M.

AT THE

WOMAN'S TRADES UNION HALL

43 East 22nd Street

ADMISSION. 15 CENTS

Card advertising one of many Goldman lectures about the recently executed Spanish anarchist and modern school educator Francisco Ferrer. (By permission of the Kate Sharpley Library)

Again, there is Sebastian Faure[6] and his Beehive. He, too, has founded a Modern School, a free, happy, and harmonious place for children. There are scores of modern schools in France, yet no other man's death will act as a fertilizing force as that of Francisco Ferrer.

Was Ferrer's influence so great because of a lifetime of devoted effort? During eight years his heroic spirit strove to spread the light in the dark land of his birth. For eight years he toiled, ceaselessly, to rescue the child from the destructive influence of superstition. One hundred and nine schools with seventy thousands pupils crowned the gigantic efforts of our murdered comrade, while three hundred and eight liberal schools sprang into being, thanks to his beneficial influence. Yet all this and more fails to account for the tremendous volcano that swept the civilized world at Francisco Ferrer's death.

His trial was a farce. The evidence against him perjured. But was there ever a time when the State hesitated to resort to perjury when dealing with opponents? Was there ever a time when it exercised justice toward those who endangered its stronghold? The State is the very embodiment of injustice and perjury. Some make a pretence at fairness: Spain was brazen; that is all.

What, then, is the secret of the phenomenon?

Driven from its omnipotent position of open crime by the world's progress, the Catholic Church had not ceased to be a virulent poison within the social body. Its Borgia methods merely became more hidden, more secret, yet none the less malignant and perfidious.

---

6. Sebastian Faure (1858–1942) was a French anarchist, journalist, and educator who ran a libertarian school called Le Ruche (The Beehive) that EG visited in 1907.

Cowed into apparent submission, it had not dared since the days of Huss[7] and Bruno[8] to openly demand a noble victim's blood. But at last, blinded by arrogance and conceit and the insatiable thirst for martyrs' blood, the Catholic Church forgot the progress of the world, forgot the spirit of our age, forgot the growth of free ideas. As of old, it was the Jesuit hand that stretched forth its bloody fingers to snatch its victim. It was the Archbishop of Barcelona who, in a statement signed by the prelates of the Church, first denounced Ferrer and demanded his life. As of old, Inquisition methods were used in the incarceration and mock trial of Ferrer. No time was to be given the progressive world to check the premeditated murder. Hastily and secretly was the martyr assassinated. Full well the Church knew that the dead cannot be saved.

In vain the frantic efforts of Church and State to connect Francisco Ferrer with the uprising at Barcelona. In vain their delirious cries defaming the character of the dead. In vain the scurrilous attacks of their harlots upon the ideas and comrades of Ferrer—attacks which have now reached even the American press.

Before the awakened consciousness of mankind the world over the Catholic Church stands condemned as the instigator and perpetrator of the foul crime committed at Montjuich. It is this awakened human consciousness which has resurrected Francisco Ferrer.

Therein lies the secret of the force of one man's death, of one solitary man in the ditch of Montjuich.

Mother Earth 4 (November 1909): 275–77.

7. John Huss (ca. 1370–1415) was the Bohemian priest and religious reformer excommunicated after attacking what he considered to be abuses by the clergy. For his denial of the infallibility of the pope, he was ultimately sentenced as a heretic and burned at the stake.
8. Giordano Bruno (1548–1600) was the Italian philosopher and early freethinker whose works attacking both Aristotelian and Christian doctrines drew the attention of Church authorities; he was tried for heresy and burned at the stake. An early proponent of rational philosophy, Bruno became an icon for freethinkers and the freethought movement.

You have made yourself perfectly plain, Ben dear. You have substantiated what I knew long ago, what I told you many times, namely, love is an unknown thing to you. What you call love, is an insatiable monster, that saps loves blood and then kicks it into the cold. Your love ~~exculd~~ excludes giving, excludes concern for the welbeing of ~~the~~ loves objects. Your love takes and takes and when it can take no more, it thrusts love aside, in a manner so cold so brutal, so inhuman as if love had never existed

Please, do not think I scold or upraid, or blame you

If I were still in that stage, I should not be so miserable. Can I blame the blind if he does not see, can I blame the deaf if he does not hear? Why then should I blame you? Besides it is not a question of ~~realization~~ blame, it is a question of coming face to face with a terrible fact

Last Thursday, on that most terrible day of my life, the day of my greatest humilliation, I came fact to face with a cruel fact

I saw, that, what you called love, was only a caprice to satisfy your every whim no matter at what expence. I saw too, that unless I continue to submit, to that whim, I have no place in your life, no place in your humanity no place in your esteeme.

Well, I do not blame you, I do not sencure you, I do not condemn you. I only know, I can never again put myself in a position that should give you the right to treat me, as you have on that black day in Boston

I can never again place my soul at your heel to be kicked and bruised until it is sore beyond endurence.

I shall not go into the reasons you give for your mood. They are too foolish and are no justification. "Packed you off." Great Heavens, have I not stripped myself of the last, that you may satisfy your fancies that you may run back and forth between NY and Chicago.

You are the first human being who has ever excused me of money considerations and if you were not so utterly swallowd up by your own childish desires, you would know, that I deserve no such accusation. If it were not ~~so funny it would be pathe~~ so pathetic, it would be funny indeed, to think that you would outrage and state your "great love for me, just because you could not see your "friends Fannies, Lydias and Heaven knows whom else. And for these these "friends my selfrespect my womanhood, my humanity had to be outraged. It's really too awful to contemplate.

No, indeed you are not usless. On the contrary, you are a wonderful worker, Ben dear

It is too bad, we did not meet, when propaganda meant more to me than everything else in the World, when I had no personal interest in people or things, when I could use everything and everybody for the sake of the cause. That time is past much to the disadvantage of my own life.

Meetings, free speech, ME are nothing to me now, if my love my life, my peace my very soul is to be mitilated. Work with you, so long as I had faith in your love, meant the greatest sweetest joy in life. That may account for my utter abandonement, my a utter dissolution to my love for you. That may also account why I, the woman who has been treated with respect by friend and foe could crouch on her knees and beg and plead with you. Yes, I believed in your love, or rather I believed too much in the power of my love to teach you, to make you see the beauty the force the greatness of love. I believe in it no longer, I have no faith in your love, and with it the joy of work with you is gone. I have no right to bring a message to people when there is no message in my soul. I have no right to speak of freedom when I myself, became an abject slave in my love. I have no right to talk of the beauty of love, when with that hidious Thursday before me. Why then have meetings. I do not wish to go to Buffalo, still less do I care to go to Chicago.[1] All is dead. Unfortunately, I too shall not die; most people live with dead souls, why not I?

I see, I have already said too much. I hope you will be as happy as you can. I shall always be your friend I am sure, always be interested in your life.

It's not a question of whether I love you well enough to stand your moods, or whether I want you, I know I shall never again endure what I have endured last Thursday never again.

Emma

ALS, IU-U. On *Mother Earth* stationery.

1. EG was barred from speaking in Buffalo in January 1910 by the chief of police. She spoke in Chicago on 17 January 1910, at the German Hod Carriers' Hall.

I got your Special only this morning Ben, dear. You addressed it to Chicago, thats why. Your wire came late last night, when I returned from the Arb ring, where I was dully installed as the 100th member.[1] Needless to say, I was very much surprised to hear, that "Chicago gives me "free speech.""[2] Free speech with police conditions, what a mockery. Still, I am quite ready to avail myself of that.

I would rather not race however. I am negotiating with Rochester and Pittsburg. The letter from R will explain. The writer is a Unitarian minister, who wrote me last week. I asked for their Hall which is connected with their Church. If I can get it, I could reach a class of people which otherwise, I could never get, I could charge 50, and 25 c[ents] admission. Besides that I can have a Jewish meeting. In Pittsburg the Arb ring asked me for two dates. I gave them only one, $15 for the lecture, $10 expences. If they exc accept, I could have an English meeting. Maybe something can be done in Buffalo with the new Mayor, since the old one does not reply. Altogether I should like to visit these cities, before I reach Chicago, also Cleveland, Toledo & Detroit. I need at least 2 weeks for that, which would bring us up to the middle of Jan. Sunday Jan 16 afternoon & evening, we can have two meeting on that day in Chicago.[3]

I do not think it advisable to try Illinois, towns, until we succeed in Chicago. Wiscon could be attended to later.

In Chicago I should like 3 English and one Jewish meetings. The first to be in a pretty large hall. The Jewish in the largest hall on the West side. If possible, tickets should sold in advance. I do not want you to cooperate with the Edelst group,[4] they are a petty lot, but get Beckie and Bill[5] to help you. Also if you have tickets you could give them out to people

---

1. The Arbeiter Ring (Workmen's Circle), founded in 1892, was a Jewish welfare, educational and fraternal organization with strong ties to the Jewish labor, socialist and anarchist movements.

2. EG spoke in Chicago on 17 January 1910 at the German Hod Carriers' Hall with the permission of Police Chief Leroy T. Steward, who took office in August 1909. He promised to allow her to speak but stated that he would maintain a police presence at all her meetings.

3. EG's 1910 tour, from 5 January to 18 June, covered cities in 25 states. She lectured in Chicago, Milwaukee, Madison, Hannibal, St. Louis, Detroit, and Ann Arbor in January and February. Then in March she lectured in Rochester, Pittsburgh, and Minneapolis before lecturing in various cities in Ohio, Iowa, Nebraska, Wyoming, Colorado, Utah, and California.

4. The Edelstadt group was a Chicago anarchist organization inspired by Yiddish anarchist poet David Edelstadt (1866–1892), founded by his brother, Abe Edelstadt, and organized by Miriam (Beckie) Yamplosky and William Nathanson.

5. EG refers to Chicago anarchist Miriam (Beckie) Yamplosky and Beckie's companion William (Bill) Nathanson.

like Dr Greer,[6] and other reliable subscribers of ME the list of which, I will send you later, also to Mrs Annie Livshitz[7] and the girls that come there. I think, by taking our time and selling tickets in advance, we could have a success. Tickets to the Engl meetings should be 50–25 reserved, if a large hall 15 c[ents] general admission. Of course, the public will have to know, that I am permitted to speak only 4 times, that will draw.

As soon, as I hear from Rochester and Pittsburg I shall let you know and ask you to go to Detroit, Cleveland, Toledo, Pittsburg and R to work up the meetings. Meanwhile you can secure halls in Chicago begining Jan 16th,[8] print tickets and give them in charge of Beckie Y also make it known that I am coming. But before everything you must have the absolute assurence that the meetings will not be stopped.

I know dear, you are impulsive, you are easily carried away, you have not yet learned that if a Mayor or chief receives you kindly, there is more reason to look out.

I have not the desire or the means to go to Chicago unless we are sure of non interference. The subjects, I would like to talk on, is Woman Suffrage, Ferrer, (of course) The White Slave trafic, new lecture (preparing to day) the Dream as a moral force. Have prepared "Strife" yesterday it is very good, I could speak on that.[9] Marriage and Love[10] is hateful to me, hateful because my faith in the power of love has been shattered. I used to think it can perform miracles, poor fool that I was. You do not seem to realize, my boy; the shock the awful shock, my love has received, one never survives after such a shock. I therefore hope, that when we meet again, you will not use the method, you employ with other women coerce me drive me force me back into a relationship. I may or may not find my way back to you, dear which ever way, will depend on you. One thing is certain, I am beyond the old way. I could not stand for that really not. Mother Earth is not out yet, who cares? I am the only one who wears her heart out, to no use. I shall have a hard day tomorrow, 3 lectures two new subjects.[11] Please dear, keep me posted, tell me the Halls you secured and what the papers say

AFFECTIONATELY

MOMMY

ALS, IU-U. On *Mother Earth* stationery.

6. Joseph H. Greer (1851–1921) was a Chicago physician, radical, and sex reformer as well as a supporter of EG, often hosting her during her stays in Chicago, contributing money to her free speech fights and one article to *Mother Earth* in November 1912. He wrote a number of books on women's sexual health including *A Physician in the House* (Chicago: M. A. Donohue, 1897).
7. EG refers to Chicago anarchist Annie Livshis.
8. EG spoke in Chicago on 17 January 1910 on "Women Suffrage."
9. During her 1910 lecture tour EG spoke often on women's suffrage, Ferrer, drama, the general strike, the Church, and anarchism.
10. EG first lectured on the topic of "Marriage and Love" on 27 September 1908, after which it became one of her staple topics and eventually appeared as an essay in *Anarchism and Other Essays* (New York: Mother Earth Publishing Co., 1910). She did speak on "Marriage and Love from an Anarchist Perspective" a number of times during her 1910 lecture tour.
11. EG spoke on "Strife" and "The New Theater" at the Women's Trade Union Hall in New York City on 19 December 1909.

CHRONOLOGY

1902

JANUARY

The Congress of Americas in Mexico, attended by representatives of many countries including the United States, passed anti-anarchist criminalization and extradition agreements.

JANUARY 2

E. C. Walker, Edward Chamberlain, Edward Bond Foote, Jr., M.D., and members of Manhattan Liberal Club, who would later form the Free Speech League, issued the first call for support of the editors and publishers of the suppressed anarchist newspaper *Discontent*.

MARCH 11

Trial of editors of *Discontent* took place after their arrest in September 1901 for "depositing lewd, lascivious and obscene materials in the mails." The judge dismissed the charge the same day.

APRIL

Evicted from her First Street apartment, EG moved to a Lower East Side tenement building on Market Street in **New York**; found work as a night-shift nurse for poor immigrants.

APRIL 3

The Criminal Anarchy Act passed in Albany, New York.

Memorial meeting for John P. Altgeld in Cooper Union, **New York**, organized by the Central Federated union and the Workingmen's Committee of One Hundred. Henry George, Jr., was the chair of the meeting; the principal speaker was Clarence Darrow. EG was in the audience.

APRIL 7

Italian anarchist Errico Malatesta was sentenced in Rome to five months imprisonment for writing articles that applauded the assassination of President William McKinley.

APRIL 8

EG spoke on "Modern Phases of Anarchism" at New Irving Hall in **New York**.

APRIL 11

New York Supreme Court upheld Johann Most's conviction for publication of "Murder against Murder" immediately preceding McKinley's assassination.

APRIL 18

Judge Charles F. MacLean, of the New York Supreme Court's appellate division, granted Johann Most a stay while his case was pending an appeal. MacLean ruled that there was a possibility of reasonable doubt.

APRIL 23

Silk workers went on strike in Paterson, New Jersey.

APRIL 30

The Criminal Anarchy Act passed in Trenton, New Jersey.

MAY–DECEMBER

EG resumes political work, conducting a lecture tour to raise funds for students and peasants under attack in Russia and for the striking Pennsylvania coal miners. Her activities were closely monitored by police detectives. Many lectures were outlawed, especially in coal-mining cities like Wilkes-Barre and McKeesport, Pennsylvania. She held successful lectures in **Chicago**; spoke in **Milwaukee** and **Cleveland**.

MAY 1

The Free Speech League was founded in New York. Members include E. W. Chamberlain, A. C. Pleydell, E. B. Foote, Jr., E. C. Walker, and Benjamin R. Tucker.

MAY 4

A farewell reception was held in honor of Johann Most at New Irving Hall in New York City; Most was to begin his prison sentence the following day. During his speech, William MacQueen yelled comments such as "To hell with the laws of America; to hell with the government." Most then took the platform and addressed the crowd in German. MacQueen and Most were arrested while a mob, acting in the two men's defense, attacked the three detectives making the arrests.

MAY 11

EG spoke on "Modern Phases of Anarchy" at Paine Memorial Hall in **Boston**, Massachusetts.

MAY 31

The Boer War ends.

JUNE 10

Johann Most's conviction for publication of "Murder against Murder" was upheld by the New York Court of Appeals.

JUNE 18

EG was invited to attend rally of striking silk-workers at Belmont Park, Paterson, New Jersey, but declined to attend. The rally became a riot. Rudolf Grossmann and William MacQueen were later arrested and charged with incitement to riot. Luigi Galleani fled to Canada to avoid arrest.

JUNE 20

Johann Most's conviction was upheld by the New York State Court of Appeals, followed by his sentencing to a third term on Blackwell's Island.

CA. JUNE 21

The Free Speech League held a dinner for Ida C. Craddock upon her release from Blackwell's Is-

land, after being imprisoned for sending obscene material through the mail. This was the first official function of the Free Speech League.

OCTOBER 10

EG spoke on "God and Religion" at the Terrace Garden in **New York**. Jay Fox and Rudolf Grossmann also spoke.

NOVEMBER 9

EG was prevented by police from speaking in **Providence**, Rhode Island.

NOVEMBER 16

EG spoke on the situation in Russia at Brand's Hall in **Chicago**, Illinois, with Rudolf Grossmann.

NOVEMBER 18

EG spoke on "The Situation in Paterson, New Jersey" at a meeting at Nevearving Hall, 214–220 Broome St., **New York**. Other speakers included Rudolf Grossmann, Moshe Katz, Joseph Barondess, and Nellie MacQueen, wife of William MacQueen, one of those arrested at Paterson.

NOVEMBER 23

Barred from Handel Hall where she originally had been scheduled to speak on "Modern Phases of Anarchism," EG spoke at the Trades Unions Hall in **Chicago** on "The Radical and the Child."

NOVEMBER 30

EG was barred by police from speaking at Aurora Hall in **Chicago**.

DECEMBER 6

A farewell reception for EG was held at Ruehl's Hall in **Chicago**.

DECEMBER 7

EG spoke on "Modern Phases of Anarchism" at Uhlich's Hall in **Chicago**. The chairman of the meeting announced that Police Chief O'Neil stated that if EG was prevented from speaking in Chicago, it was without orders from him.

DECEMBER 14

EG was scheduled to speak on the events in Russia at the Hungarian Hall in **Cleveland**, Ohio.

DECEMBER 19

Voltairine de Cleyre was shot and wounded in Philadelphia by Herman Helcher, a former pupil.

1903

JANUARY 27

Police arrested EG and Max Baginski in **New York** for no reason other than on "general principles"; they were released after questioning.

MARCH 3

Immigration Act was passed by Congress. The act named anarchists as a group barred from immigration and naturalization in the United States.

SPRING

For many weeks, EG nursed a patient ill with tuberculosis in **Liberty**, New York.

APRIL 2

Edward Brady, Austrian anarchist and former companion of EG, died in New York.

APRIL 6–8

Pogroms occurred in Kishinev, Russia.

APRIL 11

Johann Most was released from prison on Blackwell's Island two months early for good behavior.

MAY 6

EG attended a Friends of Russian Freedom meeting in **New York**.

JUNE

Cronaca Sovversiva, Italian-language anarchist communist newspaper, was founded in Barre, Vermont.

JUNE 29

EG lectured on the situation in Russia at the New American Hall in **New York**. Michael Cohn, M.D., also spoke.

SEPTEMBER 27

A pogrom occurred in Gomel, Russia, after a group of about five hundred railroad workers began a rampage through a Jewish neighborhood.

OCTOBER 19

Warrant for the arrest of John Turner, English anarchist, issued by the U.S. Secretary of Commerce and Labor.

OCTOBER 23

English anarchist John Turner was arrested after giving a lecture "Trade Unionism and the General Strike" at Murray Hill Lyceum in New York and charged with promoting anarchism and violating alien immigration law. Turner was detained on Ellis Island pending deportation. EG in attendance at the meeting.

OCTOBER 25

EG attended an organizational meeting to support the Turner case at the Radical Reading Room, 180 Forsyth Street, in **New York**.

OCTOBER 28

EG attended an organizational meeting on the Turner case at the Radical Reading Room in **New York**.

OCTOBER 29

EG attended an organizational meeting on the Turner case at the Radical Reading Room in **New York**.

NOVEMBER

The Free Speech League became the Turner Defense Committee, with Edward Chamberlain as chairman, A. C. Pleydell as secretary, and E. B. Foote, Jr., as treasurer.

NOVEMBER 2

EG spoke at a meeting on the Turner case at 83 Forsyth Street in **New York**.

NOVEMBER 4

EG attended an organizational meeting on the Turner case at the Radical Reading Room, 180 Forsyth Street, in **New York**.

NOVEMBER 5

EG spoke on the Turner case at Grand Irving Palace in **New York**. Other speakers included Joseph Barondess and Hillel Solotaroff, M.D.

NOVEMBER 7

U.S. Circuit Court judge Emile Henry Lacombe upheld the Immigration Act and Turner's deportation order.

DECEMBER

The Free Speech League issued two press bulletins, Nos. 1 and 2, both entitled *Free Speech and the New Alien Law*.

DECEMBER 3

A mass meeting was held at Cooper Union in New York City protesting the proceedings against

John Turner; chaired by John Sherwin Crosby (single-tax advocate); speakers included Henry Frank, Ernest Crosby, and John de Witt Warner.

1904

JANUARY

EG began a brief lecture tour on behalf of the Free Speech League to gain support for Turner. She spoke before garment workers in **Rochester**, New York, and miners in **Pennsylvania**.

JANUARY 4

Ricardo Flores Magón (released from prison in October 1903) and other Mexican Liberal Party (Partido Liberal Mexicano, PLM) members moved to Laredo, Texas, to escape from the Díaz government in Mexico.

FEBRUARY

Free Society moved to New York from Chicago.

FEBRUARY 4

EG spoke on "The English Propaganda" during the intermission at the play *The Jewish Sappho,* at the Thalia Theater in **New York**, a benefit for *Free Society*.

FEBRUARY 8

Japan launched a surprise attack on the Russian fleet in Port Arthur.

FEBRUARY 10

Declaration of war made between Japan and Russia.

MARCH 17

EG spoke at the International Commune celebration at the Manhattan Lyceum in **New York**. Other speakers included Pedro Esteve, J. Villalore, and H. Weinberg.

MARCH 21

Dinner organized by the Free Speech League at the Arlington Hotel, **New York**, in honor of John Turner. EG spoke. Other speakers included E. B. Foote, Jr., Joseph Barondess, and Hugh Pentecost.

MARCH 19

John Turner spoke at the Cooper Institute in New York under the auspices of the Free Speech League.

MARCH 24

John Turner was scheduled to speak at Cooper Union in New York City on "The Signs of the Times."

MARCH 27

EG attended a meeting given in honor of John Turner at the Odd Fellows' Temple, on Broad and Cherry streets, in **Philadelphia**, Pennsylvania. Turner lectured on "Signs of the times." George Brown, William Ross, James Williams, Thomas Kavanaugh, and Frank Westel also spoke.

At a meeting set to discuss "The Home and the Higher Education of Women" at the Broad Street Baptist Church in Philadelphia, Bernard Blau cited EG as an example of the highest type of educated woman. He stated that this was because she worked for the benefit of other human beings. The audience hissed at Blau until he stopped speaking.

APRIL 1

EG spoke at a reception for John Turner at Manhattan Lyceum, **New York**.

APRIL 6–7

John Turner's deportation trial was argued before the U.S. Supreme Court in Washington, D.C. Turner was represented by Clarence S. Darrow and Edgar L. Masters.

APRIL 10

EG was scheduled to speak at the Odd Fellows' Temple in **Philadelphia**, Pennsylvania. Her meeting was banned by local authorities.

APRIL 11

EG spoke on "The Struggle Between Capital and Labor" at the Grand Irving Palace in **New York**. John Turner also spoke.

APRIL 17

A meeting was held at Odd Fellows' Temple in Philadelphia to protest police activity to bar EG from speaking.

APRIL 22

John Turner spoke in Chicago at the Workingman's Hall.

APRIL 23

John Turner spoke in Chicago at the Union Hall.

APRIL 24

The meeting barred two weeks previously (April 10) at Odd Fellows' Temple in **Philadelphia**, Pennsylvania, was held. EG spoke on "The Tragedy of Woman's Emancipation."

APRIL 30

John Turner returns to England.

MAY 13

EG spoke on "The Tragedy of Woman's Emancipation" at the Manhattan Liberal Club in **New York**.

MAY 16

The U.S. Supreme Court ruled on John Turner's case that Congress had unlimited power to exclude aliens and deport those who have entered in violation of the law. They also denied the unconstitutionality of 1903 Immigration Act.

MAY 22

EG spoke on "Anarchism and the Modern Drama" at the Odd Fellows' Temple in **Philadelphia**, Pennsylvania.

MAY 25

EG spoke on "The Unpleasant Side of George Bernard Shaw" at Etris Hall in **New York**.

JUNE 15

EG spoke on "The Unpleasant Side of George Bernard Shaw" at the Liberal Art Society in **New York**.

SEPTEMBER 5

An anarchist convention was held in St. Louis, Missouri. The convention was poorly attended because of Johann Most's criticisms of the meeting in multiple anarchist periodicals. The thirteen people who attended focused their discussion on anarchist tactics and the general strike.

FALL

EG hosted two members of the Russian Social Revolutionary Party seeking to organize support for political freedom in Russia. With the American Friends of Russian Freedom, EG aided the successful tour of Catherine Breshkovskaya. EG's niece, Stella Comyn, came to live with EG in New York.

SEPTEMBER 11

EG spoke in **New York** at a large anarchist meeting in support of the Russian anarchist movement. Among other speakers were Johann Most, Abe Isaak, and Harry Kelly.

SEPTEMBER 19

EG was prevented from speaking at a picnic in the borough of **Queens, New York City**.

NOVEMBER

Running for the presidency on the Socialist Party ticket, Eugene Debs received 402,793 votes. His running mate was Benjamin Hanford. Catherine Breshkovskaya arrived in New York.

NOVEMBER 5

PLM's *Regeneración* reappeared in San Antonio.

NOVEMBER 10

EG spoke at a Haymarket commemoration meeting held at New American Hall in **New York**. Other speakers included Harry Kelly, James F. Morton, Jr., and Lucy Parsons.

NOVEMBER 11

EG spoke at a Haymarket commemoration meeting at the Broadway Labor Lyceum, on Willoughby Avenue, in **New York**.

NOVEMBER 20

Free Society ceased publication.

EG was scheduled to speak on "Modern Phases of Anarchism" at Plotz's Hall, 240 East 80th Street, in **New York**.

DECEMBER

EG opened her own business as a "Vienna scalp and face specialist" in **New York**.

DECEMBER 22

A mass meeting at Cooper Union in New York City was held for the Russian cause. Catherine Breshkovskaya, Chaim Zhitlovsky, M.D., and Robert Ely spoke.

1905

JANUARY

Kōtoku Shūsui arrested in Japan for violating publishing laws (he published a translation of the Communist Manifesto). He was sentenced to five months in prison.

JANUARY 22

"Bloody Sunday" occurred in Russia. Soldiers killed and wounded hundreds of workers and their families as they marched to the Winter Palace in St. Petersburg to present a petition to the tsar asking for better working conditions, civil liberties granted to all citizens, and a constituent assembly elected on the basis of democratic suffrage. The following day over 150,000 workers went on strike in protest. The incident provided credibility to Catherine Breshkovskaya's lectures on tsarist brutality that she delivered while on tour in the United States. EG continued to lecture and raise funds to support Russian revolutionaries.

JANUARY 23

The police prevented EG from speaking at a meeting of the Russian Socialist Revolutionaries at Clinton Hall in **New York**.

FEBRUARY 2

Ricardo and Enrique Flores Magón opened *Regeneración* office at 107 North Channing Avenue in St. Louis, Missouri, moving there after a problem with the authorities in San Antonio, Texas. First edition published 27 February.

FEBRUARY 12

EG spoke on "The Events in Russia" at Old Homstead Hall, **New York**. Other speakers included Chaim Zhitlovsky and others from PSR.

MARCH

Catherine Breshkovskaya returned to Europe. EG threw a farewell party for Breshkovskaya at her apartment at 210 East 13th Street.

MARCH 7

Farewell meeting for Breshkovskaya at Webster Hall, **New York**. EG acted as interpreter and chair.

MARCH 23

Pavel Orlenev and Alla Nazimova opened in New York with the St. Petersburg Dramatic Co.

JUNE 27

The founding convention of the Industrial Workers of the World (IWW) began in Chicago.

Attendees included William D. Haywood, Eugene V. Debs, Lucy Parsons, Daniel De Leon, Charles Moyer, Jay Fox, Julia Mechanic, and Joseph Peukert.

JULY

EG met Russian actor Pavel Orlenev in **New York**. She became the Orlenev Theater company's manager until early 1906.

JULY 19

AB was removed from Western Penitentiary to the Allegheny workhouse where he served the final year of his sentence, shortened to ten months for good behavior.

SEPTEMBER 5

Russia and Japan signed a peace treaty in Portsmouth, New Hampshire, ending the Russo-Japanese War.

OCTOBER 12

Offices of *Regeneración* in St. Louis, Missouri, raided by Pinkerton detectives (acting without warrants). Presses were confiscated, the brothers Magóns and associates arrested, charged with libel and defamation, and eventually let out on bail until December.

OCTOBER 30

Tsar Nicholas II signed manifesto providing for limited suffrage and a legislative assembly.

FALL

Renewed pogroms in Russia. In the last four months of 1904, 33 anti-Jewish riots occurred, many of them instigated by soldiers in response to antisemitic newspapers claiming that Jews were aiding Russia's enemies.

NOVEMBER 18

Orlenev Theater Company at Russian Lyceum, **New York**, in *The Brothers Karamazov*.

NOVEMBER 19

Orlenev Theater Company at Russian Lyceum, **New York**, in *Star* (matinee) and *Forests* (evening).

NOVEMBER 21

Orlenev Theater Company at Russian Lyceum, **New York**, in *Star*.

NOVEMBER 22

Orlenev Theater Company at Russian Lyceum, **New York**, in *Innocent Culprits,* a benefit for Russian Jews.

NOVEMBER 24

Orlenev Theater Company at Russian Lyceum, **New York**, in *Family Zwee.*

NOVEMBER 25

Orlenev Theater Company at Russian Lyceum, **New York**, in *Family Zwee.*

NOVEMBER 29

Kōtoku Shūsui arrived in America.

DECEMBER

Tsarist forces crush general strikes in Moscow.

DECEMBER 30

Ex-Idaho governor Frank Steunenberg killed by a bomb planted in front of his home in Caldwell, Idaho.

1906

The Free Speech League published Thaddeus Wakeman's pamphlet *Administrative Process of the Postal Department: A Letter to the President,* on the free-speech implications of the Comstock laws.

JANUARY 1

Harry Orchard was arrested for the murder of ex-Idaho governor Frank Steunenberg.

JANUARY 8

Idaho governor Frank Gooding hired Pinkerton detective James McParland to coordinate Steunenberg's murder investigation. McParland investigated the Western Federation of Miners "inner circle," including William Haywood, Charles Moyer, and George Pettibone.

EARLY FEBRUARY

EG spoke on "The Present Phase of the Russian Revolution" at the Progressive Association, **New York**. Other speakers included Max Baginski, Johann Most, and Harry Kelly.

FEBRUARY 1

Regeneración was published again in St. Louis after the raid by Pinkerton detectives the previous October.

FEBRUARY 5

Orlenev scheduled benefit performance of August Strindberg's *Countess Julia,* to raise seed money for the publication of EG's new magazine. Upon the arrest of Orlenev by creditors, rehearsals were cut short, after which the performance was rescheduled to 7 March.

FEBRUARY 12–25

EG traveled with the Orlenev troupe as its manager under the alias E. G. Smith for its two-week residency in **Chicago** at the Studebaker Theatre. She also delivered lectures on anarchism under her own name.

FEBRUARY 15

Colorado governor Jesse Fuller MacDonald honored the extradition papers for the arrest of William Haywood, Charles Moyer, and George Pettibone.

FEBRUARY 17

William Haywood, Charles Moyer, and George Pettibone were arrested and kidnapped in Denver, accused of Frank Steunenberg's murder, and illegally transported to Boise, Idaho.

FEBRUARY 26

Moses Harman, editor of *Lucifer* and 75 years old, was imprisoned for sending obscene material through the mail. He was sentenced to a year at hard labor.

Meeting of Sunrise Club in Cafe Boulevard, **New York**, attended by 400, to discuss the motion "Woman the Inconstant One," put by Hugh Pentecost. EG spoke from the audience against the motion.

MARCH 6

William Haywood, Charles Moyer, and George Pettibone were indicted on charges of conspiring to commit Frank Steunenberg's murder.

MARCH 7

Orlenev's *Mother Earth* benefit performance of Henrik Ibsen's *Ghosts* in Manhattan raised less money than anticipated, in part because the play had already been performed.

MID-MARCH

The first issue of *Mother Earth* was published. EG began a speaking tour with Max Baginski on its behalf. In *Living My Life*, she recalled large meetings in Toronto, Cleveland, and Buffalo.

Enrique Flores Magón, Ricardo Flores Magón, and Juan Sarabia paid their bail in St. Louis and fled to Toronto, Canada. The men feared that Mexican president Porfirio Díaz would arrange their extradition to Mexico through U.S. authorities. *Regeneración* was left to be edited by Librado Rivera, Antonio I. Villarreal, and Manual Sarabia even though U.S. postal authorities, at the request of the Mexican government, revoked its fourth class mailing privileges.

The Free Speech League published four pamphlets by Theodore Schroeder: *Freedom of the Press and "Obscene" Literature; Liberty of Speech and Press Essential to Purity Propaganda; Much Needed Defense for Liberty of Conscience, Speech and Press, with Special Application to Sex Discussion;* and *What Is Criminally "Obscene"?*

MARCH 16

EG, along with Max Baginski, spoke in German on "Anarchist-Communism" at the Pythian Temple in **Cleveland**, Ohio. EG's evening lecture was delivered in English.

MARCH 17

Johann Most died in Cincinnati, Ohio.

EG eulogized Most in an address at the Pythian Temple in **Cleveland**. Other speakers included Max Baginski and Walter Behlen, former president of the Cleveland Franklin Club.

MARCH 18

EG spoke in **Buffalo**, New York, in English, complying with Buffalo Police Capt. Ward, who warned that any presentation in a language other than English would be considered a felony. Max Baginski, not fluent enough in English, was unable to speak as planned.

MARCH 19

EG's second presentation in **Buffalo** was dispersed by police even before EG's arrival; doors to the hall were locked.

MARCH 20-21

EG was scheduled to speak in **Rochester**, New York.

MARCH 22-23

EG was scheduled to speak in **Syracuse**, New York.

MARCH 24-25

EG was scheduled to speak in **Utica**, New York.

LATE MARCH

EG was scheduled to speak in **Toronto**, Canada.

APRIL

EG terminated the lease on her scalp and facial massage office, deciding to devote herself full-time to *Mother Earth*.

APRIL 1

EG spoke at an afternoon anarchists' gathering at Grand Central Palace in **New York** to commemorate the life of the late Johann Most. Presided over by Abe Isaak, other speakers included Lucy Parsons, Chaim Zhitlovsky, M.D., Hillel Solotaroff, M.D., Saul Yanovsky (in Yiddish), Pedro Esteve (in Spanish), Max Baginski (in German), and Michael Cohn (in Yiddish). A collection was made for Most's children.

In the evening, EG's speech "in advocacy of anarchist principles" to a packed house at Engineer's Hall in **Albany**, New York, was interrupted by the police.

APRIL 11

EG wrote, in a letter to Joseph Labadie, about the success of the first issue of *Mother Earth* with 3,000 copies distributed in its first week, requiring an additional print run of 1,000 copies.

APRIL 29

EG was scheduled to speak in **Utica**, New York.

APRIL 30

EG spoke before the Sunrise Club at Café Boulevard, 10th Street and Second Avenue, in **New York**.

EARLY MAY

Pavel Orlenev was expected to return to Russia, possibly coming back to United States in November to repay his debts.

MAY

Enrique and Ricardo Flores Magón moved from Toronto to Montreal.

MAY 12–CA. JUNE 30

EG's lecture tour began in **Cleveland**, and continued in **Detroit**, **St. Louis**, and **Chicago**.

MAY 18

AB was released from the Allegheny workhouse, where he had served the last year of his sentence. EG and AB met in **Detroit**, Michigan, stayed with Carl Nold, and were trailed by reporters.

MAY 21

Telegram of support sent to Moses Harman in prison from EG, AB, and Carl Nold. Harman had been convicted and sentenced to one year of hard labor for sending obscene materials through the U.S. mail (in violation of the Comstock Act). He had published two articles, "The Fatherhood Question" and "More Thoughts on Sexology," in his newspaper *Lucifer, the Lightbearer*.

MAY 22

EG arrived in **Chicago** from **Detroit**.

MAY 23

EG was scheduled to speak in the afternoon to the Socialists' Club at the University of Chicago in **Chicago**. EG spoke at an evening meeting to celebrate AB's release from prison (AB was scheduled to arrive in Chicago on 29 May) at Metropolitan Hall. EG, Carl Nold, and Lucy Parsons were also scheduled to speak.

MAY 24

EG spoke to a woodworkers' union in the evening at Schimberg Hall, 235 Milwaukee Avenue, in **Chicago**.

MAY 29

AB and EG spoke in honor of the Haymarket anarchists at Brand's Hall in **Chicago**.

MAY 31

Anarchist Mateo Morral, who worked in the publishing department of the Escuela Moderna (Modern School) founded by Francisco Ferrer in Barcelona, attempted to assassinate the Spanish king Alfonso XIII at his wedding procession with Victoria Eugenia (Ena) of Battenberg, princess of Great Britain. Morral threw a bomb disguised in a bouquet, missing the king but killing 20 others and wounding about 100.

JUNE 1

EG and AB spoke in support of the attempted assassination of Alfonso XIII at a meeting in Apollo Hall (Blue Island Avenue and Twelfth Street) in **Chicago**.

JUNE 2

His whereabouts discovered by the police, Mateo Morral shot the officer who tried to arrest him and then shot himself in Torrejón de Ardoz, fourteen miles outside of Madrid.

JUNE 4

Francisco Ferrer was arrested and tortured on charges of planning the assassination of Alfonso XIII and inducing Mateo Morral to carry it out. He was confined until May 1907.

JUNE 5

Kōtoku Shūsui left America. During this period he moved even more toward anarchist communism, after an extended stay in the San Francisco Bay area where he mingled regularly in socialist and anarchist circles.

JUNE 10–12

EG lectured on topics such as "The Constitution," "The Idaho Outrage," "The General Strike," and "The False and True Conception of Anarchism" in **Pittsburgh**, Pennsylvania.

JUNE 12

Moses Harman's appeal for executive clemency was denied.

JUNE 17

EG was among a number of anarchists who spoke at Central Palace in **New York**. Two thousand people greeted AB after his release from prison. Other speakers included Saul Yanovsky, Abraham Cahan, Harry Weinberg, M. Zametkin, Harry Gordon, Michael Cohn, Max Baginski, Hugh O. Pentecost, Hillel Solotaroff, Bolton Hall, and AB.

JUNE 22

EG attended a banquet at Terrace Garden (58th Street between Lexington and Third Avenue) in **New York**, in honor of Nikolai Chaikovsky and Chaim Zhitlovsky, two delegates from the Socialist Revolutionary party of Russia.

JUNE 23

Kōtoku Shūsui arrived in Japan.

JULY 1

The formal platform of the Mexican Liberal Party (PLM) was issued.

MID-JULY

EG, AB, and Max Baginski vacationed in **Ossining**, New York.

AUGUST

EG and AB vacationed in **Ossining** until late in the month.

SEPTEMBER

EG advertised her services in the *Woman's Journal* as a "Vienna Scalp and Face Specialist," under the name E. G. Smith, even after her office had closed.

SEPTEMBER 2

Ricardo Flores Magón and other PLM members arrived in El Paso to make final preparations for revolutionary activity in Mexico. PLM organized uprisings against the Díaz government.

SEPTEMBER 15

The St. Louis offices of *Regeneración* were destroyed by police.

SEPTEMBER 17–OCTOBER 3

Second IWW convention with 93 delegates took place in Chicago, Illinois.

SEPTEMBER 23

The PLM uprisings against the Díaz government in Mexico were defeated.

SEPTEMBER 30

Ricardo Flores Magón fled to Los Angeles, California.

OCTOBER

October 1906 issue of *Mother Earth* was devoted to Leon Czolgosz, marking the fifth anniversary of his death, sparking controversy and large sales.

OCTOBER 14

AB began a lecture tour to benefit *Mother Earth*. He lectured in Albany, Syracuse, and Pittsburgh, suffered a nervous breakdown in Cleveland, abandoned the tour, and came close to suicide.

OCTOBER 27

Julius Edelsohn (Becky Edelsohn's brother), Max Moscow, and M. Rubenstein were arrested for participating in a debate about whether Leon Czolgosz was an anarchist, at the Progressive Library, 106 Forsyth Street, in New York.

OCTOBER 30

EG was arrested while attending an anarchist meeting at the Manhattan Lyceum on 66 East 4th Street in **New York**, called to protest police suppression of free speech on 27 October; charged with unlawful assembly for the purpose of overthrowing the government (under New York State's new laws on "criminal" anarchy, passed after McKinley's assassination). EG held on two charges: for articles printed in *Mother Earth* and for inciting to riot. Others arrested included Lena Sweet (called Lena Smitt by EG in November 1906 *ME*), and Julius Edelsohn, Annie Pastor, Rebecca Edelsohn, Rosie Rogin, Jacob Veltin, William Gordon, Harry Lang, and Morris Berkowitz. (Berkowitz was apparently charged separately as his name does not appear on the police report, and was sentenced to six months in the workhouse for attempting to incite a riot at, or en route to, the police station.) All charged with disorderly conduct; Julius Edelsohn and Lena Sweet also charged with inciting to riot.

OCTOBER 31

EG was arraigned in **New York** Police Court and held on $1,000 bail for further examination; released the same day with the help of Hugh O. Pentecost and Meyer London, her legal counselors.

NOVEMBER 2

EG pled not guilty to criminal anarchy charges before the city magistrate, R. C. Cornell, in **New York**.

NOVEMBER 5

The charges against EG were dropped for her 30 October arrest.

NOVEMBER 11

EG, Harry Kelly, and others scheduled to speak at 19th anniversary celebration in memory of the Chicago Haymarket anarchists, at the Labor Temple (243–247 East 84th Street) in **New York**, organized by the Freiheit Publishing Association.

NOVEMBER 23

Mother Earth Masquerade Ball at Webster Hall (119– 125 East 11th Street) in **New York**, organized to raise money for the publication, was disrupted by police, who forced the owner to close the hall.

DECEMBER

AB opened a small printing press—a short-term business venture.

Moses Harman released from prison.

DECEMBER 14

Russian Socialist Revolutionary Party member Grigorii Gershuni, recently escaped from Siberia, spoke at Carnegie Hall, **New York.** EG and AB were in the audience. EG later spent time with Gershuni in New York discussing the situation in Russia.

DECEMBER 16

EG delivered a lecture on "False and True Conceptions of Anarchism" before the Brooklyn Philosophical Association at Long Island Business College (143 South 8th Street), **Brooklyn**, on behalf of *Mother Earth.*

DECEMBER 20

*Kakumei (*Revolution*)* No. 1 was published in association with the Social Revolutionary Party of Oakland. It was influenced by Kōtoku Shūsui. *Revolution* stressed militant direct action against the Japanese imperial family.

DECEMBER 26

Theodore Schroeder wrote a letter to the New York Commissioner of Police complaining about the police harassment of the Manhattan Liberal Club, especially with regard to their right to sell *Mother Earth.*

1907

Mother Earth Publishing Association published a number of pamphlets, including EG's *The Tragedy of Woman's Emancipation;* John Coryell, *Sex Union and Parenthood and What Is Seduction;* Voltairine de Cleyre, *McKinley's Assassination from the Anarchist Standpoint;* Jay Fox, *Trade Unionism and Anarchism;* Maksim Gorky, *The Masters of Life, An Interview;* and Theodore Schroeder, *The Criminal Anarchy Law and On Suppressing the Advocacy of Crime.*

The Free Speech League publishes two pamphlets by Theodore Schroeder, *Constructive Obscenity* and *Our Vanishing Liberty of the Press.*

JANUARY

The *Mother Earth* office moved to 308 East 27th Street in New York.

JANUARY 2

Luigi Galleani was arrested for his participation in the 1902 Paterson, New Jersey, silk workers' strike.

JANUARY 3

Ernest Crosby died.

JANUARY 6

EG was arrested while speaking on "The Misconceptions of Anarchism" at an afternoon meeting of 600 people in Clinton Hall in **New York** held to organize readership and support for *Mother Earth.* She was charged with publicly uttering "incendiary sentiments." AB, 15-year-old Israel Schwartz, and John Russell Coryell, who had chaired the meeting, were all arrested on unspecified accessory charges. Police claimed that AB encouraged the audience to disobey police orders to disperse and that Schwartz refused to leave the hall.

JANUARY 7

EG and AB were arraigned in the Essex Market Court; pled not guilty (EG feigned pregnancy to the police, according to the *New York World*, 7 January 1907).

JANUARY 11

EG's hearing began in Essex Market before Magistrate Joseph F. Moss. EG's defense was postponed until the following Tuesday.

JANUARY 15

EG's legal case dismissed on grounds that she had acted within her rights to speak.

JANUARY 17

Luigi Galleani was freed on bail. AB, Harry Kelly, EG, and Max Baginski at a meeting in Turn Hall in **Paterson**, New Jersey, protested Galleani's arrest.

JANUARY 24

EG was scheduled to address an anarchist meeting at Everett Hall (31 4th Street) in **New York**, suppressed by the police.

FEBRUARY 2

Hugh O. Pentecost died.

FEBRUARY 24

EG spoke in Yiddish at an afternoon meeting organized by the Progressive Workingmen's Club at 108 Park Street in **Chelsea**, Massachusetts. EG spoke in the evening at Laster's Hall (a labor meeting hall) in **Lynn**, Massachusetts.

FEBRUARY 27

EG discussed "the coming March elections and pirates" at the opera house in **Barre**, Vermont. Luigi Galleani also spoke, in Italian.

LATE FEBRUARY

EG spoke in **Boston**, Massachusetts.

EARLY MARCH

EG asked AB to become editor of *Mother Earth,* dividing the work, as she went on tour to gather readers and support for the magazine.

MARCH

AB closed his print shop.

In *Mother Earth* EG announced that the magazine's office had moved back to 210 East 13th Street in New York.

To avoid arrest, Ricardo Flores Magón of the PLM fled to San Francisco and Sacramento before returning to Los Angeles, California.

Financial panic in United States in the wake of a sharp drop in the stock market.

MARCH 3

EG left New York City for series of lectures. She was scheduled to speak in Cleveland, Columbus, Toledo, Cincinnati, Chicago, St. Louis, Minneapolis, and Toronto.

MARCH 4

EG lectured on "Direct Action vs. Legislation" at the Perry Theatre in **Cleveland**, Ohio.

MARCH 5

EG was scheduled to speak on "The Revolutionary Spirit in Modern Drama" at Ohlsen's Hall, 1940 West 28th Street, in **Cleveland.**

MARCH 6

EG spoke in German on "Crime Against the Child" at Crystal Hall, Woodland Avenue and East 39th Street, in **Cleveland.**

MARCH 8

Massive strike of Parisian electricians surprised entire city—darkness pervaded for two nights until strikers won their demands for rights to a pension and eight-hour workday—an event that became a symbol to EG of the effectiveness of direct action, in contrast to strikes in the United States orchestrated and announced in advance.

MARCH 9

EG was prevented from speaking at a scheduled lecture at Hunt's Hall in **Columbus**, Ohio, after the landlord reneged on the rental agreement. She left on a train for Toledo, Ohio.

MARCH 12

Thanks to the intervention of local activists, including Kate Sherwood, feminist and abolitionist, Mayor Brand Whitlock of **Toledo**, Ohio, allowed EG to deliver lectures at Zenoba Hall.

MARCH 13

EG spoke on "Misconceptions of Anarchism" to a mid-sized audience at the Labor Temple in **Toronto**, Ontario, in Canada. She also spoke at two other meetings in Toronto during this period.

MARCH 16

EG's evening lecture in **Detroit**, Michigan, was blocked by police, leaving her vulnerable to the possibility of the financial failure of her tour. EG stayed with Carl Nold.

MARCH 17

EG scheduled to speak in **Detroit**, but stopped by police.

MARCH 18

EG arrived in **Chicago**, Illinois, and spoke, in Yiddish, at the anniversary and celebration of the 1871 Paris Commune, and raised support for the Idaho trial of Charles Moyer and William Haywood at a meeting of 800 Jewish anarchists at a hall on Jefferson and O'Brien streets.

MARCH 19

EG was scheduled to speak in celebration of the Paris Commune at a meeting organized by the Bohemian Anarchists in **Chicago**.

EG spoke on "The Revolutionary Spirit of the Modern Drama," at the Masonic Temple in **Chicago** to an audience of University of Chicago professors and students, lawyers, politicians and factory workers.

MARCH 25

EG spoke on "The Misconception of Anarchy" at the Schlitz Park pavilion in **Milwaukee**, Wisconsin.

MARCH 29

EG was scheduled to speak in English on "The Misconceptions of Anarchy" at Cosmopolitan Hall in **Cincinnati**, Ohio, sponsored by the Workmen's Educational and Art Society.

MARCH 30

EG was scheduled to speak on "The Education of Children" at Cosmopolitan Hall in **Cincinnati**, sponsored by the Workmen's Educational and Art Society.

MARCH 31

EG scheduled to speak in German on "Direct Action Versus Legislation" at Cosmopolitan Hall in **Cincinnati**, sponsored by the Workmen's Educational and Art Society.

EARLY APRIL

EG lectured in **St. Louis**, Missouri.

APRIL 2

A letter written by President Theodore Roosevelt, which refers to Charles Moyer and William Haywood as "undesirable citizens," is leaked to the press. Samuel Gompers, pressured by rank and file union members to take an active stance in support of Haywood, refused to rebuke Roosevelt for his remark, drawing much criticism from EG and others.

APRIL 6

EG spoke on "Misconceptions of Anarchism" at Holcomb's Hall in **Minneapolis**, Minnesota.

APRIL 7

EG lectured in German on "The Education of the Child" at Kistler's Hall in **Minneapolis**.

APRIL 10–16

EG in **Winnipeg**, Manitoba, Canada for a six-day visit. She was scheduled to deliver five lectures, three of which were to be in German: "Crimes of Parents and Education," "Direct Action versus Legislation," and "The Position of the Jews in Russia," at the Rupert Street Trades Hall, arranged by the anarchist branch of the Winnipeg Radical Club.

APRIL 22

EG lectured on "Misconceptions of Anarchy" at Social Turner Hall in **Denver**, Colorado.

APRIL 23

EG spoke in German at a hall on West Colfax Avenue in **Denver**.

APRIL 24

EG was scheduled to lecture in **Denver**.

APRIL 25–30

EG was scheduled to lecture in **Sacramento**, California.

LAST WEEK OF APRIL

Luigi Galleani was tried for alleged participation in the Paterson riots of 1902. Arrested in 1902 for inciting to riot, along with William MacQueen and Rudolf Grossmann (aka Pierre Ramus), he fled to Canada to avoid trial and lived for several years in hiding in Vermont, while Grossmann fled to Europe. Galleani's trial resulted in a hung jury and he was set free. MacQueen, who was very ill with tuberculosis and had almost completed a five-year prison sentence, was pardoned on the condition that he leave the country; he returned to England and died shortly after.

MAY

EG held meetings with the Liberty Club, the Socialist Local, and the Arbeiter Ring in **San Francisco**, California.

MAY 5

EG spoke in the evening at Walton's Pavilion in **San Francisco**, California. A portion of her lecture centered on the local cable car strike that had just begun. A violent strike in its initial weeks, it ended in defeat for the carmen's union in early November.

MAY 8

Fred Warren, managing editor of *Appeal to Reason*, was indicted by federal authorities for circulating "scurrilous, defamatory and threatening" material. In an effort to publicize the kidnapping of Western Federation of Miners' leaders from Colorado to an Idaho jail, Warren had advertised a $1,000 award for the return to Kentucky of Republican ex-governor William S. Tailor, who fled the state after he was indicted for the murder of his Democratic successor in 1900. Tailor remained in Pennsylvania and Indiana, protected by those states' Republican governors, who ignored official demands to send Tailor home to face trial.

MAY 9

EG spoke to a small audience at Turn-Verein Hall in **San Jose**, California.

William Haywood's trial began in Boise, Idaho.

MAY 10

EG was scheduled to speak on the principles of anarchism at Turn-Verein Hall in **San Jose**.

MAY 16

EG spoke in German on "The Corrupting Influence of Religion" at 677 McAllister Street in **San Francisco**.

MAY 19

EG spoke on "The Building of True Character" at Equality Hall in **San Francisco**.

MAY 23

EG spoke in the evening on "Misconceptions of Anarchism" at Burbank Hall (542 South Main Street) in **Los Angeles**, California.

MAY 24

EG spoke on "The Building of True Character" at Burbank Hall in **Los Angeles**.

MAY 25

EG spoke on "Crimes of Parents and Educators" at Naturopathic Hall (337 1/2 South Hill Street, where the Los Angeles Eugenic Society held weekly meetings) in **Los Angeles**.

MAY 26

EG spoke in the afternoon on "The Revolutionary Spirit of Modern Drama" and in the evening debated Claude Riddle on "Direct Action Versus Political Action" under the auspices of the Socialist Party Branch, Los Angeles, at Burbank Hall in **Los Angeles**. EG donated half the proceeds to the socialist paper *Common Sense*.

MAY 27

EG established a Social Science Club in **Los Angeles** to discuss a variety of social, literary, and art topics; intended as an open forum for divergent ideas and cultures, the club began with 55 charter members.

JUNE 2

EG spoke on "Direct Action vs. Legislative or Political Action" and "The Revolutionary Spirit in the Modern Drama" at the Selling-Hirsch building in **Portland**, Oregon.

JUNE 4

EG lectured in the evening on "The Spirit of Revolution in the Modern Drama" at Home Colony in **Tacoma**, Washington.

JUNE 5

EG addressed a large crowd at the Temple of Music in **Tacoma**. Several police detectives were in the audience.

JUNE 9

EG lectured on the "Misconceptions of Anarchism" at the Socialist Temple in **Seattle**, Washington.

JUNE 11

EG lectured on "Direct Action versus Political Action" at the Socialist Temple in **Seattle**.

JUNE 12

EG lectured on "The Revolutionary Spirit of the Modern Drama" at the Socialist Temple in **Seattle**.

Francisco Ferrer was released for lack of sufficient evidence from the Carcel Modelo in Madrid, after a year in prison for his alleged association with the attempted assassination of Alfonso XIII.

JUNE 16

EG lectured on "Some Misconceptions of Anarchism" at Alexander Hall in **Calgary**, Canada.

JUNE 27

EG returned to **New York** (until August 14).

JULY 28

William Haywood was acquitted on the charge of conspiracy to murder ex-Idaho governor Frank Steunenberg. EG, AB and Hippolyte Havel sent a telegram to President Theodore Roosevelt expressing their joy at the verdict.

JULY

EG selected by anarchists from many cities including Cleveland, Chicago, San Francisco, and Winnipeg as their representative to the International Anarchist Congress in Amsterdam.

AUGUST 3

EG spoke (with AB, Max Baginski, and others) about the Boise trials at the Manhattan Lyceum (4th Street) in **New York**.

AUGUST 14

EG and Max Baginski sailed to Amsterdam for the International Anarchist Congress, trailed by secret agent Maurits Hyman. *Mother Earth*'s editorial work carried by AB, with the assistance of John Coryell, Hippolyte Havel, and others, in EG and Baginski's absence.

AUGUST 23

Ricardo Flores Magón, Librado Rivera, and Antonio I. Villarreal had reunited in Los Angeles in mid-summer. They were illegally assaulted in their home office by detectives from the Furlong Detective Agency hired by the governor of the Mexican state of Chihuahua, Enrique C. Creel. They were arrested, beaten, and taken to the city jail where they were accused of resisting arrest.

AUGUST 26

EG among speakers at the opening session of the International Anarchist Congress in **Amsterdam** in the Netherlands, attended by 300 delegates. EG brought greetings from the anarchists in the United States and was impressed by the conference's positive treatment by Amsterdam city officials and the favorable coverage by the local press.

AUGUST 30

EG attended the International Anti-militarist Congress in **Amsterdam** organized by Dutch anarchists, including Ferdinand Domela Nieuwenhuis. Others present included Pierre Ramus (Rudolf Grossmann) and Luigi Fabbri.

AUGUST 31

EG chaired the International Anarchist Congress session on its last day in **Amsterdam**. Establishment of an international anarchist movement based in London was proposed and accepted. Errico Malatesta, Rudolf Rocker, and Alexander Schapiro were appointed to the secretariat of the London International Bureau. EG also addressed a gathering of Dutch transport workers, in **Amsterdam**.

SEPTEMBER

EG met with Stella Ballantine, Victor Dave, and Peter Kropotkin in **Paris**, France. She met French artist "Grandjouan" (Jules-Felix Grandjouan, 1875–1968), solicited artwork for the cover of *Mother Earth*, and attended trial of antimilitarists. She also visited La Ruche (The Beehive), Sebastien Faure's experimental and "rational school" for poor and orphaned children, located on the outskirts of Paris, in the French village of Rambouillet.

SEPTEMBER 16–24

The third annual IWW convention was held in Chicago, Illinois.

SEPTEMBER 23

In an ongoing federal investigation of EG's citizenship, the Fourth Deputy Commissioner of the New York City Police Department sent the Acting Commissioner of the New York Bureau of Immigration EG's arrest record. EG claimed citizenship through the naturalization of her former husband and her father. On 1 July, new immigration laws had gone into effect streamlining the procedures for prosecution and deportation of undesirable aliens.

SEPTEMBER 24

U.S. Bureau of Immigration and Naturalization allegedly declared that it would bar EG from re-entry, assuming she was on her way back from the Amsterdam congress.

The Commissioner-General of the Bureau of Immigration in Washington, D.C., directed the East Coast Commissioners of Immigration (in Boston, New York, Philadelphia, and Baltimore) to watch for EG's and Baginski's re-entry and examine their proof of citizenship carefully, requesting no publicity, with strict orders of confidentiality.

SEPTEMBER 29

English anarcho-syndicalist Sam Mainwaring died in London.

OCTOBER

A run (mass withdrawal of customer funds) on the Knickerbocker Trust Company wiped it out and several other banks also failed, leading to a nationwide bank panic. A national recession followed the panic, lasting well into 1908.

OCTOBER 2

Voltairine de Cleyre, AB, EG, Hippolyte Havel, and George Bauer (manager of *Freiheit*) appealed to readers in *The Demonstrator* to support the establishment of a weekly paper "to deal entirely with labor, its battles, hopes and aspirations." The appeal was also printed in the September 1907 issue of *Mother Earth* and the 14 September 1907 issue of *Freiheit*.

OCTOBER 3

EG left **Paris** for **London.**

OCTOBER 4

EG arrived in **London**, where she was apparently informed of the immigration problems she would face when she returned to the United States.

OCTOBER 7

EG spoke on "The Labour Struggle in America" at Holborn Town Hall on Gray's Inn Road, in **London**, after which she became aware of being trailed by Scotland Yard detectives.

EG scheduled to speak again in London, the provinces, and in Scotland, but the publication of *Mother Earth* and "other matters," including rumors that her re-entry to the United States would be blocked, cut her visit short.

OCTOBER 9

EG set sailed from **Liverpool** aboard a ship headed for Montreal, Canada, after she learned that she might be refused entry into the United States.

MID-OCTOBER

EG arrived in **Montreal**, Canada. She took a train to **New York.**

OCTOBER 19

Chief of Secret Service in Washington, D.C., notified Commissioner-General of the Bureau of Immigration that agent Maurits Hymans, returning to the United States, could be found "back at work" among the country's anarchists.

NOVEMBER–DECEMBER

EG reported, just five weeks after her return from Europe, lecturing in the states of **Massachusetts**, **Connecticut**, and **New York**, continuing on in 1908 to the cities of **Philadelphia**, **Baltimore**, **Washington, D.C.**, and **Pittsburgh.**

NOVEMBER 3

An "Open Letter to Mutsuhito, The Emperor of Japan, From Anarchist Terrorists" was posted on the door of the Japanese consulate and throughout public places in San Francisco on the occasion of the Emperor's birthday, probably emanating from Berkeley Japanese socialist revolutionists strongly influenced by Kōtoku Shūsui.

NOVEMBER 5

Mother Earth concert ball held in New York. Julius Edelsohn was allegedly clubbed by the police "without provocation" upon leaving.

The San Francisco cable carmen's union strike (which began on 5 May) effectively ended in defeat.

NOVEMBER 6

Monroe County, New York, certified that Jacob Kershner received his citizenship on 18 October 1884. (Document submitted as Exhibit A at Kershner's denaturalization hearing.)

NOVEMBER 11

EG was scheduled to speak at the Manhattan Lyceum (66–68 East 4th Street) in **New York** with seven others, including Max Baginski, Voltairine de Cleyre, AB, and Harry Kelly, at the twentieth anniversary meeting to commemorate the execution of the Haymarket anarchists. City police tried to prevent the anarchists' meeting, exerting pressure on the owner of the building to refuse to open his doors to anarchists, even though he had recently rented his hall to AB. Anarchists marched uptown to the Bohemian Hall (321 East 73rd Street, between First and Second avenues). Police closed doors but permitted those already in the hall to proceed with their meeting. EG addressed the crowd.

NOVEMBER 13

Commissioner-General of the Bureau of Immigration, anticipating the return of EG and Baginski from Europe, reminded the East Coast commissioners of immigration (in Baltimore, Boston, Ellis Island, and Philadelphia) to be on the alert for their re-entry.

NOVEMBER 14

The Bureau of Immigration prepared an arrest warrant for EG for violating the Immigration Act of 20 February 1907. (This act streamlined the federal government's ability to prosecute and deport undesirable aliens; the first immigration act to specifically exclude anarchists was passed in 1903.) The warrant also stated that she had entered the United States without inspection (all immigrants were questioned by immigration authorities and inspected by medical personnel upon their entry). Warrant ordered that EG be taken into custody and appear before a Board of Special Inquiry at Ellis Island "to enable her to show cause why she should not be deported in conformity with law."

NOVEMBER 16

EG was investigated by New York Commissioner of the Bureau of Immigration Robert Watchorn. Secretary of Commerce and Labor Oscar Straus issued Watchorn a warrant for EG's arrest based on the prosecutable suspicion of "being an anarchist." Authorities had intended to arrest EG at the port of entry upon her return from Amsterdam.

NOVEMBER 17

EG lectured in **Lynn**, Massachusetts.

New York Bureau of Immigration sent a memorandum regarding EG's illegal entry into the country to the Secretary of Commerce and Labor Oscar Straus in Washington, D.C., stating that evidence from her 6–15 January 1907 arrest and trial may not have been sufficient to convict her under the New York penal code, but is "probably sufficient to bring her within the class of anarchists as defined by the immigration law," informing him that a certified copy of the record of the January 1907 trial will be sent for his use.

NOVEMBER 18

EG lectured in English on "Direct Action as the Logical Tactic of Anarchism" (a discussion that encompassed labor tactics, public education, voting, and marriage) and Sebastian Faure's theories on the modern school, at Paine Memorial Hall on Appleton Street in **Boston**, Massachusetts, monitored closely by government interpreter Louis J. Domas.

NOVEMBER 17

Secretary of Commerce and Labor Oscar Straus notified the Commissioner of the New York Bureau of Immigration that EG's arrest warrant was being withheld pending an investigation of her citizenship.

NOVEMBER 20

Agent Maurits Hymans reported on his surveillance of anarchists in London and Antwerp, where he gathered useful information for the United States. He met EG and Max Baginski at Holborn Town Hall in London, but, because they knew him, was unable to follow them closely.

NOVEMBER 21

The New York Commissioner of the Bureau of Immigration sent a confidential copy of the transcript of EG's January 1907 criminal anarchy hearing in New York to the Solicitor of the Department of Commerce and Labor in Washington, D.C.

Acting Commissioner-General of the Bureau of Immigration in Washington, D.C., thanked the Boston Commissioner of the Bureau of Immigration for the recent report about EG's speaking engagement in Boston and informed him that they were carefully investigating EG's citizenship status, but "the utmost caution is being observed to prevent publicity and criticism."

NOVEMBER 22

EG attended a semi-annual reunion of the *Mother Earth* "family" scheduled to take place at a concert and ball at Everett Hall (31–35 East 4th Street) in **New York**. Readings by Sadakichi Hartmann. Julius Edelsohn and an unidentified woman were arrested without provocation upon leaving the ball at 2 A.M.

Immigration inspector in charge of the Bureau of Immigration in Chicago responded to the 19 November 1907 confidential request of the Commissioner-General of the Bureau of Immigration in Washington, D.C., to find information on Max Baginski that would lead to his arrest. Described Baginski as an anarchist terrorist, who was being investigated by E. Diehl, a secret service agent with ties to the Berlin secret service.

NOVEMBER 23

The Boston Commissioner of the Bureau of Immigration informed the Commissioner-General of the Bureau of Immigration in Washington, D.C., that EG entered the country in a French ship at the port of New York City.

NOVEMBER 25

On behalf of the Spanish Foreign Ministry, the minister of state asked a representative of the American Legation, Department of State, Madrid, for a description of EG.

DECEMBER 8

EG spoke at an afternoon meeting at 47 Center Street in **Brockton**, Massachusetts.

DECEMBER 9

EG spoke in the evening at 313 Common Street in **Lawrence**, Massachusetts.

DECEMBER 10

EG spoke in the evening in **Haverhill**, Massachusetts.

DECEMBER 11

EG spoke in the evening in English on "Trade Unionism" at Odd Fellows' Temple (84 Middlesex Street) in **Lowell**, Massachusetts.

DECEMBER 12

EG spoke in Yiddish on "Women and Anarchism" to a large crowd in Arcanum Hall (566 Main Street) in **Worcester**, Massachusetts.

DECEMBER 13

EG was scheduled to speak in the evening on "The Revolutionary Spirit in the Modern Drama" at 15 Leverett Street in **Boston**, Massachusetts. She spoke in German to a primarily Yiddish-speaking audience, causing some disappointment.

DECEMBER 15

EG was scheduled to speak in the afternoon in **New Britain**, Connecticut.

EG was scheduled to speak in the evening in **Hartford**, Connecticut.

DECEMBER 16

EG was scheduled to speak in **Waterbury**, Connecticut.

DECEMBER 20

EG lectured in the evening on "The Revolutionary Spirit of the Modern Drama" to the Harlem Liberal Alliance, at the Fraternity Hall (100

West 116th Street, corner of Lenox Avenue), in **New York**.

DECEMBER 23

EG spoke on "Anarchism, What It Really Stands For" at a hall located at 184 Main Street (the top floor above the New York Dental Parlors) in **Paterson**, New Jersey.

DECEMBER 25

EG was scheduled to lecture in the evening in German on "Direct Action as the Logical Tactics of Anarchism" at the American Star Hall (Pitkin Avenue and Christopher Street), in **Brooklyn.**

DECEMBER 27

PLM members Ricardo Flores Magón, Antonio I. Villarreal, Librado Rivera, and Lazaro Gutierrez De Lara drafted the "Manifesto to the American People" at the county jail in Los Angeles, California. The manifesto would later be published in *Mother Earth* (February 1908).

1908

EG's pamphlet *A Beautiful Ideal* is published. Mother Earth Publishing Association published EG's pamphlet *Patriotism: A Menace to Liberty* and Peter Kropotkin's *Modern Science and Anarchism.*

The Free Speech League published three pamphlets by Theodore Schroeder entitled *The Scientific Aspect of Due Process Law and Constructive Crimes, Unconstitutionality of All Laws Against "Obscene Literature Asserted in a Brief,* and *"Due Process of Law" in Relation to Statutory Uncertainty and Constructive Offences* and a pamphlet by Benjamin Flower et al., entitled *In Defense of Free Speech: Five Essays from the Arena.*

JANUARY

Effects of the recession after the Bank Panic of 1907 and stock market plunge were still felt. Market prices were down, food prices shot up, and 8 percent of the nation's workforce was unemployed.

JANUARY 3

Annual Anarchistic Ball (Baueren Ball, or the Peasants Ball) was scheduled to take place in Boston, Massachusetts.

JANUARY 4

George Pettibone was acquitted of ex-Idaho governor Frank Steunenberg's murder.

JANUARY 5

EG was scheduled to speak on "Labor Organizations" in the afternoon, and on "The Revolutionary Spirit in Modern Drama" in the evening at Turn Hall (133 Lafayette Street) in **Utica**, New York. Lectures were arranged by Abe Brandschein under the auspices of the Workmen's Circle, Branch 118.

JANUARY 6–7

EG lectured on consecutive nights in **Syracuse**, New York. During the evening on the 7th, a group meeting was held in the home of a local supporter and attended by approximately 30 people to hear EG's report on the Amsterdam anarchist congress. Police attempted to break up the meeting and EG was threatened with arrest.

JANUARY 8–12

EG gave various lectures, reported substantial audiences for "The Revolutionary Spirit in the Modern Drama" and "Woman Under Anarchism," in **Rochester**, New York.

JANUARY 12

EG was scheduled to lecture in the afternoon on "What Anarchism Really Stands For," and in the evening on "The Child and its Enemies," at Huron Assembly Hall (84 Seneca Street) in **Utica**, New York, under the auspices of the Workmen's Circle, Branch 118.

JANUARY 13

EG was scheduled to lecture in the evening on "Trade Unionism" at Eintracht Hall (371 South Pearl Street) in **Albany**, New York.

JANUARY 14

EG was scheduled to lecture in German on "The Woman in the Future" at Eintracht Hall in **Albany**.

JANUARY 15

EG was scheduled to speak on "Trade Unionism" at a meeting in **Gloverville**, New York.

JANUARY 16

EG lectured on "Syndicalism—A New Phase in the Labor Movement" in **Schenectady**, New York.

JANUARY 24–25

EG was scheduled to speak in Philadelphia but illness prevented her from going, and AB went instead to address the audience.

JANUARY 26

EG was scheduled to give an afternoon lecture on "The Revolutionary Spirit in Modern Drama" in **Washington, D.C.**, but the city's mayor and chief of police prevented her from speaking. She was also scheduled to give an evening lecture in **Baltimore**, Maryland.

JANUARY 27

EG lectured at a meeting arranged by H. Kraemer in **Pittsburgh**, Pennsylvania.

FEBRUARY

The PLM's "Manifesto to the American People" was published in *Mother Earth*.

FEBRUARY 8

Literary Evening and Ball to celebrate the second anniversary of *Mother Earth* was scheduled to take place at the Terrace Lyceum (206 East Broadway) in **New York**.

FEBRUARY 13

EG began her western tour via **Montreal, Toronto, London** (Ontario, Canada), and **Cleveland**, Ohio. She was scheduled to speak on "The Crisis: Its Cause and Remedy," "The Relation of Anarchism to Trade Unionism," "Direct Action as the Logical Tactics of Anarchism," "Syndicalism: A New Phase of the Labor Struggle," and "Woman under Anarchism."

FEBRUARY 14–15

EG was scheduled to deliver two lectures in Yiddish at St. Joseph's Hall, 182 Catherine Street in **Montreal**, Quebec, Canada. The lecture on 15 February on "The Relation of Trade Unionism to Anarchism" was organized by the *Arbeter Fraint* group.

FEBRUARY 16

EG lectured on "Trade Unionism and Anarchism" at the Montreal Labor Exchange, 123 San Dominic Street, in **Montreal**. The meeting was organized by Albert St. Martin.

FEBRUARY 17

EG lectured on "Anarchism, What it Stands For" at the Finnish Hall, 214 Adelaide Street, in **Toronto**, Ontario, Canada.

FEBRUARY 18

EG was scheduled to lecture in German at the Finnish Hall in **Toronto**.

FEBRUARY 19

EG lectured on "Straight Unionism" at Cullis' Hall (259 Wellington Street) in **London**, Ontario, Canada, under the auspices of the South Educational Society (an organization encompassing many groups, among them Canadians, English, and Jews).

FEBRUARY 20

EG lectured on "The Revolutionary Spirit and the Modern Drama" at Cullis' Hall in **London**, Ontario. Subjects included Henrik Ibsen's *The Doll House* and *Ghosts*; also George Bernard Shaw's *Mrs. Warren's Profession*.

Italian and Jewish anarchists called a meeting in Philadelphia at the New Auditorium Hall, on South Third Street, to address the issues of unemployment and economic depression. The meeting was addressed by Voltairine de Cleyre, George Brown, and Chaim Weinberg. Unemployed workers left the meeting and started to march toward city hall to demand work. A confrontation with police when the demonstrators reached Broad Street led to a riot. Four Italians—Michael Costello, Dominick Donelli, Angelo Troi, and Francesco Piszicallo—were arrested and charged with inciting to riot and assault and battery with intent to kill. Later in the day, Voltairine de Cleyre and Chaim Weinberg were arrested on similar charges and held on $1,500 bail.

FEBRUARY 21–22

EG was scheduled to lecture in German at 5217 Woodland Avenue in **Cleveland**, Ohio.

FEBRUARY 23

EG lectured in English on the subject of women, children, and marriage at the Pythian Temple (corner of Prospect Avenue and Huron Road) in **Cleveland**.

Father Leo Heinrichs was assassinated by Guiseppe Alia at the altar of St. Elizabeth's Roman Catholic church in Denver, Colorado. Alia, a recent Italian immigrant, was reported to be an anarchist by the press.

FEBRUARY 24, 25, 26

EG was scheduled to speak in **Toledo**, Ohio.

FEBRUARY 28

EG began a series of four lectures in **St. Louis**, Missouri, under the auspices of the *Freedom* and *Liberty* groups. In the evening she gave a lecture in Yiddish on "The Relation of Anarchy and Trade Unionism" at Fraternal Hall (11th Street and Franklin Avenue). Federal authorities in Chicago were considering the deportation of EG to Russia under the provisions of the immigration law. The *St. Louis Post* reported that dispatches from U.S. Commissioner of Immigration Frank P. Sargent directed federal authorities in Chicago to arrest her. After James R. Dunn, inspector for the Bureau of Immigration, Department of Commerce and Labor in St. Louis, wired Sargent for approval to arrest EG, however, the commissioner wired back to inform him to take no action against her.

FEBRUARY 29

EG gave an evening lecture at Druid's Hall in **St. Louis**.

MARCH 1

EG gave an afternoon lecture in German and an evening lecture in English at Northwest Turner Hall in **St. Louis**.

MARCH 2

Lazarus Averbuch, a Russian Jewish immigrant, was shot and killed by the Chicago chief of police George Shippy in Shippy's home. Both Shippy's son and driver were wounded and Shippy incurred a superficial stab wound. Afterwards Shippy claimed Averbuch was an anarchist, and many newspapers portrayed him as a follower and associate of EG. EG spoke about the incident in **Springfield**, Illinois, having arrived there the same day from St. Louis. She denied that Averbuch was an anarchist, claiming that no true anarchist would attack a child.

MARCH 3

At least nine people, all associates of Lazarus Averbuch, were arrested in Chicago, including Harry Goldstein, secretary of the Edelstadt Group in Chicago and reportedly the ring leader of the plot against Shippy's life.

MARCH 4

The press speculated that if EG's deportation proceedings from the United States were to begin, she would flee to Montreal for asylum.

MARCH 5

EG was scheduled to speak in a public meeting in **Chicago**, Illinois.

MARCH 6

EG was scheduled to speak at the German Hod Carriers' Hall (Harrison and Green streets) in **Chicago** under the auspices of the Edelstadt Group. Because police vow they will meet her at the train station and prevent her from speaking, barring her from all meeting halls, EG found an open air tent for her talk. Prepared for distribution to Chicago public were 50,000 copies of an appeal signed by EG.

The Anarchist Federation in New York published EG's appeal, entitled *A Letter to The Public of Chicago*.

MARCH 7

EG was scheduled to speak before the garment workers' union at Metropolitan Hall in **Chicago**. She reported that when she was prevented from speaking in a public hall, she addressed 50 wealthy Chicagoans at a mansion on Lake Shore Drive.

MARCH 8

EG was scheduled to speak on "What Anarchism Really Stands For" at the Masonic Temple in **Chicago** to the Social Science League, but the police prevented her entry.

Department of Commerce and Labor attempted to determine EG's citizenship. EG was under continual surveillance by secret service agents.

MARCH 9

EG was denied permission to speak at the Lessing Club House (447 West Taylor Street); an anarchist allegedly tried to rent the Apollo Hall in **Chicago** for her to speak but failed; when the hall was set on fire, the police blamed anarchists.

Federal authorities, trying to find grounds to deport EG, claimed they had no record of her return to the United States after attending the International Anarchist Congress in Amsterdam.

MARCH 10

EG was denied permission to attend burial of Lazarus Averbuch in Waldheim Cemetery by the Jewish Hebrew Burial Ground Association in Chicago. The group decided that anarchists should not take part in the burial.

MARCH 11

EG announced her decision not to speak at the painters' union meeting at 55 North Clark Street in **Chicago**.

MARCH 13

EG met BR at the home of Becky Yampolsky, M.D., on Twelfth Street near Ashland Avenue, in **Chicago**.

BR offered her the use of the headquarters of the Brotherhood Welfare Association (392 Dearborn Street) to serve as a lecture hall. Chicago assistant corporation counsel Holt gave nod of approval to EG to speak on anarchy if the hall was in proper condition, on the condition that she not advocate violence, the destruction of government, nor attack the police department. EG announced a series of meetings to begin that night at the storefront venue arranged by BR. Several hundred anarchists gathered but police blocked the meeting on grounds that the building had been condemned and was unsafe.

MARCH 15

EG and BR took a walk in Lincoln Park, were followed by detectives, and their budding romance became the subject of newspaper reports. EG attended a meeting of the Anthropological Society in **Chicago** in the afternoon but did not speak and left with BR. Forty officers rushed to the hall to prevent her from speaking.

MARCH 16

EG tried to speak on "Anarchy As It Really Is" at Workingmen's Hall (Twelfth and Waller streets) in **Chicago**, an event planned by the Freedom of Speech Society, presided over by William Nathanson of the Edelstadt Group. Police forcibly removed EG from the hall, with approximately 65 officers on hand. Her suppressed lecture was later published in pamphlet form as *A Beautiful Ideal* (Chicago: J. C. Hart, 1908).

AB began a lecture tour to benefit *Mother Earth*. At his first stop in Worcester, Massachusetts, AB was prevented by police from entering a hall where he was scheduled to speak, and the Reverend R. E. White, who interfered on AB's behalf, was arrested and later fined ten dollars.

MARCH 17

Chicago's assistant chief of police criticized his subordinate for ejecting EG from Workingmen's Hall, claiming he had played into EG's hands; stated EG had a right to speak and that police would not interfere unless she said something which could be construed as inciting to riot.

MARCH 20

EG was scheduled to leave Chicago for **Milwaukee**, Wisconsin.

In a letter to Attorney General Charles J. Bonaparte, President Theodore Roosevelt ordered the exclusion of *La Questione Sociale*, an Italian-language anarchist newspaper published in Paterson, New Jersey, from the mails. The president deemed the newspaper indecent and immoral because an article advocated the murder of police officers and enlisted men. Roosevelt also asked the attorney general to see if it was possible to prosecute the newspaper's editors under federal law.

MARCH 22

EG spoke on "Anarchy and What It Really Stands For" in **Milwaukee**.

MARCH 23, 24

EG was originally scheduled to speak on "The Revolutionary Spirit in Modern Drama," and "The Child and its Enemies" at the Turner Hall in **New Ulm**, Minnesota. She reported that the Turner Society (Turnverein) canceled the two lectures.

MARCH 24

EG returned to **Chicago**, Illinois; made arrangements to speak; assistant chief of police Herman Schuettler said that he would allow her to do so as long as she "obeyed the law." In 1886 Schuettler arrested Haymarket anarchist Louis Lingg and served as a witness at the trial of the Haymarket men. EG made arrangements to speak at 571 West Taylor Street and 526 Union Street.

MARCH 25

EG spoke during the evening on "the philosophical and theoretic side of anarchy" before a crowd of several hundred at Holcomb's Hall in **Minneapolis**, Minnesota.

MARCH 26

EG lectured in the evening at Dania Hall in **Minneapolis**.

MARCH 27

EG delivered her third evening address at Kistler's Hall in **Minneapolis**.

MARCH 28

EG lectured at Holcomb Hall in **Minneapolis** to a smaller crowd than her first lecture there. At an illegal demonstration of the Conference of the Unemployed of the Socialist Party, in Union Square, New York, attended by 10,000 to 25,000 people, a bomb exploded in the hands of Selig Silverstein (a member of the Anarchist Federation) after clashes between the police and demonstrators. The blast killed a bystander and mortally wounded Silverstein.

MARCH 30

EG left Minneapolis for **Winnipeg**, Manitoba, Canada, unaccompanied by BR.

AB arrested in connection to bomb-throwing incident in Union Square; released the same day.

MARCH 31

EG lectured to one thousand people on "Anarchism" at Trades Hall in **Winnipeg**, Manitoba, Canada.

APRIL

Francisco Ferrer founded the International League for the Rational Education of Children in Paris. Its international committee included Sebastian Faure, Maurice Maeterlinck, Charles Malato, and Ferdinand Domela Nieuwenhuis.

APRIL 2

EG spoke on "Trade Unionism's Relation to Anarchy" at Trades Hall in **Winnipeg**.

APRIL 3

EG was scheduled to lecture on "Why Direct Action Is the Logical Method of Anarchy" at Trades Hall in **Winnipeg**.

APRIL 4

EG attended a reception held in her honor at Trades Hall in **Winnipeg**.

APRIL 5

EG delivered an afternoon lecture on women's emancipation and an evening lecture on "The Revolutionary Spirit in Modern Drama" at Trades Hall in **Winnipeg**. She charged an admission fee (despite the Lord's Day Act in Canada ruling this illegal).

APRIL 6

EG left Winnipeg and was detained until after midnight at the **Canadian/U.S. border** by U.S. immigration officials, who eventually released her after their interrogation of her and her production of the naturalization papers of Jacob Kershner (her former husband) that secured her citizenship.

APRIL 9

In a message transmitted to Congress, President Theodore Roosevelt requested the enactment of legislation to suppress anarchist publications. His message also included a report by Attorney General Charles J. Bonaparte that declared that there was no federal statute that made such publications illegal.

APRIL 11

EG spoke on "What Is Anarchism?" at Eastman Hall in **Salt Lake City**, Utah.

APRIL 12

EG was scheduled to lecture on "Direct Action—A Logical Tactic of Anarchism" in the afternoon and "The Revolutionary Spirit of Modern Drama" in the evening at Eastman Hall in **Salt Lake City.**

APRIL 15

EG spoke on "Anarchism: What It Really Stands For" at the Pythian Castle, at Ninth and I streets, in **Sacramento**, California.

APRIL 16

EG lectured on "The Methods of Anarchism" at the Pythian Castle in **Sacramento**.

APRIL 17

EG arrived in **San Francisco**, California, accompanied by BR. Alexander Horr, EG's local agent and West Coast tour manager, reported that EG had been trailed by detectives from Sacramento. Police warned her that anarchist propaganda could not be circulated in San Francisco.

APRIL 18

EG, BR, and Alexander Horr were forced to leave the St. Francis Hotel in **San Francisco** by the management. They were given refuge in the home of anarchist sympathizer Joe (Julius) Edelsohn in the Potrero district at 248 Boutwell Street.

APRIL 19

EG was warned by police that anything of an inflammatory nature in her lecture would result in a police breakup of her meetings at Walton's Pavilion.

EG spoke in the afternoon at Walton's Pavilion in **San Francisco**.

EG spoke at a meeting in the evening encouraging the collective action fueling the success of strikes in **San Francisco**. No police interfered inside, but three arrests were made for the distribution of handbills on the street. The *San Francisco Call* reported that a "remarkable fea-

ture" of the meeting was a large presence of Japanese in the audience.

APRIL 21

EG debated socialist Nathan L. Griest on "Resolved, that socialism, and not anarchism, will solve the social problem" in **San Francisco**.

APRIL 26

EG gave her final lecture, on "Patriotism," at Walton's Pavilion in **San Francisco**. U.S. Army soldier (private first-class) William Buwalda attended the lecture in uniform and was witnessed shaking her hand. EG also presided over a meeting in which BR delivered a speech.

APRIL 28

EG spoke on "Anarchism: What It Is and What It Seeks to Accomplish" at Metropolitan Hall in **Los Angeles**, California. She also visited George A. Pettibone of the William Haywood and Charles Moyer trial during her stay.

LATE APRIL

Common Sense, a socialist paper, refused to publish *Mother Earth*'s paid advertisement for EG's lecture series in Los Angeles.

MAY 1

Demonstration was held at Union Square in New York, arranged by the First-of-May Conference. The conference consisted of "representatives from various labor organizations" and included the Anarchist Federation of New York. An estimated 10,000 men and women marched in line from Rutgers Street to Union Square. AB, the federation's chosen speaker, was met with hostility by socialists in the crowd but eventually delivered his address.

MAY 2

EG debated Kaspar Bauer on the question of "Socialism versus Anarchism" at Howell Hall (814 South Main Street) in **Los Angeles**.

MAY 14

U.S. Army soldier William Buwalda was court-martialed for violation of the 62nd Article of War—charged because he attended and "did frequently and repeatedly applaud" EG's speech, which was characterized as "an attack and criticism of the government and especially the Government of the United States and the Army and Navy" and "did . . . declare to the said Emma Goldman his sympathy with her and his approval of her remarks." Buwalda pled not guilty but was found guilty, dishonorably discharged and sentenced to five years at hard labor on Alcatraz Island, San Francisco, California.

MAY 15

EG was in **Spokane**, Washington.

MAY 17

EG debated Socialist Party member Hermon F. Titus, M.D., on "Socialism Against Anarchy" at Egan Hall in **Seattle**, Washington.

MAY 22

William Buwalda's sentence was commuted by Brigadier General Funston to three years of hard labor, in deference to Buwalda's 15 years of excellent military service and the assumption of a temporary lapse in judgment under the sway of an "anarchist orator."

MAY 23

EG was scheduled to speak in the evening on "Why Emancipation Has Failed to Free Women" at Alisky Hall (corner Morrison and Third streets) in **Portland**, Oregon. Before her arrival in Portland, she was denied access to two halls previously rented for her lectures (Arion and the YMCA).

MAY 24

EG was scheduled to speak in the afternoon on "The Menace of Patriotism" at Merrill Auditorium in **Portland**.

EG spoke in the evening on "Anarchism and What It Really Stands For" in Merrill's Hall (86 Seventh Street) in **Portland**. Introduced by Senator C. E. S. Wood, who denounced the Portland YMCA for its refusal to rent a hall to EG.

MAY 25

EG spoke on "The Relationship of Anarchism to Trades Unionism" at Alisky Hall in **Portland**.

MAY 26

EG spoke on "Patriotism" at Merrill Hall in **Portland**; local anarchists planned a protest

against the court-martial and imprisonment of William Buwalda.

MAY 27

EG was scheduled to lecture on "The Revolutionary Spirit in the Modern Drama" and "Patriotism" at Alisky Hall in **Portland**.

The Act for the Suppression of Trade in, Circulation of, Obscene Literature and Articles of Immoral Use, also known as the Comstock law, was amended to include under the category of "indecent material" "matter of a character tending to incite arson, murder, or assassination," which was to be excluded from the mails. This amendment was directly aimed to halt the circulation of anarchist publications.

MAY 29

EG was originally scheduled to lecture in **Spokane**, Washington, but the lecture was cancelled because no large downtown hall space could be secured.

MAY 30

EG held an evening press conference in the parlor of the Victoria Hotel in **Spokane**, accompanied by BR. During an interview, EG quoted a letter to her from Butte, Montana, announcing that the Reverend Duncan would be dynamited if EG were allowed to speak in his church.

MAY 31

EG spoke in the afternoon on "What Anarchism Really Stands For" and in the evening on "The Menace of Patriotism" at the Spokane Theater in **Spokane**. Evening lecture arranged by Alexander Horr. It was announced in *The Evening Chronicle* (Spokane, 30 May 1908) that soldiers and sailors in uniform would be admitted free of charge to EG's evening lecture.

JUNE 1

EG spoke in the Spokane Opera House in **Spokane**.

JUNE 3

EG was scheduled to speak in the evening on "Trade Unionism and Anarchy" at the Finnish Hall in **Butte**, Montana, but waylaid in Drummond by floods.

JUNE 4

EG was scheduled to speak again in the evening on "The Revolutionary Spirit in Modern Drama" in **Butte**.

JUNE 5

EG spoke on a wide range of topics including police and the U.S. prison system, the press, and on the existing conditions in Butte. Her first lecture took place in the afternoon at Carpenters' Hall in **Butte**, accompanied by BR.

JUNE 7

EG was scheduled to speak in the afternoon on "What Anarchism Stands For" and in the evening on "The Menace of Patriotism" at the Broadway theater in **Butte**.

JUNE 12

Alexander Horr, EG's West Coast manager, arrived in Helena, Montana, to make arrangements for her meetings. The Socialists of Butte challenged EG to debate Ida Crouch-Hazlett and had already hired an auditorium for the event, scheduled for 24 June. The Grand Army of the Republic members complained to the town council, which prompted alderman Bob Fiske, who rented out the hall, to renege on his contract. Hazlett insisted on her right to hold a meeting, and authorities stated that they would allow Hazlett to speak but not EG. Horr rented the Electric Hall in Helena for EG's other meetings.

JUNE 14

EG delivered an evening lecture on "The Aims and Objects of Anarchy" at Carpenters' Hall in **Butte**.

JUNE 18

Voltairine de Cleyre and Chaim Weinberg were tried in Philadelphia, Pennsylvania, for their involvement in the Broad Street riot on 20 February. When the prosecution's only witness failed to appear and no other evidence was presented, Judge Mayer Sulzberger directed the verdict of not guilty. In a separate trial, the four Italians who were also arrested on charges of incitement to riot were found guilty and sen-

tenced to long prison terms. Dominick Donelli, the only anarchist of the four, received a five-year sentence of hard labor. Voltairine de Cleyre and Joseph J. Cohen organized a defense committee for the men to raise funds for an appeal to the Pennsylvania Boards of Pardons.

JUNE 22–23

EG was scheduled to speak at Electric Hall in **Helena**, Montana.

JUNE 24

When EG went to the auditorium in **Helena** to debate Ida Crouch-Hazlett, she found the hall locked. Hazlett spoke to the crowd gathered in front of the auditorium, relating the facts of the case. EG tried to speak, but the police told her that she would not be allowed to continue. Socialists claimed that the debate was disrupted because the number of socialists was a growing threat to Montana's mainstream political parties.

President Theodore Roosevelt suggested that U.S. Army soldier William Buwalda's sentence be shortened to six months as it was perfectly clear that Buwalda deserved punishment for such an offense of "peculiar horror" but that the sentence as imposed was too severe and might elicit sympathy in the military ranks.

JUNE 30

In a letter to Fred C. Ainsworth, Adjutant General of the U.S. War Department, Brigadier General Frederick N. Funston recommended an executive pardon for William Buwalda. Funston, a decorated hero in the Spanish-American War who was stationed in San Francisco, asked that Bulwalda's faithful service to the United States Army and the fact that he did not hold any anarchist beliefs be taken into consideration.

JULY

American Socialists, including John Kenneth Turner and Ethel Duffy Turner, began to write articles and deliver speeches in support of the Mexican Liberal Party (PLM).

EARLY JULY

EG travels between her farm in **Ossining**, New York, and the city of **New York**.

JULY 3

Judge-Advocate General George B. Davis chose not to object to the granting of clemency to William Buwalda but not allow his release until "affairs in the Harbor of San Francisco have settled down to a normal basis." Davis also recommended that the clemency not be published until closer to Buwalda's date of release (December 31). Shortly thereafter, President Theodore Roosevelt granted clemency to Buwalda.

JULY 19

EG's article "What I Believe" was published in the *New York World*. EG received $250 for the article, which helped support *Mother Earth* through the summer months.

Mother Earth Publishing Association published EG's *New York World* article, later this year, as a pamphlet entitled *What I Believe*.

AUGUST 3

George Pettibone died in Denver, Colorado.

AUGUST 17–SEPTEMBER 14

EG traveled back and forth between the city of **New York** and her farm retreat in **Ossining**, New York.

SEPTEMBER 7

Labor Day meeting of the unemployed took place at Cooper Union, sponsored by the Brotherhood Welfare Association of New York. BR delivered a speech prepared by EG, causing a great uproar upon this disclosure. AB and Becky Edelsohn were arrested. Although Meyer London, the socialist attorney, asked to defend AB, the trial took place before any defense could be finalized.

SEPTEMBER 12

AB was released from Blackwell's Island, having served five days for his arrest on 7 September.

SEPTEMBER 13

EG spoke in German on "affinities" ("Love and Marriage") and verbally attacked the police at the Terrace Lyceum, 206 East Broadway, in **New York**, a meeting sponsored by the *Freie Arbeiter Stimme* Group, and the first in a series of Sunday lectures.

SEPTEMBER 16

The press announced EG's plan to tour Australia beginning in January 1909.

SEPTEMBER 20

EG lectured on the topic "The Revolutionary Spirit in the Modern Drama," speaking on Gerhardt Hauptmann's *Sunken Bell;* George Bernard Shaw's *Mrs. Warren's Profession;* and Henrik Ibsen's *Doll's House* and *The God Revenge,* at Terrace Lyceum, 206 East Broadway, in **New York**, as part of her Sunday afternoon Yiddish-language lecture series, sponsored by *Freie Arbeiter Stimme.*

SEPTEMBER 24

At its fourth annual convention in Chicago, the IWW delegates voted to remove all reference to political action from the preamble to their constitution, by only a three-vote majority (35 to 32).

SEPTEMBER 27

EG was scheduled to deliver the third of her Sunday Yiddish-language lectures in the evening on "Marriage and Love" at American Star Hall, Pitkin and Christopher Avenues (in **Brooklyn**), sponsored by *Freie Arbiter Stimme.*

FALL

Spokane city council passed an ordinance prohibiting "the holding of public meetings on any streets, sidewalks, or alleys within the fire limits," effective 1 January 1909, in response to the IWW practice of organizing and speaking in public spaces.

OCTOBER 3

Mother Earth "harvest ball" took place at the Terrace Lyceum, 206 East Broadway, **New York**.

OCTOBER 4

EG was scheduled to deliver the fourth of her Sunday lectures at 206 East Broadway in **New York**.

OCTOBER 11

EG was scheduled to deliver the fifth and final of her Sunday lectures in the afternoon on "The Political Circus" at the Terrace Lyceum, 206 East Broadway, **New York**.

OCTOBER 13

EG was scheduled to lecture on "The Political Circus" at the Metropolitan Saenger Hall, Pitkin Avenue and Watkins Street, in **Brooklyn**.

OCTOBER 15

EG's 13 October lecture on "The Political Circus" was re-scheduled for this date.

OCTOBER 16

EG gave a farewell lecture on "The Exoneration of the Devil" at Clinton Hall in **New York**, in anticipation of her trip to Australia.

OCTOBER 17

EG began a lecture tour to **Rochester**, **Pittsburgh**, **Cleveland**, **Omaha**, **Cincinnati**, **Indianapolis**, and she hoped, to Australia. She announced her lecture topics for upcoming tour in *Mother Earth:* "The Dissolution of our Institution"; "Puritanism, the Great Obstacle to Liberty"; "The Psychology of Violence"; "Marriage and Love"; and "Comrades, to Work!" Additional topics announced were "Life versus Morality"; "The Drama: The Strongest Disseminator of Radicalism"; and "The Political Circus and Its Clowns."

OCTOBER 18–20

EG was scheduled to lecture in Germania Hall, Clinton Avenue North, in **Rochester**, New York.

OCTOBER 21

EG lectured to a large audience on "The Political Circus and Its Clowns" at Turn Hall, Fourth Street. in **Pittsburgh**, Pennsylvania.

OCTOBER 22–24

EG lectured in **Cleveland**, Ohio. According to Hutchins Hapgood, EG addressed 3,000 people in one of the city's public squares.

OCTOBER 25–26

EG was scheduled to lecture in **Cincinnati**, Ohio.

OCTOBER 27–29

EG was scheduled to lecture on "Anarchism and What It Stands For," "The Revolutionary Spirit in the Drama," and "Patriotism" at the Propylaeum in **Indianapolis**, Indiana. The city controller informed Hutchins Hapgood, acting on EG's behalf, that the city had decided not to grant EG a license to speak; she could speak, however, without a license as long as she did not charge admission. When EG arrived at the Propylaeum ("the most 'respectable' hall in Indianapolis"), she found doors locked and the police turning people away.

NOVEMBER 1

EG lectured in the afternoon on "The Devil Exonerated," an analysis of the many recent dramatic and literary representations of the devil as a symbol of revolt and rebellion against conventions, at Druid's Hall in **St. Louis**, Missouri. William Marion Reedy, editor of *St. Louis Mirror,* presided.

NOVEMBER 2

EG lectured in **Springfield**, Missouri.

NOVEMBER 3

EG lectured in **Liberal**, Missouri. Attended mostly by farmers.

NOVEMBER 3–4

In the presidential election Eugene Debs, Socialist Party candidate, achieved 420,973 votes—2.8 percent of the total vote.

NOVEMBER 4–6

EG lectured twice in **Kansas City, Missouri**, and once in **Kansas City, Kansas**.

NOVEMBER 5

William Marion Reedy's article "Emma Goldman: The Daughter of the Dream" was published in the *St. Louis Mirror* on 5 November 1908. In *Living My Life* (p. 442), EG commented that "No finer appreciation of my ideas and no greater tribute to me had ever been written by a non-anarchist before."

NOVEMBER 7–13

EG was scheduled to lecture in **Omaha**, Nebraska; chief of police convinced owners not to allow EG to lecture in her rented hall (the Lyric Theater, located in a commercial college building). Instead, EG lectured at the Labor Temple, attracting middle-class audiences nevertheless.

NOVEMBER 11

EG participated in the first commemoration of the Chicago Haymarket anarchists in **Omaha**, with the police in full force.

NOVEMBER 14

EG was scheduled to lecture in **Council Bluffs**, Iowa.

NOVEMBER 15

EG lectured twice in **Des Moines**, Iowa.

NOVEMBER 17–22

EG was scheduled to deliver a series of eight lectures in **Minneapolis**, Minnesota, accompanied by BR.

NOVEMBER 17

EG spoke at Dania Hall in **Minneapolis**.

CA. NOVEMBER 23

EG lectured in **St. Paul**, Minnesota.

NOVEMBER 24

EG spoke in the evening on "The Dissolution of Our Institutions" at Trades Hall, James Street East, in **Winnipeg**, Manitoba, Canada.

NOVEMBER 25

EG was scheduled to speak in the evening on "Puritanism, the Greatest Obstacle to Liberty" at Trades Hall in **Winnipeg**.

NOVEMBER 29

EG lectured twice in **Winnipeg**, to an audience of approximately 1,500.

NOVEMBER 30

EG lectured at Trades Hall, **Winnipeg**.

DECEMBER

EG's article "What I Believe" was translated into Italian ("Quel ch'io Credo"), and commented on in *Il Pensiero*, an Italian anarchist newspaper edited by Luigi Fabbri, 1–16 December 1908.

DECEMBER 1

EG was scheduled to debate with socialist J. D. Houston at Selkirk Hall (owned by a Baptist church on Logan Avenue) in **Winnipeg**. Objections were raised by the pastor of the church, but the meeting took place as scheduled.

DECEMBER 2

EG lectured in **Fargo**, North Dakota.

DECEMBER 3

EG was scheduled to deliver a lecture in **Bismarck**, North Dakota.

DECEMBER 6–7

EG gave an afternoon lecture on "The Devil Exonerated," "Do Anarchists Believe in Organization?" and "Why Persons Commit Rash Acts" in **Butte**, Montana. EG helped organize a branch of the Social Science Club in the city.

DECEMBER 9–11

EG was scheduled to lecture in **Spokane**, Washington, but it appears that she was unable to secure hotel or lecture hall.

DECEMBER 10

EG arrived in **Seattle**, Washington.

DECEMBER 12

EG spoke on "Violence" at 5617 22nd Avenue, N.W. in **Seattle**, Washington, in the Ballard neighborhood. The *Seattle Post-Intelligencer* reported that the meeting attracted only 12 "reds," such poor attendance that EG cut her talk short.

DECEMBER 13

EG spoke on "Violence" at the Labor Temple in **Seattle**, in the afternoon although the local press reported that the Labor Temple was reluctant and had only mistakenly rented the hall to EG. In the evening, EG was scheduled to speak at Hibernian Hall in **Seattle**. She was locked out of the hall; one of her followers broke the lock; and police took EG to police headquarters.

DECEMBER 14

EG was denied the right to speak in **Everett**, Washington. Fraternal Hall was secured for the meeting but the hall was cancelled, so she secured a small hall on the riverside. Authorities claimed that they wanted to prevent the meeting to protect EG because vigilante types had threatened to harm her if she spoke.

In **Bellingham**, Washington, EG and BR were arrested by police and charged with inciting "treason" and unlawful assemblage.

DECEMBER 15

EG was released from jail and placed on a train bound for Canada. She had retained a lawyer to defend her from the charge of inciting to unlawful assemblage but instead agreed to leave the city when she learned she would be charged with insanity if the first charge failed. Canadian immigration officials removed her from the train but, on instructions from the Canadian government in Ottawa, released her and BR; EG and BR proceeded to **Vancouver**, British Columbia, Canada.

DECEMBER 15–16

EG lectured in **Vancouver**.

DECEMBER 19

BR arrived in Portland, Oregon, as an advance man for EG's lectures.

DECEMBER 20

EG lectured on "The Dissolution of Our Institutions" in the afternoon and on "Marriage and Love" in the evening at Alisky Hall in **Portland**, Oregon.

Goldman's father, Abraham Goldman, filed his last will and testament at the city of Rochester, Monroe County, New York.

DECEMBER 21

EG was scheduled to debate socialist Walter Thomas Mills on "Anarchism vs. Socialism" at Merrill's Hall in **Portland**.

DECEMBER 27

EG debated Socialist Party member Hermon F. Titus, M.D., on "Socialism Against Anarchy" at Labor Temple in **Seattle**, Washington.

DECEMBER 31

William Buwalda was released from prison.

1909

Mother Earth Publishing Association published EG's pamphlet *The White Slave Traffic*, Voltairine de Cleyre's *Anarchism and American Traditions*, and Francisco Ferrer's *The Modern School*.

The Free Speech League published Theodore Schroeder's pamphlet *The Conflict Between Religious and Ethical Science* and also, with The Truth Seeker Publishing Company, an anthology compiled by Schroeder entitled *Free Press Anthology*.

JANUARY 2–8

EG gave seven lectures at Burbank Hall in **Los Angeles**, California; audiences ranged in size from 200 to 600. Her meetings were managed by Claude Riddle. EG's lectures on "The Devil Exonerated" and "The Drama, the Most Forcible Disseminator of Radicalism" were attended by some of the city's leading drama critics.

JANUARY 5

EG's father, Abraham Goldman, died in Rochester, New York.

JANUARY 6

EG lectured on "Puritanism, the Greatest Obstacle to Liberty," at the Socialist Hall in **Pasadena**, California.

EG announced that one thousand dollars had been raised by anarchists for Army private William Buwalda, who was imprisoned for attending an anarchist meeting while in uniform, in **Los Angeles.**

JANUARY 8

William Buwalda wrote to President Theodore Roosevelt, thanking him for his pardon, but protesting the injustice of the charges against him, saying that the government acted as if it had "a mortgage on [his] soul."

JANUARY 9

EG lectured on "Anarchy, What It Really Stands For" at 8 P.M. at the Germania Hall in **San Diego**, California.

JANUARY 10

EG lectured on "Marriage and Love" at 11 A.M. and "Direct Action Not Political Action" at 8 P.M. at Germania Hall in **San Diego**. She left for San Francisco that night.

JANUARY 13

EG spoke on "The Dissolution of Our Institutions" at the Victory Theater (Sutter Street near Fillmore) in **San Francisco**, California, at 8 P.M.; William Buwalda, court-martialed in 1908, also spoke.

JANUARY 14

EG was scheduled to speak on "Puritanism, the Greatest Obstacle to Liberty" at the Victory Theater in **San Francisco** at 8 P.M. Both EG and BR were arrested on charges of conspiracy against the government (BR arrested in the hall—having preceded EG there, and EG upon trying to enter); both held on eight counts, each charge set at $2,000 bail, totaling $16,000. William Buwalda, who had recently been pardoned by President Roosevelt, was arrested and charged with disturbing the peace. The scheduled speech was canceled. Bail was determined at $2,000 for each meeting scheduled, each evidenced as individual counts of conspiracy.

JANUARY 15

EG and BR were arraigned on eight charges of conspiracy to incite a riot; the hearing was continued until the next morning. While in jail, EG received news of her father's death.

Protesting arrests of EG and BR, a meeting gathered at the Victory Theater in the evening. After they were ejected from the theater by police, people re-gathered on the corner of Post and Fillmore streets, where they were again forcibly moved on by the police.

JANUARY 18

EG and BR were released on bail. EG's bail reduced from $8,000 to $2,000: $5,000 raised in New York for the bails, expected to be received the following day; money received by Charles Sprading used to release EG.

JANUARY 19

EG participated in debate on "Direct Action vs. Political Action" at the Victory Theater in **San Francisco**, 8 P.M.

EG and BR were newly charged on a count of unlawful assembly; original eight charges against them were continued, and a warrant served charging them with denouncing government institutions and preaching anarchist doctrines. The defendants were released upon providing bail ($250 for charge of unlawful assembly).

JANUARY 20

EG was scheduled to speak on "The Buwalda Case" as the principal speaker at a dinner sponsored by the San Francisco Sunrise Club at the Cosmos Cafe (658 Market Street, opposite Palace Hotel) in **San Francisco**. It was scheduled as her last appearance in public before her planned departure for Australia.

JANUARY 23

EG's planned but never realized departure date for Australia.

JANUARY 28

EG's trial scheduled for the afternoon in **San Francisco**, dismissed before the case went to jury when the judge decided that it was not unlawful to denounce the government or preach anarchist doctrines, and instructed the jury to acquit EG and BR.

JANUARY 31

EG spoke to a crowd of over two thousand people on "Why I Am an Anarchist" at Dreamland Pavilion in **San Francisco**. She thanked police for arresting her and giving her free publicity.

FEBRUARY 11

The U.S. Department of Justice attempted to cancel Jacob Kershner's certificate of naturalization, stepping up their effort to deport EG.

FEBRUARY 28

EG debated socialist Walter Thomas Mills on "Anarchism vs. Socialism" on two occasions, afternoon and evening, before large audiences at the Auditorium Pavilion in **San Francisco**.

MARCH 4

Spokane City Council adds religious groups to their ordinance prohibiting public speaking (a response by the council to the IWW's charges that the ordinance was unfair, claiming that religious groups were allowed to proselytize on street corners; the IWW announced their intention to violate the ordinance until all groups are treated equally). In defiance of the ordinance, IWW member J. H. Walsh mounted a soapbox and was arrested by the police and taken to jail. Throughout March other IWW members followed Walsh's lead and Spokane's jails were soon filled with IWW members and their supporters.

MARCH 5

EG spoke on "Why I Am an Anarchist" in **Santa Barbara**, California.

MARCH 8

EG debated the sex question ("Free love without collective regulation is the only guarantee of a healthy race") in **Los Angeles** with Edward Adams Cantrell, national lecturer for the Socialist Party.

MARCH 12

EG in **El Paso**, Texas, held one meeting, in which city authorities did not allow Spanish to be spoken, for fear of losing control of a population vulnerable to EG's message. EG noted that most of the El Paso press denounced anarchism, except for the *El Paso News,* which published an "intelligent and fair editorial."

MARCH 14

EG arrived in **San Antonio**, Texas. In an interview with the local press, BR claimed this was the first time an anarchist had spoken in the South. Article also noted that she and BR were on the train that wrecked near Sanderson, Texas, though they escaped injury.

MARCH 15

EG left San Antonio for **Houston**, Texas, on the late evening train because the Trades Council refused to allow her the use of the Labor Hall, and the Beethoven Hall was available only at an exorbitant rate. It was reported that the Socialist Hall would have been available to EG, had she asked.

MARCH 16

In **Houston**, the police and mayor offered her the use of the town hall, but she arranged to rent a hall from a Roman Catholic order. When the brothers found out who she was, however, they refunded her money. Finally, single-taxers offered her their hall, the "Log Cabin" (on the outskirts of Houston).

MARCH 21

EG ended her lecture tour, giving two lectures in **Fort Worth**, Texas. In the afternoon she spoke on "Anarchy: What It Really Stands For" and in the evening on "Love and Marriage."

APRIL 6

William Buwalda sent a letter to Joseph Dickinson, U.S. Secretary of War, returning his campaign badge received for his bravery in the line of duty during the Philippine Insurrection, asserting that he had no further use for it and it would be better to give it to someone who might appreciate it.

APRIL 8

Judge John R. Hazel at the U.S. District Court in Buffalo, N.Y., canceled the citizenship papers of Jacob A. Kershner, EG's former husband, and as a result, EG's right of citizenship was also revoked.

APRIL 11

EG lectured in English on "The Psychology of Violence" at Lyric Hall (Sixth Avenue, near 42nd Street) in **New York** at 11 A.M., the first of a Sunday lecture series.

APRIL 18

EG scheduled to speak at Fraternity Hall (100 West 116th Street, corner of Lenox Avenue) in **New York** at 11 A.M. (second lecture of the Sunday series). EG scheduled to lecture in Yiddish on "The Psychology of Violence" at the Terrace Lyceum at 2 P.M., and in English on "The Psychology of Violence" at Washington Hall at 8 P.M.

APRIL 25

EG scheduled to lecture on "The Greatest Obstacle to Liberty, the Hypocrisy of Puritanism," at Fraternity Hall in **New York** at 11 A.M. (third lecture of Sunday series). EG was scheduled to speak in Yiddish on the meaning of Eugene Walter's play *The Easiest Way* at Terrace Lyceum at 2 P.M.

MAY

Ricardo Flores Magón, Librado Rivera, and Antonio I. Villarreal were extradited to Arizona Territory to be tried for breaching the neutrality laws. The three men had been arrested on 23 August 1907 and held in Los Angeles, California.

MAY 1

Mother Earth May Day concert and dance scheduled for Terrace Lyceum in **New York**. EG, Sadakichi Hartmann, and others were scheduled to speak or perform.

MAY 2

EG was scheduled to lecture at Fraternity Hall in **New York** (fourth lecture of Sunday series).

MAY 6

EG spoke at a convention of the National Committee for the Relief of the Unemployed, urging unemployed to organize, at Manhattan Lyceum in **New York**.

MAY 9

EG lectured on "The True Significance of Anarchism," at Lexington Hall in **New York** (fifth lecture of Sunday series).

MAY 10

EG was scheduled to speak on "Direct Action as a Logical Tactic of Anarchists" at 206 East Broadway in **New York**.

MAY 13

EG was scheduled to speak on "How Should Parents Raise Children" at 66–68 Essex Street in **New York**.

MAY 14

EG was scheduled to speak in **New Haven**, Connecticut, on "Anarchy: What It Stands For"; admitted into the hall by the police, who then refused to allow anyone else to enter.

Ricardo Flores Magón and two other PLM members were sentenced to eighteen months in the state penitentiary at Yuma, and later moved to a prison located in Florence, Arizona Territory.

MAY 16

EG spoke on "Minorities versus Majorities," at Lexington Hall in **New York** (sixth lecture of Sunday series).

EG spoke in Yiddish on "The Social-Revolutionary Aspects of the Modern Drama" at Terrace Lyceum in **New York**.

MAY 21

EG and AB lunched with the New Jersey Society of Mayflower Descendants at the Woman's Club in **East Orange**, invited by Alden Freeman (black sheep of the Standard Oil fortune), which came as a surprise to other guests.

EG scheduled to speak on "The Child and its Enemies" in **Brooklyn**, sponsored by the Sunday School Committee of the Friends of Art and Education, Branch 139, Workmen's Circle.

MAY 23

EG was scheduled to speak on the "Modern Drama: The Strongest Disseminator of Radical Thought" at Lexington Hall in **New York** at 11 A.M. (seventh lecture of Sunday morning series), but, according to police, she did not stick to the subject, giving them the right to break up the meeting of 200 persons, dispersing 1,000 people outside of the hall. Becky Edelsohn and Leopold Bergman were arrested and charged with disorderly conduct. EG returned in the afternoon and attempted to deliver her lecture, but the police denied all access to the hall and cleared the street with their clubs.

MAY 24

EG spoke on "The Hypocrisy of Puritanism" to the Sunrise Club (at Cafe Boulevard, Tenth Street and Second Avenue), 6:45 P.M., in **New York**, to an audience of 270.

MAY 30

EG intended to deliver her speech on the modern drama, which had been broken up by police the previous Sunday, at Lexington Hall in **New York** (as part of her Sunday morning lecture series).

LATE MAY

"A Demand for Free Speech" manifesto (signed by at least 20 prominent individuals), focused on the recent suppression of EG's free speech, was published in *Mother Earth* and circulated in radical and liberal circles. Signatories included J. G. Phelps Stokes, Rose Pastor Stokes, William Marion Reedy, Senator C. E. S. Wood, Alden Freeman, and Anna Strunsky Walling.

JUNE 8

EG was scheduled to speak at a meeting to commemorate the 100th anniversary of Thomas Paine's death in **East Orange**, New Jersey, sponsored by the Open Forum; Alden Freeman scheduled to introduce her, but police prevented her from entering the public hall (English's Hall). The crowd of 1,000 people had to regroup at a barn on Freeman's property, corner of Central and Munn avenues, where EG spoke on "The Modern Drama," the same speech the police had suppressed on May 23.

JUNE 18

EG was scheduled to speak, with AB, on unionism and anarchism, at Liberty Hall (Spring and Shippen streets), **West Hoboken**, New Jersey.

JUNE 30

A meeting was held by the Free Speech Committee at Cooper Union, New York, to protest treatment of EG by police of New York City on May 23, and to win back the right of free speech; 2,000 people attended. Leonard Abbott, John Sherwin Crosby (a single-tax advocate), Voltairine de Cleyre, Alden Freeman, and Harry Kelly spoke. EG did not attend the meeting because she felt she would be arrested if she tried to speak.

JULY 2

EG spoke on "The Drama" at 100 West 116th Street, at the hall of the Harlem Liberal Alliance in **New York**; the hall was jammed with 250 people, and police stood by without interfering. The meeting was later considered a "test" to see if EG would be allowed to lecture, even though police had tried to intimidate hall owners as a passive tactic for suppression of anarchist ideas.

JULY 23

EG spoke on "Some Misconceptions of Anarchism," at the hall of the Harlem Liberal Alliance in **New York**. No police presence; no disruptions.

JULY 26–AUGUST 1

Uprising in Barcelona initiated, later called the "Tragic Week," organized by workers group, Solidaridad Obrera.

MID TO LATE SUMMER

In Missoula, Montana, IWW skirmishes with local authorities over street-speaking rights.

AUGUST 10

The Spokane City Council revised the city ordinance on public speaking, allowing all religious groups the right to speak, but requiring all other groups to obtain permits.

AUGUST 11

EG was scheduled to speak at a meeting to celebrate the uprising in Barcelona at the Manhattan Lyceum, 64 East 4th Street, **New York**. The proprietor refused to open his door to the speakers and audience. AB, BR, and Becky Edelsohn told celebrants the meeting would be held instead on August 12 at 206 East Broadway.

AUGUST 12

EG spoke at her rescheduled meeting in **New York** to honor the uprising in Spain.

AUGUST 16

The Providence Board of Police Commissioners refused to grant EG a permit to speak if she charged an admission fee. BR was warned that any violent remarks by EG would promptly be followed by police interference.

AUGUST 17

EG spoke in the evening on "Anarchism and What It Really Stands For" at Olive Branch Hall, 98 Weybosset Street, in **Providence**, Rhode Island.

AUGUST 28

EG was scheduled to speak on "Marriage and Love" at Columbia Hall in **Newark**, New Jersey.

AUGUST 31

Francisco Ferrer was arrested near his native village of Alella in Spain. He was charged with being the "author and chief" of the rebellion in Barcelona (commonly referred to as "Tragic Week") in late July.

LATE AUGUST

EG lectured in **Boston**, **Lynn**, **Malden**, and **Brockton**, Massachusetts.

SEPTEMBER

The American Magazine began publishing John Kenneth Turner's articles on Mexico, which would later form the basis of the book *Barbarous Mexico.*

Ricardo Flores Magón, Librado Rivera, and Antonio I. Villarreal were moved to a penitentiary in Florence, Arizona Territory.

SEPTEMBER 3

EG attempted to speak in **Burlington**, Vermont. Originally scheduled to speak at the City Hall, she was not allowed to speak in any city-owned building, by rule of the mayor. When she secured another hall, he persisted in his attempts to prevent her from speaking. Without enough support to fight the mayor, she did not speak.

SEPTEMBER 4

EG and BR traveled to **Worcester**, Massachusetts, hoping to be allowed to speak there, but could not find anyone willing to rent them a hall. Mrs. Eliot White, the wife of an Episcopal minister, offered the use of her house and lawn.

SEPTEMBER 6

EG attended a meeting organized at the socialist headquarters (274 Main Street) in **Worcester** to plan a strategy for securing free speech for her, with Morris Hillquit of New York as legal representative for her case.

SEPTEMBER 7

BR and the Reverend White met with Mayor Logan of Worcester, telling him that, in the event of suppression of free speech, they would hold him responsible and take the matter to court. BR also went to Clark University to consult with university president and prominent educational theorist G. Stanley Hall.

SEPTEMBER 7–11

During this time, EG attended a Clark University lecture in **Worcester** by Sigmund Freud. She had apparently heard Freud speak in Vienna in 1896.

SEPTEMBER 8

After finding Beaver Hall in **Worcester** locked, a crowd of 300 to 400 followed EG to the Reverend Eliot White's home. Police pushed people off the sidewalk into the street. White intervened, and EG successfully delivered her lecture, "What Is Anarchism."

SEPTEMBER 18

Mother Earth ball scheduled for New York.

SEPTEMBER 24

BR asked the director of public safety in Philadelphia if the police intended to interfere with EG's upcoming lecture; when the police director announced that he would not permit EG to speak, single-taxers denounced him.

SEPTEMBER 25

Leonard Abbott arrived in Philadelphia, Pennsylvania, from New York to aid the free speech fight, bringing letters of support from prominent individuals, including Upton Sinclair, Eugene Debs, and Jack London.

SEPTEMBER 28

EG was scheduled to speak at Odd Fellows' Temple in **Philadelphia**, Pennsylvania, but prevented from entering the hall by police. BR and Voltairine de Cleyre addressed the audience, de Cleyre read the speech EG was to have given as a way to subvert the police director's mandate to review EG's proposed speech before delivering it. Some 300 to 400 police officers lined both sides of the street at the Odd Fellows' Temple.

SEPTEMBER 29

EG met with single-taxers, freethinkers, and other radicals at 1502 Arch Street in **Philadelphia** to discuss her free speech fight. Attorney Henry John Nelson drafted an injunction restraining the mayor, director of public safety, and police from further interference with EG's lectures.

LATE SEPTEMBER

The city council in Missoula, Montana, passed an ordinance making street-speaking illegal. The arrest of four IWW organizers, including Frank Little, for defying the ordinance triggered the 30 September 1909 edition of *The Industrial Worker* to call for all workers to travel to Missoula to engage in a free speech fight. Hundreds of IWW members flooded the town and were arrested.

OCTOBER 1

At a hearing before Judges Willson and Audenried for the injunction proceedings called by EG to prevent police interference with her meetings, she testified about her anarchist beliefs. She continued to hold education meetings at 1502 Arch Street in **Philadelphia**.

OCTOBER 3

EG was in **Philadelphia**, awaiting the court's decision to her appeal for an injunction to restrain the police from further prevention of her speaking; she was unable to find anyone in Philadelphia willing to rent her a hall for fear of police harassment. EG was trailed by detectives, hotels were under surveillance, and hotelkeepers put on alert by police.

OCTOBER 4

EG planned to speak on the Philadelphia City Hall Plaza in **Philadelphia** this evening if the injunction against her was granted, and hoped to reveal the names of prominent individuals who had supported her free speech efforts.

OCTOBER 6

EG's attorney Henry John Nelson and assistant city solicitor Alcorn appeared before Judges Willson and Audenried to schedule a rehearing of her case in Philadelphia. Her citizenship status prevented the judges from making a decision.

OCTOBER 8

EG's case was scheduled for rehearing; when questions about her citizenship status were raised by the judge, the hearing was continued without a formal decision.

Philadelphia anarchists held a meeting at the Labor Lyceum (6th and Brown streets), chaired by Leonard Abbott. EG, still awaiting the decision of the court, on whether aliens had a right to receive the protection of U.S. law, did not attend. EG sent a letter, read twice to the crowd, to great cheers.

OCTOBER 9

Francisco Ferrer was tried before a military court and was found guilty of directing the revolt in Barcelona in late July. He was sentenced to death by firing squad.

OCTOBER 13

Having been convicted as primary instigator of the "Tragic Week" in Barcelona, Francisco Ferrer was executed by firing squad.

OCTOBER 15

Judge Willson sustained the Philadelphia police refusal to permit EG to deliver lectures, by denying the injunction brought before the court on her behalf, and found that police had the right to prevent anyone, whether a citizen or an alien, from speaking, if the words of the speaker were likely to create a public disturbance. The judge also determined that because EG was not a citizen, she had no constitutional guarantee of right to free speech.

OCTOBER 17

EG was the primary speaker at a mass meeting called to protest the execution of Francisco Ferrer in Clinton Hall, 151 Clinton Street, in **New York**; attended by 1,000 people.

BR and Voltairine de Cleyre held an afternoon memorial meeting for Ferrer in Philadelphia, despite Police Director Clay's ruling denying their right to gather in his memory. An evening meeting at Industrial Hall (Broad and Wood streets) was prevented by police. The meeting was relocated to 424 Pine Street, and police broke up the meeting midway, when BR attempted to speak.

OCTOBER 18

EG returned to **Philadelphia** to resume free speech fight.

OCTOBER 20

EG held a private gathering to plan the forthcoming mass meeting in Philadelphia, hoping to speak without police harassment or interruption, in her room at 1502 Arch Street in **Philadelphia**. When police attempted to enter her private room, they were stopped by EG and BR, who argued their right to privacy; police then threatened to cordon off the boardinghouse to prevent anyone from entering, an action protested by the owner. A detective was stationed at the foot of the stairs to EG's room to turn away her visitors. In response to this the owner asked EG to move.

OCTOBER 21

EG and BR moved to Voltairine de Cleyre's home in **Philadelphia**..

OCTOBER 22

EG and BR traveled to **New York**. The Free Speech Committee met in evening at 120 Lexington Avenue, chaired by Leonard Abbott, to discuss free speech fight in Philadelphia and EG's report.

OCTOBER 23

EG marched in an anarchist-socialist parade of 600 people up Fifth Avenue, from Madison Square Garden to 57th Street, in **New York**. The marchers passed St. Patrick's Cathedral (50th Street and Fifth Avenue), denounced the Pope, and then met in Carnegie Hall to protest the execution of Francisco Ferrer.

NOVEMBER 1

A legal ruling denounced Spokane's ordinance banning street speaking as unconstitutional.

NOVEMBER 2

James P. Thompson, local IWW organizer, and many IWW members were arrested in Spokane and charged with disorderly conduct. IWW's headquarters in Spokane raided by police late in the evening. By end of free speech fight (March 1910), approximately 400 IWW members arrested and jailed.

NOVEMBER 5

A meeting of EG's scheduled in **Brooklyn** was prevented by Police Chief Shaw, who intimidated the hall owner. An open air meeting, attended by 3,000 people, attracted sensational press about the hall being closed to EG. BR arrested when asked to produce a permit. Judge refused to comply with Shaw's request to issue a warrant for EG's arrest.

NOVEMBER 6

BR fined $5 at Manhattan Police Court.

NOVEMBER 7

EG spoke on execution of Ferrer, and his founding of the Modern School, 8 P.M., at Frost's Hall, 107 West 116th Street, **New York**, where the Reverend Eliot White also spoke about the Worcester, Massachusetts, free speech fight.

NOVEMBER 11

EG was scheduled to lecture at a meeting at 206 East Broadway, **New York**, to honor the memory of Chicago Haymarket anarchists.

NOVEMBER 22

After a mass meeting sponsored by the International Ladies Garment Workers Union in the Great Hall of the People in Cooper Union, New York (attended by prominent labor leaders, among them Samuel Gompers, Leonora O'Reilly, Jacob Panken), a strike, inspired by Clara Lemlich, of 15,000 women shirtwaist workers would last until February 1910.

NOVEMBER 28

EG was scheduled to lecture on "Francisco Ferrer, His Life and Work" at the Women's Trades Union Hall, 43 East 22nd Street in **New York**.

NOVEMBER 30

Elizabeth Gurley Flynn was arrested in Spokane and charged with criminal conspiracy.

DECEMBER 12

EG spoke on "Will the Vote Free Woman? Woman Suffrage," 2:30 P.M., at Lyric Hall, 725 Sixth Avenue near 42nd Street in **New York**. EG characterized suffrage as a "wild goose chase." The meeting was attended by 300 women, most of whom were suffragettes. A collection was taken for Elizabeth Gurley Flynn.

MID-DECEMBER

EG attended a production of John Galsworthy's *Strife* at the New Theatre in **New York**.

DECEMBER 17

EG became the one-hundredth member of the Arbeiter Ring (Workers Circle) at a meeting in **New York**.

DECEMBER 19

EG spoke on the New Theatre and on John Galsworthy's new labor drama, *Strife,* at the Women's Trades Union Hall on East 22nd Street in **New York**. She also spoke briefly about her perception that it was the merits of the strikers' demands, not the assistance of Mrs. O. H. P. Belmont, Anne Morgan, and other "wealthy ladies" to the striking shirtwaist makers, that would win the battle.

DECEMBER 24

EG attended a ball to benefit *Mother Earth* at the American Palace Hall, 310–312 Grand Street, in **New York**.

DECEMBER 26

EG's last lecture before tour to the western United States, on "White Slave Traffic," was scheduled to take place at 8 P.M., at the Women's Trade Union Hall, 43 East 22nd Street, **New York**.

Abbott, Leonard Dalton (1878–1953) American radical and freethinker. Born and educated in England, Abbott moved to the United States in 1897. He became a socialist through the influence of William Morris and was a member of the Socialist Party of America's executive board in 1900. Abbott met EG through Ernest Crosby in the late 1890s at a meeting at Justus Schwab's saloon, organized to exert public pressure for reduction of AB's prison sentence. Abbott was an original board member of the Rand School of Social Science (1906), president of the Free Speech League after 1907, and chairman of the Free Speech Committee (1909). He contributed to the *British Labour Annual* every year from 1899 to 1901, where he reported on the progress of socialism in America. Abbott was on the editorial board and a contributor to the *Socialist Spirit* (Chicago, 1900–1903), edited the *Free Comrade* with J. W. Lloyd (1900–1902), and was associate editor of *Current Literature* for over 25 years. He also contributed to *The Comrade, Commonwealth,* and *Mother Earth* and was the author of a number of pamphlets, including *The Society of the Future* (Girard, Kans.: J. A. Wayland, 1898); *A Socialistic Wedding: Being the Account of the Marriage of George D. Herron and Carrie Rand* (New York: Knickerbocker Press, 1901), an account of the wedding presided over by William Thurston Brown; *The Root of the Social Problem* (New York: Socialistic Cooperative Publishing Association, 1904); *Ernest Howard Crosby: A Valuation and a Tribute* (Westwood, Mass.: Ariel Press, 1907); and *Sociology and Political Economy* (New York: Current Literature, 1909).

Adams, Edith Thorpe (dates unknown) "Anarchist friend" EG stays with in 1908. Adams lived in St. Louis, Missouri. She contributed an article on the Haymarket anarchists to the 4 December 1909 edition of Ross Winn's *Firebrand*.

Addams, Jane (1860–1935) American advocate of women's independence and settlement house worker. Founder of the social settlement Hull House in Chicago. Hull House, which opened in 1889 in the midst of Chicago's worst immigrant slums, became a center of social programs aimed at helping poor immigrants. Besides sponsoring clubs and social functions for immigrants, Hull House served as a base for reform efforts in child labor laws, workers' safety issues, and women's suffrage. She was one of the founders of the Women's Trade Union League in 1903. Between 1905 and 1908 Addams served as a member of the Chicago Board of Education. In 1909, she helped found the National Association for the Advancement of Colored People. A mediator in the Chicago Garment Workers' Strike of 1910, she was the first vice president of the National American Women Suffrage Association between 1911 and 1914 and a founder and the first president of the National Federation of Settlement and Neighborhood Centers in 1911. During 1915 Addams helped organize the Women's Peace Party and was elected its first chair. She presided at the International Congress of Women at The Hague in 1915. Associate editor of *The Survey* (1912), the magazine dedicated to social work, she also contributed to *The Outlook* and was the author of several books, including *Newer Ideals of Peace* (New York: Macmillan, 1907), *The Spirit of Youth and the City Streets* (New York: Macmillan, 1909), *Twenty Years at Hull House* (New York: Macmillan, 1910), *A New Conscience and an Ancient Evil* (New York: Macmillan, 1912), with Emily G. Balch and Alice Hamilton, *Woman at The Hague* (New York: Macmillan, 1915), and *The Long Road of Woman's Memory* (New York: Macmillan, 1916).

Andrews, John Bertram (1880–1943) American progressive reformer. With strong interests in labor and unemployment issues, Andrews studied with labor economist John R. Commons at the University of Wisconsin, receiving his doctorate in 1908. Beginning in 1906 Andrews served as executive secretary of the American Association for Labor Legislation, and along with his wife, Irene Osgood, who was also a student of Commons, Andrews advocated the use of social scientific expertise to formulate public policy. He published a leaflet entitled *Labor Leaders and Labor Literature* (Madison, Wisc.: 1904?).

Andrews, Stephen Pearl (1812–1886) American individualist, Texas lawyer and abolitionist, driven out of Houston for his abolitionist activities. A follower of the French sociologist and reformer Charles Fourier, by 1850, Andrews had joined Josiah Warren in advocating decentralism and individualism. He worked on a universal language he called "Alwato." In 1851, with Warren, he co-founded the Modern Times colony. An early advocate of sociology, he was the author of the *Science of Society,* nos. 1 and 2 (New York, 1852), which stressed the historical importance of the sovereignty of the individual, and *The Basic Outline of Universology* (New York, 1872), in which he sought to unite sociology with all the branches of the natural sciences. After the Civil War, Andrews became interested in the movement for women's rights, and was an associate of Victoria Woodhull. In the 1880s he was active in sex reform, speaking at a Boston meeting of the Institute of Heredity on 25 May 1882 on "Heredity, Its Place in the Scale of Subjects for Scientific Investigation." Other members present at the meeting included E. B. Foote, Sr., Elizabeth Cady Stanton, and John Quincy Adams.

Andreyev, Leonid Nikolayevitch (1871–1919) Russian author, lawyer, crime reporter, and editor. A friend and protégé of Maksim Gorky, Andreyev's first volume of stories was published by Gorky's publishing house. His works include *Savva* (1906), *King Hunger* (1907), *The Seven Who Were Hanged* (1907), and *The Pretty Sabine Women* (1912). His play *King Hunger* was featured in EG's lectures and her book *The Social Significance of the Modern Drama* (1914), and was first published in English in the quarterly magazine *Poet Lore* (1911). It was, however, his play *Anathema* (1909) that EG would later consider Andreyev's most thought-provoking work.

Angiolillo, Michele (1871–1897) Italian anarchist. Angiolillo (referred to in some newspaper accounts as "Golli") shot and killed Antonio Cánovas del Castillo, prime minister of Spain, on 8 August 1897, at the Santa Agueda baths. The son of a tailor, Angiolillo worked as a compositor before leaving Foggia in October 1883, spending time in Marseilles and Barcelona under the name José Santos. He became interested in anarchism while in Coromina, and traveled again to Marseilles and was expelled. He later frequented anarchist circles in Belgium and London. Sentenced in April 1896 to eighteen months in prison for disseminating anarchist literature, he fled to Spain before he had completed his term. During his trial, he testified that he had acted independently in the assassination of Cánovas, an act he intended as revenge for the 4 May 1897 executions at Montjuich prison of five anarchists linked by the Spanish government to the Corpus Christi Day bombing of 7 June 1896. Denied the right to speak of anarchism or the wars in Cuba and the Philippines at his trial, Angiolillo was sentenced to death by garrote and executed on 20 August 1897. He was the subject of a Voltairine de Cleyre short story, "The Heart of Angiolillo" (1898), which was reprinted in *The Selected Works of Voltairine de Cleyre* (New York: Mother Earth Publishing Association, 1914).

Austin, Kate (1864–1902) American anarchist and advocate of women's independence. Austin was born Catherine Cooper in La Salle, Illinois, and settled with her husband, Sam, on a farm near Caplinger Mills, Missouri. An early freethought and free love advocate, Austin was among those influenced by the legacy of the Haymarket anarchists and became a lifelong anarchist communist. Austin was a friend of William Holmes and Carl Nold. She and her husband arranged EG's Missouri lectures in 1897 and 1899. According to *Living My Life*, EG intended to, but was barred from, delivering Austin's report on "The Question of the Sexes," a history of the free love movement in the United States, at the 1900 Paris Congress after a French anarchist group feared "that any discussion of sex would only serve to increase the misconceptions of anarchism" (*LML*, p. 271). Austin's paper did, however, appear in the official reports of the 1900 Paris Congress in *Les Temps Nouveaux*, as well as in the Italian-American anarchist newspaper *La Protesta Humana*. In 1901 in the pages of *Free Society*, Austin joined EG in defending Leon Czolgosz's attack on President McKinley. Austin was a contributor to *Free Society, Firebrand, Lucifer, the Lightbearer*, and *Discontent*. She died of consumption in Kingman, Kansas, on 28 October 1902 while traveling to Denver. Both EG and Voltairine de Cleyre penned obituaries for Austin.

Averbuch, Lazarus (1889–1908) Russian Jewish immigrant, living in Chicago from late 1907. Killed on 2 March 1908 by Chief of Police George Shippy, who testified that he was acting in "self-defense" to thwart an assassination attempt. Averbuch was assumed, without evidence, to be an anarchist. A roundup of Chicago anarchists followed, along with an attempt to link EG to a nation-wide anarchist conspiracy.

Baginski, Max (1864–1943) German-born anarchist, editor, and co-founder of *Mother Earth*. Baginski was co-editor of *Freiheit* (1906–1910) with Henry Bauer after the death of Johann Most in 1906. Baginski moved to New York from Chicago in 1905 with his companion, Millie Schumm, and EG invited them to live on the farm in Ossining, New York, given to her by Bolton Hall. He was part of the group that planned the production of the journal that would become *Mother Earth*. Baginski accompanied EG to the 1907 anarchist congress in Amsterdam. In New York he worked as a publicist for left journals, including German-language workers' papers, *Mother Earth*, and his own short-lived journal, *Internationale Arbeiter Chronik*. His works include *Syndikalismus: Lebendige, keine toten Gewerkschaften* (New York: 1909?). Baginski was a frequent contributor to *Mother Earth* on topics ranging from syndicalism to European literature. *See also vol. 1, p. 517.*

Bakunin, Michael (1814–1876) Russian revolutionary and theorist of anarchism. Bakunin was born into the aristocracy of Premukhino, in Tver province, and was part of the Russian intelligentsia. In the circle of the Young Hegelians in Berlin in 1840, he knew Karl Marx well (he later tried to have *Das Kapital* published in Russian). He also met the anarchist Pierre-Joseph Proudhon in Paris in 1844. Bakunin was arrested in Dresden and condemned to death for his part in the revolutionary activity of 1848 and 1849, but his sentence was commuted to life imprisonment. Turned over first to the Austrian and then the Russian government, he was imprisoned in the Peter-Paul fortress from 1851 to 1857, then exiled to Siberia, from which he escaped in 1861, traveling to Japan, the United States, England, Italy, and finally Switzerland. The leading force in the anti-authoritarian opposition to Marx in the First International, Bakunin first described himself as an anarchist in the mid-1860s, and in writing in 1867. His principal works are *Statism and Anarchy* (1873) and *God and the State* (1882), the latter of which was translated into English by Benjamin Tucker (Tunbridge Wells: Science Library, 1883) and also published by Tucker in Boston. *God and the State* was published in 1896 (Columbus Junction, Iowa: E. H. Fulton, 1896) and again in 1900 by Abe Isaak (San Francisco: A. Isaak, 1900). Tucker also serialized Bakunin's *The Political Theology of Mazzini and the International*, translated by Sarah E. Holmes, in *Liberty* in 1886 and 1887. Bakunin died in Berne, Switzerland, on 1 July 1876.

Baldwin, Roger Nash (1884–1981) St. Louis-based reformer. Baldwin was born in Wellesley, Massachusetts, where his Unitarian family had strong liberal ties. He graduated with a master's degree in anthropology and philosophy from Harvard in 1905 and moved to St. Louis in 1906, where he taught at Washington University and was the director of Self Culture Hall, a settlement house serving Jewish and Irish immigrants in St. Louis. From 1907 to 1910 he was chief probation officer for the St. Louis juvenile court. Baldwin first heard EG speak in 1908; he was also acquainted with Harry Kelly while Kelly was living in St. Louis. Baldwin became secretary of St Louis's Civic League in 1910. Baldwin later attributed his founding of the American Civil Liberties Union with Crystal Eastman to the inspiration of EG.

Barondess, Joseph (1867–1928) Russian-born trade union organizer. Barondess was born in Kamenets-Podolsk, Russia, the son of a rabbi; he immigrated first to England where he was an active trade unionist, and in 1888 to the United States. Initially sympathetic to anarchism, he joined Eugene Debs and Victor Berger after they launched the Social Democratic Party in 1898. Barondess was a member of the Free Speech League from 1902 to 1903 as part of the Turner Defense Committee. In 1909 Barondess organized and led a mass funeral procession through New York City to commemorate the death of Yiddish playwright Jacob Gordin. He served two four-year terms on the New York City Board of Education after 1910. He became a committed Zionist in 1903 and was a founding member of the American Jewish Congress in 1918. *See also vol. 1, p. 518.*

Berkman, Alexander (1870–1936) Lithuanian-born anarchist organizer, editor, and author and EG's closest comrade politically as well as lifelong friend, although during this period tensions over political strategy had begun to arise regularly between them. Berkman was released to the workhouse to serve the last year of his sentence on 19 July 1905, and was finally released from imprisonment on 18 May 1906. He suffered from a severe depression after his release, during which time he corresponded extensively with Voltairine de Cleyre, who understood his depression and encouraged him to write his memoirs. Shortly after his release, an unsuccessful lecture tour in late 1906 ended when AB suffered a minor breakdown and temporarily disappeared. In January 1907, he started a short-lived printing business. Berkman was arrested in January 1907 for protesting EG's arrest at a New York anarchist lecture. At EG's encouragement, he quit his printing business and became editor of *Mother Earth* (March 1907), a job at which he excelled. At this time Berkman became the companion of Rebecca Edelsohn. He was a founder and organizer of the Anarchist Federation of

America (1908). Arrested for "inciting to riot" after the Union Square bombing (28 March 1908), all charges against him were quickly dropped due to lack of evidence. He was arrested again at a Brotherhood Welfare Association meeting at Cooper Union on Labor Day 1908, with Rebecca Edelsohn, for defending Ben Reitman, after Reitman was attacked for reading a speech criticizing Labor Day that was actually written by EG; Berkman spent five days in the workhouse for disturbing the peace. Despite ideological and tactical differences, Berkman worked with Reitman at *Mother Earth*. Berkman is the probable author of a number of small pamphlets published by the Anarchist Federation in 1908, including *How to End Panics: An Address to Poor People, Workingmen Don't Vote,* and *To The Unemployed and Homeless!!*

Bjørnson, Bjørnstjerne (1832–1910) Norwegian freethinker, poet, playwright, novelist, and theater director. Bjørnson's earlier work examined and celebrated Norwegian identity, while his later work (after 1870) addressed issues of political liberty and social inequality. A stage director in Bergen (1857–1859), he was also director of two theaters: the Oslo (1865–1867) and the Kristiania (1866–1871). Bjørnson was forced to resign his editorship of the newspaper *Aftenbladet* (1859–1860) for his reformist articles; later he was editor of the *Norsk Folkeblad* (1866–1871). Bjørnson was awarded the Nobel Prize for literature in 1903. His work was featured regularly in EG's drama lectures. Major works include *Mellem Slagene* (Between the Battles, 1857), *Maria Stuart I Skotland* (Mary Stuart in Scotland, 1864), *En Fallit* (A Bankruptcy, 1875), *Redaktören* (The Editor, 1875), *En handske* (A Gauntlet, 1883), *Over aevne, I* (Beyond Our Power, I, 1883), and *Geografi og Kjaerlighed* (Love and Geography, 1885). Bjørnson's play *Over aevne, II* (Beyond Our Power, II, 1895) addressed labor strife and the anarchist movement.

Blackwell, Alice Stone (1857–1950) American advocate of women's independence, reformer, and translator. Blackwell was the daughter of suffragist Lucy Stone and editor of the *Women's Journal*, the paper of the American Woman Suffrage Association, from 1881 until 1917, and recording secretary of the National American Woman Suffrage Association from 1890 to 1918; she was also a founding member of the League of Women Voters. Blackwell edited and distributed the "Women's Column," a regular collection of news articles about suffrage, from 1887 until 1905. She was the press committee chair for Friends for Russian Freedom; the group supported Russian revolutionaries fighting tsarist oppression. When Maksim Gorky, a romantic and heroic figurehead for Russian freedom, visited American in 1906 to raise money, she participated in the preparations for his highly anticipated visit but subsequently withdrew her support in the furor surrounding the *New York World*'s article about Gorky's "marriage" to his female traveling companion and alleged desertion of his wife and children in Russia. She was also active in the Women's Christian Temperance Union and the Women's Trade Union League during this period. She translated a number of books into English, including *Armenian Poems* (Boston: Roberts Brothers, 1896), *Songs of Russia* (Dorchester, Mass., 1906), *Songs of Grief and Gladness* by Ezekiel Leavitt (St. Louis: Press of the Modern View, 1907), and *Little Grandmother of the Russian Revolution, Reminiscences and Letters of Catherine Breshkovsky* (Boston: Little, Brown, 1917).

Bonaparte, Charles Joseph (1851–1921) Secretary of the U.S. Navy (1905–1906) and attorney general (1907–1909) under President Theodore Roosevelt. The grand-nephew of Napoleon and grandson of the King of Westphalia, Bonaparte had been a member of the Federal Board of Indian Commissioners (1902–1905) and was a personal friend of Roosevelt. Bonaparte advocated, in an August

1906 speech, the death penalty for any anarchist who sought, directly or indirectly, to take a life, and whipping and imprisonment for less serious offenses, including "seditious" speeches. Bonaparte also advocated that dissemination of anarchist literature, whether orally or through publication, should be considered a crime. His published works included *What Is Civil Service Reform?* (New York: The New York Association for Civil Service Reform, 1903) and numerous speeches, including *Concord and the American Revolution; An Oration Delivered on the 125th Anniversary of Concord Fight, April 19, 1900* (Baltimore: Williams and Wilkins, 1900), *John Marshall as Lawyer and Judge, an Oration Delivered on "John Marshall Day," February 4, 1901* (Baltimore: Williams and Wilkins, 1901), *Punishment and Pardon: A Paper Read at the Annual Meeting of the National Prison Congress, Chicago, Illinois, September 18, 1907* (Baltimore: Kohn and Pollock, 1907).

Bradlaugh, Charles (1833–1891) English freethinker, birth control advocate, and politician. Bradlaugh edited the *National Reformer* from 1862 to 1891 and co-founded the National Secular Society in 1866. He was tried and convicted between 1876–1877 on obscenity charges for publishing a book about contraception, but his conviction was overturned on a technicality. Elected to Parliament in 1880, Bradlaugh was ejected for refusing to take the oath of office on the Bible; he was re-elected several times until 1886, when Parliament accepted his terms and allowed him to serve until his death in 1891. An advocate for republicanism, universal suffrage, and the abolition of the House of Lords, Bradlaugh wrote numerous freethought pamphlets, among them *A Few Words about the Devil* (New York: A. K. Butts, 1874), *A Plea for Atheism* (New York: A. K. Butts, 1883), and *Humanity's Gain from Unbelief* (London: Freethought Publishing Association, 1889).

Bresci, Gaetano (1869–1901) Italian American anarchist. Born in Prato, Tuscany, Bresci apprenticed as a silkweaver in Milan, where he first joined the anarchist movement. Bresci settled in early 1898 in Paterson, New Jersey, where he worked as a silk weaver. He gravitated toward the *anti-organizzatori* affinity group in Paterson and became a subscriber and benefactor of *La Questione Sociale*. In May 1900, to avenge the victims of government repression in Milan and Sicily, he left his home in New Jersey to assassinate King Umberto of Italy at Monza on 29 July 1900 and died in prison the following year, reportedly by suicide. Bresci was considered a martyr of heroic significance to much of the American and European anarchist movement. *See also vol. 1, pp. 520–21.*

Breshkovskaya, Catherine (1844–1934), Russian revolutionary. Breshkovskaya joined the Narodniki revolutionaries in the 1870s, was arrested for propaganda work among the peasants, and sent to Siberia (1874–1896). After her release from exile in 1896 she founded the Social Revolutionary Party with Grigorii Gershuni and others in the winter of 1901–1902. She met EG and Alice Stone Blackwell while in the United States in 1904 and 1905, touring to gain American support for the early Russian revolutionary efforts for her party. She addressed audiences in New York, Boston, Philadelphia, and Chicago, many of which were sponsored by the Friends of Russian Freedom. Breshkovskaya was often a guest of settlement houses, staying at Lillian Wald's Henry Street House in New York, Jane Addams's Hull House in Chicago, and Helen Dudley's Denison House in Boston. She returned to Russia for the 1905 Revolution, where she supported the formation of the new Peasants Union. Breshkovskaya was imprisoned again in 1907 and exiled permanently to Siberia in 1910.

Brown, John (1800–1859) American abolitionist. Brown attacked the national government for its link to slavery. Brown led the raid on Harpers Ferry in 1859, in an attempt to secure arms and distribute them to slaves for rebellion. Brown was tried for murder, slave insurrection, and treason in the state of Virginia, for which he was hanged 2 December 1859. When he was hanged, he became for many Northerners a hero and martyr, both for his critique of slavery and his bravery during his trial. EG associated him with an undercurrent of anti-statism in the American political tradition.

Brown, William Thurston (1861–1938) American-born Christian socialist, minister, and teacher. Brown left the Congregational Church in 1902 after being expelled from two pulpits (the first in 1896) for his socialist beliefs. An organizer for the Socialist Party, he would later found a number of modern schools and become the principal of the Modern School at Stelton, New Jersey. Brown presided over the secular wedding of George Herron and Carrie Rand in 1901. An associate of Ernest Crosby, he edited *The Social Gospel* (1898–1901) with Crosby and Bolton Hall. Brown was a contributor to a number of socialist magazines, including *The Comrade, Wilshire's Magazine, Socialist Spirit* (of which he was on the executive board), and *The Wage Worker,* and the author of *After Capitalism What?* (Chicago: C. H. Kerr, 1900), *The Real Religion of Today* (Chicago: C. H. Kerr, 1900), *The Axe at the Root* (Chicago: C. H. Kerr, 1900), and *The Relation of Religion to Social Ethics* (Chicago: C. H. Kerr, 1901).

Buwalda, William (ca. 1869–1946) U.S. Army soldier who attended EG's lecture on "Patriotism" in San Francisco in 1908. Buwalda was court-martialed and imprisoned for shaking EG's hand while in uniform. His original sentence of five years at hard labor was reduced to three, and he received a pardon from President Theodore Roosevelt on 3 July 1908. Upon his release, he sent a letter to Roosevelt thanking him for his pardon but saying that, in fact, he was not guilty of any crime. He also later returned the badge he had received for his service in the Philippines. Briefly active in anarchist circles, by 1911 he was living near Grand Rapids, Michigan, caring for his elderly mother on the family farm. He remained an anarchist all of his life.

Cánovas del Castillo, Antonio (1828–1897) Spanish prime minister, historian, and writer. Cánovas was assassinated by Italian anarchist Michele Angiolillo in revenge for his ordering the execution of five anarchists and the torture of hundreds of anarchists and radicals for their alleged involvement in the 7 June 1896 bombing of a Corpus Christi Day parade in Barcelona.

Carnot, Marie François-Sadi (1837–1894) Fourth president (1887–1894) of the Third Republic of France. Carnot was stabbed to death by Italian anarchist Sante Caserio on 24 June 1894, in retaliation for his refusal to pardon Auguste Vaillant, who was executed on 6 February 1894 for attempting to blow up the Chamber of Deputies on 9 December 1893.

Carpenter, Edward (1844–1929) British author and poet, social reformer, libertarian socialist, and proponent of women's equality. Along with John Addington Symonds, Carpenter was an early advocate of homosexual emancipation. His 1908 book *The Intermediate Sex* (London: S. Sonnenschein, 1908) was adopted as the title of a frequently delivered lecture by EG on homosexuality. Other works from this period include *Prisons, Police and Punishment; an Inquiry into the Causes and Treatment of Crime and Criminals* (London: A. C. Fifield, 1905), *The Village and the Landlord* (London: Fabian Society, 1907), and *Socialism and Agriculture* (London: A. C. Fifield, 1908) with T. S. Dymond and D. C. Pedder, and *The Wreck of Modern Industry and its Re-Organisation* (Manchester: National Labour Press, 1910?).

Carrington, Charles (1857–1922) Paris publisher. Born Paul Ferdinando, Carrington was an underground Paris publisher, printer, writer, and collector of erotic literature. He was the foremost overseas dealer of English-language erotica from about 1895 to 1917 and also published French erotica. His business required him to travel between France, Belgium, Holland, and England to avoid arrest. Expulsion orders from the French government were twice issued against him, which he evaded. Carrington was acquainted with Oscar Wilde and published his *The Picture of Dorian Gray* (1908) as well as other respectable titles. His erotic publications included works of anthropology, chronicles of scandal, flagellation, original literature, and scientific works on sex, including *Lives of Fair and Gallant Ladies* (1901), *The Memoirs of Dolly Morton* (1899), and his own bibliography of erotic literature, *Forbidden Books: Notes and Gossip on Tabooed Literature* (1902). Later in life he went blind, reportedly due to syphilis, and his mistress and children allegedly robbed him of his substantial fortune in books. He died in a lunatic asylum (as they were then called) in 1922.

Caserio, Sante (1873–1894) Italian anarchist. Caserio was from Motta Visconti, near Pavia, and a baker by trade. Caserio sought to avenge the execution of Auguste Vaillant on 6 February 1894 by assassinating French President Sadi Carnot in Lyon on 24 June 1894, which led to the passage of the third of three anti-socialist "Exceptional Laws" (or what anarchists referred to as *lois scélérates*) on 26 and 27 July 1894.

Chaikovsky, Nikolai (1851–1926) Russian revolutionary. Chaikovsky, one of the most prominent members of Socialist Revolutionary Party (PSR) at this time, was a proponent, at times, of terrorism and guerrilla warfare. A political exile living in London, he visited the United States and then returned to Russia briefly in 1907, where he planned to organize guerilla warfare against the government. Arrested and imprisoned for eleven months before his bail money could be raised by his friends and supporters, Chaikovsky was acquitted after a short trial in March 1910 and thereafter became active in the Russian cooperative movement and as an opponent to Vladimir Lenin and the Bolsheviks. Wrote "The Russian Revolutionary Movement" for *The Outlook*, 28 April 1906. *See also vol. 1, p. 522.*

Chamberlain, Edward W. (ca.1843–1908) New York lawyer, freethinker, and early free-speech and free-press advocate. Chamberlain was treasurer of the National Defense Association, founded in 1878, which was the forerunner to the Free Speech League. He was the founding president of the Free Speech League in 1902, and vice president of the Manhattan Liberal Club. An outspoken critic of the Comstock Act, he protested Ezra Heywood's conviction on obscenity charges in 1878. Chamberlain was a member of the American Press Writers Association, a group whose members included Kate Austin and other liberals, freethinkers, socialists, and anarchists who monitored newspapers for bias and wrote editorials in protest to mainstream papers across the country. Chamberlain was a frequent contributor to *Lucifer, the Lightbearer,* and a thirty-year subscriber to the freethought journal, *The Truth Seeker*. He was author of the pamphlet *United States Versus Heywood: Why the Defendant Should Be Released* (New York: National Defense Association, 1891?).

Champney, Adeline (d. 1945) Boston and then Cleveland individualist anarchist. Married once for a short time; in Cleveland, Champney was the companion of Fred Schulder, with whom she had two sons, Horace and Freeman Champney. Champney was related through her brother's marriage to Benjamin Tucker's wife, Pearl Johnson Tucker. She contributed allegories and poems as well as essays to *Liberty, Lucifer the Lightbearer, The American Journal of Eugenics,* and occasionally *Mother Earth*. She was a member of the Cleveland Freethought Society and secretary-treasurer of

Propaganda for Free Discussion, a group of which E. C. Walker was the leading force. Author of the pamphlet *The Woman Question* (New York: Comrade Co-operative Company, 1903).

Channing, Walter (1849–1921) American psychiatrist and professor at Tufts University Medical School, founder and chief of the department of mental diseases of the Boston Dispensary, researched and promoted the treatment of mental illness. Channing testified at the trial of Charles J. Guiteau, who assassinated President James A. Garfield in 1881. Twenty years later, Channing and his assistant L. Vernon Briggs, M.D., were unconvinced by the conclusions of the five psychiatrists (three for the prosecution and two for the defense) who examined Leon Czolgosz, President William McKinley's assassin, prior to trial and pronounced him sane. Their own investigation led them to judge Czolgosz mentally unstable. In contrast to EG's emphasis on the larger social context for Czolgosz's act, it was Channing's opinion that Czolgosz's claim to be an anarchist was possibly a delusional aspect of his mental illness and that his act was less a result of exposure to anarchist teachings but more a convenient means for accomplishing his idea that he had a duty to perform his already-formed plan to assassinate the President. Channing explained the McKinley assassination strictly in terms of the assassin's personal history. In his 1902 article on Czolgosz, Channing quoted a report of the address Czolgosz claimed to have heard EG deliver on 5 May 1901 (see vol. 1: "Defends Acts of Bomb Throwers," Article in the *Cleveland Plain Dealer*, 6 May 1901), as well as a passage from EG's 30 November 1902 letter to *Lucifer, the Lightbearer* (entitled "Free Speech in Chicago"). See Walter Channing, "The Mental Status of Czolgosz, the Assassin of President McKinley," *American Journal of Insanity* 59 (October 1902): 233–78. He published numerous academic papers on mental health topics, such as "The Connection Between Insanity and Crime" (Utica, 1886) and "Characteristics of Sanity" (Boston: Damrell and Upham, 1897).

Chekhov, Anton Pavlovich (1860–1904) Russian short story writer and dramatist. Chekhov's major plays include *The Seagull* (1895), *Uncle Vanya* (1900), *Three Sisters* (1901), and *The Cherry Orchard* (1904). EG lectured on his works regularly and featured *The Seagull* and *The Cherry Orchard* in her *Social Significance of the Modern Drama* (1914), pp. 283–93.

Clausen, Emma (b. 1867) German-born Detroit-based anarchist, physician, and poet. Educated in Hamburg, Clausen studied to become a kindergarten teacher and emigrated at age eighteen to Canada. After a short-lived marriage, she moved with her two daughters to Detroit, where she worked as a teacher, nurse, and physician. Clausen was a member of the Detroit anarchist circle that also included Robert Reitzel, Carl Nold, and Joseph Labadie. Clausen contributed original poetry and translations to *Der arme Teufel*, including many translations of Charlotte Perkins Gilman's work and also contributed one poem to *Mother Earth* (July 1906).

Cohn, Michael Alexander (1867–1939) Russian-born Jewish anarchist, physician, and lifelong friend and financial supporter of both EG and AB. Cohn spent two years preparing to become a rabbi before deciding to study mathematics and Russian in Warsaw. Instead of graduating, he emigrated in 1886 to Boston where he worked as a tailor and began writing for the Yiddish periodical *New Yorker Volkszeitung*. Deeply affected by the execution of the Haymarket anarchists, he had become by 1890 a regular contributor to *Freie Arbeiter Stimme*. He studied medicine at New York University and in Baltimore, but remained an active anarchist. His first wife, Annie, was also a strong supporter of the anarchist movement and highly regarded by EG (in 1916 both would work with EG during the birth control fight). From 1890 Cohn practiced medicine in Brooklyn and continued to contribute intellectually and financially to the Jewish anarchist movement. He helped work for AB's release from prison. Cohn attended the 1900 anarchist congress in Paris with EG, where he gave a report on "The History of the Jewish Movement in America." Cohn contributed to *Free Society, Mother Earth,* and later the *Road to Freedom.* In later years he would take an active role in the defense of Nicola (Ferdinando) Sacco and Bartolomeo Vanzetti. He translated Peter Kropotkin's *Memoirs of a Revolutionist* into Yiddish (London: Grupe Frayhayt, 1904–1905). Cohn's publications include *Two Worlds, an Imaginary Speech delivered by Bartolomeo Vanzetti before Judge Webster Thayer: Why Sentence of Death Should Not Be Pronounced on Him and Nicola Sacco* (New York: Independent Sacco-Vanzetti Committee, 1927), *Some Questions and an Appeal* (New York: Independent Sacco-Vanzetti Committee, 1927) and he wrote the introductory biographical sketch, "Joseph Bovshover: His Life and His Work" in *To the Toilers and Other Verses, by Basil Dahl (Joseph Bovshover) with an appreciation by Benjamin Tucker, including translation from Yiddish by Rose Freeman-Ishill* (Berkeley Heights, N.J.: Oriole Press, 1928).

Comstock, Anthony (1844–1915) American reformer and founder of the Society for the Suppression of Vice in 1872. Comstock was the Post Office official charged with enforcing the obscenity law bearing his name. As a special, unpaid postal inspector, with the power to enter any post office and confiscate any material he deemed obscene, he sometimes used fictitious names when investigating in order to suppress progressive and radical publications, including works of literature, like Walt Whitman's popular *Leaves of Grass,* Leo Tolstoy's *Kreutzer Sonata,* and anything in print about birth control. Comstock's crusade was marked by conflict with anarchists and freethinkers. *Discontent, Lucifer, the Lightbearer,* and *Mother Earth* were among many papers he barred from the mail. EG sharply criticized Comstock's role as a censor in many of her later talks and essays, including "The Hypocrisy of Puritanism" (in *Anarchism and Other Essays* (New York: Mother Earth Publishing Association, 1910) and *Victims of Morality* (New York: Mother Earth Publishing Association, 1913). Comstock's only published work after 1900 was *Race Track Infamy: or, Do Gamblers Own New York State; a Scathing Exposure of How the Constitution of New York State Is Flagrantly Violated by Common Gamblers* (New York, 1904). *See also vol. 1, p. 523–24.*

Comyn, Stella (born Stella Cominsky) (1886–1961) EG's niece and one of her closest relatives. Comyn corresponded with AB in prison and performed secretarial work for EG.

Cook, Cassius V. (1879–1950) American anarchist, baker, and secretary of the San Francisco Social Science Club. Cook was secretary of the Free Speech League formed after the 1909 arrests of EG and BR in San Francisco. In 1910 Cook organized EG's lectures in Seattle. He worked in Chicago as treasurer of the Rationalist Association of North America in 1915. Cook was a contributor to the tenth anniversary souvenir edition of *Mother Earth* and a contributor to the individualist anarchist journal *Instead of a Magazine* (1916).

Cook, John H. (d. 1931) American anarchist. A socialist until his late twenties, Cook was a mainstay of the labor movement in his home city of Providence, Rhode Island, serving as secretary of the local carpenters' union for fifty years and for several years the president of the Central Labor Union, as well as being involved in the Providence Wendell Phillips Educational Club. He was the local subscription agent for, and a contributor to, *Free Society.* Arrested on several occasions for holding street meetings, he regularly arranged EG's meetings in Providence beginning in the 1890s. He was arrested in December 1901 for holding street lectures and fined $27. Arrested again in June 1902 for walking across the street in front of a street car during a street car strike, he was charged with obstructing the street cars. While Cook was in jail awaiting trial, the charges of promulgating anarchist doctrines and speaking disrespectfully of President Theodore Roosevelt were added. A defense fund for Cook was set up by local anarchists in Providence, and an appeal was published in the 6 July 1902 *Free Society*. Cook was released when the grand jury failed to indict him. He organized the 9 November 1902 Haymarket memorial meeting in Providence, at which EG was prevented from speaking.

Cornelissen, Christianus Gerardu (Christiaan) (1864–1942) Dutch anti-parliamentarian socialist and syndicalist; close associate of Ferdinand Domela Nieuwenhuis. He translated Karl Marx's *Communist Manifesto* into Dutch and helped to created the Nationaal Arbeids-Secretariaat, the Dutch syndicalist organization. After the 1907 anarchist congress in Amsterdam, Cornelissen was chosen to become editor of the syndicalist *Bulletin Internationale du Mouvement Syndicaliste*. He was also the author of the five-volume *Traite general de science economique*. He was a signatory, with Peter Kropotkin, of the "Manifesto of the Sixteen" in support of England and France in the First World War. *See also vol. 1, p. 524.*

Coryell, John Russell (1851–1924) American author, educator, and anarchist. EG describes him and his wife, Abby Coryell, as generous contributors to the movement and two of her closest American friends; both were members of the Sunrise Club. Coryell was the originator of the popular Nick Carter detective series and Bertha M. Clay romances. He was arrested 6 January 1907 at a *Mother Earth* meeting with EG and AB for "propagating anarchist ideas." Coryell lectured to the Liberty Congregation at Lyric Hall 1908 and was a frequent contributor to *Mother Earth* under his own name and one of his many pseudonyms, Margaret Grant. Coryell was part of the group that planned the publication of the journal that would become *Mother Earth*. He was a contributor to *Lucifer, the Lightbearer* (1907) and *Physical Culture* as well as the publisher and editor of a short-lived journal, *The Wide Way* (1907–1908). He wrote a number of pamphlets, including *Love and Passion* (New York: Corwill, 1907), *Making of Revolution* (New York: Corwill, 1908), *Sex Union and Parenthood and What Is Seduction?* (New York: Mother Earth Publishing Association, 1907), and *The Rent Strike* (New York: Corwill, n.d.).

Crosby, Ernest Howard (1856–1907) American social reformer, single-taxer, lecturer, and author. A leading proponent of Tolstoyan anarchism in the United States, Crosby met EG in the late 1890s around attempts to gain a pardon for AB. His numerous anti-militarist poems were printed in *Mother Earth*. From 1902 to 1905 he was co-editor with Benedict Prieth of the small literary and political magazine *The Whim*, "a periodical without a tendency." From 1905 until his death in 1907 he was a contributing editor of *The Public*, a Chicago-based weekly edited by Louis F. Post that supported the single-tax and anti-imperialist movements. His most important publications during this period include *How the United States Curtails Freedom of Thought* (New York: North American Review Publishing, 1902), an argument against the deportation of John Turner; *Swords and Plowshares* (New York: Funk and Wagnalls, 1902), his second collection of poetry; *Tolstoy and his Message* (New York: Funk and Wagnalls, 1904); *Broad-cast* (London: Arthur C. Fifield, 1905); *Garrison, the Non-Resistant* (London: Arthur C. Fifield, 1906); and the posthumous *Labor and Neighbor: An Appeal to First Principles* (Chicago: L. F. Post, 1908).

Czolgosz, Leon (1873–1901) American laborer, self-proclaimed anarchist, and assassin of President William McKinley. Born near Detroit to Polish-immigrant parents, Czolgosz was traveling under the alias "Fred Nieman" at the time of his appearance in Chicago in the summer of 1901 and of his *attentat* in Buffalo on 6 September 1901. His *attentat* was linked in the press and in his trial to the influence of EG's speech on "The Modern Phases of Anarchy," although she only met him briefly.

Darrow, Clarence Seward (1857–1938) American socialist, freethinker, single-taxer, and lawyer. A friend and associate of John Altgeld, governor of Illinois who in 1893 pardoned the surviving anarchists convicted in the Haymarket affair, Darrow gained a national reputation as a labor lawyer defending Eugene Debs and the American Railway Union during the Pullman strike in 1894 and was counsel for the coal miners in the arbitration before President Theodore Roosevelt's appointed commission in the anthracite strike of 1902. He advocated pardoning the Haymarket anarchists and was hired by the Free Speech League in 1903 to defend John Turner's case against deportation before the Supreme Court in 1903–1904. He was also a member of the 1909 Free Speech Committee. In 1907 Darrow successfully defended Western Federation of Miners' leaders Bill Haywood, Charles Moyer, and George Pettibone on trial for the murder of ex-Idaho governor Frank Steunenberg. Darrow was the law partner of the poet Edgar Lee Masters from 1903 to 1911. He contributed articles to *Everyman,* and his works during the first decade of the twentieth century include *Crime and Criminals: An Address Delivered to the Prisoners in County Jail* (Chicago: C. H. Kerr, 1902), *Resist Not Evil* (Girard, Kans.: Haldeman-Julius, 1902?), *Farmington* (Chicago: A. C. McClurg, 1904), and *The Open Shop, A Defense of Union Labor* (Chicago: Hammersmark Publishing, 1904).

Dave, Victor (1845–1922), Belgian-born anarchist writer and editor. Drawn to the libertarian wing of the First International from his student days in Liège and Brussels, Dave was an associate of Michael Bakunin, Peter Kropotkin, and Johann Most. He left Belgium in 1878 and spent much of his life in London, where he was a leading figure in the Bruderkrieg (Brothers War) and, in 1884, he briefly edited *Freiheit.* In Paris he was a contributor to *L'Humanité nouvelle* (1897). Dave met EG in Paris at the 1900 anarchist congress, which was prohibited by the Paris police. According to EG, Dave then took her to the secret Neo-Malthusian congress there. EG met Dave again at the 1907 International Anarchist Congress in Amsterdam.

Debs, Eugene Victor (1855–1926) American labor and political leader. Debs was five times the Socialist Party candidate for President of the United States, in 1900, 1904, 1908, 1912, and 1920. In 1905 he was present at the founding conference of the Industrial Workers of the World, and he was a member of the 1909 Free Speech Committee. Debs supported the IWW within the Socialist Party until 1913. Although he supported the general strike and advocated industrial unionism, he did not advocate sabotage. Debs was editor of the long-standing Socialist paper *Appeal to Reason* and the author of several pamphlets, including *The Issue* (Chicago: C. H. Kerr, 1908), *Class Unionism* (Chicago: C. H. Kerr, 1909), and *Revolutionary Unionism* (Chicago: C. H. Kerr, 1909). *See also vol. 1, p. 527.*

de Cleyre, Voltairine (1866–1912) American anarchist, freethinker, advocate of women's independence, poet, lecturer, and teacher. Together with EG and Lucy Parsons, de Cleyre was a leading anarchist spokeswoman of the period. In an appreciation published in 1932, EG called her "the poet rebel, the liberty-loving artist, the greatest woman-Anarchist of America." Based in Philadelphia, she taught English to Russian Jewish immigrants and became a mainstay of the city's radical life, acting as a link between Jewish immigrant anarchists and American-born libertarians. She lectured and took an active role in the city's Social Science Club, which she had been instrumental in starting in late 1901 and early 1902. De Cleyre was the victim of an assassination attempt by one of her former students, Herman Helcher, in 1902. Though seriously wounded, she refused to press charges. (Errico Malatesta and Louise Michel likewise had refused to press charges when they were attacked.) EG and Edward Brady helped coordinate fundraising efforts in New York to help pay for de Cleyre's medical treatment, resulting in a warming of relations between the two women. When her health improved de Cleyre traveled to Christiania (now Oslo) in June 1903, and from there to Scotland in August, and England in September. Soon after her return to the United States, she again fell ill. By November 1904 Natasha Notkin and others in Philadelphia organized the "Friends of Voltairine de Cleyre" to appeal for funds in the anarchist press for her health care. After years of serious mental and physical illness, her health temporarily improved in 1906. She corresponded with AB while he was in prison and helped him adjust to life after his release. On 20 February 1908 de Cleyre was arrested in Philadelphia and charged with inciting a riot after violence broke out following a meeting at which she had spoken. Found not guilty, she campaigned vigorously in an ensuing free speech campaign for the Italian anarchists arrested with her who had not been released. She contributed to a number of anarchist periodicals during this period, including *Free Society, Lucifer, the Lightbearer,* and *Mother Earth.* Her publications during this period include *Det Anarkistiske Ideal* (Christiania: Social-Demokraten, 1903; her lecture "The Anarchist Ideal" was delivered in Christiania in August 1903), *Crime and Punishment* (Philadelphia: Social Science Club, 1903), *McKinley's Assassination From an Anarchist Standpoint* (New York: Mother Earth Publishing Association, 1907), and *Anarchism and American Traditions* (New York: Mother Earth Publishing Association, 1909). *See also vol. 1, pp. 527–28.*

Díaz, José de la Cruz Porfirio (1830–1915) President of Mexico (1877–1880, 1884–1911), Oaxacan governor (1880–1884), and military general. Díaz gained the presidency after his initial defeat in the 1876 election to Sebastian Lerdo de Tejada; he overthrew Lerdo's government and was formally elected in 1887. His regime became increasingly dictatorial, with congress reduced to subservience and the Mexican constitution amended in 1890 to allow him an indefinite number of re-elections. His government regularly imprisoned its opponents and censored the press. As the nation advanced industrially, with massive foreign investments, mostly from the United States, the building of railroads and exports rose, along with the gap between the rich and poor. The last decade of his rule was marked with opposition and discontent; his re-election in 1910 set off a revolution. In 1911, he was forced to flee and eventually died in exile.

Dudley, Helen (1858–1932) American pacifist and settlement house worker. Dudley was head resident of Boston's Denison House from 1893 until 1912 and was one of the founders of the Women's Trade Union League in 1903. She hosted Catherine Breshkovskaya at the Denison House for six weeks during her 1904 speaking tour and remained in frequent correspondence with the "grandmother of the Russian Revolution" thereafter. In 1912, Dudley resigned her position at Denison House, fearing that her support for the IWW would alienate the settlement's more conservative supporters. During and after the First World War, Dudley was involved in international peace efforts. She died in Switzerland shortly after attending a conference held by the pacifist Women's International League.

Edelsohn, Rebecca (nickname Becky) (b. ca. 1891–1973) New York anarchist militant. Edelsohn lived at EG's home when she was a teenager. She was in her early teens when AB was released from prison and was one of the few people he felt comfortable with. She helped AB rehabilitate himself and became his companion in late 1907. Arrested in 1906 along with a number of other young anarchists at a meeting to discuss whether Leon Czolgosz was an anarchist, their arrests helped bring AB back into political activity. She was arrested again at an International Brotherhood Welfare Association meeting at Cooper Union on Labor Day 1908, with AB, for defending Ben Reitman, after Reitman was attacked for reading a speech criticizing Labor Day that was actually written by EG. Edelsohn was arrested again on 23 May 1909 with Leopold Bergman and charged with disorderly conduct at EG's Lexington Hall meeting that was broken up by the police.

Ely, Robert Erskine (1861–1948) New York reformer and leader in adult education. Ely was the director of the League for Political Education from 1901 to 1937 and secretary of the National Arbitration and Peace Congress (New York, 14–17 April 1907). Ely met and befriended Peter Kropotkin on the latter's first visit to the United States in 1897, which was the occasion of his acquaintance with EG. Ely, with other American friends, convinced Kropotkin to write his memoirs, arranging their serialized publication in the *Atlantic Monthly*. Ely wrote an introduction to Kropotkin's memoirs and helped arrange lectures for his second tour of the United States in 1901. He was secretary of the New York branch of the Friends of Russian Freedom, when the society was revived in 1904. Ely edited the proceedings of the National Arbitration and Peace Congress (New York, 1907) and published *A Beginning* (New York: Private Print, distributed by the Town Hall, 1944), a history of the League for Political Education.

Emerson, Ralph Waldo (1803–1882) American essayist, poet, and philosopher. An influential early transcendentalist, Emerson founded the Concord-based New England Transcendentalism Circle, of which Henry David Thoreau was also a member. Emerson emphasized individualism and the rejection of traditional authority. He worked with the anti-slavery movement and the movement for women's rights. For EG he was a part of the vibrant American celebration of the individual over the authority of the state. Excerpts from Emerson's works were printed in *Mother Earth* and, together with Henry David Thoreau, he was a topic of one of her lectures and often referred to in her writings. His works included *Essays* (Boston: James Munroe, 1841), *Representative Men* (Boston: Phillips, Sampson, 1850), *May Day and Other Pieces* (Boston: Ticknor and Fields, 1867), and *Society and Solitude* (Boston: Osgood, 1874).

Faure, Auguste Louis Sébastien (1858–1942) French anarchist, journalist, orator, birth control agitator, and educationalist. Faure was an acquaintance of Jean Grave, Émile Pouget, and Paul Reclus. He launched, in 1885 with Louise Michel, the weekly *Le Libertaire*, which he edited through June 1914, publicizing it through conferences and speeches. Faure was interested in neo-Malthusianism at the beginning of the century and took an active part in the French birth control movement. Between 1904 and 1917 he ran the libertarian school La Ruche (The Beehive) at Rambouillet (near Paris), visited by EG in 1907, who wrote about it in the November 1907 edition of *Mother Earth*. Faure wrote numerous books and pamphlets, including *La douleur universelle* (Paris: Savine, 1895), *Réponse aux paroles d'une croyante* (Oyonnax: Imprimerie ouvrière, 1903), *La question sociale (position de la question)* (Ardennes: La Colonie d'Aiglemont, 1906), and contributed to Gustave Hervé's *La Guerre Sociale* (1906).

Ferrer y Guardia, Francisco (1859–1909) Spanish anarchist and educator. Ferrer was the founder of the Escuela Moderna (modern school) in Barcelona (1901–1906). A significant benefactor in the development of anarchism in Spain, he founded *La Huelga General* in 1902 with Ignacio Clavia, with support from Anselmo Lorenzo and Ricardo Mella. In 1907, with Anselmo Lorenzo, Jose Prats, and Enrique Puget, Ferrer launched *Solidaridad Obrera,* which later became the organ of the Confederacion National Trabajero (CNT). He also founded the International League for the Rational Education of Children in Paris in 1908. Ferrer was suspected of involvement in anarchist assassination attempts on King Alfonso XIII in 1905 and 1906. The Spanish government executed Ferrer on 13 October 1909, on the official charge of being "author and chief of the rebellion" in the July 1909 general strike in Barcelona called by *Solidaridad Obrera,* in which churches were burnt, thousands were injured, and over 200 workers were killed. Not actually in Barcelona during the "Tragic Week," Ferrer's arrest and execution caused an international outcry from anarchist, radical, and liberal circles. The protest of Ferrer's execution led, in the United States, to the creation of the Francisco Ferrer Association and later, to Ferrer Modern Schools. By the first anniversary of his death there were twenty-five Ferrer associations in the United States, attracting a variety of political figures, including EG and AB, Leonard Abbott, William Thurston Brown, James F. Morton, and E. B. Foote, Jr. Ferrer edited *L'Ecole Renovée* (France, 1908–1909) and was the author of *The Modern School* (reprinted by Mother Earth Publishing Association, 1909) and *The Origin and Ideals of the Modern School* (London: Watts, 1913).

Fitzgerald, Margaret Eleanor (1877–1955) American radical and anarchist and EG and AB's lifelong friend. Known affectionately as "Fitzie," or "the Lioness" for her red mane of hair, Fitzgerald would become the office manager at *Mother Earth,* and later *The Blast.* She was a teacher who planned in 1898 to become a missionary for the Seventh Day Adventists. She became interested in anarchism and the labor movement in 1901 and 1902, speaking regularly on the plight of imprisoned labor leaders. Fitzgerald was an early lover and friend of BR.

Fleming, J. W. (nickname Chummy) (1863–1950) Australian anarchist activist who emigrated from England in 1884. Fleming invited EG to tour Australia in 1908, losing money when the tour was cancelled. He was a regular correspondent to *Mother Earth* (which he also distributed in Australia) and to a wide variety of other international anarchist papers.

Flores Magón, Ricardo (1873–1922) Mexican anarchist revolutionary, founder of the Mexican Liberal Party (Partido Liberal Mexicano, PLM), and journalist. As a law student in Mexico City, Magón participated with his brothers, Jesus and Enrique, in the liberal opposition to Porfirio Díaz. He continued his opposition as a journalist and aided in the publication of the paper *Regeneración.* It is likely that he came into contact with anarchist ideas at this time. In 1903 he fled, with Enrique and some of their liberal comrades, to the United States. These men began publishing *Regeneración* again, and moved from city to city, attempting to avoid harassment by Mexican authorities and their hired detectives. In 1905 the founding of the PLM was officially announced from St. Louis, Missouri, with Ricardo as president. Although it has been widely reported, there is no evidence that Ricardo came into contact at this time with EG. Nonetheless, during this period Ricardo and the PLM's leadership were moving from a liberal position to an anarchist one, although they scrupulously avoided use of the word at Ricardo's insistence. In August 1907 police and detectives arrested Ricardo, Modesto Díaz, Librado Rivera, and Antonio Villarreal in Los Angeles. At first it was unclear for what reason they were being held, but soon they were indicted for violations of the neutrality act and extradited to Arizona Territory. The American left rallied behind the imprisoned men, but despite this broad support they were tried and sentenced to eighteen months imprisonment, not to be released until August 1910.

Foote, Edward Bliss (1829–1906) American physician, birth control advocate, father of Edward Bond Foote, Jr. Born in Cleveland, Ohio, Foote worked as a newspaper editor before studying medicine. An early advocate of public hygiene and the general dissemination of physiological knowledge, Foote opposed the professionalization of medicine as anti-democratic. His first book, *Medical Common Sense* (1858), was a home guide, written in a vernacular style, that dealt especially with sexual problems from a social as well as medical point of view. It sold very well and was reprinted many times (an enlarged version came out in 1870 under the title *Plain Home Talk, Embracing Medical Common Sense*). Its success made possible Foote's financial support of the Free Speech League, among other organizations and individuals. He also published his own journal, *Dr. Foote's Monthly* (New York: Murray Hill Publishing, 1876–1896), wrote books for children (including a five-volume saga of Sammy Tubbs, the boy doctor, published in 1875 as an introduction to anatomy), and issued various pamphlets. In 1874 Foote was one of the first to be arrested under the new Comstock Act. He was found guilty in 1876 but only fined, not imprisoned. In 1894, he ran unsuccessfully for U.S. Congress as a Populist.

Foote, Edward Bond, Jr. (1855–1912) American physician and prominent free speech and birth control advocate. He founded and edited *Dr. Foote's Health Monthly* (New York, 1876–1896) with Edward Bliss Foote, his father. Foote, Jr. was an advocate of single tax, freethought, prison reform, sexual freedom, eugenics, and especially free speech. He was one of the original founders of the National Defense Association, the Manhattan Liberal Club and the Free Speech League. Foote was the guiding spirit of the Free Speech League from its founding, offering the League financial backing as well as serving first as treasurer and in 1909 as president. He was treasurer of numerous other organizations, including the Thomas Paine National Historical Association and the American Secular Union. Foote also regularly gave his financial support to EG and *Mother Earth,* as well as other anarchists and papers, including *Lucifer.* His publications include *The Radical Remedy in Social Science; or Borning Better Babies through Regulating Reproduction by Controlling Conception* (New York: Murray Hill Publishing, 1886) and *Comstock versus Craddock* (New York, 1902), which reviewed the case of Ida Craddock, one of the first cases to be taken up by the Free Speech League when it was formed in 1902. Like his father, he first met EG at the Manhattan Liberal Club in the 1890s and later worked with her in the Free Speech League.

Fox, Jay (1870–1961) Irish-born American anarchist, labor organizer, and syndicalist. Present at the 1886 Haymarket riot, Fox was one of several prominent Chicago anarchists. He played a major part in the publication of *Free Society* in Chicago, and was one of those arrested in 1901 after the McKinley assassination. Fox was a delegate at the 1905 founding IWW convention. He contributed to *The Demonstrator* (editing it for a short time) and *Mother Earth,* and authored the pamphlet *Trade Unionism and Anarchism* (Chicago: Social Science League, 1908), later published by Mother Earth Publishing Association. *See also vol. 1, p. 530.*

Frank, Henry (1854–1933) American rationalist, reformer, and writer. Frank founded the Metropolitan Independent Church in New York City in 1897 (which was renamed three years later the Rationalist Society of New York) and the Society for Psychological Study in 1899. He founded and edited two journals: *Rostrum* at Jamestown, N.Y. (1887) and the New York City *Independent Thinker*

(1901); he was a member of the Sunrise Club, a freethought/anarchist discussion group begun by E. C. Walker. He authored books on rational Christianity (or "scientific metaphysics"), including *The Evolution of the Devil* (Chicago: C. H. Kerr, 1896); *The Doom of Dogma and the Dawn of Truth* (New York: G. P. Putnam, 1901); *Modern Light on Immortality* (London: T. F. Unwin, 1900); and *Psychic Phenomena, Science and Immortality* (Boston: Sherman, French, 1911). Frank moved to San Francisco in 1917, where he founded and was leader of the Peoples' Liberal Church.

Freeman, Alden (1862–1937) American political reformer; son of the treasurer of the Standard Oil Company. Freeman was an organizer and secretary of the reform group Citizens Union of East Orange, New Jersey (1902–1908). Freeman attended a 1909 lecture by EG on the playwright Henrik Ibsen, which was broken up by the police. Outraged by the suppression of free speech, he invited EG to his estate to give the lecture, which led to friendship between the two. Freeman signed the 1909 Free Speech Committee letter. He was also a substantial contributor to the *Mother Earth* Sustaining Fund (1909–1913) and an occasional contributor to the magazine. His works include *A Year in Politics* (1906) and *The Fight for Free Speech: A Supplement to Law-Breaking by the Police* (East Orange, N.J.: East Orange Record Press, 1909), a pamphlet that documented the suppression of EG's meetings in 1909.

Frick, Henry Clay (1849–1919) American industrialist. Frick was a coal mine owner, whose company, Frick Coke, was established in 1871 and controlled 80 percent of the coal output in Pennsylvania. Frick became partners with Andrew Carnegie, and in 1889 became chairman of the Carnegie Company; he played a central role in organizing Carnegie Steel, established in 1892. Frick's decision to lower the piecework wage rate to increase profits, led to the 1892 call to strike by the Amalgamated Iron and Steel Workers Union. His strong anti-union policies during the Homestead strike and his decision to employ 300 Pinkerton strikebreakers, leading to the death of nine workers, was the impetus for AB's *attentat.*

Funston, Frederick N. (1865–1917) Brigadier General of the U.S. Army. Funston entered the military as a colonel in 1898, served in the Philippines until 1901, where he participated in the capture of Emilio Aguinaldo, the Filipino leader. Funston's military actions were castigated by many, including Mark Twain and EG. He was appointed brigadier general in 1901. During the 1906 San Francisco earthquake Funston took command and, with his troops, assisted firemen and patrolled the city. He published a 1906 article entitled "How the Army Worked to Save San Francisco" (*Cosmopolitan Magazine* vol. 41, no. 3, July 1906) and *Memories of Two Wars; Cuban and Philippine Experiences* (New York: C. Scribner's Sons, 1911).

Galleani, Luigi (1861–1931) Italian anarchist militant, organizer, lecturer. Galleani was editor of *La Questione Sociale* (1901–1902) and founder and editor of *Cronaca Sovversiva* (1903–1906; 1907–1919). Educated as a lawyer, Galleani was an active revolutionary in Europe until he was arrested in 1894 in the wave of repression following the assassination of French president Sadi Carnot. Galleani spent over five years under house arrest before escaping in 1900. By October 1901 he arrived in Paterson, New Jersey, where he became the editor of *La Questione Sociale*. In June 1902, he was shot and wounded during a clash between the city's police and silk factory strikers during a strike in the city's silk factories. He escaped to Canada to avoid arrest for inciting to riot, staying briefly before slipping back into the United States under a pseudonym to live and work in Barre, Vermont, where he became a leader in the Italian-speaking anarchist community. Galleani was tried and acquitted in 1907 after his identity was discovered; he returned to anarchist propagandizing, until his deportation from the United States in 1919. Galleani defended Gaetano Bresci, and acts of political violence, arguing that a violent overthrow of the existing order was necessary for revolution. Under the pseudonym Mentano, he wrote *Foccia a foccia (o) nemico: croncche siudiziarie dell anarchismo militante* (Face to Face with Your Nemesis) (East Boston: Edizione del Gruppo Autonomo, 1914).

Garrison, William Lloyd (1805–1879) American abolitionist and reformer. Garrison helped organize the New England Anti-Slavery Society (1832) and American Anti-Slavery Society (1833). Believing that every man had the God-given right to be free from bondage, he renounced the church and state, calling the U.S. Constitution a "pro-slavery document." Garrison co-edited *The Genius of Universal Emancipation* (1821–1839) and later published the anti-slavery paper *The Liberator* (1831–1865). For his anti-statist beliefs, EG considered Garrison a courageous and principled American whose position on religion and government resonated with what she considered the essence of the anarchist tradition. In 1903, his son, William Lloyd Garrison, Jr., would support the Free Speech League.

George, Henry (1839–1897) American economist, writer, and leader of the single-tax movement. The co-founder of the *San Francisco Evening Post* (1871–1875), George also authored several books on economics and politics, including *Progress and Poverty* (San Francisco: W. M. Hilton, 1879), the best-selling book on economics to that date; and *The Irish Land Question* (New York: D. Appleton, 1881). George ran unsuccessfully for secretary of state for New York in 1887 and 1897. EG and other anarchists, including Benjamin Tucker, who wrote a pamphlet published in 1896 on the matter *(Henry George, Traitor)*, were bitterly angered by George's renunciation of support for the executed Haymarket anarchists during his 1887 campaign.

Goldsmith, Marie (aliases M. Isidine, M. Korn) (1873–1933) Russian anarchist and scientist living in Paris. Goldsmith was an associate and regular correspondent of Peter Kropotkin after 1897. Her father, Isidor, published radical journals in St. Petersburg and after her mother, Sofia, completed medical studies the family joined proscribed associations. The family fled Russia in 1884 and Isidor died in 1896 in Paris where they had settled. EG probably met Goldsmith during her visit to Europe from 1895 to 1896. Goldsmith was awarded a doctorate in biology at the Sorbonne in 1915 and published numerous scientific papers. She was an active and well-respected figure in Russian anarchist circles who maintained strong relationships with the broad Russian revolutionary movement. She wrote regularly for the anarchist press, often under the pseudonym M. Korn, in English, French, Italian, and Russian, and in the Yiddish periodical *Freie Arbeiter Stimme*, and wrote a number of pamphlets. The Paris apartment she shared with her mother was an important meeting place for Russian anarchists of the city. EG met her in 1900.

Gompers, Samuel (1850–1924) English-born American labor organizer. Gompers was president of the American Federation of Labor, a body of craft unions open to skilled workers (1886–1894, 1896–1924). During this period, Gompers traveled extensively, visiting Puerto Rico in 1904 and undertaking a tour of Europe in 1909, where he addressed the General Federation of Trade Unions, the International Secretariat of National Centers of Trade Unions, and the Trade Union Congress. He was also active in American politics, co-writing and presenting labor's Bill of Grievances in 1906, which called for better enforcement of the Chinese Exclusion Act and protested the nullification of the eight-hour labor law and the formation of the House Committee on Labor, which he saw as hostile to labor interests. He also appeared before the platform committee of the Democratic national convention in 1908. Gompers was also occupied with his own legal proceedings, having been found in contempt of court in 1908 for issuing a "do not patronize" notice against the Buck's Stove Company despite a court injunction. The case was not settled until 1911, when the U.S. Supreme Court reversed the 1908 contempt ruling. Gompers's publications of this period include "The Limitations of Conciliation and Arbitration," in *Annals of the American Academy of Political and Social Science* (Philadelphia: American Academy of Political Science, 1902); *Open Shop Editorials* (November 1903–August 1904; Washington, D.C.: American Federation of Labor Bureau of Literature, 1908); *Organized Labor: Its Struggles, Its Enemies, and Fool Friends* (Washington, D.C.: American Federation of Labor Bureau of Literature, 1906); *Organized Labor's Attitude toward Child Labor* (New York: American Federation of Labor Child Labor Committee, 1906); *Free Press and Free Speech Invaded by Injunction Against the AFL, A Review and a Protest* (Washington, D.C.: American Federation of Labor, 1908); and, with Herman Gustadt, *Meat vs. Rice: American Manhood Against Asiatic Coolieism, Which Shall Survive?* (San Francisco: American Federation of Labor, 1908; appears as Senate Document 137 in 1902 and is reprinted with an introduction and appendices by the Asiatic Exclusion League).

Gordon, Harry (1866–1941) Lithuanian-born Jewish American anarchist and machinist. Born to a prosperous family, Gordon settled in Pittsburgh. EG described him as "one of our best workers, a faithful and enthusiastic friend." Gordon served as secretary and treasurer of the Berkman Defense Association, and in 1901, was the first person allowed to visit AB in prison in nine years. Gordon moved to Chicago and then New York with his companion, Lydia Landau.

Gorky, Maksim (pseudonym of Aleksey Maksimovich Peshkov) (1868–1936) Russian novelist and a conceptual founder of Russian socialist realism. *Mother Earth* occasionally reprinted his work. By the time of his visit to America in 1906, Gorky had become a heroic symbol of the Russian revolutionary movement; the announcement of his visit evoked considerable public enthusiasm and a series of lectures, engagements, and dinners were scheduled in his honor. Participants included Mark Twain, William Dean Howells, and Jane Addams. Only a few days after his arrival, an article was published in the *New York World* averring that Gorky was not married to his female companion and had deserted his wife and children in Russia. Attempts to explain the complexity of Russian Orthodox divorce and the common practice of common-law marriage failed to ameliorate the firestorm of negative opinion. Controversy surrounded publication of the *New York World* article. It was alleged by some socialists to be a plant by the Russian embassy, which had tried unsuccessfully to prevent Gorky's entry. The newspaper allegedly knew Gorky's personal situation before he landed but only published the article after learning that Gorky had given exclusive publication rights to the Hearst newspaper corporation, with which the *New York World* had a longstanding feud. News of Gorky's telegram of support to Western Federation of Miners organizers Bill Haywood, Charles Moyer, and George Pettibone, on trial for their alleged involvement in the murder of ex-Idaho governor Frank Steunenberg, may have exacerbated the matter. In the September 1906 *Mother Earth*, Voltairine de Cleyre called Gorky's subsequent public seclusion and departure cowardly. Major works include the classic novel of revolutionary Russia, *Mother* (New York: D. Appleton, 1907), *A Confession* (London: Everett, 1910), and *My Childhood* (New York: The Century Co., 1915). His short story *The Masters of Life* was printed in *Mother Earth* in 1907 and issued as a pamphlet by the Mother Earth Publishing Association the same year. EG discussed his play *A Night's Lodging* (Boston: Poet Lore, 1905) in her *Social Significance of the Modern Drama* (1914).

Grave, Jean (1854–1939) French anarchist communist, participant in the Paris Commune, writer, and editor. A shoemaker by trade, Grave became an anarchist activist around 1878. Although not a syndicalist, Grave corresponded with Pierre Monatte, a Confederation Géneral du Travail (CGT) organizer, and often lent his support to syndicalist actions. Grave refused to attend the Amsterdam International Anarchist Congress in August 1907, decrying all forms of organization as suspect. He met EG in 1907. Grave wrote fiction, including *Malfaiteurs!* (Paris: Stock, 1903) and *Terre Libre* (Paris: Librairie des Temps Nouveaux, 1908), and children's books, including *The Adventures of Nono* (Paris: Stock, 1901), which was used in Ferrer's Modern School. In June 1909, Grave married Miss Mabel Holland Thomas, a wealthy Englishwoman and short story writer for *Les Temps Nouveaux*. *See also vol. 1, p. 532.*

Grossmann, Rudolf (aliases Kl. Morleit, Fr. Stürmer, and Pierre Ramus) (1882–1942) Austrian anarchist, orator, and editor of *Der Zeitgeist*. After speaking on 18 June 1902 in Paterson, New Jersey, Grossmann was arrested along with Luigi Galleani and William MacQueen for "inciting to riot" during a strike in which police opened fire on workers. Jumping bail a short time after, Grossmann fled first to England and then to Vienna. There he continued his political work under the pseudonym Pierre Ramus. He was active in the birth control movement in Vienna. Grossmann edited *Die freie Generation* (1906–1908) and *Wohlsrand für Alle* (Wealth for All, 1907–1914). He was an early correspondent of EG and corresponded with both AB and Hippolyte Havel during this period.

Hall, Bolton (1854–1938) Irish-born American single-taxer, social reformer, lawyer, and Tolstoyan anarchist. Hall came to the United States in 1868, graduated from Princeton in 1875, and Columbia Law School in 1881. He co-founded the American Longshoremen's Union in 1896. An associate of Henry George, Hall met EG through Ernest Crosby. Though not always in political agreement with EG, Hall remained her loyal admirer and supporter. In the aftermath of the McKinley assassination, he lent her money to start her Vienna scalp and facial business in December 1904, and provided EG with the shelter of a farm in Ossining, New York, in 1905. As part of the "back to the land movement," he promoted vacant-lot gardens in Philadelphia and New York, and in 1909 founded and donated the seed money for Free Acres, a cooperative single-tax colony in New Jersey. An official of the Free Speech Committee (1909), he contributed to the single-tax paper *Justice* (published in Delaware and Philadelphia), was on the National Executive Committee of the Single Tax League with G. Frank Stephens in 1895, and was also a frequent contributor to *Mother Earth*. His works include *Three Acres and Liberty* (New York: Macmillan, 1907), *A Little Land and a Living* (New York: Arcadia Press, 1908), *The Game of Life* (New York: Arcadia Press, 1909), *The Garden Yard: Handbook of Intense Farming* (Philadelphia: D. McKay, 1909), and *Making Money in Free America* (New York: Arcadia Press, 1909). He also wrote poetry, books promoting agricultural colonies, and studies of social reform, most notably *Free America* (Chicago: L. S. Dickey, 1904).

Hapgood, Hutchins (1869–1944) American journalist, author, social critic, bohemian, and radical. Hapgood worked as a journalist under Lincoln Steffens at the *New York Commercial Advertiser* and the *New York Globe*. Hapgood married the author and playwright Neith Boyce in 1899. His major works were informed by a literary theory that merged journalism with fiction. Hapgood contributed articles to *Mother Earth*, maintained a flirtatious relationship with EG, and was a drinking companion of Ben Reitman. His publications include *The Autobiography of a Thief* (New York: Fox,

Duffield, 1903), *The Spirit of Labor* (New York: Duffield, 1907), *The Spirit of the Ghetto: Studies of the Jewish Quarter in New York* (New York: Funk and Wagnalls, 1902), *An Anarchist Woman* (New York: Duffield, 1909), and *Types from City Streets* (New York: Funk and Wagnalls, 1910). In October 1908 he helped arrange EG's lectures in Indianapolis.

Harman, Lillian (1870–1929) American free-love advocate and anarchist editor, daughter of Moses Harman. She assisted her father in publication of *Lucifer, the Lightbearer* and *Our New Humanity* (1895–1897) and took over editorial and publishing duties for *American Journal of Eugenics* after his death but published only one issue, "Memorial to Moses Harman" (30 January 1910). No longer able to continue the publication, Harman transferred the subscriptions of the *American Journal of Eugenics* to *Mother Earth*. Harman also edited *Fair Play* (1888–1891) with E. C. Walker and contributed to *The Adult* (1898). In 1897 she was elected president of the Legitimation League in England. Her writings include *Some Problems of Social Freedom, etc* (London: Office of the Adult, 1898), *Marriage and Morality* (Chicago: M. Harman, 1900), and *The Regeneration of Society* (Chicago: M. Harman, 1900).

Harman, Moses (1830–1910) Midwestern sex radical, anarchist, editor, and publisher. Harman was a prominent early free-love, women's rights, and "family limitation" (birth control) advocate and was arrested many times for obscenity violations under the Comstock Act of 1873. He never fully recovered from his final imprisonment in 1906 at the age of 75 for articles published in *Lucifer, the Lightbearer* the previous year, including one that cautioned women against sexual relations during pregnancy. His journal *Lucifer, The Lightbearer*, renamed *The American Journal of Eugenics* in 1907, continued until Harmon's death in 1910. His daughter, Lillian Harmon, also a free love anarchist, helped edit both journals. His writings during this period include *A Free Man's Creed: Discussion of Love in Freedom as Opposed to Institutional Marriage* (Los Angles: American Journal of Eugenics, 1908). *See also vol. 1, p. 533–34.*

Hartmann, Sadakichi (1867–1944) Avant-garde writer, poet, and critic. Hartmann was born in Nagasaki, the son of a Japanese mother and a German father, grew up in Hamburg, and came to the United States in 1882. EG met him in New York in the 1890s. He contributed critical and creative work to *Camera Work* and *Mother Earth*. Hartmann also wrote *Moderne amerikanische Skulpturen* (Berlin, 1902), *A History of American Art* (London: Hutchinson, 1903), *Japanese Art* (Boston: L. C. Page, 1904), *Iaponskoe iskusstvo: perevod s angliiskago O. Krinskoi* (St. Petersburg: R. Golike i A. Vilborg, 1908), *Composition in Portraiture* (New York: E. L. Wilson, 1909), and an article for *Essentials in Portraiture* (New York: Tennant and Ward, 1909).

Hauptmann, Gerhardt (1862–1946) Silesian (now Poland) writer, playwright. Hauptmann received the Nobel Prize for literature in 1912. EG discusses his plays in her *Social Significance of the Modern Drama* (1914), including *The Weavers* (1892), an indictment of the poverty caused by industrialization that Max Baginski helped him to research, *Lonely Lives* (1898), and *The Sunken Bell*, which was first published in *Poet Lore* (1898).

Havel, Hippolyte (1869–1950) Czech-born anarchist communist, journalist, and propagandist. When EG returned to America following the 1900 Paris anarchist conference, Havel accompanied her, settling in Chicago. In 1906 he worked with EG to found *Mother Earth* and was an editor during the first years of the publication, contributing regularly to the journal on a variety of topics.

Haywood, William D. (nickname Big Bill) (1869–1928) American labor organizer. Haywood played an integral role in the Western Federation of Miners (WFM) and was secretary-treasurer of WFM from 1901 to 1907. Haywood and union members adopted violent tactics, often engaging in shootouts with replacement workers and state militia. A leading spirit in the movement to create the IWW, Haywood was chairman of the 1905 founding convention, the Continental Congress of the Working Class. In 1906, Haywood, along with Charles Moyer and George Pettibone, was charged with conspiracy to commit the 1905 murder of ex-Idaho governor Frank Steunenberg. In what Eugene Debs called "the greatest legal battle in American history," Haywood and the others were acquitted, with the aid of attorney Clarence Darrow. Their case was enthusiastically supported by EG. Haywood drifted away from the IWW, believing it ineffective by 1906. He ran unsuccessfully for governor of Colorado on the Socialist ticket during his trial in 1906. After his release the Socialist Party of America elected him to its National Executive Committee. By April 1908, Haywood was forced out of the WFM. The union left the IWW at the same time and rejoined the AFL in 1911. Haywood was contributing editor to *International Socialist Review* (1906–1913) and a regular contributor in *Solidarity* and the *Industrial Worker*. Haywood would return to IWW activity in 1911.

Herron, George D. (1862–1925) American clergyman and Christian Socialist. A Congregational minister before becoming a professor at Iowa College, Herron became the most public Christian Socialist in the country. In 1905 with Carrie Rand, he co-founded the Rand School of Social Science for the advancement of socialism. He was a member of the 1909 Free Speech Committee and contributed financially to the Free Speech Fund. Ousted from his professorship for his unmarried relationship with Rand, they subsequently moved to Florence, Italy, where he was initially a critic of the First World War. Herron contributed once to *Mother Earth* in 1912.

Hillquit, Morris (born Moses Hilkowicz) (1869–1933) Russian Jewish immigrant socialist, trade unionist, politician, and labor lawyer. Hillquit was founder of the United Hebrew Trades Organization (1888) and a founding member (1901), key strategist, and leader (1906–1908) of the Socialist Party of America. He ran unsuccessfully for Congress and also for mayor of New York City several times and served on the executive committee of the Second International (1905–1914). His works during this period include *The History of Socialism in the United States* (New York: Funk and Wagnalls, 1903) and *Socialism in Theory and Practice* (New York: Macmillan, 1909). *See also vol. 1, p. 534–35.*

Horr, Alexander (1871–1947) Hungarian-born anarchist. An early single-tax supporter, he lived in Wilmington, Delaware, until 1896, when he briefly returned to Hungary. In 1904, EG lived with Horr and his wife at 210 East Thirteenth St., New York, which became the home base and office of *Mother Earth* after Horr moved to the West Coast. Horr supported Theodore Hertzka's utopian philosophy outlined in *Frieland* (*Freeland*, 1890); he joined the Equality Colony in Bow, Washington in 1904, which later in that year became Freeland, under Horr's leadership. Horr distributed *Mother Earth* in Seattle before moving to San Francisco. In 1908 he acted as EG's San Francisco advance lecture agent. Horr was a member of the New York (1901) and later the San Francisco Social Science leagues. He was arrested in December 1908 while delivering an open air lecture, his case precipitating a free speech fight in San Francisco that led to the arrest of EG and BR in January 1909. Horr appears to have been the subject of a government deportation attempt after his arrest. With the socialist William McDevitt, Horr was proprietor of the Liberty Bookstore on

Golden Gate Avenue, and briefly secretary of the local San Francisco jitney drivers union. Horr was editor of the journal *Freeland* (Bow, Wash., 1904 and San Francisco, 1909). He contributed to *Mother Earth* an article on EG's San Francisco visit in 1908 and was author of *Fabian Anarchism* (San Francisco: Freeland Printing and Publishing, 1911). Horr ran for governor of California on the Socialist Party ticket in 1922.

Ibsen, Henrik (1828–1906) Norwegian-born dramatist and poet. Ibsen's drama often centered around middle-class characters and presented an intense psychological analysis of their reaction to social pressures. Ibsen worked as stage director in the Norwegian Theater in Bergen (1851–1857) and artistic director of the Kristiania Theater (1857–1862). He went on to found the Norwegian Company with his friend and colleague Bjørnstjerne Bjørnson in 1859. Major works include *Brand* (1866), *A Doll's House* (1879), *Hedda Gabler* (1890), *The Master Builder* (1891), and *Ghosts* (1881). Ibsen's character Dr. Stockman in *An Enemy of the People* was seen by some anarchists, such as EG, to epitomize individual resistance against the state. In the March 1908 *Mother Earth*, Ibsen's volume of letters was favorably reviewed.

Isaak, Abe (1856–1937) Russian-born American anarchist, editor. Isaak was forced to flee Odessa in 1889 for anti-tsarist activism. Isaak was editor of the anarchist newspaper *Firebrand* (1895–1897) and *Free Society* (1897–1904) and was an occasional contributor to *Mother Earth* and later, *The Blast*. In 1901, Isaak, his wife, Mary, and two of his children were arrested because Leon Czolgosz had spoken briefly with EG and Isaak a few months prior to President McKinley's assassination. In fact, Isaak had suspected Czolgosz of being a police spy and issued a warning in *Free Society*. After *Free Society* ceased publication in 1904, Isaak worked in Max Maisel's bookstore in New York City. In 1909, Isaak founded, and settled in, an anarchist cooperative, the Aurora Colony, near Lincoln, California, with his family.

Jefferson, Thomas (1743–1826) Third president of the United States. Jefferson founded the Republican Party to limit the power of federal government, anticipating the power of the emerging nation-state. Jefferson, a drafter of the Declaration of Independence, was a wary supporter of the Constitution in 1787 and opposed strong central government. He wrote a letter in 1787 to Madison warning that the Constitution created too much national power. Jefferson also drafted the 1799 Kentucky Resolution advocating power to local government and nullifying actions of the national government that violated constitutional rights. Jefferson was often evoked by EG to locate anarchism within the undercurrent of anti-statism in the American political tradition.

Jonas, Alexander (1834–1912) German American socialist, immigrated to the United States in 1869. He joined the Socialist Labor Party (SLP) in 1877 and co-founded and edited the daily *New Yorker Volks-Zeitung* from 1878 to 1889; he remained on its editorial board until his death. In 1883 he was one of a few prominent SLP members who unsuccessfully proposed consolidation with the International Working People's Association. Though he spoke almost no English at the time, he was the SLP's candidate for mayor of New York City in 1878, 1888, and 1892, for state senator in 1891, and for state assemblyman in 1894. His writings include *Reporter and Socialist: An Interview Explaining the Aims and Objects of Socialism* (New York: Wetzel and Oehler, 1885).

Katz, Moishe (1864–1941) American Jewish anarchist. Katz, a member of the Pioneers of Liberty in New York City, which was the first Jewish anarchist organization in the United States, helped found

Freie Arbeiter Stimme (1890–1894); he helped to select Morris Winchevsky as editor and took part in a lecture tour to raise money for the venture. Katz was also literary editor of *Der Vorwärts*, a New York socialist weekly paper that ran from 1897 to 1932, was on the editorial board *Varhayt* (Truth), the first Yiddish-language anarchist periodical in America, and a contributor to *Di Fraye Gezelshaft*. Katz translated several anarchist books into Yiddish, including Peter Kropotkin's *Conquest of Bread* (1906, with A. Frumkin), Jean Grave's *The Anarchist Society* (1894), and Alexander Berkman's *Prison Memoirs of an Anarchist* (2 vols., 1920–21, also with A. Frumkin).

Kelly, Henry May (known as Harry) (1871–1953) American anarchist, printer, and lecturer. Kelly was a founder of the Ferrer Association in New York and the Modern School at Stelton, New Jersey. Kelly was a lifelong friend of EG and loyal member of the *Mother Earth* group. In London, where he came in 1898 as a representative of his union, he joined the *Freedom* group, helped publish its paper, and assumed the role as liaison between European and American anarchism, often writing about the American movement in *Freedom* and the English and European movement in *Free Society*. He returned to New York in 1904. In 1906, he joined EG at a New York protest meeting against police repression of anarchists, and was part of the group that planned the production of *Mother Earth*. Kelly worked with Alexander Berkman between 1906 and 1909 as a Sunday school teacher for the Workingman's Circle (Arbeiter Ring). Kelly worked as a traveling salesman while living in St. Louis in 1909, where he was a friend of Roger Baldwin. A member of the 1909 Free Speech Committee, he contributed regularly, under the bylines "Harry Kelly," "Henry May," and "H.M.K," to *Freedom* and to *Mother Earth*. In his unpublished memoirs, *Roll Back the Years*, he wrote of EG, "Emma Goldman was ahead of her time, a crime which humanity cannot forgive until the offender is dead." *See also vol. 1, pp. 536–37.*

Kennan, George (1845–1924) American journalist, lecturer, and a leading authority and commentator on Russia and Siberia. After a fifteen-month investigation of the Russian government's system of Siberian exile of political prisoners in 1885–1886 (which included meetings with Russian émigrés in London), Kennan reversed his earlier stance of support for the regime in an influential series of articles for *Century* magazine, beginning in May 1888, and later published in book form under the title *Siberia and the Exile System* (New York: The Century Co., 1891). On this trip Kennan met, among other political prisoners and refugees of the tsarist state, Catherine Breshkovskaya and Peter Kropotkin, then in exile in Siberia and London, respectively. Although Kennan's greatest influence on Russian affairs was before the turn of the century, he continued to report and offer commentary on Russian events. He covered the growing domestic unrest in Russia between 1903–1905 and reported on the Russo-Japanese War of 1904–1905 from the Japanese lines for *Outlook*, a paper Kennan would continue to contribute to through the First World War. *See also vol. 1, p. 537.*

Kershner, Jacob A. (also Kersner) (ca. 1865–1919) Russian-born tailor and EG's first husband. Kershner settled in Rochester, N.Y. In 1884, based on the belief that Kershner was born on 1 April 1863 and that he had lived in the country for five years (since 1879), the U.S. government granted him citizenship. EG married Kershner in 1887 and divorced him in 1888, remarrying him the same year. During the 1890s Kershner was convicted twice for grand larceny; he served an eighteen-month sentence at Onondaga County Penitentiary from 1894 to 1895, and a three-year sentence at Auburn in 1899. After his release from prison, Kershner lived with his parents in Rochester. In 1907 he relocated to Chicago where he assumed the alias "Jacob Lewis" and worked as a tailor.

The U.S. government initiated an inquiry regarding the legitimacy of Kershner's naturalization in 1908 "for the purpose of depriving Emma Goldman of her rights of citizenship." Although Kershner never appeared in court to defend himself and the evidence does not offer a consistent date of birth or emigration, Judge John R. Hazel concluded that Kershner was born in 1865, emigrated to the United States in 1882, and was therefore underage and had lived in this country less than the required five years when he was granted citizenship. On 9 April 1908, Jacob Kershner's citizenship was revoked, thereby nullifying EG's citizenship as well. This ruling would become a central issue in EG's deportation from the United States in 1919. *See also vol. 1, p. 537.*

Kirk, Ernest E. (1872–1950) California socialist attorney. Kirk served in Brigadier General Frederick Funston's regiment during the Spanish-American War. By this time a socialist living in San Francisco, Kirk successfully defended EG and BR in their 1909 San Francisco free speech fight. Later involved in the IWW's free speech fight in San Diego, Kirk was charged with "conspiracy to violate the anti-street-speaking law" in 1912. Kirk remained close to EG, and acted as both EG's and BR's personal attorney during the 1912 San Diego free speech fight.

Kropotkin, Peter (1842–1921) Russian revolutionary, geographer, geologist, and principal theorist of anarchist communism. By 1902 Kropotkin was living in exile in London. His interests had shifted from the strategy and tactics of the social revolution to the theoretical problems facing the future anarchist society, and the focus of his revolutionary concerns shifted from western Europe back to Russia, his homeland. Concerned by the increasing popularity of Marxism and the Social Democratic parties, he tried to combat this influence by encouraging James Guillaume to publish his letters and notebooks on the International Working Men's Association. By August of 1903, Kropotkin was facilitating the publication of the Russian paper *Khleb i Volia* (Bread and Liberty), edited by Georgii Gogelia and his wife, L. V. Ikonnikova, in Geneva. Kropotkin served as an advisor and contributed to fund-raising efforts, although he never assumed a leadership role in the publication. (His involvement with the paper diminished in 1904 due to disagreements with Gogelia, whom he believed had glorified terrorism.) Kropotkin later edited a successor to *Khleb i Volia,* called *Listki, Khleb i Volia* (Leaflets of Bread and Liberty; London, 1906–1907). Kropotkin became absorbed with events in Russia, convinced that they signaled a mass and leaderless revolution. In addition to his writing, Kropotkin participated in anarchist organizing meetings—in December 1904 (London), September 1905 (Paris), October 1906 (London), and January 1907 (Paris)—intended for the coordination and cooperation between the anarchist movement in Russia and the anarchists in western Europe and America. Mother Earth Publishing Association published the second English-language edition of Kropotkin's *Modern Science and Anarchism* in 1908 (the first English translation was published by the Social Science Club of Philadelphia in 1903). In the summer of 1909 Kropotkin wrote a series of articles for *Les Temps Nouveaux* exposing the errors and dangers of European social democracy. Kropotkin's published work during this period also included *Russian Literature* (New York: McClure, Phillips, 1905), *The Conquest of Bread* (New York: G. P. Putnam's Sons, 1906), *The Great French Revolution* (London: Heinemann, 1909), and *The Terror in Russia* (London: Methuen, 1909). He was for EG a revered correspondent and mentor, although rather skeptical of her involvement in free speech issues. *See also vol. 1, pp. 538–39.*

Kropotkin, Sophia (1856–1938) Companion of Peter Kropotkin. The daughter of a well-to-do Jewish family, she met Peter Kropotkin in Geneva in 1878 while studying biology at the University of

Berne. They married the same year. While she held strong political convictions in her youth, after her marriage she devoted herself almost entirely to Kropotkin and his political work.

Labadie, Joseph Antoine (1850–1933) American individualist anarchist, printer, labor organizer, editor, journalist, and civil servant of the Detroit water board. Labadie was a participant in a wide range of radical campaigns and organizations. He helped organize EG's Michigan lectures. Between 1909 and 1911, however, Labadie expressed discomfort with EG's activism on issues of sexuality and her outspoken defense of Leon Czolgosz. From 1885 until 1910, Labadie's column, "Cranky Notions," was syndicated in the Knights of Labor–affiliated *Labor Leaf,* Benjamin Tucker's *Liberty,* the *Industrial Gazette* (jointly the official paper of the Michigan Federation of Labor and the Detroit Trades Council), the *Detroit News, Winn's Firebrand,* and a host of other papers. His popularity in Detroit instigated a protest in 1908 against the Detroit water board; he won his job back after the board had dismissed him for his anarchist beliefs.

Lee, Algernon (1873–1954) American Socialist and New York City alderman (1918–1922). For over forty years Lee was the chief administrator of the Rand School of Social Science. With Joseph Barondess, among others, Lee was on the executive committee of the Free Speech League in 1903–1904. He became editor of the New York socialist weekly *The People* in 1899, which eventually became the *New York Call;* Lee edited the *Call* from 1908 to 1909. Lee served as a delegate to the Stuttgart International Socialist Congress of 1910. Initially supportive of the Russian Revolution, he later became an outspoken anti-Communist. Lee wrote several books and various pamphlets on socialism, including *Lectures on the Development of Society* (Minneapolis, Minn.: The Socialist Educational Club, 1898), *Labor, Politics, and the Socialist Press* (New York: Socialist Co-operative Publishing Association, 1901), and the introduction to *The Essentials of Marx; the Communist Manifesto* (New York: Vanguard Press, 1926).

Livshis, Annie (1864–1953) Russian Jewish anarchist. The companion of Jake Livshis and a friend of both EG and Voltairine de Cleyre, Livshis was active in the *Free Society* Group in Chicago between 1901 and 1904. She had been a member of an Am Olam colony in Kansas in the 1880s and had helped form a clock-makers union in Chicago in 1890.

Livshis, Jake (dates unknown) Russian Jewish anarchist, cigar maker, and companion of EG's friend Annie Livshis. Livshis was active in the *Free Society* Group in Chicago between 1901 and 1904.

London, Jack (1876–1916) American novelist and socialist. London met and befriended EG during her 1908 San Francisco tour. A member of the 1909 Free Speech Committee, London wrote a protest letter on EG's behalf during the Philadelphia free speech fight in 1909. Among his many works, *The Iron Heel* (New York: Macmillan, 1908) was especially important in radical circles. *Mother Earth* reprinted an excerpt from his *White Fang* in February 1907.

London, Meyer (1871–1926) Russian-born American Socialist leader and labor lawyer. London was born in Kalvarie, Poland (Russia), and immigrated to the United States in 1891. He was a member of Eugene Debs's Socialist Party of America. London was active in supporting members of the Bund, the Russian revolutionary organization of Jewish workers, who were in exile due to the pogroms in Russia and the 1905 revolution. From 1905 until his death, London was legal advisor to the Arbeiter Ring (Workmen's Circle); he was also the legal counsel for EG, AB, and John Coryell after their arrest in 1907 and to AB and Becky Edelsohn after their arrest at Cooper Union on Labor Day 1908. London was a member of the 1909 Free Speech Committee and leader of the garment workers' strike of 1910 in New York City. London ran unsuccessfully for Congress in 1910 and 1912, and was elected in 1914. He was the second Socialist Party member to be elected to Congress (Victor Berger was the first) and the first from New York state; London was elected again in 1916 and 1920.

Luccheni, Luigi (1873–1910) Italian anarchist. Luccheni assassinated Empress Elizabeth of Austria in Geneva on 10 September 1898, stabbing her to death with a sharpened file. Luccheni supposedly had planned to assassinate the Duke of Orleans, who was to be visiting Geneva, but when he did not come Luccheni decided instead to assassinate the Empress, who happened by coincidence to be in town. In a letter to the *New York World,* EG repudiated Luccheni's act, pointing out that because the Empress was not a political enemy of anarchism, the violence was senseless and reflected badly on anarchists in general. Luccheni, who was sentenced to life in prison, hung himself in 1910.

MacQueen, William (1875–1908) Scottish-born anarchist, writer, publisher of the *Free Commune* (Leeds, 1898–1899), and an associate of John Kenworthy. EG first met MacQueen on her tour of England in 1895. One of the few anarchists actively opposed to the Boer War, MacQueen came to New York City in 1902, where he published *Liberty* (1902). Fluent in German, he was invited to help organize German silk workers in Paterson, New Jersey, after a strike broke out in June. MacQueen spoke at meetings, wrote a manifesto in *La Questione Sociale* calling for a general strike, and was arrested for "inciting to riot" with Luigi Galleani and Rudolf Grossmann after the 18 June riot. MacQueen jumped bail and fled to England but later returned to stand trial. He was released in 1907 after Luigi Galleani's acquittal, but having contracted tuberculosis in prison, MacQueen died the following year in England. H. G. Wells visited MacQueen in prison, and a very sympathetic account of MacQueen appeared in Wells's *The Future in America* (London: Chapman and Hall, 1906).

Maisel, Max N. (1872–1959) American publisher and bookseller. Maisel owned a bookshop at 424 Grand Street in New York City where he published and sold anarchist works, European and Yiddish literature, and various Yiddish translations. He was also a New York agent for anarchist periodicals including *Free Society* and *Mother Earth* and sold tickets for EG's lectures in New York. After *Free Society* ceased publishing, Abe Isaak worked in Maisel's bookshop.

Malatesta, Errico (1853–1932) Italian anarchist. Born in Santa Maria Capua Vetere (Caserta), Malatesta joined the International Working Men's Association (IWMA) in 1871 and met Michael Bakunin in Switzerland in 1872. Malatesta advocated insurrection as the primary strategy for the realization of anarchy; after taking part in several such actions he was forced into exile in 1878. Traveling widely, he met Peter Kropotkin and Élisée Reclus, and lived in London between 1881 and 1883 before returning to Italy. From 1888 to 1889 Malatesta edited *L'Associazione;* he later edited *L'Agitazione* from 1897 to 1898. Arrested in 1898, he escaped from his island prison in 1899 and traveled to the United States, where he edited (anonymously) *La Questione Sociale* in Paterson, New Jersey, from 1899 to 1900. Malatesta then moved to London where he worked as a mechanic. He played a central role in the International Anarchist Congress in Amsterdam (1907). At the congress, while endorsing the syndicalism of the French delegates, Malatesta encouraged a more comprehensive approach to achieving anarchism. He had a considerable impact on American anarchist communist theory through his pamphlets *Anarchy* (London: C. M. Wilson, 1892) and *A Talk About Anarchist Communism Between Two Workers* (San Francisco: Free Society, 1898). *See also vol. 1, p. 541.*

Malmed, Leon (born Leon Bass) (1881–1956) Russian-born Albany, New York anarchist and owner of a delicatessen. Mistakenly named Malmed, his half-brother's last name, by a U.S. immigration officer, he appears as Leon Bass in EG's *Living My Life*. Malmed was a member of the Albany Germinal Group, a Jewish anarchist group taking its name from the influential Émile Zola novel. He and the group arranged meetings for EG and others and distributed literature in Albany, New York, including *Mother Earth*. Malmed met EG in 1906 and sparked a flirtatious friendship that foreshadowed their later affair.

Manning, Henry Edward (1808–1892) English theologian. Manning joined the Roman Catholic Church in 1851, became Archbishop of Westminster in 1865, and a cardinal in 1875. Manning acted as intermediary in the London dock strike of 1889. In response to the Trafalgar Square "Bloody Sunday" deaths on 13 November 1887, he wrote: "Necessity has no law, and a starving man has a natural right to his neighbour's bread" ("Distress in London: A Note on Outdoor Relief," *Fortnightly Review* 49, January–June 1888; London: Chapman and Hall, 1888). Anarchists, including Charles Mowbray and Voltairine de Cleyre, as well as EG in *Living My Life*, cite Manning as the inspiration for EG's words during the 1893 unemployment demonstrations in New York City. Manning's works include *The English Church* (London: J. G. and F. Rivington, 1835), *The Rule of Faith* (London: J. G. and F. Rivington, 1838), *The Unity of the Church* (London: J. Murray, 1842), *The Grounds of Faith* (London: Burns and Lambert, 1852), and *England and Christendom* (London: Longmans, Green, 1867).

Maryson, Jacob Abraham (1866–1941) Jewish American anarchist and physician. A member of the Pioneers of Liberty, Maryson was on the editorial board of *Varhayt,* was editor of *Freie Arbeiter Stimme* for a short time, and edited *Dos Freye Vort* in 1911. He contributed to both Yiddish- and English-language anarchist papers including *Di Freye Gezelshaft, Solidarity* (under the name F. A. Frank), and *Mother Earth*. He translated works of radical literature into Yiddish, including Karl Marx's *Capital* (New York: Kropotkin Literature Group, 1917–1918), Max Stirner's *The Ego and His Own* (New York: Kropotkin Literature Group, 1916; introduction and biographical sketch by Maryson), and Thoreau's *Civil Disobedience* (New York: Max Maisel, 1907). Maryson's other works included *Anarchism and Political Activity* (New York: Max Maisel, 1907), *Mother and Child: Practical Advice for Mothers on How to Take Care of Themselves During Pregnancy and How to Rear Children* (New York: Maisel, 1912), a four-volume *Physiology* (New York: Educational Committee of the Arbeiter Ring, 1918–1925), and *The Principles of Anarchism* (New York: Arbeiter Ring, 1934, trans. 1935).

McKinley, William (1843–1901) President of the United States from 1897 to 1901. McKinley was shot by Leon Czolgosz on 6 September 1901, in Buffalo, New York. Before serving as president, McKinley was a congressman from Ohio (1877–1891) and served two terms (1892–1896) as governor of Ohio. While governor, he formed a state board to regulate labor disputes and became friends with millionaire industrialist Mark Hanna, who managed his 1896 presidential campaign. McKinley is credited with being the first president to make the United States an imperial power, principally because, as a result of the Spanish-American War of 1898, the United States gained the territories of Puerto Rico, Guam, and the Philippines. While giving a speech at the Pan American Exposition in Buffalo, New York, President McKinley was shot twice by Leon Czolgosz and died from complications of his wounds on 14 September 1901. Two collections of his speeches were published: *Speeches and Addresses of William McKinley from His Election to Congress to the Present Time* (New York: D. Appleton, 1893) and *Speeches and Addresses of William McKinley from March 1, 1897 to May 30, 1900* (New York: Doubleday and McClure, 1900).

Metzkow, Max (1854–1945) Berlin-born anarchist and follower of Johann Most. Metzkow was imprisoned twice in Germany for his activities before leaving for London; in 1888 he emigrated to the United States, where he worked as a typesetter. By 1900 he decreased his activity in the anarchist movement, although in 1904 he was the Brooklyn agent for *Free Society*. He also helped EG during her 1909 free speech fight. *See also vol. 1, pp. 542–43.*

Michel, Louise (1830–1905), French anarchist, teacher, and writer. Michel was a heroine of the Paris Commune who transferred her activism to anarchism. She joined the *La Revolution Sociale* circle in Paris and contributed to *Les Temps Nouveaux* and *Le Libertaire*. Michel wrote essays, novels, poetry, history, and an opera, as well as her memoirs. EG met Michel in London in 1895, where they spoke on the same platform. *See also vol. 1, p. 543.*

Minkin, Helene (b. 1873) Russian-born Jewish anarchist, then communist, then social democrat. Helene Minkin immigrated to the United States in 1888 with her father and her sister Anna. She and Anna lived with EG, AB, and Modest Stein between 1889 and 1891 in New York and New Haven. In 1892 she became Johann Most's companion. She worked as a bookkeeper for *Freiheit* and assumed much of the responsibility for keeping it afloat after Most's 1901 imprisonment. Despite a temporary separation, their relationship continued until Most's death in 1906. She and Most had two sons, Lucifer and John Joseph. In 1932, responding to the publication of *Living My Life*, Minkin published her own memoirs in fourteen installments in the New York Yiddish-language paper *Forverts*.

Morton, Eric B. (d. ca.1930) Norwegian-born American anarchist. Morton was codenamed both "Eric the Red," after the hero of an Icelandic saga, and "Ibsen," after the Norwegian playwright, in AB's *Prison Memoirs of an Anarchist*. At EG's request, Morton attempted to dig AB's escape tunnel in 1899–1900. He fled after the plot was discovered and after poisonous fumes in the tunnel infected his blood and erupted dangerously into a skin disease. EG nursed Morton back to health in Paris. Morton, on the recommendation of EG, smuggled guns into Russia during the Revolution of 1905 for Catherine Breshkovskaya and the Russian Socialist Revolutionaries.

Morton, James Ferdinand, Jr. (1870–1941) New York anarchist, lawyer, and freethinker. Morton lived at the Home Colony in Washington until 1904. He was an early member of the NAACP. Morton moved in 1904 to New York, where he practiced law, worked for the *Truth Seeker* (the journal of the American Secular Union), and lectured on the single tax. He was a member of the 1909 Free Speech Committee and associate editor of the *Truth Seeker* (1909–1915). Morton contributed articles to *To-morrow* (1905) and in 1906 briefly edited *The Demonstrator* (1903–1908), contributing articles from 1903 to 1908. Morton wrote and self-published *Do You Want Free Speech?* (Home Colony, Wash., 1903) and *The Curse of Race Prejudice* (New York, 1906). He contributed an occasional article to *Mother Earth* on free speech and wrote an appreciation and obituary for Moses Harman that appeared in the March 1910 issue of *Mother Earth*. *See also vol. 1, p. 544.*

Most, Johann (1846–1906) Bavarian-born anarchist communist propagandist, imprisoned several times for his speeches and publications. Notorious for his defense of violence, Most's writing was among the best and wittiest of the German labor movement. He died during a propaganda tour in Cincinnati on 17 March 1906 and was memorialized by Max Baginski in the March 1906 and March 1911 issues of *Mother Earth*. For a more detailed account of Most's relationship with EG and the American anarchist movement, *see vol. 1, pp. 544–46*.

Moyer, Charles H. (1866–1937) American labor leader. Born in the coal mining community of Moingana, Iowa, Moyer became involved with the Western Federation of Miners (WFM) in 1887 in South Dakota and was its president from 1902 to 1916. Moyer engaged in several labor disputes, and while the WFM was known for its militant radicalism, Moyer often advocated moderation and negotiation. He was arrested along with Bill Haywood and George Pettibone for the murder of ex-Idaho governor Frank Steunenberg, but was eventually released in 1908 after both Haywood and Pettibone were acquitted. Moyer emerged from prison much more conservative. Although present at the 1905 founding convention of the IWW, Moyer withdrew the WFM from the IWW in 1908 because it was too radical. Also, after at one time being very close to Haywood, he removed Haywood from the WFM in 1908 and became more sympathetic toward American Federation of Labor strategy, reaffiliating the WFM to the AFL in 1911.

Nathanson, William (1883–1963) Chicago anarchist, physician, writer, philosopher, translator, and organizer of the Edelstadt Group. A regular speaker at meetings, Nathanson was the companion of Miriam Yampolsky, M.D. He helped EG prevent a riot after her Chicago arrest, on 17 March 1908.

Nazimova, Alla (born Mariam Edez Adelaida Leventon) (1879–1945) Russian-born Jewish actress. Nazimova immigrated to the United States in 1905 as the leading actress in Pavel Orlenev's theater troupe, for which EG served as tour manager as well as friend. During her run with the Orlenev group, Nazimova received critical acclaim and became popular with American audiences as an actress and as an intriguing free spirit, which allowed her to embark on a successful stage and film career after the Russian group left the country in 1906. She made her film debut in *War Brides* (Herbert Brenon Film Corp., 1916), and became a popular silent film actress.

Nettlau, Max (1865–1944) Austrian-born anarchist writer and historian. His inherited wealth enabled him to devote himself to collecting and studying anarchist history. He was acquainted with EG, Peter Kropotkin, Errico Malatesta, Rudolf Rocker, Victor Dave, and Élisée Reclus, among others. Nettlau wrote for the London *Freedom*, including most of the international notes and the annual "Reviews of the Year." He prepared and edited the revised edition of Michael Bakunin's *God and the State* (London: Freedom Press, 1910). *See also vol. 1, p. 547.*

Nieuwenhuis, Ferdinand Domela (1846–1919) Dutch freethinker and socialist, then anarchist. After a career as a Lutheran pastor, Nieuwenhuis left the church and in 1879 founded the socialist and pacifist journal *Recht voor Allen* (Right for All; Amsterdam, 1898–1900), which was followed by *De Vrije Socialist* (The Free Socialist, 1898–1919). In 1881 he helped found a Dutch Socialist League and was a founder of the Dutch Social Democratic Party; in 1888 he became the first socialist member of the Dutch parliament (1881–1891). Nieuwenhuis moved to anarchism after his disillusionment with parliamentary politics. He published numerous pamphlets, including *Mijn afscheid van de kerk. Twee toespraken* (Amsterdam: Drukkerij "Excelsior", 1894), *Het Internationaal Kongres te Londen in 1896* (Amsterdam?, 1897), *Mijn ofscheidsgroet aan de arbeiders* (The Hague: B. Liebers, 1887), *Hoe ons land geregeerd wordt op papier en in de werkelijkheid* (Gravenhage: Liebers

1891), *Vrijheid-blijheid!* (Haarlem: W. C. de Graff, ca. 1881), *Les divers courants de la démocratie socialiste allemande* (Bruxelles: Veuve Monnom, 1892), *L'éducation libertaire conférence/par Domela Nieuwenhuis* (Paris: Aux bureaux des *Temps nouveaux,* 1900), *Socialism in Danger* (London: J. Tochatti, Liberty Press, 1899?), and *The Pyramid of Tyranny* (London, *Freedom* Office, 1901).

Nold, Carl (1869–1934) German-born anarchist. Nold was imprisoned with AB from 1894 to 1897. Nold settled in Detroit, where he became an active force in the anarchist community and continued to work for the reduction of AB's sentence. He was an associate of Joseph Labadie. Nold contributed to various anarchist publications, including *The Demonstrator, Discontent, Free Society,* and *Mother Earth. See also vol. 1, p. 548.*

Notkin, Natasha (b.1870) Russian-born anarchist and pharmacist. EG met her on her first trip to Philadelphia in 1893. Notkin's activism in Philadelphia included distributing *Free Society, Freedom,* and *Mother Earth,* and other anarchist literature, raising money for the Berkman Defense Association, and participating in the Ladies Liberal League as well as the Social Science Club, an anarchist reading group formed in 1900 by Voltairine de Cleyre.

Orlenev, Pavel Nikolayevich (1870–1932) Russian actor and head of the St. Petersburg Players. Orlenev's 1905 American tour, which included performances of works by August Strindberg, Henrik Ibsen, Fyodor Dostoyevsky, Leo Tolstoy, and Maksim Gorky, introduced the naturalist style of the Russian drama to American audiences. His troupe's leading actress was Alla Nazimova. In the fall of 1905 EG, under the pseudonym E. G. Smith, became tour manager for his troupe's second tour of the United States. Orlenev and the St. Petersburg Players gave a benefit performance to help launch *Mother Earth* in 1906 before their return to Russia.

Paine, Thomas (1737–1809) English writer, freethinker, and humanitarian. Paine was influential in shaping public opinion during the American Revolution and an active participant in the French Revolution. His major writings include *Common Sense* (1776), *The Rights of Man* (1791–92), and *Age of Reason* (1794, 1796). Many anarchists and freethinkers, including Leonard Abbott, James F. Morton, and individualist anarchist E. C. Walker, joined the Thomas Paine National Historical Association. EG and other anarchists identified with both Paine's hostility to established religion and his attempt to keep government as small as possible.

Parsons, Lucy E. (1853–1942) American anarchist, labor activist, speaker, writer, editor. Parsons, the widow of Haymarket anarchist Albert Parsons, participated in the founding convention of the IWW in 1905, where she called for a program of "revolutionary socialism." Parsons began publishing the *Liberator* (1905–1906) from Chicago amidst complaints from Jay Fox that the paper should be published from the Home Colony in Washington state. The controversy subsided and Parsons wrote on a wide range of issues, including women's rights and birth control, an attack on the election process, and a series of articles entitled "Labor's Long Struggle with Capital." Following the arrest of Bill Haywood, Charles Moyer, and George Pettibone, Parsons became active in their defense effort through articles in the *Liberator* as well as lectures. She engaged in a series of lecture tours between 1908 and 1911. During this time, she reprinted *Life of Albert Parsons: With a Brief History of the Labor Movement in America* (Chicago: L. E. Parsons, 1903; first published in 1889). She contributed twice to *Mother Earth,* once in January 1909, and once in November 1909, although Parsons's relations with EG were often contentious.

Pentecost, Hugh Owen (1848–1907) American lecturer, author, single-taxer, Congregationalist minister, and co-editor of the *Twentieth Century* (New York, 1888–1892). Pentecost was sympathetic to anarchism in the 1890s and also a supporter of Henry George's single tax. Richard Croker nominated him for assistant district attorney in New York City in 1894. Pentecost worked with Clarence Darrow on John Turner's deportation defense in 1903. With Meyer London, Pentecost acted as legal advisor for EG after her arrest at the 30 October 1906 meeting called to protest the arrest of the speakers at the meeting three days earlier, which had been called to discuss whether Leon Czolgosz was an anarchist. Pentecost's ideological perspective changed several times in his life, from single-taxer to socialist. He ran for assistant district attorney of New York City, during which time he reneged on his former support for the Haymarket anarchists, which predictably angered many anarchists, including Voltairine de Cleyre (see her obituary of Pentecost in *Mother Earth*, March 1907). Publications include *What I Believe* (Newark, N.J.: author, ca. 1890), *Evolution and Social Reform. The Anarchist Method* (New York, 1891), *A Good Man Sent to Prison* with E. B. Foote (Boston: James H. West, 1890), and *The Little White Slave Trade: An Address Delivered in the Berkeley Lyceum, New York, Sunday, June 22, 1902* (New York, 1902).

Perovskaya, Sophia (1853–1881) Russian revolutionary and populist. Perovskaya was a member of the Chaikovsky Circle and later a leader of Narodnaya Volya (People's Will), a clandestine socialist group that emerged out of a split in the populist Zemlya i Volya (Land and Liberty) and which embraced assassination as a political strategy. On 13 March 1881, Perovskaya stationed her co-conspirators in Narodnaya Volya along the route of Alexander II and signaled them when the Tsar was in range of their bombs. Arrested 22 March 1881, she was hanged on 15 April 1881, the first woman political prisoner in Russia to be executed. In *Living My Life* (p. 362), EG describes Perovskaya and other Russian revolutionaries as being "my inspiration ever since I first read of their lives."

Pettibone, George (d. 3 August 1908) American justice of the peace and a union official in Coeur d'Alene, Idaho, in the Western Federation of Miners. Pettibone was one of the many arrested in the Coeur d'Alene miners' strike in 1882. Pettibone and other union officials were convicted on conspiracy charges but were later released by the U.S. Supreme Court on a technicality. Pettibone became an official for Western Federation of Miners and a businessman in Denver. He was charged, along with William Haywood and Charles Moyer, with the 1905 murder of ex-Idaho governor Frank Steunenberg but was later acquitted of all charges. Pettibone died of stomach cancer shortly after his release from prison in 1908. EG wrote a poignant and admiring obituary of Pettibone in the August 1908 issue of *Mother Earth*.

Phillips, Wendell (1811–1884) American abolitionist, orator, and women's rights and labor advocate. In 1837 Phillips gave up his practice as a lawyer to dedicate himself to the abolition movement. He worked closely with William Lloyd Garrison, writing for Garrison's *The Liberator*. Phillips was the critical cohesive force behind the Anti-Slavery Society until the Fifteenth Amendment was passed. He then put his energies into advocating prohibition, women's suffrage, abolition of capital punishment, currency reform, and labor rights. In 1870 Phillips ran for governor of Massachusetts representing the Prohibition and Labor Reform parties, and won almost 15 percent of the vote. To EG he was an heroic fighter for justice within the American political tradition. *Mother Earth* published "Wendell Phillips, the Agitator" by Max Baginski in the November 1911 issue. Wendell

Phillips societies emerged across the United States, including a Providence branch in which anarchist John H. Cook was the secretary.

Pleydell, Arthur C. (1872–1932) American single-taxer. Pleydell was editor of the Delaware and Philadelphia, Pennsylvania, single-tax paper *Justice* until November 1901, secretary of the Free Speech League, and a member of the Turner Defense Committee.

Post, Louis Freeland (1849–1928) Chicago lawyer, single-tax editor, and civil servant. Post was a friend of Henry George and founded and edited the *Public* (Chicago and New York, 1898–1919), a liberal single-tax journal that reported sympathetically on EG, defending her and her free speech fights. Post was a member of the 1909 Free Speech Committee. He was appointed to the Chicago school board by Edward F. Dunne (1905). His works in this period include *Ethics of Democracy* (New York and Chicago: Moody Publishing and Dickey, 1903), *Ethical Principles of Marriage and Divorce* (Chicago: The Public Publishing Co., 1905), *Our Despotic Postal Censorship* (Chicago: The Public Publishing Co., 1906), and *Social Service* (New York: A. Wessels, 1909).

Pouget, Jean Joseph (known as Émile) (1860–1931) French anarchist, syndicalist, author, and editor. Works include *Grève générale réformiste et Grève générale révolutionnaire* (The Reformist General Strike and the Revolutionary General Strike, 1902) and *Comment nous ferons la révolution* with Emile Pataud (1909; *How We Shall Bring About the Revolution,* trans. Fred and Charlotte Charles; Oxford, 1913). Other works translated into English include *The Basis of Trade Unionism* (London: Freedom Press, 1908) and *Sabotage* (trans. Arturo M. Giovannitti, Chicago: C. H. Kerr, 1913). *See also vol. 1, p. 552.*

Ramus, Pierre, see Grossmann, Rudolf.

Ravachol (pseudonym of François-Claudius Koenigstein) (1859–1892) French anarchist. Ravachol bombed the homes of the judge and prosecuting attorneys of the anarchists arrested at an 1891 May Day parade outside Paris. He was executed on 11 July 1892 for his 1891 murder of a rich elderly man. Ravachol, fearless in the face of death, idealized his crimes and was elevated to the stature of a hero by many anarchists, artists, and intellectuals.

Reclus, Jean-Jacques Élisée (1830–1905) French anarchist communist and geographer. Born into the family of a dissident Protestant pastor, Reclus was a leading theorist of anarchist communism. His approach to anarchist communism was distinguished by unusual tolerance and generosity to other anarchist tendencies. Originally a follower of Pierre-Joseph Proudhon, he became closely involved with Michael Bakunin in the 1860s, and also Jean Grave. Reclus was imprisoned after the Paris Commune (1871) and sentenced to ten years banishment, which he spent in Switzerland writing his monumental *Nouvelle géographie universelle* (published as *The Earth and Its Inhabitants;* London: J. S. Virtue, 1876–1894). Reclus placed particular emphasis on the free associative action of individuals, and in *Le Révolté* he advocated propaganda by the deed, but was dismayed by the "verbal violence" rife in the anarchist circles of Paris and Lyon. Reclus wrote numerous works on anarchism, including the widely translated and reprinted pamphlets *An Anarchist on Anarchy* (Boston: B. R. Tucker, 1884) and *Evolution and Revolution* (London: W. Reeves, 1884). From 1894 on he lived in Belgium, teaching at a university founded in his honor.

Reedy, William Marion (1862–1920) American single-tax editor and publisher. Reedy was editor of *The St. Louis Mirror* (1893–1920); known as "Reedy's Mirror," the paper played an important role in

American letters, opening its pages to a wide variety of writers and thinkers, including first publishing the poetry of Edgar Lee Masters. Reedy introduced EG to many influential people in St. Louis during her visits in 1908, 1909, and 1911. He was a member of the 1909 Free Speech Committee. Reedy wrote *Emma Goldman: The Daughter of the Dream* (St Louis, 1908), first published in the *Mirror* on 5 November 1908, in which he asserted that "There is nothing wrong with Miss Goldman's gospel that I can see, except this: She is about eight thousand years ahead of her age."

Reitman, Ben (1879–1942) Chicago physician, flamboyant civic presence, and hobo, Reitman was EG's "grand passion." She introduced Reitman to anarchism, and he served as her tour manager and advance agent for her lectures. In 1906 he became involved in the International Brotherhood Welfare Association, founding a Chicago branch of the Hobo College and serving as its president (1907–1908). Reitman was known in Chicago for leading and being beaten at a march of unemployed workers on 23 January 1908. He met EG in March 1908; when she was unable to find a lecture venue, Reitman offered her the Hobo College hall. He introduced EG to emotional and physical passions hitherto unknown to her. A skilled organizer and promoter, Reitman dramatically increased the size and reach of EG's audiences. He also acted as business manager of the *Mother Earth* office. He contributed tour reports and articles regularly to *Mother Earth,* although he and AB often disagreed on politics and tactics. EG remarked later in her life to AB that "Ben during ten years dedicated to me and my work as no other man ever had, making it possible for me to do the best and most extensive work I had done up to my meeting him"(EG to AB, 14 May 1929, *EGP* reel 21). And BR wrote to EG that the ten years with her were not only the best years of his life, "but if ever I amount to a damn, if ever I give anything worthwhile to society, it will be because you loved me and worked with me" (BR to EG, 20 July 1928; *EGP* reel 20).

Reitzel, Robert (1849–1898) German-born American anarchist, poet, critic, and translator. Reitzel came to the United States in 1870, finally settling in Detroit. He was founder and editor of the radical literary journal *Der arme Teufel* (The Poor Devil, 1884–1900). Reitzel was a staunch supporter of the imprisoned Haymarket anarchists and later of AB during his confinement. *Der arme Teufel* was the only radical serial AB was allowed to receive while in prison. In the 1890s, Reitzel became friends with EG, who visited him shortly before his death. His posthumous publications include *Das Reitzel-Buch einem Vielgeliebten zum Gedachtniss,* ed. Martin Drescher (The Reitzel-Book: In Memory of a Loved-One; Detroit, 1900), *Abenteuer eines Grunen* (Adventures of a Greenhorn: An Autobiographical Novel; Chicago: Mees, Deuss, 1902), and *Des Armen Teufel,* ed. Max Baginski (That Poor Devil; Detroit: Reitzel Klub, 1913).

Riddle, Claude (d. 1914) Los Angeles socialist, physician, and president of the local chapter of the IWW in 1906. Riddle was suspended from the Socialist Party in Los Angeles in 1908 for acting as an advance agent for EG, organizing her meetings. Persuaded by EG during a 1909 public debate on anarchism versus socialism to work for and speak on anarchism, he was expelled from the Socialist party. Riddle was a member of the Los Angeles Social Science League and the Los Angeles Liberal Club, serving one term as president. He contributed a report, "Propaganda in California," on EG's Los Angeles lecture tour to *Mother Earth* (February 1909). Riddle was a friend of Charles T. Sprading, who wrote Riddle's obituary in the August 1914 *Mother Earth.*

Rockefeller, John D. (1839–1937) American industrialist, founder of Standard Oil. In 1859, with $1,000 he had saved and another $1,000 borrowed from his father, Rockefeller started his career in Cleveland. By 1870, he organized the Standard Oil Company, which prospered, putting Rockefeller on the list of the world's twenty wealthiest people by the end of the decade and prompting Rockefeller's decision in 1882 to merge all his properties into the Standard Oil Trust. At this time the Standard Oil Trust controlled 95 percent of the oil refining business in the United States as well as interests in iron ore mines, lumber tracts, manufacturing plants, and transportation.

Rocker, Rudolf (1873–1958) German anarchist historian, writer, and activist. Rocker was a lifelong comrade and correspondent of EG and early follower of Peter Kropotkin. A member of the German Social Democratic Party, Rocker became an anarchist in 1891 at the Second International Congress, as divisions between libertarian and authoritarian socialism were growing. Forced to flee Germany in 1893 for illegally distributing anarchist newspapers, Rocker went first to Paris, then settled in London in 1895, where he worked as a bookbinder and met Milly Witkop, his lifelong companion. In London's East End, he learned Yiddish and joined the Jewish anarchist and trade union movement. Rocker met EG during her first trip to London in 1895. In 1906, Rocker established the Jubilee Street Association to educate workers in English, history, literature, and sociology. He was a delegate at the International Anarchist Congress at Amsterdam in 1907, representing the English federation of Jewish anarchist groups. Rocker was a contributor to *Arbeter Fraynd* (Worker's Friend) from 1896, the weekly central organ of Yiddish activism in London, and founded *Germinal,* a theoretical and literary monthly that same year. Rocker edited the weekly *Dos Freie Vort* (The Free Word) and became editor of *Arbeter Fraynd* in 1898.

Roosevelt, Theodore (1858–1919) President of the United States from 1901 to 1909. As Vice President to William McKinley, Roosevelt ascended to the presidency following McKinley's assassination in 1901. Three years later, Roosevelt was voted into office by the American electorate. Known as a "trust-buster," Roosevelt built his reputation as an anti-monopolist and a friend of the common laborer. During his presidency, Roosevelt used the Sherman Anti-Trust Act of 1890 to bring suit against 44 large industrial monopolies. Demonstrating his hostility toward "big business" in the 1902 Pennsylvania coal strike, he forced mine owners to negotiate a settlement with strikers by threatening to seize the mines. In spite of his pro-labor reputation, in his private correspondence Roosevelt described labor leaders, including Eugene Debs, Charles Moyer, and William Haywood, as "undesirable citizens." During McKinley's campaign for the presidency, Roosevelt's suggestion for handling labor's opposition to federal jurisdiction over strikes was to gather a dozen of its leaders and, as with the leaders of the Paris Commune, "stand them against a wall and shoot them dead." Roosevelt also actively suppressed anarchist activism, supporting the passage of a 1903 act forbidding the immigration of anarchists.

Ruskin, John (1819–1900) English writer, art historian, and social critic. Ruskin's views were rooted in the ideas of reformer and socialist Robert Owen (1801–1877). Ruskin inspired the founding of the English Labour Movement and influenced many radicals of his day, including artist and socialist William Morris. Ruskin taught at the London Working Men's College, founded in 1854 by Christian Socialist F. D. Maurice, and his book *On the Nature of Gothic Architecture—and Herein the True Functions of the Workman in Art* (London: Smith, Elder, 1854) became the school's manifesto. Other influential works include *Unto This Last: Four Essays on the First Principles of Political Economy* (London: Waverley, 1862) and *Sesame and Lilies: Two Lectures Delivered at Manchester in 1864* (London: Smith, Elder, 1865), which proposed social reforms such as labor organizing and a minimum wage.

Schlüter, Hermann (1851–1919) German-born American socialist, journalist, and editor. Born in Elmshorn, Holstein, Schlüter was in Chicago in 1873 where he helped found *Vorbote,* organ of the Illinois Workers' Party. He was secretary of the IWMA's Chicago section until 1876 when he returned to Germany, there editing the Dresden organs of the *Sozialistische Arbeiterpartei Deutschlands.* Arrested several times, Schlüter was finally forced to leave Dresden in 1883. In Zurich he headed the Socialist Democratic Party publishing firm *Schweizerischer Volksbuchhandlung.* His articles in *Der rote Teufel* led to his expulsion from Switzerland in 1888. After a year in London Schlüter came in 1889 to the United States and there edited the *New Yorker Volkszeitung* from 1891 to 1919. In 1905 he was named to the Board of Directors of the Rand School of Social Science. Schlüter wrote *Die Anfänge der deutschen Arbeiterbewegung in Amerika* (The Beginnings of the German American Labor Movement in America; Stuttgart, 1907).

Schulder, Fred (1874–1961) Cleveland philosophical anarchist and single-taxer. Schulder was the companion of Adeline Champney. He served as sales representative for Benjamin Tucker's *Liberty* and helped organize meetings for EG in Cleveland. Schulder wrote the pamphlet *The Relationship of Anarchism to Organization* (Cleveland: Horace E. Carr, 1899; reprinted, 1907).

Seldes, George S. (1860–1931) Russian-born freethinker, revolutionary utopian, single-taxer, and anarchist. Seldes attempted to establish a utopian collective farm in Alliance, New Jersey, but failed due to lack of local interest. After moving to Philadelphia, he became a druggist and studied law. Extremely well-read, Seldes was fluent in eleven languages. A prominent member of the Friends of Russian Freedom, he supported the 1905 uprising against the Tsar and corresponded with such notable revolutionaries as Peter Kropotkin and Leo Tolstoy. Seldes was also an ardent advocate of rational education.

Seldes, Nunia Berman (dates unknown) Pittsburgh friend and correspondent of EG. Nunia Seldes was a financial supporter of anarchist causes, including the *Mother Earth* Sustaining Fund. She married George Seldes, becoming his second wife. EG offered her advice and support when she began an affair, and appeared to have seen Nunia Seldes as a confidant.

Shapiro, Meyer (dates unknown) Friend and financial supporter of EG and anarchist causes. Shapiro hosted EG in London, Ontario, Canada, during her 1906 speaking tour.

Shaw, George Bernard (1856–1950) Irish playwright and literary critic. Benjamin Tucker may have been the first to publish American editions of Shaw's work in 1885. EG admired Shaw primarily for his unmasking of the hypocrisy of Christianity. She regularly featured him in her lectures and analyzed two of his plays, *Mrs. Warren's Profession* and *Major Barbara,* in her *Social Significance of the Modern Drama* (1914) pp. 175–95.

Shippy, George (1855–1913) Chicago police chief (1907–1908). Shippy alleged he was the victim of an anarchist assassination attempt by Lazarus Averbuch in March 1908, claiming he killed his attacker in self-defense. Shippy resigned his position within two months of the affair and died of syphilis five years later.

Solotaroff, Hillel (1865–1921) Russian-born physician and anarchist lecturer and writer. Solotaroff was an important figure in the Yiddish-speaking anarchist movement from the mid-1880s when he was a principal activist in the Pioneers of Liberty, the first Jewish anarchist group in the United States. EG heard Solotaroff lecture in New Haven in 1888, and sought him out when she arrived in New York City the following year, and it was he who introduced her to AB. Solotaroff, along with Moshe Katz, edited *Fraye Arbeter Shtime* after David Edelstadt's death in 1892. Solotaroff contributed to various other Yiddish papers, including *Der Tog* and *Tfileh Zakeh* (nos. 1–5, New York, 1889–1893), an anti-religious journal. In 1897 he hosted a gathering for Peter Kropotkin during his first visit to the United States, and later joined the executive committee of the Kropotkin Literary Society, founded in 1912. Solotaroff became an advocate of Zionism. His publications include *Serious Questions* (London: Tseinistisher Arbayter Forvets, 1903; reprinted from *Freie Arbeiter Stimme*) and *Collected Works* (New York: Dr. H. Solotaroff Publication Committee, 1924). It was Solotaroff who, after the McKinley assassination, helped find work for EG as a nurse. He also was part of the group that planned the production of the journal that would become *Mother Earth*. See also vol. 1, p. 556.

Spielman, Jean E. (dates unknown) Minnesota syndicalist and labor organizer. Spielman was a partner in the International Bookbinding Company, Chicago, which advertised in *Mother Earth* during 1907. At the end of 1907 he wrote to *Mother Earth* arguing against EG's contention that the IWW was not a revolutionary organization. Spielman helped organize the Flour and Cereal Mill Workers Local Number 1 in Minneapolis (1901–1909), was secretary of the Minneapolis IWW in 1911, and helped organize textile workers in 1912. In later years he lectured to the Social Science League of Minneapolis, and contributed to *The Toiler* (1914) and *Free Lance* (1916).

Sprading, Charles T. (dates unknown) Los Angeles-based libertarian and freethinker. Sprading made substantial donations to the Free Speech Fund (1906–1908). He was president of the Los Angeles Liberal Club.

Stirner, Max (born Johann Caspar Schmidt) (1806–1856) German individualist. Stirner exerted a powerful influence on individualist anarchism both in the United States and internationally through his *Der Einzige und Sein Eigentum* (The Ego and His Own; trans. Steven T. Byington; New York: Benjamin Tucker, 1907), which proclaimed enlightened self-interest as the only valid and compelling motivating force for human conduct (in a philosophy known as "egoism"), and adopted by Benjamin Tucker around 1891. The book was given an equivocal review by Max Baginski in the May 1907 *Mother Earth*.

Stokes, J. G. Phelps (1872–1960) American Socialist. Stokes became interested in progressive reform and in the settlement house movement in his late twenties, and served on the board of directors of the University Settlement House on New York's Lower East Side from 1897 until 1903. He was a founding member and vice president (1905–1907) and president (1907–1917) of the Intercollegiate Socialist Society. He was elected to the National Executive Committee of the Socialist Party in 1908, and resigned from the Socialist Party in 1917 over its opposition to American entry into the First World War.

Straus, Oscar Solomon (1850–1926) American lawyer, merchant, diplomat, and presidential cabinet member. After working as a lawyer and subsequently as a crystal and glass merchant, Straus served as U.S. minister to Turkey from 1887 to 1889 and 1898 to 1900, after which time he was made an advisor to Theodore Roosevelt, who later appointed him Secretary of Commerce and Labor in 1906. Straus served from 1906 to 1909, becoming the first Jewish cabinet member, in which capacity he enforced administrative proceedings against anarchists, including efforts by the Bureau of Immigration to deport EG. Straus was later appointed by President William Howard Taft ambassador to Turkey, the first U.S. ambassador to the Ottoman Empire (1909–1910), ran unsuccessfully on the Progressive Party's ticket for governor of New York in 1912, and served as chairman of the Paris Peace Conference in 1919. He wrote several political and historical works, including *Roger Williams: The Pioneer of Religious Liberty* (New York: The Century Co., 1894), *The Origin of Republican Form of Government in the United States of America* (New York: G. P. Putnam and Sons, 1885), and *National Solidarity and International Unity* (New York: League to Enforce Peace, 1917; and New York: National Security League, 1918).

Thoreau, Henry David (1817–1862) American writer, poet, abolitionist, and philosopher. A naturalist, Thoreau lived the doctrine of New England Transcendentalism as expressed by Ralph Waldo Emerson. He began work as a teacher, but resigned when asked to use corporal punishment on his students. In 1838, Thoreau opened a private school in Concord based on the principles of Transcendentalism. In 1845, Thoreau went into seclusion at Walden Pond for over two years, and in 1854 he published *Walden* about his experience. He came to town once during this time, and was arrested for intentionally refusing to pay the poll tax, an experience that prompted him to write "Resistance to Civil Government" (1849), later known as "On the Duty of Civil Disobedience." Thoreau supported John Brown and the abolition movement. EG considered him a vital part of the undercurrent of anarchist thinking in the American political tradition. Along with Emerson, Thoreau was the topic of one of EG's lectures and was often referred to in her writings.

Tolstoy, Leo (Count Lev Nikolayevich) (1828–1910) Russian writer. Tolstoy is best known for his literary works, including *War and Peace* (1869), *Anna Karenina* (1877), and *The Death of Ivan Illyich* (1884), and his later philosophical essays, including *Confession* (1884), *What Then Must We Do?* (1886), *The Kingdom of God Is Within You* (1894), and *The Slavery of Our Times* (1900), and for his attempt to combine both in his more polemic fiction, including *Master and Man* (1895). His *Kreutzer Sonata* was banned under the Comstock Act. A portion of the profits from his last novel, *Resurrection* (1899–1900), were donated to Jane Addams's Hull House. Anarchists admired Tolstoy's compassion for the poor and his anti-feudal sentiments, recognizing that he was a pacifist and antimilitarist who condemned all acts of violence including revolutionary activity; they also celebrated his rejection of institutionalized religion despite Tolstoy's advocacy of Christian love as the primary vehicle for improving society. Tolstoy's ideas were popularized in the United States by Ernest Crosby and Benjamin Tucker, among others. An article by Tolstoy, "America and Russia," was published in the March 1909 *Mother Earth*.

Traubel, Horace L. (1858–1919) American journalist. In his monthly magazine, *Conservator* (Philadelphia, 1890–1919), which consisted primarily of his own articles, and in his books, including *Chants Communal* (1894), *Optimos* (1910), and *Collects* (1915), Traubel espoused a blend of socialist, humanitarian, anarchist, and libertarian ideas. Traubel was secretary of the Fellowship for Ethical Research of Philadelphia in 1896. A friend and the literary executor to Walt Whitman, Traubel devoted much of his life to tending the poet's literary reputation. In *Living My Life,* EG recalled meeting Traubel at a Whitman celebration in 1903.

Tucker, Benjamin R. (1854–1939) American individualist anarchist. Tucker was the founder, editor, and publisher of *Liberty* (Boston, 1881–1892; New York, 1892–1908). He was a member of the Turner Defense Committee in 1903. By the beginning of the twentieth century, with American individualist anarchism on the decline, *Liberty* appeared erratically, although Tucker continued to play a role in the movement, In 1906 he opened Tucker's Unique Book Shop in New York, frequented by the young Eugene O'Neill, among others, including his future wife, Pearl Johnson. In January of 1908 his warehouse was consumed by fire and his printing press and extra stock destroyed, a devastating event that effectively ended Tucker's lengthy publishing career. The last U.S. edition of *Liberty* was published in April of 1908. Tucker and his wife left the United States the following November after the birth of their daughter Oriole, never to return. The family spent the next 17 years in France and then 13 in Monaco, where Tucker died on 22 June 1939.

Turgenev, Ivan (1818–1883) Russian writer, dramatist. Turgenev wrote novels instead of plays to answer the tsarist policy of censoring controversial performances. The main character in Turgenev's novel *Rudin* (1855) was based on Russian anarchist Michael Bakunin. Other works include *A Sportsman's Sketches* (1852), *A Nest of Gentlefolk* (1859), *On the Eve* (1860), and *Fathers and Sons* (1862), whose character Bazarov is both a revolutionary agnostic and nihilist. *Mother Earth* reprinted "The Reporter" and "The Beggar" in 1906.

Turner, John (1864–1934) British anarchist, lecturer, journalist, and founder of the Shop Assistants' Union. Turner visited the United States from October 1903 to 1904 for the second time, and became the first casualty of the 1903 Immigration Act, passed in response to the assassination of President McKinley, which specifically excluded alien anarchists. Turner's arrest and deportation order prompted EG's involvement and co-operation with the Free Speech League. The League and EG raised funds for Clarence Darrow and Edgar Lee Masters to defend Turner and take the case to the U.S. Supreme Court. Turner returned to England in early 1904, before the case was decided (the Court upheld the Immigration Act and mandated his deportation). His sister, Lizzie, also an anarchist, was the companion of Thomas H. Bell, a Scottish-born associate of EG. Turner was the printer and publisher of *Freedom* (1895–1907), helped publish *Voice of Labor* (1907), and contributed to *Mother Earth* in 1907. *See also vol. 1, p. 560.*

Umberto (1844–1900) King of Italy. Umberto was assassinated in 1900 by Italian anarchist Gaetano Bresci. After ascending the throne in 1878, Umberto was the target of three assassination attempts. The first two attacks, presumed to be the result of anarchist conspiracies, prompted inconclusive investigations.

Vaillant, Auguste (1861–1894) French anarchist. Vaillant threw a bomb from the public gallery into France's Chamber of Deputies on 9 December 1893, injuring about eighty people. He was executed on 6 February 1894. At his trial Vaillant declared "the deputies are responsible for all society's afflictions." After his death Vaillant's daughter Sidonie—"the crown princess of anarchy"—was entrusted to Sébastien Faure. Vaillant's action led to the passage of anti-anarchist laws (known as *lois scélérates*) and inspired Sante Caserio's assassination of Sadi Carnot. The argument he presented to the court was widely circulated in pamphlet form and reprinted by Benjamin Tucker in *Liberty*, 24 February 1894; Émile Zola featured him in his novel *Paris* as the anarchist character Salvat.

Wald, Lillian (1867–1940) American nurse and social worker. Wald founded the Henry Street Nurses' Settlement (later known as the Henry Street Settlement) in New York in 1895. The daughter of a wealthy German Jewish merchant, Wald was raised in Rochester, New York. She received her nursing diploma from the New York Hospital Training School in 1891, and entered the Women's Medical College in New York. During this training she volunteered to teach health classes on the

Lower East Side, an experience that inspired her to found the Henry Street Settlement. She remained on Henry Street her entire life and became an integral part of the Lower East Side community. She was one of the founders of the Women's Trade Union League in 1903. As vice president of the Friends of Russian Freedom, Wald spoke and wrote frequently on behalf of Russian political prisoners. Her friendship with Catherine Breshkovskaya began during the latter's first visit to the United States in 1904–1905 and continued through correspondence thereafter. In 1909, the Henry Street buildings housed the constituent meetings of the National Association for the Advancement of Colored People. Supported by wealthy patrons including Jacob Schiff, and closely linked through her friendships with Jane Addams, Florence Kelley, Felix Adler and Jacob Riis to a nationwide network of progressives and reformers, Wald worked on behalf of various causes benefiting women and children, including the Women's Trade Union League. Wald was also an important figure in the movement to professionalize nurses. She helped establish Columbia University's nursing school and served as president of the National Organization for Public Health Nursing.

Walker, Edwin Cox (1849–1931) American anarchist individualist and atheist, bookseller. Walker was founder of the Sunrise Club discussion group (1890–1931) and New York agent for *Mother Earth*. EG spoke several times at the club. At times Walker was critical of EG's actions, especially what he considered her support of terrorism. He edited *Lucifer* from 1882 to 1888 with Moses Harman and *Fair Play* from 1888 to 1908 with Lillian Harman, contributed to *The Adult* (1898), *American Journal of Eugenics* (1906–1908), and was an editorial contributor to *Liberty* (1906–1908). Walker's works include *Variety vs. Monogamy; an Address Before the Ladies' Liberal League of Philadelphia* (Chicago: Lucifer Library, 1897), *Our Worship of Primitive Social Guesses* (New York: Fair Play Publishing, 1899), *Vice, Its Friend and Its Foes* (New York: E. C. Walker, 1901), *Who Is the Enemy: Anthony Comstock or You?* (New York: E. C. Walker, 1903), *Liberty vs. Assassination* (New York: E. C. Walker, 1907), and *A Sketch and an Appreciation of Moncure Daniel Conway: Freethinker and Humanitarian* (New York: Edwin C. Walker, 1908).

Warren, Josiah (1798–1874) American anarchist, inventor, author, editor, musician, and music teacher. Warren was a pioneer writer on individualism, voluntary cooperation, and the labor theory of value. Although he admired Robert Owen, Warren placed a greater emphasis on individuality, a belief he linked to security of each person and his or her property. Especially interested in applying his theories, Warren founded several colonies and stores based on the concept of "labor exchange," in which products were exchanged for the hours necessary to produce them. He founded the Cincinnati Time Store (1827), the Utopia colony (1847), and, with Stephen Pearl Andrews, the Modern Times colony (1851). A prolific author and editor, he wrote, among other works, *A New System of Musical Notation* (New Harmony, Ind., 1884), *Equitable Commerce* (New Harmony, Ind., 1846), *True Civilization* (Boston: J. Warren, 1863), and *The Emancipation of Labor* (Boston, 1864), and edited *The Peaceful Revolutionist* (Cincinnati, 1833; Utopia, Ohio, 1848) and *The Periodical Letter* (Long Island, N.Y.; Boston, 1854–1858).

Watchorn, Robert (1858–1944) U.S. Commissioner of Immigration at Ellis Island from 1905 to 1909. An English-born coal miner, Watchorn had served as president and secretary-treasurer of the Pittsburgh division of the National Trades Assembly, #135, Knights of Labor and as first secretary-treasurer of the United Mine Workers of America. One of the pioneers in sweatshop and child labor reform in Pennsylvania, he also served as chief clerk to Robert E. Pattison, governor of Pennsylvania.

As U.S. Commissioner of Immigration he is credited with practical and humanitarian reforms in the registering and treatment of immigrants. After 1909 he pursued a career in the oil industry, later founded his own company and eventually became a renowned philanthropist.

Wess, William Woolf (1861–1946) Lithuanian-born British labor organizer, orator, and anarchist. The brother of Doris Zhook (1874–1954), Wess was among EG's closest London anarchist friends. He was smuggled out of Russia (ca.1881) to avoid military service. Wess was a member of the London Socialist League and secretary of the Tailors Strike committee in London's East End (1889). His command of Yiddish, Russian, and English enabled Wess to act as a liaison between the various radical groups in London. In 1894 he played an active role with Saul Yanovsky in the formation of a Jewish co-operative bakery. He worked as a printer at *Freedom* until 1894 and from 1895 to 1896 he edited the Yiddish-language periodical *Arbeter Freynd*. Wess returned to the *Freedom* Group in 1896, remaining active in London anarchist and union circles until his death.

Whitman, Walt (1819–1892) American poet, journalist, and essayist. Whitman is best known for his collection of poems, *Leaves of Grass* (1855), revised and reissued in three different editions in his lifetime. The collection was often banned on grounds of obscenity under the Comstock Act, especially the poem "A Woman Waits For Me," which figured in cases against *The Word* and *Firebrand*. Whitman held numerous jobs while writing and editing for periodicals, including *The Brooklyn Eagle* (1846–1848) and *The Brooklyn Times* (1857–1858). During the American Civil War, Whitman worked first as a clerk in Washington, D.C., and then as a nurse, tending to both Union and Confederate wounded. He later worked as a clerk in the Department of the Interior and in the Attorney General's office. A paralytic stroke in 1873 forced Whitman to give up his work. At the time of his death, his poetry was more popular in Europe than in the United States.

Whitman's work had enormous influence throughout the American freethought and radical movements of the late nineteenth and early twentieth centuries. Robert Ingersoll, his friend, delivered a passionate oration at Whitman's funeral. Benjamin R. Tucker was an early champion of *Leaves of Grass,* and EG had originally planned to name *Mother Earth* (itself a Whitmanesque title) *The Open Road* after Whitman's influential poem of the same name. Whitman's works include *Sequel to Drum Taps* (1865), *Democratic Vistas* (1871), and *Specimen Days and Collect* (1882–83). A ten-volume edition of his complete writings was published in 1902.

Wilde, Oscar (1854–1900) Irish playwright, libertarian socialist author. His works *The Soul of Man Under Socialism* (1891) and *The Ballad of Reading Gaol* (1898) were influential in radical circles. *Mother Earth* reprinted an extract from his *De Profundis* in 1906.

Wood, Charles Erskine Scott (1852–1944) Portland lawyer, writer, poet, social reformer, former military colonel, and philosophical anarchist. Wood contributed to the Max Stirner memorial fund in 1906, was a member of the 1909 Free Speech Committee, and was a substantial donor to the San Francisco Free Speech Defense Fund the same year. Wood often chaired EG's meetings when she was in Portland and was a prolific contributor to journals, including *Liberty, Everyman,* and *Mother Earth,* where among other contributions his poem in "In Memory of Francisco Ferrer," was published in the November 1909 issue.

Yampolsky, Rebecca Miriam (dates unknown) Chicago anarchist and physician. Yampolsky was an organizer of the Edelstadt Group and an early advocate of birth control. She treated EG's sudden illness in 1908 and arranged, with Ben Reitman, for the use of the Hobo College hall. Yampolsky was a member of the Chicago Social Science Club and the companion of William Nathanson, M.D.

Yanovsky, Saul (1864–1939) Jewish anarchist, lecturer. Yanovsky was a founder of the Jewish anarchist group Pioneers of Liberty and editor of the Yiddish-language papers *Di Abend Tsaytung* (The Evening Newspaper, 1906), *Freie Arbeiter Stimme* (1899–1919), and *Di Fraye Gezelshaft* (1910–1911). He was perceived by EG as "despotic" and by AB as rigid and "dictatorial." However, *Freie Arbeiter Stimme* did sponsor some of EG's lectures. A capable administrator and organizer, he put *Freie Arbeiter Stimme* on a sound financial footing. Under his editorship the paper published many prominent European writers as well as spotlighting new Yiddish writers. It also moved to a more conciliatory and less anti-religious anarchism.

Zola, Émile (1840–1902) French novelist, naturalist, and social critic. In *Germinal* (1885), Zola's character Souvarine epitomizes the nihilist and *attentater*. In *Paris* (1898), the anarchist character Salvat is closely based on Auguste Vaillant. Zola's major work was a twenty-novel history of the Rougon-Macquart family (1871–1893). He was also a vigorous defender of French army officer Alfred Dreyfus.

Appeal To Reason Kansas City, Mo., Kansas City, Kans., Girard, Kans.: 6 August 1895–4 November 1922, mostly weekly. Independent socialist newspaper founded and edited during this period by Julius Augustus Wayland; strongly supportive of Eugene V. Debs and the Socialist Party. An enormously popular paper that promoted itself aggressively, its circulation had risen to 275,000 by 1907. Supportive of the Mexican Liberal Party (PLM) before the Mexican revolution. Supported EG's right to free speech but drew a distinct line between socialism and anarchism. Contributors included Debs, Kate Richards O'Hare, Charlotte Perkins Gilman, Upton Sinclair, and Ernest Untermann.

Common Sense Los Angeles, Calif.: 20 August 1904–7 August 1909, weekly. Continuation of *Los Angeles Socialist* (12 November 1901–20 August 1904). A socialist paper originally published by the Los Angeles Socialist Party and then by Common Sense Publishing Co. Edited by John Murray, Jr., Kasper Bauer, Chas. R. Ross, Edgar B. Helphenstine (later known as Edgar B. Helfenstein), W. A. Corey, Frank I. Wheat, W. S. Bradford, and W. Scott Lewis with German anarchist Alfred G. Sanftleben as circulation manager and translator. Contributors included L. T. Fisher, Jack London, John A. Morris, J. Stitt Wilson, E. G. Severance, Florence Kelly ("Christmas Cruelties," 10 December 1904), and John Kenneth Turner. Commonly published pieces by Eugene V. Debs, as well as William D. Haywood and Maksim Gorky. Published the booklet *Appreciations* (1907), written by Sanftleben and Corey, with a chapter of accolades about EG's work, and also reported favorably on EG's Los Angeles visits, while refusing to publish a paid advertisement for EG's April–May 1908 lecture series in the city. L. T. Fisher published an article entitled "Emma Goldman: A Study of Noted Woman Anarchist and Her Views" (8 June 1907), which spoke favorably of her as a speaker but criticized her adherence to anarchism as confused. The paper sponsored a debate between its editors and EG in May 1908.

The Commonweal February 1885–October 1894, mostly weekly.

Cronaca Sovversiva: Ebdomadario anarchico di propaganda rivoluzionaria (Subversive Chronicle: An Anarchist Weekly of Revolutionary Propaganda) Barre, Vt.: vol. 1, no. 1 (6 June 1903)–vol. 10, no. 5 (3 February 1912), weekly; Lynn, Mass.: vol. 10, no. 6 (10 February 1912)–vol. 16, no. 18 (18 July 1918); Washington, D.C.: vol. 17, no. 1 (March 1919)–vol. 17, no. 2 (May 1919); some later issues in Italy. Italian-language anarchist communist newspaper, edited anonymously by Luigi Galleani, who published under various pen names, including Grigi Galleani, Luigi Pimpino, Mentano, and Tramp. Associates included Andrea Salsedo, Carlo Valdinoci, and Constantino Zonchello; contributors included Umberto Colarossi, Raffaele Schiavina, and, later, Bartolomeo Vanzetti. Published translations of articles by EG and news of her lectures tours.

Current Literature New York: July 1888–May 1925, monthly. Journal edited by Edward J. Wheeler with associate editor Leonard Abbott from 1905 to 1925. Included frequent features on modern European literature and favorably reviewed EG's work. It was from her reading of *Current Literature* (along with *Poet Lore*) that EG was introduced to much of the modern European literature that would become the subject of many of her lectures.

The Demonstrator Home [Colony], Wash.: vol. 1, no. 1 (11 March 1903)–vol. 2, no. 14 (26 October 1904), weekly; vol. 2, no. 15 (16 November 1904)–vol. 5, no. 15 (19 February 1908), semi-monthly; subtitled *A Weekly* (later *Semi-Monthly*) *Periodical of Fact, Thought and Comment*. Continuation of *Discontent*. Intended especially for the Home Colony community, *The Demonstrator* was nonetheless the only English-language anarchist newspaper in the United States following the close of *Free Society*. First edited by James F. Morton, Jr., then by Jay Fox; and then by Lawrence Cass, the editor of *The Emancipator*, which merged with *The Demonstrator* in July 1907, and finally by the *Demonstrator* Group, whose notice was signed by Gertie Vose. Under Jay Fox, the paper took a more labor-oriented and international tone, and began displaying the IWW emblem and running "International Notes" by Andrew Klemencic. Included positive reports on EG and in the 2 October 1907 issue printed a solicitation from EG and George Bauer, AB, Voltairine de Cleyre, Hippolyte Havel, and Harry Kelly for seed money to fund a labor-oriented anarchist weekly. Contributors included Moses Harman, Lizzie M. Holmes, C. L. James, Joseph Labadie, Jules Scarceriaux, and Horace Traubel. On 18 December 1907, a call for funds to improve the press was issued, but the paper folded two months later. See *Discontent,* below.

Discontent: "Mother of Progress" Lakebay, then Home [Colony], Wash.: vol. 1, no. 1 (11 May 1898)–vol. 4, no. 31 (30 April 1902), weekly. Anarchist communist newspaper published by O. A. Verity, the Discontent Publishing Group, and others at Home Colony. James F. Morton, Jr., became editor after *Free Society* moved to Chicago. Contributors included Cassius V. Cook, Lizzie Holmes, and C. L. James. Following the assassination of President McKinley in 1901, the paper faced increased harassment, including an unannounced suspension of mailing in Tacoma, Washington, the indictment and arrest of associates for obscenity, and the eventual closing of the Home post office. The paper was suspended and continued by *The Demonstrator*.

L'Era nuova (The New Era) Paterson, N.J.: no. 1 (13 June 1908)–no. 455 (29 October 1917), weekly. Successor to *La Questione Sociale* (see below); continued by *Il Bollettino de L'Era Nuova*. Italian-language anarchist periodical edited by Camillo Rosazza, Ludovico Caminita, Franz Widmer, and others. Suppressed after U.S. entry into the First World War. Contributors included AB, Jay Fox, and Saverio Merlino.

Everyman Los Angeles, Calif.: 1906–1909, 1913–1919, monthly. Also known as *The Golden Elk* and *Luke North's Everyman*. Published by the Single Tax League of Los Angeles and edited by Luke North. Contributors included Clarence Darrow, EG, Harry Kelly, and William C. Owen.

Fraye Arbeter Shtime See *Freie Arbeiter Stimme*.

Freedom London: October 1886–December 1927, monthly. Principal English-language publishing organ for the theoretical development of anarchist communism; founded by Peter Kropotkin and

Charlotte Wilson, among others. Editors during the first decade of the twentieth century were Alfred Marsh and Thomas Keell. Regularly published news of EG's activities, lectures and publications.

Free Society San Francisco: 14 November 1897–December 1901, weekly; Chicago: February 1901–1904; New York: 27 March–20 November 1904. Succeeded *The Firebrand*. Anarchist communist newspaper edited by Abe Isaak. *Free Society* was the principal English-language forum for anarchist ideas in the United States at the beginning of the twentieth century. Contributors included Kate Austin, Voltairine de Cleyre, Michael Cohn, Jay Fox, Lizzie Holmes, William Holmes, C. L. James, Harry Kelly, James F. Morton, Jr., and Ross Winn.

Freie Arbeiter Stimme (Free Voice of Labor) New York: July 1890–1894, weekly; 1899–1977. Yiddish-language anarchist communist newspaper edited at this time by Saul Yanovsky. Included labor news, literary and cultural criticism as well as poetry and translations of novels. Advertised EG's lectures but was critical of some of her actions and statements regarding Leon Czolgosz and the Union Square bomb of 1908. Among the paper's contributors were Peter Kropotkin, Johann Most, Max Nettlau, Rudolf Rocker, and poet Morris Winchevsky; the paper also provided translations of Leonid Andreyev, Henrik Ibsen, Octave Mirbeau, George Bernard Shaw, Ivan Turgenev, and Oscar Wilde.

Freiheit (Freedom) Principally London and New York: 4 January 1879–13 August 1910, weekly. German-language social democratic, then anarchist newspaper, edited primarily by Johann Most, and by Max Baginski and Henry Bauer following Most's death in 1906. Once the most powerful and popular German-language anarchist paper, its influence was waning during the first decade of the twentieth century. Although hostile to EG under Most, following his death *Freiheit* advertised EG's lectures and supported her free speech fights.

International Socialist Review Chicago: July 1900–February 1918, monthly. Independent socialist journal, originally a theoretical journal aimed at intellectuals and hostile to anarchism. Published by Charles H. Kerr and edited by Algie Martin Simons until 1908, then edited by Kerr, under whom the paper took a less theoretical and more agitational form. Contributors at this time included Leonard Abbott, Clarence Darrow, Eugene V. Debs, Bolton Hall, Covington Hall, Karl Kautsky, Kōtoku Shūsui, Wilhelm Liebknecht, Jack London, Tom Mann, Anton Pannekoek, Upton Sinclair, and William English Walling.

Khleb i Volia (Bread and Liberty) Geneva and London: no. 1 (August 1903)–no. 24 (November 1905); London and Paris: n.s. no. 1 (March 1909)–no. 2 (July 1909). Its masthead cited Michael Bakunin's "The urge to destroy is also a creative urge." Published between 1906 and 1907 as *Listki, Khleb i Volia*. Russian-language anarchist journal founded by Georgian anarchist Georgii Gogelia, his wife, and a group of Russian and Georgian students. Peter Kropotkin was both an inspiration for and a frequent contributor to the journal. The journal published pamphlets by Bakunin and Kropotkin and Russian translations of works by Jean Grave, Errico Malatesta, and Élisée Recus as well as other European anarchists. However, after an article by Georgii Gogelia in the 5 December 1903 issue calling for and praising mass violence as necessary for real change, Kropotkin broke with the journal in early 1904, criticizing its concentration on terror as the sole tactic for revolutionary change. The journal ceased publication in 1905 when Gogelia returned to Russia to take part in the revolution. EG read the paper, albeit critically, and it helped her, through Kropotkin and Marie Goldsmith, to become aware of the growing Russian anarchist movement.

The Liberator Chicago: vol. 1, no. 1 (3 September 1905)–vol. 1, no. 30 (15 April 1906), weekly. Newspaper "devoted to revolutionary propaganda along lines of anarchist thought,"edited by Lucy E. Parsons. Contributors included Lizzie M. Holmes, C. L. James, Andrew Klemencic, "Rex" (possibly Jay Fox), and Jean Spielman. Printed the works of Clarence S. Darrow, Viroqua Daniels, Eugene V. Debs, Enrico Ferri, Maksim Gorky, Peter Kropotkin, Dyer D. Lum, Wendell Phillips, Élisée Reclus, T. P. Quinn, Horace Traubel, and William E. Trautmann. The paper was especially oriented toward class struggle and highly supportive of the nascent IWW; it also published articles on the "sex question" and supported Moses Harman. In addition, the newspaper reprinted many works on anarchism, the speeches and memorials of the Haymarket anarchists, a series by Parsons on "Labor's Long Struggle with Capital," popular essays on science and nature, and news of labor in the United States and Europe, as well as information on the Russian revolution of 1905. The paper also reprinted the International Working People Association's Pittsburgh Manifesto of 1883, an announcement for *Mother Earth,* and a black-bordered memorial for Johann Most.

Liberty: Not the Daughter but the Mother of Order Boston: vol. 1, no. 1 (6 August 1881)–, biweekly; vol. 2, no. 16 (17 May 1884)–; vol. 7, no. 3 (7 June 1890)–, associate editor Victor Yarros; vol. 8, no. 7 (25 July 1891)–vol. 8, no. 36 (13 February 1892), weekly; New York: vol. 8, no. 37 (30 April 1892)–, without Yarros; vol. 9, no. 45 (August 1893)–, monthly; vol. 9, no. 47 (24 February 1894)–, biweekly; vol. 10, no. 10 (22 September 1894)– vol. 17, no. 1 (April 1908), frequency varied. Anarchist individualist newspaper founded and edited by Benjamin R. Tucker. The thought of Pierre-Joseph Proudhon, Herbert Spencer, and, later, Max Stirner were major influences in its pages. Influential internationally, it was instrumental in introducing the work of Friedrich Nietzsche, Pierre-Joseph Proudhon, George Bernard Shaw, and Leo Tolstoy to America. Contributors included Adeline Champney, E. H. Fulton, Joshua K. Ingalls, Joseph Labadie, Dyer D. Lum, John Beverly Robinson, George Schumm, C. E. S. Wood, and Victor Yarros (also for a time its associate editor). Although it maintained its criticisms of EG and anarchist communists in general, as a rule the paper extended its support to them when arrested. During the first decade of the twentieth century it became less influential and was published erratically. In January 1908, fire destroyed *Liberty*'s publication office, and the paper ceased publication.

Listki, Khleb i Volia (Pages of Bread and Liberty) London, Paris, Geneva: no. 1 (30 October 1906)–no. 18 (5 July 1907). See *Khleb i Volia,* above. Russian anarchist communist newspaper edited by Peter Kropotkin, Marie Goldsmith, Ivan Knishnik, and Vladimir Zabrezhnev

Lucifer, the Lightbearer (various subtitles, including *A Journal of Investigating and Reform* and *Devoted to the Emancipation of Women from Sex Slavery*) Valley Falls, Kans.: 1883–1896; Chicago: 8 May 1896–6 June 1907. Mostly weekly newspaper founded and edited by Moses Harman; co-editors included Lillian Harman and Edwin C. Walker; published articles on anarchism, atheism, and free speech, but became especially well known for open discussions of sexuality, marriage, and feminism. Advertised EG's meetings and regularly reported on her; in turn, *Lucifer* was regularly advertised in *Mother Earth* and EG spoke at various *Lucifer* circles. Supported efforts to release AB. Contributors included Kate Austin, Voltairine de Cleyre, Edward Bliss Foote, Edward Bond Foote, Jr., C. L. James, Abe Isaak, James F. Morton, Jr., and Emil Ruedebusch. Was dated from the death of Giordano Bruno in 1600 (E.M., or Era of Man) rather than the birth of Jesus. Became the *American Journal of Eugenics* (Chicago, 1907–1908; Los Angeles, 1908–1910). In December 1907 *Mother Earth* offered its readers a joint subscription with the *American Journal of Eugenics.*

Mother Earth New York: March 1906–August 1917, monthly; subtitled *Monthly Magazine Devoted to Social Science and Literature.* Anarchist journal published by EG and edited variously by EG, Max Baginski, AB, and Hippolyte Havel. Baginski was the usual author of the "News and Comments" section. Contributors included Leonard Abbott, Adeline Champney, John R. Coryell, Voltairine de Cleyre, Floyd Dell, Jay Fox, Alden Freeman, Bolton Hall, Sadakichi Hartmann, Lizzie M. Holmes, William Holmes, C. L. James, Harry Kelly, Peter Kropotkin, William C. Owen, BR, Lola Ridge, Theodore Schroeder, John Kenneth Turner, Charles Erskine Scott Wood; also printed some letters of Francisco Ferrer.

New Yorker Volkszeitung (New York People's Newspaper) New York: 28 January 1878–12 October 1932, daily. German-language socialist newspaper published by the Socialistic Co-operative Publishing Society, and at different times the official organ of many trade unions and groups. Contained news, editorials, announcements, and poetry, all from a socialist viewpoint. A weekly edition was titled *Vorwärts* (Forward).

Poet Lore Boston: 1889–. Literary journal edited by Helen A. Clarke, Paul H. Grunmann, Edward J. O'Brien, and Charlotte Porter. Included works by Bjørnstjerne Bjørnson, Alice Stone Blackwell, Georges Duhame, Gerhardt Hauptmann, James Oppenheim, and August Strindberg. Read regularly by EG and, with *Current Literature,* introduced her to much of the modern European literature that would become the subject of many of her lectures.

The Public Chicago: 1898–1919, weekly. Liberal and single-tax paper edited by Louis F. Post; associate editors included Bolton Hall, Lincoln Steffens, and C. E. S. Wood. Defended free speech and advocated the importance of understanding radical ideas; it supported EG in her conflicts with the police over her right to speak. Contributors included Hutchins Hapgood and Joseph Labadie.

La Questione Sociale Paterson, N.J.: vol. 1, no. 1 (15 July 1895)–vol. 5, whole no. 127 (2 September 1899), biweekly; n. s. no. 1 (9 September 1899)–vol. 14, n. s. whole no. 419 (21 March 1908). Italian-language anarchist newspaper. Editors included Pietro Gori, Guiseppe Ciancabilla, Errico Malatesta (from 1899 to 1900, anonymously), and Luigi Galleani. Gaetano Bresci, Ludovico Caminita, and Pedro Esteve all worked with the paper. Malatesta was influential in its founding—his papers in Florence (1883–1884) and Buenos Aires (1885–1886) bore the same name. It suffered from factional conflict among local anarchists as well as harassment by the authorities. Banned from the mails in 1908, it reappeared the same year under the title *L'Era nuova* (see above).

Regeneración (Regeneration) Mexico City: 1900–; San Antonio, Texas: 1904; St. Louis, Mo.: 1905–1906; Los Angeles, Calif.: 1910–1918. Spanish-language Mexican liberal opposition, then anarchist paper, edited by the Mexican revolutionary Ricardo Flores Magón at times with Juan Sarabia, Librado Rivera, and Antonio Villarreal. The English-language section was edited first by Alfred Sanftleben, then by Ethel Duffy Turner, and finally William C. Owen. Featured EG, regularly reported on her lectures, and acknowledged in print the donations it received from her meetings.

The Truth Seeker Paris, Ill.: 1873; New York: 1874–1964; San Diego, Calif.: 1964–. Freethought journal edited at this time by Eugene Montague Macdonald. In 1909, George E. Macdonald succeeded E. M. Macdonald as editor. Contributors included Leonard Abbott, C. L. James, and BR.

Vorwärts (Forward) See *New Yorker Volkszeitung,* above.

The Wide Way New York: vol. 1, no. 1 (December 1907)–vol. 1, no. 2 (January 1908), monthly. Edited by John R. Coryell, in essense his personal publication (his articles were sometimes published in the magazine under the pseudonym Margaret Grant). Advertised in and supported by *Mother Earth*. Contributors included Floyd Dell and Edwin C. Walker.

Woman's Journal Boston and Chicago: 1870–1912; Boston: 1912–1917, weekly. Newspaper supporting temperance, women's suffrage, and suppression of vice. Founded by members of the American Women Suffrage Association. Edited at this time by Henry Blackwell and Alice Stone Blackwell. Contributors included Charlotte Perkins Gilman and Carrie Chapman Catt. Advertised EG's scalp and facial massage business.

American Society of the Friends of Russian Freedom The American Society of the Friends of Russian Freedom was established in Boston in 1891 by the Russian Socialist Revolutionary Party exile Boris Kravchinskii (aka Stepniak), who had formed the English Society of the Friends of Russian Freedom in April 1890. The American group was always small, the membership never numbering more than two hundred, and consisted primarily of wealthy liberals who supported the work of the Russian Revolutionaries against the Tsarists in Russia. Founding members included such prominent figures as Samuel Clemens (Mark Twain), William Lloyd Garrison, and George Kennan. Kennan (1845–1924), a journalist, lecturer, and a leading American authority on prisons in Russia and Siberia, was instrumental in bringing the plight of Russian political prisoners to the attention of the American public. Kennan wrote several books and a host of magazine articles on the subject, and contributed to the monthly organ of the Friends of Russian Freedom, *Free Russia* (London and New York, 1890–1894).

According to *Free Russia* (July 1891), "the object of the Society of Friends of Russian Freedom is to aid by all moral and legal means the Russian patriot in their efforts to obtain for their country Political Freedom and Self-Government." Also, "the work will be extended most successfully if those who have taken the Russian question to heart will unite in forming a society in order to do systematically and permanently what has been done hitherto by individual efforts—namely, to obtain and spread authentic information about the condition of Russia, to organize lectures, meetings, debating societies, and to use all other legal and honorable means of influencing public opinion in America, and to promote similar societies in other free countries."

By the mid-1890s the Friends of Russian Freedom had virtually disappeared; *Free Russia* terminated publication in July 1894. Only a small number of sympathizers in New York kept the group alive until it was resurrected in 1904. As Russian exiles began to tour America more frequently in search of funds and support and as news of various pogroms filtered into the country, the Friends of Russian Freedom helped to plan itineraries and arrange lectures and dinners in major cities across the country.

EG's involvement with the Society of the Friends of Russian Freedom consisted of helping the group with the visit of Catherine Breshkovskaya, the sixty-year-old Russian Socialist Revolutionary known affectionately as Babushka. The Society of the Friends of Russian Freedom sponsored a U.S. speaking tour for Breshkovskaya in 1904 and 1905, the purpose of which was to raise funds and to arouse public sentiment for the Socialist Revolutionaries. An initial meeting between Breshkovskaya and the Friends of Russian Freedom was brokered by EG, who was also instrumental in the formation of the New York branch of the group, headed by the Rev. Minot Savage, and to which Robert Ely also belonged. The group occasionally met in EG's apartment.

Anarchist Federation At the 1907 International Anarchist Congress in Amsterdam, an Anarchist International Federation was created, composed of anarchist groups and federations as well as individuals, with the intent of bringing the various different groups into closer contact with each other. A bureau of correspondence was also created, composed of five individuals, led by Alexander Schapiro, for the purpose of maintaining communication. In February–March 1908 the first issue of the *Bulletin de L'Internationale Anarchiste* appeared. The bulletin was from London, in French, and contained extracts from the reports of delegates at the 1907 Anarchist Congress and information on the state of the anarchist movement in various countries.

Based in New York, founded in 1908, and organized by treasurer Alexander Berkman and secretary J. C. Behr, the American Anarchist Federation is identified variously as the Anarchist Federation of America, Anarchist Federation of New York, and simply the Anarchist Federation. The first announcement of the Anarchist Federation appeared in the January 1908 *Mother Earth*. The purpose of the organization, according to the announcement, was to bring together anarchist individuals and groups, act as an educational bureau, propagate anarchism through bulletins, seek "participation in the every-day social life of the people," involve itself in labor unions, propagate direct action and the general strike, and serve as a collection center for funds to defend radical political prisoners. The American Anarchist Federation affiliated itself with the International Anarchist Federation. In 1908 the American Anarchist Federation published *To the Unemployed and Homeless!!* (New York: Anarchist Federation of America, 1908), *How to End Panics: An Address to Poor People* (the pamphlet was found at the home of 1908 Union Square bomber Selig Silverstein and published in the January 1908 *Mother Earth*), *Down with the Anarchists* (printed in the March 1908 *Mother Earth* as "To Our Enemies"), and *To the Public of Chicago*, written by EG and others as a response to the killing of Lazarus Averbuch.

On 22 January 1908 an International Federation of Chicago was organized, linking the various anarchist groups in Chicago. Twenty-five people representing three groups met at the Edelstadt Club to organize the local federation, with Theodore Appel serving as secretary. By February 1908, New York anarchist groups including *Mother Earth,* Progressive Library, Weckruf, Licht für Frauen, Freir Entwicklungs-Verein, Group Freiheit, and Anarchistisches Lese-Zimmer had affiliated themselves with the American Anarchist Federation, as had Group Arbeiter Fraint of Montreal, Group Freiheit of Patterson, New Jersey, and individuals from Atlantic City, New Jersey.

In March 1908 the American Anarchist Federation held a mass meeting for the unemployed (also commemorating the Paris Commune) and participated in the May Day demonstration and conference organized by various labor groups, held in Union Square, New York.

Edelstadt Group The Edelstadt Group was a Chicago anarchist organization inspired by Yiddish anarchist poet David Edelstadt (1866–1892), founded by his brother, Abe Edelstadt, and organized by Miriam Yamplosky and William Nathanson. Its secretary, Harry Goldstein, was arrested in 1908 in connection with the shooting of Chicago Police Chief George Shippy. Documents confirm he was a government police spy. In 1908, when twenty-five anarchists, representing three groups, formed the International Federation of Chicago, they met at the Edelstadt club rooms in Chicago.

Free Speech League The Free Speech League, formed in 1902, had roots in the liberal and freethought movements of the late nineteenth century, particularly the National Defense Association, a radical splinter group of the National Liberal League, established in 1878 to fight the Comstock Acts of 1873 and 1876 and defend those "unjustly assailed by the enemies of free speech and free press."

Following the 1901 McKinley assassination, widespread fears of violence led to the quick passage of anti-anarchist legislation and a resurgence of the use of the Comstock Act to harass anarchists through their publications, especially targeting the paper *Discontent*. On 24 September 1901, C. L. Govan, James W. Adams, J. B. Larkin, and G. Morong were arrested under the Comstock Act for an article by Rachel Campbell, "Prodigal Daughter," first published in the late 1890s, which addressed the "sex question," and argued that legal marriage is the cause of prostitution. James F. Morton, Jr., published a formal protest in *Discontent* and *Lucifer*. A defense committee for the *Discontent* publishers formed, of which Morton was secretary, taking on the issue of freedom of the press and focusing their efforts on the *Discontent* case. The 2 January 1902 issue of *Free Society* reprinted the protest letter from the defense committee, signed by Edward Chamberlain, E. B. Foote, Jr., E. C. Walker, and J. William Lloyd, among others. Calls for organized protests spread to the pages of the *Demonstrator* (the successor to the suppressed *Discontent*), to *Lucifer* (where an editorial by Moses Harman vigorously called for the formation of a group to fight the anti-anarchist laws), and to a freethought paper, *The New Age,* which united in the battle against anti-anarchist legislation and in defense of freedom of the press and of the mails.

On 1 May 1902, the Free Speech League was formed at a meeting of the Manhattan Liberal Club. Edward Chamberlain and E. B. Foote, Jr., prominent members of the Manhattan Liberal Club, and previously president and secretary respectively of the National Defense Association, assumed the role of president and treasurer of the newly formed League. Arthur Pleydell, a prominent single-taxer, served as the League's secretary, along with several well-known anarchists on the executive committee, including E. C. Walker, Benjamin Tucker, and J. A. Maryson. The League's first event was a dinner honoring the release of Ida Craddock, who was imprisoned for mailing her instructional sex booklet, *The Wedding Night,* deemed obscene under the Comstock Act. Craddock, who was soon re-arrested, committed suicide in 1903 because of Anthony Comstock's relentless persecution against her.

The year 1903 also marked the first formal alliance between the Free Speech League and EG, mobilized by the 23 October arrest of English anarchist John Turner. Turner was arrested on grounds that he had violated the new alien immigration act passed by Congress in March of that year, excluding the entrance of alien anarchists into the country. EG, under the auspices of the Free Speech League, temporarily renamed the Turner Defense Committee, collected money and organized meetings to protect Turner's rights, and limit the effect of the law on others. Members of the Turner Defense Committee of the Free Speech League included Benjamin Tucker, Joseph Barondess, George MacDonald, E. C. Walker, Moses Oppenheimer, H. Gaylord Wilshire, W. F. Doll, J. A. Maryson, David Rousseau, Alexander Jonas, Herman Schlüter, Charles Oberwager, William Graven, Algernon Lee, and Peter E. Burrowes. Although in the end Turner left the country, the episode initiated a partnership between EG and the League that continued into the next decade.

Around 1905, attorney Theodore Schroeder became the Free Speech League's secretary and driving force, devoting himself to developing legal and political arguments for unrestricted speech, and writing articles, pamphlets, and books documenting the suppression of free speech. To operate the League and finance Schroeder's full-time work, E. B. Foote, Jr., devoted a fund, first created in his father's will, to protect free speech. Schroeder resisted tying the League to any political position, and cautioned Leonard D. Abbott, the League's new president and a friend of EG as well as a participant in anarchist activities in New York, against political affinities. Other new members including Lincoln Steffens and Gilbert Roe were also close to EG and her circle. Schroeder focused his energies on legal analysis and the writing of briefs, rarely entering the courtroom; Roe acted as the League's trial attorney. For the next decade, the League provided legal and financial support to political activists, sex radicals, and a variety of freethinkers.

The League was critical to EG's ability to reach large audiences, especially as she traveled across the country, and it responded quickly to repressive city and state government attempts to stop her from speaking. In 1909 alone, so many of her lectures were blocked, eleven in the month of May, that a special committee of the League—the 1909 Free Speech Committee—was organized by prominent liberals, socialists and anarchists, united in their devotion to securing EG's rights. Alden Freeman, a member of the Free Speech Committee, published the pamphlet *The Fight for Free Speech: A Supplement to Law Breaking by the Police* (East Orange, N.J.: East Orange Record Press, 1909). The pamphlet documented police suppression, including an incident in East Orange in which Freeman provided the private space for EG's lecture after the city had barred her. The pamphlet also included the letter of protest signed by over seventy Free Speech Committee members. Regional free speech leagues affiliated and supported by the New York organization emerged across the country as the need arose, including one in San Francisco in 1909 formed just after the suppression of EG's meetings in the city.

The League sponsored meetings and lectures, organized free speech legal defense, and, under Schroeder's direction, published and circulated educational and political literature on free speech. EG, appreciative of the work of, and closely associated with the Free Speech League, often contributed the proceeds of her lectures to the League, solicited donations through *Mother Earth*, and worked to raise public awareness of the critical importance of the Free Speech League.

See Selected Bibliography for a list of the publications of the Free Speech League during this period.

Industrial Workers of the World (IWW) The Industrial Workers of the World was formed in 1905, based on the principles outlined in the Industrial Union Manifesto, written at the Chicago Conference of Industrial Unionists on 2 January 1905. The manifesto emphasized the role of craft unions in segregating workers from each other and was widely circulated among workers and unions following the conference; all those in agreement with the outlined principles were invited to a convention in Chicago on 27 June 1905 to form an organization based upon those principles. The conference was attended by two hundred delegates, representing various organizations including the Western Federation of Miners, American Labor Union, and the Socialist Trade and Labor Alliance. In spite of Samuel Gompers's denouncement of the conference and the prospective industrial union, representatives from several chapters of the American Federation of Labor, as well as Lee Grant, a representative sent by Gompers to make personal confidential reports about the conference, attended. Also present at the founding meeting of the IWW were Eugene V. Debs, William D. Haywood, Lucy Parsons, William Trautmann, Father Thomas Hagerty, Daniel De Leon, Joseph Peukert, Jay Fox, and Mary Harris Jones (known as "Mother Jones"). In his opening words to the convention, William D.

Haywood stated, "We are here to confederate the workers of this country into a working class movement that shall have at its purpose the emancipation of the working class from the slave bondage of capitalism." A primary point of unity among the parties at the conference was a general criticism of the inadequacy of the AFL and of the importance of a union that emphasized the class struggle.

During its initial years, the IWW worked both to develop its own membership as well as to propagandize for industrial unionism. Whereas the AFL had excluded, by design or default, many workers from its ranks, including women, new immigrants, migrant workers, and workers without specialized skills, the IWW specifically sought to include these workers.

The initial official publication of the IWW was *The Industrial Union Bulletin*, first published in 1906, which was followed by the *Industrial Union Bulletin*. Later publications included *Solidarity* and the *Industrial Worker*, both founded in 1909. Though not an official organization publication, Lucy Parsons's Chicago-based paper *The Liberator* was a strong supporter of the IWW and represented the more anarchistic side of the IWW.

The early years of the IWW were hampered by factionalism and disagreements about the best approach to reach the goals of industrial labor, namely the issue of political action. Though it was agreed at the founding convention that the IWW would use political, as well as economic, means to accomplish its goals, the issue caused continual disagreement. The IWW's political factionalism was criticized in the "Observations and Comments" section of the October 1907 issue of *Mother Earth*. While lauding the goals and intentions of the IWW, *Mother Earth* expressed dismay that the group seemed too mired in politics and factionalism to accomplish its goals. In 1908 the faction in favor of political action, affiliated with Daniel De Leon, was expelled from the IWW and the political action clause was removed from the organization's preamble.

In 1906, shortly after the IWW was founded, the group was involved in the campaign to defend three labor leaders, one of whom was a key IWW organizer, falsely implicated in the murder of Idaho's former governor Frank Steunenberg. The main organizers of the Western Federation of Miners, William D. Haywood, Charles Moyer, and George Pettibone, were indicted for conspiracy to commit murder; Haywood's trial began on 4 June 1907 in Boise, Idaho, with Clarence Darrow as defense counsel.

IWW members frequently made public orations on street corner soapboxes as a propaganda tactic, and when the right to make such speeches began to be threatened, free speech fights ensued in many cities. The initial free speech fights occurred in Missoula, Montana, in 1909, and Spokane, Washington, in 1909–1910. When IWW members would start to speak, they were quickly arrested by the police. The tactic devised to respond to the continual arrest of IWW speakers was to cause the arrest of even more members, flood the jails, and demand individual jury trials for each arrested IWW member, causing a backlog of legal work and a tedious process for authorities. The IWW free speech fights continued in other cities in the years to follow.

International Brotherhood Welfare Association   The International Brotherhood Welfare Association (IBWA) was primarily an educational association that sought to establish social bonds and solidarity for transient workers. James Eads How, the "millionaire hobo" and socialist who denounced his inherited wealth and became a hobo, was the founder of the International Brotherhood Welfare Association in 1905 and also organized "Hobo Colleges," which he described as the migratory workers' universities. Lectures at Hobo colleges were given on a variety of subjects from philosophy and industrial law to politics and health, and were designed to educate hobos in the rudiments of economics, social sciences, and public speaking. The colleges also served as gathering place and cultural center, and were a political pressure group to reform vagrancy laws, improve municipal lodging facilities, demand pay for work done in jail, and improve the conditions for the itinerant laborer. In May 1913 the IBWA issued *The Hoboes Jungle Scout* (1913–1915), later renamed the *Hobo News* (1915–1923), a regular journal on issues relating to the hobo community.

By 1919 the association, headquartered in Cincinnati, had local branches and colleges in fifteen cities. After visiting How and the St. Louis Hobo College in 1907, BR opened a Chicago branch of the International Brotherhood Welfare Association and founded the Chicago Hobo College in 1907, the largest of the locals. BR led a "march of the unemployed" on 23 January 1908, during which he was clubbed and arrested by Chicago police. In March 1908, BR offered EG the Chicago Hobo College hall for her lectures after she had difficulty obtaining a venue in the city. BR and the IBWA also sponsored a meeting on the unemployed at New York's Cooper Union on Labor Day 1908, where he delivered a speech prepared by EG, with AB in the audience. Following BR's admission that EG had prepared the speech, a small riot ensued between anarchists and "anti-anarchists," and both AB and Becky Edelsohn were arrested by "anarchist watchdog" detectives. On 31 March 1908, BR was denounced by fifty men who had helped him found the IBWA in Chicago, on grounds that he had abandoned their cause in favor of anarchism and EG.

Liberal Clubs The Liberal movement, organized on the principles of freethought, was devoted primarily to countering and protesting the dominant role of organized religion in state affairs. The national movement was organized at the first Centennial Congress of Liberals, in Philadelphia on 4 July 1876, ratifying a constitution that promoted the adoption of a religious freedom amendment to the U.S. Constitution, along with a platform that included advocacy of public control of railroads, cessation of the sale or grant of public land, and legislation championing the right of workers to organize. Attempts to form a national party, however, were short-lived, due to internal disagreement about its proposed platform and overall doubts about the practicality of a Liberal Party. The constitution called for the formation of "local auxiliary chapters of the National Liberal League," which led to the formation of many smaller organizations, including the Liberal Alliance, the Women's National Liberal Union, and many local Liberal leagues, unified by a common adherence to the principles outlined in the group's national constitution and to a "liberal ideology." In 1884, the National Liberal League split into two factions, divided on whether to sustain and further its involvement in a variety of social and political initiatives or to limit itself strictly to work toward the secularization of the state. Following this split, one faction of the Liberal League renamed itself the American Secular Union, with its own constitution and organizational structure, leaving those who favored a broader social agenda to work through regional and local Liberal clubs.

The New York Liberal Club, also known as the Manhattan Liberal Club, was founded in 1869 as an open forum on politics. The club sold radical literature including *Lucifer* and *Mother Earth*. Founding members included the Rev. Stickney Grant, socialist Charles Edward Russell, and muck-raker Lincoln Steffens. For the club's twenty-fifth anniversary celebration, the New York group published *The Manhattan Liberal Club: Its Methods, Objects and Philosophy* by E. B. Foote, Jr. and Thaddeus Wakeman, an organizational history commissioned in 1884 by the *Truth Seeker*, a leading freethought paper and supporter of the Manhattan Liberal Club. In *LML,* EG recalls attending weekly meetings of the Manhattan Liberal Club from 1894 on, and despite the controversy in the club about her after the McKinley assassination, in 1903 she was invited to discuss the arguments in opposition to the bill legalizing the exclusion and deportation of alien anarchists. In 1902 the Manhattan Liberal Club was instrumental in the formation of the Free Speech League, and many of its members had previously been active in the National Defense Association.

Liberal clubs often provided EG a sheltered venue for her lectures. In Philadelphia, the membership of the Ladies' Liberal League and the Friendship Liberal League included anarchists. The Friendship Liberal League, a freethought organization that sponsored lectures primarily on secularism, had among its members Voltairine de Cleyre, James B. Elliott, and others who successfully lobbied the group for discussion of a broad range of topics, including anarchism. The Ladies' Liberal League was an 1892 offshoot of the Friendship Liberal League of Philadelphia. Under the guidance of Voltairine de Cleyre and Natasha Notkin, it quickly outgrew its origins as a women's auxiliary and sponsored lectures on a wide variety of subjects, becoming an important forum for radical and feminist activity in Philadelphia. Anarchists, including Charles Mowbray, John Turner, Harry Kelly, and EG, spoke before the two groups during the late 1890s, and EG spoke before the groups again in 1901.

In New York, among the active liberal organizations was the Harlem Liberal Alliance, where both EG and Voltairine de Cleyre lectured. The Brooklyn Philosophical Association and the Sunrise Club, founded by E. C. Walker, also hosted EG's lectures.

Mexican Liberal Party (Partido Liberal Mexicano, PLM) In 1905 Ricardo Flores Magón and a small group of Mexican exiles in St. Louis announced the formation of the Junta Organizadora del Partido Liberal Mexicano (Organizing Board of the Mexican Liberal Party) to work toward the overthrow of the regime of Mexican president Porfirio Díaz. Its board consisted of Ricardo Flores Magón as president; Juan Sarabia as vice-president; Antonio I. Villarreal as secretary; Enrique Flores Magón as treasurer; and Librado Rivera, Manuel Sarabia, and Rosalío Bustamante as committee members. The newspaper *Regeneración* became the PLM's official organ. Under constant harassment from Mexican authorities, *Regeneración* moved its operation to San Antonio, Texas, and published its first American issue on 5 November 1904, before moving again in February 1905 to St. Louis.

On 1 July 1906, the PLM's manifesto was published in *Regeneración*. advocating, among other things, the limitation of the term of the president to four years with no re-election, the nationalization of Church lands, the return of land to indigenous tribes, and labor reforms including the eight-hour work day and a minimum wage. The manifesto was translated and printed in the February 1908 *Mother Earth*.

The PLM organized local clubs and military units, with which they planned two failed uprisings in 1906 and 1908. By 1907 there were approximately 44 clandestine guerilla units and over 350 PLM clubs across Mexico. By 1908 the junta had allied itself rather secretly to anarchist communism, although Ricardo Flores Magón argued strongly for the organization's public identification with the phrase "liberal" to attract wider support for its program.

Although the political structure of the PLM centered around the junta, the local clubs and members provided the financial and military support for PLM activities. Local clubs and members sometimes corresponded directly with the junta, but there were also *militantes medios* who helped to co-ordinate activities. These members were important in maintaining communication between the junta and the clubs; they included Tomás and Manuel Sarabia, Antonio de P. Arjuo, and Aaron Lopez Manzano. The PLM military structure was based upon the guerilla unit, which elected their *jefe* and *subjefe*, the two of whom communicated with and were directed by the *delegados* of each of the five zones into which the PLM had divided Mexico. The *delegados* were appointed and directed by the junta.

Throughout the first decade of the twentieth century, the PLM junta was subject to increasing U.S. harassment, including arbitrary detention. Ricardo Flores Magón, Villarreal, and Rivera were arrested without warrant in Los Angeles in 1907 by agents from the Furlong Detective Agency that had been hired by Enrique Creel, the Mexican ambassador to the United States. Extradited to Tombstone, Arizona Territory, they were charged with violation of the neutrality law. In response, labor organizations rallied behind the PLM, and in 1908 the Western Federation of Miners voted to offer financial support. In addition, the United Mine Workers (at the urging of Mother Jones) along with the American Federation of Labor passed supportive resolutions culminating in the symbolic public gesture of Samuel Gompers presenting a letter to President Roosevelt on behalf of the imprisoned men. Eugene V. Debs also corresponded with Ricardo Flores Magón and championed the PLM's cause. *Mother Earth* reported regularly on their case and devoted considerable space to Mexican affairs, as did the socialist paper *Appeal to Reason*. Despite this support, Ricardo Flores Magón, Villarreal, and Rivera were found guilty, sentenced to eighteen months imprisonment, and not released until August 1910.

Russian Socialist Revolutionary Party (PSR) The Socialist Revolutionary Party was formed in the winter of 1901–1902 from a unification of a number of existing groups. The PSR drew its ideological inspiration from Russian populism, a socialist movement that emerged in the last half of the nineteenth century, was distinguised by an emphasis on the peasantry and agrarian issues, and was the predominant form of Russian socialist thought before the rise of Marxism. Prominent members of the party included Catherine Breshkovskaya, Victor Mikhailovich Chernov, Grigorii Andreevich Gershuni, and Mikhail Rafailovich Gots. The party's main periodicals were *Revolutsionnaya Rossiya* (Revolutionary Russia) edited by Chernov and Gots, and *Vestnik Russkoi Revoliutsii* (Messenger of the Russian Revolution) edited by N. S. Rusanov and I. A. Rubanovich; both papers were actually founded prior to the organization of the PSR. The program of the party was not adopted until the party's first congress at the end of 1905. The 1905 congress adopted a draft of the party program submitted by Chernov, the party's most prominent theorist. Along with various constitutional reforms, the focus of the program was the socialization of agricultural land. The PSR was the largest socialist political party in Russia until after the February 1917 Russian Revolution.

In Russia at this time political parties were illegal, and party activity, organized by local groups, chiefly centered around the production of propaganda and terrorism. In 1902 the "Battle Organization of the PSR" was organized and carried out the assassination of D. S. Sipiagin, minister of the interior. Leaders of the combat organization included Gershuni, Boris Viktorovich Savinkov, and Evno Fishelevich Azef, who in 1908 was discovered to be a double agent for the tsarist police. The party's combat organization was very active in carrying out assassinations, including in July 1904 the minister of the interior V. K. von Plehve and in February 1905 Grand Prince Sergei Aleksandorovich. The assassinations were intended to agitate the population, defend the party's interests, and destabilize the government.

The PSR was active in the 1905 revolution in both the city and countryside and was active in the Moscow and St. Petersburg Soviets. The PSR boycotted the 1906 Duma, with 34 (of 448) members of the Duma identifying themselves as Socialist Revolutionaries. After the dispersal of the first Duma, the PSR called off its boycott and participated in the second Duma, to which 37 Socialist

Revolutionaries were elected (of 518), which was again dispersed. The PSR resumed its boycott for the third and fourth Dumas (1907–1917).

The PSR produced two significant splinter groups: the Popular Socialists (or legal populists), and the Union of Maximalist Socialist Revolutionaries. The Popular Socialists rejected revolution, supported state ownership of the land, and participated in the Duma of 1906, which the PSR boycotted. The Maximalists supported the "maximal" program of the party: immediate revolution, the socialization of agricultural land and factories, decentralization, attacks on landowners, anti-parliamentarism, robbery, and economic terrorism. The tactics and beliefs of the Maximalists led the group to be confused with anarchists, though the group strictly denied anarchist affiliation.

The PSR was supported in America by people of diverse political affiliations, including anarchists and socialists. In New York, Russian immigrants, mainly Jews, organized a U.S. branch of the PRS. In addition, prominent Americans, through the American Society of the Friends of Russian Freedom (see above), extended their support to members of the party. In 1904 a number of prominent Russian Social Revolutionaries visited America, including Catherine Breshkovskaya, Chaim Zhitlowsky, and two others known only as Nicolaev and Rosenbaum. Breshkovskaya, who met with and for some time stayed with EG in New York, was particularly well received by the public. Breshkovskaya's speaking tour helped raise nearly $10,000 for the PSR, some of which, with the help of EG, was turned over to Eric B. Morton, who used the money to purchase arms and smuggle them into Russia.

EG joined the Directing Committee of the New York branch of the PSR, although she did not agree with all of its programs and left the group in 1905 (see EG to Marie Goldsmith, 14 May 1905, *EGP* reel 2, and EG to Catherine Breshkovskaya, 14 May 1905, *EGP* reel 2). AB's uncle, Mark Andreyevich Natanson, was also a member of the PSR.

Single Tax Single-tax doctrine is based on the idea that private land ownership is the fundamental source of social and economic injustice, and also on a critique of the fact that the majority of wealth accrued to landlords rather than those considered the productive classes, workers and capitalists. Single-taxers advocated eliminating the existing system of taxation in favor of a "single tax" on land intended to end land speculation, create common land ownership and abolish private property. Lifting the weight of taxation on productive industry would also increase wages, according to single-taxers. The movement achieved limited legislative success, although its theories retained their popularity for decades.

The single-tax movement emerged under the leadership of Henry George and Father McGlynn (who was expelled from the Catholic Church for his support of single tax). Single-tax theory had taken root before George, but he specifically proposed single tax as a solution to the land question and popularized the theory in two books, *Our Land and Land Policy* (San Francisco: White and Bauer, 1871) and his landmark *Progress and Poverty* (San Francisco: W. M. Hilton, 1879). Bolton Hall, G. Frank Stephens, A. C. Pleydell, and George Seldes linked the theories underlying the single tax to those of anarchism. Supporters included mostly middle-class intellectuals and some Populists and wealthy individuals.

Among the first single-tax organizations were the San Francisco Single Tax Club—whose members included George and James G. Maguire—and the Free Soil Society, founded in New York in 1883, to which George also belonged. Single-tax organizations would prove most successful on the local level; despite persistent efforts, there were not many national organizations, and most single-taxers often preferred to work through local groups or through organizations not solely focused on single-tax issues. Among the most influential national organizations were the Single Tax League of the U.S. (founded 1890) and the American Single Tax League (1907). Among the local groups were George's Land Reform League of California (1878), the Free Soil Society (1883), various Land and Labor clubs and Henry George clubs (1880s), Anti-Poverty societies (late 1880s), and the Henry George Lecture Association (1899). Single-tax clubs blossomed nationwide between 1888 and 1889, beginning with the Manhattan Single Tax Club founded by Bolton Hall, Thomas Shearman, and Lawson Purdy; and the Chicago Single Tax Club founded by journalist Warren Worth Bailey. Among the 131 single-tax clubs formed by 1889, strongholds were in New York, Ohio, Pennsylvania, New Jersey, Indiana, California, Colorado, Illinois, Texas, and Iowa. Many of these, notably those in Philadelphia, Detroit, and Houston, arranged meetings for EG.

The first and largest single-tax colony, in Fairhope, Alabama, was first inhabited by colonists in 1894–1895 and incorporated as a municipality in 1908. It lasted until 1954. Fairhope residents attempted to shift the incidence of some state and local taxes from labor and capital to land, but were unable to fully implement the single-tax doctrine. Another colony, in Arden in Delaware, was founded in 1900 by the sculptor G. Frank Stephens and the architect Will Price. The novelist Upton Sinclair and the anarchists George Brown and Mary Hansen were Arden residents.

Single-tax newspapers included the *Single Tax Review*, the *Courier* (Fairhope), *Justice* (Philadelphia and Wilmington), and George's *The Standard* (New York).

Henry George ran unsuccessfully in the New York City mayoral campaigns in 1886 (aided by the Central Labor Union) and in 1897. During his 1888 presidential campaign, George wrote an editorial for the *Standard* in which he retracted his support for the Haymarket men, calling the court's decision to execute them just. Critics suspected that the shift was politically motivated and many, including EG and Benjamin Tucker, denounced George as a traitor.

Single-tax organizations formed in Europe in this period as well, including the Land Restoration Society in Scotland, the Land Values League in England, and the Land Reform League in Germany.

Social Science Clubs "Social Science" was a generic term used to describe any study of social issues. From around the beginning of the twentieth century, the term would be used by anarchists to reinterpret and study social issues from an anarchist perspective. Many early Social Science clubs had strong anarchist ties and influences without strictly defining themselves as anarchist clubs, and all seemed dedicated to open and free discussion. A Social Science club in New York was active from 1898, offering weekly free lectures and discussions, involving many American-born anarchists. Also in 1898 a weekly Social Science club was started in San Francisco for "free discussion on all questions." Advertisements for both clubs' meetings were placed in *Free Society*. In 1900, *Free Society* also advertised a weekly Social Science club in Chicago. An anarchist reading group called the Social Science Club began in Philadelphia in 1901, started by Voltairine de Cleyre, and modeled after a reading and study group that she and Dyer D. Lum had belonged to in the early 1890s. In an announcement in *Free Society* in 1900 she wrote, "Let us take up the work as quiet students, not as disputatious wrangles . . . let us saturate ourselves with the facts concerning anarchistic tendencies in society; then we may hope to convert others" (*Free Society*, 30 September 1900). Its first members, including George Brown, Mary Hansen, Pearle McLeod, and Natasha Notkin, met every Sunday evening. The club sponsored lectures and published Mary Hansen's *A Catechism of Anarchy* (1902). Hansen suggested in *Free Society* that although she had written the first draft, the essay was in fact a group effort of the Social Science Club; she explained that the club was not named as author because its members were not uniformly self-identified anarchists. The New York club also published Voltairine de Cleyre's *Crime and Punishment* (1903) as well as the first English edition of Peter's Kropotkin's *Modern Science and Anarchism* (1903), which was translated by David A. Modell, a doctor, Philadelphia anarchist, and member of the Philadelphia Social Science Club.

In December 1901, the New York Social Science Club sponsored a series of lectures, including "Anarchism and Communism" by Rudolph Grossmann, "Discipline" by Elizabeth Ferm, and "Anarchists and Anarchism: Their Principles and their Tactics" by Alex Horr. The Boston Social Science Club lecturers included Adeline Champney, whose "The Woman Question" was later published as a pamphlet (New York: Comrade Co-Operative Press, 1903). The Chicago Social Science League, whose members, including William Nathanson, Miriam Yamplosky, Edith Adams, and Jake Livshis and Annie Livshis, published Jay Fox's *Trade Unionism and Anarchism* (Chicago: Social Science Press, 1908). In Los Angeles Claude Riddle was chair of a Social Science league. Alex Horr and Cassius Cook were members of a San Francisco Social Science league, which organized a series of eight lectures and two debates in San Francisco for EG beginning 13 January 1909, and then took an active part organizing the Free Speech League set up to fight the arrest and suppression of EG and Ben Reitman in San Francisco.

The many local Social Science clubs linked the phrase "social science" with anarchism, broadening the definitions for a more inclusive agenda. By 1906 the masthead of *Mother Earth* read "Monthly Magazine Devoted to Social Science and Literature," and the masthead of *Revolt* (1915–1916), a Chicago Swedish-anarchist paper edited by Theodore Johnson, read "A Monthly Swedish Journal Devoted to Social Science and Revolutionary Thought."

SELECTED BIBLIOGRAPHY

Abad de Santillán, Diego. *Historia de la revolucion mexicana*. Mexico City: Frente de Afirmacion Hispanista, 1992.

Adamic, Louis. *Dynamite: The Story of Class Violence in America*. Gloucester, Mass: Peter Smith, 1960.

Addams, Jane. *Twenty Years of Hull House with Autobiographical Notes*. New York: Macmillan, 1962.

———. *Jane Addams Papers*. Ed. Mary Lynn McCree Bryan and Peter Clark. Ann Arbor, Mich.: University Microfilms International, 1985.

American Labor Press Directory. New York: Rand School of Social Science, 1925.

Anderson, Carlotta R. *All-American Anarchist: Joseph A. Labadie and the Labor Movement*. Detroit: Wayne State University Press, 1998.

Anderson, Nels. *On Hobos and Homelessness*. Chicago and London: University of Chicago Press, 1998.

Arbdt, Karl J. R., and May E. Olson. *German-American Newspapers and Periodicals, 1732–1955: History and Bibliography*. 2nd rev. ed. New York: Johnson Reprint, 1965.

Archer, William. *The Life, Trial, and Death of Francisco Ferrer*. London: Chapman and Hall, 1911.

Ashbaugh, Carolyn. *Lucy Parsons: American Revolutionary*. Chicago: Charles H. Kerr, 1976.

Avrich, Paul. *The Russian Anarchists*. Princeton: Princeton University Press, 1967. Reprint, New York: W. W. Norton, 1978.

———. *An American Anarchist: The Life of Voltairine de Cleyre*. Princeton: Princeton University Press, 1978.

———. *The Modern School Movement: Anarchism and Education in the United States*. Princeton: Princeton University Press, 1980.

———. *The Haymarket Tragedy*. Princeton: Princeton University Press, 1984.

———. *Anarchist Portraits*. Princeton: Princeton University Press, 1988.

———. *Sacco and Vanzetti: The Anarchist Background*. Princeton: Princeton University Press, 1991.

———. *Anarchist Voices: An Oral History of Anarchism in America*. Princeton: Princeton University Press, 1995.

Bakunin, Michael. *Statism and Anarchy*. Ed. and trans. Marshall S. Shatz. Cambridge: Cambridge University Press, 1990.

Berkman, Alexander. *Prison Memoirs of an Anarchist*. New York: Mother Earth Publishing Association, 1912. Reprint, New York: Schocken Books, 1970.

Bettini, Leonardo. *Bibliographia dell' anarchismo. Vol. 1: Periodice e numeri unici anarchici in linguq italiana*. 2 parts. Florence: CP Editrice, 1972.

Biagini, Furio. *Nati Altrove: Il movimento anarchico ebraico tra Mosca e New York*. Pisa: Biblioteca Franco Serantini, 1998.

Blackwell, Alice Stone, ed. *The Little Grandmother of the Russian Revolution: Reminiscences and Letters of Catherine Breshkovsky*. Boston: Little, Brown, 1917.

Blatt, Martin Henry. *Free Love and Anarchism: The Biography of Ezra Heywood*. Urbana: University of Illinois Press, 1989.

Bloomfield, Maxwell H. *Alarms and Diversions: The American Mind Through American Magazines, 1900–1914*. The Hague, Paris: Mouton, 1967.

Bookchin, Murray. *The Spanish Anarchists*. San Francisco: AK Press, 1998.

Brissenden, Paul. *The IWW: A Study of American Syndicalism*. New York: Russell & Russell, 1957.

Brommel, Bernard J. *Eugene V. Debs: Spokesman for Labor and Socialism*. Chicago: Charles H. Kerr, 1978.

Brown, Marshall G., and Gordon Stein. *Freethought in the United States: A Descriptive Bibliography*. Westport, Conn.: Greenwood Press, 1978.

Bruns, Roger. *The Damndest Radical*. Urbana: University of Illinois Press, 1987.

Buhle, Mari Jo. *Women and American Socialism, 1870–1920*. Urbana: University of Illinois Press, 1983.

Cahm, Caroline. *Kropotkin and the Rise of Revolutionary Anarchism, 1872–1886*. Cambridge: Cambridge University Press, 1989.

Camp, Helen C. *Iron in Her Soul: Elizabeth Gurley Flynn and the American Left*. Pullman: Washington State University Press, 1995.

Carey, George W. "La Questione Sociale, An Anarchist Newspaper in Paterson, N.J. (1895–1908)." In *Italian Americans: New Perspectives in Italian Immigration and Ethnicity*, ed. Lydio F. Tomasi. New York: Center for Migration Studies, 1985.

Carpenter, Edward. *My Days and Dreams*. London: George Allen and Unwin, 1916.

Carpenter, Mecca Reitman. *No Regrets: Dr. Ben Reitman and The Women Who Loved Him*. Lexington: Southside Press, 1999.

Cohen, Naomi W. *A Dual Heritage: The Public Career of Oscar S. Straus*. Philadelphia: Jewish Publication Society of America, 1969.

Conlin, Joseph R., ed. *The American Radical Press, 1880–1960*. Westport, Conn.: Greenwood Press, 1974.

Cottrell, Robert C. *Robert Nash Baldwin and the American Civil Liberties Union*. New York: Columbia University Press, 2000.

Cowan, Geoffrey. *The People v. Clarence Darrow*. New York: Times Books, 1993.

Daniels, Roger. *Not Like Us*. Chicago: Ivan R. Dee, 1997.

Davis, Sally, and Betty Baldwin. *Denver Dwellings and Descendants*. Denver: Sage Books, 1963.

De Cleyre, Voltairine. *Selected Works of Voltairine de Cleyre*. Ed. Alexander Berkman. New York: Mother Earth Publishing Association, 1914.

Debs, Eugene. *The Letters of Eugene V. Debs*. Ed. J. Robert Constantine. 3 vols. Urbana: University of Illinois Press, 1990.

Deutrich, Mabel E. *Struggle for Supremacy: The Career of General Fred C. Ainsworth*. Washington, D.C.: Public Affairs Press, 1962.

Drinnon, Richard. *Rebel in Paradise: A Biography of Emma Goldman*. Chicago: University of Chicago Press, 1961.

Drinnon, Richard, and Anna Drinnon, eds. *Nowhere at Home: Letters from Exile of Emma Goldman and Alexander Berkman.* New York: Schocken Books, 1975.

Dubofsky, Melvyn. *We Shall Be All: A History of the Industrial Workers of the World.* New York: Quadrangle/New York Times Book Company, 1969.

———. *"Big Bill" Haywood.* Manchester: Manchester University Press, 1987.

Duden, Arthur Power. *Joseph Fels and the Single Tax Movement.* Philadelphia: Temple University Press, 1971.

England, George Allan. *The Story of the Appeal.* Girard, Kans.: Appeal Publishing, 1915.

Falk, Candace. *Love, Anarchy, and Emma Goldman.* New York: Holt, Rinehart and Winston, 1984; rev. ed., New Brunswick, N.J.: Rutgers University Press, 1999.

Fink, Gary M., ed. *Biographical Dictionary of American Labor.* Westport, Conn.: Greenwood Press, 1984.

Fishman, William J. *Jewish Radicals: From Czarist Stetl to London Ghetto.* New York: Pantheon Books, 1974.

Foner, Philip. *History of the Labor Movement in the United States. Vol. 3: The Policies and Practices of the American Federation of Labor, 1900–1909.* New York: International Publishers, 1973.

———. *History of the Labor Movement in the United States. Vol. 4: The Industrial Workers of the World, 1905–1917.* New York: International Publishers, 1973.

———. *My Fellow Workers and Friends: I.W.W. Free-Speech Fights as Told by Participants.* Westport, Conn.: Greenwood Press, 1981.

Frost, Richard H. *The Mooney Case.* Stanford: Stanford University Press, 1968.

Gallagher, Dorothy. *All the Right Enemies.* New York: Penguin Books, 1989.

Galsworthy, John. *Justice.* New York: Charles Scribner and Sons, 1920.

Geifman, Anna. *Thou Shalt Kill: Revolutionary Terrorism in Russia, 1894–1917.* Princeton: Princeton University Press, 1993.

Glenn, Susan A. *Daughters of the Shtetl: Life and Labor in the Immigrant Generation.* Ithaca: Cornell University Press, 1990.

Goldman, Emma. *Anarchism and Other Essays.* New York: Mother Earth Publishing Association, 1910; 2nd rev. ed., 1917. Reprint, with introduction by Richard Drinnon, New York: Dover Publications, 1969.

———. *Emma Goldman: A Guide to Her Life and Documentary Sources.* Ed. Candace Falk, Stephan Cole, et al. Alexandria, Va.: Chadwyck-Healey, 1995.

———. *Emma Goldman Papers: A Microfilm Edition.* Ed. Candace Falk, Ronald J. Zboray, et al. 69 reels. Alexandria, Va.: Chadwyck-Healey, 1991–1993.

———. *Living My Life.* 2 vols. New York: Knopf, 1931. Reprint, New York: Dover Publications, 1970.

———. *The Social Significance of Modern Drama.* Boston: Richard G. Badger, 1914.

Goldstein, Robert J. "The Anarchist Scare of 1908, a Sign of Tensions in the Progressive Years." *American Studies* 15, no. 2 (Fall 1974).

Gompers, Samuel. *The Samuel Gompers Papers.* Ed. Stuart B. Kaufman, Peter J. Albert, Grace Palladino et al. 8 vols. Urbana: University of Illinois Press, 1986–2000.

Gordon, Linda. *Woman's Body, Woman's Right: A Social History of Birth Control in America.* New York: Penguin Books, 1974.

Graham, John, ed. *Yours for the Revolution: The Appeal to Reason, 1895–1922.* Lincoln: University of Nebraska Press, 1990.

Guérin, Daniel. *No Gods No Masters: Books One and Two.* Trans. Paul Sharkey. San Francisco: AK Press, 1998.

Hapgood, Hutchins. *A Victorian in the Modern World.* New York: Harcourt, Brace, 1939.

Harrison, Royden, Gillian B. Woolven, and Robert Duncan. *The Warwick Guide to British Labour Periodicals, 1790–1970.* Atlantic Highlands, N.J., and Hassocks, Sussex: Humanities Press and Harvester Press, 1977.

Hildermeir, Manfred. *The Russian Socialist Revolutionary Party Before the First World War.* New York: St. Martin's Press, 2000.

Holtzman, Filia. "A Mission that Failed: Gor'kij in America." *The Slavic and East European Journal* 6 (Fall 1962): 227–235.

Hoffman, Frederick J., Charles Allen, and Carolyn F. Ulrich. *The Little Magazine: A History and a Bibliography.* Princeton: Princeton University Press, 1946.

Hong, Nathaniel. "Free Speech Without an 'If' or a 'But': The Defense of Free Expression in the Radical Periodicals of Home, Washington, 1897–1912." *American Journalism* 11, no. 2 (Spring 1994).

Hug, Heinz. *Peter Kropotkin (1842–1921): Bibliographie.* Grafenau: Edition Anares in Trotzdem-Verlag, 1994.

Hunsberger, Willard D. *Clarence Darrow: A Bibliography.* Metchuen, N.J.: Scarecrow Press, 1981.

Hunt, William R. *Body Love: The Amazing Career of Bernarr Macfadden.* Bowling Green, Ohio: Bowling Green State University Press, 1989.

———. *William J. Burns and the Detective Profession, 1880–1930.* Bowling Green, Ohio: Bowling Green State University Press, 1990.

Jones, Mary. *The Autobiography of Mother Jones.* 2nd ed. Chicago: Charles H. Kerr, 1972.

Kairys, David. "Freedom of Speech." In *The Politics of Law: A Progressive Critique,* 3rd ed. Ed. David Kairys. New York: Basic Books, 1998.

Kaun, Alexander. *Leonid Andreyev: A Critical Study.* New York: B. W. Huebsch, 1924.

Kautsky, Karl. *Karl Kautsky: Selected Political Writings.* Ed. and trans. Patrick Goode. London: Macmillan Press, 1983.

Kershaw, Alex. *Jack London: A Life.* New York: St. Martin's Press, 1997.

Kipling, Rudyard. *Rudyard Kipling's Verse.* Rev. ed. London: Hodder and Stoughton, 1933.

Kipnis, Ira. *The American Socialist Movement, 1897–1912.* Westport, Conn.: Greenwood Press, 1968.

Lambert, Gavin. *Nazimova: A Biography.* New York: Knopf, 1997.

Lane, Anne J. *The Brownsville Affair: National Crisis and Black Reaction.* Port Washington, N.Y.: National University Publications, Kennikat Press, 1971.

Lang, Lucy Robins. *Tomorrow Is Beautiful.* New York: Macmillan, 1948.

Ledbetter, Rosanna. *A History of the Malthusian League, 1877–1927.* Columbus: Ohio State University Press, 1976.

LeWarne, Charles Pierce. *Utopias on Puget Sound, 1885–1915.* Seattle: University of Washington Press, 1975.

Loughery, John. *John Sloan: Painter and Rebel.* New York: Henry Holt, 1995.

Lukas, J. Anthony. *Big Trouble.* New York: Simon & Schuster, 1997.

Macdonald, George E. *Fifty Years of Freethought: Story of The Truth Seeker from 1875.* 2 vols. New York: The Truth Seeker Company, 1929, 1931. Reprint, New York: Arno Press, 1972.

MacLachlan, Colin M. *Anarchism and the Mexican Revolution: The Political Trials of Ricardo Flores Magón in the United States.* Berkeley: University of California Press, 1991.

Madison, Charles A. *Jewish Publishing in America: The Impact of Jewish Writing on American Culture.* New York: Sanhedrin Press, 1976.

Maitron, Jean, ed. *1871–1914. De la Commune à la Grande Guerre.* Part 3, vols. 10–15 of *Dictionnaire biographique du mouvement ouvrier français.* Paris: Les Éditions Ouvrières, 1973–1977.

Marsh, Margaret S. *Anarchist Women, 1870–1920.* Philadelphia: Temple University Press, 1981.

Martin, James J. *Men Against the State.* DeKalb, Ill.: Adrian Allen Associates, 1953.

Melancon, Michael. *'Stormy Petrels': The Socialist Revolutionaries in Russia's Labor Organization, 1905–1914.* Pittsburgh: Center for Russian and East European Studies, University of Pittsburgh, 1988.

Miles, Dionne. *Something in Common: An IWW Bibliography.* Detroit: Wayne State University Press, 1986.

Miller, Martin A. *Kropotkin.* Chicago: University of Chicago Press, 1976.

Mitchell, Barbara. *The Practical Revolutionaries.* New York: Greenwood Press, 1987.

Moritz, Theresa, and Albert Moritz. *The World's Most Dangerous Woman: A New Biography of Emma Goldman.* Vancouver, Toronto: Subway Books, 2001.

Mott, Frank Luther. *A History of American Magazines. Vol. 5: Sketches of 21 Magazines, 1905–1930.* Cambridge, Mass.: Belknap Press of Harvard University Press, 1968.

Nettlau, Max. *A Short History of Anarchism.* Ed. Heiner M. Becker, trans. Ida Pilat Isca. London: Freedom Press, 1996.

Patsouras, Louis. *Jean Grave and the Anarchist Tradition in France.* Middletown, N.J.: Caslon, 1995.

Patten, John, ed. *Yiddish Anarchist Bibliography.* London: Kate Sharpley Library, 1998.

Perry, Lewis. *Radical Abolitionism: Anarchy and the Government of God in Antislavery Thought.* Ithaca: Cornell University Press, 1973.

Poole, David, ed. *Land and Liberty: Anarchist Influences in the Mexican Revolution.* Sanday, Orkney: Cienfuegos Press, 1977.

Poole, Ernest. "Maxim Gorki in New York." *Slavonic and East European Review* 22 (May 1944): 77–83.

Putnam, Samuel P. *400 Years of Freethought.* New York: The Truth Seeker Company, 1894.

Rabban, David M. *Free Speech in Its Forgotten Years.* New York: Cambridge University Press, 1997.

Rauchway, Eric. *Murdering McKinley.* New York: Hill and Wang, 2003.

Ringenbach, Paul T. *Tramps and Reformers, 1873–1916.* Westport, Conn.: Greenwood Press, 1973.

Rogoff, Harry. *An East Side Epic: The Life and Work of Meyer London.* New York: Vanguard Press, 1930.

Rosemont, Franklin. *Joe Hill.* Chicago: Charles H. Kerr, 2003.

Roth, Walter, and Joe Kraus. *An Accidental Anarchist.* San Francisco: Rudi Publishing, 1998.

Rowbotham, Sheila. *A Century of Women.* New York: Penguin Books, 1991.

Rowbotham, Sheila, and Jeffrey Weeks. *Socialism and the New Life: The Personal and Sexual Politics of Edward Carpenter and Havelock Ellis.* London: Pluto Press, 1977.

Sack, A. J. *The Birth of the Russian Democracy.* New York: Russian Information Bureau, 1918.

Salerno, Salvatore. *Red November, Black November: Culture and Community in the Industrial Workers of the World.* New York: State University of New York Press, 1989.

Salvatore, Nick. *Eugene V. Debs: Citizen and Socialist.* Urbana: University of Illinois Press, 1982.

Sanborn, Alvan F. *Paris and the Social Revolution.* Boston: Small, Maynard, 1905.

Sanger, Margaret. *The Papers of Margaret Sanger.* Ed. Ester Katz et. al. Columbia, S.C.: Model Editions Partnership, 1999. Electronic version, http://adh.csd.sc.edu/ms/ms-table.html.

Schroeder, Theodore. *Free Speech for Radicals.* New York: Free Speech League, 1916.

———. *Free Speech Bibliography.* New York: H. W. Wilson, 1922.

Sears, Hal D. *The Sex Radicals: Free Love in High Victorian America*. Lawrence: Regents Press of Kansas, 1977.

Sprading, Charles T., ed. *Liberty and the Great Libertarians*. Los Angeles: Golden Press for the author, 1913.

Thompson, Arthur W. "The Reception of Russian Revolutionary Leaders in America, 1904–1906." *American Quarterly* 18 (Autumn 1966): 452–476.

Thompson, Fred, and Patrick Murfin. *The IWW: Its First Seventy Years*. Chicago: IWW, 1970.

Tridon, André. *The New Unionism*. New York: B. W. Heubsch, 1913.

Venturi, Franco. *Roots of Revolution: A History of the Populist and Socialist Movements in Nineteenth Century Russia*. Trans. Francis Haskell. New York: Universal Library, 1966. Revised ed., London: Phoenix Press, 2000.

Warren, Sidney. *American Freethought, 1860–1914*. New York: Columbia University Press, 1943.

Watchorn, Robert. *Autobiography of Robert Watchorn*. Ed. Herbert Faulkner West. Oklahoma City: The Robert Watchorn Charities, Ltd., 1958.

Wexler, Alice. "Emma Goldman on Mary Wollstonecraft." *Feminist Studies* 7, no. 1 (Spring 1981): 113–33.

———. *Emma Goldman: An Intimate Life*. New York: Pantheon Books, 1984.

Whitman, Walt. *The Complete Poems*. Ed. Francis Murphy. New York: Penguin Books, 1996.

Woodcock, George. *Anarchism: A History of Libertarian Ideas and Movements*. Cleveland: Meridian Books, 1962.

Woodcock, George, and Ivan Avakumovic. *The Anarchist Prince: A Biographical Study of Peter Kropotkin*. London: T. V. Boardman, 1950.

Young, Arthur Nichols. *The Single Tax Movement in the United States*. Princeton: Princeton University Press, 1916.

Zipser, Arthur, and Pearl Zipser. *Fire and Grace: The Life of Rose Pastor Stoke*. Athens: University of Georgia Press, 1989.

PUBLICATIONS BY EMMA GOLDMAN

A Beautiful Ideal. Chicago: J. C. Hart, 1908.

A Letter to the Public. New York: Anarchist Federation, March 1908.

A New Declaration of Independence. New York: Mother Earth Publishing Association, 1909. First published in *Mother Earth* 4, no. 5 (July 1909).

Patriotism: A Menace to Liberty. New York: Mother Earth Publishing Association, ca. 1908. Also published in *Anarchism and Other Essays* (New York: Mother Earth Publishing Association, 1910), with many wording differences.

The Tragedy of Woman's Emancipation. New York: Mother Earth Publishing Association, ca. 1907. First published in *Mother Earth* 1, no.1 (March 1906); also published in *Anarchism and Other Essays* (New York: Mother Earth Publishing Association, 1910; 2nd rev. ed., 1917), with minor differences. Published in French as *La Tragédie de l'Émancipation féminine* (Orléans: Ed. de l'Ere nouvelle, n.d. [1908?]); published in Japanese as *Fujin Kaihó no Higeki*, in *Seitó* 3, no. 9 (September 1913).

What I Believe. New York: Mother Earth Publishing Association, 1908; 2nd ed., ca. 1910. First published in *New York World*, 19 July 1908. Published in Italian as *Quel ch'io credo* ("*Intervista avuta il 19 luglio 1908 dalla autrice con un reddatore del Wolf [sic], e da questo giornale pubblicata,*" in *Cronaca Sovversiva*, 8 August 1908) (Rome: Bibliothèque de la Gioventú libertaria, 1908).

The White Slave Traffic. New York: Mother Earth Publishing Association, ca. 1909. Published in *Mother Earth* 4, no. 11 (January 1910), with the name "Dr. Ploss" replaced by "Dr. Bloss"; published in *Anarchism and Other Essays* (New York: Mother Earth Publishing Association, 1910) as "The Traffic in Women," with many changes.

PUBLICATIONS OF THE MOTHER EARTH PUBLISHING ASSOCIATION

Coryell, John. *Sex Union and Parenthood and What Is Seduction.* 1907.

De Cleyre, Voltairine. *McKinley's Assassination from the Anarchist Standpoint.* 1907. First published in *Mother Earth* 2, no. 8 (October 1907).

———. *Anarchism and American Traditions.* 1909. First published in *Mother Earth* 3, nos. 10–11 (December 1908–January 1909).

Ferrer, Francisco. *The Modern School.* 1909.

Fox, Jay. *Trade Unionism and Anarchism.* 1907. First published in *Mother Earth* 2, no. 9 (November 1907).

Gorky, Maxim. *The Masters of Life, An Interview.* Trans. M. Zaslaw. 1907. First published in *Mother Earth* 1, no. 11 (January 1907), with minor typographical differences.

Kropotkin, Peter. *Modern Science and Anarchism.* 1908. First published in *Mother Earth* 1, nos. 6–10 (July–December 1906), with minor typographical differences. Originally published in Russian as *Sovremennaja nauka: anarcizm.* London: Russian Free Press Fund, 1901.

Schroeder, Theodore. *The Criminal Anarchy Law and On Suppressing the Advocacy of Crime.* 1907. First published as "On Suppressing the Advocacy of Crime," *Mother Earth* 1, no. 11 (January 1907).

PUBLICATIONS OF THE FREE SPEECH LEAGUE

Flower, Benjamin Orange, Theodore Schroeder, Louis Post, and Rev. Elliot White. *In Defense of Free Speech; Five Essays from the Arena.* 1908.

Free Speech and the New Alien Law. Press Bulletins No. 1 and No. 2. December 1903.

Schroeder, Theodore. *Freedom of the Press and "Obscene" Literature: Three Essays.* 1906.

———. *Liberty of Speech and Press Essential to Purity Propaganda. An Address Prepared for the National Purity Conference and to be Delivered October 10th, 1906.* 1906.

———. *Much Needed Defense for Liberty of Conscience, Speech and Press, with Special Application to Sex Discussion.* 1906.

———. *What Is Criminally "Obscene"? A Scientific Study of the Absurd Judicial "Tests" of Obscenity.* 1906.

———. *Constructive Obscenity.* 1907.

———. *Our Vanishing Liberty of the Press.* 1907.

———. *The Scientific Aspect of Due Process Law and Constructive Crimes.* 1908.

———. *Unconstitutionality of All Laws Against "Obscene" Literature Asserted in a Brief.* 1908.

———. *"Due Process of Law" in Relation to Statutory Uncertainty and Constructive Offences, Giving Much Needed Enlightenment to Legislators, Bar and Bench. . . . 1908.*

———. *The Conflict Between Religious and Ethical Science.* 1909.

Schroeder, Theodore, comp. *Free Press Anthology.* New York: Free Speech League and The Truth Seeker Publishing Company, 1909.

Wakeman, Thaddeus. *Administrative Process of the Postal Department: A Letter to the President.* 1906.

EMMA'S LIST

The Emma Goldman Papers Project thanks our sustaining sponsors and the following additional donors, who have led Emma's List, for their vote of confidence and material support over the years.

IN REMEMBRANCE

BELLA ABZUG is remembered by Gloria Steinem.

LYDIA AND GEORGE ARONOWITZ, loved for their wit and passion. May their goodness and sparkle—like Emma's—live on. Remembered by Merrill, Andrew, Todd, and Adam Stone, and by Candace Falk.

ROGER BALDWIN, civil liberties champion, is remembered by his goddaughter, Katrina van den Heuvel.

STELLA COMINSKY BALLANTINE, Emma's "favorite niece" and aide, and her two sons, IAN BALLANTINE and DAVID BALLANTINE, are remembered by Roy Kahn.

ANNA BARON is remembered by Prof. Millicent and the late Eugene Bell.

LEONARD BASKIN is remembered by Lisa Baskin.

WILLA BAUM is remembered by Nancy Mackay.

THOMAS H. BEADLING is remembered by Patricia A. Thomas.

SARAH BELLUSH, who loved and taught him to admire Emma Goldman, is remembered by her son, Bernard Bellush.

SUSAN PORTER BENSON is remembered by Judith E. Smith.

WARREN K. BILLINGS, dignified friend and colleague of Alexander Berkman, sentenced to life imprisonment in association with the 1916 Preparedness Day bombing, is remembered by his niece, Marguerite Joseph.

BEN AND IDA CAPES, Emma's dear friends and comrades, are remembered by David and Judith Capes, their grandchildren; by Bonnie Capes Tabatznik, their daughter; and by Susan Chasson and Albert Chasson, their niece and nephew.

ALICE CHECKOVITZ MAHONEY is remembered by her niece, Susan Wladaver-Morgan.

STEFANIE CHECKOVITZ WLADAVER (1920–2001) is remembered by her daughter, Susan Wladaver-Morgan.

MARLENE CAROL CLEMENS is remembered by her parents, Mary and the late Alan Dietch.

SARAH T. CROME, who helped found the Emma Goldman Papers, is remembered by Andrea Sohn, her niece; the late Esther and Eugene Revitch, her sister and brother-in-law; and by her friends Victoria Brady, Dale Freeman, Ken Kann, Stephanie Pass, Lyn Reese, and Judy Shattuck, and by her ever grateful colleague and friend Candace Falk.

SOPHIE AND JOE DESSER, Emma's dear friends and comrades, are remembered by their daughter, Mildred Desser Grobstein.

CHANELE (ANNA) SCHILHAUS DIAMOND, Emma Goldman's seamstress, is remembered by her son, the late David Diamond.

FRANK AND EDITH EIVE are remembered by Gloria Eive.

ALICIA EINWOHNER'S beloved mother is remembered by Bonnie Glaser.

WALTER AND LILLY ELSON are remembered by Eleanor Lee and Ronald Elson.

REBECCA FEILER (1982–2004), spirited young member of the Emma Goldman Papers, is remembered by her parents Debbie and Michael Fieler, Rabbi Arnold and Linda Levine, Cecelia (Aunt Seal) Polan, Miriam Polan, Ruth Polan and Fred Protopapas, Stephen Tobias and Alice Webber, and by Candace Falk and Barry Pateman of the Emma Goldman Papers.

JUDITH ANN FEINBERG is remembered by her mother, Sally Brown.

THE FERRER COLONY AND MODERN SCHOOL OF STELTON, NEW JERSEY, are remembered by Sally Brown.

MARTHA FREEDMAN is remembered by Estelle Freedman.

RACHEL FRUCHTER is remembered by Susan Reverby.

EMMA GOLDMAN was remembered by the late Art Bortolotti with gratitude for fighting "her last battle with the authorities, a battle that lasted until her last breath," on his behalf.

EMMA GOLDMAN is also remembered by the late David Diamond with gratitude for encouraging him in his youth to pursue his love of music and the violin and "Kling in de ganze Velt" (play for the entire world).

SAMUEL GOMPERS is rememebered by Grace Palladino.

DOROTHY R. HEALEY is remembered by Carol Jean and Edward F. Newman.

ELSIE HILLMANN is remembered by Robert Hillmann and Olivia Crawford.

SYLVIA KAUFMAN is remembered by Linda Kerber.

ISIDORE KIVIAT, a contemporary and fellow anarchist with Emma Goldman, is remembered by his grandson J. David Sackman.

BARBARA KRAUTHAMER is remembered by Alice Hall.

SHIRLEY KRAVITZ is rememebered by Susan Laine.

ESTHER LADDON, who gave Emma a home in Canada during her exile, is remembered by her daughter, the late Ora Laddon Robbins.

ORA LADDON (ROBBINS), who shared her many Emma stories with good humor and generosity, is fondly remembered by Candace Falk.

SARAH LAZAR is remembered by Shirley van Bourg.

AUNT FAYE LEVY—a great lady!—is remembered by Marrill Stone, by her nephew Neil Solomon and family, and by her niece Candace Falk, whom she counseled over the years to "let Emma Goldman rest in peace, already."

PETER LISKER is remembered by William and Rae Lisker.

RELLA LOSSY, who captured Emma's spirit in her plays, is remembered by Frank T. Lossy.

OSVALDO MARAVIGLIA is remembered by Louis Maraviglia.

HENRY MAYER, friend and fellow biographer, is remembered by Candace Falk.

JANE MAVERICK WELSH is remembered by Beá Welsh Weicker.

ESTHER MERCER is remembered by Mecca Reitman Carpenter.

JESSICA MITFORD is remembered by her daughter, Constancia Romilly.

JESSICA MITFORD AND BOB TREUHAFT are remembered by Peter Stansky.

CURTIS W. REESE, who delivered Emma's last eulogy at her gravesite, is remembered by his son, Curtis W. Reese Jr.

BEN REITMAN, Emma's road manager and lover, is remembered by his daughter, Mecca Reitman Carpenter.

SOPHIA LEVITIN RODRIGUEZ is remembered by Catherine Pantsios.

ZITHA ROSEN TURITZ is remembered by her niece, Nancy Chodorow.

ARTHUR LEONARD ROSS, Emma's lawyer and friend, is remembered by his sons, Ralph and Edgar Ross.

MARSHALL ROSS is remembered by Matthew Ross and Gloria Lawrence.

MARICARMEN RUIZ-TORRES is remembered by Linda Gort.

IRMA SHERMAN, aunt, soul-mate and respected member of Emma's List, is remembered by her daughter, Valerie Broad, Alfred and Joan Miller, and by her niece Candace Falk.

JENNY SIDNEY, comrade and mother, is remembered by Barry and Paul Pateman.

RABBI XARRY J. STERN is remembered by Stephanie S. Glaymon.

EMANUEL B. TISHMAN is remembered by his son, Don Tishman.

CARLO TRESCA is remembered by Rudolph J. Vecoli.

JULIE VAN BOURG is remembered by her mother, Shirley van Bourg.

NATHANIEL WALROD is remembered by his father, Mr. Stephen Walrod and the Love Cultivation Assets Fund.

LEON WALTER, of the Stelton community, is remembered by his daughters, Linn Walter Solomon and Ruth Walter Croton.

NORMA WIKLER is remembered by her siblings, Marjorie Senechal and Daniel Wikler, and by her friend Candace Falk.

KATE WOLFSON is remembered by her daughter, Irene Schneiderman.

CARLOS WUPPERMANN is remembered by Valerie Yaros.

REGGIE ZELNIK, our "Prince Kropotkin," is remembered by Zelda Bronstein and by many members of the Emma Goldman Papers who benefited form his wisdom and wit.

IN HONOR OF THOSE WHO CONTINUE TO KEEP EMMA'S SPIRIT ALIVE

ANTONIA, who embodies Emma's spirit, is honored by her father, David Madson.

LOIS BLUM FEINBLATT is honored by the Malino family, Candace Falk, and the Emma Goldman Papers for her remarkable presence and generosity.

JANE M. BOUVIER is honored by her daughter, Virginia Bouvier.

TALIA ROSE BRAND is honored by Susan and Jeffrey Brand.

MARY BURTON is honored for her sixtieth birthday by her son James O'Neil.

DANIEL BURTON-ROSE is honored by Peter Rose.

DAVID CAPLAN is honored by his father, Michael Caplan.

SUSAN CHASSON is honored by Syliva F. Scholtz.

MRS. RUTH DUBOW is honored by Merrill, Andrew, Todd, and Adam Stone.

ELEANOR ENGSTRAND AND MARGE FRANTZ are honored by Carol Jean and Edward F. Newman.

CANDACE FALK is honored by Allida Black and Judy A. Beck, Carol Brosgart, Yvette Chalom and Paul Fogel, Rabbi Ferenc Raj and Paula L. Wolk, Lois Schiffer, Peter Stansky, and Rudolph J. Vecoli.

JANE FALK is honored by Neil Goteiner and N. Joseph, by Merrill, Andy, Todd, and Adam Stone, and by her sister, Candace, who all wish her continued good health and happiness.

SARAH FINK is honored on her sixteenth birthday by Sandi L. Wisenberg.

JOSEPH FRIEDMAN is honored by his son, Larry Friedman.

R. BONNIE GLASER is honored by Rose Weilerstein, Hildegard Berliner, and Susan Thompson.

SARAH BARRINGER GORDON is honored in recognition of her work and support of the legacy of Emma Goldman.

LINDA HIRSCHORN is honored for her song, "Dance a Revolution," which carries on the spirit of Emma Goldman, and by Nancy Shimmel and Claudia Morrow.

BEN AND GINNY KENDALL are honored by Sheldon Rovin.

HANNAH KRANZBERG is honored by Michael Goldhaber and Candace Falk.

CAROL LASSER is honored by Cathy Kornblith.

LYNN LERER LAUPHEIMER is honored by Angeleen Campra.

LEON LITWACK is honored by William M. Tuttle Jr. and all the Emma Goldman Papers staff for his generous guiding hand and advocacy of the history of dissent.

LIVER ORGAN DONORS are honored by William C. Rosa.

EDITH LOBE is honored by Lori Marso.

LAUREN MCINTOSH is honored by Alice Hoffman.

BARRY PATEMAN is honored for his ongoing support and research of the Emma Goldman Papers by Michael Caplan.

UTAH PHILLIPS is honored by Nancy Lenox.

GAIL REIMER of the Jewish Woman's Archive is honored by Shelly Tenenbaum.

KIERSTEN AMANDA ROESEMANN is honored by her father and mother, Douglas N. Roesemann and Marla Erbin-Roesemann, and by her grandmother, the late Audrey Roesemann.

EMMA SAMELSON JONE'S graduation is honored by Renee Samelson.

JORDAN AND COREY SCHER are honored by their mother, Christine Sorensen for future choice and freedom of expression!

EMMA SHAW CRANE is honored by Susan Shaw and Thomas W. Crane.

EMMA AND ALEXANDER SIPE are honored by Gary Doebler.

FRED THOMPSON is honored by David Roediger and Jean Allman.

TIM WARDEN-HERTZ is honored by David Hertz and Mary Ellen Warden.

EMMA ARIELLE WEINSTEIN, named after Emma Goldman, is honored by Jessica Litwak.

VERA WEISS is honored by Barbara Bloch.

JEAN WILKINSON is honored by her friend Lyn Reese.

ARI WOHLFEILER is honored by Dan Wohlfeiler.

EMMA WOLF is honored by her parents, Louis Wolf and Dolores Newman.

ANTONIO F. YOON is honored by Eric A. Isaacson and Susan K. Weaver.

JOSEPH ZELNICK is honored by Carl N. Degler.

INSTITUTIONAL DONORS

Action Democrats
American Council for Learned Societies
The William Bingham Foundation
California Council for the Humanities
Chadwyck-Healey, Inc.
The Catticus Corporation
The Commonwealth Fund
Congregation Beth El
Emma Goldman Clinic
The Ford Foundation
The Funding Exchange
Furthermore: A Program of the J. M. Kaplan Foundation
George Gund Foundation
Hunt Alternatives Fund
Kimo Campbell of the Pohaku Fund

Lerach Coughlin Stoia Geller Rudman & Robins, Attorneys at Law
Lois and Irving Blum Foundation
The L. J. Skaggs and Mary C. Skaggs Foundation
Lucius W. Littauer Foundation
The Los Angeles Educational Partnership
Milken Family Foundation
Mills College
The Murray and Grace Nissman Foundation
Price Waterhouse Coopers, Ltd.
The Rockefeller Foundation
Samuel Rubin Foundation
The San Francisco Foundation: Love Cultivating Assets Fund
The Streisand Foundation
Sun Microsystems
The Vanguard Foundation
Earl Warren Chapter of the American Civil Liberties Union
H. W. Wilson Foundation
Women's Studies Program at Middle Tennessee State University

INDIVIDUAL DONORS

Anonymous
Mark Aaronson and Marjorie Gelb
Martha Ackelsberg
Herb Adelman
Janet Adelman
Harriet Alonso
Meryl Altman
Lisa D. Alvarez and Andrew Tonkovich
Carol Amyx
Ron Anastasia and Kim Anway-Anastasia
Elizabeth Anderson and the late Henry Mayer
Bill Andrews
William L. and Charron F. Andrews
Joyce Appleby
Jeffrey Travis Atwood
Bob Baldock and Kathleen Weaver
Lisa Baskin
Rosalyn Baxandall
Alan Becker
Helen Becker
Jonathan Becker
Pessl Beckler-Semel-Stern
Prof. Millicent Bell and the late Eugene Bell
Bernard Bellush
Marlou Belyea and Zachary Taylor
Lenni Benson
Richard Berger and Judith Derman

Estelle and Howard Bern
Carmina Bernardo
Anne Bernstein and Conn Hallinan
Elizabeth Berry
Mary F. Berry
Hilton Bertalan and Michele Donnelly
Stephen Berzon
Sheila Biddle
Rebeccalyn Bilodeau
Nancy Bissell and Robert Segal
Allida Black and Judy A. Beck
Katharine and Charles Blackman
Barbara and Arthur Bloch
Jack Block
Paul Bluestone and Susan Sanvidge
Carolyn Patty Blum and Harry Chotiner
Herman and Margaret Blumenthal
Bailey Coy Books
Lynn A. Bonfield
Anne Borchardt
Danice Bordett
Eileen Boris and Nelson Lichtenstein
The late Art Bortolotti
Virginia Bouvier
Jo Ann Boydston
Victoria Brady
Julie Brammnick
Susan and Jeffrey Brand
Marion Brenner and Robert Shimshak
Carroll Brentano
Ramsay Breslin
Valerie and Richard Broad
Bill Broderick and Bea Kumasaka
Addy and Merle Brodsky
Sunny and Philip Brodsky
Zelda Bronstein
Carol Brosgart
Michael Brown and Laura Malakoff
Sally Brown
E. Wayles Browne
Robert Browning and Linda Maio
June and the late Abe Brumer
Paul Bundy
Julianne Burton-Carvajal
Angeleen Campra
David and Judith Capes
Bonnie Capes Tabatznik
Jane Caplan
Michael Caplan
Mortimer Caplin
Mecca Reitman Carpenter
Scott Carpenter

Candace M. Carroll
Clayborne and Susan Carson
JoAnn Castagna
Joseph and Susan Cerny
Mariam Chamberlain
Marlene and Albert Chasson
Susan Chasson
Nupur Chaudhuri
Robert Cherny
Leah and the late Marvin Chodorow
Nancy Chodorow
Noam Chomsky
Harry Chotiner
Joy Christenberry
Pat Cody
Natalie Cohen
Elizabeth Colton
William Connell
Charles and Beverly Connor (Harriette Austin Writers)
Scott Conover
Blanche Weisen Cook
J. Scott Corporon and Josie Porras
Margaret Corrigan and Larry Gibbs
Maureen Corrigan and Richard J. Yeselson
Nancy Cott
Patrick Coughlin
Carole M. Counihan and James M. Taggart
Victoria Crane and Matthew Engle
Matthew, Linda, and Ellen Creager
Fred Croton
Christina Crowley and Peter Hobe
Naomi Dagen and Ronald L. Bloom
Suzanne K. Damarin
The late David Diamond
Tom Debley and Mary Jane Holmes
Carol DeBoer-Langworthy
Carl N. Degler
Edward DeGrazia
Anna DeLeon
Michael Denneny, Andrew Miller, Robert Weil (formerly of St. Martin's Press)
Cleo Deras and Carlos Hernandez
Mary and the late Alan Dietch
John P. Diggens
Christine Distefano
Jill and Martin Dodd
Gary Doebler
Conrad Donner
Shawn Donnille
Janet Drake and Kevin Lee
Martin Duberman

Thomas Dublin and Kathryn Kish Sklar
Robert Dunn
William Dunn
Jack Edelman
Samuel and Hope Efron
Diane Ehrensaft and Jim Hawley
Robin Einhorn
Laurel and Eugene Eisner
Gloria Eive
Robert Elias and Jennifer Turpin
Roz Elms and Donald Sutherland
Barbara Epstein
Edwin M. Epstein
Shelly Errington and Leo Goodman
Jane Fajans and Terry Turner
Jane Falk
Deborah Farrell
Claire Feder
Debbie and Michael Feiler
Lois Blum Feinblatt
Ovina Maria Feldman
Laura Fenster and Jon Rosenberg
Kathy Ferguson
Emily Filloy and David Weintraub
Joseph A. and Elizabeth Fisher
Barbara and Robert Fishman
Bruce Fodiman
Shirley Jean Foster and Christopher Barnard
    Foster
Steve Fortuna
Nancy Fox
Mary Ann Frankel
The late B. Franklin and the late Joan F. Kahn
Suzanne E. Franks
Marge Frantz and Eleanor Engstrand
Donald and Dava Freed
Estelle Freedman
Dale C. Freeman
Marilyn French
Larry Friedman
Mark Friedman and Marjorie Solomon
    Friedman
Robert and Ann Friedman
James and Dianne Fristrom
William Lee Frost
Lisa Fruchtman and Norman Postone
Lisa Ganung
Judith Gardiner
Daniel Garrison
Dan C. George and Erica L. Marks
Donald Gibson and Dai Sil Kim-Gibson
Patricia Gill

Christina and John Gillis
Abigail Ginzberg
Bonnie Glaser
Ruth Glaser
Peter Glassgold and Suzanne Thibodeau
Stephanie S. Glaymon
Traci Gleason
Susan Glenn and James Gregory
Burton Gold
Neil Goldberg and Hagit Cohen
Sam and Maria Goldberger
Michael Goldhaber
Janet Goldner
Rick Goldsmith and Susanna Tadlock
Sherry L. Goodman
Nancy Gordon (Koret Gallery, Palo Alto, Calif.)
Nancy Gordon and Associates, Inc.
Nancy Gordon and Ken Kirsch
Richard Gordon and Meredith Miller
Sarah Barringer Gordon
Ralph Gorin
Linda Gort
Neil Goteiner
The late Joanne Grant and Victor Rabinowitz
Edward de Grazia
Marty Nesselbush Green
Janet Greenberg
Eleanor Greene
Ronald Grele
Susan Grigg
Mildred Desser Grobstein
Richard Grosboll
Denyse Gross and Kenneth Morrison
Rachael J. Grossman and John Doll
Susan Groves and Eric Anderson
Erich Gruen
Gay Gullickson
Mary Gutzi
Roland Guyotte
Alice Hall and Michael Smith
David and Joan Halperin
Robert Hamburger
Larry Hannant
Donna J. Haraway and Rusten Hogness
Louis R. and Sadie Harlan
James Harrell
Nina Hartley
Martin O. and Professor Barbara S. Heisler
Stuart Hellman
Linda J. Henry
Leroy J. Hertel
David Hertz and Mary Ellen Warden

Frederick Hertz and Randolph Langenbach
Katrina van den Heuvel
Nancy Hewitt and Steven Lawson
Barbara Hill
Ronald Hill
Robert Hillman and Olivia Crawford
Sally Hindman
Adrienne Hirt and Jeff Rodman
Barbara Hoffer
Alice Hoffman
Deborah Hoffmann and Francis Reid
Ronald W. Hogeland
Patricia Holland
Catherine W. Hollis
Lorraine and Victor Honig
Chris Hoofnagle
David A. Horowitz and Gloria T. Myers
Frank Hunter
Scott A. Ickes and Mary T.B. Currie
Isbel Ingham and Lorraine Kerwood
Eric Alan Isaacson and Susan Kay Weaver
Elizabeth Jameson
Susan Jarratt
Dr. Thomas E. Jeffrey
Philip M. Jelley
Mary Jennings and Donald Sarason
Carole Elizabeth Joffe and Fred Block
Judy Johnson
Marilynn Johnson, Daniel Zedek, and Rosa
    Margurite Joseph
Erica Jong and Ken Burrows
Marguerite Joseph
Henry Kahn and Mary Gillmor Kahn
Jane Kahn
Kathy Kahn
Lorraine Kahn
Peggy Kahn
Roy Kahn
The late Wu Ke Kang
Kenneth L. Kann and Stephanie Pass
Timothy Kantz and Simone Levine
Doris Kaplan
Susan Kaplan
Michael Katz
Deborah Kaufman and Alan Snitow
Bruce Kayton
Meaghan Keegan
The late Frances Richardson Keller and the
    late William P. Rhetta
Loretta Kensinger
Richard E. and Linda K. Kerber
John Kessell

Shirley Kessler and Bill Jersey
Alice Kessler-Harris
Kristina Kiehl and Bob Friedman
Allen and Hannah King
Kathleen King
Barbara Kingsolver and Stephen Hopp
Jessie and James Kingston
Betty Klausner
Harvey Klein
Heather and Scott Kleiner
Gerald M. Kline and Julie Florinkline
Maurice Knoepler
Brigitte Koenig and Mark Christopher Garman
Cathy Kornblith (The People's Eye)
Hannah Kranzberg
Julia Kraut
Stephan Krug
Uldis and Ann Kruze
Jay Kugelman
Mark Kulikowski
Susan Laine
Robin Lakoff
Russell and Carol DeBoer Langworthy
Arthur Charles Leahy and Mary Kathryn Leahy
Eleanor Lee and Ronald Elson
Madeleine Lee
Elaine Leeder
John Leggett
Jesse Lemisch and Naomi Weisstein
Nancy Lenox
Gerda Lerner
Paula Goldman Leventman
Cornelia and the late Lawrence Levine
Rabbi Arnold and Linda Levine
Rhonda Levine
Simone Levine and Timothy Kantz
Lynda and Carl Levinson (Max and Anna
    Levinson Foundation)
Rita Lewis and family
Jody Lewitter
Doris H. Linder
Steven and Judith Lipson
Rae and William Lisker
Jessica Litwak
Frank T. Lossy
Kristin Luker and Jerome Karabel
Zella Luria
Jordan Luttrell
Nancy Mackay
David J. Madson
Sarah and Jonathon Malino
Jeffrey A. Mandel and Wendy Lichtman

Peter Theodore Manicas
J. Louis Maraviglia
Louis Maraviglia
Maeva Marcus
Victor and Katalin Markowitz
Erica L. Marks and Dan George
Daniel Marschall
Lori Marso
Mary Ann Mason and Paul Ekman
Antje Mattheus and David Kairys
Anne Mattina
Lary and Elaine T. May
Judith McCombs and Ernst Benjamin
Pamela McCorduck and Joseph Traub
Mary Lynn McCree Bryan
Dennis McEnnerny and Bryant 'Tip' Ragan Jr.
Maggie McFadden
Blaine and Virginia McKinley
Peter Alexander McNamara
Jennifer Mei and Han Min Liu
Russell Merritt
Muffie Meyer
Suzanne Meyer
Diane Middlebrook and Carl Gerassi
Alfred and Joan Miller
Fredrika V. Miller
Jesse Miller
Maya Miller
Sally Miller and Peg Keranen
Sigrid Miller and Robert Pollin
Herbert Mills
Ruth Milkman
The late Jessica Mitford and the late
    Robert Treuhaft
Dominic Montagu and Diep Ngoc Doan of the
    Nepheli Foundation
Marie Morgan
James Mullins
Carol Murphy
Victor Navasky
Marty Nesselbush Green
Dolores Neuman and Lois Wolf
Dolores Newman
Ed Newman and Carol Jean Newman
Jeffrey Nichols
Brian Norman and Greg Nicholl
Mary Beth Norton
Thom Nosewicz
The late Morris Novik
C. Benjamin Nutley
Bob O'Dell
Karen Offen

Kaoru Ohara
Philip O'Keefe, M.D.
James O'Neil
Philip Owh
Nell Painter
Grace Palladino
Catherine Pantsios
Keith Park
Pamela Parker
Stephanie Pass and Ken Kann
Barry and Paul Pateman
Thomas Peabody
John Peck
Mary Elizabeth and Ralph Perry III.
Joan K. Peters and Peter Passell
Agnes F. Peterson
Frances Pici
Janice Plotkin
Cecelia H. Polan
Miriam Polan
Ruth Polan and Fred Protopappas
Linda Post and Eugene Rosow
Ruth Price
Carl Prince and family
Jacoba Prins
The late Adele Proom
Leslie and Merle Rabine
Victor Rabinowitz and the late Joanne Grant
Rabbi Ferenc Raj and Paula Wolk
Harold Ramis
Alan Ramo
Charles H. and Carolyn J. Reese
Curtis W. Reese Jr.
Joan, Robert, and Heather Reese
Lyn Reese
Marylin B. Reizbaum
Susan Reverby
The late Esther and the late Eugene Revitch
Hon. Jennie Rhine and Tom Meyer
Brenda Richardson
Leonard Rico
Thomas Riggio
The late Ora Laddon Robbins
Victor Roberge
Dennis Roberts
Morton S. and Josephine T. Roberts
Renée Robin and Scott McCreary
David Roediger and Jean Allman
Doug Roesemann, Marla Erbin-Roesemann
    and Kiersten Amanda Roesemann, and the
    late Audrey Roesemann
Florence Roisman

Rachel Eleah Roisman, M.D.
Shelly and Coleman Romalis
Constancia Romilly
Steve and Suzy Ronfeldt
William C. Rosa
Joanna Rose
Peter Rose and Daniel Burton Rose
Ruth Rosen and Wendel Brunner, M.D.
Shale Rosen
Carolyn Cavalier Rosenberg
Erica Rosenfeld and James Wilson
Florence Rosenstock and James van Luik
Roy Rosenzweig
The late Marshall Ross
Matthew Ross and Gloria Lawrence
The late Ralph and Edgar Ross
Steven Rosswurm
Elizabeth Rotundo
Sheldon Rovin
Sheila Rowbotham
Ronald Rowell
Lillian and Hank Rubin
The late Maricarmen Ruiz-Torrez and
    Linda Gort
Marcia and the late Lucio Ruotolo
The late Prentice Sack and Paul Sack
Jeffry and Jerolyn Sackman
Harriet Sage
Samuel Salkin and Frankie Whitman
Renee Samelson and Richard Jones
Ann Elizabeth Samuelson
Ethel Sanjines
Susan Sarandon and Tim Robbins
Camille Saviola
Jaymie Sawyer
The late Virginia Scardigli
William Schechner
Seth Schein and Sherry Crandon
Danny Scher
Lois Schiffer
Nancy Schimmel and Claudia Morrow
Lillian Schlissel
Jim Schmidt
Ann and Richard Schmidt Jr.
Ann M. Schneider
Irene Schneiderman
Syliva F. Scholtz
Herb Schreier
Donna Schulman
Ann Schultis
Constance Schultz
Jane and Jerome Schultz

Marilyn and Harvey Schwartz
John and Kathleen Scott
Robert Segal and Nancy Bissel
The late Jules and the late Helen Seitz
Martin Selig
Mary Selkirk, Lee Balance, and Zoe
Marjorie Senechal and Daniel Wikler
Juliet Shaffer
Judy Shattuck
Susan Shaw and Thomas W. Crane
Richard and Martha Sheldon
Julius and the late Irma Sherman
Valerie Sherman and Richard Broad
Michelle Shocked
Hannah Shostack
Alix Kates Shulman
Elizabeth Sibley
Barbara Sicherman
Stephen Silberstein
Harriet F. and John Simon
Kitty Sklar and Thomas Dublin
Arlene and Jerome Skolnick
Janet Small
Deborah L. Smith and Lucas E. Guttentag
Judith Smith
Yvon Soares
Carol Soc
Andrea Sohn
Margaret E. Sokolik
Linn Walter Solomon
Mark Solomon
Naomi Solomon
Neil Solomon and Paula Birnbaum
Nancy Caldwell Sorel and Ed Sorel
Christine Sorensen
Claire Sotnick
Daniel Soyer and Jocelyn Cohen
Robert Grayson Spillers
John Spragens Jr.
Judith Stacey
Christine Stansell and Sean Willentz
Peter Stansky
Randolph and Frances Starn
Brenda Start and Charlene Lofgren
David Steichen
Gloria Steinem
Pessl Beckler Semel Stern
The late Philip M. Stern
Joanne Sterricker
Judith Stiehm
Eric Stone and Eve Eilenberg
Jean Stone

Merrill, Andrew, Todd, and Adam Stone
Landon Storrs
Susan Strasser
Craig Syverson and Christina Allen
Evelyn and Norman Tabachnick
Suzanne Talmachoff
Nancy and Robert Taniguchi
Marcia Tanner and Winsor Soule
G. Thomas Tanselle
Reesa Tansey
Dickran L. Tashjian and Ann Hulting
Jill Taylor
Judith Nissman Taylor
Sydney Temple and Sarah Kupferberg
Shelly Tenenbaum
Nancy Terrebonne
Patricia Anne Thomas
Sally Thomas
Irene Tinker
Ted J. Tipton
Barbara Tischler
Donald Tishman
Stephen Tobias and Alice Webber
Joseph Traub and Pamela McCorduck
George L. Turin
William M. Tuttle Jr.
Elaine Tyler and Lary May
Laurel T., Gael, and Amy Ulrich
Carol and Steven Unger
Patricia Valva
Shirley van Bourg
Jill and Rudolph Vecoli
Maria Vullo
Nora Wagner
Richard Walker
Judith and Daniel Walkowitz
Stephen Walrod
Bridget Walsh and Louis Plachowski
Susan Ware
Deborah and Dan Waterman
Bruce Watson and Julie Kumble
Brenda Webster and Ira Lapidus
Jill Weed
Bonnie Lynn Weimer
Beá Welsch Weicker
Rose Weilerstein, Hidegrad Berliner, and
    Susan Thompson
Lila Weinberg
Lynn Weiner and Thomas Moher
Neil and Myra Weiner
David Weintraub and Emily Filloy
Cora and Peter Weiss

Janet Corey Weiss and Jeffrey Conrad
Susan Wengraf and Mark Berger
Marcia Whitebook
Ann Whitehead
Blanche Wiesen Cook
The late Norma Wikler
Margy and Tony Wilkinson
Carol Williams
Beverly Dean Williams and Norman Francis
John Alexander Williams
Victoria Williams
Brigitte and John Williams-Searle
Elsbeth Wilson
Vickie Wilson (Alfred A. Knopf)
Elizabeth Wingrove
Martha Winnacker
Barbara Winslow
Priscilla Winslow
Sandi L. Wisenberg
Susan Wladaver-Morgan
Roz and Leon Wofsy
Dan Wohlfeiler
Louis Wolf
Margery J. Wolf and Kieth M. Marshall
Elizabeth A. Wood
Ann Wrixon
Laura X (Shaw Murra)
Mormoru Yamaguchi
Susumu Yamaizumi
Valerie Yaros
Fay Zadeh
Rhonda Zangwill
Naomi Zauderer
Martin Zelig
Margaret Zierdt
Arthur and Charlotte Zilversmit
Roslyn and Howard Zinn
Joan Zoloth
Carol Zullman and Eric Taub

* * *

*And special thanks to our many donors who chose
to remain anonymous and the literally thousands
of others whose contributions, large and small,
have been absolutely critical to the survival of the
Emma Goldman Papers Project. We also honor
the memory of the recently deceased friends who
were near and dear to us. We hope our volumes
reinforce the spirit of continuity between the past,
the present, and the future.*

ACKNOWLEDGMENTS

Collaboration is the core component of the Emma Goldman Papers Project. For over twenty years, many hands have created what has become a secular cathedral to the remembrance of things past and almost forgotten. Every effort, large and small, built the structure, added complexity and nuance to the work, and confirmed the importance of situating the advocates of free expression into the historical record as a lasting tribute to courageous spirits.

Emma Goldman's amazing foresight and daring, her insistence that both political and personal freedom are realizable—no matter how difficult the struggle or intangible the outcome along the way—remain an inspiration. The work of preserving and publishing the written artifacts of Goldman's active life has elicited an almost unmatched outpouring of generosity and enthusiasm from those whose determination and vision resonate with Goldman's essential daring.

Perhaps it is not surprising that the controversial side of Goldman—the anarchist deported from the United States, the woman feared for her challenge to organized government—also provoked storm clouds around the historical research for this documentary edition. Ironically, as we prepared the manuscript for *Making Speech Free,* the office of the vice chancellor for research at the Berkeley campus of the University of California chose to censor two relatively benign Goldman quotes from the Project's 2002 holiday solicitation, considering them direct statements of opposition to the then-impending war in Iraq. The first quote, taken from Goldman's essay entitled "Free Speech in Chicago" and written in 1902, warned American citizens that they too might soon be subject to the restrictive laws against alien anarchists enacted after President McKinley's assassination: "We shall soon be obliged to meet in cellars or in darkened rooms with closed doors, and speak in whispers lest our next door neighbors should hear that free-born citizens dare not speak in the open." In the second quote, taken from "Preparedness, The Road to Universal Slaughter" and published in 1915 in her magazine, *Mother Earth,* prior to U.S. entry into the First World War, Goldman urged the public "not yet overcome by war madness to raise their voice of protest, to call the attention of the people to the crime and outrage which are about to be perpetrated on them." The absurdity of banning 100-year-old quotes was not lost on the *New York Times.* The paper considered the controversy front-page news twice in the same week (14 and 17 January 2003), headlining the first article "At Berkeley A New Dispute Over Words From Long Ago." And the lead-in to Aaron Brown's cable television show raised the question, "Just how much trouble can a dead anarchist's words make?" The public outrage against the university's censorship touched a nerve in the nation, and the Emma Goldman Papers Project received hundreds of support letters, e-mails, and even contributions. The fear-factor turned—with university administrators suddenly worried that suppressing a growing movement against the war might make *them* the subject of ridicule worthy of front-page news. Berkeley's chancellor, Robert Berdahl, a historian of Germany during the First World War, agreed that there were in fact horrifying similarities between then and now, took a principled stand, and publicly overturned the decision of his vice chancellor. We are hopeful that the benefits of taking a stand against censorship helped protect others, perhaps more vulnerable and less outspoken. This experience was living proof that "making speech free" is a constant struggle, meriting vigilance and the rallying of support from a community of wide-ranging ideas united in a principle that ultimately protects us all.

We have also weathered a backlash and lapses in both financial support and editorial continuity. Yet, always an individual or institution has risen to the occasion, made an extraordinary effort on our behalf, and the Project, like Emma Goldman herself, has survived. That her papers and these volumes, so full of scholarship and insight into a world whose tracings are rare and whose importance has often been obscured by political prejudice, are now an indelible part of the historical record is the shared accomplishment of literally hundreds of people over the years.

Many of our extended family of friends and colleagues can assert with great authority and confidence that their individual efforts helped bring the project to publication and made all the difference. Every bit of research over the past twenty-four years added to the subtlety of our work—small details gradually linked to present a complex picture of Goldman's world. Others supported us by creating a foundation for our efforts, a frame for public history and meticulous research, providing archival sources and funding resources, cushioning us with kindness. In the mountain of words and ideas that comprise our work, none can express fully the depth of our appreciation for the devotion and selflessness showered upon us, sanctioning our perseverance, in spite of all odds, to preserve the written legacy of Emma Goldman.

It would be impossible to name all those associated with the Emma Goldman Papers Project over the years whose remarkable solidarity and support have sustained us. I, who have facilitated the Emma Goldman Papers Project from the beginning, have been privileged to spend so much of my life poring through Emma Goldman's papers in the company of those, past and present, drawn to the many facets of her exalted and complex vision.

IT IS A GREAT PLEASURE to thank the extraordinary people and institutions without which publication of the selected edition of the Emma Goldman's papers would have been impossible.

First and foremost, a great tribute is due to the Project's editorial staff, whose tireless and creative work gave life to a time and a movement otherwise hidden from history. Barry Pateman, a scholar and archivist of anarchist sources, in his five years with the Project has transformed the raw coal of our more than twenty years of archival research into diamonds of scholarship. His association with the Emma Goldman Papers, which began in the Project's early years of searching through archives and private collections in England, came full circle with his arrival in California in 1999—when he became "the fastest study in the West." As a colleague—every step of the way from daily administrative tasks to intellectual engagement in the writing of the introductory essays—and as an enthusiastic mentor to students and aficionado of anarchist history, Barry Pateman's efforts are unmatched. It is largely to his herculean efforts that we owe the timely and accurate recording and contextualization of Goldman's American years.

The editorial group that has shepherded to completion the volumes covering Goldman's American years also stands out in the history of the Emma Goldman Papers Project as the very best. Jessica Moran came to the Project when she was a student at the University of California, Berkeley, and over time has assumed a critical role in coordinating, maintaining, and researching many crucial components of the volumes—including the biographical and organizational directories—and managing a plethora of incredible detail with amazing grace. In the process of her work at the Goldman Papers she found her passion for the archival world, which will, no doubt, benefit from her energy and insight.

As the work of the Emma Goldman Papers Project evolved, from the earliest days of searching for Goldman's correspondence, writings, newspaper reportage, legal and government surveillance reports, and photographic images for the comprehensive microfilm edition to the production of these volumes documenting Goldman's American years, every aspect of the public history outreach generated by the Project bears the mark of historian Robert Cohen and illustrations editor Susan Wengraf.

Robert Cohen began his association with the Project when he was a graduate student studying the history of student movements, especially of the 1930s. With his constant focus on free expression and education, he has followed the thread of his interests from the early years of the twentieth century with Emma Goldman on to the radicals of the 1930s and to the activists of the free speech movement of the 1960s on the University of California, Berkeley, campus. An enormously generous and insightful colleague and friend, he collaborated on the selection of the documents and offered rare intellectual camaraderie as he critiqued the introductory essays, encouraging me to take a longer view on Goldman, to face her limitations even as I celebrated her grand achievements. And when, midstream in the Project's work, I faced a life-threatening illness, he was among the most devoted to the work, and his unwavering kindness to me during that harrowing time created a shield of support.

Susan Wengraf's impeccable visual sensibility and fascination with Goldman and her time graced the Project with an ever-increasing photographic archive that allowed us to attend to the edition's artistic form as well as historical content. Wengraf created a parallel narrative comprised of facsimiles of original documents from newspapers, magazines, government documents, and personal correspondence gathered from a wide variety of sources—complementing and distilling the volumes' daunting abundance of historical texts. Barry Pateman, in his other role as curator of the Kate Sharpley Library, generously added his original visual material. In the final hours, Wengraf was assisted by John Blaustein and Andrea Sohn, who generously gave of their time and technical expertise. Wengraf began the search for Goldman-related images more than twenty years ago—building our visual archive and helping to create a "family album" that evolved into a wonderful traveling exhibition. She continues to assist me, as I prepare to speak on Goldman at campuses across the world, by creating the Project's slide show and streamlining it for local color and historical context.

The University of California Press, a place where scholarship and public interest meet, has been the perfect publisher for the Goldman volumes, from the day Stan Holwitz solicited the manuscript more than twenty years ago, to the wonderful experience of working with Director Lynne Withey, a woman whose flexibility, compassion, and intelligent guiding hand is largely responsible for the publication of these volumes. Every step of the way, the Project enjoyed the privilege of the remarkably skilled editors at the press. Most spectacular of all is Kathleen MacDougall, who has been immersed in all details of production as well as line-editing and questioning facts—elements of the publication that when done well make a book appear invisibly seamless and clear. We are grateful for her persistence and remarkable editorial sensibility and talent, and also for her belief in the social and political value of publishing this selected edition of Goldman's papers, which made our professional tie a wondrous collegial and comradely fit. Our A-team included the prize-winning designer Nicole Hayward and assistant managing editor Erika Búky.

Indeed, the Emma Goldman Papers has been fortunate to have had the benefit of publishers who never wavered in their commitment to the work—from the gracious and intelligent publisher of the 1991–1993 microfilm edition and the 1995 analytic guide, Sir Charles Chadwyck-Healey and his associates, first Mark Hamilton and then Doug Roesemann, whose personal enthusiasm has never waned, to the stellar editors at the University of California Press. We thank them all for their part in inscribing Emma Goldman's life and times indelibly into the historical record.

Among the historians devoted to the history of dissent and to recording the violent underside of the nation's response to issues of race and labor unrest is the revered Leon Litwack, indefatigable and captivating Morrison Professor of American History at the University of California, Berkeley, and chair of the very generous Faculty Advisory Board of the Emma Goldman Papers Project. He stood by the Emma Goldman Papers tirelessly and, with compassion and enthusiasm, gave us his astute advice over the past decade of the Emma Goldman Papers Project. To have the camaraderie and respect of one who embodies the challenging spirit of Emma Goldman has been an honor. We thank him for his generosity and his willingness to go the extra mile even with his overflowing schedule, without which the Emma Goldman Papers Project could never have come this far—and for all that he has done for so many, with his characteristic combination of modesty and force. He held us together when we were drifting—as did the many members of our faculty advisory board.

A pattern of resilience, determination, and never turning back was set with the aid of two significant research companions—the magnificent and practical political visionary the late Sarah Crome and the multi-talented public historian and Web-archivist Sally Thomas. Crome joined me upon her retirement from teaching and, although she initially cringed at the impracticality of Emma's politics, developed a fascination for the history of the anarchists, eventually becoming known among younger anarchist and anti-nuclear activists as "cosmic Sarah." Thomas worked with the Project in many different roles over a fourteen-year period and helped set a tone and direction that has remained our hallmark. Flanked by our muses the three Women for Peace—June Brumer, Rae Lisker, and Beth Wilson—the "volunteers" whose weekly dedication for more than fifteen years to absolutely anything that needed to be done, added radiance and ingenuity to our work and contributed to the Project's ability to weather occasional storms of uncertainty.

The Emma Goldman Papers Project was conceived in an era of resurgence of interest in women's history. The initiator of the Emma Goldman Papers Project was the National Historical Publications and Records Commission of the National Archives. The NHPRC was mandated by Congress in 1934 to sponsor documentary editing projects to collect, organize, and publish the papers of the Founding Fathers. By the 1970s there was a groundswell of interest among historians in expanding the definition of the nation's finest leaders to include women, labor, and civil rights activists. The Emma Goldman Papers, sometimes labeled in jest as one of the "Destroying Mothers" projects, began quietly in 1980, only to be silenced briefly by budget cuts during President Reagan's administration. The NHPRC has been the Emma Goldman Papers Project's most consistent supporter—setting an unparalleled standard of excellence and respect for documentary editing and laying the foundation for the abundance of high-quality historical editions in American history published in the twentieth century. The irony of a federal agency becoming the deported Emma Goldman's primary source of support was not lost on the NHPRC's longtime officer, Roger Bruns, now retired, who often mused that perhaps Goldman was mistakenly identified on the commission's list of mandated subjects for projects. Bruns jested that they might have presumed they were funding a great "archivist," rather than a feared "anarchist." Piercing through such speculation was the NHPRC's genuine belief in free expression as a crucial element of the identity of America, which propelled the commission and its remarkably kind and engaged staff to value Goldman's contribution to American history and sustain the long scholarly quest to document her life and work. In addition to the compassionate, modest, and erudite Roger Bruns, who not only guided the Emma Goldman Papers through the years but also provided critical feedback as I wrote the introductory essays, the Project was fortunate to have the support and clever counsel of Ann Newhall and the kind support of her successor, Max Evans, fprmer director of the NHPRC. On the commission staff, Tim Connelly impressively tended to the myriad of detail, proving that the best administrative work is done with kindness and intellectual engagement in the task at hand. A host of NHPRC associates shepherded us through our work over the years, including the empathetic Mary Giunta, who saw us through many of our hardest times, and the remarkable late Sara Jackson, a kindred spirit, who took pride in her contact with the Goldman Papers, declassifying government documents for the collection and even entrusting us with records of racial lynching to place in the hands of scholars who shared our belief that historians can make a difference by exposing and correcting the documentary record. Over time, the NHPRC staff became our most consistently involved colleagues—we especially thank Richard Sheldon, Nancy Sahli, J. Dane Hartgrove, Mike Meier, and our true-blue "emmasary" enthusiast and ethicist extraordinaire Suzanne Meyer, as well as the many others who extended themselves over and over again on our behalf.

My appreciation extends to those who played an integral part in the history of the Emma Goldman Papers Project over the past twenty-four years—from staff members, volunteers, archivists, librarians, scholars in the United States and across the globe, students, grant administrators, and the many university and community facilitators of our work. While the editors who brought these volumes to completion in the last three years, checking and re-checking facts, writing and re-writing annotations, framing and re-framing the texts, and pushing themselves to the max with great equanimity and kindness to meet incredibly stringent deadlines, clearly deserve the lion's share of appreciation, others before them worked very hard to help lay the foundation for what is now the documentary history of Goldman's American years. Various configurations of the edition, ranging from one to three, and ultimately to four, volumes for the American years, have left tracings of different editorial styles—some of which were eventually abandoned and some absorbed. The volumes have benefited from the talents of each editorial group as they improved on the fine efforts of the one before it.

During 1998 and 1999, a small group of graduate students in history at the University of California, Berkeley, valiantly attempted to bring the early configuration of this documentary history to completion. Carl Prince, professor of history at New York University and longtime documentary editor, generously took a "busman's vacation" during his frequent junkets from New York to California and spent months editing annotations. Many of the Project's student editors over the years had been trained in the field of documentary editing by Stephen Cole, who coordinated the early research as an associate editor in the formative stages of the American years' edition and was especially attuned to editorial principles and practices; although the Project has since changed course and content, we are grateful for Cole's preparatory efforts on the volumes. Crossing over during this time was Sally Thomas, the longest-standing member of the Emma Goldman Papers Project, who worked first as an administrative assistant and public programs specialist and then as an editor, performing the initial transcription of the almost illegible prison letters. Among the many ways in which she helped shape the Project's mission, her vision of broad Web access has become reality—in large part, through her hard work.

For a fuller account of the hundreds of people who worked with us over the years, especially as we collected material for the microfilm and guide, please see *Emma Goldman: A Guide to Her Life and Documentary Sources* (Alexandria, Va.: Chadwyck-Healey, 1995) for the lists of editors, administrative and program staff (especially the army of graduate students), research associates, production editors, editorial assistants, international search coordinators, international researchers, research assistants and translators, the hundreds of contributing library institutions, and donors. Among those who worked at the Project and helped set the path, we thank especially Ronald J. Zboray, the microfilm editor for the first six years; Daniel Cornford for his short but important year as associate editor; Thomas Peabody, who extended his research interests to serve as a key writer of the narrative notes for the microfilm edition; Alice Hall, who coordinated the government document series; Kurt Thompson, coordinator of the early computerization of our work; Dennis McEnnerney and Vivian Kleiman, who assisted in the very early domestic and international search; and the late Brenda Butler, our European and Asian search coordinator. Rebecca Hyman, Barbara Loomis, and Robert Cohen very wisely built our newspaper collection, always cognizant that the public perception of Goldman was a critical complement and counterpoint to our collection of her personal letters. To all those from near and far who came to work with us, even briefly, we extend our thanks. We hope that you can see the imprint of your work in this documentary edition and recognize the many facts that you tracked down years ago, now integrated into the historical fabric of these volumes.

For a more extensive collection of the sources from which much of the documents in this edition were selected, researchers may consult *Emma Goldman: A Comprehensive Microfilm Collection* (Alexandria, Va.: Chadwyck-Healey, 1991–1993). Though a remarkable number of new documents were found in the process of working on the annotations for the American years' edition, the material already in the Emma Goldman Papers Project microfilm collection, brought together from over a thousand archives and private collections, sets a broader documentary context (in raw form without the scholarly apparatus of annotations). The search for documents and their organization, identification, and publication in the microfilm archive laid the foundation for the book edition and took almost fifteen years. I thank the many people who worked with the Emma Goldman Papers in its early years, when its mission seemed more ephemeral, its tasks somewhat more mundane—and for the result, an archive that is a quiet gift to scholars and political activists for posterity.

A very spirited and talented group of undergraduate research assistants helped us pull the final details together, provided a fact-checking safety net, and shared our enthusiasm for expanding the scope of our documentary history to include a history of the anarchist activity in America and Europe that motivated and informed Goldman's work. This task required remarkable detective work and tenacity. Guided by Barry Pateman and Jessica Moran, the office has been buzzing with the excitement of discovery, the thrill of working with primary sources, and the sense that the time has come to fill this gap in the historical record—a mission the Emma Goldman Papers Project has been primed for and working toward for more than twenty years. Among the many students who helped with background research for the annotations and appendices and performed critical fact checking for the volumes, we thank especially Eric Hetzner and Nicole Waugh for their ever-refined research and annotation skills, as well as Katherine Allen, Rajeev Ananda, Jennifer Beeson, Christie Blakely, Ryan Boehm, Esther Byum, Theresa Chen, Rebecca Cohen, Evan Daniel, John Elrod, Hanni Fakhoury, Karen Rodriguez G', Jennifer Guth, Karen Hannah, Emily Hass, Stephen Higa, Lisa Hsia, Mary (Mollie) Hudgens,

Alexandra Kemp, Jenny Lah, Hillary Lazar, Rebecca Martinez, Tamara Martinez, Dennis Marzan, Shani McElroy, Sanaz Mozafarian, Jenny Mundy, Sara Newland, Emma Pollin, Heather Reese, Sara Smith, Mariyan Solimon, Emily Spangler, Sayuri Stabrowski, Kristin Stankiewicz, Rachel Starr, Sarah Stone, Andrea Valverde, Ehssan Vandaei, Billy Vega, Angeline Young, Nicole Zillmer, and Kenyon Zimmer, among others. Sadly we mourn the death of the reflective, gentle Rebecca Feiler, who came to the work later, and was snatched from life before her time. On the staff was Gabriella Karl who transcribed documents, performed background research for the annotations and directories, and helped coordinate the work of the students, and tended to the Project's administrative tasks. The administrative coordination of such a research project is enormous—and we thank especially the generous-spirited Joanna Sterricker and Georgia Moseley for keeping the plethora of forms and budgets and grants and paychecks moving, allowing the book edition to move forward as well. And in this age of rapidly aging computers and dwindling finances, we thank Michael Katz for his years and years of frugal technical problem solving and Jason Jedd for coming to our rescue so effectively over this past year of all-too-frequent computer crashes; and Nancy Gordon and Donna Lesh of Nancy Gordon and Associates, who donated their time to update and refine our ever-increasing mailing list of friends and supporters; and Erik Hetzner, the ultimate "Mr. Fix-It.".

The Project was also graced with the generous talents of translators Paul Sharkey (for French, Italian, and Spanish), the late Eli Katz (for Yiddish and German), and Lisa Little and the late Reginald Zelnik (for Russian). We thank them all for their steady availability, linguistic and political intuition, and enthusiasm for our work. We are grateful for the many outside researchers who took an interest in our work and led us to new documents—among whom, we especially thank Robert Helms for the kind sharing of his extensive knowledge of Philadelphia anarchists, Julia Kraut's shared focus on the early twentieth-century anti-anarchist laws, Yamaguchi Mamoru, who continues to share anarchist documents from China and Japan, and the many archivists who pored over their holdings on our behalf, answering our queries and sending us their discoveries.

Every writer and historian needs a sounding board, constructive criticism, and people on the outside of the work willing to jump in and pretend to be the average reader, especially in the final hours when clarity is of the essence. Writing the introduction to *Making Speech Free* was more difficult than I ever imagined. It was written during a time when the world—especially the United States—seemed ever more mired in violence. The task of setting the analytical frame for documents that cast new light upon the shadow side of the multi-faceted Emma Goldman raised questions that remain both unsettling and vital. I present the work with the humbling recognition that although the life and activities of a public historical figure whose clandestine involvements were integral to her political vision can never be fully revealed, it is now possible to read the silences between the documents as well as the documents themselves with more insight and clarity.

I thank my many friends who functioned as outside editors and personal advisors—spending hours reading through drafts and re-drafts of the various configurations of this edition as well as the proposals, letters, and ancillary public history material. First and foremost among those who gave so generously of themselves and their talents are Lorraine Kahn, filmmaker, humorist, cultural theorist, round-the-clock editing maven and sounding board whose editorial efforts consistently encompassed work well beyond the volumes; Julianne Burton, artful editor, professor of Latin American literature and film, local historian of Monterey, California, and biographer; Daniel Burton Rose, generous, multi-talented political and cultural consultant, and an ever-challenging thinker and writer for a new generation of activists; Joan K. Peters, professor of English and author of dazzling books on women and work, and Ruth Butler, professor of psychology at Hebrew University, whose attunement to language, ideas, and the complexity of living in and around violence while holding steadfastly to a vision of peace and coexistence, give me the confidence to offer a more philosophical coda to the introduction—on issues of "war or peace." All of these friends have showered me with love and meticulous attention to the detail of the work, and deserve much credit for the good within it. I also thank my fellow biographers, especially Ramsey Breslin, art critic, and poet, whose careful reading of the introduction to the first volume made all the difference and whose talent as an editor, thinker, and good-natured friend shepherded me through the nightmarish task of cutting and pasting, changing the format of the introduction to the second volume in ways that I could never have faced without her. I will always be grateful for the way in which she submerged herself during those final days before submission of the manuscript. This introduction marked a painful but necessary deconstruction of Emma Goldman. She, along with colleagues in the psychobiography study group, particularly Marilyn Fabe, film critic, Stephen Walrod, psychotherapist and art collector, and Alan Elms and William McKinley Runyan, leaders in the field of psychobiography, added depth to my understanding of the interaction between the historical and psychological conditions that shape individual experience not only of one's subject but of the biographer's relationship to that subject as well. I am also grateful for the heartfelt enthusiasm of Pia Lundberg, the remarkable visual anthropologist from Denmark who arrived at my doorstep just when I needed the constancy of an intelligent eye and the supportive friendship of another focused writer in the house. Remi Omodele, dear friend, neighbor, and scholar of the theater, not only brightened my daily life, wrapping family and work seamlessly together, but imparted her tremendous insight into the political history of the theater and Goldman's relationship to it as well as her piercing political understanding of the global dynamic of the struggle for freedom against injustice. Harriet Sage, modest force, staunch friend, and appreciator of books and of people, shared her keen psychological insights into the inner Goldman, and stood by me through sickness and health with wisdom and generosity.

Librarians and archivists are at the core of almost every dimension of our work. The foundation of all documentary editions are the primary sources and the books that provide an accurate historical context. A documentary editing project could simply not exist without the assistance of archivists and librarians, whose quiet, persistent, meticulous dedication makes all research possible. We thank you all. Fine anarchist collections are especially rare, and the Emma Goldman Papers Project has been fortunate to work on an almost daily basis with Julie Herrada, who succeeded Ed Webber and Katherine Beam as curator of the Labadie Collection at the University of Michigan; Herrada shared her material and her expertise with utmost generosity. The International Institute for Social History in Amsterdam, where Goldman placed both her own collection and Berkman's after his death, allowed much of its extensive Goldman archive to be integrated into our comprehensive microfilm collection and has continued to assist the Emma Goldman Papers Project, graciously filling in for previous omissions from her early political years, including rare Berkman items, and offering access to the many difficult-to-find journals and photographs preserved in its archive. We thank especially those who worked at IISH when the Project began—including Rudolf de Jong, Thea Djuiker, Kees Rodenburg, Mieke Ijzermans, and then-director Erik Fisher—and the current director, Jaap Kloosterman, for his ongoing assistance. We also honor the memory of Deborah Bernhardt, director of New York University's Tamiment Institute and Robert F. Wagner collections, who graced our project with archival sources and true friendship and camaraderie, and we thank those who followed her great example.

Fortunately for the Emma Goldman Papers, associate editor Barry Pateman is also the curator of the Kate Sharpley Library, the largest collection of English-language anarchist material in the U.K. Especially for the material on Goldman's early years and for full-run copies of rare anarchist journals, his collection cannot be matched. It has been remarkable to have access to a breadth of material, literally at our fingertips, deepening the Project's understanding of the anarchist movement and refining the historical research for the books.

The Project is also privileged to be part of the University of California, Berkeley, an institution with one of the most extensive research libraries in the nation. With over a thousand books circulating from their stacks to our office, a steady stream of interlibrary loan requests, almost constant use of the newspaper microfilm reading room, and frequent trips to the Bancroft Library's archival collection—we are deeply indebted to all who have facilitated our work, graciously approving the multitude of proxy cards in my name, patiently taking our orders, respecting our work, and even restoring rare manuscripts given to the Project. We thank Beth Sibley for expanding the collection on our behalf, Gillian Boal for her careful restoration, the staff at the circulation desk, especially Joyce Ford, a longtime colleague from afar, all the staff at the Interlibrary Loan Service, and all the staff in the Microfilm Reading Room, especially Vicki Jourdan. We especially thank and honor former director of the library the late Peter Lyman for his generosity to the Emma Goldman Papers, and we honor current University Librarian Tom Leonard, and especially the director of the Bancroft Library, Charles Faulhaber, who has helped garner financial and administrative support for the Project. In the process of working on these first volumes of the documentary edition, we have had the help of many talented archivists and librarians at "Cal" and across the nation. As kindred book people, we salute your work, and thank you for your assistance over the years.

We would like particularly to acknowledge the pioneering work of the historian Richard Drinnon, who in 1961 (twenty-one years after her death) published *Rebel in Paradise,* the first biography of Emma Goldman. His book presaged the free speech movement on the Berkeley campus and the women's movement. The publication of Drinnon's work may have fanned the flames of protest as organizers welcomed the discovery of a resonant historical spirit. The Drinnons helped me years ago, when I was pregnant with child and also with great hopes as I embarked on the writing of the biography *Love, Anarchy, and Emma Goldman.* Although we came to the Berkeley campus at very different times, it seems that Richard Drinnon carved the space for Goldman there, and led the way for "Emmasaries" everywhere.

There are no books at the Project's office as worn from our daily use as those written by the late Paul Avrich, the renowned scholar of multiple volumes on the history of anarchism, who also has generously helped us with innumerable queries over the years. For his careful reading of our texts, cumulative knowledge, and camaraderie, we remember him with profound respect and appreciation. His dignity and fine work continue to be an inspiration and our guide.

THE STORY OF THOSE WHO HELPED sustain the work of the Emma Goldman Papers deserves a book in itself. Like all good projects without a secure financial base—including Goldman's magazine *Mother Earth*—we have relied on the generosity of our friends and our kindred spirits to pull us through. Over time, our "Emma's List," a group of donors who have helped us bring Emma's words into libraries and bookstores (and the counterpart to "Emily's List," a fund focused on electing women into public office), has evolved into a strong community bound together by a desire to preserve the courage of those who, like Emma Goldman, dared to challenge hypocrisy and to affirm what she considered everybody's right to a world of economic and social liberty. Our staunch Emma's List supporters at all levels have surrounded us with kindness, affirming the significance of our work and replenishing our resilience and perseverance. We thank you all.

Like Goldman's own circle of political theorists, writers, journalists, and creative thinkers on the burning issues of her time, the wide array of professional and personal paths represented on Emma's List is a tribute to the all-encompassing hope and inspiration the story of her life continues to evoke. It is important to note, however, that Emma's List contributors by no means all agree on every aspect of Goldman's political trajectory. The unifying principle of their support is the belief that the history of the early battles for free expression and the story of courage of individuals like Emma Goldman deserve a permanent place in the nation's documentary record.

Among the most compassionate and generous of our sustaining contributors is Lois Blum Feinblatt, whose modest dignity and concern for every aspect of the Project's well-being has grounded us in love. Her commitment to the promotion of mentoring in the schools and her own work as a psychotherapist combined to bestow upon us all the wisdom, tolerance, and open-mindedness that characterizes Emma's List. The matriarch of a remarkably generous and politically impressive family, all of whom have contributed to the Emma Goldman Papers, Lois Blum Feinblatt has been the sweet soul who at various times underwrote the cost of our office space and whose constancy and faith in the value of long-term research allowed us to push on. Her daughter, Carolyn Patty Blum, a dear friend and colleague, is a lawyer who has championed human rights and protected political exiles and whose work—in the spirit of Emma—puts fear into the heart of torturers everywhere. She not only contributed to our material well-being but also was a brilliant reader for the introductory essays, especially on issues of human rights so integral to Goldman's work. And we thank also Patty's husband, Harry Chotiner, a historian, remarkable teacher, unflinching enthusiast, and long-time friend, for enriching our work with a veritable library of books and ideas over so many years. Lois's daughter-in-law, Judith Smith, an insightful historian of gender and race, sent the Emma Goldman Papers Project the royalties from her book on urban history to promote our work; and her sister, Sarah Malino, also a women's historian, added her contribution as well. Lois's cousin, Sunny Jo Brodsky, quilted beautiful wall hangings with photographic images of Emma to adorn the halls of our Project and even designed a pot-holder of Goldman's invitation for sharing some of her famously delicious "blintzes."

Cora Weiss, an Emma Goldman in her own right, proclaimed that "You don't have to be an anarchist to want Emma Goldman resources readily available. Women need role models on how to be effective advocates, and how to make a perfect blintz." Weiss is one of the most consistent, persevering nongovernmental advocates for world peace and the rights of women and girls in our time—her accomplishments and force of character have had a remarkable impact on the movement against war and for global harmony and freedom. With her leadership, the Samuel Rubin Foundation, committed to the promotion of work for peace and justice, graciously stretched their guidelines for many years to honor the importance of the documentation of the lives and activities of those in our past whose courage and vision laid the groundwork for the well-being of present and future generations across the world. One can only hope that the Rubin Foundation, and Cora Weiss too, will consider documenting their own impressive history as an example of how individuals can, in fact, make an enormous difference. We have been honored to have their support.

The most remarkable recent rescue of the Emma Goldman Papers Project came from Stephen Silberstein, a librarian and developer of computer systems who advanced the field of digitized access and catalogue information retrieval and was a supporter of the University of California, Berkeley's free speech movement. Working with others, Silberstein ensured that the history of that dramatic time in the 1960s would be a point of pride on the Berkeley campus. His contribution to the Emma Goldman Papers Project followed the path blazed by his generous establishment of the Free Speech Movement Cafe in Moffitt Library and a free speech archive at the Bancroft Library that is also part of the California Digital Library, available via the Internet to students of all ages all over the world. We thank him for extending his support to the documentation of Emma Goldman's early battles for free speech, thus anchoring our work as part of the legacy of those who fought to uphold the right of free expression on college campuses across the nation.

The J. M. Kaplan Fund, through its project "Furthermore," has also contributed generously to our work, helping us get closer to publication and sharing our commitment to the documentary history of the long and arduous struggle for freedom as well as an appreciation for the feisty and courageous Emma Goldman. Like bookends, the L. J. and Mary C. Skaggs Foundation, that helped launch the Goldman Papers microfilm edition, has now come back, upon the encouragement of Charles Faulhaber of the Bancroft Library, to contribute to the completion of the book edition—as did Jean Stone, whose husband, Irving, wrote many biographies with her help on prominent figures in Goldman's circle; and Kimo Campbell of the Pohaku Fund, also a supporter of our fellow editing colleagues at the Mark Twain Papers.

A large proportion of our supporters, though by no means all, are people I've known for a very long time who generously stretched their friendship to encompass the Emma Goldman Papers Project. The constant thread that ties this extended family of friends is our belief in the possibility of change—the ongoing quest for social and economic ethics, the blossoming of individual creativity, and the readiness to question authority in the name of social justice. Kernels of such values are evident in the myriad of activities and life choices of many on Emma's List.

The generous contributions of Judith Taylor, elegant poet and loyal friend, include her finely honed literary sensibilities—and the willingness to make the judgment call at midnight for a sentence fix, to rein in excess, and to extend to the Project her compassion for the arduous process of years of small victories and minor setbacks. For her belief in the value of work outside conventional norms and her acceptance and tolerance for both "the good *and* bad Emma"—icon and complex political figure—we thank her.

Hannah Kranzberg, a soulful spirit and friend, who has helped give voice to the progressive Jewish community, to a vision of peace and justice, and to the arts, gave graciously of herself in my moments of despair—like Emma herself, Hannah is grounded in her culture and reaches beyond it, in the name of freedom.

My long-lost, energetic cousin Marjorie Solomon, cutting-edge research practitioner in psychology, and her husband, Mark Friedman, creative "urban revivalist," have contributed generously to the Emma Goldman Papers.

Extraordinary documentary filmmakers and friends Bill Jersey and Shirley Kessler contributed generously to the Emma Goldman Papers Project over the years as kindred spirits in the challenging quest to make the history of the struggle for freedom accessible, piercing, and visually inviting. Their talents for celebrating the rituals of life have deepened my own understanding of the link between private and public history.

Among those friends whose contributions to the Project extended into the actual writing and research, are the magnificent Marge Frantz, radical historian, and Eleanor Engstrand, veteran librarian, both women for peace and pillars of the community, who saw me through the very beginnings of the Emma Goldman Papers Project and spent endless hours discussing nuances of history and musing about whether or not the world had in fact moved forward. They, along with the eloquent biographer of William Lloyd Garrison, the late Henry Mayer; the insightful historian of the "comrades and chicken farmers" of the Petaluma area, Ken Kann; and the modest Emma Goldman-like Sarah Crome, my closest early associate at the Project, invited me to join the Chamakome ranch, a cooperative retreat named after an earlier Native American village on the same ridge along the north coast of California. Surrounded by beauty and rare quiet, the Chamakome ranch has become for me a sacred space for finding the focus so vital to the writing and editing of the Goldman volumes. (I often wonder whether Goldman's ability to put her early thoughts in writing could have been attributed in part to Bolton Hall, who gave her "the farm," her country retreat up the Hudson River in Ossining, New York, and later, to Peggy Guggenheim, who gave her "Bon Esprit" in St. Tropez, France, where she wrote her autobiography.) For the privilege of solitude and the solace of community, I thank my Chamakome-mates, many of whom have also generously extended the ranch spirit of mutual aid to Emma's List.

I especially thank the John Simon Guggenheim Foundation for granting me the time for my own writing, the honor of being in the elevated company of its very impressive history of "fellows," and for the encouragement to develop aspects of my work that diverge slightly from the path of the Goldman Papers to include personal and political reflections upon these many years of editorial engagement with Emma.

One of the most gratifying aspects of Emma's List support has been the great privilege of receiving contributions in memory of those who lived in Emma's spirit and in honor of those who continue keep her legacy alive. Most touching of all are the contributions from the families of Goldman's nearest and dearest friends—a gesture of continuity that has grounded our historical research across time, across generations. The first of such contributions came years before the volumes had even begun. The late Art Bortollotti, the Italian anarchist jailed in Canada under the repressive laws of the pre–World War II era, won his freedom largely due to what was Goldman's last political battle— arousing public opinion on his behalf. In homage and appreciation to his dear friend and comrade, Bortollotti sent his generous contribution of funds for the preservation of Goldman's papers and the documentation of her political work with a note written on the Goldman stationery that he had saved for over forty years.

Mecca Reitman Carpenter, the daughter of Goldman's wayward lover and road manager, Ben Reitman, embraced the Project with great ideas especially for our public outreach and funding, as her father had done for Emma for over a decade so many years before. Giving generously of her own resources, she weathered our struggles and celebrated our victories. Years ago when I wrote *Love, Anarchy, and Emma Goldman,* the very graphic, erotic story of Goldman's complex and passionate relationship with Mecca's father, I feared the censure of members of the Reitman family who might take offense at the sexual themes of the book. Instead, I found the compassionate Mecca, who had worked through her own relationship to her father in the unusually accepting biography of his many loves, *No Regrets: Dr. Ben Reitman and the Women Who Loved Him,* never shunning the raw complexity of the clash of love and anarchy between her father and Emma. Even when her own health has failed her, Mecca Reitman Carpenter has not faltered in her support of the Emma Goldman Papers.

The same devotion that propelled the friendship between Goldman and Ida and Ben Capes extended to the Capes children, grandchildren, nephews, and nieces to support the Emma Goldman

Papers—one of the most moving outpourings of friendship across generations and across the continents. In a similar extension of camaraderie, we have received contributions from the sons of Goldman's witty lawyer, Arthur Leonard Ross; the daughter of Goldman's Canadian friends, Sophie and Joe Desser, who in her youth had also assisted Goldman with her secretarial work; the son of Curtis Reese, who delivered an oration at Goldman's funeral; the daughter of Esther Laddon, who provided Goldman a home base in Canada; and the daughter of Goldman's friend Kate Wolfson. The late David Diamond, composer and violinist, and son of Goldman's Rochester, New York, seamstress, Chanele (Anna) Schilhaus, sent his contribution with a remembrance of Goldman standing on a footstool with pins in her skirt as she cheered on his musical career as a violinist—"Kling in de ganze Velt" (Play for the entire world)—as the smell of her rosewater perfume suffused the air. Warren Billings, a friend of Alexander Berkman, who was jailed in connection with the 1916 Preparedness Day bombing in San Francisco, was remembered by his niece, who also contributed many of Billings's books by Goldman to the Project. The Ferrer Colony in Stelton, New Jersey, was remembered by many of the children of its members, including the late Helen Seitz, who as a child sat on Emma's lap when she visited the colony (Helen remembered being scared and repelled by the sweaty embrace of this anarchist celebrity); she told us that her parents met at a soiree in New York City given in Goldman's honor. Another dear friend of the Project is Amy Olay Kaplan, whose grandfather Maximiliano Olay was one of Emma Goldman's Spanish translators; together we uncovered her grandparents' hidden past. Others who joined Emma's List grew up in anarchist circles in Chicago, Toronto, New York, and London. The late Wu Ke Kang (Woo Yang Hao), a member of the Chinese anarchist circle living in Paris and translator of Goldman's works, was one among many who sent his support and recollections of Goldman's influence on China's early revolution—especially on the revered author the late Ba Jin. The late Arthur Weinberg, who attended Goldman's funeral services in Chicago, kindly corrected the reminiscences of others interviewed by the Project about the event. Many who grew up in the circle of Chicago anarchists that supported Emma Goldman have also extended their affectionate attachment to their colorful past through their support of the Goldman Papers' current work—among whom is the magnificent Evelyn Tabachnick and her husband, Norman, who have carried the anarchist respect for the development and flourishing of the individual into their work in the field of psychology and psychiatry. Free-speech-advocate Roger Baldwin's god-daughter Katrina vanden Heuvel, the magnificent editor of *Nation* magazine, remembered his bedtime stores of Emma's courageous resolve and run-ins with the police. One contributor found a chance notation in his mother's diary chronicling her attempt with a baby buggy to mount the stairs of a crowded hall in San Francisco, anxious to hear Goldman lecture. These and other stories add life and texture to our work, and the sweetness of human contact (see Emma's List Remembrances).

Contributors with personal contact to Goldman in her lifetime added their recollections to the Project's reminiscence file, which contains interviews with Goldman associates now deceased, ranging from Roger Baldwin, the co-founder of the American Civil Liberties Union, to Mollie Ackerman, one among many of Goldman's young secretaries and friends. Ahrne Thorne, editor of *Fraye Arbeter Stimme,* spent hours sharing his ideas and commiserating about the mammoth task I had taken on. Albert Meltzer, the London anarchist whom Goldman referred to as "a young hooligan," opened his heart to the Emma Goldman Papers Project, sharing his ideas and his books, widening his circle to include us and our work. Federico Arcos and his late wife, Pura, inspired by Goldman in their youth in Spain, opened their home in Canada and displayed their collection of Goldman's books and even her suitcases.

Most basic to the actual publication of Goldman's works has been the generosity and friendship bestowed upon us by Goldman's nephews and literary heirs—David and the late Ian Ballantine. I remember Ian Ballantine, the publisher of Bantam (and Ballantine) Books, sitting behind a desk in a very tall office building in New York and boasting, "Aunt Emma never believed in restrictions of any kind, so why should I?" Over the years, David Ballantine, an author and collector of antique guns, shared with the Project various items his aunt had secreted away, including the ledger documenting those who contributed to her work, her legal fees, and the cost of incidentals for her magazine and lecture tours. Without their sanction, the written legacy of Emma Goldman could never have been as extensively preserved—and accessible.

Parents, children, and friends—all have been honored on Emma's List. The group as a whole is a remarkable blend—joining together political thinkers Howard Zinn and Noam Chomsky; pioneers of the women's movement, most notably Gloria Steinem, and of women's research, such as Mariam Chamberlain, Gerda Lerner, and Naomi Weisstein, among many others; and stellar literary figures including E. L. Doctorow, Barbara Kingsolver, Marilyn French, Erica Jong, Ken Burrows, Dianne Middlebrook, Peter Glassgold, Brenda Webster, and the late and witty muckraking author Jessica Mitford, who was completely in thrall to issues raised by Emma's life but thought it "deadly boring" to brave organizing anybody's papers, no matter how great they were.

Among the more theatrical figures on Emma's List drawn to Goldman's life are Susan Sarandon and Tim Robbins, Harold Ramis, and documentary filmmakers Vivian Kleiman, Rick Goldsmith, and Coleman Romalis (whose film on Emma Goldman in Canada includes an interview with the Emma Goldman Papers Project as well). Others include Pacifica Radio commentator and filmmaker Alan Snitow and Deborah Kauffman, who founded with Janice Plotkin the San Francisco Jewish Film Festival. The late Rella Lossy wrote a wonderful and playful theater piece on Ben and Emma. We have worked with several actresses who played Emma in the theatrical adaptation of E. L. Doctorow's book *Ragtime,* especially Camille Saviola and Mary Gutzi. Years ago, the actress Adele Proom impersonated Emma, pretending to break into what was an inspired benefit performance by the spirited singer and songwriter Michelle Shocked—a gathering of remarkable community and university activists who also read from the Goldman letters and speeches that most matched their own work. The political satirist and illustrator Ed Sorel once identified Emma in a cartoon as one of the "messy" characters with which a certain kind of political activist feels at home—a sentiment to which we all concur. Also among Emma's List supporters is Nina Hartley, feminist and pornographic-film actress, proudly carrying on the legacy of Goldman's celebration of sexuality and campaign against Puritanism.

Among the contributors to Emma's List are many who have devoted their lives to the documentation of the struggle for freedom. Most generous and enthusiastic among women's historians is Nancy Hewitt, who believes that much of what has shaped America is "wisdom from the margins." In her article published in *Voices of Women Historians* (1999; edited by Eileen Boris and Nupur Chaudhuri), Hewitt has claimed us all as the keepers of "Emma's Thread" of commutarian values and global visions. In a touching gesture of solidarity, over the years Hewitt has made contributions to the Project in honor of many of her students; when they earn their doctorates, they receive an archival photograph of Emma Goldman writing at a desk adorned with lilies, printed by Richard Gordon—the Project's donor gift to keep the inspiration flowing! We are honored by the financial support and intellectual vote of confidence from historians across the nation—Martha Ackelsberg, Harriet Alonso, Eric Anderson, Elizabeth Berry, Eileen Boris, Virginia Bouvier, Robert Cherny, Harry Chotiner, Blanche Weisen Cook, Nancy Cott, Carol DeBoer-Langworthy, Carl N. Degler, John P. Diggens, Martin Duberman, Tom Dublin, Bob Dunn, Robin Einhorn, Robert Elias, Marge Frantz, Estelle Freedman, Susan Glenn, Jim Gregory, Susan Groves, Robert Hamburger, Louis Harlan, Francis Richardson Keller, Linda Kerber, Alice Kessler-Harris, Ira Lapidus, Jesse Lemisch, Lawrence and Cornelia Levine, Lary May, Sally Miller, Nell Painter, Carl Prince, David Roediger, Ruth Rosen, Carol Rosenberg, Florence Rosenstock and James Van Luik, Roy Rosenzweig, Sheila Rowbotham, the late Lucio Ruotolo, Lillian Schlissel, Harvey Schwartz, Alix Shulman, Barbara Sicherman, Kitty Sklar, Daniel Soyer, Christine Stansell, Peter Stansky, Randolph Starn, G. Thomas Tanselle, Barbara Tischler, William Tuttle, Jr., Elaine Tyler, Laurel Ulrich, Susan Vladmir-Morgan, Daniel and Judith Walkowitz, Lynn Weiner, Barbara Winslow, Yamaguchi Mamoru, Yamazumi Susumu, and Martin Zelig, among others—and from our colleagues among scholarly documentary editors, especially Rudolph Vecoli of the Immigration History Project, Maeva Marcus of the Documentary History of the Supreme Court, John and Harriet Simon of the Ulysses S. Grant and of the John Dewey Papers, respectively, and my dear friends Clayborne and Susan Carson of the Martin Luther King, Jr., Papers—all of whose historical work resonates with Goldman's and makes a difference—today. We are grateful for the research assistance and documentary record of the Consortium for Women's History—the Margaret Sanger Papers, the Elizabeth Cady Stanton and Susan B. Anthony Papers, and the Jane Addams papers, led by the soulful pioneer of women in documentary editions, Mary Lynn McCree Bryan. The newest, and perhaps most spirited member of our women's consortium, Allida Black, the editor of the Eleanor Roosevelt Papers, has illuminated the present as well as the past in her very timely work. We also appreciated the members of the Emma Goldman Papers faculty advisory board who answered our queries and validated our work among colleagues across scholarly disciplines. Led by Leon Litwack, they include, among others, Lawrence Levine, whose historical studies on race, the unpredictable past, and the dignity of a lowbrow culture in a pretentious world created an affinity to the people and ideas in and around the project; the late Reginald Zelnik, generous Russian scholar, who advanced his commitment to free speech through history and action; Susan Schweik, the literary scholar (who named her daughter Emma), whose work on women's poetry of war and leadership in the affirmation of the dignity and fight against isolation of the disabled brought her closer to the ideas and culture of the anarchists; and the late Michael Rogin, whose appreciation was familial and dated back to 1906, when his great aunt Rosie Rogin was arrested with Emma Goldman.

Emma's List has elicited an unusual gathering of supporters for whom Goldman's story taps into both their desire to promote the social good and their own streak of rebelliousness and daring. These desires are expressed in the way they live their lives and in the manner in which they choose and perform their work—and are the common denominator of this outstanding group. It has been an honor to be in their midst, and to have their support. Members of Emma's List come from a wide range of occupations—from workers in methadone clinics, psychotherapists, and doctors, to retired women who send $18 each year to signify "chai" or "life" in Hebrew. Many are archivists and anarchists, students, teachers, librarians, social scientists, university administrators and community activists, labor leaders, publishers, editors, journalists, newscasters, radio personalities, economics analysts, philanthropists, foundation officials, professors from an amazing array of scholarly disciplines, anthropologists, secretaries, flight attendants, architects, designers, photographers, public health advocates, environmental activists and arborists, scientists, statisticians, tennis and soccer moms and dads, Pulitzer prize winners, progressive religious leaders, gourmet cooks, computer whizzes and mathematicians, artists, actors, progressive business executives, and a large contingent of progressive attorneys.

Among those who welcome our calls for help is garden preservationist, photographer, and friend Marion Brenner, who continues to grace us with her photoscanning time and talent. The critical-realist photographer Richard Gordon and graphic designers Andrea Sohn (the niece of the Project's co-founder Sarah Crome) and Lisa Roth on our outreach public-history materials have maintained the level of excellence in the Project.

San Diego consumer advocacy attorney Eric Isaacson, who found us through the Emma Goldman Papers website, single-handedly determined that he would change the bad reputation of his city in which Goldman's lover and manager Ben Reitman was driven into the desert—tarred, sagebrushed, and sexually attacked by a band of high-level city officials acting as vigilantes—as part of the incredibly brutal San Diego free speech fight of 1912. Recently, Eric Isaacson organized support for the Emma Goldman Papers Project, rallying his partners and friends to come to our aid in a moment of deep financial crisis. There is a kind of poetic justice underlying this outpouring of support for the Emma Goldman Papers from advocates for consumer and stockholders' rights who have chosen to share a portion of the proceeds of their victories with those who are documenting the papers of one of the great foremothers of the battle against corporate greed.

Our research base has always been the University of California, Berkeley. By far the most compassionate and forward-thinking members of the university's administrative team have been Joseph Cerny, the former vice chancellor for research, and his core staff, associate vice chancellor Linda Fabbri, and director of budget and personnel Susan Hirano—all of whom recognized the value of the kind of research that didn't fit neatly into the established categories of the university. These volumes are a tribute to their belief and support, and to the quiet but critical efforts of others who add courage and vision to the mix of administrative duties. More recently, it has been professor Edwin M. Epstein, chair of Peace and Conflict Studies, and John Lie, Dean of International and Area Studies who have been our champions and rescue team when the gates of universities' beneficence to those outside the mold has been rapidly closing.

Briefly under Chancellor Robert M. Berdahl, the Emma Goldman Papers Project has enjoyed periods of relative security that allowed the work to move forward—and without which these volumes could never have been published with such care.

We are grateful to the National Endowment for the Humanities for the intermittent support—including a one-year grant toward the editing of the volumes. More than ten years ago, NEH support solidified the Project's work with a three-year grant that coincided with parallel support from both the Ford and the Rockefeller Foundations. Those early grants helped create the base from which these volumes on Goldman's American years were written, and are greatly appreciated. We thank especially Sheila Biddle, formerly of the Ford Foundation, whose dedication and generosity continues to be a source of affirmation and camaraderie.

There are many anarchist archives across the globe in which all the work of processing the material is voluntary and completely run as a cooperative. Their staffs, unlike our varied group, all share the same anarchist political perspective. The idea of applying for government grants and constantly jumping through administrative hoops, or even accepting corporate funds, would be abhorrent to them. We revere their tenacity, devotion, and ability to merge the form and content of their work. We have benefited from their sources, and from their wisdom, and hope that they too value our efforts, recognize the validity of our struggles, and will reap the benefits of the Emma Goldman Papers' remarkable depth of research—now available to all.

To our vast range of contributors, material and spiritual, the ever-generous members of Emma's List—and the many small donors with large spirits, unnamed in the volume but whose combined support has carried us through our sparsest times, to those who stood by us during our own free speech battle—we send our appreciation and respect and hope that you will take pride in having contributed to a work intended for posterity. We have also been showered with gifts that are intangible—gestures of support from friends, family, and community which signal that this very long process is worth the effort.

We thank the many institutions, foundations, and individuals who have lent their names and generous spirit and talent to the Emma Goldman Papers over the years—and laid the foundation for the comprehensive reach of the volumes. While we appreciate your support, we relieve you of responsibility for factual mistakes or errors of omission on our part. We are also grateful to our extended family of friends and colleagues, unnamed here but not forgotten, without whom this work would never have come this far.

EMMA GOLDMAN and the Emma Goldman Papers Project have been fixed constellations in my immediate family, looming over and around us with a constancy that has been both reassuring and disconcerting at times—a long-term relationship that has deepened with time. It has been more than twenty-five years since the day my husband-to-be and I browsed in a guitar store in Chicago's Hyde Park with my dog "Emma"—a rambunctious Irish setter–Golden retriever who burst into the shop after us. From the moment my friend John (son of the late and magnificent Ruth and Merlin Bowen), who worked at the shop, asked her name, my personal history was transformed forever. Scratching his head as he stroked the dog, Bowen remembered that he had seen back in the storeroom a box of letters that bore the large scrawl "E. Goldman" on the envelopes' return addresses. Within minutes, a boot box of old, yellowed letters appeared, and we were overtaken with the torrent of passion and torment between Emma Goldman, the great heroine of personal and political freedom, and the wayward and promiscuous Ben Reitman, her talented road manager and lover. It was not long before I embarked on the first of many challenging attempts to draw together and interpret the complexities of Goldman's all-encompassing spirit. For me, a young student in my twenties and very much a part of the women's movement and counterculture "love" generation, reading letters Goldman had written when she was thirty-eight years old seemed like prying into the surprising vulnerabilities of a very old woman. Many people helped me muster the confidence to write a respectful biography of the struggle to balance her exalted vision with her conflicted experience of intimacy and love. After more than twenty-five years of living with the papers of Emma Goldman, the perspective of age has became an important overlay and my concerns have shifted and broadened to include more of the historical context and detail of Goldman's circle od supporters and detractors. All through my intense engagement with the issues in and around Goldman's life, the love and constancy of my family and friends kept me from losing myself to the past, from losing track of my own trajectory and parallel entitlement to a full life. For this, and more, I especially thank my husband, Lowell Finley, there from the very first discovery of Emma's letters, master of titles, editorial sounding board, advocate of free speech and political justice, shield of caring and love; my daughter, Mara, an eloquent young woman who combines compassion for the rights of workers and the love of the written word, and son, Jesse, a creative young man with a vision—who have all allowed Emma to be a positive presence in their lives and have respected the preemptive demands of work on the Emma Goldman Papers Project with remarkable patience and affection.

When I was pulled by illness all too abruptly into a treacherous and tenuous realm of life and death, my family, friends, colleagues, and talented healers rallied to my support. I am forever grateful to have survived that harrowing time. That my children's lives were cradled in kindness and the momentum of the work of the Emma Goldman Papers hardly faltered, is a tribute to an extraordinary community for whom the desire to repair the world extends to caring for each other. Among the many who were at my side at that time, I thank especially Norma Blight, mother-in-law extraordinaire; Cornelia Sherman, cousin and soul-mate; and my dear friends Nancy Bardacke, Yvette Chalom and Paul Fogel, Ruth Butler and Arie Arnon, Joan K. Peters and Peter Passell, Remi Omodele and Ric Lucien, Meredith Miller and Richard Gordon, Cleo Deras and Carlos Hernandez, Deborah Hirtz Waterman, and my sister, Jane Falk, linguist and writer whose caring actions have spoken louder than words, and the aunts, uncles, cousins, various in-laws, and adopted family across the country—all of whom never faltered in their caring and love. And where else but in the Bay Area can one find such remarkably forward-thinking restorers of health? I am profoundly grateful to my doctors Debu Tripathy and Laura Esserman, who combine amazing compassion with cutting-edge research, and to Michael Broffman (and his compassionate assistant Louise Estupinian), doctor of acupuncture and complementary medicine, whose creativity and willingness to step away from the dominant paradigm is in the spirit of Emma herself. I thank also Adele Schwarz, Eileen Poole, Donna La Flamme, and Neil Kostick, whose intuitions about the intersection of the mind and the body gave me hope in my darkest hours, and to doctors Philip O'Keefe (and his compassionate associates Deborah Graves and Suoan Sullivan), and Charles Jenkins and Risa Kagan, whose caring attention to detail literally saved my life, and to my sweet soulful support group—the "bosom buddies" Denyse Gross, Barbara Hoffer, the late Anja Hübener, and the late Jeannie McGregor.

Ultimately, the Emma Goldman Papers Project too could not have survived without a community of support—scholars, donors, political activists, and ordinary people whose imaginations were sparked by Goldman's daring. The unique and intrepid City of Berkeley has honored Emma Goldman "as a major figure in the history of American radicalism and feminism . . . early advocate of free speech, birth control, women's equality and independence, union organization" and commended the Project for its "perseverance" and for inspiring the "collaboration of scholars, archivists, activists, students, and volunteers, both in Berkeley and around the world." In 1998, the city council proclaimed May 14—the day of Emma Goldman's death—as Emma Goldman Papers Project Day. With the publication of these volumes, we hope to mark a rebirth of interest in Goldman as "a voice crying out against injustice and oppression, wherever it has existed"—and we honor all those who helped make our work possible.

WITH APPRECIATION AND RESPECT,

CANDACE FALK

INDEX

Page number in italics indicate illustrations; page numbers immediately followed by the abbreviation Ital. indicate documents in the Italian language; other abbreviations used include EG (Emma Goldman) and AB (Alexander Berkman).

American Revolution, 176–77, 323, 448n9

American Secular Union, 522

American Single Tax League, 564

American Society of Friends of Russian Freedom: Breshkovskaya's tour and, 148, 494; Chicago branch of, 149n1; description of, 555–56; as liberal rallying point, 26; meetings of, 471, 512; members of, 511, 520, 542, 546; PSR support from, 563

American Woman Suffrage Association, 511, 554; journal of, 48

Am Olam (Eternal People) colonization movement, 158n2, 532

anarchism: as absence of State, 341–42; anarchy distinguished from, 153; and Jewish culture, 15; censorship of Czolgosz question and, 38–39; chronology of EG's speeches on, 469, 470, 476, 479, 480, 481, 483, 487, 488, 490, 491, 492, 493, 494, 496, 498, 500, 501, 502; definitions of, by government, 16–17, 115n1, 434; definitions of, by sympathizers, 21–22n47; direct action as fundamental to, 276; as doing preparatory work of destruction, 80, 173; EG's speeches on, 227, 273–77, 291–94; growth of interest in, 226–27; ideals of, 4–5, 7, 13, 37, 40, 273, 274, 282; misunderstandings about, 52, 72–73; police ignorance of, 455; as process and as protest, 340; reform of, 133; self-defense taught in, 95. See also anarchist communism; anarchists; anarchist/socialist/liberal alliance; anarcho-syndicalism; anti-anarchist laws; *A Beautiful Ideal* (EG); socialism vs. anarchism; *What I Believe* (EG)

anarchist communism: Bauer on, 318; development of, 550–51; EG and development of, 60; EG's approach to, 41, 54; ideals of, 5, 263, 294, 341; Reclus's approach to, 539. See also Kropotkin, Peter

Anarchist Federation: AB's role in, 44n79; description of, 556; founding of, 282n4, 510–11; May 1 demonstration and, 492; publications of, 489; Silverstein as member of, 297n4, 298, 299

Anarchistic Ball (Baueren Ball, Peasants Ball), 258, 487. See also *Mother Earth* (New York): fund-raising balls of

anarchist individualism: assassination and, 205; decline of, 544–45; Stirner's role in, 162n1, 543; Tucker's book on, 263. See also egoism; individual

anarchist pacifism, 14n27, 544

Anarchist Red Cross, 258n2

anarchists: Averbuch portrayed as, 281–82; barred from immigration and naturalization, 471; caricatures of, 2, 79; convention of, 473; Czolgosz as or not, 2, 8, 9, 10–11, 95, 197, 200–204, 324, 425n4; differences of opinion among, 6; dissatisfaction felt by, 173; EG's alliance with militant, 2–3; executions of Spanish, 509, 513; first Jewish U.S. organization for, 529–30; number of, 357–58; Turner's case and, 18–20

anarchist/socialist/liberal alliance: appeal to, 404; context of, 2–3; EG's acceptance in, 24; formation of, 20–21; in free speech fight, 49; goals in, 104; for supporting Mexican political exiles, 63–64; synergies in, 3–6

anarcho-syndicalism, 19, 60. See also syndicalists and syndicalism

Anderson, Margaret, 41n74

Andrews, John Bertram, 263, 508

Andrews, Stephen Pearl, 211, 508, 546

Andreyev, Leonid Nikolayevitch, 401, 508

Angiolillo, Michele: biographical summary on, 508–9; Cánovas assassinated by, 347, 351, 508, 513; mentioned, 128

Anthropological Society (Chicago), 490

anti-anarchist laws: anarchism defined in, 16–17; context of, 2–3, 79; EG's understanding of personal effect of, 66–67; expansion of, 67n98; in France (*lois scélérates*), 545; free speech implications of, 6–8, 79; Kropotkin on, 127–28; legal precedent for, 21; in New York, 16–17, 38–39, 197n3, 200, 434n12, 469; organization to fight, 557–58. See also Immigration Act (1903)

anti-militarism: growth of, 243; impetus for,

381; international solidarity in, 381–82; support for, 59–60; of Tolstoy, 14n27, 544. *See also* patriotism

Anti-Poverty League, 220n12

anti-Semitism, 27, 79, 164n2. *See also* Russian Jews

anti-statist tradition in U.S., 448n9, 513, 529

anti-war rallies, 43n77

Appeal to Reason (Kansas City), 482, 518, 549, 562

Appel, Theodore, 556

Arbeiter Freund (London), 541, 547

Arbeiter Ring (New York): EG as member of, 466, 505; lawyer of, 532; schools of, 152n5, 530

Arbeiter Ring (San Francisco), 482

Arbeiter Zeitung, 108n3, 125n3

Arbeter Fraint group (Montreal), 488

Arbuthnot, John, 415n1

Arden (Del.): single-tax colony in, 564

Der arme Teufel (The Poor Devil, Detroit), 138, 515, 540

arrests (of EG): in Bellingham (Wash.), 53, 497–98; documents concerned with, 67, *198*, 254–55, 485; for incitement to riot, 470, 490, 492, 499, 523, 526; interrogation in, 282n5; in New York, *198*, 200, 204n3, 208n5, 225, 403n2, 425n2, 471, 478–79, 479–80; possibility of, in St. Louis, 278–79; publicity from, 499; queries about, *232*, *233*; in San Francisco, 403–9, 499

Art Commission (New York), 123n14

Articles of War, 328n2, 331n5

Ashdown, James Henry, 391n1

assassination: congressional debates on, 17–18n34; EG's disavowal of, 204, 210–11, 436; Most's advocation of, 19n40; motivations for, 346–47, 351, 458; as political strategy, 538; public response to McKinley's, 2–3, 9–10; reforms due to, 350–51; support for, in Russia, 27–28. *See also* propaganda by deed (*attentats*); *specific people*

assassins: government stereotype of, 17

Astor, John Jacobs, 266n7

Astor, John Jacobs, III, 266n7

Astor, John Jacobs, IV, 266n7

attentats. See assassination; propaganda by deed

Audenried (judge), 504

Auger, Charles L., 91, 93

Aurora Colony (Calif.), 529

L'Aurora (Springfield, Ill.), 11n21

Austin, Kate: biographical summary on, 509; death of, 108n1; organizational activities of, 130n6; periodical contributions of, 551, 552

Austin, Sam, 108n1, 509

Australia tour (EG): departure set for, 418; funds for, 390; planning for, 368n2, 371; postponement of, 421

Austria: birth control movement in, 526

Averbuch, Lazarus: biographical summary on, 509; burial of, 490; death of, 281–82, 284, 489, 542; fund to investigate death of, 286; legacy of, 72–73

Azef (Azev), Evno Fishelevich, 351n11, 563

back to the land movement, 526

Baginski, Max: arrests of, 17, 471, 486; barred from speaking in German, 187; biographical summary on, 509; as delegate at Anarchist Congress (Amsterdam), 59, 230, 238–39, 358, 483; editorship of, 43, 208, 551, 553; EG's relationship with, 9; family of, 162n3; mentioned, 428; Most memorialized by, 476, 536; as *Mother Earth* contributor, 220, 223; on Phillips, 539; at Progressive Library meeting, 197; publishing skills of, 44; resolution on Russia and, 244; speeches of, 262, 475, 476, 477, 480, 483; as suspicious of Czolgosz, 437n21; vacation of, 478

Bailey, Warren Worth, 564

Baker, Robert, 124n1, 125n6, 454n2

Baker, Rosie, 209

Bakunin, Michael: associates of, 349n7, 518, 539; biographical summary on, 509–10; as influence on EG, 52, 551; Malatesta's meeting of, 533; Turgenev's character based on, 400n14, 545; works: *God and the State*, 536

Bund (Russian revolutionary organization of Jewish workers), 532
Bunker Hill Company, 248n4
Burlington (Vt.): EG barred from speaking in, 503
Burrowes, Peter, 117, 122, 557
Bustamante, Rosalío, 561
Butte (Mon.): EG's speeches in, 494, 497
Butterick Publishing Company, 264n1
Buwalda, William: arrests of, 53, 403n1, 409, 499; biographical summary on, 513; character of, 342–43; charges against, 328; court-martial of, 50–51, 492–93, 494, 495; crime of, 379–80; EG's references to, 321–22, 326–27, 333, 352; EG's relationship with, 50–52, 328–29; Funston's letter concerning, 335–36; medals returned by, 51, 500; pardon for, 51, 338, 498; Roosevelt on sentence of, 51, 337, 338, 494, 495; sentencing of, 330–31; speeches of, 498

Cahan, Abraham, 117n7, 158n2, 477
Calgary (Alberta): EG's speeches in, 483
California. *See specific cities*
Calvert, Bruce, 168n1
Calvia, Ignacio, 521
Camera Work, 527
Campbell, Rachel, 557
Canada: EG's entry to, 68, 430; immigration authorities in, 391. *See also specific cities*
Cánovas del Castillo, Antonio, 347, 351, 508, 513
Cantrell, Edward Adams, 500
capitalists and capitalism: abolishment of, 242, 317; Church linked to, 52; as despotic imperialism, 246; as first invaders, 319; individual suppressed by, 80, 450; injustice of, 93–94; Kropotkin on, 23; militarism as bulwark of, 51–52, 381, 382, 450; piracy of, 238; as thieves, 52–53; trade unionism's approach to, 265–66; war to protect interests of, 77, 376; workers' conditions under, 320. *See also* State
Cardwell (East Orange mayor), 446, 447
Carlyle, Thomas, 275, 375

Carmen's Union (San Francisco): strike of, 264–65, 482, 485
Carnegie, Andrew, 347, 523
Carnegie Steel Co., 347n15, 523
Carnot, Marie François-Sadi, 347, 513, 514
Carpenter, Edward, 46, 114n10, 216, 217, 513
Carr, Walter W., 307–13
Carrington, Charles, 157, 513–14
Caserio, Sante: biographical summary on, 514; Carnot assassinated by, 347, 513; execution of, 435n15; influences on, 545
Cass, Lawrence, 550
Catholic Church, 461, 462–63
Catt, Carrie Chapman, 554
censorship: of Czolgosz question and anarchism, 38–39; definition of, 79; inconsistency in, 76–77; of materials on free love and free speech, 20–21; publicity generated by, 300, 304; in Russia and U.S., 177, 545; targets of, 36. *See also* Comstock Act; speech, written and spoken
Centennial Congress of Liberals, 560. *See also* Liberal Clubs
Century (magazine), 530
Chaikovsky, Nikolai, 25, 274, 478, 514
Chaikovsky Circle of Russian revolutionaries, 538
Chamberlain, Edward W.: age of, compared to EG, 24n53; biographical summary on, 514; in free speech fight, 20, 557; in Free Speech League, 469, 470; on Turner Defense Committee, 117n5, 122, 471
Champney, Adeline: biographical summary on, 514–15; companion of, 542; meetings likely organized by, 187n4; periodical contributions of, 552, 553; speeches of, 565
Champney, Freeman, 514
Champney, Horace, 514
Channing, Walter, 13–14, 95–96, 515
Chapelier, Émile, 236, 244
Charter of Amiens, 235nn6–7
Chekhov, Anton Pavlovich, 34, 270, 400, 515
Chelsea (Mass.): EG's speech in, 480
Cherkezov, Varlaam N., 25

Chernov, Victor Maikhailovich, 562

Chernyshevsky, N. G., 24, 137n6

Chicago: anarchist circle in, 282, 556; anarchists framed by police in, 299; Breshkovskaya's speeches in, 149; EG barred from speaking in, 97–99, 282, 284, 286, 300, 304, 344n8, 362n5, 470, 489–90; EG nearly arrested in, 68; EG's criticism of, 186–87; EG's speeches in, 223, 466, 470, 475, 477, 481; IWW conventions in, 474, 478, 483, 495, 537; police brutality in, 290, 304; police chief shooting in, 72–73, 281–82, 284, 286, 489, 509, 556; police harassment and surveillance in, 97–99, 284, 286, 489–90

Chicago Daily Journal: EG interviewed in, 71, 290; on police chief shooting, 281nn2–3; text of EG's speech in, 291–94, 300

Chicago Daily News, 203

Chicago Inter Ocean: EG interviewed in, 71, 284–87; on police chief shooting, 281n2

Chicago Tribune, 297, 298, 299

childbirth as metaphor, 70, 386

childhood education: AB on, 152; criticism of, 238, 259, 275; EG's speech on, 481; experimental schools for, 61, 141n1, 152n5, 230n2, 259, 461, 483, 485, 498; influences on EG's approach to, 61–62; league concerned with, 491; militarism in, 382. *See also* Ferrer Modern Schools

childrearing: in context of free love, 387–88; in context of marriage and love, 346; EG's speech on, 501

Chinese Exclusion Acts, 21

Chirikov, Evgenii Nikolaevich, 33, 269n2, 269–70

Chirikov Society, 34, 191n4

Christian anarchism, 14n27

Christianity: misunderstanding of early, 324, 340

Christian socialism, 528

Christmas: commercialism of, 418

Church: as barrier to individual freedom, 211n4; commercialism of Christmas and, 418; condemnation of, 461, 462–63; EG's beliefs about, 52, 344–45; emancipation from, 451; failure of, 258; invasiveness of, 345, 388; rejection of, 324–25; teachings of, 266–67. *See also* religion

churchism: use of term, 324–25

Ciancabilla, Guiseppi, 11n21

Cincinnati (Ohio): EG's speeches in, 481, 496

Circulo de Trabajores, 376n11

Citizen's Alliance, 322n3, 380n21

citizenship, U.S. (EG's): annulment of Kershner's and, 416, 417, 425–27, 429–30; basis for, 485, 491, 530–31; free speech hearing and, 504; inquiries about, *232, 233,* 280, 288–89, 307–13; revocation of, 66–67, 68–69, 500; state and federal investigation of, 484, 485, 486; through father and husband, 278n5, 305, 311 (*see also* Kershner, Jacob A. [EG's husband]). *See also* deportation investigation; State

Citizens Union of East Orange, New Jersey, 523

civil rights. *See* free speech; right to privacy

Clarke, Helen A., 553

Clark University, 503

class: crossing boundaries of, in free speech fight, 75–76; EG's and AB's approach to, 37, 60, 78; of European anarchists, 211; focus on intelligent middle, 153

Clausen, Emma, 138, 221, 515

Clay, Henry, 454n2

Clemens, Samuel (Mark Twain), 26, 525, 555

Clement, Leon, 243–44

Cleveland: anarchists in, 48, 187n4; EG's speeches in, 8, 187, 436n21, 470, 476, 477, 480, 488–89, 496; EG welcomed in, 209, 210; meetings organized in, 542

Cleveland Freethought Society, 514

Clough, David, 392n1

Cohen, Joseph J., 459n3, 494

Cohn, Annie, 515

Cohn, Michael Alexander: biographical summary on, 515–16; at Most's commemoration, 476; periodical contributions of, 551; speeches of, 471, 477

9, 10–11, 95, 197, 200–204, 324, 425n4; biographical summary on, 517–18; censorship of discussing, 38–39; citizenship of, 17; defenders of, 509; EG's meeting of, 436–37; electrocution of, 13; McKinley assassinated by, 2, 7, 10–12, 534–35; mental status of, 12, 13–14, 95n1, 515; *Mother Earth* issue on, 38–39, 196n1, 200–201, 204n3, 220, 248, 478; statements of, 457

Daltich, William, 285

D'Annunzio, Gabriel, 401

Darrow, Clarence Seward: biographical summary on, 518; and commerce clause, 23n50, as Haywood and others' lawyer, 528, 559; periodical contributions of, 550, 551; speeches of, 469; as Turner's lawyer, 22–23, 122–23, 472, 538, 545

Darwin, Charles, 45

Dave, Victor: associates of, 536; biographical summary on, 518; EG's meeting with, 230n2, 250, 251, 483; letters to, 62–63, 359–60; mentioned, 157

Davies, Daniel D., 395

Davis, George Breckenridge, 328–31, 495

Dawson, Oswald, 114n9

Deasy (judge), 406–7, 408

Debs, Eugene Victor: associates of, 510; biographical summary on, 518; Crosby's relationship with, 217; free speech supported by, 503; IWW and, 55, 474, 558–59; lawyer of, 518; periodical contributions of, 549, 551; PLM support from, 562; presidential candidacy of, 415n2, 423n6, 473, 496; reputation as orator, 35; support for, 549; as "undesirable citizen," 231n1, 541

Declaration of Independence: call for new, 344; EG on, 52, 59; EG's rewriting of, 64–65; right of rebellion against tyranny in, 60, 310, 323; soldiers' orders vs., 379. *See also* "A New Declaration of Independence"

de Cleyre, Voltairine: AB's correspondence with, 510; as anarchist, 17–18n34; on Angiolillo, 509; appeals for funds for, 144; arrest

of, 344n8, 362n5, 454n1, 488; associates of, 532; biographical summary on, 518–19; Ferrer memorial meeting and, 504; at free speech meeting, 502; on Gorky, 26n61, 525; health of, 227; home of, 505; on labor newspaper, 484; library work of, 459n3; on Manning, 534; organizational activities of, 561; on Pentecost, 538; periodical contributions of, 208, 220, 361, 551, 552, 553; reading group of, 537, 565; reputation as orator, 35; shot by student, 470; speeches of, 76, 262, 460, 503; trial and not-guilty verdict for, 494; works: *Anarchism and American Traditions*, 361n3, 498; *Crime and Punishment*, 565; *McKinley's Assassination from the Anarchist Standpoint*, 258n1, 479

De Leon, Daniel, 474, 558–59

Delesalle, Maurice Paul, 235

Dell, Floyd, 553, 554

Delmotte, Clementine, 244

Democratic Party: EG's opinion of, 420

The Demonstrator (Home Colony, Wash.): AB's appeal for weekly in, 59, 246–47; contributors to, 522, 537; description of, 550; editor of, 535; IWW coverage in, 56; *Mother Earth* compared with, 190

Denison House (Boston), *146*, 512, 519

Denver (Colo.): EG's speeches in, 481; priest shot in, 324n2

deportation investigation (of EG): context of beginnings of, 49–50; fight against, as concession to State, 430; insufficient information for, 278–79; lengthy process of, 66–69; newspaper reports on, 489; Straus on basis for, 256–57; tactics in, 499. *See also* citizenship, U.S.; Kershner, Jacob A.

Des Moines (Iowa): EG's speeches in, 497

Detroit (Mich.): anarchist circle in, 515, 537; EG barred from speaking in, 218, 481; EG's speeches in, 477; EG's visit to, 190; Water Board in, 532

Detroit News, 532

devil: EG's speeches on, 496, 497, 498; EG's views of, 384–86

Díaz, Modesto, 521

Dick, Charles W. F., 380n22

Dick Act (1903), 380–81

Diehl, E., 486

direct action: Anarchist Congress (Amsterdam) and, 59–60; centrality of, 276; EG's evasiveness in defining, 259–60; electricians' strike as exemplar of, 259, 265, 480; as logical tactic (EG's speeches on), 77–80, 258, 485, 487, 491, 492, 501; political action vs. (EG's speeches on), 227, 480, 481, 482, 483, 498, 499. *See also* strikes

Discontent (Lakebay and Home Colony, Wash.): Comstock's targeting of, 97n1, 516, 557; contributors to, 509, 537; description of, 550; editors of, on trial, 20, 21, 469; Free Speech League and, 122n3

divorce proceedings (EG's), 430

documentary editing: approach to, 81–85; context of, 1–2, 31

Doll, William Frederick, 122, 122n7, 557

Domas, Louis J.: letters from, 258–61, 264–72; reports on EG by, 52–53, 57–58, 67, 485

Donelli, Dominick, 488, 494

Donnegan, William, 419n4

"do not patronize" notice, 525

Dos Freye Vort, 534, 541

draft (military), 329, 381

Draper, John William, 228

dreams: EG's speech on, 467

Dreyfus, Alfred, 127n7, 401n22, 548

Dudley, Helen, 145–46n4, 164n1, 512, 519

dueling, 397–98

due process, 22n49, 23, 288

Dugro, Philip Henry, 447

Duncan, Lewis, 325, 326, 493

Dunn, James R., 278–79, 489

Dunne, Edward F., 186, 539

Dunois, Amédée, 236, 237, 239, 240, 242

Duse, Eleanora, 182, 401n19

Dutch Social Democratic Party, 536

Dutch Socialist League, 536

Dyker Heights Children's Neighborhood Playhouse and Workshop, 141n1, 155n5

Earle, Ferdinand P. ("Affinity"), 446, 447

Eastman, Crystal, 510

East Orange (N.J.): citizens' organizations in, 523; EG barred from speaking in, 75, 443; EG's speech in Freeman's barn in, 446–48; lunch meeting in, 75, 501; Paine commemoration in, 441–42n4, 446, 502

L'Ecole Renovée, 521

economic panic and recession (1907–8), 366n2, 480, 484, 487

Edelsohn, Julius (Joe or Ike): arrests of, 197, 199, 200, 202n2, 204n3, 262n5, 478; attack on, 485; biographical note on, 197n2; EG assisted by, 492; at *Mother Earth* reunion, 486; released on bail, 225n4

Edelsohn, Rebecca (Becky): AB's relationship with, 197n5, 369, 510, 520; arrests of, 197, 204n3, 363–64, 365n1, 431n1, 478, 495, 501, 511, 560; biographical summary on, 519–20; lawyer of, 533; living situation of, 197n2, 355

Edelstadt, Abe, 466n4, 556

Edelstadt, David, 466n4, 543, 556

Edelstadt Group (Chicago): activities of, 536, 547; description of, 556; EG's opinion of, 466; mentioned, 424; police spy in, 395; speeches arranged by, 489, 490

education, rational, 542. *See also* childhood education

Educational Alliance, 125n4

Educational League, 125n4

egoism: discussion of, 237–38; EG's reading about, 45–46; introduced to *Liberty* group, 162n1; journal associated with, 543; organization and, 239–40. *See also* anarchist individualism; individual

eight-hour day movement, 265

Der Einzige und Sein Eigentum (New York), 543

Elizabeth (empress of Austria), 533

Elliott, James B., 561

Ellis, Havelock, 114n9, 378–79

Ellis Island: Turner imprisoned on, 121, 130, 137

El Paso (Texas): EG's speech in, 419, 500

El Paso News, 500

Ely, Robert Erskine: biographical summary on, 520; Kropotkin on, 127; letters to, 111, 148; organizational activities of, 26, 556; speeches of, 473

Emerson, Ralph Waldo: as anarchist, 40, 210n2, 273, 283, 455; associates of, 544; biographical summary on, 520

Emmanuel movement, 435

Engel, George, 253n5

English language: anarchist literature needed in, 359, 361; and EG's audience, 40, 79; EG's militancy in, 79

equality: EG's vision of, 386–87; superficial type of, 178; in wages, 318. *See also* women's emancipation

equal opportunity: socialist view of, 319

L'Era nuova (Paterson, N.J.), 550

erotica publishing, 513–14

Esperanto (artificial language), 236, 244

Esteve, Pedro, 472, 476, 553

Etiévant, George, 350

Europe: anarchist trade-unionism in, 62; industrial unionism in, 55; single-tax organizations in, 564; syndicalism in, 59; U.S. compared with, 209, 210

Evening Chronicle (Spokane), 493

Everett (Wash.): EG barred from speaking in, 53, 392, 497. *See also* police harassment and surveillance

Everett Morning Tribune, 392–93

Everyman (Los Angeles), 518, 547, 550

Fabbri, Luigi, 236, 244, 483, 497

Fairhope (Ala.): single-tax colony in, 564

Fair Play, 527, 546

family: EG's chosen, 9–10; Roosevelt's ideal, 70, 103, 388

Fargo (N.Dak.): EG's speeches in, 497

Faure, Auguste Louis Sébastien: biographical summary on, 520; experimental school of (La Ruche), 61, 230n2, 259, 483, 485; organizational activities of, 491; Vaillant's daughter and, 545

Federal Reserve Bank, 366n2

Feiss-Amoré, Henri, 235

Fellowship for Ethical Research, 544

Ferm, Alexis, 141n1, 155n5

Ferm, Elizabeth, 141n1, 155n5, 565

Ferrer Modern Schools, 61, 152n5, 498, 521

Ferrer y Guardia, Francisco: arrests of, 477, 502; biographical summary on, 520–21; EG's speeches on, 462, 467; execution of, 61–62, 243n29, 459, 504; experimental school of, 152n5, 498; league founded by, 491; letters of, 243, 553; memorialized, 62, 333n9, 459, 461–63, 504, 505, 547; released from prison, 483. *See also* Francisco Ferrer Association

Field, Sara Bard, 41n74

Fielden, Samuel, 253n5

The Fight for Free Speech (comp. Freeman), 444

Figner, Vera, 10, 10n17

Firebrand (Portland, Oreg.), 507, 509, 529, 532

First-of-May Conference, 492

Fischer, Adolf, 253n5

Fiske, Bob, 494

Fitzgerald, Margaret Eleanor (Fitzie), 439n2, 521

Flaubert, Gustave, 349n8

Fleming, J. W. (Chummy), 368n2, 371, 442, 521

Flores Magón, Enrique: bail for, 409n5; education of, 229n24; EG's relationship with, 63–64; move to Canada, 476, 477; move to U.S., 521; periodical of, 472, 474; PLM activities of, 561

Flores Magón, Jesus, 521

Flores Magón, Ricardo: arrest and extradition of, 500–501, 562; attack on, 483; biographical summary on, 521–22; editorship of, 472, 474, 553; education of, 229n24; EG's relationship with, 63–64; imprisonment of, 503; and Kropotkin, 63; manifesto of, 487; move to California, 480; move to Canada, 476, 477; PLM activities of, 478, 561–62; sentencing of, 501; support for, 63–64

Flour and Cereal Mill Workers Local Number 1, 543

Flower, Benjamin, 487

IWW fights for, 57–58, 499–500, 502, 503–4, 505, 531, 559–60; manifesto on, 447n8, 501; periodical on, 553; perseverance in, 75–76, 78–79; in Philadelphia, 503–5; police ignorance of constitutional right to, 75, 187, 282; in San Francisco, 531; support for, 549; in Worcester (Mass.), 503, 505. *See also* anarchist/socialist/liberal alliance; Free Speech League; speech, written and spoken

Free Speech Committee: formation of, 429n1, 442n4; manifesto of, 447n8; meetings of, 502, 505; members of, 507, 518, 526, 528, 530, 532, 533, 535, 539, 540, 547

Free Speech Fund (Philadelphia), 459n6

Free Speech League: court fight supported by, 454n2; and Craddock, 122n3, 470, 557; description of, 557–58; EG's acceptance in, 24; EG's lecture tour for, 472; first official function of, 470; founding of, 20, 97n1, 117n5, 122n3, 469, 470, 514, 522; funds for, 522; Harman assisted by, 194n1; lawyer of, 518; letterhead of, *140*; members of, 6n8, 507, 510, 516, 532, 539, 545; publications of, 129n3, 475, 476, 479, 487, 498, 573. *See also* Free Speech Committee; Turner Defense Committee

Free Speech League (Calif.), 317n1

Free Speech League (San Francisco), 197n2, 408n3

freethought movement, 46, 202n1, 463n8, 514. *See also* Liberal Clubs; National Defense Association

Freethought (San Francisco), 122n5

Freie Arbeiter Stimme (New York): AB's request for, 172–73; contributors to, 515, 524; description of, 551; editors of, 534, 543, 548; on EG's reports on anarchist congress, 357n3; founding of, 530; funds for, 130; on Progressive Library meeting arrests, 200

Freie Arbeiter Stimme group: attacks on, 11n21; criticism of, 66, 357–58; EG's speeches sponsored by, 495; origins of, 108n3

Freiheit (London and New York): assassination advocated in, 19n40; description of, 551; editors of, 509, 518; management of, 535

Freiheit Publishing Association, 479

Freud, Sigmund, 503

Frick, Henry Clay: AB's *attentat* against, 8–9, 25n56, 43, 108, 347, 435n15, 523

Friedeberg, Raphael, 236, 243

Friendship Liberal League (Philadelphia), 561

Friends of Russian Freedom. *See* American Society of Friends of Russian Freedom

Funston, Frederick N.: biographical summary on, 523; Buwalda's arrest and, 51, 321, 331, 379–80, 493, 494; letters from, 335–36, 342, 343; regimental members and, 531

Furlong Detective Agency, 483, 562

Galleani, Luigi: arrest of, 243n28, 479, 526, 533; biographical summary on, 523–24; editorship of, 103n1, 549, 553; flight to Canada, 470; released on bail, 480; speeches of, 91n1, 480; trial of, 481–82

Galsworthy, John, 505–6

gambling, 411

Garfield, James A., 515

Garrison, William Lloyd: as anarchist, 21–22n47, 210–11, 455; associates of, 538; biographical summary on, 524; as influence on EG, 10; organizational activities of, 555

Garrison, William Lloyd, Jr.: at Breshkovskaya's speech, 145n3; father of, 524; letter from, 124–25n4; organizational activities of, 26; Turner's defense and, 124n1

gender: EG's challenges to conventions of, 9; individual as more important than, 47–48, 178; Roosevelt's view of, 70, 103; as topic in *Mother Earth*, 75. *See also* free love; sexuality and sex question; women's emancipation

genius: insanity linked to or not, 349–50

George, Henry, Jr.: Altgeld memorial meeting and, 469; associates of, 526, 539; biographical summary on, 524; reversed opinion of Haymarket affair, 21n43, 428; as single-taxer, 220n12, 563–64. *See also* single-tax movement

Gould, Jay, 291n4

Govan, Charles L., 557

government. *See* State

governmentalists: use of term, 125

Grand Army of the Republic (GAR), 494

Grandidier, Louis, 244n34

Grandjouan, Jules-Felix: cartoons of, 268n8; EG's meeting with, 230n2, 483; *Mother Earth* cover by, 257, 267–68

Grant, Lee, 558

Grant, Margaret (pseud.). *See* Coryell, John Russell

Grant, Stickney, 561

Grave, Jean: associates of, 520, 539; biographical summary on, 526; translation of, 530; writings of, 350n9

Graven, William, 557

Great Britain: John Bull figure in, 415; military expenditures in, 374–75; Walsall anarchists in, 113. *See also* London (England)

Great White Fleet, 377n14

Greenwich Settlement (New York), 164n1

Greer, Joseph H., 467

Greiffuelhes, Victor, 235

Griest, Nathan L., 492

Die Grosse Kundes, 449

Grossmann, Rudolf (aka Pierre Ramus): on anti-militarism, 243; arrest of, 13, 243n28, 470, 533; bail for, 225; biographical summary on, 526; as delegate at Anti-militarist Congress, 483; flight to Europe, 481–82; speeches of, 91n1, 470, 565

Grunmann, Paul H., 553

Guillaume, James, 531

Guiteau, Charles J., 515

Gutierrez De Lara, Lazaro, 487

habeas corpus. *See* due process

Hagerty, Thomas, 558–59

Halbe, Max, 398

Hale, Edward Everett, 325

Hall, Bolton: associates of, 111, 513; bail provided by, 204n3, 225, 363, 365n1; biographical summary on, 526; editorship of, 553;

EG's reading of, 46; farm given to EG by, 29, 162, 509; free speech manifesto signed by, 447n8; letter to, 162–63; mentioned, 197, 199, 440; single-tax movement and, 21n43, 564; speech of, 477; Turner's defense and, 122; writings of, 45n81, 551, 553

Hall, G. Stanley, 503

Hall, Thomas C., 124n1

Hamon, Augustin, 42

Hanford, Benjamin, 423, 473

Hanna, Mark, 534

Hansen, Mary, 564, 565

Hapgood, Hutchins: biographical summary on, 526–27; on EG's Cleveland audience, 496; mentioned, 424; periodical contributions of, 553

Harlem Liberal Alliance: EG's speeches for, 486–87, 502, 561

Harman, Lillian: arrest of, 114n9; biographical summary on, 527; editorship of, 202n1, 546, 552

Harman, Moses: biographical summary on, 527; editorship of, 20, 546, 552; in free speech fight, 97n1; imprisonment of, 36, 194n1, 475, 477; letter to, 194; periodical contributions of, 550; released from prison, 479; on sexuality, 114n9; support for, 552

Harriman, E. H., 231n1

Harris, James Thomas (Frank), 114n10, 411

Harrison, Carter H., Jr., 98n5

Hartford (Conn.): EG's speeches in, 486

Hartley, Roland, 392n1

Hartmann, Sadakichi: biographical summary on, 527; distribution of writings of, 45; as *Mother Earth* contributor, 553; *Mother Earth* events and, 423n3, 486, 501; symbolist plays of, 157

Hauptmann, Gerhardt: biographical summary on, 527; EG on work of, 271, 398, 399, 495; mentioned, 431, 433; plays of, performed, 271n6

Havel, Hippolyte: AB's arrest and, 363; biographical summary on, 527; correspondents of, 132, 526; editorship of, 43, 220, 223, 247n1,

34, 46; on liberty, 340; mentioned, 431, 433; plays of, performed, 164n4, 182n5, 207n1, 475; on social issues, 177; Stockman as idealistic character of, 237, 239

IBWA. *See* International Brotherhood Welfare Association (IBWA)

Idaho: strikers held in bull pens in, 204–5, 380; WFM's militancy in, 248n4

Ikonnikova, L. V., 156n3, 531

ILGWU (International Ladies Garment Workers Union), 505

Illinois Workers' Party, 542

illnesses (EG's): "inverted womb" or endometriosis, 32; mentioned, 103, 488; tiredness and fatigue as, 129–31, 135, 304, 460; Yampolsky's treatment of, 548

immigrants and immigration: "alien," use of term, 256n2, 311; birth rate of, 103n2; fear of, 9; motivation of, 210; naturalized citizenship of, 288n1, 311n6; political ideology as issue in, 3; repression of, 14

Immigration Act (1891), 256n1

Immigration Act (1903): alien as used in, 256n2, 312; anti-anarchist provisions of, 6–8, 17–18, 67, 210, 485, 541; EG's arrest possible under, 66–67, 278; enforcement of, 18–20, 22–23; free speech endangered by, 6–8; passage of, 471; political beliefs as restricted in, 17n32, 21; Turner's prosecution under, 115–16, 117n5, 545; as unconstitutional, 122; upheld by Supreme Court, 473; warrant for EG's arrest issued under, 254–55

indecent: Comstock's definition of, 21n42

Independent Thinker, 522–23

India: British colonial rule in, 415

Indianapolis (Ind.): EG barred from speaking in, 52, 390, 496; Turner's speech in, 114

individual: Church and State as barrier to freedom of, 211n4; criticism of reliance on, 237; dignity of, 71; direct action of each, 276; EG's focus on, 4, 47, 158; Emerson as exemplar of, 520; government's invasiveness of, 204–5, 293; as more important than gender, 47, 178; motives of, 291; organization in con-

text of, 238–39; self-development of, 47–48, 185, 387, 456; supremacy of, 153, 216, 238, 319–20, 450–51; work character/conditions determined by, 341. *See also* anarchist individualism

Industrial Gazette, 532

Industrial Union Bulletin (Chicago), 559

Industrial Union Manifesto, 558

Industrial Worker, 503–4, 528, 559

Industrial Workers of the World (IWW): conventions of, 474, 478, 483, 495, 537; criticism of, 56, 253; description of, 558–60; free speech fights of, 57, 499–500, 502, 503–4, 505, 531; goal of, 55; Haywood's role in, 528; leadership of, 540; Minneapolis section of, 543; red neckties of, 407; socialists and anarchists in, 55–56; support for, 518, 552; WFM withdrawn from, 536

Ingersoll, Robert, 547

insanity: genius linked to or not, 349–50; as grounds to detain EG, 391

Instead of a Magazine, 516

instincts: social and individual, 291–92

Institute of Heredity, 508

Intercollegiate Socialist Society, 543

International Anarchist Congress (Amsterdam): anti-militarism discussed at, 243; Bureau of Correspondence discussed at, 240–41; delegates to, 228, 230, 483, 509, 518, 541; direct action discussed at, 59, 60; EG interviewed about, 284–86; EG's description of, 234–45; EG's report to, 56, 65; Grave's refusal to attend, 526; individual and egoism discussed at, 238–40; Malatesta's role in, 533–34; militant undercurrents of, 59–60; overview of, 234n1; resolution on Russia, 244–45; session chaired by EG at, 243–45; syndicalism discussed at, 241–42; terrorism discussed at, 242–43

International Antimilitarist Association, 244n33

International Anti-militarist Congress (Amsterdam), 483

International Bookbinding Company, 543

Lang, Harry, 204n3, 478

Lang, Lucy, 29n64

Larkin, J. B., 557

Lawrence (Mass.): EG's speeches in, 486

laws: as capitalist's friend, 23, 52–53, 266; due process, 22n49, 23, 288; eighty cent, 276; emancipation from, 451; of nature, 23, 384; popular opinions and, 352; as tyranny, 432; wealthy protected by, 6, 274–75, 276. *See also* anti-anarchist laws

League for Political Education, 111, 520

League of Human Rights, 127

League of Women Voters, 511

Leavitt, Ezekiel, 170n3

lecture hall keepers: Criminal Anarchy Act provisions on, 434n12; police harassment of, 16, 429, 433–34, 443

lecture tours (EG's): fund-raising in, 58; growth of interest in anarchism and, 226–27; ideals encoded in, 79; increased attendance at, 43n77; for *Mother Earth*, 72, 476; organizing as function of, 152; travel reports on, 48–49, 186–88, 300–302, 314–16, 333n9; venues for, 16, 73

Lee, Algernon: biographical summary on, 532; organizational activities of, 557; Turner's defense and, 117, 122, 125

Legitimation League (England), 114n9, 527

Leishman, J. L., 108

Lemlich, Clara, 505

Lenin, Vladimir I., 26n58, 514

letters to the editor (EG's): in *Lucifer, the Light-bearer*, 97–99; in *Metropolitan Magazine*, 40–41; in *Philadelphia Public Ledger*, 454–58

A Letter to The Public of Chicago (EG), 489

Levine, Louis, 197n6

Levy (letter from), 244

Liberal Club (Cleveland), 436n21

Liberal Club (Los Angeles), 540, 543

Liberal Club (New York). *See* Manhattan Liberal Club

Liberal Clubs: description of, 560–61

Liberal (Mo.): EG's speeches in, 496

liberals and liberalism: anarchists working with, 20–21, 79; EG's speeches to, 5, 76–77; as indifferent to free speech violations, 429; meanings of term, 3n5; on violence in Russia, 27–28. *See also* anarchist/socialist/liberal alliance

The Liberator (Chicago): contributors to, 537, 538; description of, 552; as IWW supporter, 56, 559; *Mother Earth* compared with, 190; publisher of, 524

Libertaire Communist Colony, 236n11

Le Libertaire (Paris), 520, 535

liberty: free speech linked to, 5, 97; government's invasiveness of, 204–5; hypocrisy of U.S., 6–7, 21–22n47, 199, 364; militarism as evidence of decay of, 343; struggle for, 79, 340

Liberty (Boston and New York): contributors to, 514, 532, 545, 546, 547; demise of, 545; description of, 552; egoism and, 162n1; on EG's speech about AB's *attentat*, 435n15; on George's reversal, 428n3; publisher of, 533, 544; sales of, 542; Vaillant's speech in, 350n9

Liberty Bookstore (San Francisco), 396n2, 528

Liberty Club (San Francisco), 482

Liebknecht, Wilhelm, 319

Lingg, Louis, 253n5, 282n5, 491

Listki, Khleb i Volia (London, Paris, and Geneva), 228, 531, 552

Little, Frank, 503–4

Living My Life (EG): on AB's appeal for weekly, 247n1; on AB's depression, 196n1; on aftermath of McKinley assassination, 11–13; on children and childbirth, 31–33; on covert activities, 29n64; on Czolgosz, 12; on love life, 31–32, 189n5; on pact with AB and Stein, 8; on Manhattan Liberal Club, 561; on Manning, 534; on medical education, 143n3; on *Mother Earth*'s name, 168n1; on Reedy, 496; on Reitman, 73; on Schlippenback (Russian consul), 188n6; on speaking tour for *Mother Earth*, 476; on Traubel, 544

Livshis, Annie, 223, 467, 532, 565

Livshis, Jake, 223, 532, 565

Lloyd, J. William, 557

Lombroso, Cesare, 349

London (England): cooperative bakery in, 547; dock strike in (1889), 113, 534; EG's speeches in, 60–61, 248, 252–53, 484; Socialist League of, 547; Trades Council of, 112; Working Men's College of, 541

London (Ontario): EG's speeches in, 488, 542

London, Jack: biographical summary on, 532; Crosby's debate with, 216; free speech supported by, 503; periodical contributions of, 549, 551

London, Meyer: as AB's lawyer, 299n5, 363, 365n1, 495; biographical summary on, 532–33; as EG's lawyer, 478, 538; free speech manifesto signed by, 447n8

Lorenzo, Anselmo, 521

Lorulot, André, 244n34

Los Angeles (Calif.): debates in, 500; EG's speeches in, 227, 418, 482, 492, 498; explosion in newspaper building in, 186n2; Great White Fleet in, 377

Los Angeles Times, 186n2

Loubot (letter from), 244

love: EG's beliefs about, 5, 69, 71, 184, 345–46; EG's disillusionment with, 467; and marriage: EG's speeches on, 467, 495, 498, 500, 502; maternal, 5, 31–33; as *Mother Earth* topic, 47. *See also* free love; sexuality and sex question

Lowell (Mass.): EG's speeches in, 57–58, 264–68, 486

Luccheni, Luigi, 533

Lucifer, the Lightbearer (Valley Falls, Kans., and Chicago): appeal for funds for de Cleyre in, 144; barred from mails, 516; Comstock protests in, 557; contributors to, 509, 514, 517, 519; description of, 552; distribution of, 561; editors of, 475, 527, 546; funds for, 522; letters to editor (EG), 97–99, 194; masthead of, 98; on Progressive Library meeting and arrests, 202n1; suppression of, 36, 129, 477; on Turner defense rally, 124n2; on Turner (EG), 112–14

Lum, Dyer D., 253n5

lynchings, 50, 64, 65

Lynn (Mass.): EG's speeches in, 480, 485, 502

Maasch, F. W. C., 273–77

Macdonald, Eugene Montague, 122n5, 553

Macdonald, George E., 122, 122n5, 553, 557

MacDonald, Jesse Fuller, 475

MacLean, Charles F., 469

MacQueen, Nellie, 470

MacQueen, William: arrests of, 13, 243n28, 470, 526; bail for, 225; biographical summary on, 533; imprisonment and death of, 481–82; speeches of, 91n1

Maeterlinck, Maurice, 491

Maguire, George, 564

Maguire, James G., 564

Mahoney, John J., 290

Mainwaring, Sam, 484

Maisel, Max N., 45n81, 228, 529, 533

Malatesta, Errico: associates of, 236n14, 536; biographical summary on, 533–34; editorship of, 553; EG's reading of, 46; EG's relationship with, 60; on Ibsen's Dr. Stockman, 239, 529; on International Correspondence Bureau, 240n23; organizational activities of, 483; resolution on Russia and, 244; sentencing of, 469; sketch of, 298; speeches of, 239, 240, 245; on syndicalism, 241–42

Malato, Charles, 491

Malden (Mass.): EG's speeches in, 502

Malmed, Leon, 168n1, 189, 534

Manhattan Liberal Club: EG's speeches at, 473; founding of, 522, 561; free speech fight and, 12–13n23, 21, 557; members of, 514; police harassment of, 479; support for *Discontent* editors, 469

Manhattan Lyceum (New York): EG's speeches at, 472, 478, 483, 501, 502; Haymarket commemoration at, 260; Progressive Library meeting and, 204n3

"Manifesto of the Sixteen," 517

"Manifesto to the American People" (PLM), 487, 488

minorities vs. majorities: anarchism and, 243, 319–20; EG's speech on, 501

Mirbeau, Octave Henri Mari, 401–2

Missoula (Mont.): free speech fight in, 57, 560; ordinances against public speaking in, 503–4

Mitchell, John, 252n3, 253, 279n6

modern drama: chronology of EG's speeches on, 480–83, 486–88, 491, 493, 494, 495, 496, 498, 501, 502; EG interview focused on, 35–36, 396–402; EG's speeches on, 167n1, 227, 269–72, 442n4, 447; in France, 401–2; in Germany, 397–99; in Russia, 400–401; Russian free-theater movement and, 33–34; seeds of radicalism in, 1, 433. *See also Social Significance of Modern Drama* (EG); theater

Modern School movement, 62, 444, 461

Modern Times colony, 546

Monatte, Pierre: correspondent of (Grave), 526; as delegate at Anarchist Congress (Amsterdam), 234–35; on syndicalism, 241, 242

monopolies: opposition to, 541; State's support of, 293, 319, 341

Montreal (Quebec): EG's speech in, 488

Morales, Mateo, 61

Morgan, Anne, 506

Morgan, John Pierpont, 266n7

Morgan, Julius Spencer, 266n7

Morong, G., 557

Morral, Mateo, 477

Morris, William: distribution of writings of, 45; as influence, 217, 507; organizational activities of, 112; Ruskin as influence on, 541

Morton, Eric B., 29n64, 158n1, 535, 563

Morton, James Ferdinand, Jr.: biographical summary on, 535; editorship of, 550, 557; organizational activities of, 130n6, 537; periodical contributions of, 551, 552; speeches of, 459, 473

Morton, Thomas, 183n8

Moscow, Max, 197, 199, 202n2, 204, 478

Moscow Art Theater, 34, 164n5

Moss, Joseph F., 480

Most, Johann: on anarchist convention (St. Louis), 473; assassination advocated by, 19n40; associates of, 518; biographical summary on, 535–36; companion of, 535; conviction and appeal of, 469, 470; death of, 476; editorship of, 551; on education, 152n5; EG's disagreements with, 18n37; EG's names for, 137n9; followers of, 535; Hauptmann's plays and, 271n6; imprisonment of, 470; as influence on EG, 18; memorialized, 50n83, 552; mentioned, 223; periodical contributions of, 551; released from prison, 471; speeches of, 475

Mother Earth (New York): on AB's disappearance, 196; advertisers in, 543; announcement of founding (as *The Open Road*), 168–69; announcements in, 496, 556; appearance of, 42, 483; book reviews in, 529; as censorship target, 36, 516; contributors to, 26n61, 30, 58, 361, 507, 514, 515, 516, 517, 519, 522, 523, 526, 527, 529, 530, 535, 537, 538, 547; covers of, *176*, 230n2, *226*, *257*, *267–68*, *301*; Czolgosz issue of, 38–39, 196n1, 200–201, 204n3, 220, 248, 478; Declaration of Independence (rewritten) in, 65, 450–51; description of, 41–43, 47–48, 553; distribution of, 42, 208, 521, 533, 534, 537, 546, 561; editorials in, 175–77, 207–8; editorials of, 49–50; editors of, 17n31, 43–44, 480, 483, 510, 527; as EG's child, 356, 411; on EG's citizenship, 425–27; Emerson's work in, 520; on Ferrer, 461–63; finances of, 58–59, 225, *226*, 355–56, 357, 390, 418, 449, 495, 522; first issue of, 47, *176*, 476; free speech manifesto in, 447n8, 501; fundraising events for, 164n5, 208, 423, 475, 479, 485, 488, 490, 495, 503, 506, 537; on gender and politics, 75; Gorky's work in, 26, 171n3, 525; on International Anarchist Congress (Amsterdam), 234–45; internationalism of, 62–64; on IWW, 56, 559; on Labor Day, 365–67; London's work in, 532; mailing privileges for, 189; "Manifesto to the American People" in, 487, 488;

nursing: as EG's occupation, 29, 30, 103, 129–30, 469, 471, 543; professionalization of, 546

Oberwager, Charles, 364, 557
O'Brian, William, 113n7
O'Brien, Edward J., 553
occupation (EG's): functions of, 29–30; nursing, 29, 30, 103, 129–30, 469, 471, 543; theater group management, 33–34, 155, 400, 474, 537; Vienna scalp and face specialist, 29–30, 48, 143, 195, 473, 476, 478, 526, 554
October Manifesto, 382n25
O'Hare, Kate Richards, 549
Ohio State Journal, 40, 209–12
Oliver, Frank, 391
Oliver, Robert Shaw, 338
Omaha (Nebr.): EG's speeches in, 496–97
O'Neill, Eugene, 545
Open Forum (East Orange), 502
The Open Road (Ind.), 168n1
Oppenheimer, Moses: biographical note on, 122n8; in free speech fight, 21–22; organizational activities of, 122, 557
Orange (N.J.): EG's speeches in, 75–76
Orchard, Harry, 205n7, 475
O'Reilly, Leonora, 505
Orlenev, Pavel Nikolayevich: arrangements by, 164; arrest of, 191n4; biographical summary on, 537; EG and, 33–34; financial difficulties of, 191–92; mentioned, 174; return to Russia, 192n5; status of, 400; theater group of, 155n1, 207n1, 474, 475, 476, 536; travels of, 170n1. *See also* St. Petersburg Dramatic Co.
Osgood, Irene, 508
Ossining (N.Y.): EG's farm in, 29, 162, 357, 478, 494, 495, 509, 526
Our New Humanity, 527
Our Home Rights, 130n6
The Outlook, 508, 514, 530
Owen, Robert, 541, 546
Owen, William C., 550, 553

pacifism, 14n27, 79, 544
Paine, Thomas: biographical summary on, 537; commemoration of, 76, 441–42n4, 446, 448, 502; and French Revolution, 448n9, 537; as influence on EG, 41; mentioned, 175; on State, 458
Pallás, Paulino, 435n15
Palmer, Sophia French, 143, 155
Panken, Jacob, 505
Paris (France): electricians' strike in, 259, 265, 480; experimental school in, 483; Russian anarchists in, 524
Paris Commune (1871): anti-militarism and, 382; commemoration of, 223, 459n3, 481; participants banished after, 292, 539; participants in, 526, 535
Paris Peace Conference (1919), 544
parliamentarianism, 236, 243, 536
Parsons, Albert, 10, 253n5, 537–38
Parsons, Lucy E.: biographical summary on, 537–38; editorship of, 552; on Harris's book, 411n2; IWW and, 55, 474, 558–59; at Most's commemoration, 476; speeches of, 473, 477
Pasadena (Calif.): EG's speech in, 498
Pastor, Annie, 197, 199, 204n3, 478
Pastoriza, J. J., 420
Paterson Guardian, 91–93
Paterson (N.J.): Bresci in, 512; EG's speeches in, 273–77, 480, 487
Paterson silk workers' strike: arrests of speakers and, 13, 225n3, 479, 523–24, 553; beginning of, 469; description of, 91n1; EG's article on, 13, 91–94; EG's dream about, 13; rally turned to riot in, 470
patriotism: as all or nothing, 380; appeal to masses through, 377; chronology of EG's speeches on, 492, 493, 494, 496, 513; EG's critique of, 46, 328–29; EG's definition of, 51, 77; EG's speeches on, 321–22; government's definition of, 275; limits of, 381–83; logic of, 377–78; religion compared with, 372–74; requirements of, 375–76; Roosevelt's link of family to, 70, 103. *See also* State

Scott, W. D., 391

Seattle Post-Intelligencer, 497

Seattle (Wash.): debates in, 498; EG barred from speaking in, 392; EG's speeches in, 483, 493, 497; Great White Fleet in, 377

Seldes, George S.: biographical summary on, 542; mentioned, 191n1, 192, 193; single-tax movement and, 21n43, 564

Seldes, Nunia Berman, 191–93, 542

Self Culture Hall (St. Louis settlement house), 452–53, 510

settlement house movement: in Boston, *146*, 512, 519; in Chicago, 507, 512, 544; EG's relationship with, 186n2; leadership in, 543; in New York, 512, 545–46; in St. Louis, 452–53, 510

Sevastopol (Crimea): mutiny in, 382n25

sexuality and sex question: arrest of authors of materials on, 114n9, 194n1; Campbell's pamphlet on, 557; Czolgosz discussion compared with, 203; discourse on, 4, 69–71, 38; harmony in, 69, 178; as *Mother Earth* topic, 47; soldiers' lives and, 378–79. *See also* free love; love

Seymour, Henry, 114n10

Shapiro, Meyer: biographical summary on, 542; letters to, 355–58, 390, 411–12

Shapiro, Sophie, 356, 357, 390, 412

Shaw, George Bernard: biographical summary on, 542; EG on, 271–72, 473, 488, 495; organizational activities of, 114n10; on religious piety, 385n5

Shearman, Thomas, 564

Shepard, Edward M., 124n1

Sherman Anti-Trust Act (1890), 541

Sherwood, Kate, 480

Shippy, George: biographical summary on, 542; Reitman beaten and arrested under, 323n1; shooting of, 72–73, 281–82, 284, 286, 489, 509, 556

Shippy, Harry, 28n1, 282

Shop Assistants' Union (England), 19, 112, 113, 545

Silverstein, Selig: as Anarchist Federation member, 297n4, *298*, 299; bombing by and death of, 44n79, 358n5, 491; EG on, 297; sketch of, *298*

Simkhovitch, Mary Kingsbury, 164n1

Simkhovitch, Vladimir Gregorievich, 164

Simon, Charles, 91, 93, 164n3

Simons, Algie Martin, 55, 551

Sims, Edwin W., 280, 288–89

Sinclair, Upton, 503, 549, 551, 564

Single Tax Club (Chicago), 564

Single Tax Club (San Francisco), 564

Single Tax League, 526, 564

single-tax movement: cooperative colony of, 526; definition of, 21, 563–64; EG's opinion of, 420; Houston hall of, 420, 500; leadership of, 524; lecturers on, 535; periodicals of, 220n11, 550, 553; support for, 538

Sipiagin, Dmitrii, 350, 351n11, 563

Slotnikoff, Pauline, 197. *See also* Schlechtinger, Pauline

SLP (Socialist Labor Party), 117n6, 529

Smith, Charles Sprague, 124n1

Smith, J. Blair, 46

Smith, Shirley D., 307, 310–11, 312

Smitt, Lena (or Smith or Sweet), 197, 199, 204n3, 478

social democracy, 531

Social Democratic Federation (England), 112n2

The Social Gospel, 513

socialism vs. anarchism: Breshkovskaya's and EG's differences on, 28–29; debates on, 54, 317–20, 492, 493, 498, 499, 540; on equal wages, 318; mutual rejection between, 62–63; organizational division of, 108n3

Socialist Democratic Party (Switzerland), 542

Socialist Labor Party (SLP), 117n6, 529

Socialist League (England), 112

Socialist League (Philadelphia), 118

Socialist Local (San Francisco), 482

Socialist Party of America: conference and (1907), 216n2; Conference of the Unemployed of, 491; founding of, 528; leadership of, 528, 543; members of, 507, 532; organizers of, 513; publication of, 117n6;

on religious belief, 344–45n9; Riddle suspended from, 227n11; support for, 549. *See also* Debs, Eugene Victor

socialists and socialism: criticism of, 216; EG's reading of, 46; libertarian and authoritarian divisions in, 541; and protective legislation, 54; scientific, 106, 420. *See also* anarchist/socialist/liberal alliance; socialism vs. anarchism

Socialists' Club (Chicago), 477

Socialist Spirit (Chicago), 109n7, 507, 513

Socialist Trade and Labor Alliance, 55–56

Social Revolutionary Party of Japanese in America, 229n28

Social Science Club: description of, 564–65

Social Science Club (Boston), 565

Social Science Club (Butte), 497

Social Science Club (Chicago), 286, 548, 565

Social Science Club (Los Angeles), 482, 540, 565

Social Science Club (New York), 564, 565

Social Science Club (Philadelphia), 459n3, 519, 537, 565

Social Science Club (San Francisco), 516, 528, 564–65

Social Science League (Minneapolis), 543

The Social Significance of Modern Drama (EG): on Chekhov's work, 270n3, 400n16; on Gorky's work, 269n1, 341n4; on Hauptmann's work, 271n6, 398n6; on Holz's work, 397n3; on Ibsen's work, 177n3, 270n4, 271n5, 399n9; on Shaw's work, 271n7, 542; on Strindberg's work, 399n11; on Sudermann's work, 397n4

social wealth: production of, 340–41

Society for Psychological Study, 522

Society for the Suppression of Vice, 516

soldiers: sexual behavior of, 378–79; workingman's suffering due to, 382. *See also* Buwalda, William; militarism

Solidaridad Obrera, 61, 459n1, 502, 504, 521

Solidaridad Obrera group, 243n29, 459n1

Solidarity (New York), 528, 534, 559

Solotaroff, Hillel: AB's view of, 106; biographi-

cal summary on, 542–43; as EG's doctor, 32; letter to, 156; at Most's commemoration, 476; *Mother Earth* planning and, 42; as nationalist/Zionist, 172–73; periodical contributions of, 361; speeches of, 471, 477

South: EG's perception of, 418–19

South Educational Society, 488

Spain: anarchism's development in, 520–21; assassination in, 347, 351, 508, 513; experimental school in, 61, 461; "Tragic Week" in, 459n1, 502, 504, 521

Spanish-American War (1898): Buwalda's service in, 330; motives for, 376; U.S. imperialism and, 534–35; wealth made in, 266n7

Spanish language: barred from meeting, 500

Spargo, John, 216n2

Sparks, John, 274

speech, written and spoken: belief in power of, 45; inconsistent suppression of, 76–77; questions about impact of, 111n19. *See also* free speech

Spencer, Herbert, 45n81, 340, 552

Spielman, Jean E., 56n85, 200–201, 539, 543

Spies, August, 253n5

Spiritual Biblical Brotherhood, 125n3

Spokane (Wash.): EG barred from speaking in, 53, 392; EG's speeches in, 323–27, 493; free speech fight in, 52, 57, 560; IWW office raided in, 505; ordinances against public speaking in, 495, 499–500, 502, 505. *See also* police harassment and surveillance

Spokesman-Review (Spokane), 69, 323–27

Sprading, Charles T.: associates of, 540; bail provided by, 409, 499; biographical summary on, 543; EG-Bauer debate chaired by, 317

Springfield (Ill.): EG's speeches in, 489; race riot in, 419

Springfield (Mo.): EG's speeches in, 496

Stäel, Mme de (Anne Louise Germaine Necker), 178

The Standard, 220n12, 428n2

Standard Oil Company, 186, 266n7, 541

Standish, Miles, 432

Stanislavsky, Constantin, 34, 164n5

State: anarchism as absence of, 341–42; as arbitrary institution, 77, 238; as barrier to individual freedom, 53, 211n4; centralization of, 293–94; criticism of, 329; definitions of, 293; divorce proceedings as concession to, 430; EG's beliefs about, 341–42; executions by, 351–52; failure of, 258; injustice embodied by, 462; invasiveness of, 204–5, 345, 388; Jewish culture and, 15; love as off-limits to, 47, 325–26; monopoly supported by, 293, 319, 341; October issue of *Mother Earth* confiscated by, 248; Paine on, 458; socialist vs. anarchist views of, 54, 318; wealthy protected by, 52–53, 274–75. *See also* citizenship; militarism; patriotism; right of rebellion against tyranny

Statue of Liberty: hypocrisy of, 21–22n47, 199, 364

Steffens, Lincoln, 526, 553, 558, 561

Stein, Modest, 8–9, 25, 137n8, 535

Steinhauser: EG's references to, 334

Stephens, G. Frank, 454n2, 459n3, 526, 564

Stetson, Charlotte Perkins. *See* Gilman, Charlotte Perkins

Steunenberg, Frank: assassination of, 50, 205n7, 475, 483, 487, 528, 536, 538; martial law declared by, 205n5

Stevenson, Robert Louis, 396

Steward, Leroy T., 466n2

Stirner, Max: biographical summary on, 543; EG's reading of, 45–46; as influence on *Liberty*, 552; memorial fund for, 547; philosophy of, 162n1, 239–40; translations of, 534

Stokes, Anson Phelps, 216

Stokes, Helen, 216n2

Stokes, J. G. Phelps, 145, 216n2, 501, 543

Stokes, Rose Pastor, 216n2, 447n8, 454n2, 501

Stone, Lucy, 511

Stowe, Harriet Beecher, 447n4

Straus, Oscar Solomon: biographical summary on, 543–44; Breshkovskaya's meeting with, 147; on deporting EG, 67–68, 256–57; letters from, 288–89, 410; telegram to, *280*;

warrant for EG's arrest issued by, 22n49, 254–55, 485

strikes: of cable carmen, 264–65, 482, 485; of cigarmakers in Cuba, 376; of electricians (Paris), 259, 265, 480; of garment workers (1910), 533; general, 93–94, 241–42, 492; of iron and steel workers, 523; merits of demands in, 506; of miners, 205n5, 274, 322, 380, 518, 523; of printers, 264; of shirtwaist workers, 505; support for, 61. *See also* Paterson silk workers' strike

Strindberg, August, 34, 207n1, 399, 475

Sudermann, Hermann: EG on work of, 397–98, 399, 402; mentioned, 431, 433

suffrage and suffrage movement: EG's criticism of, 47–48, 69–70, 259; EG's speeches on, 467, 505; limited effects of, 180

Sulzberger, Mayer, 494

Sunrise Club: EG's speeches for, 436, 445, 476, 499, 501, 561; founder of, 546; members of, 517, 523; motion on women as inconstant before, 475; Oppenheimer's speech for, 122n8

The Suppression of Free Speech in New York and New Jersey, 442n4

The Survey, 508

Suttner, Bertha von, 397–98

Sweet, Lena (aka Lena Smitt), 197, 199, 204n3, 478

Switzerland: anti-militarism in, 243; socialist publications in, 542

Symonds, John Addington, 513

syndicalists and syndicalism: discussed at Anarchist Congress, 241–42; EG's exposure to, 46; EG's speeches on, 488; in Europe, 59, 517; support for, 234–35n3. *See also* trade unionists and trade unionism

Syracuse (N.Y.): EG's speeches in, 188, 476, 487

Tacoma (Wash.): EG's speeches in, 482; Great White Fleet in, 377

Taft, William Howard: election of, 415n2; letter to, 328–31

Tailor, William S., 482

Tailors strike committee (London), 547

Taylor v. United States, 256n2

Les Temps Nouveaux (Paris), 235n6, 236n10, 531, 535

Terrace Garden (New York): EG's speeches at, 470

terrorism: discussed at Anarchist Congress, 242–43

Tfileh Zakeh (New York), 543

theater: fire in Chicago, 286; Russian censorship of, 545; Russian naturalist style in, 164n5, 537; Yiddish, 125n3. *See also* modern drama; *The Social Significance of Modern Drama* (EG)

Thomas, Mabel Holland, 526

Thomas Paine National Historical Association, 522, 537

Thompson, Charles Willis, 431–37

Thompson, James P., 505

Thoreau, Henry David: as anarchist role model, 21–22n47, 40, 211, 273, 283, 455; associates of, 520; biographical summary on, 544; as influence on EG, 10; translations of, 534

Timmerman, Claus, 8–9, 25

Titus, Hermon F., 493, 498

Der Tog (New York), 543

Toledo (Ohio): EG's speeches in, 480, 489

Tolstoy, Leo: as anarchist, 14, 216; biographical summary on, 544; on Church, 325, 345; correspondents of, 542; EG on work of, 400–401; mentioned, 215; and militarism, 14n27, 544; on patriotism, 372; plays of, performed, 34; on soldiers, 342; on state executions, 351–52; works: *Kreutzer Sonata,* 516, 544

Tomorrow, 535

Toronto (Ontario): EG's speeches in, 187–88, 476, 480, 488

Toronto Star, 226

"To the Strikers of Paterson" (EG), 13, 91–94

trade unionists and trade unionism: criticism of, 57, 243, 258–59, 264–66; EG's appeal on behalf of unemployed , 57–58, 267; EG's

speeches on, 486, 488, 491, 493; Industrial Union Manifesto on, 558; recommendations for, 267. *See also* syndicalists and syndicalism

"The Tragedy at Buffalo" (EG), 95n3

The Tragedy of Woman's Emancipation (EG): contradictions on mothering, 33; cover of French ed., *179;* EG's talk on, 473; description of, 4–5, 47–48; influences on, 46; publication of, 479; text of, 178, 180–85

"Tragic Week" (Barcelona uprising), 459n1, 502, 504, 521

Transcendentalism, 520, 544

Traubel, Horace L., 100, 544, 550

Trautmann, William, 558–59

Troi, Angelo, 488

The Truth Seeker (Paris, Ill.): description of, 553; editors of, 122n5, 535; on Progressive Library meeting, 202–6; subscribers to, 514

Tucker, Benjamin R.: on anarchist individualism, 263; biographical summary on, 544–45; editorship of, 162n1, 552; egoism adopted by, 543; family of, 514; in free speech fight, 20, 21–22; on George's reversal, 428n3; organizational activities of, 470, 557; Shaw's work published by, 542; support for, 459n6; Tolstoy popularized in U.S. by, 544; translations by, 401n20, 510; Turner's defense and, 122; on Whitman, 547. *See also Liberty*

Tucker, Pearl Johnson, 514, 545

Turgenev, Ivan, 349, 400, 545

Turner, Ethel Duffy, 494, 553

Turner, John: appeal of, 22–23, 121–23, 125, 130, 136, 472, 473; arrest and deportation of, 19–20, 22, 115–16, 471–72, 557; biographical summary on, 545; candidacy for Parliament rejected by, 23n51; deportation order for, 136n2, 473; EG's biographical sketch of, 112–14; EG's London visit and, 60–61, 248, 252, 484; on International Correspondence Bureau, 240n23; Kropotkin on, 127–28; lawyers of, 472, 518, 538; as legal precedent, 21–24; letter from, 124; released on bail, 137n4; U.S. visit of, 110, 111, 472, 561

Turner, John Kenneth: periodical contributions of, 549, 553; on support for PLM, 494; works: *Barbarous Mexico*, 503

Turner, Lizzie, 545

Turner Defense Committee: correspondence on, 117–18; EG authorized to collect funds for, 139–40; formation of, 22, 117n5, 121n2, 557; meeting place of, 125n2; members of, 122, 471, 510, 539, 544; opposition to, 132–33; rally of, 122–25, 128n8, 471–72; reports of, 129n3; significance of, 23–24

Twain, Mark (Samuel Clemens), 26, 525, 555

The Twentieth Century, 220n11, 538

Typographical Union No. 6, 264n1

Umberto (king of Italy), 11n19, 347, 512, 545

UMW (United Mine Workers of America), 546, 562

unemployed: call to organize, 366–67; capitalism as cause of, 450; EG's appeal on behalf of, 57–58, 267; mass meeting of, at Cooper Union, 363–67, 495, 520, 560; organization for, 422–23; Philadelphia meeting of, 454n1

Union of Maximalist Socialist Revolutionaries (Russia), 563

Union Square (New York): bomb explosion in, 44n79, 73, 297, *298*, 299, 358, 491; First-of-May Conference demonstration at, 492; 1893 meeting of unemployed in, 403n2, 425n2

Unitarian Church, 466

United Hebrew Trades Organization, 528

United Mine Workers of America (UMW), 546, 562

United States: criticism of, 204–5; Europe compared with, 209, 210; growth of, 293–94; military expenditures in, 374–75; Russia compared with, 26, 49, 123, 275, 321, 448; Russification of, 14–16, 53, 98–99

U.S. Bureau of Immigration and Naturalization: Board of Special Inquiry's examination of EG, 307–13; caution of, 68, 288–89; commissioner of, 279n6, 395n1, 546–47;

EG detained by, 491; on EG's reentry to U.S., 233, 484, 485; establishment of, 256n1; Straus's report to (on EG), 256–57; Turner arrested by, 115n1

U.S. Congress, 533. *See also* Immigration Act (1903)

U.S. Constitution: commerce clause in, 23n50; on free speech, 6, 7, 22–23, 75–77, 187, 443, 445, 447, 454; on right to petition government to redress grievances, 310n4

U.S. Justice Department, 499

U.S. military: cost of, 374–75; court-martial by, 492–93; "legalized murder" by, 328; standing armies and, 375–77; surveillance ordered by, 315n4. *See also* Buwalda, William; militarism; soldiers

U.S. Secret Service: surveillance by, 61, 68, 288; Turner arrested by, 115n1

U.S. Steel Corporation, 347n15

U.S. Supreme Court: on eighty cent law, 276; Turner's case before, 22–23, 121–23, 125, 130, 136, 472, 473

United States v. Aultman, 256n2

United States v. Jacob Kersner, *416*, 426

University of Chicago, 186

University Settlement house (New York), 543

Untermann, Ernest, 549

Utica (N.Y.): EG's speeches in, 476, 487

Vaillant, Auguste: biographical summary on, 545; as character in Zola's novel, 548; execution of, 435n15; revenge for execution of, 347, 513, 514; speech of, 350; violent acts of, 127n6

Vaillant, Sidonie, 545

Vancouver (B.C.): EG's speeches in, 498

Vanderbilt, Cornelius, 266n7

Vanderbilt, William Henry, 266n7

Vanderveer, George W., 333n4

Vanzetti, Bartolomeo, 516, 550

Varhayt (Truth), 530, 534

Verity, O. A., 550

Victoria Eugenia (princess of Great Britain), 477

World War I, 519, 543, 550

WTUL (Women's Trade Union League), 507, 511, 519, 546

Yampolsky, Rebecca Miriam (Becky): biographical summary on, 547–48; companion of, 536; mentioned, 395, 490; organizational activities of, 466, 467, 556, 565

Yanovsky, Saul: associates of, 547; biographical summary on, 548; editorship of, 357n3, 358, 551; letter to, 156n4; at Most's commemoration, 476; as nationalist/Zionist, 172; on Progressive Library meeting, 200; sketch of, *192*; speeches of, 477

Yarros, Victor, 552

Yiddish Free People's Theater, 125n3

Yiddish language: books translated into, 530, 534; in England, 237; as "jargon," 193; lecture series in, 495; theater in, 125n3

Yonkers (N.Y.): EG barred from speaking in, 443

youth: arrest of, 197, 199–200, 204n3. *See also* Progressive Library meeting

Yvetôt, Georges Louis François, 244

Zabregneff, Vladimir Ivanovich, 244

Zamenhof, "Ludovic" Lazar Markovitch, 236n12

Zametkin, M., 477

Der Zeitgeist, 526

Zemlya i Volya (Land and Liberty), 538

Zhitlovsky, Chaim: banquet honoring, 478; at Most's commemoration, 476; U.S. speaking tour of, 473, 474, 563

Zhook, Doris, 547

Zionism, 15, 172–73, 510, 543

Zitlen, Jacob (also Veltin, Dillem, Dillon), 204n3, 478

Zola, Émile: biographical summary on, 548; characters of, 545; genius and sanity of, 349; as influence, 534; plays of, performed, 182n5

The University of Illinois Press
is a founding member of the
Association of American University Presses.

_____

University of Illinois Press
1325 South Oak Street
Champaign, IL 61820-6903
www.press.uillinois.edu